Managing Residential Construction Projects

Managing Residential Construction Projects

Strategies and Solutions

Derek Graham

McGraw-Hill

New York   Chicago San Francisco Lisbon London Madrid
Mexico City   Milan   New Delhi   San Juan Seoul
Singapore Sydney Toronto

The **McGraw·Hill** Companies

Cataloging-in-Publication Data is on file with the Library of Congress

Copyright © 2006 by The McGraw-Hill Companies, Inc. All rights reserved. Printed in the United States of America. Except as permitted under the United States Copyright Act of 1976, no part of this publication may be reproduced or distributed in any form or by any means, or stored in a data base or retrieval system, without the prior written permission of the publisher.

1 2 3 4 5 6 7 8 9 0 DOC/DOC 0 1 2 1 0 9 8 7 6

ISBN 0-07-145934-0

The sponsoring editor for this book was Cary Sullivan and the production supervisor was Richard C. Ruzycka. It was set in Century Schoolbook by International Typesetting and Composition. The art director for the cover was Margaret Webster-Shapiro.

Printed and bound by RR Donnelley.

This book is printed on acid-free paper.

McGraw-Hill books are available at special quantity discounts to use as premiums and sales promotions, or for use in corporate training programs. For more information, please write to the Director of Special Sales, McGraw-Hill Professional, Two Penn Plaza, New York, NY 10121-2298. Or contact your local bookstore.

Contents

Preface

Opulent magazine spreads of lavish apartments, appointed with fine finishes—every month, periodicals are bursting with them. But if you venture behind the scenes, things are seldom as pretty as the picture, which also may pale at closer examination. To be sure, the aesthetics of published work tend to run only skin deep. Any seasoned architect or contractor will tell you that a large percentage of projects are invariably wrought with mistakes, acrimony, and innuendo, not uncommonly, *ad nauseum*. The terms *Kafkaesque* and *Murphy's Law* come to mind; and finally—*Comedy of Errors*. These seemingly extravagant and complex projects tend to be so ridden with the dual strife of being over budget, and behind schedule, that to finally finish them is a Pyrrhic victory. Why is the construction industry, particularly the residential sector, so prone to such failure? There is no simple answer.

This book intends to enlighten the layman and scholar alike, as to the modern thinking and skills required to be successful in a field that is extremely problematic, resistant to change, with a low margin of success. Through facilitation and empowering knowledge, this book will show the way to a healthier residential contract management perspective. Finally, it is hoped that someday, the process can catch up with some of the more successful end-products, that is, both being bona fide works of art.

To the two thousand years of scientists, engineers, and workers whose labor made possible the modern city, and to the scientists, engineers, workers, and good citizens of today and tomorrow who will make the cities of the future centers of health, ease of living, beauty, and peaceful activity.[1]

Endnote

1. Harry Granick, *Underneath New York* (New York: Rinehart, 1947), dedication page.

Acknowledgments

Thanks is due the following persons and entities:

David Smotrich, David Smotrich & Partners

Suzanne Harness, The American Institute of Architects

Bruce D'Agostino, The Construction Management Association of America

Phil Warner, FMI Management Consulting

Preston H. Haskell, for his paper *Construction Industry Productivity: Its History and Future Direction*

And special thanks to

Walton Graham

Professor Wendy Graham, Vassar College

Professor Emeritus James Williams, Hunter College

Pierre Crosby, Uberto Construction

Chris Clark, Clark Construction

Warren Ostroff, Ostroff Electric

Bojan Petek

Roger Kasunic, McGraw Hill

John Schwarz

Author's Note

The author has composed this text in a somewhat unorthodox fashion for a "technical book," in that general conclusions are presented based on experience, and that research corroborating these conclusions was resourced *subsequent* to the findings of the text, as opposed to before—the traditional approach. Experience informs most of the author's aspect, and research mostly reiterates it. In this way, he believes he has come about his information honestly. The author's experience involved extended examinations of over twenty different general contractors, as well as his own general contracting experiences.

Available research and statistics on construction is relatively sparse, and not all reliable. Much of the research is contradictory. Research before 1975 or so still lacks relevance. The BLS (Bureau of Labor and Statistics) maintains a database on things such as production rates, but they do not track this database, hence, it isn't reliable. Moreover, it has only been surveyed for 5 years. For that reason, it is generally not particularly useful. Additionally, the construction industry is fragmented into an enormous number of sectors, which makes research difficult. Nonetheless, special thanks is due the *Construction Users Roundtable* (CURT), and the *Joint Center for Housing Studies of Harvard University* (JCHS) in particular, for their exemplary efforts to isolate and interpret difficult and esoteric areas of study, without whose excellent work there would be precious little research on my subject.

While the text will make use of available research on the subject, it must be said that with a few exceptions—especially the aforementioned, by and large, most available research pertains to *large scale commercial, industrial, and institutional projects*. These statistics should be interpreted with the notion that demonstrable trends will be *exacerbated* in the residential sector, which is the focus of this book. Additionally, it must be understood that there is a whole other discipline pertaining to the science of interpreting statistics called "epidemiology," which has perhaps more relevance to the study of statistics than any other related field. By and large, studies that don't take epidemiological factors into consideration, or research that isn't correctly interpreted, must be approached with a measure of skepticism. For this reason, one must be vigilant in qualifying a given study's means and methods. For more information related to epidemiology, refer to *Appendix C*.

The text will continually refer to "high-end residential" or "residential construction." The distinctions are that:

- The residential sector is unique to the construction industry and merits special consideration.

- An enormous quantity of residential work is done "under the radar" or below acceptable standards of quality, code compliance, and legality. The nature of this work will not be considered for our purposes; however, the point at which it does become relevant is forever elusive. As part of the text we will try to define this boundary.

- The term "residential construction" refers to any *qualifying* housing, remodeling, and repair work, based on the parameters set forth in the text, chiefly, single-family residences, or individual units within multiple family dwellings. Developer work will be treated as a subcomponent.

- The term "high-end residential," and its connotations are specifically defined in Chap. 2.

I am guilty, should I be charged (as I usually am), of a prevailing pessimistic tendency toward arguable conclusions on my subject, such that one might wonder if things are as I say they are. All I can say is I defy doubters to prove me wrong, and in fact, would be pleasantly surprised if they did. In that vein, it must be said that although the majority of the residential remodeling industry makes a mockery of its purpose, there are some good eggs that nobly ply their trade. I have the utmost respect for such people, whether it is a hard working, proud laborer, or an eccentric ingenious project manager. There are some extraordinary architects and (to a lesser extent) small contractors. It is such people that we can look to for guidance in preparing for the future. On the other hand, the case studies of patent failures perpetrated by specific contractors in the text are not meant to unduly criticize any particular contractor, for there is nothing unusual about their behavior that would distinguish them from legions of their peers.

Introduction

The annual home remodeling market is now nearly a one-quarter trillion dollar industry ($233 billion). Expenditures for the remodeling industry tripled between 1970 and 1980, and jumped another 250% between 1980 and 1990. Between 1995 and 2003, such expenditures increased by 40%. In 2003, the remodeling market accounted for about 2% of the overall economy. The average age of existing homes stands at 32 years and is rising, thus the expectation is that remodeling expenditures will continue to increase for some time, at about 3% annually.[1] Between 1994 and 2003, almost 30 million homes were significantly upgraded.[2] Clearly, there is an enormous and formidable workload coming down the pike for the remodeling industry.

The art of operating a small construction company is enigmatic. There is clearly no consensus on methodology, and no two circumstances are alike. There isn't even agreement on what constitutes success. There are guidelines for different companies, and guidelines for these companies in a given market. This being the case, the limited amount of available literature on the subject varies widely. However, much of it is too broad or general, outdated, or just uninformative. This is especially true as it pertains to the residential building industry.

Too broad or general: The one-size fits all approach. Depending on the author's background, the information may reflect only the author's particular experiences in a given market, typically, large-scale construction, which should be differentiated from other types of construction. While there is some crossover of theories, large and small-scale constructions differ considerably. Resultantly, a jaundiced view emanates. There seems to be a great need for publications that focus on residential construction, particularly, high-end.

Outdated: Like so much information, no sooner is it in print than it seems to become obsolete. Like much old theory, this information is simply that—old, and, old-fashioned, out of step with current events. This material is easy to identify. It is full of common, rigid, old-school theories, which have little to do with today's fast modern times, and simplistic axioms meant to streamline a process which takes years to learn. Many authors write their books when they retire, recalling old experiences that have no bearing on today's practice.

Uninformative: Construction management is an applied science. Literature on the subject should at least attempt to treat it thus. While some publications are more scholarly than others, many take the layman's approach, condescending to what they perceive as a uniformed or even uneducated audience. Perhaps this assumption is passed down from times when tradesmen went to trade school, not finishing high school or college, and authors felt a need to talk down to their audience's level. Suffice it to say, times have changed, and many colleges in fact offer degrees in construction management (more about that later).

Many publications are stark for their lack of imagination and creativity. They have nothing new or interesting to tell us, just regurgitation of old ideas: tried, but not necessarily true, and certainly static. Good for automatons, but not for the thinking man. So immersed in theory are they that there is no reasonable practicum. Boring and unstimulating, and most importantly, nonempowering: not encouraging or facilitating people to think for themselves, a necessity of the successful operator.

Another consideration is the notion that some authors seem to lack field experience, or haven't "worked the tools." This is the complaint of many field personnel of their upper managers that the latter are office personnel or "paper-pushers," not construction people like themselves. What is ultimately missing is a focused aspect, or distillation from a combination of office and field, and finally, the wherewithal to put such knowledge into a cohesive form.

Finally, for lack of a better resource, many of today's managers seem to get their training on the job. In of itself, such knowledge can be useful; however, field experience alone will not yield the comprehensive tools required for the job. This is especially true of the open shop (nonunion) and private sectors. It would appear that this sector has only itself to blame for its woes:

> Less than 10 percent of all funds now going into construction craft training are directed toward open shop training. Likewise, less than 10 percent of those individuals completing construction craft training are in open-shop programs.
>
> If the open-shop sector remains at the present level of 60 percent without a significant increase in its training, there could be a long-term deterioration in the quality and productivity of the construction workforce.
>
> There is a need for recognized and accredited training curriculum that can be utilized by open-shop contractors to train craftsmen for industrial work by modern skill related methods, particularly in the specialty trades. Such a curriculum is not available at this time.[3]

Many of these open-shop programs attract large numbers of recruits; however, the annual completion rate is only 10% to 13%, with a drop-out rate of 50% to 60%. While the same rate applies to union-sponsored training, it is unacceptable.[4] Nevertheless, for a few pennies on the dollar, the private sector could do infinitely better in cultivating its resources. The unions pass on these costs to their customers, which they should, by increasing hourly rates through their collective bargaining agreements. Perhaps the lower rate of turnaround for union companies is an incentive to invest in their workers. Regardless, it's sad to see people toiling away at the same company for years, and their employer never making any investment in their potential.

As the above referenced report indicates, there is certainly "deterioration in the quality and productivity of the construction workforce." Although the data is 15 years old, it is still as relevant as it ever was. This dilemma is exacerbated by the current trend of the last 15 years—the rapidly growing high-end sector, where more skills are required. The high-end sector is indeed the fastest growing sector:

According to the Survey of Consumer Finances (SCF), while the number of all households grew by only 14%, and that of all homeowners grew by 21%, (between 1989 and 2001), the expensive housing market grew by about 120% to 170% (120% for houses > $500,000, and 170% for houses > $1,000,000). Even though this sector represents only 11% of the housing stock, it accounts for over 90% of growth in overall improvement spending between 1995 and 2003[5] (Table 1.1). Spending on home improvements in this group increased from $8 billion annually, to over $40 billion annually, in the same period. The average income of the million-dollar house owners was $900,000 (SCF). These houses account for some 27.8% of all homes, and 91.6% are owned by the top quintile of household income (80% for half-million-dollar homes).[6] The median price per square foot of all such homes was $462.[7] These figures do not take into account apartment houses and condos. For single-family homes represent only 1.8% of all owner-occupied housing in Manhattan.[8] On the whole, California represents a whopping 40.99% share of all million-dollar units. The next largest share belongs to New York, 7.12%. With the exception of Michigan and Illinois, the remainder of the top ten states was all on the east coast.[9]

Even before this rapid growth took place, there were already projections of skilled labor shortages as early as 1990. The increase in the required labor force from 2002 to 2012 was then projected at 15%. We will examine the effect of labor supply problems on the high-end sector more fully in Chap. 2. The other dilemma for the building industry is the fact that production rates are not proportionate to gains in other industries: particularly nonagricultural productivity, which outpaces the building industry by over 2:1.

> Two independent methodologies demonstrate that total construction productivity has increased during the past 37 years, on the order of 33%, or .78% per year[10] . . . however, (that) is less than one-half that of U.S. nonagricultural productivity gains during the same period, which averaged 1.75%[11] annually between 1966–2003.

This book is written to facilitate the residential construction company sector with a new sensible approach to what at times seems dauntingly confusing—simplifying business operations, and upgrading services. It is also intended to create criteria for understanding and cooperation between contractors and the design industry, and finally, the end-user stands to gain a keen insight into the process that often will define one of the biggest investment decisions he will ever have to make.

There is a Zen observation of what is elementally wrong with much of the industry. What is regarded as complex is really simple, what is taken for granted as simple, is really more complicated, or in Western terms: "the good ones make it look easy." The average company functions on shaky foundations, which preclude a healthy life cycle. Just a little common sense could upgrade such companies' performances significantly.

That is why this book begins with the notion of establishing a mission statement, or philosophy, as being the first step in starting a new business, or changing an existing one.

Endnotes

1. Joint Center for Housing Studies of Harvard University (JCHS), *The Changing Structure of the Home Remodeling Industry* (2005), pp. 2–3. These are JCHS's tabulations of 1995–2003 American Housing Survey and the U.S. Department of Commerce Survey of Expenditures for Residential Improvements and Repairs.
2. Upgrade expenditures >50% of the value of the home.
3. The Business Roundtable, *Training Programs in Open Shop Construction, Report D-4* (1990).
4. *Ibid.*
5. JCHS 10.
6. Zhu Xiao Di, *"Million Dollar Homes" and Wealth in the United States,"* Joint Center for Housing Studies (2004).
7. *CNN Money*, July 31, 2003, http://money.cnn.com/2003/07/29/pf/yourhome/milliondollarbuyers/
8. Robert L. Bennenfield, "Home Values: 2000," *Census 2000 Brief,* May 2003. http://www.census.gov/prod/2003pubs/c2kbr-20.pdf
9. 2000 Census, Table H74.
10. Preston H. Haskell, *Construction Industry Productivity: Its History and Future Direction* (December 2004). The study concentrates on the building sector of construction, which is a rare and important distinction and focus, however, single-family residential construction was not measured; although Haskell's measures of multiple-family dwelling industry productivity serve as a benchmark, the more specialized single-family and high-end residential would be an exacerbated factor of the multiple-family dwelling rate.
11. BLS, *Private Nonfarm Business: Productivity and Related Indexes 1948–2003.*

Managing Residential Construction Projects

Mission

*When we build, let us think that we build forever.
Let it not be for the present delight, nor present use
alone. Let it be such work as our descendants will
thank us for; and let us think, as we lay stone to
stone, that a time is to come when those stones will
be held sacred because our hands have touched
them, and that men will say, as they look upon the
labor, and wrought substance of them, "See! This
our father did for us."*

JOHN RUSKIN

There is a need to better understand the nature of the residential construction industry, how it is unique from other building sectors, and how different companies function within this framework. Understanding your position within this structure should be a prerequisite to starting any construction company. For established companies, these ideas can be discussed retroactively and considered for the future well-being of the company. To understand a company's place in today's market, it is necessary to define the structure of this market.

Construction companies are a dime a dozen, especially since the eighties' building boom, and the subsequent recession which reoriented projects back into a cost-driven market. Vestiges of the old boom still remain—the market was demand heavy and the need for more contractors was great. To satisfy this need, it seemed that new companies were coming out of the woodwork. Many of these companies were unlicensed and lacked experience. To this day, we are still tearing out their handiwork and marveling at the degree of ineptitude that characterized the 1980s. There was a considerable shakeout in the recession of the early 1990s, but judging from what the industry now produces, not enough. Again, the work speaks for itself. There never really was a "back to grassroots" movement, wherein the industry self-corrected itself to return to a more quality-oriented mentality, as it once was regardless of supply and demand. It was merely a Darwinian shakeout: Bigger companies made do, and smaller companies tanked. However, a lot of the old perpetrators still persevere—perhaps they were young and belonged to lower management then, but now they are executives at large firms, doing more damage than ever.

> It doesn't take experience to make money and be considered successful in the construction business.

Read the above statement again. There are a few considerations regarding this statement:

1. Experience and quality don't necessarily translate to profitability, nor does a lack of it preclude profitability.
2. Because the above statement reflects the nature of today's industry, there are many players who excel merely based on their profitability record. These people also reside at the top and are calling the shots for much of the industry.

And then consider the following:

> Success has always been the greatest liar.[1]

This observation maintains that success, or the appearance of it lacks a suitable definition, such that it is often measured by any number of misinformed rubrics. For example:

> If they've been around this long, they must be doing something right. If they act or appear to be successful, they probably are. Apparent success implies that they are otherwise trustworthy and competent.

Thus people are inclined to measure success based on the perception of image alone, as opposed to actual deeds. A lack of discernment and attention span is to blame for such ignorance. More important, feigned success betrays inherent shortcomings of character—specifically, a lack of those attributes that would form the basis for *real* success.

Assuming you aspire to more than just making money, you need to ask yourself "What other incentive is there for pursuing a career in residential construction?" and "Do I have what it takes to realize these goals?" If your only goal is to make money, then you don't really belong in the business; the sector is already saturated with residential contractors who fail to recognize that they are in a service-oriented industry that demands more motivation from its participants than just profit. You may have a brilliant background, maintain a strong measure of good faith, be better than the competition, and still not be successful. On the other hand, your company may produce substandard quality, yet persevere in the marketplace, even profit. These are seemingly contradictory realizations that beg deeper insights:

- The straight and narrow path could lead to a profitable, yet miserable company, whereas a humble well-intended company happily toiling away by the book may take forever to evolve. This is an ethical dilemma.
- The market's response to this conundrum perpetuates it; the criteria for success do not seem to be meritocratic but nepotistic, superficial, and sometimes inscrutable.

- If a company is profitable, albeit incompetent and/or unethical, there can be little motivation to shake things up.

Remodeling Market

According to the U.S. Census Bureau, in 1997 there were 350,000 residential contracting firms with payrolls. Add to that number 198,600 self-employed contractors and legions of contractors under the radar, and you get an idea of the size of the sector. Primarily, about half of them were new homebuilders and the other half were remodelers. About 50% of all firms reported that most of their revenue came from home improvements or repairs. Of these firms about 80% had annual receipts <$500,000 (Table 1.1). A small handful—8.8%—collected a little over 51% of the total share of billings. Thus, the largest market share was realized by a tiny minority or subgroup.

Enormous growth in the remodeling sector generated a 52% growth rate between 1987 and 1997 (Table 1.2). However, 90% of this growth is attributable

TABLE 1.1   The Remodeling Industry

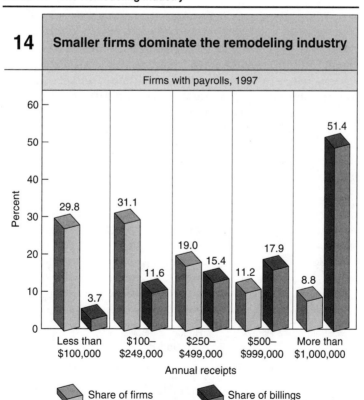

14   Smaller firms dominate the remodeling industry

Firms with payrolls, 1997

Share of firms   Share of billings

Source: Joint center tabulations of the 1997 census of construction industries.

TABLE 1.2   The Number of Remodeling Firms

The number of remodeling firms climbed by half between 1987 and 1997			
	1987	1992	1997	Change 1987–97
General	56,668	52,694	62,405	10%
Specialty	55,832	64,692	109,139	95%
Total	112,500	117,386	171,544	52%

Source: Unpublished tabulations of the 1987, 1992, and 1997 census of construction industries.

to specialty firms, whose focus is on infrastructural upgrades and replacement projects, such as heating systems and electrical systems. Despite a flourish of growth in the sector, home improvement firms were first on the list of top consumer complaints in 2001 and 2003–2004,[2] and have been in the top three for the past 5 years. Suffice it to say the market takes notice of the low quality of performance by the industry.

Players

Today's industry is a hodgepodge of characters: some well intended and successful, some neither, some with business and construction experience, and some lacking in one or both. Among the smaller to midsize companies that dominate the residential sector there is an exorbitant rate of ineptitude such that it is hard to take the majority of them seriously. To find such shortcomings in the high-end residential sector is to expose serious flaws and gross misrepresentations; often the only difference between so-called high-end contractors and their inferior counterparts is their price structure. Let's explore some of the more familiar types of players in the industry:

Power plants and refrigeration

Straight size elbows

Reducing elbows
Elbows

45° Elbows

Cast iron fittings. Commercial fittings for joining the separate lengths of pipe together are made in a great variety of forms, and are either screwed, or flanged; the former being generally used for the smaller sizes of pipe up to 3½ in., and the latter for the larger sizes 4 in. and above. Harding and Willard, *Mechanical Equipment of Buildings, Vol II: Power Plants and Refrigeration* (New York: John Wiley & Sons, 1918).

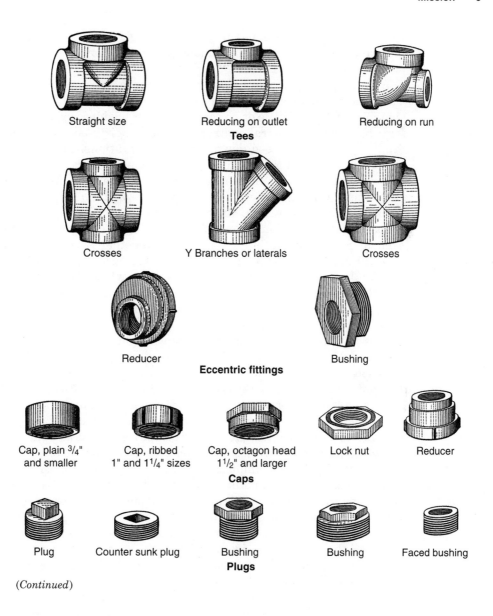

Straight size   Reducing on outlet   Reducing on run

Tees

Crosses   Y Branches or laterals   Crosses

Reducer   Bushing

Eccentric fittings

Cap, plain 3/4" and smaller   Cap, ribbed 1" and 1 1/4" sizes   Cap, octagon head 1 1/2" and larger   Lock nut   Reducer

Caps

Plug   Counter sunk plug   Bushing   Bushing   Faced bushing

Plugs

(*Continued*)

Single proprietorships and new ventures[3]

Most residential contractors start out alone or as single proprietorships. If they accumulate enough work, they will take on employees as they have need for them. Soon enough, they will have a little construction company. As they grow, they will make slow and deliberate changes to the company structure in order to facilitate that growth. When a single proprietor is successful and growing, the logical next step is to incorporate or take on a partner; however, this isn't always the case, as we will discuss in Chap. 8, Single Proprietor Syndrome. In the home building and remodeling industry, about 26% of surveyed members were single proprietorships.[4]

What is odd about today's residential sector is its composition of contractors. The building boom of the eighties offered such promise of fortune to aspirants that many who had little or no construction or business experience entered the fray. Historically, general contractors knew their business. Often they were family businesses passed down through generations. This was beginning to change. In the eighties, the industry was becoming saturated with inexperienced general contractors. Quality and safety were regularly compromised to an indecent extent. Cost-driven and low-end projects with no skill requirements perpetuated this phenomenon. Much of this had to do with the real estate boom—property values were increasing and changing hands so rapidly that it didn't seem to matter how the buildings were put together. All the owners needed was a Certificate of Occupancy. Most of these hacks, learning the hard way, have gone back to the livery or art studio occupation from which they had deviated. There are a few vestiges of this era remaining "above the line" established in this text, and they serve as useful examples of one sort of folly that is to be discouraged, that is, dilettantism.

Growth of small, single proprietorship companies seems never to be without pain and frustration, especially when it is experienced under the control of a tenacious company leader. Think of the rearing of a difficult preadolescent—the development of the company is critical at this stage, as it will likely be a strong determinant of the company's future. It is important to understand why new ventures are so prone to failure,[5] and how they fail, in order to avoid a similar fate, and also to gain some insight on your competition, and how they function.

The larger a company becomes, the greater the opportunity for mishap, or what I call "implosion." Implosion is the antithesis of explosion; however, it is no less messy. Many companies have no center and the negative pressure experienced by the company structure can implode. Other's experiences may more resemble a rocket ship slowly disintegrating as it reenters the earth's atmosphere, shedding its thin skin in little chunks, the crew inside oblivious to this fact until the vehicle vaporizes into jet trash. This condition may go undetected for years, especially if someone is "cooking the books," or if accounting is inscrutable. But for small companies, once the center collapses, everything around it falls on top of it. This may become evident the minute the company experiences its first substantial change. From this milestone, the fate of the company can take one of several directions:

They are, in order of frequency:

- Cease and desist
- Continue half-cocked until it no longer is feasible to go on
- Continue half-cocked regardless of whether it is feasible to go on or not
- Roll with the punches: adapt, persevere, and grow

None of the above are without consequences; only the last has a chance of a positive outcome. Companies fail for a number of reasons. Sometimes a client gets behind on payments, or declares bankruptcy, leaving the general contractor holding the bag. Other times, general contractors get behind in their payments to creditors who inevitably never do get paid. Unfortunately, there is a propensity toward denial regarding failure; this denial is a character flaw. This is a vanity that takes its toll on the industry in wasted capital, lawsuits, and even accidents and fatalities.

To summarize, most failing new ventures should, by every right, cease and desist within the first 5 years of operation, before they can do any more damage. The majority of the balance will find a way, usually tortured, to survive a market even when they are incompetent, uncompetitive, or crooked. From that subgroup will emanate a shakeout to yield a small survival rate. These companies, whose existence seems to be extremely tenuous, are ubiquitous; yet there seems to be no palpable reason why any of these surviving companies have market staying power, but many do.

There are a number of reasons for the high failure rate of start-up ventures:

- Construction is an industry in which many people underestimate the skill level necessary to be successful. People see others, like themselves, not particularly ingenious, evidently successful, and they think, "If they can do it, I can do it." So many people believe this that the playing field is now saturated with incompetence. We all know how a project with an incompetent contractor will turn out.

- Many start-up ventures are led by people who lack some critical aspect of running a business, such as controlling cash flow, basic business administrative skills, or people skills, or they simply might be incompetent builders. If they don't swim fast enough, it will be just a matter of time before they sink.

- Most companies, especially start-up ventures, which are invariably flawed, are dysfunctional in at least one way or another. Over time, as they fail to make the necessary adjustments to change, they founder under the weight of calamity, whether it is negative cash flow or an inability to operate—failure is the fate of the majority of the industry.

Many companies are given a chance— they may get that "big job" they've been hoping for, or they may get a flurry of several smaller projects. This advent can be a turning point in their career. The company's future is predicated on how they handle such growth. If they are not careful, rapid unchecked "growth" will render their efforts insignificant. It is not uncommon for companies to take on more work than they can handle, to the extent that they cease to function effectively. Thus the meaning of the term *growth* becomes skewed; instead of denoting maturity, success, and sophistication, it merely refers to an increase in revenue. Merely landing contracts does not substantiate a good builder. Only the value of work in place quantifies production not the contract value. A crude artist cum builder I knew had some $40 million in high-end commissions to be built over a 2-year period. Most of these he had charmed his way into, as opposed to earning them on merit. At the time he seemed well positioned, having the infrastructure and good resources. However, after 1 year he had put only about $4 million of the work in place, —about 10% of his target; he had the work, but for a number of reasons, couldn't build it. This was about 6 years ago. *Mirabile dictu*, his company yet thrives in the same fashion, albeit as a bottom-feeder. Sad to see, and not pretty, sometimes it can take 2 or 3 years for the death throes of a bad project or dying company to play out. Worse is that a failed general contractor can drag down his creditors with him.

Other new ventures simply wither under the impetus of the flawed "single proprietor syndrome," a sort of systemic debilitating affliction brought on by the presence of one overbearing individual affecting all operations. This problem is easier to analyze than other maladies, as the afflicted company will wear its heart on its sleeve being so small and centralized, problems are systemic and companywide—all or most of the blame can be attributed to one or two people. This will be further discussed in Chap. 8.

Small to midsize firms

Small to midsize firms lend themselves well to residential construction. Large unwieldy corporations have a hard time being competitive in the small specialized residential sector, and tend not to undertake such work. Midsize firms (twenty to sixty employees)[6] have a lot of advantages over their larger and smaller competition—chiefly, maneuverability. They can be more versatile and more flexible than their bloated competition. They can downsize without mass layoffs and restructuring programs. Unlike the smaller companies they can withstand more challenges.

Being small, but not so small that infrastructural changes and upgrades can't be adequately facilitated, fits the ideal of "lean and mean." Systemic changes at smaller companies are easier to make, whereas changes at large companies can be a daunting task, requiring restructuring, expense, and training. This is a major inhibition to real growth, regardless of profits. Efficient small corporations don't have as much overfeed as their larger cousins; they can putter along with one or two small projects at a time for years.

Smaller entities do have their limitations. For one, they can only take on so much work at a time before they have to pass up prospects because they are too busy. Business tends to be cyclical, so it is often feast or famine, neither of which are they suited to operate accordingly. Also, the playing field is still Darwinian wherein the bigger players get most of the market share. Also on the downside, having less capital and shallower pockets, it is difficult for them to weather prolonged adverse market conditions or droughts. The larger corporations simply downsize, whereas downsizing at a small company can easily halve that company's staff. If a high-level manager leaves a small company, he could leave a substantial hole in their infrastructure.

In addition to adverse market conditions, the plight of the small contractor can be threatened by these factors:

Overbooking

Taking on too much workload can inundate and spoil a small corporation in much the same way that small single proprietorships wither under oppressive neurotic tyranny. At first, companies may deem it counterintuitive to turn work away. After learning that overbooking is a bad policy, some companies may adjust accordingly. It can be a lot of work to climb out of such a hole because from there you must weather the storm without sinking further. One problem with gauging workload is the consideration of market conditions. Companies must keep this in mind while planning. If a drought is envisioned, a company may take all the work they can handle, and then some, for fear of a prospective market downturn.

There is an art to gauging how much and what particular sort of work a given company can handle. For example, you may have one very large project and five smaller projects. The aggregate contract value of the five smaller projects is less than the one larger. If the larger project was made up of five smaller projects, the same company would have ten projects and would be hard pressed to coordinate them all; not having the infrastructure. Thus, the company can generate the workload of six projects, but could not perform the work spread over ten projects.

Cash flow and working capital will also dictate how much work a company should take on. Unfortunately, the effect cash flow has on a company tends to generate a reactive response; in other words, businesses have a very hard time estimating how much cash they will have, how much will be needed, and when the cash must be in hand—their bookkeeping is by and large shooting from the hip. A cash flow projection might direct a company as to what work they should take on or help them plan. Without this consideration a company must succumb to the whims and caprices of their clients' payments. A company that has a lot of work, yet makes payroll late and pays subcontractors late, may be having a good year in terms of its revenue; however, they will be scrambling around between payments to make ends meet.

Absenteeism and Turnover

People come and go so quickly here!
FROM THE WIZARD OF OZ

Turnaround, especially at the management level, is high in the construction industry. In fact, construction industry turnover at the rate of 25.4% was second only to the retail industry at the rate of 31.2%.[7] Small companies are prone to suffer the most because they are often hard-pressed to bring in a replacement for a recent vacancy. They usually run a help-wanted advertisement as opposed to preferably bringing in another individual already at the company; one of the choices larger companies usually have. Since residential construction is such a small sector, the supply base becomes even more limited; it follows that it is more exigent for small companies to minimize employee turnaround, as for them consequences can be imminent.

TABLE 1.3   Reasons for Absence

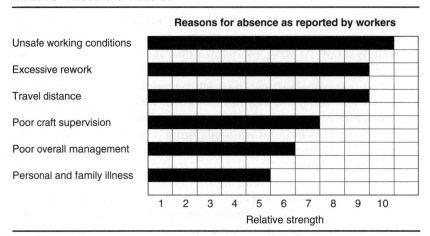

Reasons for absence as reported by workers

The rate of employee traffic is an important consideration for any size company. For one, they will have to absorb the retraining costs of the new hire. If the late employees file for unemployment, their insurance rate will increase. In the big picture, employee turnaround makes it difficult to establish and maintain company wide systems. Add to this a high rate of absenteeism, and you have a real problem. And with the team always changing, there will always be a readjustment period. Turnaround of field personnel is also a problem. A recent study showed losses of up to 9%—"a conservative estimate of the direct costs of absenteeism and turn over, based only on clearly identifiable costs, indicates that a 9% reduction in project labor costs is attainable on a typical job."[8] In the eyes of your client, turnaround is a sign of instability. They will be especially anxious if a new manager is introduced to the project midstream.

In fact, employee turnaround in the industry is so rampant that many companies have abandoned any hope of implementing infrastructural systems to any extent greater than the bare essentials because of the investment of time and expense of orienting and training new personnel. This is a reality to which today's contractors must realize and adapt accordingly. To do so one must understand the reasons why absenteeism and turnover are commonplace on their projects. A 1982 survey (Table 1.3) confirms some obvious observations but also presents some new interesting ones:

Absence

- Not surprisingly, projects with poor safety programs were the biggest incentive for people to skip work.

- Excessive rework was the second leading reason for workers to skip. This indicates that workers are sensitive to tear-out and redo work. It is understandable that they would be sensitive to this work but it is surprising that it is the second leading reason why they would not show up for work. As residential work involves much tear-out and redos, imagine how much of a negative impact it must have on its workers. In fact, rework gripes may eclipse safety complaints on residential projects, as the incidence of accidents is much smaller there than in the rest of the industry.

- Absenteeism attributable to perceived excessive workloads and type of work (other than redo) does not appear on the survey. I believe that this complaint is a moderate factor of absenteeism rates not represented in the survey. Perhaps interviewees were reluctant to admit this.

- The most salient data in the chart is the measure of personal and family illness, as being the last reason given. I expect that most of these workers call in sick, as they would be loath to indicate one of the other reasons on the survey, which are the predominant or real reason.

- If most absences are attributed by employers as illness related, there must be a good deal of ignorance regarding upper management's perceptions, such that it perpetuates the problem—ironically, there's nothing they can do to reduce illness-related absences which they believe is the biggest factor of absenteeism, whereas the real complaints could all be addressed by a little remediation in the workplace.

Turnover

- Relationship with boss was the leading indicator of incentives to ditch. This is another instance where the real problem was cloaked by calling in sick. Once the worker leaves, the jig is up, and the real reason for earlier absences becomes evident. While some problems can be mitigated, you can't change people. Workers will regard their relationship with a boss they resent, as an untenable condition. It is inevitable that the relationship will end badly. This is a theme that will be examined in more detail in this text, as it is a determinant of the level of employee satisfaction.

- Other than overtime available on another job,which could also be construed as leaving for better pay, most of the other complaints also focused on psychological factors such as poor overall management, and excessive surveillance by the owner. These data would denote that the job market was healthy enough that workers could up and leave for any reason; workload not even being cited as a factor.

The factors of absenteeism and turnover's indirect cost to the industry can be broken down into components that inform one of how such costs are distributed:

Indirect impacts of absenteeism

- Increased man power complement to meet staffing needs
- Loss of revenue from not meeting project schedules (due to lack of man power)

- Administrative costs to recruit and train new employees
- Lost efficiency in work crews attributable to new or inexperienced members
- Underutilization of capital investments (tools, equipment, and the like)
- Interruption of work flow and task execution
- Misallocation of skills and talent of employees
- Increased demand for administrative time and resources for planning and rescheduling
- Increased overtime and employee fatigue
- Lower morale[9]

The survey points to some direct impact and costs of absenteeism and turnover that are measurable:

Direct impacts of absenteeism

- Time spent by crew members (others) waiting for replacements
- Time spent moving replacements from other work locations
- Time lost by supervisory personnel in reassignment of work activities and locating replacements

Principal costs of turnover

1. All of the absentee-costs described above
2. Payroll and clerical costs associated with terminating and hiring
3. Exworkers' nonproductive time (portions of the first and last day)
4. Disruption of other workers on the job site[10]

Thus, it is easy to see how such factors can affect a company's performance. Some of these factors are measurable, most are not. The survey suggests an average of 9% decrease in performance; however, it must be considerably higher for residential projects.[11]

Large Corporations/Developers

The large corporate structure seems almost inevitably fated to being incongruous with the high-end residential construction industry. For the most part, large companies realize this and avoid such work; however, there are exceptions. For example, consider the tale of a misguided developer:

Sensing something amiss with their newly purchased condominium, a client asked me to conduct a quality control survey of the developer's handiwork. The space was located in a prewar building in an exclusive neighborhood in New York City's posh Lincoln Center district. The building prospectus promised opulent appointments and touted premium workmanship and the price of the units reflected that sentiment. The builder was a real estate developer who had partnered with a semi-large scale builder to retrofit the interiors of the entire building. Since there was really little or no corework on the project, the contractor was there to install fit-out or interior partitions and finishes, as well as branch mechanical electrical and plumbing (MEP) work. It was their work I came to inspect.

First, let it be said that there is now a ubiquitous term for such endeavors—it is called *developer work*, and it implies that (a) such work is limited to real estate ventures, particularly redevelopment, (b) it tends to be nondescript, understanding that it is a waste of time to customize or highly detail a space, in which the new owner will want to do for himself along with his own contractor,[12] and (c) that the customary level of finish work of most developers is far beneath acceptable levels of high-end quality, hence, they generally avoid it, or only install the core work, leaving the finishes to others. This project was an exception.

Apparently, this developer and contractor violated the criteria of (b) and (c), by attempting to deliver a high-end product, a task they were incapable of or unwilling to do. The substandard work by this contractor was perpetuated by either their ignorance, or denial of it; otherwise, corrections would have been made. The defects I found tended to be epidemic and of a nature that would make one think unskilled workers were installing the work. Whether they were skilled or not, the level of workmanship was so poor that it should have been an embarrassment and shameful experience for the developer. Not to speak of high-end work, it was difficult to even substantiate it as medium quality work. Nevertheless, the developer, not about to lose face, never conceded that he was incompetent; in fact, he unsuccessfully tried to remediate the problems but still, after several attempts, was unable to pass the minimum quality control requirements. Realizing the futility of his remedial efforts, he offered the client a concession off the sale price.

Larger corporations seldom are adaptable to smaller endeavors that generally require infrastructural overhaul on their part. As befits a large company, they have in place systems that are tailored to fit the needs of firms with large projects and payrolls. They are slow to change with the times, as that requires Herculean effort. They are better suited to large volume projects like core work and developer work. Occasionally, a large company will become enamored of the large price tag, or the generous price per square foot ($/SF) of a big residential project and often are successful at bullying their way in. Such enterprises I have seen yield extreme examples of folly and waste. On other occasions, larger companies' corporate clients may ask them to also build their country homes and apartments. They may take these jobs as they feel obligated to; however, they normally would not seek out such work.

Larger companies pursue like-sized projects. The projects, being large, are generally claimed and built by union help. Some union subcontractors have more skills than others and thus they can install high-quality work, but they tend to be the exception, as general contractors rightly shy away from specialized residential projects, for which their men are not trained to do. On the other hand, if a midsize to large project built by a private small company needs man power in a hurry, they will invariably be strapped for resources. Unions are never unable to find more workers, even if it means sending workers with no skills, such as the shaky hands that wave the picket signs outside "scab" buildings. Sometimes a small company goes up against a significantly larger company. Some clients feel the smaller companies will be more competitive, as they have less overhead and probably need the work more. The client will presume more leverage with the smaller company. Also there is some tacit sense of provincialism one gets when working with a small concern—that the contractors will have more direct involvement with them or will pay special personal attention to their wants and needs. This may or may not have been true at one time; however, this concept serves no purpose in today's market as there are simply too many parameters to measure besides price and quality.

There will always be a battle over the middle ground of the residential sector between smaller and larger companies, with the larger companies typically coming out ahead, at least in the beginning; however, though the larger companies win the battle, they will invariably lose the war simply because they are out of their element, that is, core work. It will take a long time for the lesson to be learned as large companies are notoriously slow to recognize problems and make corrections. Until then the market will likely continue to claim such companies as liabilities. The nature of the relationship of small and large companies regarding longevity is illustrated in the following finding:

Age and size exert especially strong influences on dissolution probabilities. In the Northeast, for example, the probability of dissolution varies from 46.2% for establishments 10 years or older to 66.9% for establishments less than 2-years old. Expected 5-year dissolution rates vary from 29% for those with $1 million or more in receipts to 72.1% for those with less than $100,000 in receipts.[13]

We will talk more about the structure of different companies and how to find your place in the market in Chap. 6.

What It Takes

As we discussed above, success in today's market should be defined by more than just assets or market share. As I have said, there are many large companies plodding along inconveniently, waiting only for evolution to take its natural course as it did for the herbivorous dinosaurs—strong survive the short run, but inability to adapt will be the long-term fate of a rogue company. However, because they only aspire to be profitable, without that consideration many such companies would have nothing to recommend themselves. This is a one-dimensional approach that in the large scheme of things renders most companies' significance negligible. Such companies are only interested in their bottom line, caring little for the welfare of the industry as a whole, save for its relationship to them. This is a malignant force in our economy and in the long run will play out in lost market share on a global basis in much the same way that the industry is becoming over reliant on immigrant workers and because there is such a dearth of American skilled construction workers.

One purpose of this book is to set parameters for a more intuitive and more modern approach to business practices and ethics in the construction industry, so as to gear the industry more toward the future, not the past. And to make the industry more like a team than a bunch of overpriced free agents looking for a big contract. For demonstration purposes, I shall create a hypothetical company that I will refer back to throughout the course of this book. This company shall be known as Modern Builders Inc.

The genesis of this company would have been concocted by a one-time carpenter/millworker who aspired to a higher station in his career path. He will have some college, but no degree. In other words, he is a pretty average specimen. The first thing he will do is establish a *raison d'etre* for his company or a purpose other than merely making money.

Finding a Niche in the Modern Marketplace

Before diving in, he needs to find his place in the market. He will query himself the following questions:

1. How big a company can he hope to initiate now, and how much growth does he aspire toward?
2. What will be his specialty?

That's really all there is to Step 1. But when you think about it, if you asked most owners the same questions, you would be amazed how unexamined their answers will be. Truth is, they may really not know, have lost site of their goals or simply function mechanically or reactively, without any forethought other than the instinct for making more money.

By establishing goals and never losing sight of them, our man will have a plan in mind. Let us say he will form a small *S* type corporation, specializing in high-end residential construction, with the average contract value of $250,000, with no job exceeding $1,000,000 (in his first year) and the aggregate of his first year's revenue no less than $2,500,000. Within his self-conceit as a high-end residential contractor he will find the foundation of his mission statement. Within his financial goals he will have established his level of comfort.

Level of Comfort

Every businessperson knows what being uncomfortable feels like. He feels uncomfortable when work is slow, when cash flow is poor, or when a job turns into a loser. However, it is the shrewd business manager who can identify and negotiate problems in flush times; when there is plenty of work, as during these periods, they believe they live a charmed life. However, when companies lose money, instead of taking preventative measures so as not to repeat themselves, they look to finance their loss or find money on another project to offset the loss. This is how they play the game of survival—dollars and cents, as opposed to good business practice and common sense. When things go wrong, the mistake commonly made is to treat the symptom and not the cause.

Simply by adding workload to a foundering enterprise, a contractor is not going to make his company more successful. He may increase revenue, but if he only adds more work he is simply compounding the problem, not eradicating it. This is a rut in which countless contractors find themselves. Their livelihood may become predicated on a "rob Peter to pay Paul" cash flow position. Even though a company has a high rate of failure, they may persevere by finding one cash cow, thus breathing new life into the company in vain, for they will endlessly repeat the process. To some, in their minds, mere perseverance and survival substantiates success.

In our case, Modern Builders Inc. is a new enterprise and has the advantage of preplanning its first year's growth (as discussed earlier) and the infrastructure needed to facilitate it. It is therefore unlikely that in the beginning it will have too much work and too few employees, or too many employees and not enough work.

Success Story?

I met a contractor whose family-run business was founded some eighty years hence. I admired photos of crude site-machinery and immigrant Depression Era workers from the company's early years, wearing old denim overalls stopping briefly for a glum photo op, lining the walls of his office. I was impressed with the fact that his company had been around so long and mistakenly assumed, based on this longevity, that it was a successful company (other than profitable, as this book defines the meaning of success). This is a common assumption made by people that if the company has staying power it must be a good company. The other assumption is that there is inherent quality in "old-school or traditional" businesses.

In truth, this particular company rested on its laurels, for its present status was dubious as the company was smallish with two or three project managers and six or seven superintendents. One of the family members served as vice president and general manager. One of the chief problems was with the company's infrastructure or lack of one. Below the project manager level there was virtually no control and no system. However, there was a good reason for this as the employee turnaround was so radical that the company had neither the time nor the incentive to develop its new hires, who typically left sometime before their first project ended. A 1-year project might burn through four different superintendents and at least one project manager.

The company posted a help-wanted advertisement for superintendents in a major newspaper for about 40 weekends out of the year, 2 years consecutively; however, apparently in that time the company neither increased its revenue nor its workforce; they were merely going through people. At the end of the day the only thing old school about this company is that their ability to conduct business never improved throughout the company's long history.

Mission Statement

Having chosen a market niche and a level of comfort it is now time to form a mission statement. The mission statement should not merely be a marketing tool; in fact, it should primarily be an in-house instrument; however, it will improve your company's public image. Considering the inscrutable and unpredictable behavior of most construction companies a mission statement is highly recommended for a new or restructured venture. If they had to form a mission statement, it would read something like: "make money, not friends," or "it's not what you know, but who you know." According to a recent survey only 17% of the sample indicated that they had a written mission statement. Of the same sample, only about 15% utilized a written operating budget.[14] With no written mission or operating budget, indeed to some degree, the majority of the residential building sector must be flying by the seat of their pants. Typically, a mission statement merely takes the form of some hackneyed motto, or simple sales pitch.

> You dream it; we build it
> Builders to the Stars
> Fine general contractors
> Interior Specialists
> High-end residential general contracting
> Residential Construction Managers
> Commissioned Private Residences

With the exception of the first two, all of the above phrases seem relatively benign; however, upon further inspection of a given company's operations, betray themselves as empty rhetoric. If you are able, abstain from using such devices.

The mission statement essentially will describe what and who the company is, what service they provide, and how they provide it. It will also describe their long-term goals. It should constantly be referred back to for compliance and to monitor the company's progress toward meeting goals.

Mission Statement of Modern Builders Inc.

1. We are builders specializing in residential high-end construction. We aspire to deliver a level of work that legitimately constitutes high quality.

2. Because we excel above our competitors, we aspire to contract our work through referrals and return business. This is evident in our work.

3. Although we strive to be competitive, we wish to engage in negotiated bids as much as possible, forgoing the competitive bid process.

4. We strive to achieve win-win outcomes. If our customers are not satisfied, we are not. We are here to serve the community.

5. We are a company built on integrity, and we will not tolerate impropriety or any other form of dishonesty.

6. We wish to improve the quality of the workforce and the way things are done by setting examples that we believe can help the industry as a whole.

7. We believe that respect is the key component of any relationship.

8. We place a priority on employee and client satisfaction, and believe happy employees will always work better and harder.

9. We hope to establish better rapport with the design industry as partners, not adversaries.

Short of a company-wide mission statement drilled into everyone's head, upper-level management must espouse the basic ideals of the mission statement and as its apostles, make it so in the marketplace. This includes design professionals, clients, and colleagues. A company whose mission statement exists in a vacuum will never manifest its vision into the marketplace. The vision must be translated into action. Merely putting up awareness posters in the workplace does not substantiate a mission statement. Some companies have reasonably sound mission statements; however, they fail, because they neglect to manifest their ideals into action.

In reality, it is apparent that most companies do not have a mission statement. It is not difficult to discern a company without a mission statement or a failed mission statement; the company seems to have no center, ethically or professionally. There seems to be no unity of purpose or perhaps not even a sense of purpose besides survival. People are moving in whatever direction they feel necessary to fit the small picture, as the big picture becomes further obfuscated.

Sources of Work

Residential construction is generally designed by architects and interior designers. Being the source of the work, these are the people who will most likely solicit bids from your company. There are numerous media marketing tools available as well, and if you have the resources, you should pursue an appropriate program. Direct marketing is not easy and the returns are small, maybe less than 1%. For example, if you send a thousand sales letters, you may be lucky to get fifty responses. Out of those fifty you may net one or two sales for a return of 0.1%. Nevertheless, even at those odds it is good to have a marketing program, if not to generate sales then at least to get your name circulated.

There are other sources of work, but to get to them entails some creativity and energy: Public information is published on all home sales as a matter of record. A database or registry will show information describing the property location and description, sales price, buyer and seller, and mortgagor. Realtors are informed of this information before it is publicly recorded and as such can be a potential source of referrals. "For sale" signs that either have a "sold" sticker applied to them, or that are removed, may indicate a new home owner who will likely need upgrades or changes to his new asset. A moving van (moving in or out) in the street may point the way to a residential project.

In apartment buildings, especially conversions, once the core work and general conversion is complete, the units will go to market; in fact, even before. These units often are sold to new owners who will then fit out the space, which typically involves an architect, drawings, and a contractor. The conversion market is supplied only insofar as such buildings become available and there is a limited supply; however, for the next 10 years, there will continue to be a substantial number of residential projects generated from these conversions. Typically, the core and shell work takes place and the general contractor moves on to the next project, paving the way for an interior contractor. Keeping abreast of conversions can help you resource future sales.

Embossed glass. This design may be embossed on simple white glass by drawing an exact outline of the size required. Placing this underneath the sheet of plate glass, take a sable pencil and paint in the background carefully with Brunswick black and turpentine, accurately tracing the lines of the design and keeping the glass rigidly free from grease. When this glass is ready to receive the acid, fix the wax around the edges and pour the dilute hydrofluoric acid quickly over the surface, allowing it to remain until the design required is sufficiently etched. Then, pour off the acid, wash the plate freely, and remove the wax. This was composed of three parts beeswax, and one part burgundy pitch, fused together and forming a soft putty, resisting any acid. *A Treatise on Architecture and Building Construction, Volume IV* (Scranton: The Colliery Engineer Co., 1899).

A lot of time and money can be spent looking for work. The thing to keep in mind is the notion that merely one or two projects generated from your efforts can make the whole endeavor worthwhile, especially for a small company. Architects are leery of contractors in general and therefore tend to be very loyal, to a fault, to those whom they already approve of; having established relationships with them. The fault is that they can be overly tenacious in maintaining their relationships with general contractors, to the extent that they will not disengage before the burnout stage—sort of like not selling falling stock shares in time to minimize losses. But if things continue to go right, a good experience can evolve into a positive long-term relationship. Such long-term relationships lend themselves well to *partnering*, an underutilized working relationship that I highly advocate.

In addition to the marketing strategies above, I believe the best long-term way to find work is by networking. Networking can also help your company in other ways.

Networking

Networking, as mentioned here, refers to the involvement a company has within a business community. Sales are not the only goal of networking. By networking, a company can generate information to the community about what they do. Equally important, networking is used to acquire information about other members of the community such as your competition and recommendations of good vendors, suppliers, and subcontractors. In other words, networking focuses on long-term perspectives and opportunities. It is not a one-time or a temporary endeavor; it should be a mainstay of your marketing program and interaction with the community you service.

You should network with as many people as possible—contractors, architects, designers, realtors, suppliers, vendors, manufacturer representatives, even people on the street or people in other sectors that might connect with construction such as banking, real estate, facility, and management. In your day-to-day activities, you probably network quite a bit without even realizing it. There are many and diverse arenas for networking at your disposal. Some examples:

- Conferences and trade shows
- Showrooms and supplier spaces
- Bidder's walk-throughs
- Visiting public work sites, and private sites on request
- Chance meetings

Speaking with people who aren't the source of work can be an excellent indirect way to network, and to find work opportunities. Workmen, suppliers, drivers, doormen, and sales representatives almost all know something that can be useful to you. Always have your eyes and ears open for networking opportunities.

In networking, you will want to spend time talking up and referring members of your network to other interested parties in the hope that another node on the network is connected. Hopefully, your peers in the network are doing the same for you. The thing to keep in mind is: be selective. Just as you choose your friends carefully, choose your network partners carefully. You don't want to recommend a company whose acumen and performance you are not sure of; at least without a caveat. By the same token, take contractor referrals with a grain of salt; there are more credentials required to demonstrate competence than merely being recommended by someone.

Passive networking

Recommending vendors is a good way to network; however, if you aren't 100% sure of them, don't recommend them without the proper limitation(s):

> I saw a tin knocker on a project, he was really good but a bit slow. I can give you his number.

You make it clear what your caveat is with this referral and that your endorsement is predicated on summary information. You only want to make such a recommendation when asked. It is not appropriate to make an unsolicited recommendation of someone whom you don't wholly endorse. Why would anyone go out of their way to do that? Understand that no referral is going to be 100% fail-safe but do not let this be a hindrance to recommending others.

Active networking

> The installers were great, their detailer was sharp and the work went in on time. You should definitely talk to . . .

You are giving two thumbs-up rating because you have no reservations about this company. You don't fear a callback with a complaint about them. This is the sort of advice you would like others to give about your company. Word will surely get back to them that you were extolling their virtues, and they will appreciate and reciprocate the gesture.

Keep your networking information up-to-date by asking around how "so and so" is getting on, especially if you are referring them or solicit bids from them. Recently, I knew of a struggling millworking shop. They were fairly large and set up for production. The residential project I met them on was a contract of about $.5 million, a project they likely took just for cash flow. Having good machinery and some talented old school installers, they executed the project fairly well and I was prone to refer them for certain projects. As it turned out, 1 year after the end of this project, I saw a posting for a bankruptcy auction of their assets. Wasn't it a good thing I kept my eyes and ears open? Imagine what would have happened if I had continued to recommend them?

Ethics

The following is a discussion on the subject of ethics which some may feel has no place in a book on construction; however, I beg to differ, and assert that a firm understanding of some of the simpler concepts of ethics should be a prerequisite to becoming a successful person or businessperson. The industry suffers from a well-deserved tarnished image. One hears countless stories of the ineptitude, deceitfulness, greed, and general malevolence, to the extent that many companies have to live down this reputation before they even earn it whether it is deserved or not. Positive mission statements and codes of ethics are so loosely defined or jaundiced that an industrywide reassessment is sorely needed.

Referring back to the mission statement above, you will see that I place a high value on respect, honesty, and integrity. These priorities are not limited to the residential construction industry. If you lead a reasonably principled and ethical existence, it should not be too much of a stretch to incorporate these qualities into your professional behavior and attitude. You will constantly be challenged on this set of ethics and will be treated by others accordingly.

Respect

You should enter into any business relationship with as much expectation of respecting your peers as possible. If you do not, you are already handicapping yourself and setting the scene for future problems. If you expect not to respect someone, you will not. Once a person realizes you do not respect him, the road becomes all uphill from there to get back into their good graces, should you wish to. Some people are extremely sensitive about how they are treated and consider even small breaches of respect as major affronts, for which they will often retaliate or bear a grudge. If people have a choice as to whom they work with, they will elect not to work with people who are disrespectful toward them. Respect is a prerequisite to liking someone, though not a prerequisite to success can certainly go a long way. If your client and members of your job team dislike you, your work will become extremely difficult, as the bar will be set higher. Your goal should be to maximize positive relationships, and minimize negative ones.

Respect should not be limited to your benefactors, but applies to your colleagues, peers, and especially your subcontractors and vendors, and your employees, for these are the lifeblood of your production system. Judging from what I see and from talking to hundreds of laborers and mechanics, I get the overall impression that disrespect, especially from superiors, is rampant. It seems as if the only notion of respect is that which is feigned by owners and upper management toward the client or architect. This is an extremely unhealthy condition, and must be eradicated for the good of the industry. You should advocate and insist on a respectful environment on all your projects, among all team members.

Honesty

We always think of financial propriety when we think of honesty, especially in construction. However, honesty must encompass all of your professional behavior. There is no exigent need here to describe the nature of being honest, except to point out that people are quick to rationalize it by qualifying some as being more honest than others, which is merely the inverse of saying that some are more deceitful than others, either way, an equivocation. The fact of the matter is: either you're honest, or you are not.

Disrespect is no more prevalent in the construction industry than in others and it will have diverse effects. As an assimilated social trait and variably accepted quirk of human nature it will also be tolerated; however, consider dishonesty to be a deal breaker, because in business relationships it invariably has financial implications. However, it can be manifested otherwise, but it should be tolerated no more than impropriety. Needless to say, honesty is mandatory for your business interactions. To a lesser degree, you will want others to be honest, even though you expect the opposite; that is human nature. Surprisingly, contractors regard honesty and integrity as "the (*second*) most important factor to the success of a business."[15]

Just like respect, honesty and trust are distinctions of behavior that you want to emphasize within your company. It will lay the foundation for healthy relationships and, more importantly, give representatives of your company the positive image that you wish to project to your clients. This is always an uphill battle, as contractors typically must overcome society's stereotypes of them as being dishonest.

Integrity

Like honesty, integrity is also becoming a subjective term. Many contractors would be hard put to even define integrity. It would appear that some have never even entertained the prospect. Integrity, just like respect, cannot be feigned, and a lack of it will be readily detected. Either you have it, or you don't. If you don't, consider getting another to act in your place as your company's public representative until such time as you can train yourself accordingly to be presentable. Meantime, you can be humble and say, "take me as I am," but under no circumstances do you want to pretend you're something you're not. Yet that is precisely what so many people do only to generate false perceptions. Then there are those well-meaning individuals who do have integrity, yet because they have difficulty conveying it, are misunderstood.

In the construction industry, there is a tacit presumption that most of its constituents to varying degrees are lacking in integrity, by dint of sheer association with the industry: for example, "They're construction guys—what do you expect?" Integrity is an abstract concept, but one that is readily assessed in peoples' behavior and attitude. The measure of integrity is based on a qualification of the following attributes:

- Honesty
- Respect
- Tolerance
- Discipline
- Fortitude
- Fairness
- Clarity
- Prudence
- Conviction

The above are attributes of character that will generally be noticed, and gain the respect of others. Conversely, a shortfall in them will be assessed accordingly.

Integrity is unlike honesty in that you may be lacking in some component of integrity, and still have some integrity. For instance, you may not always communicate well and you may be thought of as sheepish or calculating. Or perhaps you have to use rigid disciplinary methods to reel in a misbehaving employee, which behavior is later construed as overly strict. While these may or may not be true assessments, neither behavior will necessarily vanquish all one's integrity, whereas the notion of dishonesty tends to be static and immutable; you can't have "some" honesty. Dishonesty is a deal breaker. The local construction industry is a small world, even in large cities. Bad eggs are subject to wholesale criticism and scrutiny. However, many operators don't seem to care about or consider the consequences of their actions.

Trust

One of the most elemental and problematic factors of any relationship is trust. Greed and narcissism are the driving forces of untrustworthiness—we expect others to be out only for themselves. Trust is especially elusive in business relationships because money is involved. The construction industry suffers from a well-publicized tarnished past of misdeeds and corruption that contractors are forever trying to live down—one is *expected* to be untrustworthy. Owners and architects are on their guard for signals from their contractors that would betray such attitudes. A developer or other constant builder can get burned once or twice and perhaps find a way to recover, but a one-time builder such as a homeowner is more at risk; thus he will take fewer chances—keep his contractor on a short leash. If the project has a lot of money at stake—for example, a high-end gut renovation, there is much more opportunity for a client to get overcharged or not get his money's worth. The high price tags of the biggest projects can induce contractors to engage in illegal and unethical practices such as bid rigging and kickbacks. Adding to the possibility of underperformance by the contractor, clients are indeed an anxious hypersensitive lot.

The trust factor goes down the line and affects all relationships. The relationship of subcontractor to contractor is a vital one, as good subcontractors are hard to find. Like wise, trustworthy general contractors are hard to come by for aspiring subcontractors. They are fond of retelling the exploits of inefficient and unethical general contractors whom they no longer work for. Either they don't want to get burned (again), don't want to be associated with them, or both. Thus, distrust can manifest itself in any number of ways on a project. Distrust precludes positive working relationships, and translates into poorly done works and deeds. To be ignorant of this dilemma is to increase the likelihood for failure.

Teamwork

Finally, the skill which *should* most determine your level of success in residential construction is your ability to work with others. I use the word should, because many companies achieve success with the bare minimum of social skills required for teamwork. Historically, the image of the construction industry doesn't lend itself to this idea—the stereotypical construction person may be presumed as uneducated, déclassé, gruff, or any other unbecoming aspect by his assumed superiors and benefactors. There seems to be little common ground for clients and contractors to rub elbows, and architects and contractors seemingly will always be at odds. As a response, some contractors imagine themselves as above the fray, or as *prima donnas*. This is an affectation put on to impress clients and will generally be regarded with skepticism.

Any company that emphasizes healthy working relationships will have a leg up on the competition. Partnering with, rather than working for or against, the design team is one long-term goal of companies that have a future. At your own company, it is unlikely that any one individual will possess the skills needed to relate to everyone, but it is impractical that any one person should be the nexus of all interaction. There are many different relationships between job team members that require different people using various people skills. They are in order of importance:

- Clients
- Architects
- Employees
- General public
- Subcontractors
- Vendors and manufacturer's representatives

Clients

Client-contractor relationships are a special consideration in residential construction for a number of reasons:

The project is typically the client's personal or living space. He will be much more sensitive to how the project is handled as opposed to say a real estate developer. Often being hypersensitive, there tend to be many more conflicts on residential projects. We will go into more detail regarding the nature of such conflicts, and how to avoid them in Chap. 8.

Residential projects often require a lot of hand-holding and person-to-person interactions between the contractor and client. Typically, the relationship is a teacher (contractor) to pupil (client) relationship, where the client is a little leery of the advice he is given considering conflicts of interest. However, the client must be educated in order to understand the mechanics of the operation, and to gain answers to his questions. This understanding will improve immeasurably once a healthy level of trust is established. Then there are those clients who have been through the process before and know what they want. They may insist on having as much control as they deem necessary. Sometimes, such a client can be a nuisance, while other times, it can be a relief to do business with someone who understands what they are buying. In between lies the grey area of the client who thinks he knows all the angles, but really doesn't. Nevertheless, he wants control. This sort of character can make life exceedingly difficult for a contractor and his team.

Because you are working in someone's home your company's relationship with the client may become personal. Understanding this and taking it into consideration can be a great advantage to your relationship with the client on the whole, for there will be countless opportunities to service the client, making him happy without great expenditure. One of the most sensitive issues for clients regarding their homes is the level of cleanliness and hygiene maintained on the work site. To the men, the work site may be regarded as merely a dirty sweat lodge like any other construction site, but to the client, it will always be home. If he sees unkempt areas or senses an air of apathy to his concept of hominess he may take offense—personally. Keep this well in mind. Appoint someone to maintain the level of cleanliness and organization on the site. Be extra aware to comments made by the client regarding these issues; you will reap a great return for a relatively small investment. Your attitude says to them: "I want you to be happy and to let me know if you are unhappy." In other words it means you care. It is difficult to be successful on a project when your client believes you don't care about him or the job, especially if he is right. Therefore, take extra pains to show empathy and a caring attitude; be conscientious.

Optimally, you want to have a person who relates well to the client on all of your projects, even if you have to create a job title just for this purpose. If a client feels he has no one else he can talk to he will always defer to his advocate—the architect, when you would prefer him to come to you directly. However, this is the customary relationship, because so few contractors relate to, or have positive relationships with their clients. In construction management projects particularly, it is critical that the contractor-client relationship is a positive, trusting one, because of the high degree of interaction that they will have together, and the leap of faith the client must take based on the contractor is sometimes blind trust. In this special contractual relationship, the construction manager is, in fact by definition, the client's advocate. We shall discuss the role of the construction manager and client psychology further, in Chap. 8.

Architects and Interior Designers

The traditional relationship between architects and contractors has long been regarded by many as being adversarial in nature.[16] Though both may no longer understand how or why this is so, it is an encumbrance on countless projects that inhibits the cooperation necessary to work together in a civil fashion. Some architects will be reluctant to back down from a standoffish attitude, which can make for a rough ride. Frequent dissatisfactions with builders in their past have made them gun-shy. This was not always the case. Architects really didn't become involved with home building until about the 1850s. Owners and builders got along just fine without them. Some of the perceived shortcomings of these early architects are still sensed by today's builders.

> Architecture was not practiced as a business but was considered an art, and it was carried out by gentlemen, not by journeymen, and more often than not by skilled but untrained amateurs—dilettantes.

Even some of today's trained architects and especially interior designers, bear a striking resemblance to the nineteenth century dilettante.

> Houses were built one at a time, and since the architect was not a contractor, he was not in a position to introduce substantive innovation to the building process.

There were no established precedents or standards for architects to follow— every project was one-off, and the builder was calling the shots as he was the expert. Even with the standards at architect's disposal, contractors will always be at odds with architects who imply or detail means and methods to their designs—tell the contractor how to do his job.

> Unlike the cabinetmaker who controlled all aspects of production, from building to marketing, the architect was primarily a draftsman who prepared drawings for work carried out by others.

This reductive view of an architect's purpose is that they are merely draftsmen, that they have no place in the building process, they are forever trying to live down, and are frequently met with resentment should they voice their opinion regarding building means and methods.

> As a result he developed theoretical knowledge that was based not on construction, but on a study of history and historical precedents. In any case, architects were then, as they are now, interested more in the appearance of buildings than in their functioning. They were not prepared, by either training or inclination, to involve themselves in such mechanical matters as plumbing and heating.[17]

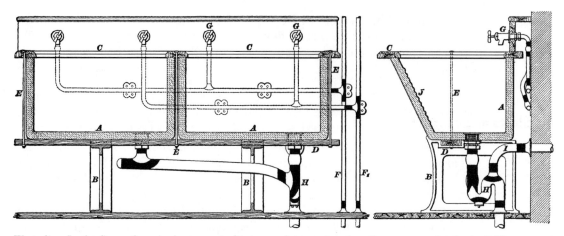

Waste line. In the figure there is shown a set of two porcelain or glazed earthenware wash tubs A, A. They are set upon two cast-iron stands B. An ash frame C is bolted to a hardwood strip D by long bolts E. Branches are taken from the hot and cold lead water pipes F, F, to supply the tub cocks G. One of the tubs has part of its inner surface corrugated as at J. This is often used as a scrub board.

A Treatise on Architecture and Building Construction, Volume IV (Scranton, The Colliery Engineer Co., 1899)

And still today, degree wielding architects seem to be taught little in the way of building practicum, which they regard as the stuff of engineering, of which few architects pay attention to. Nevertheless, they continue to detail engineering work for which they are seldom qualified or licensed to do. The tacit understanding of an architect is that in order to master his craft he should, in fact, be literate in building means and methods. Without such knowledge there is a tendency for him to be perceived as the mid-nineteenth century artsy sideman.

Architects in the residential sector are in the minority. Despite the growth of expenditures in the residential sector only 5% of architectural firm revenue is from the design of single-family residences, and only 11% of these billings were from private individuals[18] who largely comprise residential construction revenue. It is interesting that such a small group of architectural firms can generate such considerable consumer spending figures (see Foreword).

Having positive relationships with the project architect and architects in general is a critical requirement for the longevity of your company, for architects and designers are invariably the source of most of your work. Once a general contractor gets in an architect's good graces, the architect will likely become very loyal to him because dependable contractors are rare. The architect will offer him his best work and negotiate contracts whenever possible. You should hope to build a repertoire of architects with whom you have established working relationships, for repeat work and referrals. Not everyone subscribes to this dictum, and resultantly, architect/contractor relationships can be extremely strained, especially when there is no incentive to get along, which there often is not—self-interest being the inhibition. Because of a predisposition to adversity the majority of architect/contractor relationships result in divorce after the first project.

Generally, your first experience with an architect will be on a project that you were awarded by either referral, or as competitive bidder. Whatever the case, there will be a feeling out phase and subsequently a relationship that will continue for at least the remainder of the project. For architects whom you would like to get repeat work from, you will make extra efforts to satisfy. For others, you may just want to make it through the project. Finally, there will be architects whom you may find no common ground with, such that you may want to terminate a contract. Your relationship with the architect on a project will tend to vacillate. In the beginning of a project most architects seem reserved, or reluctant to be optimistic. An architect's level of contentment is relative to how much he is getting his way; some of which is reasonable—build the project in a timely and workmanlike manner, and some unreasonable—engage design changes and extra work without the proper protocols. Apart from that, they tend to be malcontents, ultimately dissatisfied and discontent with the industry as a whole. This is the chip which they carry on their shoulder. The formation of this distinction isn't always under your control, but there are things you can do to drive their perceptions.

It helps to understand your architect's position in relation to you and the client before you begin to negotiate or become familiar. Typically, the architect is the client's agent and in that capacity he might be conflicted in terms of behaving graciously toward someone who he is expected by the client to control, so don't be surprised if he doesn't appear too chummy in your early interactions with him and especially in subsequent negotiating.

Care should be taken in your dealings with your architect, especially when the client is present, such as at job meetings as they often are. At such times, both contractor and architect, whether consciously or not, may engage in garnering the client's favor, often at the expense of the other team member. For instance, it is common for an architect and a contractor to argue over whether or not a change order is legitimate, with the expected outcome likely to leave one of the parties blameful of negligence. Such discussions can quickly become malevolent. The discussion may be necessary, but it need not take place before the client, unless it is mutually irresolvable—airing out dirty laundry, as it were. Unpleasant discussions should be undertaken with discretion. You should endeavor to have any change order approved by the project architect before it is presented to the client because there are few architects who will approve a change order upon first sight. Otherwise, you run the risk of a face-losing confrontation in front of the client. There will be revisions. If there is disagreement, it should be handled in private. Once a change order is negotiated, it can then be presented to the client by the architect. Only as a last resort should the client sit in judgment of the validity and accountability of a change order; this is not his bailiwick. Besides, more often than not, he will side with his architect who is programmed to represent his best interests, even if it means being wrong-headed.

In short, you want to stay on good terms with the architect or designer; whether you like him or not, or whether or not you desire future work from him.

Do what you can to keep him happy without compromising your own interests. Find out what his likes and dislikes are and use this information to your advantage. You will find many architects aren't receptive or simply aren't interested in nurturing a relationship with you. This is typical and no cause for alarm. A last word, one can't underestimate the advantage of being well liked by the architect. This mere condition can set the stage for future interactions and negotiations to your benefit. A lot of it has to do with luck and chemistry, but it can't hurt to try.

A close relative of the architect, but certainly not a replacement for him, is the interior designer. It is very common for an interior designer to detail a project, using an architect of record in order to file the job. This is often done so to keep the design budget to a minimum as licensed architects generally charge more than their lessers. Except for a few seasoned firms, these projects invariably betray the fact that the architect of record did not or will not:

a. Detail the architectural components of the work

b. Detail the MEPs (often done without an engineer)

c. Monitor the construction of the work

d. Manage quality control and code issues

e. Administrate the contract in a general sense

Nevertheless, they continue to prosper and are a fact of life for the building industry. This arrangement is an area of concern for general contractors because:

- Inferior design documents will translate to losses of time and money.
- A nonlicensed detailer can put the builder and owner at risk.
- Interior designers who detail architectural components typically do not have an architect's degree, license, or expertise, thus doing the industry, architects especially, a disservice by publishing inferior design documentation.

Therefore, builders must take the necessary precautions when constructing projects with only an architect of record. If interior designers actually did involve the architect of record in the design and construction process, perhaps there would be less incidence of project failure. Because design fees are so competitive, the architect of record is summoned only as a last resort. Naturally, if clients didn't skimp on design budgets, they would have an architect design the project, leaving the designer to his business of aesthetics.

Employees

Unless you are a one-man show, or principle in a partnership, you will have employees. Depending on how much construction you do, and how much management you staff, you will have the necessary complement of both workmen and middle managers. Depending on your day-to-day involvement in the company your interactions with your employees will be variable. For small and start-up companies, company owners spend a fair amount of time with all their employees and need to learn to "speak their language," assuming they don't already.

To them, you will always be *Boss*. Being boss you have special responsibilities toward them that are unique to any of their colleagues. Your relationship with them will generally be patriarchal, as you are their master, guide, and benefactor. Historically, this relationship is perceived as one-sided, and many stereotypes have emanated from that observation. Unfortunately, this set of circumstances is more or less the standard employee/employer relationship in our society, and is inbred into our collective consciousness. These dynamics pose a special problem in terms of workplace interrelations, an idiosyncrasy that is taken for granted as being immutable, and generates unhappiness among the workers.

That is a shame, for think how much more efficient is a person who is happy in his work and gets on with his employer. This being said, you should endeavor to attain employee satisfaction as part of your mission statement. This means more than your relation to your employees; it also includes your workers' relationships with one another, and their superiors. You should also gain an understanding as to why employees may have high absentee and turnover rates. A study[19] (Table 1.4) shows that "relationship with (the) boss" is the chief motivation for leaving a company. Unsafe working conditions, followed by excessive rework, were to blame for high absentee rate. Therefore, no one is in a better position to change things than the owner, and his managers. Some of the reasons for turnover are controllable while some are not. The results of a survey of worker motivators and demotivators (Table 1.5) aptly points in the direction of some of the strategies that a company can adopt to keep their people happy. Such a program should be a mainstay of any decent workplace. Circulating this survey in questionnaire form to your employees will also be a valuable exercise.

TABLE 1.4   Reasons for Turnover

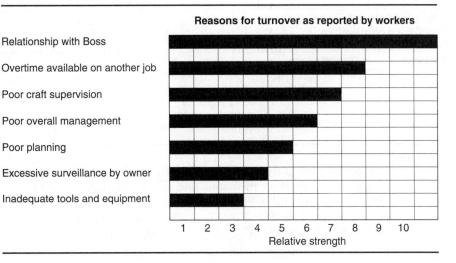

TABLE 1.5 Motivators and Demotivators

Survey results of motivators on twelve construction projects												
	Projects											
Motivators	A	B	C	D	E	F	G	H	I	J	K	L
Good craft relations			1*			2	2		1	1		
Good orientation program	3	3	1		1	1	1	2				2
Good safety program		1*	1	1*	2*	3		2*	2			
Work itself	2		2	2	2		3					2
Overtime					3		3					
Pay			2	1	1	2	2	2	2		2	2
Recognition				1*	1*							
Goals defined				1	1	1		1				
Open house & project tour	2	1		2								
Well-planned project						2*	2*	1*				
Suggestions solicited			1*		1*	1		2*	1			
Survey results of demotivators on twelve construction projects												
	Projects											
Demotivators	A	B	C	D	E	F	G	H	I	J	K	L
Disrespectful treatment		3	3	2		1			3	3		2
Little accomplishment			1		2					2		
Material availability	2	2	2		3	1	1	2	1	2	1	2
Tool availability	2	1	2		2			1	1	1	1	2
Redoing work	1	1	1	1	1				1	1	2	2
Crew discontinuity	1		2		1		2					2
Project confusion	1	1	1	1	1	1	1	1	1	1	1	1
Lack of recognition	2	2		1*	1*		1	1		1		
Productivity urged, but no one cares	1	1	1							2		2
Ineffective utilization of skills	1	1					2	1		2		
Incompetent personnel	1	1	1	1	1		1	1	2	2	2	2
Lack of cooperation among crafts	1		1*					1			3	3
Overcrowding		1			1							
Poor inspection programs		1		1					1	1		
Communications breakdown	1	1	1	1	1	1		2	2	2	2	2
Unsafe conditions	1	1*		1*	2*		2	1*		2		2
Lack of participation in decision making	1	1	2*	1	1*			1				

Key 1 Somewhat important
2 Major importance
3 Extremely important
* Motivator and demotivator

You will invariably be called on to referee disagreements between employees, they will tell you their problems and ask you for raises. And you will act accordingly in your role as company patriarch. If you or another in your place does not serve this function, the company is like a ship full of mercenaries without a captain; a squadron without a commanding officer, and will eventually founder. Your ability to negotiate your way through difficult situations can be a show of pluck and mettle—something many workers respect in their boss. Sadly, few small companies take time to consider their employees interests, probably because in large part they don't care about them, and don't believe morale management to be a good investment of their time. If they make waves, they'll likely simply be laid-off.

Workers Today and the Work Ethic

The art of working with one's hands has been lost in modern times; some will applaud recognition of this notion as they embrace technological advances that lead to the replacement of human creations. Most advocates of advancement in manufacturing technology are those who stand to gain the most from them— business owners. Some workers surely don't approve, as technology results in lost jobs for them. Other workers are nostalgic for the days when most of their work was hand-done. Clearly, the workplace of 50 years ago bears little resemblance to today's workplace; the men are still the same, but now the tools they use do much of the work they used to do by hand, and much product that used to be handmade is fabricated in factories and then sent to the site. We now know that such developments increase worker's rate of production,[20] which is good for the owners, but is it good for the men? I doubt it. I believe there is a dehumanizing effect, and devaluation of worker's abilities within the notion of replacing them with machines. An unskilled worker can now use a machine to do work that otherwise might require a highly skilled tradesman. Few workers will appreciate how well someone can use a machine, but they will always celebrate good old-fashioned hand workmanship, which ironically they have more control over. I believe that the creeping modernization of much of the production aspect of the construction industry creates an underlying melancholy in worker's attitudes toward their occupation. This notion was anticipated as far back as the nineteenth century, and is continually revisited in the present day. Even in the predigital twentieth century a dim prognosis was entertained:

> It (the book) proposes that new tools and technologies cause social changes; that they shift ways of production, possessions, wealth and power; yet though the inevitable logic of new technologies, offering new advantages for labor saving and profit making, is willingly accepted on pragmatic intellectual terms, it is stubbornly opposed in the emotional sphere where man clings to obsolete standards and empty conventions of the past, unapproachable by logical argument, and often against his best interests.[21]

The implication being that technological advancement will run roughshod over any human emotional response, which it indeed has. This statement also alludes to the senseless nostalgia some people hold for any of the "old ways" a reactionary sentiment antithetical to any sort of progress. Thus, any reference to the old ways of doing things is classified as nostalgic, and not relevant to the corporate ethic that prioritizes machines over men. Accordingly, it would follow that many workers cannot be effective and happy at the same time. The choice has been made for them.

As I have said, people happy in their work turn out a better product. That sounds simplistic, but it is a concept that has been complicated by years of change in people's attitudes and work ethics. In general, few people enjoy doing work at all, especially work they dislike; they either associate work with the sensation of pain, or equate work as antithetical to pleasure. This is an elementary Freudian observation; however, its significance must not be underestimated. What it denotes is that an individual's avoidance of displeasure must be overcome in order for him to become a productive worker; otherwise, he will do as little as possible. Think of the saying "better a bad day of fishing than a good day's work" and you will begin to understand man's natural sedentary leanings. While that is no great epiphany, it begs the question: What are the factors that caused and are perpetuating what Freud might say is an infantile response to life's obligations? Before you answer that, you must put the question into context. How is this relevant to present conditions in the American labor market in particular? The answer lies within our sociopolitical landscape. It must first be understood that conditions have changed drastically over the past 50 years, and will continue to change. Therefore, it will be helpful to compare present day conditions with those of the past.

Today's native workers begrudgingly slog through their quotidian as if they were doing someone a favor. You can see it in their eyes and mannerisms. They work slowly, take as many breaks as possible, and gripe and complain constantly. Their level of skill and quality is invariably lower than it needs to be, and they likely do not care about what they produce, only that they earn a day's pay. Is this a work ethic imported by immigrant labor as well? Often it is not; only an individual may be compelled to adopt poor work ethics just to fit in. For example, a hardworking youngster in the union will be discouraged by work rules and other workers against putting in an "honest day's work"[22] oxymoronic and antithetical terms for organized labor. Production rates are strictly enforced within organized labor; overachievers are discouraged, perceived as making others look bad, and instill the apprehension that owners will take notice of their efforts and wonder why everyone doesn't put out the same. This ethic doesn't lend itself to improving rates of production in any industry. On the other hand, union workers tend to be better trained than their private sector counterparts; they simply may not work if they don't have the skills. However, union schools don't really focus on the high-end residential sector, as there is not a great union presence or constituency there, but should a private company become large enough, land a huge commission, or work in one of *their* buildings or areas, the union will start paying attention and will likely present a contract to the builder. In other words, residential contractors can have their piece so long as it doesn't get too big. Otherwise, the union wants to stick their beak in.

I like to compare today's average worker and old-school practitioners to the movie extras of old Hollywood to modern Hollywood. Take a close look at the actors in the background of an old black and white movie; they don't just stand around looking tacky; they act their part to the letter no matter how insignificant their role is. They may or may not have had training, but it's hard to tell.

It looks like they were trained. They are legitimate supporting actors. In today's movies, extras are merely used as motif to fill up the scenery. This means that they aren't really supporting actors, just eye-candy. They have no formal training. Over time, the quality of performance by these extras began to flag. Directors realized this, and soon began creating graphic backdrops of peopled landscapes, which evidently did not cause an outcry for the reestablishment of live extras. In today's movies, these one-dimensional landscapes are being replaced by digital effigies. It's almost surprising that the Screen Actors Guild has not picketed movie sets with an overabundance of vector trash. It's disheartening to see this, and makes one nostalgic for the old days. The residential construction business seems to have taken a cue from the same playbook. In the old days, whether you were union trained or not, you needed to be skilled in order to become a tradesman who could put out, and you were held accountable for your work. You couldn't "skate" like you can today; people would notice right away. Nowadays, contractors are lucky to find one or two mechanics with a decent set of skills on the same project. They will do most of the brain work and the rest of the crew will perform the mindless grunt work. These crews, who should be skilled, often are not, and are a considerable drain on productivity as they frequently don't have the requisite skills. Why can't they simply perform the role they have advertised as being qualified to do?

You might say this is an unqualified insinuation; that there are no statistics to support this theory. However, if you take a look behind the walls during the demolition phase of a project you can get a pretty good idea of the workmanship on the preexisting installation. Tear-out of work installed in the last 50 years will evidence that quality steadily deteriorated over that time. Recent tear-outs show that much work done in the past decade is utterly inferior to installations beginning in the postwar period. We judge the acumen of a mechanic by his works. There is no place to hide from the trained eye. If managers and supervisors knew what things to look for, and actually looked, perhaps quality control wouldn't be such an epidemic hazard, and we wouldn't feel so nostalgic when work is done correctly.

Another factor affecting residential construction is the nature of high-end construction budgets. The market trend nowadays is cost-driven to the point where there are not enough resources to pay for the exclusive level of talent necessary to do the work. The demand side of the market is mostly to blame for this because if high-end projects were adequately funded more contractors would be motivated to produce at a higher level of quality. There is a high rate of denial of this fact as workers who are not highly skilled are often put in the position of doing work they are not qualified to do. The problem is that they often are passed off as having superior skills or skills far above their actual competency. This is a borderline fraudulent business practice. The contractors in question will invariably insist that they are up to the task, and as a defense, may criticize real talent (the higher bidder) as *prima donnas*, merely because their skill level vastly eclipses their own. They will say they can do the job as well as anyone, and for less money.

Why are there so few skilled workers around? There are a number of reasons economists and sociologists point to, but their findings require further interpretation. For example, to generate a given number of skilled workers today, you might require 30% more candidates than you would have a century ago. A further increase in worker shortage will be exacerbated by the disproportionate number of "baby boomer" generation workers, who will be next to age-out of the industry. Advances in manufacturing and production in the last century have resulted in some job loss in the industry, as machines are taking the place of people. In 1900, about 38% of the labor force worked on farms. Today, the number stands at 3%; by and large, fewer people work with their hands today. This trend will continue for as long as technology progresses; however, the rate of the trend over the past 20 years has been exceptional, thanks to the development of computer science. Even though the overall labor force of the United States increased sixfold in the last century, the component of the labor force in goods producing industries (including construction) slowed from 31% to 19%. A majority of these workers entered service industries leading to an increase from 31% in 1900 to 78% in 1999. The last major wave of immigration to the United States, about ten million people, was between 1990 and 2000; however, the post World War II housing boom brought the last substantial group of skilled construction workers. Many who came were skilled craftsmen, and plied their trade to the postwar building boom housing shortage. They typically passed on their skills to their children, baby boomers who carried forth, but many of whom are now aging out of the industry.

Had mid-twentieth century immigration continued at the rate of eight to ten million every 10 years, as it did before 1920, many more skilled workers would have entered the labor force between 1929 and 1965. Due to quotas established by the National Origin Act of 1929, between 1930 and 1940 immigration dropped to less than 100,000 per year. Today's immigrant workforce is a diminutive subset of this last influx of skilled and semiskilled labor. The economic and social factors in force now are very different than they were in the postwar period. Life, in general, is much more complicated, especially for young adults entering the workforce. Young folks today have little stomach for manual labor, or work in general; they would much rather watch television all day or play computer games. Distractions are everywhere. This ethic was borne, and is perpetuated by pandering big media and manufacturers who stand to gain the most from such distractions. These changes have disposed this new generation to different ambitions, and left a hole in the manual labor workforce. In 1900, child labor, 10 to 15 years old, comprised 6% of the labor force,[23] most of them because they had to help their families survive. Of course, child labor is outlawed today, and with good reason. On the downside, young people today have no idea of what an honest day's work feels like; they have no desire whatsoever to work with their hands.

This vacuum in the workforce is again being filled by immigrants, who leave their native country for higher wages in the United States; however, they do not appear to have the level of skill that their predecessors—the postwar immigrants—brought with them; call it Old World workmanship, if you will. Today, immigrants make up 19.9%[24] of the total national construction workforce. They are concentrated in urban areas; for example, immigrants comprise 58% of New York City's workforce.[25] What does seem painfully apparent is the difference in their general attitude toward work, compared to Americans. Instead of viewing a job as a right, or entitlement, they perceive it as a privilege or at least an opportunity. I have observed immigrants' work habits next to their host's for 24 years, and I denote a pronounced gap in the work ethic between the two. Evidently, people are used to working much harder, and at the same time getting paid less in other countries. If the visitors are not successful, they may have to return home. U.S. citizens can either find new work, or apply to an entitlement program. The exceptions are workers coming from jobs in Communist bloc countries, which paid poorly, and did not require them to work very hard.

The American Dream used to be a good-paying job, and then ownership of a home. After World War II, there still seemed to be some nationalistic pride evident in the expansion of a postwar America. Nowadays, we suffer from a collective narcissism that asserts well-being for the masses, but really only prioritizes the welfare of certain individuals and big businesses. This failing of democracy was foretold by de Tocqueville over 150 years ago: "In democratic societies, each citizen is habitually busy with the contemplation of a very petty object, which is himself." The modern ethic is: first "win the lottery, and then buy the house." Once achieved, a life's work is complete or one is successful. The American icon of achievement is the grinning cretin sipping a pina colada on a raft in his oversized swimming pool in the backyard of his mansion. The proliferation of poor work ethics is affecting new arrivals as well. Over the past 15 years or so the motivation of immigrant labor seems to be on the wane and on an analog with their new sponsors—the Americans. This sentiment is encouraged by State and Municipal governments who not only sponsor such lotteries but also market them hyperaggressively. Lotteries are a considerable source of revenue for the government, but are a debilitating factor on working-class constituent's incomes and work ethics. Thus, the lotteries are a poor return on investment. If there must be lotteries, why not offer decent paying jobs as the prizes, or at least training programs.

Outsourcing is also commonplace in many business sectors, and is beginning to take hold in the construction industry. It began when cheap overseas manufacturing costs lured companies away from the superior, but more expensive workforce. The market is now flooded with poor quality product made by cheap labor, using inferior materials, and substandard production machinery. Our government responds with sanctions, tariffs, and subsidies to prop up failing industries. With cheaper labor outside the United States as an incentive, the decision to outsource is a no-brainer for shrewd entrepreneurs; however, in the long term, our skilled workforce will become less globally relevant. Until the U.S. economy can be more competitive in the manufacturing sector, business will continue to shift overseas.

Substandard work ethics are to blame for many poorly executed projects, but the blame is not limited to the workmen. If managers have a poor attitude, or simply aren't effective, their men will also be rendered insignificant; however ineffective, the men don't necessarily have poor work ethics. With fewer managers having hands-on experience, the industry is as prone as it ever was to dysfunction. Project managers are often required to have a college education, sometimes even a civil engineering degree. While the latter is a superfluous appendage in residential work, education, or lack of it, has vast implications. There are many project managers who lack the proper education to meet the requirements that their job description dictates. Some of them are to blame for their own ignorance, while the industry, which invests precious little in education, and the degeneration of the K-12 and college curriculums, are mostly to blame for producing uneducated managers. Many of such managers command six-figure salaries, yet can't use a computer, write a cohesive memo, or do simple geometry or algebra.

Subcontractors and Subcontracts

Relationships with subcontractors and suppliers are less complicated than others. Basically, the success of your relationship will be measured on how well you get along, how well they work for you, and how timely you pay them. Though relationships with subcontractors are simpler than others, they are nonetheless equally prone to dysfunction. For the residential sector, qualified subcontractors are becoming scarce. Subcontractors, like general contractors, are also affected by the underskilled laborforce. The result is that fewer and fewer qualified subcontractors are qualified to work in the residential market. Thus, qualified subcontractors are in high demand, and typically charge a considerable premium for their work, even if it is simple work.

Subcontractors are as important, if not more important, as your employees, for they also will be a key factor in determining the integrity of your end product. Your code of ethics should also apply to them, as they, albeit indirectly, represent your company. This concept will be difficult to enforce. As the subcontractor's men don't work for you directly, they won't feel obliged to observe certain rules such as playing loud music, smoking, cursing, or even drinking. There will be only so much your field people can do to control their behavior. In the event that there is a problem with one of your subcontractor's men, you should direct your complaint to the person's immediate superior, whenever possible.

Realizing the value of a worthy subcontractor or vendor is critical as such, a small percentage of them merits that distinction. General construction tradesmen are more plentiful; however, most of the specialty trades are in high demand and low supply. Thus, if you find a good one, treat him well. Good subcontractors in demand have their choice of general contractors they will work for. These are generally the ones who treat them well, and pay on time.

Subcontract management can be tricky, and one must be careful in choosing what instrument he will use as a basis for agreement with his subcontractors. Aggressive contracts will scare many vendors away whereas passive contracts may be ineffective. Using American Institute of Architects' (AIA) A201 *General*

Conditions of the Contract for Construction as a benchmark, it would follow that each line item of a *Continuation Sheet* (itemized invoice) represents monies that will be paid to respective parties:

> The Contractor shall promptly pay each Subcontractor, upon receipt of payment from the Owner, out of the amount paid to the Contractor on account of such Subcontractor's portion of the Work, the amount to which said Subcontractor is entitled, reflecting percentages actually retained from payments to the Contractor . . . (9.6.2)

But this is rarely the case. A general contractor will pay out the least that he can, regardless of what he has billed the client. The "amount paid to the Contractor on account of such Subcontractor's portion of the Work" refers to a value entered on the *Continuation Sheet*—not just the general contractor's, but the subcontractor's, which should be of the same value as the general contractor's. General contractors pay the full amount to a subcontractor about as often as the subcontractor issues a *Continuation Sheet*, which is a rare occurrence. However, the A201 includes language expressly forbidding such actions:

> Such applications may not include requests for payments for portions of the Work for which the Contractor does not intend to pay a Subcontractor or material supplier . . . (9.3.1.2)

This means that the contractors bill against their subcontractors' work, but don't always pay out what they've billed against, but use the monies elsewhere. The above general conditions are virtually never exercised in contractual agreement between residential prime and subcontractors. The terms set forth above are intended to protect the owner. Even so, they are seldom referenced even by those who would seemingly benefit from them. Probably for two reasons: (1) they are micromanagerial in nature, and (2) they are invidious. For these reasons, and others, which we discuss further on, the A201, *status quo*, does not adequately serve all the needs of the residential industry.[26]

It doesn't take much to taint your relationship with your subcontractors—for example, they may not be manning your projects adequately, or with the appropriate level mechanics and foreman. The delays they cause may affect your work and other subcontractors' work. You will often argue over whether or not given scope was part of their base contract, or if it constitutes a change order. These differences are commonplace, and often irreconcilable, and for that reason, many contractors will go through an army of subcontractors. On the other hand, subcontractors can become disenchanted too, after one or two bad experiences with a general contractor, the subcontractor may decline to bid further work for him. Subcontractor burnout afflicts many general contractors, who have themselves to blame. If a subcontractor bids work for a general contractor all the time, but is seldom awarded a contract, he will soon become reluctant to continue bidding work. Subcontractors become unhappy on dysfunctional projects as well. Too many loser projects, and they will be ready to leave. If a general contractor is delayed on part of a project, he can often shift gears and work on another scope. The delayed subcontractor seldom enjoys the same luxury as he has to leave and come back when his turn comes up again, a circumstance for which many feel cheated by. As always, payments should be timely; subcontractors won't hesitate to man other projects, or look for other sources of work that pay better.

For the duplex project we will discuss, the contractor didn't have the appropriate level subcontractors to do the work, because (a) he and his resources had never done such a project, and (b) because his resources were substandard. In this regard, he was at risk. He decided to solicit bids from contractors whom he had never met but were listed in the Blue Book. The only qualification made was a low bid. In the event a subcontractor failed to deliver, he could terminate them, and hold on to their payments, using them to finance the next victim. It didn't matter to the contractor that he was making enemies and burning bridges, for he figured, just like strangers on the street; he would never see them again. Such practice is considered below any ethical standards of the industry, but is surprisingly commonplace. A simple perusing of publicly posted mechanic's liens will testify to the degree of conflict epidemic in contractor–subcontractor relations.

You don't want to be put into the position where you are working with a completely unknown quantity; however, at times, you will have no choice. This doesn't mean that you solicit bids from anyone; it means that you will have to do some homework, and exert a higher level of scrutiny in the selection process than you normally would. Suffice it to say, the stakes are appreciably higher in the high-end residential sector, where there is little or no tolerance for error. Subcontractor–contractor relations will be explored again in Chap. 2.

General Public

I have often marveled at how an aggressive or dangerous driver literally drags his company's name and driving complaint contact phone number about town on the side of his truck, oblivious to the fact that he is embarking on a negative advertisement campaign for his company. The perception of a company's image to the general public is typically the furthest thing from a contractor's mind, for there is little incentive apparent to him, to consider it. This attitude is by no means confined to the residential sector, but because residential construction is a public oriented industry, there is considerable interaction with the public. For this reason there are countless policing and monitoring agencies set to the task of contractor watchdog. If there were not, the building industry would literally build their works on top of the unsuspecting public. Many contractors are careless in this regard, being inconsiderate and generally unsympathetic. They may be inconsiderate of noise levels, housekeeping, or even personal conduct. They may flout the law by engaging in remedial work illegally, such as asbestos or lead paint removal.

There are other reasons to act with integrity toward the public, such as when a friendly act is returned in kind, or perhaps, your kindness is rewarded with a business prospect. On the downside, being unfriendly, a contractor is more subject to consumer and neighbor complaints than is the friendly company. Remember—residential construction is a people oriented industry.

Resident Entities and Pet Contractors

Those contractors and vendors who are mandated to a project by the owner I call "resident entities, or pets." They may be:

- Chosen from a preferred vendor list
- Named in the specifications
- Brought in by the owner

Under these circumstances a contractor typically concedes leverage, even if he contracts directly. I have found such relationships to be so problematic, that I suggest that a conflict prevention program be implemented as a preventative for any such occasion; special meetings and keeping such resources on a very short leash are in order. However, always give the pet contractor the benefit of doubt—treat him as you would any contractor. I suppose some of these subcontractors, not feeling beholden to the general contractor (which is a rare position for them) take the opportunity to flaunt their newfound independence, or exact revenge, albeit misdirected, for former grievances. When such a relationship goes bad, you can lose money through their retaliatory actions, and have no leverage for recourse.

There is a custom hardware manufacturer who is often designated in architect's specifications. Because they are the only source for the merchandise, which is custom-made to order, they seem to take certain liberties in their dealings with contractors, such as issuing unacceptable pricing information, not generating samples, or not making delivery dates. When confronted with these issues, there was always denial and apathy. After experiencing this behavior on about twelve different projects I was convinced that this vendor required special handling; for any future project where this vendor was preselected, a disclaimer for any component of their performance and service was to be written into the contract as a rider.

Of course, in the large scheme of things, resident entities are of little consequence—feeling entitled to their share of work they lose the incentive to please the general contractor. Nevertheless, there is not much you can do to stop clients from using them, but you can allow for their involvement in your game plan.

The Interdisciplinary Approach

Working knowledge from several aspects or experience is the notion that denotes what I call the *interdisciplinary approach* to construction management. In the past, it was sufficient that you merely knew the construction business. I suppose things were simpler then. Business could be done on a handshake, and the concept of construction management didn't exist. There were fewer monitoring agencies, and fewer lawsuits. Many in the industry still cling to the idea that you only need know your work. For today's complicated business world more tools are needed if you are going to be successful in terms of the parameters set forth herein this text. We have discussed many of them in this chapter. I will summarize skills already discussed—following are the resources or tools required to realizing your goals and ensuring success:

- Mission statement: a definitive outline and constitution of your company's purpose
- Ethics: a sense of, and respect for sound morals and values within the business community, and the ability to manifest this in your organization
- Quality and proficiency: the ability to execute and deliver projects on at least a professional level that is commensurate with what you contract to deliver
- Consistency: a track record of achievement, and a measure of stability within your company's structure, and the industry
- Communication and people skills: the ability to deal with people from different walks of life, often on personal terms, and the skills necessary to cope with conflict. This includes the general public.

Within these five parameters you should be able to form a strong foundation for your organization, one which you can build on. Arriving at, or satisfying these requirements *in toto*, is where you will invoke skills from areas other than construction practice and theory; that is, other disciplines.

Mission Statement

In order to create a substantial and relevant mission statement, certain clarity of mind is essential and not a little wisdom. For most of us, this realization or epiphany is a lifelong process, one seldom attained, but a basic mission statement for a business can be created once one has a clear vision of purpose. The ability to convey this to other individuals and to make it happen is a never-ending process requiring great energy, perseverance, and diligence. Think of your mission statement as a castle that you must defend against an invading army. A company's mission statement need not be a written manifesto; in fact it has more relevance when it is conveyed through action. If someone has a vision they want to incorporate into their company as a group vision, they will have to take the initiative through whatever vehicle there is available, whether it be word of mouth, or written.

The hypothetical mission statement we have created would strike some as idealistic. Not that the ideas are untenable or unreasonable, but that it would be such a daunting task for most organizations to implement, if they were ever to think of it, that it would quickly be forgotten. That's fine, for most people; however, those who hope to excel at what they do will do everything they can to keep to their mission statement.

Thus I equate the invocation and application of a mission statement as central to an organization's success. I also consider that the most difficult of the interdisciplinary approaches, because it requires a great measure of self-knowledge, intuition, and visualization, all rare qualities that comprise the primary discipline of a focused and positive organization. Forming a mission statement is an elusive undertaking, one that you won't find the answer to in any book.

I once knew a contractor who created a mission statement in the form of a one page credo of empty rhetoric entitled "Service America." It was manifested as a crude copy of the contractor's epiphany hastily adhered to the wall somewhere in his office, and vaguely eluded to at "pep rallies" or the company's job meetings. Yes, it was as ridiculous as it sounded, and not a valiant effort. What I learned from that experience was just how clueless some people are to the concept of forming a mission statement. To some, it is simple idealism—you only need to think it to make it so.

As if the formation of a mission statement weren't difficult enough, it is a tiny undertaking in proportion to what it takes to see the vision through, and make it your companywide credo. For that, you need a dedicated and committed team. Instilling your views in others is an endless process, and the task is further compounded by apathy and employee turnaround, especially if men feel they are underpaid. On the other hand, too much theory will start to smack of hypocrisy and pretension. You don't want to turn people off before they even find out what you're all about. Consider the following new age rhetoric in another company's mission statement:

> From the moment you walk through our front door you'll feel an energy that is quite unlike anything you've probably felt before. There is something in the air that is both energizing and motivating. We refer to it as . . . and it lives within each employee. Everyone brings a unique energy and passion to their job that makes (us) feel more like a second family or home than a place of employment. People enjoy coming to work every day and doing their part to make (us) a better place.

Turned off yet? And you only just walked in the door.

Ethics

I believe the practice of a good set of ethics requires acumen independent of specific hands-on skills, and that is why I include them in the discussion of the interdisciplinary approach. From this standpoint, the discussion of ethics refers to your personal *weltanschuang*, and how well you convey it to others. The foundation of one's sense of ethics is generally formed early on—in childhood. You will later embellish and manifest these beliefs into your worldview, which will finally dictate how you set store as a player in the industry. It is one thing to have a sense of ethics; it is another to manifest them into your daily life and company operations. Because people have different priorities, cultural and social differences, ethics seem to be perpetually clashing. There will never be a one-sided victory in an argument where the adversaries each hold strong convictions that are counter to their rival.

The biggest component of mastering your ethical standpoint is an understanding of human nature. This is part psychology, part intuition, and part life experience. The more interactions you have with people, the better you should become. That assumes that you are a scholar of the subject. Nothing is learned by those who pay no attention. The next important aspect of human nature recognition is an understanding of how people will perceive you, and what you do and say. It is necessary to continually stand outside oneself and put oneself in another's shoes. You may think one thing, and they another. For example, what you perceive as a gesture of generosity, a client may take offense at if they believe they were already entitled to what you consider a gift. Or a friendly inquiry into a worker's hobbies may appear to him condescending.

People continually stand in judgment of one another, especially when they feel they are vulnerable, as they believe that their record won't stand up to harsh scrutiny. In contracts, this sizing-up process begins at the first interview, and will continue for the duration of the project. If you want people to think well of you and your company, you should be vigilant about the image you project. This topic will be discussed further in Chap. 8.

Quality and Proficiency

We discussed some of the prerequisite ethical skills above that I feel are necessary to start and maintain a thriving company, but what about practical skills? What are the sets of practical skills required for an individual or group to operate a residential construction business? Legally, they differ for each municipality and in some cases, virtually no skills at all. Some governments require licensing (66%), while others (33%)[27] do not. It is a moot point whether such licensing increases standards of practice for the industry. To be sure, more licensing will facilitate more complaints; however, unlike engineering and architecture, you don't need a degree to build. Individuals and companies who do not have a license use other's licenses. This is a common ploy employed by subcontractor that further complicates accurate statistics.

Some talented individuals have both the technical skills, and the business skills needed to run a construction company; however, at smaller companies, these skills are distributed among a group of two or three individuals. In many cases, a company may be lacking in both. These companies seemingly would have skipped the regimen of proper training, preparation, and organization, going right to the operation stage. However, when the going gets tough, they become dysfunctional. Simple projects, where the degree of skill required is minimal, do not require highly proficient people to do the work. Such projects are best suited to those companies who are lacking in proficiency from the top on down and there are plenty of them. Some of these people will realize the allure of the especially lucrative high-end residential market, and often set their sights there; they honestly believe that they can produce high-level work but they are kidding only themselves.

Architects today are pretty savvy in judging a general contractor's acumen, and will be loath to sponsor an unqualified company. The exception would be projects with overly aggressive budgets. If you know who else is bidding a project (ask your subcontractors) you can get a pretty good idea of the budget, and how your company is perceived by the architect. If the bottom feeders are flocking to the bid field, or if there are more than five bidders, you will begin to have your doubts. You also won't be pleased to find your company in the same bid pool as the riffraff. It's interesting to see companies who wish to be appraised more highly in their rank but who won't or can't do what it takes to get there. We will discuss just such a company in the course of this book—in short, a low-end, low proficiency commercial contractor who dared to enter into a high-end duplex addition project, with an aggressive schedule and insufficient budget. The reason for repeated reference back to this contractor and project is that the lessons to be learned from it should be repeated again and again. This particular project will be treated as a case study, as it seems to cover a broad spectrum of behaviors and practices to be avoided. Thus, the author is thankful for the existence of this company to serve as a model. We will later discuss many specific instances of failure and dysfunctions of this project to serve as example of what not to do. For general purposes, we can take the antitheses of what went wrong with this project, and set them in contradistinction to correct approaches. This tendency reinforces my credo "learn from other's mistakes."

Insofar as quality and proficiency are concerned, these are two attributes that must be accurately assessed before entering the market. First, it goes without saying that you should be proficient in your work. You can later decide what niche you will specialize in, if any. The contractor building the duplex may have been proficient in simple designs, where quality was not an issue; however, he was completely unprepared for the intended duplex project. In terms of high-end residential projects, the required level of craftsmanship is higher than any other construction discipline. While there are degrees of proficiency, and various contractors suitable to a level of quality, meeting the minimum requirement is becoming a more and more elusive goal. Quality oriented contractors have extreme difficulty filling management positions, as qualified individuals are in short supply. If they don't have qualified vendors and subcontractors then they will find it even more difficult to produce quality work. This condition can have debilitating effects on a contractor who has the work, but no one to facilitate it.

The bottom line here is that you should know your business. Don't pursue projects or markets where you have no experience, resources, or projects that are over your head. If you aspire to a certain aptitude, you must first learn the discipline. Nowhere is this distinction more critically made than when you start your business. Seek a level of work that is commensurate with your skill set.

We discuss the attributes of quality and proficiency here in Chap. 1 because they are essential to the process of becoming a successful residential contractor. Because quality and proficiency are subjective terms, there are many who mistakenly appraise their company's proficiency higher than it should be, perhaps based on their own fancies. Inaccurate self-assessment and overqualification is an irresponsible exercise in vanity that many companies fall into, sometimes to the extent that the action is tantamount to gross misrepresentation or fraud. It will be just a matter of time before a self-aggrandizing contractor shows his true colors. An honest self-assessment is a valuable exercise; however; there are some objective measures of quality that you can use as a benchmark in assessing your acumen.

Professional organizations, such as Sheet Metal and Air Conditioning Contractors National Association (SMACNA), Architectural Woodworking Institute (AWI), and Construction Specification Institute (CSI), publish standards of practice, means and methods, and tolerances for their respective industries. Many specifiers either refer to these publications, or insert their criteria directly into their project manuals. By familiarizing oneself with industry standards, you put yourself in the realm of objectivity. Knowledgeable architects (should) assess your work based on these standards, and their own standards, which they will also include in their specifications. However, don't wait for the architect to tell you your work is not up to snuff. Rather, gain a comprehensive understanding of what constitutes quality work, and institute the means and methods to facilitate quality work within your company before you contract yourself to perform such work. When you are ready to go to work, take an honest assessment of your company's ability, and based on that, pursue a level of work within your means.

You should constantly reassess your level of proficiency and quality, as it may change for better or worse. Solicit comments from objective parties whose opinion you respect. Pay special attention to constructive criticism made by your clients, architects, and especially the workmen on the project. Such advice can be helpful in making adjustments in your company or the way you do business. Remember, in this business it's not how proficient you think you are, or how proficient you are perceived to be by your clients. It is how proficient you *really* are.

Consistency

In the beginning, you may start with your mission statement, and self-examination. You may have all sorts of ideas and practices that you wish to establish, efforts that will require a lot of energy and attention. You will then find a level of comfort where you will set your sight on prospects. After a time, you will want to reassess, and consider your efforts according to the goals you originally set forth. This is called "remembering where you came from," a lifelong lesson in humility. Once you lose sight of your humble roots, you lose the benchmark that was the nascence of your company; for everything you do is measured in relation to the goals you set forth in the creation process, not just your bottom line.

Inefficiency is a sign of inconsistency in that it signifies a deviation from your game plan. No one plans to fail. Problems tend to be treated symptomatically; however, in the long run, the cause may remain and continue to malinger. A good manager will get to the root of the problem, and seek a treatment for it such that the behavior is reoriented back to the mission statement and game plan. By being focused on maintaining your goals, you are performing in a consistent manner, one that will make you more successful. Your clients will take note of your sound methods, and you will be respected and rewarded accordingly, just as you will be punished for not delivering as advertised.

High employee turnaround is another sign of inconsistency. Your clients and your peers will take note of it. It is a clear indication of dissatisfaction with your company that you should endeavor to resolve. You also hear what a "small world" the construction market is, especially in the tiny residential sector. This is generally true. People tend to talk and gossip; therefore, you hope they don't have something unbecoming to say about your company.

A company with poor payment habits is at best inconsistent, and will not make a lot of friends. Once word gets out that a company doesn't make timely payments, their field of influence becomes limited; many contractors refuse to work for them. High employee turnaround, and botched jobs, all contribute to business failure. You may hear now and then, of a given company's shortcomings from a disgruntled colleague; however, no reputation is more fatal than the contractor who doesn't pay—this information is circulated widely among the subcontractors and vendors, and has an inconvenient way of getting around. Your most esteemed model of consistency will be prompt payments—nowhere will your efforts be more appreciated, or lack of effort result in calamity.

People Skills

In order to smooth over relations and develop necessary tools to constructively work through difficulties with others you will want to have a fair command of some of the following abilities and skills:

- Ability to genuinely empathize with people
- Clear communication
- Willingness to admit mistakes
- Appreciation of other people's feelings and basic respect for them
- Open-mindedness, in terms of listening to what people have to say
- Ability to relate to culturally and socially diverse peoples
- Tolerance for people that don't fit the *ideal*
- Patience in dealing with delicate or volatile issues

The above considerations apply to relating to people, especially at difficult times. Equally important is your attitude toward friendship and camaraderie with people you work with. There is always room for conflict, but forging positive relationships can be a real challenge, especially if there isn't any real incentive for both parties. Today's workforce is more diverse than it ever was. It is not unusual to hear four or five languages used on a single small project. A recent project with only forty or so production team members featured the following languages and cultures: Polish, Ecuadorian, Jamaican Patois, Italian, Colombian, Puerto Rican, and American. It was a real challenge to connect at all with some of them, as they all didn't speak English. In addition to language barriers, cultural barriers were just as prominent.

Nevertheless, there is a universal *lingua franca* of friendliness, and you want to be fluent in it such that you exude a positive, approachable image—someone people feel they can talk to and who will listen. Few upper management personnel take the time to take a vested interest in workers beneath them. They find it difficult to relate to their workers socially. They lose on two fronts: for the company, and for themselves. Just about everyone has something to offer.

Insofar as your client and architect are concerned, you will want to be aware of what will inhibit the establishment of a positive relationship. It also helps to be able to relate to them. Typically, contractors are cut from a far different cloth than their architect and client. This leaves little common ground for discussions other than those concerned with building. However, if you have some knowledge or interest that you think you might share with them, they may appreciate the effort, or even engage you.

Communication

Therefore is the name of it called Babel; because the Lord did there confound the language of all the earth.

GENESIS XI9

Despite all the advances in telecommunication and information technology, the quality of communication in our society is on a seemingly endless down spiral. People cannot, do not, or will not say what they feel or mean. The result is miscommunication, logorrhea, and conflict. In business, this combination is deadly, and contributes to failure about as much as any other factor. Succinct communication is at the heart of any good construction management program. In order to be successful in the residential sector, one should have a sophisticated, or at least accurate and consistent level of communication. Without coherent communication, a company has no business professing to be a construction manager. It isn't enough that just the principle or sales people are coherent—the production team must be no less sharp than the sale's team; else the client is in for a letdown.

But communication efforts must include the entire project team, if the project is to operate efficiently. Indeed, improving communication and collaboration ranks at the top of issues concerning owners. Respondents to FMI/CMAA[28] survey indicate what they think would improve these issues. They were, in order of importance:

- Provide a clear contact for decisions and approvals
- Openly share project information
- Assemble the project team early and meet frequently
- Meet with service providers to share mission and goals for the project
- Delegate communication and collaboration responsibility to the project manager or construction manager[29]

People skills can be challenged in face-to-face confrontations; however nowadays, with the exception of meetings, most architect-contractor interface happens over the telephone, or by e-mail. Written correspondence that used to be mailed or faxed is now frequently sent over the Internet. The point is developments in technology have raised the bar on the level of communication skills needed to effectively administrate a project. However, there will still be plenty of face time spent with team members despite the advent of e-mail, faxes, and phone calls.

Chitchat aside, what must be kept in mind in any form of communication is that it all should be held to the same level of scrutiny. You therefore will want to establish controls regarding who is authorized to send what level of communication to whom. As often happens, architects and owners will issue verbal directives to production team members in the field. Evidently, the AIA contract (A201: 3.9.1) condones this intercourse; however, this is the sort of discussion that you would want to discourage, as it will inevitably complicate matters. Make your protocol clear to all job team members by identifying the chain of command that communication must follow. This includes the owner and members of the design team.

Forms of communication can be broken down into a number of categories, each requiring a separate set of skills:

- Face-to-face
- Telephone
- E-mail
- Written

Face-to-face

If you are generally in the office you will have less direct contact with your client. Direct discussions should be conducted with a number of considerations kept in mind, some of which we have discussed here, others in Chap. 8. The most important notion to keep in mind is the fact that during owner/architect/contractor face-to-face discussions, you can expect a fair amount of hypersensitivity and scrutiny, for which you should be prepared. This is due to the attendant apprehension evident in most clients at the start of a project. Notwithstanding self-awareness books in print, I will offer my own guidelines for personal meetings:

- Avoid affectation and disingenuousness. This vain and unnecessary behavior can be disconcerting to nervous clients, or those who expect you to be more serious
- Establish eye contact when speaking or spoken to
- Try to engage as many people involved in discussions as you can, but avoid free-for-alls
- Strive to get consensus on issues. Don't make unpopular decisions unless there is no reasonable alternative

- Do not address or continue to talk to people who are not paying attention
- Avoid confrontation: de-escalate provocative issues
- Do not attend meetings by yourself; always bring a partner. You can bail each other out of treacherous waters, and take turns discussing matters

In addition to these considerations you will want to be diligent in the following matters:

Attention to posture, tone, and body language. Any or all of these can influence other's perception of you. If it should, let it be for the better. For example, a contractor who walks into a meeting plunks down in a chair on an angle, slumps, and casts his glances aside does not pose a very engaging counterpart to discussion. This behavior will offend some people, even if no words have been exchanged. On the other hand, if you have some bad news, you can couch it in a positive way: sitting up straight in your chair, speaking clearly, with a pleasant voice. Likewise, your good news will be received that much better.

Certain discussions should only take place in a forum designated for that purpose—a production meeting should not digress into a design meeting; working out conflicts with the design team should not be done in front of the client; and haggling over change orders should be done one-on-one with the architect, to name a few. All of these eventualities you will have to provide an arena for, lest they should fall into a catchall meeting as they so often do. Should these issues creep into your job meetings you should indicate that a separate time should be established for such business to be negotiated.

The most important thing to keep in mind when communicating is to be a good listener. People will tend to tell you what they want to know or hear. If they don't, you will want to find out by asking questions. This will save everyone time and aggravation. If you show to be a good listener, people will be pleased, and respect what you have to say in return that much more. They appreciate your interest in their point of view. Some people will not appear to be engaging when you need them to be. Try to develop strategies to "draw them out" accordingly, even if it means explaining to them the importance of their involvement.

One of the pitfalls of face-to-face is that you have to think fast in order to keep the conversations moving, try to be mindful of the messages you are sending out unconsciously or not. The way to do this is to take time and think about what you are about to say before you say it. Often, you will find that you don't have a ready answer, which is okay; being very eager, clients often will solicit (and insist on) pricing information on the spot. To answer straight away is almost always disadvantageous. Advise them that you require additional time to process the request and issue newly requested pricing information.

Telephone

I dislike conducting business over the telephone, especially official business, such as that which must be documented, such as request for information (RFI) and request for proposals (RFP). Complex information solicited over the phone has a small chance of materializing into required hard copy directives. Moreover, accurate records of telephone conversations are rarely documented. Assuming most discussion between you and your architect will mostly be business, it goes without saying that such discussions should be documented.

However, out of necessity, much conversation takes place over the telephone, yet, if one waited for every piece of information to be documented, there would be little building done. Therefore, the *soliciting or directing party* is obliged to document what information they require, or are issuing, which we will discuss further and in Chap. 8. One should therefore attempt to minimize the number of telephone discussions that pertain to items that must be documented, presenting such information otherwise, such as in a job meeting, or a memo.

You would like to be able to evaluate your comportment and performance when it is important for you to know how you are coming across to others. Of course, the telephone handicaps your ability to observe responses in your partner. There is also an absence of the fluidity that direct conversations naturally have. Therefore, certain conversations, especially sensitive or complicated ones, should be confined to either direct interface or documentation.

Like e-mail, telephone tends to lower inhibition, thus people sometimes forget themselves, or become looser. In of itself, this is not problematic; however, you don't want to lower your standard of communication, or become informal when it isn't appropriate.

E-mail

E-mail can be a fabulous tool. Insofar as technical skills, e-mail may necessitate many, depending on what it is used for. If you carry a palm top and type match-head size tiles with your thumbs then you will not appreciate lengthy e-mails, and attachments will be difficult or impossible to use. By the same token, avoid sending large messages, or attachments to other personal digital assistant (PDA) users. You will send a lot of two- and three-word responses. Naturally, this interface requires little intuition.

As we shall discover in Chap. 6, electronic data are more than commonplace in industry correspondence today; in fact, it is becoming the norm. However, it is the quality of, and what one does with, the information coming in and out that will determine just how much use you are getting from e-mail. Chapter 6 will also describe ways to use the Internet to maximize the potential of e-mail and its attachments. Suffice it to say, without being computer literate, and having the use and working knowledge of the programs generating your e-mail attachments, you just as well may stick to typing with your thumbs.

Many use e-mail as an end of itself—that is, messages are sent, read, and directly disposed of. This type of usage tends to be antithetical to what a construction manager needs to do with his information, which is to process it, and archive it for future reference. For a palm top user, instant disposal is typical, and there isn't much of a choice. However, many palm top users have other accesses to their e-mail. The beauty of e-mail is that not only does it communicate, but it also documents the correspondence at the same time. Since your e-mail will be a written record, you want to treat it as such; avoid writing anything that you wouldn't otherwise disclose in a memo or other document.

There are some basic protocols to be aware of, but if you stick to the principles of good writing (see below) your e-mail will be just as professional as all your documentation:

- If you are going to e-mail documentation, get in the habit of including the documentation as an attachment, on your company's letterhead, as opposed to the text window of the e-mail.

- Avoid becoming too informal or familiar, as you would with a friend or your family. E-mail has a tendency to lower the bar on formality.

- Just as you do your written correspondence, be judicious in whom you choose to cc on your e-mail—some people shouldn't see some things, and others won't want to see them.

- Your e-mail and word processing programs have a spell-checker, which you should set on automatic. There's no excuse for typos with a spell-checker. Short of a spell-checker, proofread your outgoing correspondence. Even with a spell-checker, a last going-over will often turn up mistakes, especially grammatical ones. Spreadsheets with calculations must absolutely be checked before being issued.

- Certain documentation should never be e-mailed, such as that which requires a signature or stamp—for example, a contract, or change order. Scaled drawings should always be issued by hand; never by fax or e-mail. Many discussions are more appropriately presented face-to-face, especially those which may elicit an emotional response. Complicated matters should be avoided in e-mail communications. Once they get engaged such matters can take on a life of their own, where the threads of the message multiply to the extent that the issue can't be isolated.

If you are issuing a document via e-mail, it doesn't hurt to solicit a "read receipt" from the recipient, which verifies that they have received the message. Short of "read receipts," you should always follow-up with hard copy of the documentation.

Written

Written documentation includes e-mail; however, I shall here refer to it as written documentation other than e-mail text, which we discussed above.

Coherent writing is one of the most elusive skills in professional business, for that matter, in any correspondence. Many managers with high-level degrees often do not know how to write. As communication is at the heart of construction management, and writing and documentation are the crux of communication, one can't stress enough the importance of writing skills. Nowadays, more and more correspondence is being delegated to the administrative level people who might not have good writing skills either. This further compromises the integrity of communications.

What often happens is that contractors continually do themselves a disservice by under or miscommunication; they may neglect to effectively issue important information, because they aren't able to put their ideas into writing. Often they may think they've been clear, only to find out their correspondence was ambiguous. This sort of dilemma is a great detriment to project facilitation, and is to blame for a majority of management failures. Additionally, as we shall discuss in Chap. 8, a project should end in arbitration or litigation, documentation will play a key role in tracing accountability; therefore, a lack of accurate documentation could then put one at a disadvantage.

As I said above, there is a tacit stereotype of many contractors that they tend to be not as literate as the rest of the business world. While you can take that sentiment at face value, long experiences confirm that the bar isn't set very high for the level of communication in the construction industry to begin with, thus in some measure, evident illiteracy is a self-fulfilling prophecy—clients don't expect a lot. But imagine if you were on the short-list of companies that were held in high esteem for their literate and informative documentation? Not such a bad prospect.

Nonetheless, lack of formal education may have little bearing on one's communication acumen. Fortunately, the industry provides forms for just about any standard document—contract, change order, RFP, RFI, proposal, transmittal log, and so forth. These are readily available—the AIA forms are nearly universally recognized by architects and are often mandated as vehicles within a contract. However, a fair amount of documentation won't neatly fit into a prefab form. Although there are some templates in circulation meant to be used to notify an architect of such things as a late condition, or preexisting condition, these forms tend to be generic, incomplete, and not very professional looking. For that reason, there are many books in print that illustrate business writing. Nevertheless, most contractors typically generate their own custom document family.

In addition to documents that only furnish data, there are many correspondences which require a critical or analytical approach, such that would necessitate coherent writing skills as well as high-level construction management skills. Like any other issue, you will also be judged on the integrity of these documents. We will discuss documentation further in Chap. 4. One of the most difficult memos to write is the explanation of a schedule—particularly, of why a given schedule is delayed, and what the effect the delay has on subsequent tasks. We will address this particular dilemma in Chap. 3.

Notes

The zen of residential construction general management

- *Learn from other's mistakes*
- *Be proactive, not reactive*

- *If you can't build it right, don't bother*
- *There's no such thing as a half-hour lunch . . .*
- *If it ain't broke; don't fix it, but if it never worked right in the first place, it probably isn't broken, it was just done wrong*
- *Less is more—expensive*
- *Take care that offering a solution doesn't become the problem*
- *Bosses are seldom right, that's why they're bosses*
- *The smaller the payment, the harder you will work for it*
- *You don't always get what you pay for, especially if you don't understand what you're buying*
- *The writing is always on the wall—if you can't see it, maybe you need glasses*
- *Difficult things in the world must have their beginnings in the easy; big things must have their beginnings in the small.*

LAO TZU

10 keys to effective communicating

- Ability to genuinely empathize with people
- Clear communication
- Willingness to admit mistakes
- Willingness to apologize
- Appreciation of other people's feelings and basic respect for them
- Open-mindedness, in terms of listening to what people have to say
- Ability to relate to culturally and socially diverse peoples
- Tolerance for people that don't fit the "ideal"
- Patience in dealing with delicate or volatile issues

Above all, be a good listener:

Empathetic listening is so powerful because it gives you accurate data to work with. Instead of projecting your own autobiography and assuming thoughts, feelings, motives, and interpretation, you're dealing with the reality inside another person's head and heart. You're listening to understand.[30]

Endnotes

1. Friedrich Nietzsche.
2. NACAA/CFA, *Thirteenth Annual Consumer Complaint Survey Report 2003–2004* (2005).
3. Also see Chap. 8.
4. D. Mark Hutchings and Jay P. Christofferson, *Management Practices of Residential Construction Companies Producing 25 or Fewer Units Annually* (2004). The survey was conducted of a sampling of 1020 NAHB members. Although the main source of revenue for the sample group was from the sale and construction of new homes, the majority of the remainder

of NAHB builders (about one-third total NAHB membership, which was 220,000 in 2004) were the remodelers. Indeed 40% of all the residential construction spending were remodeling expenditures. Thus, the sample group survey can offer a reasonable analog to the residential industry as a whole.

5. For the purpose of this discussion, the term *failure* denotes insolvency, bankruptcy or other termination of operation. However, for the remainder of this book it also describes the state of companies, many of them prosperous, who by their mismanagement and misrepresentation, *fail* to make a positive and healthy contribution to the industry, or in their mission statement.

6. This range applies only to the residential and high-end sector.

7. Bureau of Labor and Statistics.

8. The Business Roundtable, *Absenteeism and Turnover, Report C6* (1989).

9. *ibid.*

10. *ibid.*

11. Although the survey indicates estimated costs for its control group—nuclear power plant, petrochemical, and refinery projects, the equations generating the data are not necessarily transposable to other projects, but do justify further research.

12. This is beginning to change as boutique architects are partnering with developers to offer furnished or finished units as a special incentive to prospective buyers; typically those with deep pockets.

13. Eric Belski, Mark Calabria, and Alfred Nucci, *Survivorship and Growth in the Residential Remodeling Industry* (Joint Center for Housing Studies of Harvard University, 2001), p. 16.

14. D. Mark Hutchings and Jay P. Christofferson, 36.

15. D. Mark Hutchings and Jay P. Christofferson, *ASC Proceedings of the 37th Annual Conference, Denver, CO, April 4–7, 2001, 263–270; Factors Leading to Company Success: Perceptions of Small Volume General Contractors.* Hutchings and Christofferson point out that their survey indicates that "strategic planning," which should be a top priority ranked only twenty-first out of a total of seventy-eight possible responses. This fact has some interesting connotations and the author considers it an anomaly of the survey. There seems to be significant cross-over in some if the other responses, such that many fit the criteria of some aspect of "strategic planning."

16. For more, see excerpt by Tracy Miller, at the beginning of Chap. 5.

17. Witold Rybczynski, *Home*, (New York, Viking, 1986), 126–127.

18. *The Business of Architecture*: The 2003 AIA Firm Survey, Copyright 2003, The American Institute of Architects.

19. The Business Roundtable, *Absenteeism and Turnover, Report C6* (1989).

20. Although not on par with other industries (see Preface).

21. Laszlo Moholy-Nagy, *Vision in Motion* (Illinois: Paul Theobold and Company, 1947), p. 5.

22. The meaning of "an honest day's work" has special ramifications within organized labor. It isn't a measure of a given individual's abilities and potential to generate an effort that is morally and substantially acceptable to his employer. It merely is a dilution from the ideal that organized labor defines—a day's work is defined by the measured output a union believes is proportionate to its labor contract or current relationship with contractors. Even though workers have varying degrees of production potential, they are all expected and required to do no more than is mandated by their labor contract, or their shop steward.

23. Donald M. Fisk, *American Labor in the 20th Century* (Bureau of Labor and Statistics, 2003). All statistics in this paragraph are attributed to the above-referred publication.

24. Bureau of Labor and Statistics.

25. *ibid.*

26. The AIA does not intend the A201 to fit every project in its present form, that is, the A201 is a foundation that can be added to or subtracted from. The AIA offers the following synopsis of its A511, a guide to modifying the A201. *"Upon retainer and request, contract lawyers of all stripes will provide supplemental language as necessary."* The author suggests consulting the *American Institute of Architects Legal Citator*, 2005 Edition, by Stephen G.M. Stein, edited by Matthew Bender, updated annually, published since 1996. The *Citator* is a case finder for key state and federal interpretations of AIA documents.

   A511-1999 Guide for Supplementary Conditions for use in considering changes to the A201. The A511-1999 is a guide for modifying and supplementing *A201-1997, General Conditions of the Contract for Construction*. It provides model language with explanatory notes to assist users in adapting A201 to local circumstances. Although A201 is considered as a keystone in the legal framework of the construction contract, as a standard document it cannot cover all the particulars of a specific project. Thus, A511 is intended as an aid to the users of A201 in modifying A201 or developing supplementary conditions. Excerpting of the model text is permitted by the AIA under a limited license for reproduction granted for drafting the supplementary conditions of a particular project.

27. NAHB (1996).
28. FMI is a management-consulting group for the construction industry. CMAA is the Construction Managers Association of America.
29. FMI/CMAA *Fifth Annual Survey of Owners* (2004), p. 11. The survey queried members of CMAA, COAA, and a "randomly selected cross-section of owners." 44% of the sample were private organizations; the biggest single group represented in the sample. While there were some general contractors and construction managers within the sample, most of the respondents were demand side owners. The distinction between the owners of the sample group, and owners as referred to in this text, is that the owners in the survey have little in common with homeowners. These owners are people at large corporations who the survey classifies as "constant builders"—such as industrial facility, water/waste water companies, and transportation builders. Such companies have in-house construction managers and project managers seeing to their needs. These owners have much in common with professionals in the construction sector, and their responses to the survey are an excellent analog for the residential sector. Their survey responses would certainly be corroborated by their peers in the residential sector with the help of general contractors and construction managers.
30. Stephen R. Covey, *The 7 Habits of Highly Effective People* (New York, Fireside, 1990), p. 241.

2

Valuation

*The greatest of all gifts is the power to estimate
things at their true worth.*
                    Francois de la Rochefoucauld

Construction cost estimating is at the heart of any successful construction business, as it will ultimately determine a company's fate. Nowhere is estimating more difficult than in the residential sector, particularly, high-end remodeling. The margin of error can be considerable. Even one seemingly minor mistake or oversight can sink a project.

For every contractor, each project will begin with the cost estimate. Estimating is a tricky business that many contractors, especially small firms, are loath to entrust to a third party; they do their own estimating. Others will hire an estimator. The trick is to find the right estimator for the type of work you do. I have interviewed many estimators for residential work, but found that very few really knew the work from an estimator's standpoint. It is not uncommon to receive over one hundred responses to a want-advertisement for an estimator, only to find that none of them were suitable. Why is this sort of incompetence so commonplace? I suppose, at a certain point in time, those who figured jobs were known as something such as cost-analysts or appraisers, or there was a tacit understanding that costs were hard and accurate. As the degree of exactitude diminished, these people became known as "estimators"—sort of a caveat title in of itself, but apt to the purpose.

Nowadays, there are three types of estimators—those who learn a trade and work their way up, those who are taught by a colleague, or someone else in the business such as a relative, and those who learn through an educational institution. The former should have a leg up on the latter; there is no replacement for hands-on experience. However, a good formal estimating curriculum will tend to yield a more management or administrative oriented person; therefore, an estimator brought up through the ranks should also have some theoretical and administrative skills. If nothing else, he should have some business skills. This is a good rule of thumb to follow for subcontractors; however, an estimator for a general contractor should have knowledge of all the trades that he estimates. It follows that an estimator with some hands-on experience in addition to a formal education would be the optimum candidate.

Since good estimators are in such short supply, it is often the company owner, or a staff member who has held his own company, who becomes the *de facto* estimator. As many contractors do their own estimating in addition to their other duties, they tend to be overworked, and complain that they are inhibited from doing their real job, that is, sales. This phenomenon we shall discuss later in the single proprietor syndrome section of Chap. 7. Once the estimating work is finally parsed out to an estimator, it will then be scrutinized by the owner nevertheless.

Many estimators get their information out of commercially available cost guides. While some of these guides provide some useful information, this information can only be used to supplement an estimator's knowledge in assembling his bid. There are inherent advantages and disadvantages to using such guides:

- Guides give accurate material and man per hour calculations for typical constructions for given tasks; however, they cannot factor in the limitations and special circumstances that apply to residential construction, or custom installations.

- Calculations are based on production tasks, and don't take into consideration the higher unit price that piecework or small production runs have, because of the proportion of setup and other overhead costs, in relation to the output.

- Costly coordination work, work between trades, and magnified general conditions are not adequately represented or analyzed.

A few examples can exemplify the limitations of estimating guides:

1. The installation of an interior custom door and door frame is estimated as taking up to 1.2 man/h.[1] If this were a special or custom door, with pivot or Soss hinges, an average duration might be about 6 to 8 man/h. Installation of a mortise lockset for such a door is estimated at 1 man/h. This task typically takes about 1.5 to 2 man/h, unless the door and frame have been pre-mortised in the door fabrication process. This sort of mistake is a gross oversight that does not take into account the comprehensive door installations, or allow for varying complexities. Many doors will be installed and removed several times for things such as fit, finishing, protection, and hardware installation, and thus one must add the cost of repeated efforts.

2. Installing a square foot of 25 g metal stud partition is estimated at 0.019 man/h. If there were 5000SF of framing on the project, the partition should take 90 man/h to frame or a two-man team just over one week. At $50 man/h, and $0.50/SF material, the work would be estimated at about $7000. The SF estimate to install 5000SF of gypsum board at the rate of 0.017 man/h brings the total partition cost to $11,250. If the partition was an unimpeded straight

run, this estimate may be accurate; however, the average residence seldom has unimpeded straight runs of wall over 20 ft. There may be corners, reveals and beads, niches, half walls, angles, curves, door openings, cutouts, access panels, holes for mechanical electrical and plumbing (MEP) installations, and so forth. What's more, the work will be constantly stop-and-go so as to allow for the necessary coordination, and especially demobilization and remobilization for the repeated setting up and breaking down of work areas. Given such complexities, residential partitions of this type may cost anywhere from $7.50 to 12.50/SF. Using $10/SF as an average, the same 5000SF of partition on a high-end residential project will average about $50,000, or about 4.4 (440%) × the book value. Discrepancies of this magnitude are unacceptable, and preclude the effective use of commercial cost guides for the residential sector.

3. The installation of a square foot of wood strip flooring is estimated at 0.047 man/h. At that rate, a mechanic would finish a 10 ft. × 10 ft. bedroom in little over half a day. Including materials ($4/board ft. for cherry or maple), this floor would cost about $600, or $6/SF. Typically, the same installation in a high-end residence would cost between $12 and $18/SF. The average room would then cost $1500, or about 2.5 (250%) × the book value.

Finally, the material quantities for book estimates tend to be accurate; however, the labor estimates, when applied to residential construction, are useless. Perhaps this is obvious to the publishers of these guides, as they seldom seem to address residential work, unless they are specifically geared toward that sector, in which case publications are sparse and limited in relevance. Either they feel the residential sector is too small, they don't know enough about it, they understand that it would be futile to standardize residential estimating, or all of the above. Whatever the case, a residential estimator is not going to learn his trade reading estimating guides.

Before undertaking any project, you must ensure that you (a) have the resources to do the project (personnel and proficiency), and (b) you are not taking on an unacceptable level of risk in doing so. In order to make money, you should first understand why most companies fail. Given proper qualification, most loser projects could be avoided.

Key Causes of Loser Contracts

- Undervaluation of base contract
- Undervaluation of general conditions
- Overly aggressive schedules
- Poor cash flow
- Unskilled or inappropriate level production
- Unknown subcontractors and vendors
- Difficult architects and clients

Undervaluation of base contract

If a project is underbid, you will know, whether before or after the fact. If you never know, something is wrong. You hope you know beforehand, as you still have time to make changes. Once in contract, it is too late. There are many reasons, some deliberate, but most unintentional as to why a given contractor may underbid a project. Often contractors will deliberately underbid, or "low-ball" a project when they are hungry for work. While this tactic can sometimes be effective in securing work for a company, it also tends to have a negative effect on the industry by driving prices up and quality down. Alternatively, if they are flush with work, the same company might bid high on the same project. In order to do either, you need to know what the market value of the work is.

However, projects tend not to be underbid deliberately. The work may be undervalued by the estimator for any number of reasons. For example, the scope of work is incorrectly calculated, the duration of the project is underestimated, a "B" company is secured to do "A" level work; even a typo could be the culprit. One elusive cost factor in estimating is general conditions—a black hole phenomenon that we will discuss below. Then there are the gray areas, for example, work needed to facilitate the subcontractors, including joint trade tasks. Although work, such as chopping, patching, cutting, and cleaning, may be intrinsic to facilitating their scope of work, subcontractors seldom do their own coordination and general conditions related tasks, and the general contractor is expected to use his own men. This is always the job of the estimator to quantify. It can be difficult to do, especially if the estimator does not have any hands-on experience. Often, it's not enough to know how a thing goes together. One must comprehend the indirect costs such as subtasks necessary to facilitate the main task.

Finally, one of the most common and misunderstood causes of underbidding is the underestimated general conditions and overhead. Without going into the breakdown of direct and indirect costs you can still begin to understand this concept. The longer the project lasts, the greater the general conditions and overhead expense will be. The more complex or refined the project is, the greater the general conditions, and finally, the more labor intensive the project, the greater the overhead. While different projects have different general condition factors, there are some basic provisions necessary to facilitate even the smallest project, which is just as subject to go over budget as any other.

Undervaluation of General Conditions: Overhead and Indirect Costs

Office administration

Bookkeeping. Managing payroll, payables, and receivables are critical tasks of any project. Payroll can be outsourced to a service rather quickly and efficiently, unlike bookkeeping, which can be extremely time-consuming, especially if an efficient system is not in place. Decent bookkeepers are difficult to find, especially with a construction background. Disorganization further compromises their performance. Some of the common challenges of construction bookkeeping are as follows:

- Keeping track of payments to vendors and suppliers; especially after the first payment
- Negotiating with subcontractors and vendors who insist on getting paid before their payment is due
- Organizing paperwork, such as invoices and receipts
- Tracking petty cash flow
- Managing bank and credit accounts
- Generating AIA *G702 Application and Certificate for Payment*, and its accompanying worksheet *G703 Continuation Sheet for G702*
- Managing *Release of Lien Waivers*
- Filing withholding and unemployment tax reports
- Closing out projects—negotiating full payment, outstanding change orders, and so forth

The above job description can quickly become untenable for an unsound bookkeeping department. Extra time will be given to some matters and other work will simply not get done, or will only be partially done. The bookkeeper may be blamed, or it may be his employer, who saddles him with an unrealistic workload, or both. In the end, it is the contractor's responsibility to ensure that bookkeeping is efficient and record keeping is organized. Not uncommonly, administrators or office managers are the *de facto* bookkeepers, who in that capacity will typically only accomplish the bare minimum of requirements. Another problem for small companies is that they can't afford to hire a full-time bookkeeper, thus their bookkeeper is a part-timer, who is more often than not, without enough time at his disposal to do a complete job.

Administrative Assistant or Secretary

Most companies have them; however, they often do other work. For problem projects, the extra amount of time and energy spent running around in circles can prevent people from being efficient, and end up costing money. That is why low-priority tasks are delegated to the administrative level, as their wages are the smallest. A certain amount of discretion must be exercised to assure that only appropriate level tasks are delegated, and that priority tasks must have checks and balances. It is in the practice of checks and balances that most administrations fail. Supervisors tend to delegate work and forget about it until they need it; thus, they consider task delegation an end in itself. Efficient administrators are typically underpaid and difficult to find, despite being a valuable asset. It is a pity that companies do not better reward good efforts.

The consequences of failure at the administrative level are not evident in the payroll records, as they might be on the job-site; they manifest themselves at the next level, or the resulting fallout from a given misdeed. For example, a vital document may not be copied to the required parties, or an important follow-up call was never placed. These are the kind of mistakes that can confound things down the line. A crooked wall can always be repaired, usually at a nominal cost; however, administrative mistakes can create scenarios where there is no fix such as loss of time and the monies associated with that loss.

Project Management

In residential projects, except for very large ones, there is seldom a need for a full-time project manager; however, there will always be a need for someone to be responsible for project manager level tasks. Experience will dictate how much involvement the project manager will invest in a given project, and how he will divide his time between the office and the field. An accurate measure of the workload of a given project's management requirements is critical to running the job efficiently, and to managing resource allocation. The right level of site supervision and project management must be considered. Too little project management will result in the typical retinue of problems, while too much time will steal away resources from other projects. The only thing worse than running overbudget in project management expenses is to run overbudget and still not be able to facilitate the project. If this should happen once, the project should be evaluated so that the same mistake should not be repeated. If it should happen continually, there are likely systemic flaws in the company structure. Chapters 4 to 6 will discuss at length various management structures to suit different types of projects.

Scheduling

On smaller projects formal schedules are not mandatory; however, milestones and critical paths must be strictly monitored. This can be done easily enough with memorandums, meetings, and e-mails. Any other project should have at least a basic schedule. If a general contractor does have a bona fide scheduler (a rare circumstance) who generates, tracks, and distributes schedules, his time will accumulate in the general conditions budget. If tracked scheduling services are not provided (which they usually are not), then the expense is not a consideration. The majority of residential contractors either do not seem to use schedules, use them in a constructive fashion, or the schedules they do use are neither critical path, nor trackable (see Chap. 3). Although there is a need for a proper scheduling program, most general contractors do without it, and thus eschew the expense.

To many contractors, a schedule is a service they must provide as part of the contract's general requirements. Judging by what is published; contractors either are inept at the task, dislike it, or both. The irony is that contractor schedules are meant to be used as a constructive tool to facilitate their own work; if they don't make it happen, they're only hurting themselves. Given that, it's hard to understand why they have to be pressured by architects and owners in order to produce schedules.

Field Personnel

Field staffing, especially management, is a notorious sap for cost cutting by companies with tight budgets. Few companies can boast a bona fide project manager and superintendent for each project, whether they should, or not. Many general contractors fall into the habit of managing their projects poorly up until the last minute, then they labor to stanch the hemorrhaging fallout of their neglected project. This is a typical "siege operation" response discussed at length in Chap. 7.

Superintendent: On smaller projects, a working foreman can play the role of superintendent. However, more complex and larger projects should have at least a part-time field superintendent. Too often contractors don't man the site with a legitimate superintendent because either they don't have money in the job for one, or because they are trying to cut costs. Such contractors simply don't belong in high-end residential construction.

Project management: On smaller projects, a superintendent is used in lieu of a bona fide project manager, often, in addition to his superintendent duties. The same holds true as it does for the working foreman cum superintendent; however, the production level tasks are likely to suffer more than the management level tasks, on which a superintendent will have better control than a working foreman. We will discuss this particular hybrid conundrum further in Chap. 6.

Driver: A driver, who circulates from project to project, moving tools, material, and men, can be a huge asset to even very small companies. There should be a provision for such a person on any project. Without him, every day can become a challenge. Especially in metropolitan areas where chunks of time are lost in travel and commuting delays. All but the tiniest of companies will hit a breakeven point, wherein they realize that their diverse courier and delivery expenses could be better used to pay one driver who can do all the work for them.

Laborers: Every project should have at least one full-time laborer. Clean up happens every day, and it is their bailiwick. On residential projects it is a constant concern. Otherwise, there seem to be infinite opportunities available to keep a laborer on task. Good laborers probably yield the highest return of investment of all employees. I believe this is due in part to the fact that they are poorly paid, and thus may be eager to put out and learn skills as a way to move up the food chain. From the contractor's standpoint it is the responsibility of the superintendent or project manager to monitor and control the number of laborers on a project, as needs tend to fluctuate. Too few laborers and work will go undone. Too many laborers, they will slow down their pace to adjust for the lighter workload until someone notices. Don't expect them to come running to the superintendent to tell him that they need work to do. For one, they may be fearful of being laid off, as they see the workload diminishing. They may figure that the extra men on the site aren't there to boost manpower, but because there isn't enough work to go around.

Shipping and handling: Moving materials, opening and closing material, sorting, debris removal, et. al. are all requirements of any project, though they are seldom elucidated in the design documentation—they are taken for granted. They are sometimes alluded to in the specifications; however; the following tasks will be exigent, regardless of mention.

- *Protections of completed work, and owner or building property*:   Damage to completed work is always a concern, as residences tend to allow fewer square feet of working space to the workers such that the risk of accidents due to congested conditions can be very high.

- *Daily protections*:   Protection and cleaning such as common area floor and wall coverings. Typically, this is a laborer's work. In residential construction this scope of work can be endless; it is quantified by how much a given general contractor is willing to spend.

- *Cleaning*:   You never can have a job site too clean and organized. Daily sweeping and debris consolidation or removal is a minimum requirement. Any laborer, if doing nothing else, should have a broom or cleaning rag in his hand.

Quantifying General Conditions

Perhaps one of the most difficult estimating tasks is to have an understanding of the entire project lifecycle in order to accurately assess a project's general conditions. In order to correctly quantify general conditions, you must first understand the difference between general conditions, overhead, and tasks that are taken in for other scopes of work. A simple (and early) definition of general conditions is provided and is still as relevant as ever:

> The general condition clause, which should precede the description of the work and material required by every specification, is introduced as a precautionary measure, to cover all those details and conditions that are likely to arise in the progress of building erection, and that cannot be foreseen and provided for under the classified headings of the different parts of the specification.[2]

The above definition illustrates that as early as the late nineteenth century builders were struggling to define general conditions, and were to some extent winging it when they quantified them. The phrases "cannot be foreseen" and "precautionary measure," would imply that at least some component of early factoring was a contingency number, whereas "likely to arise" denotes a strong probability that a certain expense will be encountered. Evidently, these engineers had given up on trying to affix a meaning to the term general conditions. This was an unacceptable circumstance then as it is now. When a contractor affixes a percentage to general conditions, he is using the most popular, but least accurate method. Companies who can't control, or don't understand general conditions lose money. Because general conditions tend to be indirect costs, intangibles, they are difficult to substantiate to clients. This being so, when companies lose on general conditions, they tend to absorb such costs alone. General conditions are particularly costly in executing change order work, and should be factored independently of the base contract rate. An owner may ask for the contractor to conduct general conditions at the same rate as the base contract. This arrangement can generate losses for the contractor, and he should protect himself from losing money in this way. This will further be discussed in Chap. 8. Cost-plus and projects with reimbursable expenses are exceptions; however, a guaranteed maximum price (GMP) clause is often invoked as a safeguard to the client.

General conditions are at their highest during premium time work (overtime, holidays, nights, and so forth), and accelerated schedules. Such costs are the most difficult of all general conditions to quantify, especially if conditions are unplanned.

As we shall see, each project's general conditions must be assessed independently, and each will vary such as smaller jobs may require the same staff, but fewer man-hours. Some projects will require extensive submittal and inspection processes that have nothing to do with the contract value, but they will affect the workload of the superintendent and project manager. These requirements will generally be found in the architect's specification book; however, for some projects, they should be done whether indicated or not. By the same token, every project has minimum staffing requirements. These will be reflected in the general conditions budget. It is not uncommon for a contractor to skimp on general conditions to hone his costs. As discussed above, he may forgo a project manager by saddling the superintendent with a project manager's responsibilities in addition to his own, and vice versa. In either case, the integrity of management level responsibilities tends to be compromised. Integrity is also compromised when underqualified staff is deployed. They may be underqualified as a consequence of cost cutting, or they simply may not know their work. In a competitive market, both are commonplace conditions.

For many architects, there are a minimum set of general requirements that are expected to be met, regardless of budget or schedule. On smaller projects, general conditions may be proportionately skewed to such an extent that you may not want to tender a bid for a project. For example, a project with a contract value of $1,000,000 may have a minimum of $100,000 in general conditions, whereas on a project of $500,000 in value you may need $75,000 in general conditions. Traditionally, contractors make very little profit on general conditions; rather, they tend to lose money on them. For that reason, they begin cutting costs there.

Aggressive Schedules

While some companies are able to survive the Darwinian world of compressed schedules, most find themselves ill-equipped. After all, it's hard enough for them to produce work on a normal schedule. Builders of retail space must specialize in expedited production, as high commercial rents are often absorbed during the production process. But they are not the only projects with carrying costs. Once a lease, any lease, is signed, the clock starts ticking for the owner. The more competitive the real estate market is, the more pressure is put on contractors to provide expedited schedules. Often, projects are awarded solely based on promised completion dates. Because of this, as we shall see, contractors won't hesitate to blindly compress a schedule in order to win a contract.

However, it is the implementation of an expedited schedule on a project that has already been awarded or begun predicated on a naturally paced schedule, which carries the most problematic conditions. Being unplanned, it is difficult to assess the impact of this change on an existing project, and thus assess the cost. When a project becomes (or is perceived to be) late, the owner may insist on the contractor expediting the work. Depending on the reason why the project is late, a client may or may not be willing to pay extra for this service. And if it is the same scope of work, the client may not feel obligated to pay extra to speed things up, especially if he feels the contractor is to blame for the delay. There are several reasons why an expedited schedule will increase costs:

- Additional shifts and premium time wage rates
- Out of sequence operations, which create more work to coordinate and execute
- Red-label shipping and factory production up charges
- Lags on production due to site overcrowding
- Lower quality workmanship due to rushing, overcrowding, fatigue, and general stress. Tear-out work may be warranted
- Change orders and back-charges from subcontractors

It should be said that the likelihood of safety lapses increase with the rate of a production on a given project, especially if it is an unnatural rate.

If a project must be expedited, it should be understood from the project's inception, and at that time be incorporated into the job logistics. To do this, you need to be informed that the project is, in fact, to be on an expedited path. Sometimes, the design team or owner will state this condition up front. Otherwise, it is the contractor's job to realize this, and make it apparent to the client before bidding the project; if either the project duration is not able to be shortened, or the client is not willing to finance the shortening of it, you may not want to entertain the prospect. If you know from the beginning of a project that the project is expedited, you can take steps and prepare. It is when this condition is thrust upon you in midstream that life becomes problematic. Generally speaking, clients don't want to hear that they are paying a premium to the contractor in order to make a deadline. If there is a premium, it is better left unmentioned, as the client can usually find another contractor who claims he can complete the work on time without a premium. Managing compressed schedules will be discussed in Chaps. 3 and 7.

Most companies are unable to produce quality work at an expedited pace, and should therefore avoid such work. They typically lack the infrastructure to manage such work, and melt down under the pressure. Larger projects, with union workers, have less of a challenge manning the work; but they will likely have the same quality control issues. It isn't always the general contractor who can't step up the pace, but his smaller subcontractors as well. Accordingly, a general contractor should know the strengths and limitations of his various resources. Too often, a general contractor will spoil a project by stretching his subcontractors too thin; getting them to agree to terms they can't possibly meet.

Poor Cash Flow

Construction is a cash business. Cash flow plays a key role in the efficacy of most projects. For this reason, you must ensure that there is, and will always be, operating capital for a given project. Typically, a deposit is given, with progress payments billed monthly. Assuming the work ensues as planned, and timely payments are made from the client to the contractor, and from the contractor to the subcontractors, work will proceed smoothly. It is when there is a lapse in cash flow that problems begin. If a client is not timely with his payments, a contractor may service other projects, which have a better cash flow. Likewise, subcontractors may not man a project with weak cash flow. The AIA *G702/3 Application and Certificate for Payment and Continuation Sheet*[3] is used on American Institute of Architect's contracts as an instrument for invoicing against work put in place. Your billing department should have the document in digital form, which is sold by the AIA. The G702/3 is designed to reflect the progress of a project for a given billing period, against the overall contract value. The architect and contractor will negotiate the value of completed work from which a retainer is subtracted. Contractors are supposed to receive a copy of the G702/3 each month from each of their subcontractors; however, smaller subcontractors rarely provide it, especially if an AIA subcontract form is not being used. Sometimes, delays by one trade can affect the cash flow to others—if a given trade is not performing, his work can't be billed. If his work is a big component of the overall scope, other contractors won't be able to perform either. Even if cash flow has dried up for one trade, the other trades must carry on, and be paid nonetheless. This is problematic when one trade's work is contingent on the completion of another's, and that work is behind schedule. It is also a problem when money taken for one purpose is spent for another—"robbing Peter, in order to pay Paul." Contractors don't always do that deliberately; however, they often have no choice.

In the long scheme of things, poor cash flow on even one project is bad for business. It can adversely affect your reputation in the industry when subcontractors compare notes regarding who pays, and who doesn't, which they are wont to do quite often. An experienced general contractor will understand the nuances of a given project's cash flow, and will negotiate payments accordingly to ensure that he doesn't get "behind the eight ball." He will also make the necessary inquiries, decisions, and adjustments to deal with issues that threaten to upset the progress of the project, and its cash flow, before and as they arise (after is usually too late).

Unskilled or Inappropriate Level Production

Assuming good quality material is used, having skilled workers is the key to quality control. There are many levels of skill, and they should be factored into the cost of a project accordingly. First, you want to have the appropriate level of skill for the quality level of a given project—if it is an A level job, don't send B workers, and vice versa. If you send overskilled workers, you will likely waste your money on overskill, whereas if workers are under-skilled, you will lose money on low production rates, and poor workmanship. You also may be compromising safety. In the former instance you may lose money, which you can make back, but in the latter, you compromise your reputation, something very difficult to redeem.

After assessing the level of quality, it is up to the estimator to solicit bids from the appropriate level contractors. The bidders' field selection process is where quality control begins on a project. Essentially, the project is made or broken depending on the outcome of this exercise. Some of the mistakes made in this early prequalification process are:

- The estimator and/or the subcontractors have over or underestimated the level of quality mandated by the design.

- The contractor and/or the subcontractor believe they can cut corners—sometimes this is deliberate. A "B" skilled worker may be working in lieu of an "A" level worker, with the company owner benefiting from the offset in wage rates. In the public sector, prevailing wage statutes are intended to control this problem by making this practice illegal. If your subcontractors are tried and true, they likely won't do this to you.

- The subcontractor overrates his company's performance and abilities, or aspires too highly.

- The subcontractor, unbeknownst to the general contractor, parses out the job to another—a cheaper subcontractor. This is known as "bait and switch."

- The in-house (superintendent and project manager) field personnel are not qualified.

Quality issues may be detected by the design team, or by the owner. Ideally, they should be detected by the general contractor, while he is still in a position to take corrective measures, and before the fur flies. Typically, such deficiencies are most apparent in the finishes, and obvious layout mistakes. Infrastructure and MEP are intractable determinants of the integrity of the final project. These trades must be scrutinized in order for subsequent trades to do their work effectively. If they are not, it will be difficult to repair infrastructure, especially after the finishes have begun. The MEP trades require the most mechanical know-how, yet mistakes are not as readily detected there, such as a mar on a wood veneer might be, or scuff on the floor would be evident in the finish phase. You and your production people must understand all the MEP trades in order to be in control of overall quality. Most importantly, a firm understanding of how infrastructure can dictate the final package. This topic will later be discussed in Chap. 4.

In a cost-driven market, it is often difficult to deliver top quality while remaining competitive; the two concepts are evidently antithetical. Quality costs money. On the other hand, paying top dollar does not guarantee top quality. It is the educated client, and the capable contractor who will understand these concepts. Typically, neither can be described as such. Responsible architects have a general sense of quality requirements, and the approval of work is rightly their bailiwick. Poor quality disputes usually end up in tear out, or redo work being undertaken, or worse, monetary concessions, or even litigation. Often a contractor will ditch a project or be terminated because he cannot perform.

Before entertaining any prospect, be sure that you have the resources necessary to perform the work. Your reputation and livelihood are on the line. Keep your subcontractors happy, and pay them on time, and they will service you accordingly. This goes for your employees as well. Introduce checks and balances to assure that work is being executed correctly. Most importantly, don't kid yourself. You're not fooling anyone but yourself if you take on a project that you cannot deliver.

Unknown Subcontractors and Vendors

In a sellers' market, subcontractors will be loath to take on a project that has an aggressive schedule, and/or low profit margin, since there are easier ways to make a living in flush times. Unlike general contractors, subcontractors are rarely slow, even in a down-market. When general contractors find out that their mainline of subcontractors are not interested in a given project, they become hard pressed to buy the job out, and they may "put the job on the street," or become willing to give the work to just about anyone who expresses an interest in it. Architects do this too, especially when they know the project is overbudget. Companies may be selected from a local publication such as a circular or Yellow Pages, Blue Book, or even a name gleaned from the side of a truck. Without a working relationship with the general contractor, there is not a lot of promise in this arrangement. This occurred on the duplex project described in Chap. 4. Those subcontractors performed poorly, and either quit or had their contracts terminated. To the trained eye, this arrangement is readily apparent, but it can be easy for a general contractor to hide this defect from the owner, as the owner typically has little interaction with the subcontractors. Needless to say, a client would and should be alarmed that his general contractor's resources have no prior relationship with their benefactor. In larger projects, a list of subcontractors is often requested by the architect for qualification purposes. For residential contracts, architects may want to prequalify the finish trades before agreeing to work with them. This practice sometimes helps to eradicate the problem of contractors gambling on unknown quantities. Although an architect may not necessarily be able to mandate that a certain subcontractor not be used, he can force the issue by not approving his submittals.

The Low Bid

(Savvy) owners seldom take the low bidding general contractor anymore, although they may use his bid as leverage with another contractor to negotiate him down to a lower price. Unlike many governmental contracts owners are not required to take the lowest bidder. This they learned the hard way, through years of poor service. Ironically, many general contractors don't follow the same rule. Their project may be so underbid or cost-driven that they either must take the lowest subbids, or take a hit. If the lower bidders have less ability they will underdeliver and create more trouble than they're worth. In the large scheme of things, it almost never pays to take the lowest bid without a comprehensive qualifying process. Architects are also aware of this phenomenon and will often insist on approving subcontractors before they join the job team, if they know them to be low bidder; however, they aren't always privy to this information.

Difficult Architects and Clients

I have been in on the ground floor of countless projects that I knew should have been passed up by the prospective contractors. How did I know? By intuition. If asked, and sometimes not, I would indicate my misgivings to the contractor, only to remind them in the future again and again: "I told you so." Although they tired of hearing that phrase, they seemingly never took it to heart and continued the behavior. The allure of profit can blind one's eyes to the inherent malignancies of an untenable working relationship, or more simply put: "some people will do anything for a buck."

Difficult clients and architects can spoil an otherwise promising project, or they can predispose it to becoming a loser. Some common maladies are:

- Indecision: failure to issue a complete set of working drawings
- Constant design changes
- Slow issuance or lack of important information
- Nervous design team
- Constant price haggling
- Poor payment history
- Poor attitude that affects the contractors' morale
- Continual dissatisfaction with performance

None of the above can be assessed in the first meeting; however, most of these signals can be perceived before a bid is tendered; while there is still time to bail out. Indecision, nervousness, price haggling, and sometimes a poor attitude can be detected early in the game, while there is still time to opt out. We will talk more about this further in this chapter and in Chap. 8.

Often, if you are a "good cop," (see Chap. 8) the one who only has a polite and accommodating relationship with the client, you may not learn about problems which could have been earlier detected. Your people—estimator and project manager—should be continually advising you of any such developments, before or during the project. At such times concessions and client coddling are in order.

The Winning Story of "*The One That Got Away*"

The restoration of a landmark limestone town house was to be a phased project beginning with demolition and salvage, and then under separate contract, the build-out. An architect who specialized in restoration was spearheading the design team effort.

The contract was let for the demolition and salvage phase of the contract. The demolition was simple except where salvage was involved, which generally consisted of setting aside some choice items. However, it soon became evident that the architect was unsatisfied with the ongoing salvage effort, which was loosely defined in the specifications. It should be said that the mere presence of demolition operations unleashed group hysteria on the part of the architect. This manifested itself in several unfortunate scenes, where the architects rallied under the banner of "historic preservation." It was difficult for the contractor to dignify most of these complaints, and soon malevolence became evident.

In response to his perception that the contractor was not performing, the architect made unreasonable directives, such as packaging and cataloguing hundreds of worthless hinges and screws, and insisted that the contractor unpack protected objects to prove that they were not broken or damaged. These seemed minor eccentricities to the project manager who did not feel it appropriate to mention to his superiors.

During the budget period for the build-out, about 3 months into the demolition and salvage phase, the contractor sat in a meeting with the architects, estimator, and project manager. In this meeting he sensed an air of pettiness and anality on the part of the architects, that he hitherto had not been exposed to, which gave him pause. On the way out of the architect's office, he solicited the opinions of his estimator and project manager, who conveyed their misgivings. The conversation lasted all of 3 minutes, after which the owner directed his office to withdraw his proposal, a contract of eight million or so. Regardless of the contract value, the contractor sensed the job would turn into a headache, and probably a loser, and rightly turned it away.

Lack of Leverage in Contract

Having the low end of the stick in a contract is a disadvantage. Small or inadequate deposits, passive payment schedules, aggressive production schedules, and overly strict criteria for payment and quality releases are all typical of weak contract positions. Such arrangements are not uncommon;

for if a contractor wants a project badly enough, he will forgo some leverage. Often the award of a contract is contingent on the contractor making some "good faith" concessions. If it is, this will be a recurring theme on the project, such as when he may be asked to absorb the cost of extra work, for which he normally wouldn't be liable. The art of negotiation should take a front seat here.

When people eat at restaurants they expect service for their money. They want to be calling the shots, and to be pampered. All they have to do is pay a fixed sum of money—little else is required on their part save for an optional gratuity. Often they make this same presumption when entering into a construction project. There is a tacit understanding by many clients that because they are paying out money, they are in essence sponsoring their contractor by helping him earn a living, and many passive general contractors will "wear out their knee pads" in tribute to the gesture; however, on dysfunctional projects, this understanding becomes less obvious. Because they may feel that they are the benefactors, the client may naturally assume the upper hand in negotiations, feeling that it is his prerogative to do so. Many contractors will give concessions to overcontrolling clients only to then find out they have been manipulated. This will become evident soon enough during the course of the project. To defend against this, always keep in mind how far you are willing to negotiate before you sit down to talk—set the bottom line, and remember, when negotiating always think *quid pro quo*. Once a passive negotiating position is assumed, it is very difficult to change. By the same token, to always take and never give will generate resentment from your client.

Often, the contractor will cede concessions, only to later turn around and recoup his losses with inflated change orders. At some point, he must make a decision as to if and when he will engage this strategy. For when he does, his stock with the architect and client may begin to irrevocably plummet. After having made too many concessions, he may no longer care, as he realizes he's been had. Some contractors plan to assault the owner with a barrage of change orders—usually low-ballers, while others take that course of action reactively, for example, as a response to offset their foolish generosity. Many contractors are duped into absorbing the cost of performing extra work gratis; work for which they are not responsible, such as an architect's omissions, usually at the prospect of future work, which is a ploy more commonly known as "waving the carrot." Unscrupulous contractors will expect their subcontractors to be equally charitable at the same dubious prospect.

To reiterate, this text cites seven chief reasons for weak positions in residential contracts as being:

- Undervaluation of base contract
- Undervaluation of general conditions
- Overly aggressive schedules
- Poor cash flow
- Unskilled or inappropriate level production

- Unknown subcontractors and vendors
- Difficult architects and clients

While there aren't a lot of statistics to substantiate these assertions, findings in surveys in other construction sectors do corroborate and shed some more light on them. The FMI and Construction Managers Association of America (CMAA) have conducted an annual owner's survey for 5 years now, which shows some interesting corollaries. Forty percent of the survey group was involved in the General Building sector, the rest in larger industrial and institutional projects. The respondents indicated the following top five reasons for cost overruns:

- Incomplete drawings[4]
- Poor preplanning process
- Escalating cost of materials[5]
- Lack of timely decisions by owner
- Excessive change orders[6]

The distinction that the author makes between the two lists is that with the exception of "difficulty in working relationships with the client or architect," the text also refers to the causes which are controllable from the supply side (general contractors and construction managers), whereas the survey respondents indicate their clients and architects as the source of the problem. Part of the survey group included members of the CMAA, therefore the survey has great implications for the construction management sector, which we will discuss in Chap. 5.

100 Acre Wood[7]

This is the euphemism I describe for the sites of those projects that languish into a state of torpor. It is a dire circumstance; subcontractors have left to service projects that they are able to work on, or the contractor may have demobilized most of his forces. The site is quiet and feels empty. Quietude and emptiness are anathema to the building process. They also come with a price. No project sits idle in midproduction without someone bankrolling the hiatus. Things have to get pretty bad to get to this point, in fact, egregious. Nonetheless, it happens all the time. It happens to projects that have not been taken seriously, or involve incompetent contractual parties including the client.

However, a project need not cease altogether to resemble 100 Acre Wood. Some projects are undertaken with such a level of incompetence that they simply can't be taken seriously. We are, in fact, talking about high-end residential projects—the frequency of incompetently managed and constructed projects in this sector is astounding and alarming because there is no justification for it. To find such incompetence where the highest level of performance is required and routinely advertised as being such is wholly unacceptable.

THE UNIFORM CONTRACT.

FORM OF CONTRACT
ADOPTED AND RECOMMENDED FOR GENERAL USE
BY THE
AMERICAN INSTITUTE OF ARCHITECTS
AND THE
NATIONAL ASSOCIATION OF BUILDERS.

_____

ARCHITECTS.

This Agreement, made the_____day of

_____in the year one thousand eight hundred and ninety_____

by and between_____

_____

_____

_____

_____

_____party of the first part

(hereinafter designated the Contractor), and_____

_____

_____

_____

_____

_____party of the second part

(hereinafter designated the Owner),

Witnesseth that the Contractor, in consideration of the fulfillment of the agreements herein made by the Owner, agrees with the said Owner, as follows:

ARTICLE I. The Contractor under the direction and to the satisfaction of

_____ Architects,

acting for the purposes of this contract as agents of the said Owner, shall and will provide all the materials and perform all the work mentioned in the specifications and shown on the drawings prepared by the said

Architects for the_____

_____

_____

_____

_____

_____

_____

_____

_____

_____

_____

_____

_____

which drawings and specifications are identified by the signatures of the parties hereto.

ART. II. The Architects shall furnish to the Contractor, such further drawings or explanations as may be necessary to detail and illustrate the work to be done, and the Contractor shall conform to the same as part of this contract so far as they may be consistent with the original drawings and specifications referred to and identified, as provided in Art. I.

It is mutually understood and agreed that all drawings and specifications are and remain the property of the Architects.

AIA 1899

Contracts

Every project should have a signed prime contract between the client and general contractor. There is plenty of work that takes place on a handshake, but such agreements are rare when any substantial amount of money is on the line. Without a signed contract the general contractor is at a disadvantage, if he should not get paid, he would have little leverage in litigation.

The parties to different contract structures are variable. At minimum, there are the owner and the contractor (Fig. 2.1a). As the work becomes more involved, a design team is retained by the owner, and subcontractors by the general contractor (Fig. 2.1b). Until the twentieth century, for the most part, the impact of architects on the industry was not really being felt—contractors did without them. Nowadays, only design/builders do without an outside architect, only because they themselves offer the design services with their own architects. Additionally, more complex projects may require another tier of designers, engineers, and consultants, as well as subcontractors (Fig. 2.1c). Finally, the owner may decide on a construction management contract,[8] where either the owner contracts the subcontractors directly (Fig. 2.1d) or he contracts with a construction manager as constructor (Fig. 2.1e), substituting "project manager" with "construction manager." However, as we shall see, construction managers are virtually nonexistent to the residential sector, save for new construction.[9]

Contract structures

There are several contract structures that are available to owners and contractors wishing to do business together. Different contract structures distribute leverage and risk between parties in a variety of arrangements. Table 2.1 illustrates the allocation of risk between owner and contractor based on given contract structures. Risk and leverage in the contract structure will affect the way the contractor approaches the project financially.

Competitive bid/stipulated sum

Competitively bid projects are essentially cost-driven, with the project typically being awarded to the lowest, or one of the lower bids, and/or the bidder who promises the earliest delivery. It is the most common arrangement, and places all risk with the general contractor—set scope of work, for a set fee. Any deviation from the protocol will necessitate a change order, or as I like to say the contractor "comes a-begging," given the poor margin contractors typically realize for their change orders. For clients, the lump sum contract has traditionally been the most preferred instrument. The AIA synopsis of A101 is as follows:

> A101[TM]-1997 Standard Form of Agreement Between Owner and Contractor where the Basis of Payment is a Stipulated Sum.[10] This is a standard form of agreement between owner and contractor for use where the basis of payment is a stipulated sum (fixed price). The A101[TM]-1997 document adopts by reference and is designed

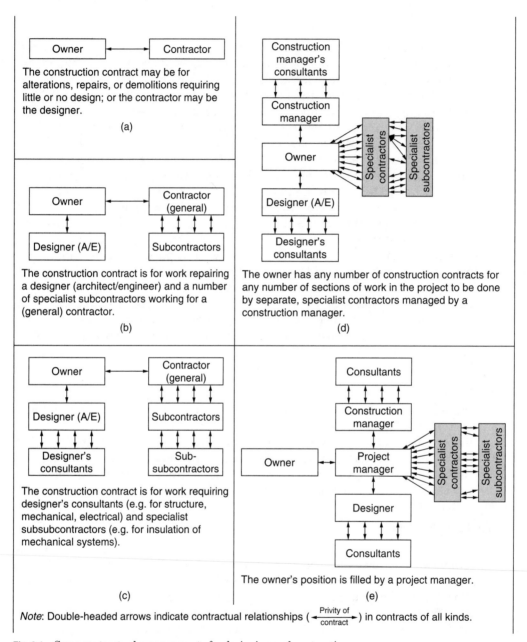

Fig. 2.1   Some contractual arrangements for designing and contracting.

for use with A201™-1997, *General Conditions of the Contract for Construction*, thus providing an integrated pair of legal documents. When used together, they are appropriate for most projects. For projects of limited scope, however, use of A107™-1997 might be considered.

TABLE 2.1   Scale of Contractual Risk Distribution

	(1)	(2)	(3)	(4)	(5)	(6)	(7)
Owner	Risk	Risk	Risk	Risk	Risk	Risk	Risk
Con-tractor	Risk	Risk	Risk	Risk	Risk	Risk	Risk
Contract type	Lump-sum contract (No changes in contract)	Lump-sum contract (Some changes in contract)	Lump-sum contract (Many changes) (Or) (Maximum cost-plus-fee)	Maximum cost-plus-fee contract with sharing-clause (50/50)	Maximum cost-plus-fee contract with sharing-clause (75/25)	Cost-plus-fixed-fee contract	Cost-plus percent-fee contract

Notes:
(1) Only slight risk to owner.
(2) Some changes in contract change nature of lump-sum contract and introduce more risk of loss for owner.
(3) Many changes in contract may alter nature of contract and risk distribution considerably.
(4) Theoretical (not practical) distribution of risk about equal (50/50).
(5) Variation in risk distribution depends on many things, including level of maximum cost, distribution in sharing of savings/losses, etc.
(6) Some risk to contractor. (i.e., is fixed fee adequate if scope of contract increases?)
(7) Only slight risk to contractor. (i.e., is percent fee adequate?)

As stated above, in addition to the above contracts, an AIA general conditions document will generally be incorporated into the contract; in fact, the contracts are designed with that in mind, and all cross-reference the A201. Interestingly enough, the A201 is a 38 page document that evidently eclipses the scope of the A101, while the main contract indicates the basics—contract sum, schedule, contractual parties, description of the work, the A201 is exhaustive in its treatment of the language, dictating the administration, and finer points of managing the base contract. The AIA synopsis A201 is as follows:

> A201™-1997 General Conditions of the Contract for Construction. The General Conditions are an integral part of the contract for construction. They set forth the rights, responsibilities, and relationships of the owner, contractor, and architect. Though not a party to the contract for construction between owner and contractor, the architect does participate in the preparation of the contract documents and performs certain construction phase duties and responsibilities described in detail in the general conditions. A201™ is typically adopted by reference in certain other AIA documents, such as owner-architect agreements, owner-contractor agreements, and contractor-subcontractor agreements. Thus, it is often called the "keystone" document.
>
> Since conditions vary by locality and by project, supplementary conditions are usually added to amend or supplement portions of the General Conditions as required by the individual project. Review the model language provided in A511™-1999, *Guide for Supplementary Conditions*, as a basis for creating supplementary conditions to A201™.

After a prolonged negotiation period between general contractors (represented by the American General Contractors Association), and architects' associations;

the A201 was revised in 1997 to include a number of changes, most notably, the Article 4 section, which provides a mediation process before arbitration, as well as mutual waivers of consequential damages. Every general contractor should be familiar with this document as its language has strong ramifications for him, some of which we will address in the course of this text. Some general contractors feel that portions of this language are so strongly biased toward the interests of the architect and owner that they refuse to sign it. Indeed, owners' attorneys routinely find objectionable language in the A201. The complicated and often nebulous language of the A201 has fostered a thriving industry of alternative language developers—attorneys who draft riders and addenda modifying the A201. Even the prospect of the replacement of a single word in the document could summon every construction lawyer within the contiguous United States to filibuster the merits of the consideration. That notion is a testament to the pervasiveness of the document. The AIA is aware of this issue, and felt it necessary to publish the *Commentary on AIA Document A201-1997*, a 101-page guide to the A201 as a reference for those who are baffled by the A201 (which is most of us).

Resultantly, contractors and their lawyers often insist on either excluding the A201 from the contract agreement, or provide substitute clauses to better represent their interests. Of course these opinions vary widely, depending on which party's attorney is consulted; however, this text shall refer to Joseph A. McManus, Jr.'s 1998 paper *"Contractors" Amending AIA A201-1997: General Conditions of the Contract for Construction.*[11] McManus essentially classifies the A201 clauses into three categories:

- Those which should remain without change
- Those which require change, for which substitute language is presented
- Those which should be removed

Of this latter group, there are several clauses that McManus finds as being unacceptable to the contractor. They are:

> 1.1.7; 1.5.2; 3.2.1; 3.3.2; 3.10.1,2; 3.12.4; 3.12.6; 3.12.8; 3.12.10; 4.3.2; 4.4.2-4; 4.6.4; 4.6.5; 5.4; 6.2.3; 9.3.1.2; 9.5.1.4; 9.6.3; 11.5.2; 12.2.5; 14.2.1.2; 14.2.2.1; 14.2.2.2.

Some of the language McManus objects to, with good reason, is as exemplified below. He recommends considerable modifications to many of the A201 clauses to the extent that one wonders if the AIA isn't unduly preoccupied with legalities. However, that conclusion would be a simplistic (and erroneous) view of a complex document. It should be said that the American Institute of Architect's mission statement does not focus unduly on litigation, or on their public advocacy position:[12]

AIA Mission Statement

The American Institute of Architects is the voice of the architecture profession dedicated to:

- Serving its members
- Advancing their value
- Improving the quality of the built environment

However, judging from some of the language of the A201, it follows that attorneys and insurance companies had more input than any architect would ever stop to consider. The reasons why McManus, and anyone giving a close read, would find certain A201 clauses objectionable are:

- The unfair allocation of risk, especially to owners
- The inequitable shifting of responsibility
- The possibility for abuse of certain language
- Controversial language
- Confusion
- Creation of extra responsibilities

Some examples he gives are as follows:

Re 9.5.1

The Architect may withhold a *Certificate for Payment* . . . to protect the Owner from loss for which the Contractor is responsible.
Delete subparagraph 9.5.1.4 in its entirety.
9.5.1.4: reasonable evidence that *the Work* cannot be completed for the unpaid balance of the contract sum.

> It is illogical for a general contractor, who is struggling to finish a project, to be punished by allowing the architect to decline certification of the remaining funds available for completion. To the contrary, it is in the owner's best interest to ensure that the contractor is promptly paid all earned and available funds to provide the necessary incentive to finish the work.[13]

The behavior of predatory attorneys and exculpating insurance companies in the industry evidently necessitated an A201 article to keep them at bay. Regarding residential construction, the A201 11.3.3 contains important language affecting that industry:

> 11.1.3 The Owner shall not require the Contractor to include the Owner, Architect, or other persons or entities as additional insureds on the Contractor's Liability Insurance coverage under Paragraph 11.1.

AIA commentary:

> Some owners have required contractors to name them as additional insurers under the contractor's liability policy. While some additional protection may be gained in this way, it ultimately increases the cost of insurance to the contractor without measurably reducing the risk of disputes on the project.

It is often the custom for residential contracts to require additional insured coverage by the contractor. The range of individuals requiring indemnification can be endless, especially within urban areas and apartment buildings. Whether or not the A201 language precludes the requirement, contractors are typically pressured into providing the coverage if they want the project. As the AIA says, this practice has an effect of increasing contractor's insurance overhead; however, contractors merely pass these costs on to their clients.

McManus goes on to say that:

> Not all projects are suited for an unamended A201. For example, smaller projects, and projects on which a long-standing Owner-contractor relationship exists do not need the complexity of the A201. A201 places on owners and contractors many responsibilities that may not be unwillingly assumed by a smaller organization.[14]

Well put; in fact, the vast majority of residential renovations fit or come close to this criteria.

According to the AIA, despite its perceived leanings, the A201 was meant to be a balanced document—one that represents each contract party equally. At least that was the intent of the AIA. Apparently, it does not always achieve its purpose; however, in its pursuit of balance it incorporates many clauses that are fair and helpful. Thus, it is not uncommon that the A201 can be a negotiated document that is amenable through riders or supplemental conditions, just as its creation was. According to the AIA A201 Commentary:

> A201 is intended to be modified. It is designed for general use, and cannot include all the requirements applicable to a specific project and location.

The AIA's position regarding the A201 is: (1) that it will always be a work in progress; one that is duly updated every 10 years[15] to reflect changes in the industry. It will next be updated again in 2007, (2) the document will never make everyone happy; there will always be someone who believes his best interests are not represented, and (3) as the synopsis above indicates, the A201 is intended to comprise only the foundation of the overall agreement, to which is routinely added supplementary conditions. It is a balance of representation that the AIA truly aspires to create in this document because the pursuit of this balance is an endless windfall for countless law firms. Again, this was not the AIA's intention. In fact, the opposite is true: the document is meant to be as unambiguous as possible, and courts have historically found that the (unmodified) language of the A201 is unambiguous. This is somewhat of a paradox; while the articles of the A201 are held to be unambiguous by the courts, they are routinely modified with riders by attorneys to fit different purposes. Such riders render the document into an instrument subject to reinterpretation. Legal documents should be mutable, not static.

Alternatively, to the A101, the AIA offers the A107:

> A107[TM]-1997 Abbreviated Standard Form of Agreement Between Owner and Contractor for Construction Projects of Limited Scope Where the Basis of Payment is a Stipulated Sum

A107-1997 is intended for use where the basis of payment is a stipulated sum (fixed price). The document contains abbreviated general conditions derived from A201-1997 and is appropriate for construction projects of limited scope not requiring the complexity and length of the combination of documents A101™-1997 and A201™-1997, *General Conditions of the Contract for Construction.* A107™ is appropriate for use when the owner and contractor have established a prior working relationship (for example, a previous project of like or similar nature), or where the project is relatively simple in detail or short in duration.

As indicated, the abbreviated general conditions are intended to simplify the contractual agreement. This document can be very appropriate for the smaller residential industry. However, as the synopsis indicates, this document is not for everyone.

Budget

Cost-driven projects with fixed or limited funds to spend may require an estimator to furnish a budget and schedule without design documentation, i.e., conceptually. Theoretically, any designer should design within a given budget; however, there are typically so many unknowns at this early stage that budgeting becomes too difficult for your average designer, who will typically seek the aid of a general contractor. Conceptual budgeting requires a special individual indeed to attain any degree of accuracy. The design is then executed within the parameters of the budget by the architect with the assistance of the estimator. Often, a gross maximum price, or GMP, is invoked to jump-start such a project. In this way, the contract can be let before the design is complete. Budget projects are invariably underfinanced, and a contractor may be asked to "sharpen his pencil," or offer a discount. This is not value engineering the work in order to meet the budget. Not enough projects are set aside during this phase, even when it is apparent that there is not enough money in the budget to achieve the design intent.

It used to be the responsibility of the architect to design within the budget, and to secure the contractor to build within that budget. Any shortfalls were the responsibility of the architect, who typically tried passing them down to the contractor. Nowadays, a contractor is still likely to be asked to take responsibility for such shortfalls; however, the architect is seldom held to account by the contractor for not designing within the budget. If the proposals come in too high, the architect will often attribute blame on the contractors bidding the work. I have seldom heard an architect chastised by the client for overdesigning, or underbudgeting a project. A good architect will realize the owner is over budget before the project he designs it, not after working drawings are distributed. Otherwise, he must be advised by his contractor, he should also advise the client that the project is over budget; not necessarily that contractors bid the job high. Therefore, as a contractor it is good practice to notify your architect that a project is over budget. The problem is that the contractors seldom know what the budget is; therefore, they are unaware of shortfalls. Suffice it to say, budgeted projects can be volatile.

As the numbers are loose and unfixed in a budget contract, it would seem most, if not all, the risk is saddled with the client, ostensibly a windfall for the contractor; hence, the GMP is often invoked. Another safeguard clients use against getting hosed in a budget contract is to underfinance it; not uncommonly, to a point making it impossible to execute. Of course, that is not the intention, but invariably the end result generates a budget, which is so meager it can't possibly be manipulated. Even so, with these safeguards, few clients have the stomach for this arrangement.

However, many negotiated contracts are drawn from budgets. For this kind of work, a contractor will want to be very specific in what he is budgeting, in fact, more specific than he would be in a stipulated-sum contract, because as I have said, he will likely be brought to task to substantiate glaring variances. A contractor would ideally want to have about a 90% degree of exactitude between budgeted and actual costs. That is the mark of an expert. For stipulated-sum contracts, a contractor should be no less than 95% accurate; else he is likely to cut into his profit margin.

So, it is somewhat misleading to say all the risk is saddled with the client in an unfixed price contract. Although a project may come in overbudget, and the contractor is duly paid, he risks compromising future prospects with his architect and client, and possibly his reputation; he could be marked as a low-baller. What may at first be perceived as a windfall is in fact, a death knell.

Construction management

A construction manager can act as both constructor and construction manager, or simply as advisor. Budget and cost-plus fee projects lend themselves well to this contract structure, as do large or complicated projects. This subject will be treated at length in Chap. 5, where construction management contract structures will also be discussed.

Fast track

A schedule-driven contract, wherein work commences before the design documentation is complete, is often called a "fast track" project. The remaining design documentation follows just ahead of each stage, or substage, of the production schedule. This arrangement is intended to reduce the overall schedule—design through buildout. It is typically invoked in order to reduce carrying costs, or owner downtime. They are popular in commercial work where the design of the project is not too complex, and lead times are short. These sorts of projects enjoy a flexibility unknown to the residential builder.

In high-end residential markets, you will sometimes be requested to embark on a fast-track project, but it will never be advertised as such. In fact, the offending party may not even realize this nuance. You may be told on a schematic project that once the work begins, the balance of the documentation will follow. Such endeavors are nearly always failures, as complex high-end residential projects don't feature the fluidity necessary to build in this fashion. Either, designers don't deliver documentation on time, the production windows are squeezed beyond reason, or both. However, certain broken-out components of a project may be fast-tracked, or have to be, in order to facilitate a schedule, which can accelerate a project along, provided the timeline is kept to by the design team. For instance, paint colors won't be needed until well into the build-out phase. The walls will go up regardless of there being a paint specification. But things such as infrastructure cannot be put off to the last minute, especially if they are critical path tasks (see Chap. 3).

To expedite a fast track project, components of the work are often ordered ahead of time, i.e., lead times should not play a factor in so far as timing is concerned, as ideally materials are procured in advance, and then stored until such time as the project is ready for them. For example, an exotic stone may take a year to quarry and machine. This lead time could impact the overall duration of the project. The job team will want to procure this material as soon as possible, and arrange to seamlessly integrate it into the work without holding up to wait for its delivery. Because high-end projects often use exotic and custom materials with long lead times, and intensive labor factors, fast track does not tend to facilitate your average high-end project. However, should a long lead order needed for a critical path task not arrive on time, the entire fast-track schedule could be threatened.

The fast-track arrangement requires a good deal of teamwork, especially between the design and production teams. Depending on things such as risk and carrying costs, things can get dicey real fast, as delays tend to be magnified, given the aggressive schedule. You will need a strong project manager to generate and track documentations, as the flow of information is the key to keeping this type of project moving. Deadlines tend to be minimal—a much-needed drawing may arrive at the last minute, leaving the contractor no review and preparation time, and no production window.

Negotiated bid and high-end

Negotiated bid contracts are popular when there is a shortlist of contractors to bid a given contract, or when the contractor is nominated before having issued a proposal (prequalified). They tend to leverage the contractor, as he has been sought out, or preselected. They are common in high-end residential work, where the bid-field may be limited, and with repeat customers, wherein a positive working relationship has been preestablished. The understanding is that the contractor is highly suited to the project, and only the price and schedule need be negotiated. These types of contracts are becoming more and more popular. There are a number of reasons for this:

The concept of the negotiated bid aspires to produce a win/win scenario for the owner and contractor. Negotiation is more upfront and open-ended compared to stipulated sum contracts. The negotiated bid process also lends itself well to developing the budget and design concept of projects still in preconstruction. Because of the high rate of project failures in the industry, some owners are willing to pay a premium, or make a leap of faith, if they are secure in their knowledge that they will be working with a contractor who can deliver on time and within budget. They understand the concept that cost-driven incentives are antithetical to high-end work, and that value is measured in quality, not in dollar savings. Having learned from their past mistakes, savvy owners realize the value of paying a little more now, than a lot more later. In the high-end sector, as there is typically a narrow playing field of qualified general contractors, there is likewise a shortage of skilled trades, and specialty trades. The contractors who specialize in this work have access, sometimes exclusively, to these tradesmen, as monopolization is in their best interests—the more work they give them, the more they control them. These subcontractors tend to be very loyal, straying from their main source only at a premium incentive. However, they will always favor their prime accounts. Some of these subcontractors are given so much steady work by two or three general contractors that they have no incentive to entertain overtures from new accounts.

It takes a good track record, negotiating know-how, and in high-end, a special set of skills to master negotiated bid contracts, but it is a worthwhile goal to pursue. It is much more pleasant to work in an environment where there is mutual trust between the owner and the contractor than it is to work in an atmosphere of adversity. The difference between competitive and negotiated bid is that you are wanted because of your good works, not merely needed because of your low prices.

Design-build

Design-build is an arrangement wherein the owner hires a company that provides both design and production services, which are traditionally contracted separately. Typically, an architect and engineers are on the staff. These firms make up only a tiny segment of the industry unless you want to count developers. In high-end construction, design-build firms are rare, with most of this type of design talent opening their own design firms. Yet, it is not uncommon for a contractor to design-build portions of the work, especially if it is to be mostly developed by their tradesmen. The AIA offers the A191 as an instrument for this purpose:

> A191^{TM}DB-1996 Standard Form of Agreement Between Owner and Design/Builder Two agreements for use in sequence by an owner contracting with one entity serving as a single point of responsibility for both design and construction services. The first covers preliminary design and budgeting services, while the second deals with final design and construction. Although it is anticipated that an owner and a design/builder entering into the first agreement will later enter into the second, the parties are not obligated to do so and may conclude their relationship after the terms of the first agreement have been fulfilled. The AIA will retire this document on August 31, 2006 (see below).
> A141^{TM}-2004, Agreement Between Owner and Design-Builder
> A141-2004 replaces A191-1996 and consists of the Agreement and three exhibits, Exhibit A, Terms and Conditions, Exhibit B, Determination of the Cost of the Work, and Exhibit C, Insurance and Bonds. Exhibit B is not applicable if the parties select to use a Stipulated Sum. A141 obligates the Design-Builder to execute fully the Work

required by the Design-Build Documents, which include A141 with its attached exhibits, the project criteria and the design-builder's proposal, including any revisions to those documents accepted by the owner, supplementary and other conditions, addenda and modifications. The Agreement requires the parties to select the payment type from three choices: (1) Stipulated Sum, (2) Cost of the Work Plus Design-Builder's Fee, and (3) Cost of the Work Plus Design-Builder's Fee with a Guaranteed Maximum Price. A141 with its attached exhibits forms the nucleus of the Design-Build Contract. Because A141 includes its own Terms and Conditions, it does not use A201-1997.

Cost-plus or fee based

This arrangement refers to when the contractor works for a set fee, or percentage of the final cost of the work, which is typically unknown at the time of contract. This is an unusual arrangement, which appears to put all risks with the owner, the exception being the invocation of a guaranteed maximum price clause. When it is used, an "open book" system is generally implemented, wherein subcontractor invoices are part of the billing package, and all financial statements are available for the client's inspection. Few contractors work cost-plus without a high level of scrutiny. Because of the obvious potential for abuse, it is therefore only rarely used; however, it is common practice for a construction manager to base his fees on the percentage of the base contract, especially if he is not the constructor. Often, to control costs, unit prices are part of the cost of the work. There are two types of cost-plus fee based AIA contracts. Following is an AIA synopsis for both:

> A111™-1997 Standard Form of Agreement Between Owner and Contractor Where the Basis of Payment is the Cost of the Work Plus a Fee with a Negotiated Guaranteed Maximum Price
> This standard form of agreement between owner and contractor is appropriate for use on most projects requiring a negotiated guaranteed maximum price, when the basis of payment to the contractor is the cost of the work plus a fee. A111™ adopts by reference and is intended for use with A201™–1997, General Conditions of the Contract for Construction, thus providing an integrated pair of legal documents.
> A114™-2001 Standard Form of Agreement Between Owner and Contractor Where the Basis of Payment is the Cost of the Work Plus a Fee without a Guaranteed Maximum Price
> The A114™-2001 is appropriate for use on projects when the basis of payment to the contractor is the cost of the work plus a fee, and the cost is not fully known when construction begins. A114 adopts by reference and is intended for use with A201™-1997, *General Conditions of the Contract for Construction*, thus providing an integrated pair of legal documents.

The use of a cost-plus fee contract indicates that there is not sufficient design information available at the time the contract is signed, in order to create a fixed-sum contract. A general contractor should inform the owner regarding how costs will be determined, and should bill according to that structure. A standard cost-plus fee structure is shown in Figure 2.2. Essentially, the costs of the work are divided into two categories—direct costs and indirect costs.[16]

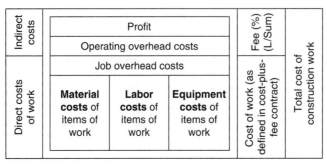

Fig. 2.2 Costs of work: the classes and their relationships. (*Keith Collier, Construction Contracts, 2nd Ed. (New Jersey) Prentice Hall.*)

Unit price

A unit price contract is a contract wherein set prices are issued for specific quantities, or units. Often, unit prices are solicited as part of a stipulated sum contract. The intent is for the owner to control costs if additional work is necessary. When change orders are introduced, the cost for the same scope of work typically increases, and the contractor may have to build-in safeguards against such occurrences, depending on the circumstances. For the most part, unit prices are not helpful in the negotiation of residential projects, one reason being that there generally are not enough quantities involved to negotiate a preferred rate. Another reason is that, especially in high-end work, much custom work is involved or it is labor intensive, involves exotic material, or requires a learning curve, all of which are difficult costs to control, not conducive to unit pricing. Custom residential work is not production oriented. The set-up costs are a much larger percentage of the production cost than in large-scale production (see Special Considerations).

Subcontracts

The AIA publishes the *A401 Contractor-Subcontractor Agreement*:

> A401™-1997 Standard Form of Agreement Between Contractor and Subcontractor This document is intended for use in establishing the contractual relationship between the contractor and subcontractor. It spells out the responsibilities of both parties and lists their respective obligations, which are written to parallel A201™, General Conditions of the Contract for Construction. Blank spaces are provided where the parties can supplement the details of their agreement. A401™ may be modified for use as an agreement between the subcontractor and a sub-subcontractor.

The implementation of this instrument for smaller residential projects is problematic. Perhaps on larger projects, it must be used, as well as the AIA *G702 Application and Certificate for Payment*, and its accompanying worksheet *G703 Continuation Sheet for G702* can also be used. The subcontract also includes the general requirements and AIA A201 portion of the prime contract, which must be appended to it in order for the subcontract to be correctly executed. However, many smaller subcontractors prefer not to use the AIA subcontract, or G702/3, as they are difficult to use without AIA software, and the data entry and tracking to utilize it: a system few subcontractors have the infrastructure to manage. Additionally, they dislike the notion that they are tethered to the prime contract; especially the general conditions portion, for these reasons, they may even settle for a mere signature on their proposal, rather than sign an A401. If you have good standing relationships with your subcontractors, contract instruments aren't a sticking point. However, if the A401 is implemented the general contractor/subcontractor contractual relationship will have critical legal obligations that would not otherwise be enumerated in a simpler document. Where the work is cut-and-dried, and there can be no misinterpretation, a purchase or work order can be an acceptable method. At minimum the instrument must indicate:

- The scope of work
- The contract documents (named drawings)
- The schedule requirements

While there are only three requirements for the purchase order, incorrectly executed purchase orders are epidemic, causing endless arguing and negotiating over what should be a simple process.

Purchase Orders

Scope of work and named drawings

Short of a subcontract, purchase orders, or work orders are issued to subcontractors in order to authorize their work, in lieu of the AIA A401. Of course, without the A401 agreement, the relationship of the subcontractors to the prime owner, and the architect will not be a traditional one, wherein the A201 General Conditions would state specific requirements, specifically the Article 5. Nevertheless, this arrangement is commonplace, and architects are resigned to it. And, as we shall discuss further, the A201 has requirements that are too stringent for the average residential project. So long as the terms of payment, schedule, scope of work, and drawings are referred to, a purchase or work order should be sufficient for most subcontracts.

A subcontractor, who is bidding the drawings, in his proposal is taking ownership of the means and methods, and design and (to some extent) intent of what the drawings show. In this way, anything not fitting that criteria is likely a change order. General contractors must bid the work in this way, and so should their subcontractors. Nevertheless, many subcontractors insist on, or prefer, enumerating their scope of work in their proposal. Many general contractors will accept that, thinking such a proposal will be more specific. While the proposal may be more specific, it certainly isn't more comprehensive; in fact, it does not adequately incorporate the project documentation. By specifically enumerating what they are going to do, it almost seems as if subcontractors are more concerned with emphasizing what they do not propose to do, or their qualifications. Given that, some subcontractors will name the drawings and give a scope of work. This practice too is problematic, as there is a tacit understanding that the subcontractor's interpretation of the drawings is represented in the scope of work; therefore, by signing such a purchase order, the subcontractors can always defer to their scope of work, or the drawings, whichever is more convenient.

Schedule Requirements

Most projects have a basic schedule. However, it may only consist of a start and end date of the overall project. To issue such a schedule to a subcontractor serves little purpose other than to inform him of these dates. It will say little or nothing specific about how and when his work must be started and finished. Part of the terms of every subcontract must state the respective subcontractors' start and end dates. Otherwise, the only requirements they can be held to are the overall start and end dates. Regrettably, as we shall see in Chap. 3, the quality and depth of information of most schedules will not have this information, or will not state it coherently.

If the schedule does not show accurate subcontractor information, the proposal or subcontract that references the schedule won't be accurate either. This can be just as troublesome a problem as defining the scope of work incorrectly; if people can't do what you need them to do when you need them, the subcontract work could become out-of-sequence, late, or not get done at all. This notion alone should be incentive enough to make a proper schedule, and refer it in each respective subcontract.

The scheduling of subcontractors can become a sticking point when projects are delayed or out of sequence. Often, a subcontractor is not in a position to change his schedule, or perhaps he even turned work away in order to do the work at hand first. A common mistake is for the general contractor to saddle his subcontractors with the responsibility of adjusting to ever-changing conditions, which is unfair, and bad for business. At minimum, it should be a joint effort. In many cases the general contractor is not blameful for the delay that caused the subcontractor a problem. Under this circumstance a subcontractor should be given more latitude; however, that is seldom the case. They are typically told to make the adjustment without a fuss. However, a subcontractor performing on a contract that does not specify his start and end dates will not be obliged to make any adjustment or concessions to accommodate delays or changes.

The problems associated with subcontractor schedule in the residential sector cannot be underestimated. Subcontractors tend to be small companies with limited resources. If one project is delayed, they may pull off to service another project. Then, when asked to return to the delayed project, they may not be able to, as they are now involved with another project. If the work is part of the critical path, the postponement of it will create delays in the schedule, or it will delay other trades and scopes of work. The general contractor must then decide if he will wait until the subcontractor can get back on task, or if he will keep moving, albeit out of sequence. On an aggressive schedule, he will have no choice but to keep moving.

Special Considerations:
The Perils of High-End Construction

Residential high-end construction is one of the most difficult construction sectors to master. It is extremely problematic, with lots of risk, and anxiety. The client, architect, and contractor must all be informed in order for a project to be successful. First, the idea of just what constitutes high-end varies widely. To some, high-end is a $/SF value. In other words, any project over $x$$/SF is in the high-end range. To others, it is a level of quality and the type of program that dictates the higher square foot price, each contingent on the other. And to others, it may merely be the renown of the designer or architect, or the exoticness of the materials. Suffice it to say, high-end is a subjective term even within small parameters. For example, one company may charge twice the unit price of another for the exact same product. Although the design criteria are the same, each perceives the work differently, and would deliver according to his assumptions. Unfortunately, the quality of work is not always commensurate with the cost of the work, and this is the crux of endless disputes, which we shall discuss in Chap. 8.

The important thing to keep in mind is what constitutes high-end work. This is no simple consideration. A client with unlimited resources may hire an architect who is unfamiliar with his client's ideals. The money may be spent on expensive materials, but the design and skilled labor may fall short. The current lexicon of today's high-end residential designs includes, but is by no means limited to, the following:

- Labor intensive finishes, such as French polish and Venetian plaster
- Exotic species of wood and stone
- Custom profiles and fabrications: wood, plaster, stone, metal, glass, tile, and so forth.
- Artisan materials and fixtures
- Architectural and ornamental metals and glass
- Custom hardware
- Oversized finish stock
- Epicurean kitchen appliances
- Dimming systems
- Touch screen controls
- Audiophile audiovisual installations
- Digitally controlled Heating, Ventilation, and Air Conditioning (HVAC) systems
- Reveal and quirk details

If you find several of the above on a bid set of drawings, there is a good chance the project is high-end. Then ask yourself: "Can you really cut the mustard?" Many answer "yes," and to them, if there is enough money, they assume they can always find someone to do the work right. Unfortunately, residential construction is not structured that way any more than is any other industry; you don't always get what you pay for, especially if you don't understand what you're buying and selling.

A lot of contractors will take on high-end work, even though they do not have the resources to deliver it. They may figure that with the anticipated budget, they can't possibly lose. Since high-end residential projects tend to load up with expensive finishes, which are fit-up in the latter part of the project, it may not be until then that a project's glaring infrastructural shortcomings become apparent. This often happens because many contractors don't attach the same significance to infrastructure quality control as they do to finishes.

As a consultant, I often rate companies by my own scale; for example, company A may be qualified to install up to $250/SF, whereas company B may be qualified up to $650/SF. You should perform this evaluation for your own company. Make a graph of each completed project's $/SF on one axis, on the other, a success factor of one to ten. The success factor should be comprised of a combination of profitability, schedule diligence, and customer satisfaction. Find the benchmark where your company's overall rating seems to slip at a rate of x $/SF (Table 2.2). Setting the bar no lower than the *minimum acceptable rate of efficiency* will dictate what projects are within your abilities and which are not. The biggest mistake companies make is setting this bar too low: accordingly, the degree to which they overestimate their abilities will correspond with their failure rate.

Unfortunately, it is difficult to regulate quality on merits other than work installed. Optimally, a walk through of one of a prospective contractor's installations

TABLE 2.2   Performance Capability Graph

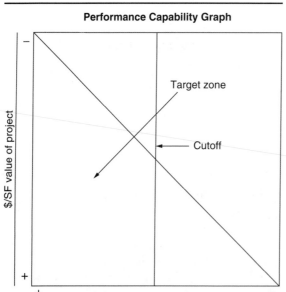

would be ideally fit to the purpose; however, homeowners, as a rule, won't appreciate groups of people traipsing through their home for a show-and-tell, in fact don't bother asking. Resultantly, general contractors rely on their portfolios, references, and braggadocio. Qualifying general contractors is a difficult and risky business, especially when the majority of high-end residential players are in over their head. Additionally, there are a host of companies who stray from their regular graze to take on a high-end project, thus complicating matters. There are publications that attempt to classify construction companies' acumen; however, they do not appear to be any more useful than restaurant guides. One such guide relies on "interviews with thousands of clients, extensive research and consultations with industry experts." Nevertheless, every contractor receives a rave review from the publisher. The publisher claims, "The result is a guide to the most reliable and professional home service providers that no homeowner should be without," despite the fact that it claims, "ratings and comments published do not convey any recommendation or endorsement of any specific providers." I have seen many companies listed that have no business being given high ratings, and some of the better companies escaping any mention whatsoever. At the end of the day, all the contractors in the book are "great," despite the claim that the publishers will "help you avoid the worst." Unfortunately, unsuspecting clients sometimes refer to these guides, much like they might look for a new restaurant they have never been to. While the publisher understands the need to simplify choosing a contractor, they do the industry and their readers a disservice by overselling and underdelivering their product.

The demand for high-end work evidently eclipses the supply of practitioners, and the situation will likely worsen over time. Statistics indicate some interesting trends:

> The number of owner households with annual incomes exceeding $120,000 has risen . . . up 73 percent between 1995 and 2001.
> High-value homes ($400,000>) represent just 11 percent of the total owner occupied housing inventory, but their owners completed over 800,000 room additions in 2002–3—contributing 43% of total expenditures in this category.
> Owners earning over $120,000 per year more than doubled their home improvement expenditures from 1995 to 2001, contributing almost 66 percent of inflation adjusted growth. In contrast, households with incomes under $80,000 accounted for only 16.4 percent of the growth . . . but only 3% of the increase in homeowner improvement spending.[17]

These trends indicate rising growth in the high-end sector, and the industry will have to rise to the occasion to meet the demands. Until recently, high-end work was the exception, and only a handful of contractors could do it. Now, it is becoming much more commonplace, despite the same shortage of skilled labor.

As an estimator, it is necessary to have a definite idea of what the design criteria are, and what it takes to deliver a given project. If he is bidding for different levels of work, he will need to invoke a sliding scale to his methods. This is done for each appraisal through the design or bid documentation; discourse with the design team, and from experience. Very little in the way of estimating guides can help. On the client/architect side, it must be understood that for the most part, high-end residential projects do not lend themselves well to cost-driven contracts. Think of the maxim "you can't have your cake and eat it too." This notion is continually flaunted, and many projects have been known to suffer because of it. The assumption associated with established contractors is that in at least some measure, the contractor is a known quantity who will perform to the level commensurate with the budget, or "you get what you pay for." However, it should be said, that some projects will not be built right no matter how much money is pumped into them. Architects know this. Many have been burned by not getting what they pay for. Their experiences make them gun-shy, and thus they continue to negotiate costs aggressively for fear they will be shortchanged. Contracts that are not cost-driven tend to be negotiated. Such contracts are becoming scarce. It can be said, that owners, design professionals, and general contractors alike all share the blame in the devaluation of high-end projects.

Gilding
Figure presents us with a door proposed to be finished in white and gold. When the paint is thoroughly hard, the parts to be gilded are judiciously selected (*a–q*). We may in passing remark that the transom light in the engraving bears a heraldic design, which should be embossed on the glass. *A Treatise on Architecture and Building Construction, Volume IV* (Scranton: The Colliery Engineer Co., 1899).

Less Is More[18]

When Mies van der Rohe coined the aphorism "less is more," he was referring to his dogma of an orthodox *Minimalism*; however, his observation carries over into our discussion, albeit in another context:

- Less is more—*work*
- Less *costs* more
- The less there is meant to be seen, the more (regrettably) defects stand out

Let's define these parameters:

The details inherent to the current lexicon of modernist and minimalist designers and architects dictates a high level of exactitude that requires more skill, greater clarity, and perfection of point, line and, plane, the geometric basis of these schools of thought. Straight, even, plumb, parallel, and level are all terms associated with degrees of exactitude. There is no such thing as "straighter," "more level," or "more plumb" as these are mere equivocations. When everything shows, a thing either is, or it is not straight, level, and plumb. Modernist and minimalist designs feature sharp lines and bold geometric planes as the defining elements of form and statement with little or no detail other than a quirk or reveal here and there. Think of the architect's inspection as a strip search. Adornment, trim and finishes, which historically is a means for a contractor to cover up mistakes, is eschewed in deference to severity and simplicity. The following elements of building are not part of the high-end modernist vocabulary:

- Molding: base, casing, cove, chair rail, cornice, shoe, and so forth
- Fillers
- Scribes
- Caulking
- Flange
- And quite often, texture

The above means and methods all give a contractor the ability to hide crudely executed substrates, poor jointing methods, and defects in general.

Look at the corners and spaces behind removed crown moldings and base boards and you will see just how little attention is typically given to these details by builders. If these spaces were to be finished and painted, they would seldom hold a line. It is just this severity and simplicity that is the bane of the production-oriented contractor, who ordinarily pays little heed to such nuances. It is always easier to achieve clarity with manufactured products than it is with hand-tooled; specifically, walls and ceilings, whereas automated machinery does not stray from the datum. The concept of perfection of point, line, and plane is anathema to most builders. They either can't produce it, or they can't do so efficiently. To do this builders must take great pains; sometimes moving at a fraction of the pace they are used to, and even then they may fail to hit the mark.

For example, the elevation and straightness of a long soffit in the ceiling of a school building can vary considerably without anyone taking notice, whereas the same detail in a high-end residence must be kept within strict tolerances; the contractor who did the soffit in a public school could never install the same work satisfactorily in a residence, and the high-end contractor could not compete with the low-end contractor's price for the school, especially his cost of labor—same detail, yet completely different ramifications. Consider their methods:

The school builder may construct the soffit using a 48-in. level projecting a level line along the length of it, or simply measure it down from the ceiling at a few equidistant points and connect them. The framing may go very quickly. He may even use a laser level, yet still frame the soffit crookedly, because the tool is poorly crafted and calibrated, or he can't keep to a line. Once the soffit is dry walled, the corner bead may be applied with a mallet and crimper—an attachment method that does not seem to take the concept of alignment very seriously. This tool will nearly always yield a crooked line, especially if its parts are not constantly tightened.

For the same soffit in a residence, the contractor will likely use a laser level or a jet line to align the framing. For a corner bead, he will not use the every-day extrusion, which as opposed to a sharp edged bead, has a rounded corner edge that invariably yields an unpleasant result. He will use the laser level or a jet line again, to align this corner bead. He will likely use ribbed panel nails to attach the bead, as opposed to a crimper, or drywall screws, which invariably twist the bead off its axis as it secures it to the substrate. The end product should be a perfectly straight knife edge detail.

What is the point of this comparison between high and low end? The criteria of what constitutes *standard levels of practice* have become so skewed, that most contractors have no idea of their legitimate standing in the hierarchy of performance. Much of what they consider high-end work is merely a standard practice and much of what they consider standard practice is far below any measure of acceptable tolerance.

High-End Hi-Jinx

It is awe inspiring just how far apart the cost of some architects' designs stray from clients' working budgets. Of course, it should be the responsibility of the architect to design within a client's budget; however, if he doesn't have all the criteria from his client, he must provide a contingency. As I said, early home architects had to design within the owner's budget. This may work for design/build firms, but for high-end construction it is a futile undertaking. It is equally remarkable how completely different the visualization of the end product is in everyone's eyes, as is the actual end product. Both of these discrepancies are extremely common on high-end projects.

An architect, contractor, or client unfamiliar with the nature of high-end work can contribute greatly to project failure. At minimum, the architect and contractor should be fluent in designing and building such projects. The average project would feature an architect and a contractor who have only some experience in their work. This is far from optimum; however, it is the reality of the industry. The real high-end players do exist. However, they are the exceptions. They tend to band together—quality architects with quality contractors.

For high-end construction, the general contractor must take the lead in guiding constructability issues, and the architect design issues. What tends to happen is that there are a number of grey areas that creep up on every job. Customary services are exacerbated in the breadth of their scope, yet are, just as often, not taken for by any party. This happens because of a general lack of foresight on the part of both parties to identify all the project's needs, and ensure that they will be met. In other words, the recipe for a disaster can be readily observed, upon close inspection, even before the first dollar is spent.

Unfortunately, there is often a third party to blame—the client. Clients are often guilty of being ignorant of the building process. They may mistakenly believe that because their project is so well endowed that it will be a "turnkey" operation; all aspects of the project will be seen to by one party or another, but never him. He only has to sit back and watch the process. It is the responsibility of the architect to educate his client as to his responsibilities in the process:

> Innocently and unknowingly, the Owner, usually on advice of counsel, a board member, a peer or friend, uses standardized contract agreements that are not coordinated or custom produced agreements. These uncoordinated and custom (sic) agreements most often result in duplication and gaps in services and eventually lead to some sort of conflict on the project. Adding to this dilemma, the parties, long before any contract was spoken of, lobbied the Owner during the selection phase, for more scope—more services equals more profit. But which party is supposed to do what, and what does "more" scope mean? This is the crux of the issue.[19]

Surprisingly, the above statement refers to projects that have a construction manager, who would ostensibly be onboard to iron out wrinkles. Even with the construction manager on the team, nebulous and uncoordinated contractual arrangements will lead to client dissatisfaction and its ensuing conflicts.

For architects, the problem may lie in the fact that the design budget is underfinanced. They are loath to point this out to the client, lest he take his business elsewhere. Some architects simply don't understand their responsibilities, or are unable to perform them to the level of detail that high-end demands, which is often considerable. They may be used to working with contractors whose detailers do their work for them. I don't believe that contractors do this because they are required to, but out of necessity because most interior architects don't have a comprehensive understanding of means and methods, especially in regard to mechanical electrical and plumbing (MEPs). If the detailers didn't design, little would ever get built. If there is enough capital in a project, the contractor will be happy to assume design responsibility; however, such services must be considered part of the means and methods as most contractors and their subcontractor's detailers are not licensed architects or engineers. If the design budget is underfinanced, chances are the construction budget will also fall short, thus creating dual strife. Again, the architect may have realized the construction budget was too small, but kept quiet about it.

For contractors, several other sets of dynamics are at play in assessing the integrity and value of a given project. Many contractors don't really understand what constitutes high-end. To them, only the material expense or contract value is a qualification. Conversely, any program with inexpensive materials likely would constitute a budget[20] project: wrong on both counts. Some larger firms that do large-scale core and shell work are often asked to do residences for their corporate clients. They don't hesitate to take on this work, although there is certainly an argument to turn it away; large general contractors are ill-prepared to do expensive, small scale, difficult and time-consuming projects. They generally don't have the experience, and the structure of their company can't adequately facilitate its special needs. They may do it because they feel obligated toward a valuable client, which is understandable. Even if the project is a loser, it can be typically written off as a loss by a large contractor. What can't be justified is the contractor who believes that because his company is big, his resources are endless—he can build anything. When the time comes to hashing out details with the architect, he will be surprised that he wasn't given working drawings at the start of the project as he is used to getting. He will be unfamiliar with the level of interaction and input, which the architect requires on his part. He simply won't be able to do it right. Even with good material and good subcontractors, his product will be compromised because his work is uncoordinated, and the contract administrated poorly on his part.

An otherwise excellent mill worker on a high-end union project was having difficulty with his installation. He was given hold[21] dimensions that were taken from axes lines on the floor established by the general contractor, and fabricated based on this information. The work was shipped (overseas, as it were) and stored until the project was ready for the work to be installed. Before substrates were applied to the walls, he came to install his grounds for his paneling. At this time he wanted to verify his dimensions; however, he was told that the axes lines had, since he last surveyed, been relocated and the framing set to the revised layout. Lines used for his hold dimensions were no longer relevant. Due to the change in dimensions, work fabricated too wide had to be scribed or refabricated. Work that was too narrow had to be refabricated. These are the perils of working with nonguaranteed hold dimensions.

More importantly, contractors unfamiliar with the tolerances and quality guidelines for high-end work are a drain on the industry. They may not even acknowledge or understand what the shortcomings of their work are even when it is right under their nose.

A stone setter I met on a project was having quality control problems. The gaps between the walls and his stone were exceedingly large, as were the joints between slabs, which he proceeded to pump up with buckets of grout; as if they were sidewalk joints. The site was always shrouded in a mountain of dust from the grinding and sanding needed to rework his mismatched stone joints. The designer was horrified and ordered the offending work to be removed. As the general contractor explained this to the stone setter it became clear that the stone setter did not agree with the designer's quality assessment. To him, it was simply implausible to assert that his work was substandard—he, having some 20 years' experience, and also recently completing a large installation of the lobby of a large scale "nut house," could not possibly produce substandard work. He was above such practices.

Aside from architects and contractors being unsuitable for a given project, there are many other things that can go wrong later in the process, when it is difficult to remediate them. Some of the more common maladies are discussed, in the following:

The intent of the work is misinterpreted: There can be a world of difference between what two different entities perceive as high quality. As a rule, the guidelines for quality are enumerated in the specification book, yet many of them are difficult to visualize or demonstrate. In any case, contract quality requirements are frequently ignored, or misinterpreted. As pertains to finishes, specification noncompliance is particularly problematic because often the problem goes undetected until it is too late. If the wrong vendor is on the project, you hope you find out at an early time, such as the qualification or submittal process, not when the work is delivered and installed. That is why you should never take chances with subcontractors you are not sure can execute the level of work you need.

Often, important and costly details are not part of the bid documents, and will be distributed after the contract is negotiated. It is your estimator's responsibility to identify any work which is unclearly detailed, especially if it has financial implications, and either provide a contingency for it, or qualify it. Another problem is work that is not shown in the drawings. An architect will generally indicate that missing details were implied by intent, or that the work is part of the means and methods. Consider some typical examples:

Because an architect did not detail window sills, the contractor has installed none. The architect argues that most windows have sills. Therefore, by drawing the window, he has implied that there should be a sill; for as he said, windows should have sills. Both architect and contractor should have known better.

Another architect had drawn a horizontal line across an elevation. Although there was no ceiling or section detail for this design, and no other reference to it, he insisted that the line in question constituted a drop ceiling, which he was entitled to at no extra cost. Depending on the value of the work, the contractor could have taken issue with that sentiment, or simply done the work and kept quiet about it. However, when there is a substantial degree of nebulous design information, there is likely to be bickering and change order conflicts.

If the project has a generous budget, the contractor may do a bit of extra work for free. But on a project that was aggressively negotiated, with horse-trading and credits for removed scope, the contractor may no longer be in any position to make such a concession. Smart contractors will flush out the hazy details of design drawings and either account for them in their bid, advise the architect, or take into consideration the fact that he will, to a certain degree, have to cover for the architect.

There is no consensus on the quality requirements: Even the tolerances set forth in a specification book leave some room for argument. A contractor may try to skimp on quality by using substandard material, and alternatively, an architect may raise the bar, making the requirements untenable. The finish trades; architectural millwork and metalwork, painting, plastering, glazing, stone and tile, are all notorious battlefields for quality compliance. MEP trades tend to receive less scrutiny than the finish trades, especially by architects unfamiliar with engineering, who although must sign off on the work, may not have a clue as to what they are looking at. Where there is uncertainty or room for misinterpretation, a control sample (for finishes) should be generated by the design team for bidding purposes because then, there can be no misunderstanding. For customized products, which are very common in the high-end, there often is no written criteria for quality, thus quality becomes subjective. The bar will invariably be set higher for custom work, as a builder has much more control over the end product than he would over a factory issued product.

Although the contractor and vendors understand the tolerance criteria, it won't necessarily trickle down to the mechanics in the field. Diligence in these matters is the crux of a good quality control program. Unbeknownst to those who don't peruse it, the specification manual for most projects will include industry standards for each trade set forth by their respective professional organization, for example, Architectural Woodworking Institute, Sheet Metal and Air Conditioning Contractors National Association, Underwriter's Laboratory, National Association of Home Builders (NAHB), Institute of Electrical & Electronics Engineers, National Association of Architectural Metal Manufacturers, Construction Specifications Institute (CSI), and many others. The only thing worse than not reading this part of the specifications is to be otherwise unfamiliar with the industry standards set forth. Many contractors mistakenly believe they are fluent in such matters, until proven wrong, which is unfortunate. Some contractors are well aware of performance criteria; however, this knowledge in of itself will not guarantee any level of quality, yet without such knowledge they would be hard put to meet such criteria.

There is a lack of skilled workers to perform the work: This is the bane of the high-end residential industry; there simply aren't enough workers of high skill level available to fit the demand. True craftsmen are a dying breed. Trade schools offer little in the way of specialized training, and even if they do, there would be a dearth of willing applicants dedicated enough to spend the time to master a trade. Trade schools have an enormous dropout rate, which would indicate a general lack of motivation in the workforce. Fewer people are encouraging and participating in the artisan crafts brought over by the immigrants than they once did, and fewer craftsmen are bringing their skills to this country as they once did. Part of the problem is that, over the years, labor costs have become prohibitive, especially union work, in such a way that training in the finer arts, labor intensive work, have not been adequately financed; evidently most clients are unwilling to pay the extra money for skilled work. Another problem has to do with occupational choices and work ethics in this country—manual labor has little appeal for a generation reared on media distraction, entitlement programs, and social subsidies. The last century saw labor trends morph from agrarian to industrial to technical and service workers. Resultantly, the truly talented tradesmen are in high demand; many, being smaller firms, are easily monopolized by one or two general contractors, as they can appreciate how hard it is to find talent. Despite talent being hard to find, it is out there. Unfortunately, there are pretenders as well. Some of them know they are underqualified, some of them don't. The result is the same; overaggressive premiums are often imposed on top of the highest skilled contractor's rates of compensation.

High-end residential is an extremely lucrative market, and the fastest growing home building and remodeling market (see Chap. 1). A local market with an average residential remodel price of $175/SF may have a high-end range between $600 and $700/SF, a prospect few are loath not to pursue, regardless of their capabilities. A smallish company can land a larger contract than a company in another market sector with twice the personnel. Thus, there are always contractors who want, or claim to deliver, high quality. The margin for error in this sector is so great, that failures can be extremely exaggerated. If a contractor isn't proficient in a given market sector, he should not participate or offer his services in it.

Nevertheless, the prospective rewards are so high that there will always be a mass of wannabes champing at the bit of high-end project opportunities. The demand side bargain hunters of the market continue to bankroll these losses by hiring low bidders, or others, who are incapable of delivering quality work. To quote astronaut Alan Shepherd:

> It is a very sobering feeling to be up in space and realize that one's safety factor was determined by the lowest bidder on a government contract.

It has become commonplace for the next highest bidder to be asked to come in to replace the lower bidder, who was unable to perform the work to a satisfactory level. Some owners have learned this lesson, and as a response, invoke other methods such as using the lowest bidder as a wedge to negotiate the next highest bidder downward. Invariably, the client pays much more than he would have, had he hired the next highest bidder at the asking price, from the get-go.

High-End Residential Quality Control

- There is a shortage of skilled workers in the residential construction sector.
- Workers are not adequately trained.
- Specialty and high-end craftsmen are in high demand and short supply.

While all the above statements ring true, they do not fully inform us as to why the average quality of work is so poor. First, one must consider what facilitated the poor work—was it inexperience or lack of skill, or laziness, which would include apathy, and not using common sense. The distinction is important; an inexperienced or underskilled mechanic can only improve his performance through more training and experience. Short of that, a contractor with more skilled mechanics could be retained. For aesthetically sensitive scopes of work such as floor finishes and wood veneer finishes, a higher degree of quality is mandated than that of infrastructure, or what lives behind the walls. There is very little tolerance for high-end finishes. Patience, fine motor skills, and experience will generate quality work. Rushing, cutting corners, and lack of skill will yield substandard products.

But for most infrastructures—concrete, partition and ceiling framing, and most MEPs, patience, fine-motor skills, and experience are not critical, nor are they required to the extent that they are for finishers; the chief reason being that such work will not be exposed in the end product; therefore, it has low aesthetic tolerances. Only gross motor skills are required. This does not mean that things can be installed incorrectly and covered up; it only means that although they may not look pretty, they must be done correctly. If they are not, whatever program connects to them will also be incorrect, or will have to be tweaked. Before the tweaking takes place, it is likely the contractor will redo the work in question correctly, rather than saddle the next worker with the problem. Infrastructural mistakes will continue to occur due to inexperience; however, a great deal of mistakes made in infrastructural construction could be significantly reduced if just a few simple concepts were observed:

Common sense: Most residential infrastructure work is semiskilled, and only requires a little common sense, and the ability to work the tools. The majority of mistakes made could be avoided with a little forethought and precaution. Too often, mechanics are taught to only do what they are told and not think for themselves. Hence, they are effectively rendered automatons. On the upside, if creative thinking was encouraged (and financed) for most of these individuals, they might make fewer mistakes.

Apathy: Some mechanics don't care about their work. It may be because they feel they are underpaid, or perhaps they wouldn't care even if they were well paid. This attitude is betrayed in obvious simple mistakes such as not reading a tape measure correctly, not double-checking a measurement, using wrong or inferiority tools, or performing work that they aren't sure is correct. These mistakes have nothing to do with competency. It is easier to negotiate a lack of common sense than apathy. Common sense is skill related, whereas apathy pertains to worldviews and values held by the workers. You can teach someone to think, but you can't teach him or her to care.

A typically designed project's production was struggling to progress—the problem was that the gypsum board partitions and ceilings were repeatedly built out of level or plumb, and were not coplanar (flat). The correct installation of such partitions is not rocket science. The superintendent investigated several instances to identify a pattern. He first identified the process, then the mistakes that happened along the way. What he discovered was that regardless of the degree of complexity (none) there were a multitude of easily avoidable mistakes that could and did go wrong.

Sequence of gypsum board partition installation

Locate line of plate or track in relation to axes lines

Affix the plate to floor

With plumb bob or laser level, transfer line of floor plate to ceiling

Affix top plate to ceiling

Install studs 16 in. on center.

After MEP program is complete, install gypsum board

Install paper tape, spackle, and corner bead as required

The above represents a process requiring little skill, and mild experience. Nevertheless, here are some of the problems the superintendent encountered:

Partitions located incorrectly in regard to axes lines and correct placement

Partitions not plumb

Partitions not in continuous planes (flat and even)

Crooked corners

Bulges in the gypsum board from screw heads below surface

Gaps around cutouts of openings

Cutouts in incorrect locations

Overapplication of wallboard compound

What went wrong?

Locate line of plate or track in relation to axes lines.
  Plate located in wrong place, or off the line
Affix plate to floor.
  Plate not attached securely
With plumb bob or laser level, transfer line of floor plate to ceiling.
  Transfer of marks inaccurate. Misreading of instruments
Affix top plate to ceiling.
  Plate not attached securely
  Transfer of marks inaccurate
Install studs 16 in. o.c.
  Misalignment of studs
  Studs not fastened
  Studs bent or damaged

After MEP program is complete, install gypsum board

  Incorrect layout of cutouts

Install corner bead as required

  Incorrect fastening method

  Failure to straight-line edge

The particular reasons as to why these mistakes happened were myriad, but petty in nature; not worthy of consideration. The point of this exercise is not to emphasize the possibilities of failed drywall installations, but to illustrate how even simple tasks are subject to a great margin of error. However, consider the margin of error for more complex tasks; what if margin for error increases proportionately to degree of difficulty? Then, the ensuing error would be magnified to an unsettling level of incompetence.

Despite this particular drywall project requiring a high-end contractor, the simplest of installations were plagued with inefficiencies. Perhaps because the partitions seemed so simple, the mechanics failed to realize that these installations would dictate the accuracy of all work referenced to them, which would by association also be incorrect. Regrettably, it often would not be until the subsequent work in the area was mobilized that the mistake(s) was realized. At that time, tear-out of installed work was ordered, and the subsequent work postponed.

Using this example to classify installations of similar complexity tells us that there is an enormous amount of poor quality work and tear-out work that need not take place, had the installers simply cared a little, and exercised a little common sense. This phenomenon has a debilitating effect on the industry by driving up the costs of basic skills, and thus high-level skills to unreasonable levels. Why it perpetuates is another story.

Material Shortages/Price Fluctuations

Sudden price fluctuations and shortages are becoming more and more of a problem for the building industry. They can come with little or no warning, and be so dramatic as to either temporarily stop work, or shut down a project altogether. To guard against this, contractors have historically qualified their proposals for a fixed number of days subsequent to its issuance, typically, 30 days. However, even with this safeguard, if materials aren't secured at the right time, they may evaporate. 2004 was a stand-out year for material price increases as well as overall construction cost increases. Prices for iron and steel rose 35% in 2004, while the cost to construct a building rose over 10.5%.[22] Those caught unawares experienced extra long lead times and price increases for such staples as heavy gauge metal stud and track, as well as concrete. Again 2005 was a record year for hurricanes, and plywood prices shot up accordingly, just like gasoline.

Other shortages occur for specialty items such as rare veneer or dimensional stone, for which there is often a limited supply. If it is known beforehand that there are limited supplies, this fact should be shared with the job team, and perhaps a plan should be implemented to guarantee the securing of the goods. Sometimes, a shortage is predictable. For example, a few years back, wenge wood was all the rage among the design elite. Inventories were quickly emptied, and forests leveled. Similarly, a few years before that, anigre was in fashion. The demand was created by media exposure to projects utilizing these species.

Unfamiliarity with Materials, and Learning Curves

Much to the chagrin of the building industry, it has always been fashionable for designers and clients to ask for the latest in cutting-edge materials, or one-of-a-kind custom designs and installations. Contractors bidding projects with exotic materials, or experimental, or radical designs generally exact a premium for such work. It doesn't help that clients have a hard time understanding why these premiums seem to be so exorbitant. Indeed, it's hard enough to teach them the value of the construction dollar even for average work. Custom and special treatments require additional attention, especially for the procurement and submittal process. The exercise of issuing prototypes and samples may start to resemble a design and development process—anathema to the general contractor. When it does, the effect can be felt as an increase in general conditions. Insofar as tasks that require trial and error or experimentation, clients will not want to finance any effort other than the final product itself; they will assume you already have working knowledge of all work on the project, or that the preconstruction effort is your responsibility. Moreover, you will be either embarrassed or feel guilty in asking your architect for assistance, especially if you have told him that your company "specializes" in custom work—a trademark of the high-end contractor. For work that requires a lot of D&D input on your part, you may want to include an upcharge in your budget indexed general conditions.

An artist cum contractor I knew had an interesting concept for his company. They fancied themselves as customization specialists in the sense that they offered support, often gratis, for nearly any sort of beta design, experimental designs and materials, all of which entailed egregious architect coddling on their part, efforts for which they were seldom remunerated. As there were other artists at the company, they seemed particularly well suited to the endeavor. While it's true that there is a great need for this type of service, it is not well financed by the industry. For example, if an architect wants to invent something, he sketches it out, and asks the contractor to do the legwork for free. It doesn't matter how ill-conceived or eccentric the idea is. Besides losing money in these endeavors, this contractor assumed responsibility for inherent flaws.

You should be able to flag underdeveloped work at the bidding stage, and establish budgets for D&D in addition to the work itself—this is not unreasonable; however, clients will balk at the prospect of endowing a contractor with a D&D budget, or for paying anyone other than his architect for design services period, unless this was his intention from the beginning. Alternatively, liberal allowances should qualify undeveloped scopes of work. As always, target dates or deliverable milestones for these designs must be given to the design team by the contractor, as details are often put off to the last minute. Problems often arise when a detail shows up too late, thus creating a delay. If the contractor had not targeted a date for the design deliverable, the design team can plead ignorance. Of course that isn't fair, but as regards the client, it is a moot point. However, a construction manager should be in the business of not missing any such details.

It is important that all production members function at the appropriate level for high-end projects, as such work has the least margin of error, and highest tolerances of exactitude. There is a *lingua franca* for the high-end job team. It mandates a fluency in the expertise of installing high quality workmanship, and exotic finishes. Any member not versed in this concept will be a lag on the project. This also will be discussed in Chap. 4.

Therefore, high-end work should be less cost-driven than it is quality driven. Sometimes this is not observed. For example, a low-balling (intentionally low bid) contractor may be awarded a project based on his winning low bid, or overtures to over deliver on the schedule; however, subsequently, the owner loses because he will either redo much of the work, which is of poor quality, or he will be hit with a barrage of change orders. This latter tactic is a hallmark of the low-baller, who bids the base contract at a preferred rate, only to later make up the difference in inflated change orders.

Successful Projects

We have discussed a great deal about problem projects, not out of a creeping pessimism, but because this knowledge is exigent for survival in the marketplace. You should have a pretty good idea how to spot a loser project, and equal discernment in selecting what projects to pursue. It must be understood that contractors, architects, owners, and third parties all have a different rubric for measuring success. Additionally, what people say are their priorities, and what they really are can bear little resemblance to each other. Their perceptions form an interesting scenario when juxtaposed.

Architect

The architect is chiefly concerned with looking good to the client, getting paid, and (joy of joys) having the job published. What's behind the walls isn't nearly as important as the visible end product. Budget and schedule are not a concern, unless there are ramifications for them such as waiting to get paid.

Engineer

Alternatively, engineers care little about the finishes. Their concern lies in the quality of execution of the MEPs and/or structural work—from a liability standpoint; that it is done correctly, and from a financial standpoint, that they will be paid on time.

Contractor

Contractor's attitudes vary considerably among different companies; however, first and foremost will be the financial picture;— that a project is profitable, and that they get paid on time, or at all. From there, it's anybody's guess what contractors prioritize and what they don't. Of course, they enjoy compliments about the quality of their work, as they can expect additional referrals thanks to their efforts.

Subcontractors

An overlooked, undervalued asset: subcontractors' experiences are crucial to the big picture, as they are driving labor and material costs as well as budgets and schedules. They tend to be treated as passive team members, and often given short shrift. They often are not invited to job meetings, or might not receive project documentation. Nevertheless, their contribution is one of the most critical determinants of the success of a given project. They will care about their quality control to varying degrees, will be reluctant to work on unhappy projects, and as always, want and need to get paid on time.

Clients

"On-time/within budget." Insofar as what's behind the walls—they could care . . . Follow the money.

Different parties and their competing priorities always put undue stress on interrelationships, which translates to strife on the project. Smart contractors realize this, and will make an effort to strike a balance in pursuit of the highly elusive win/win scenario.

Others

Media, friends, anyone with an opinion will chime in with their two cents. However, insignificant to a given project, media—periodicals, magazines, and newspapers control the flow of information to the world at large, as most people have no other gauge which to measure from. By and large, the opulence and physical character of a completed project is the only rubric used. It doesn't matter that a project may be 100% over budget and late. This is typical of how publishers wish to control and manipulate information to their readers—; by emphasizing superficialities, they teach people to undervalue all other aspects of the building process. They only want to report the good news, as bad news is bad for subscription revenues. Such business does an extreme disservice to the industry. Thankfully, there are enough trade publications and professional organizations to offset such propaganda; however, they aren't geared to the layman, and aren't nearly circulated widely enough.

Positive Experience

Always an afterthought, the nature of the quality of the experience of building a project is last on everybody's list. Few people seem to make a concerted effort to make a project run more pleasantly, or improve personal relations among the job team. There always seem to be too many contentious issues to be negotiated before barriers can be lowered so to allow for positive interactions—issues that have more important ramifications than who is happy and who is not, such as budget and scheduling factors. Alas, the industry seems too distracted by the oppressive stress load of the rigors and complexities of the building process to concern itself with peace of mind. From this aspect, it will be difficult to put a positive spin on the experience of building a home.

Aside from having a good introduction or striking a good rapport with your clients, there are other signals of a promising prospect that you can discern early in the bid phase.

Negotiated Bid

In projects involving negotiated bids, the understanding is that the project team is precertified, or prequalified, wherein either the architect or client likely has a working relationship with the contractor, or the contractor was given an extremely high recommendation. The team can forgo the tedious exercise of the competitive bid process. There is a mutual feeling of trust established from the start that is critical to the moral health of the project. It is a very proud contractor whose clients request negotiated bids. You can cheerfully involve your subcontractors and vendors in the development processes as you already own the project; they will be more motivated than were you bidding competitively against other general contractors.

The Drawings and Specifications Are Thorough

A project is only as good as the sum of its parts: the design, on the one hand, construction on the other. Since design is a prerequisite to construction, it follows that it will be the earliest determinant of a given project's success. Estimators know pretty early before they even conduct their quantity takeoffs, of the general state of the design documents. Depending on their perception they will assess a risk factor to their estimating. The more informative the designs are, the less the risk assessment. Table 2.3 illustrates the relationship of risk to the amount of design information a contractor has about a given project.[23]

There is a wide grey area between what architects and owners consider biddable drawings, when compared with acceptable terms. It is within this gray area in which the majority of bid-drawing sets find themselves, not complete enough to bid accurately, and past the window of opportunity to involve the contractor in the design phase. Regardless, frequently estimators put numbers to such drawings, without having adequate opportunity to facilitate the process. It is largely up to architects when to decide that drawings are biddable or buildable.

TABLE 2.3   Risk and Information in Bidding and Contracts

Maximum information — Assuming total knowledge (Superhuman prescience)

Information (Design and experiential)

Probable

Theoretical

Zero

Theoretical

Assuming total ignorance

Risk (of financial loss)

Probable

Maximum risk

Risk of a total loss →

Typically, drawings are put out to bid missing too much information, and ground is broken before proper construction drawings are prepared. This dilemma was long ago recognized by the rest of the industry that now uses construction managers to overcome such obstacles while at the same time advancing the schedule. Chapter 5 discusses the concept of bringing construction management to the residential sector where it has little presence, despite a great need for it.

Solid Design Team

Many architects will stick their beak into projects where they have no experience. They fail to realize the necessary fragmentation and specialization that different building sectors feature. There are plenty of qualified design professionals literate in high-end interiors to go around—there is no excuse for an experimental design team. Many architects make assumptions about high-end residential that translate into unsuccessful undertakings. Their work tends to be vain and superficial; perhaps expensive materials are used, but they are installed in a poorly executed fashion. The end product seldom translates into a fluid design concept, rather a disconnected hodgepodge.

General contractors will most favor work that:

- Comes from repeat business; people who he has worked with.
- Comes from reliable sources. Although he hasn't worked with them, he is comfortable working with them based on their reputation and track record.
- He is familiar with.

These three criteria will significantly lower his exposure, and thus increase his prospect for success. The client will be rewarded as well with an experienced job team that needs little maintenance.

Familiarity with the Program

If you are comfortable with the scope of work, have done similar work, and don't have a lot of questions, then you should have an auspicious starting position. Nevertheless, every custom residential project is different. In theory they are the same; however, each requires that the general contractor familiarize himself with the specific goals and challenges of each project on an individual basis. Once a contractor is confident with the design program, he can then look to qualifying the schedule and budget.

It is difficult for a contractor to feel comfortable with the scope of work of a project when the bid set is schematic. There is a fair amount of risk associated with that position. Again, such projects seem to lend themselves better to construction managers. Nonetheless, contractors are reluctant to point out that a project is not biddable, and it would occur to precious few of them to suggest something as novel as a construction manager. However, they will almost certainly complain when the project begins without an acceptable level of design documentation—if they had spoken up earlier they might not be in that position.

Adequate Schedule

Seldom is a project given enough time to be built at a natural pace. Allowances must be made for change orders, mistakes, *forces majeure*, and so forth. High-end projects require a higher degree of scrutiny and attention to detail than the average project, thus making them longer by their nature. Clients are always in a hurry to get in to their new home, and their anxiety can inspire a rushed schedule. Understandably, they have no concept of what comprises a construction "minute". It is the experienced client and architect who will understand why a high-end project should take longer to build. If they don't understand that, they likely misunderstand other important concepts such as the value of a construction dollar, or why change orders cost so much. However, often the schedule criteria may already be fixed by the client, or your scheduler determines that it will take longer than you thought. Many will likely not speak up; for fear they lose the prospect.

Reasonable Client and Architect

The project may have all of the above positive attributes, and still be a dubious enterprise. If the client and architect do not seem reasonable in your mind, you may want to turn away the work. We visited this topic earlier in this chapter when discussing losing prospects, and also described a particular instance where a contractor turned away an otherwise seemingly healthy prospect. It is difficult to tell early on if you are dealing with difficult people because, in the beginning, people will put on airs. You would like to know the stripe of your client and architect before you sign the contract. There should be ample time for you to form some impressions based on the following:

- How aggressive is the budget and schedule?
- What kind of rapport was struck with the architect and owner?
- Is the contract negotiation process litigious and drawn-out?
- Was your interface with the architect positive and informative?
- Was there a tortuous value-engineering process, wherein several rebids and breakouts were required?
- Did the design drawings change drastically from the bid set to the contract set?

The answers to these and other questions can help you set the stage early for how you want to approach a given project. While all the elements of what constitutes a successful prospect may seem ideal, think of them as variant determinants; different projects will have varying degrees of promise in each of their elements. It is the aggregate of each project's elemental components that will determine your level of motivation.

Synopsis of Bid Development

For our purpose, let us assume that no two residential projects are alike; therefore, for each project a separate approach must be taken. This assumption would exclude repetitive work such as that done by developers. The first thing to consider is the type of contract that will be implemented. This will dictate the structure of the proposal, as well as cash flow, overhead, and general conditions. It is common practice to factor fixed general conditions and overhead percentage for all projects. It is also common to tweak these numbers in order to hone the overall total. The tenet is usually dictated by what the market will allow, or a number based on subjective experience. Neither strikes me as particularly scientific. I believe one must do the math—come about the number honestly. At that time, if it must be adjusted, it is done without speculation. The exceptions are for contracts that reimburse for these expenses, such as a construction management and cost-plus fee projects. An owner will typically want to know up-front, what the percentages will be, especially if the budget is not fixed.

Once bids are solicited from subcontractors and vendors, they are typically incorporated into a spreadsheet, reviewed, and folded into a proposal, which can vary from a one page to twenty pages, or more. The general requirements of the specifications will usually indicate the form of the proposal, often with line items, or breakout numbers. This makes it easier for the owner to compare bids from competing contractors, in a word—apples to apples. This requirement can pose a dilemma for contractors whose estimator will likely have a set method, and many are not able, or will not conform to a requested proposal structure. This is because the owner and the contractor often see the project through different lenses. For instance, the owner may want to see a room-by-room breakout or a breakout by job phase (if the job is to be built in stages). This bid structure can create more work and confusion for an estimator. Likewise, subcontractors will not want to be bothered, or they may not be able to disseminate a proposal in this fashion. Vendors often issue lot prices, which are not broken down, and they will be reluctant to enumerate each line item if asked, for fear you will shop the job.

Ideally, an estimator will have full knowledge of the entire composition of any project he bids before he tenders a bid. This is achieved by taking the following measures.

Review All Design Documentation and Specifications

Construction drawings, specifications, and other design information will all be named as contract documents in the main contract. Especially read the general requirements and specification book, as there resides the fine print that should be perused, lest it should rear its ugly head at an inopportune time. Remember, your proposal should also be named in the contract documents, so be sure that its contents represent your interests in every way. As you review, begin making a list of qualifications. The AIA *A201 General Conditions of the Contract for Construction*, should be the first to go, or be amended. Many design documents are issued for bid, only to be revised one or more times even before the bidding process is complete. This can be a red-flag that the project may have developmental problems, and may not even be realized at all, especially if the scope of work decreases with each issue. This can be trying on your estimator, and your subcontractors, who likely have better prospects bidding other work; therefore, you will want to consider if rebidding is worth the investment. In a hectic market, subcontractors will avoid general contractors who have them bid a lot of work, only to see it awarded to a competitor. However, when rebidding revised drawings it is important not only to name these revised documents in the proposal, but also to distribute them to your subcontractors, having them also name the documents in their bids.

It is at this time that you will be able to gauge the acumen of the project documentation. You will now know the full flavor of the design intent. This will dictate the field of subcontractors you wish to include. If there are a lot of holes in the design documents, they should now become apparent. You can now consider what you are working with, and what the ramifications of that are:

- Is the job underdesigned for lack of funds, lack of knowledge by the design team, or both? If so, a risk assessment must now be weighed. If you are flush with work, you may only want to bid the work at a premium, or turn it away altogether. To be sure, if the design documentation is vague, your subcontractors will pad their bids or make wholesale exclusions in order to protect themselves.

- Is the job underdesigned because there was simply not enough time allotted to the design phase? This is a common excuse with assurances given that all information will follow in a timely manner, which essentially means, the rest of the project design will likely come in the form of sketches. If there wasn't sufficient time to design the project, there will likely be similar constraints on the construction schedule. Suffice it to say, a risk assessment should also be weighed.

- Are the MEPs developed by an engineering firm, or by a designer or an architect? If there are no engineer's drawings on a project involving MEPs, you will want to be wary. This is a common cost-cutting ploy by clients as well as architects looking to minimize the design budget. On the other hand, many projects have MEP work that isn't subject to inspection such that architects feel they can detail the work. They may get by legally; however, MEPs are a notorious weakness for most architects. In many localities, architects are, in fact, not licensed to generate MEPs. In most jurisdictions, someone will have to generate a building department set of drawings with an engineer's stamp, often subject to controlled inspection(s); again, depending on the nature and scope of the work. Because of the proliferation of litigation in construction contracts, design professionals are often eschewing liability by asking the contractor to take responsibility for designs for which they have traditionally been responsible. If the contractor is responsible for these services, he should check with his insurance carrier to ensure that his policy has coverage for such services, and of course, charge accordingly. Although engineers may have detailed the MEP work, that fact in no way assures any level of integrity: engineer's drawings must be held to the same level of scrutiny as any architect's or designer's drawings.

- Thus, if the project will be built, additional design information will be needed. The timing of this information is critical. If it does not arrive early enough, the job will be delayed, or you will have to expedite it. If the information comes in the form of hastily rendered sketches, these will also generate problems for you. In either case, the job begins to resemble the "fast track" type project mentioned above, and as I have said, this method lends itself poorly to difficult high-end remodeling projects. It is your estimator's responsibility to identify these holes, and ask for the information early.

- Does the project aspire too highly? If there are exotic designs and materials, yet, you get the impression that there are insufficient funds to design or build such creations, then indeed, the design team may have designed over budget, or the project may be a parasite. It used to be the responsibility of the design team to design within the budget; however, at the prospect of turning away work, many professionals will indicate that they believe they can design within the client's budget rather than lose a prospect; they may even believe this fantasy themselves. The same holds true for a contractor who promises a completion date that he knows is highly implausible. So long as no guarantee is made, they can't effectively be held to their erroneous forecasts.

Much of the above information you may not be apprised of until it is brought to your attention by a subcontractor. If you have a strong following, your vendors will go the extra mile, and notify you of what is missing from the bid documents rather than keep it to themselves, and pad their bid. This information you will direct back to the design team in the form of requests for information (RFIs).

It is imperative for the estimator to have full knowledge of the scope of work. This knowledge should also include intangibles, or conditions not readily apparent such as restricted working hours, restrictions on power tools, restrictions on noisy work, restrictions on elevator usage, and restrictions on shutdowns. Any of these factors can add cost to a project. Intangible conditions may involve slower production rates due to overcrowding, long lead times that don't work with the production schedule, incomplete design documentation, and inexperienced design team members. The intangibles are hard to valuate, and the owner will not readily understand them, or may not want to understand why they substantiate an increase in cost.

One of the biggest mistakes an estimator will make is to not fully review the project documentation. Sometimes, the bid window is so aggressive, typically 2 weeks, that he may not have the time for a full review. This is one of the reasons general contractors can be so overreliant on their subcontractors to cover them, and be responsible for omissions. Particularly, the specifications are where a good deal of information can be buried. Some design professionals use a boilerplate specification book, or a book drawn by a specifier. The same book is used on all their projects; only some of the finishes and schedules may be altered. Ideally, it is the estimator's responsibility to review the specifications book. The general requirements portion of the specification book, in particular, is a notorious source of conundrums for contractors. It is often drawn by an attorney, and is intended to indemnify the client and the designer, often at the expense of the contractor. Whether the client or the contractor draft the contract, the general requirements will be named in the contract documents. Should a project head for litigation, this section will invariably be invoked. There is a dilemma for the estimator in calling attention to such language—the owner might sense an air of litigiousness, and become wary of the contractor. Even though it is perfectly reasonable and sensible to draw attention to such language, few contractors do it; therefore, it is the exception. Typically, the architect will dismiss objections to their general requirements, saying the language is part of a boilerplate, not intended for general use. Therefore, it is sometimes prudent to not voice your objections until you are negotiating for the contract—merely a question of timing.

Sample Estimator Job Description

Title: Estimator

Report To: GM

Objectives:

Preconstruction

1. Intake new jobs, and enter into log
2. Review plans and specifications: identify long lead items
3. Determine schedule duration
4. Walk-through of the site with client/architect
5. Identify vendors and suppliers, and prepare drawing distribution log
6. Interface with staff to facilitate the bidding process
7. Send out for blueprint copies
8. Prepare bid packages, including specifications, and due date
9. Distribute bid packages
10. Walk-through with vendors/subcontractors
11. Process subcontractors' and in-house RFIs thru architect/engineer
12. Prepare quantity takeoffs, area SF: walls, floors, ceilings, by room and trade
13. Set up job folder on network, and hard copy
14. Process incoming subbids to spreadsheets
15. Qualify subbids
16. Assemble main bid
17. Create scope of work and drawing manifest
18. Format bid, and generate cover page
19. Present to GM with backup for approval

Construction

1. Assemble full (project management) PM job books
2. Assist in buyout of base trades and long lead items: clarify that all bidders cover full scope of work
3. Facilitate creation of job directory
4. Organize job kickoff meeting
5. Assist project manager in issuing job change orders through office and field

From the above sample job description, you can see that most of the estimator's work on a project is complete before the construction phase. Once construction begins in earnest, he should only be involved in reviewing change orders. For example, if additional expenses are charged on a budget project, he may be asked to issue a budget update. However, strong project managers should assume the responsibility of keeping records of budget updates for their own projects. It should not be the estimator's responsibility.

Visit Site

Take note of existing conditions, and access to site. If the project is in an apartment building, there will likely be building work rules and an alteration agreement that must be reviewed. Some contracts will even reference the alteration agreement even though the contractor is not a party to it. If it is a building with other people's apartments directly abutting the job site, you will want to take photographs of these areas to document their condition prior to commencing your work. These photographs may be necessary to counter a prospective damage claim. You also may want to photograph, or even videotape conditions of your worksite for the same reason. It is not uncommon for a disgruntled neighboring tenant to blame earlier damage on a contractor's current operations, in pursuit of reparations he isn't entitled to.

Preexisting conditions: Preexisting conditions are those existing before a project is commenced. Many such conditions may not become apparent until after demolition; for example, a branch valve may leak or not exist at all, or there may be asbestos lagging on steam pipes requiring remediation. Not having been apprised of preexisting conditions may not be enough to eschew the responsibility of correcting them, as most general requirements will insist that the contractor has familiarized himself with all existing conditions, and duly notified the design team. Many general requirements state that a mere site inspection visit denotes that the contractor should have been aware of any preexisting conditions. If a contractor is aware of such conditions, failure to notify the architect may result in assuming responsibility for them. Of course, it would have to be proved that he was, in fact, aware of them. Therefore, have a working knowledge of what some of the possible existing conditions may be that may constitute additional work not enumerated in the design documents on each particular project. Inspect the site for such conditions, and take the trouble to qualify or exclude the execution or remediation of any work not explicitly called out in the drawings. As you may have guessed, this phenomenon raises interesting legal conundrums, and it will further be discussed in Chap. 8.

Meet with Architect and Client

Prebid meetings with the architect and client are crucial fact-finding exercises for the estimator, and also present a good opportunity to introduce the prospective job team. Hopefully, you will initiate a positive relationship with them, establishing a rapport that will carry the team through the life of the project. First impressions are everything. In this first meeting you will make most of your assumptions regarding the client's expectations, character, and integrity, just as he will.

Understand the architect's relationship with the client—have they worked together before? Do they seem to have a good rapport? Or is this their first job together. Does the architect seem to want to prematurely gain your confidence? If so, he may be in a pickle with the client, perhaps he overdesigned, and being over budget is buttering you up for some concessions. The contract will likely appoint the architect as the client's agent, thus the man representing his best interests. The owner/architect relationship can greatly influence the execution and outcome of the project in many ways, including financially.

What about the client? What sort is he? Is he easy going, or tends to be nervous? Getting a good read on his personality will help you have a leg up in negotiating with him, and also for conflict resolution. Residential work usually involves someone's home, typically, the owner's, and you must understand that this is a sensitive topic for people, and they tend to become emotional and irrational. The ramifications of this notion must not be underestimated, and will be further discussed in Chaps. 7 and 8.

Quantity takeoffs and Bid Outline

Sometimes called a "bill of assemblies," it is a comprehensive list of every component necessary to assemble the project. Check these against your subcontractor's takeoffs. Once a project is awarded, these should be passed on to the production personnel. When vague work descriptions and allowances are invoked, the takeoffs will not be comprehensive. Nevertheless, like any other work, they must be tracked and accounted for.

Quantity surveys in residential construction are not as critical to estimating as they are in some other sectors such as industrial construction. Because residential work has significantly lower production rates than other sectors, it tends not to be quantified in units, but in time and materials. For example, an apartment with 5000 ft^2 of gypsum board ceiling may take 3 weeks to close, whereas the same area in a warehouse may take one-third the time, or 1 week.

However, a given scope of work on a specific project may be estimated by a unit price, compiled from the composite number of labor and materials, a rate, such as man/hour, crew/hour, or day rate, for that task. The sum of the costs of the tasks can then be combined into groupings by trade. This is how your in-house estimators should figure costs; however, subcontractors and vendors methods will vary, and few will get as specific as task breakdowns. The organization of this information should form the outline of your proposal. A sample quantity takeoff is shown in Table 2.4.

There are commercial estimating computer programs available, some which use a digitizer to record lines and areas. These I find not to be intuitive, or helpful in the analysis of the finer points and nuances typical of high-end residential projects, especially with their tendency toward custom trimmings. The nature and complexity of residential construction precludes the objective quantification of its

TABLE 2.4   CSI Sample QTO

09200 Plaster				
Description of Work	Quantity	Unit	@	Extension
Veneer plaster				
Veneer plaster at ceilings, to be painted:				
5th Floor	3,200	sf	13.5	43,200
6th Floor	3,200	sf	13.5	43,200
Specialist plaster				
5th Floor				
Plaster Type 1 (specialized) walls at:				
East Corridor walls	565	sf	25	14,125
West Corridor walls	400	sf	25	10,000
6th Floor				
Plaster Type 1 (specialized) walls at:				
West Corridor	570	sf	25	14,250
Ornamental				
Plaster Crown—East Corridor	36	lf	150	5,400
Total				130,175

value by commercial estimating guides; in fact, renders them irrelevant. A case in point: only about 18% of residential builders use such programs.[24]

General contractors favor various bid outline structures, but most would agree that less detail in their bid translates to less risk. However, an architect's general requirements may insist on a bid structure that is either very detailed, or broken down for comparison to other general contractors' bids in such a way that is antithetical to how an estimator bids work. Not uncommonly, many estimators are not able to, or simply will not agree to perform this task, as it is inconvenient and uncomfortable for them. For purposes of this book, a Construction Specification Institute (CSI) outline structure will be utilized.

Solicit and Qualify Bids from Multiple Vendors

This includes qualifying the acumen of a subcontractor:

- Does he have the infrastructure and manpower necessary?
- Is his price in the right place (too high or low are both a bad sign)?
- Is he accustomed to the quality level of work required?
- Will he guarantee the schedule?

These and other questions will come to mind, as there is certainly more to qualifying subcontractor bids than merely comparing bottom lines. Once the subcontractors are qualified, their bids are compared, and a shortlist will be made. The contractor may negotiate with his subcontractors at this time. However, negotiation at this stage should only be done for the purposes of clarifying the subcontractor's proposal. In other words, this is not a negotiation to improve either party's profit margin or leverage position. Such negotiations serve a different purpose, and are appropriate only after the contractor is ready to award the work. As we have discussed, in order to effectively qualify subbids, an estimator must have a comprehensive working knowledge of the project; perhaps he may even need a bill of assemblies or quantity takeoffs. Often, subcontractors will issue their proposals in different formats, requiring transposing for comparison.

Bid Models

There are three types of cost calculations: *independent, dependent, and interdependent*. In independently estimating a project, an estimator will valuate the project himself, worrying about sourcing qualified subbids for later. This is the most difficult and riskiest type of estimating, requiring the most estimating skill. About one-third of residential builders use in-house detailed quantity takeoffs,[25] which they then may or may not base their proposal on.

Typically, bid packages are distributed, and bids are solicited from the subcontractors and vendors. After collecting the bids, these may or may not be qualified. They are then parsed into the bid package. This method is quite common, and I will call it the *dependent* method. A little less than 30% of residential builders quantify their bids this way.[26] However, using this method, the additional step taken of vetting or qualifying the subbids is the key to valuating the project. Typically, a spreadsheet is generated, from highest to lowest, and a candidate, usually a lower bidder, is selected. This is not yet a qualified subbid. Only after review of scope of work, and comparison to other bidders, is it qualified. The low bidder may be omitting scope of work unintentionally, or he may have qualifications, or exclusions. He may have workers below the criteria of the skill level. Whatever the case, it is critical to understand why not just a low bid, but any bid being used must be carefully evaluated. If you do sponsor the bidder, consider what may happen if he withdraws his bid—what then? Often, the lower bidders have omitted scope, whether knowingly or not, and not made this clear to the contractor until it is too late.

The *interdependent* method is a hybrid of the dependent and independent methods. Subcontractor's bids—qualified and unqualified, are solicited and incorporated into the contractor's proposal. Other scopes of work are valuated by the estimator. Many companies have their own workforces doing the general construction, or other work, and the in-house estimator will have to valuate his own costs, merging them with the subbids. About 7% of residential builders use the interdependent method.[27]

A contractor I knew had an interesting method, which was roughly 95% dependent, and 5% interdependent, the bids were solicited to all trades required on the project. No in-house takeoffs were done. The bids were entered into a spreadsheet, and shown to one of the owners of the company. He then would discount each trade according to some intuitive method, which only he knew, or typically, some factor down the line. Even on projects with multiple trades and millions of dollars at stake, his review process took all of 5 minutes. His logic was that regardless of what their proposals indicated, each contractor was responsible for all work in their trade by virtue of them naming the drawings in their bid. In my mind, this method precludes the need for an estimator, and only a data entry person is required. There is no intuitive work to be done for an estimator using this method. However, one of the priorities of his method was the subcontractor's ownership of the work, regardless of margin.

The interdependent model is an effective method, especially when subbids are qualified. To go one better, an estimator will do his own quantity takeoffs, quantifying his own scope of work for subcontracted work, with the subbids. When the bids come in, not only can he compare them to his own, but also can make the necessary adjustments. When it comes time to negotiate, or value engineer, he can now speak from an informed point of view rather than just slash or raise prices. Nevertheless, whatever method is used, all are at risk of undervaluation. The intention of a comprehensive bid package is to minimize risk.

In addition to the three methods described above, best-guess estimates informed 9% of the average estimate, and allowances accounted for about 8%.[28] Finally, due to the vagaries that plague most architects' drawings, it is sometimes good practice to attach a 10 to 15% contingency to schematically designed residential projects, as they invariably go over budget, or have change orders due to errors and omissions (E&O). The client may not agree to this contingency; however, merely raising the issue should be a point well taken, especially when the project changes. Architects designing large projects are now starting to purchase E&O insurance to protect themselves (from themselves), but the insurance isn't catching on just yet for the residential sector.

RFIs/Clarifications

RFIs, requests for information, or questions for the architect clarifying the work are sent to the architect for comment, and then returned to the bidders. In many cases, the architect's response to a bidding stage RFI will inform costs. In fact, most subcontractors bid stage RFIs concern cost. If your estimator has no questions on a complex bid package, either something is wrong, or he or she is omniscient. The architect may also generate clarification sketches, which address the RFIs. Estimating departments must be diligent in distributing any such information to all bid applicants. Following are some sample RFIs issued for clarification in the bidding stage of a project:

1. The drawings do not seem to indicate required funnel drains and trap primers for air-handling unit (AHU) condensate lines. Both are required for the condensate runoff from all air handlers, unless they should spill into a slop sink or floor drain. Unless advised otherwise, the plumber will not provide for them.

2. The drawings show neither a secondary containment system (drip pan) nor a sensor alert system for the fan coils. We typically install these systems on all high-end interiors so to protect finishes and program below as well as adjacent installations and furnishings.

We are in receipt of an advanced copy of the revised dimming control schedule. The schedule seems to affect seventeen zones, with eight of them being additional, all of them now "smart" switches. They each call for a load capacity of 1350 W on a single circuit. Please clarify that this is the correct intention—1350 W is a maximum circuit load, and will necessitate the costly and space taking integration of power boosters. If this is the design intent, we will then request rebids from our electricians and equipment vendor. We also will want to know where we should locate the power boosters.

The above are RFIs that clearly can affect the budget. The contractor has rightly issued them in the bidding stage.

If the estimator is unsure, or feels that some of the design information is vague, he must apply to the architect for clarification. Not addressing these issues from the bidding stage can later generate problems; in a sense, an unaddressed item can become an open checkbook, wherein you may find yourself liable for more costly work than you have allowed for. Often, either the architect has no immediate answer for bid stage RFIs, or the contractor chooses not to issue RFIs for lack of time, or interest. If you do not RFI the architect then the work in question should be clarified in your qualifications and exclusions.

Subsequent to the architect's responses to RFIs, the estimator should have the maximum possible knowledge of the scope of work, and any other considerations necessary to begin the task of assembling his bid package.

Select Bidders to Sponsor

The most highly qualified bidders will be selected, and their estimates incorporated into the main proposal. The low bid is not the most qualified, or necessarily least qualified. The qualification process is a distillation of the subcontractor's proficiency, cost estimate, proposed production schedule, and how his bid compares to other bids. Also, consider his track record with your company, and your negotiating position, or leverage—if he is from your "A" list, he may give you a preferred rate. It is the composite of these considerations that will inform your decision as to whose bid to sponsor—the best resources for the project. Often, on high-end projects, there isn't much control over the price, especially if top quality is desired; however, that doesn't mean that one need not understand the value structure of a given subcontractor's bid. If you are a high-end general contractor, you need to be fluent in the valuation of pricing that involves premiums and other intangibles, as your client will likely ask for an explanation. With several bidders estimating the same work, an average of their prices is sometimes taken and used as the contractors bid for that trade.

Assemble Bid

This is best done as an in-house team process. By now, several conversations should have passed between the owner, design team, and contractors. Do the math, and check it twice. Mathematical errors in your favor will generally be detected, and have to be corrected, but it is bad business to inform a client that you have miscalculated in his favor, and that you wish to correct the mistake. As important as peer reviews are (see below), assume that there will not be one. Accordingly, you must generate the most comprehensive bid document possible, without help. The text highly advocates peer review; however, there often isn't sufficient time in the bid window for one, or there simply isn't anyone else to consult.

The assembly of the bid can be made according to your own bid structure, or according to the architect's requirements. Architects often request a format to follow that makes for easy comparison, but also to give them a negotiating edge. In a sense, they ask you to tip your hand. However, to accommodate every such request can be a lot of work; often too much, and it can also force you to divulge information that you normally wouldn't. Even if a bid structure is indicated in the general requirements, it will often go ignored by the contractor because he doesn't have time or resource to accommodate the terms of the request. The exception would be requests for alternates. Alternates are supposed to represent costs of optional scope in the base contract; however, architects sometimes request alternate pricing as a means to extract proprietary information.

Qualifications and Exclusions

Qualifications are a critical component of any proposal. They indicate what work or provisions are not included in your base contract. As such they are intended to indemnify the contractor against costs not expressly indicated in their proposal. They come in many forms. An allowance, or budget, may be used, if there is not enough information to generate a stipulated sum. Often, a designer will ask for this number, knowing that the contractor will not be able to accurately valuate a given scope of work. However, such a contingency number exists only as placeholder until a fixed number can be assessed. The less information given in the design documentation, the more qualifications and exclusions will be implemented.

Exclusions are scopes of work and conditions for which a contractor will indicate that he will not be responsible for. Common exclusions are remedial work, for example, lead or asbestos abatement, overtime, and union labor. It is not unusual for an owner to contract certain work directly with his preferred tradesmen, in which case, the prime contractor will exclude such work. However, an estimator may need to factor in costs to facilitate such work, as there are typically costs involved such as moving material to clear work areas, removing debris, and coordinating installation, i.e., general conditions.

Just as general contractors have exclusions, so do subcontractors. As part of the bid qualification process the estimator must note any such exclusion and either carry them through to the main proposal, or make provisions for them elsewhere. There are some grey areas where a subcontractor may not state that certain work is, in fact, not included in their proposal. This may become evident when it is time to execute the work, and is often the cause of disputes. Having knowledge of such grey areas, a good estimator will ask if certain work not directly called out is included in their proposal or not.

Just as a general contractor should, it is equally important to general contractors that all subcontractors and vendors name the design documents from which their bid is based. Otherwise, technically, their scope of work can be construed as only that which is referenced in their proposal. In the event of a dispute, you will be no more understanding than your architect would be if you excluded work after the contract was ratified.

During the qualification process is the time to realize the value of the work. If a bid comes in underbudget because a sub is hungry, or owes you a favor, there is no reason to blindly pass the savings on to the client, it belongs to you—, as a baseline, you should charge no less than market value. If there are incentives to charge less, weigh them accordingly. An example would be a construction manager who, as part of his contract, is sometimes awarded a percentage of below-budget actual costs.

Peer Review and Proofreading

Bid deadlines tend to be aggressive, and the pressure is on the contractor to produce. Quite often, the estimator needs all the allotted time to compose his proposal, leaving only sparse time for peer review. For this reason, the peer review often does not take place, and the proposal is reviewed only by the sales staff, and then summarily by upper management. This is unfortunate, and the practice leads to oversights, putting the contractor at risk in the form of E&Os. If at all possible, allow for at least one layer of peer review. It is always wise to have someone review another's work, and is the hallmark of a sound checks and balances system. If you think about it, your typical estimator may be hard pressed to make a bid deadline. In the eleventh hour he may be stressed or fatigued, and, more prone to error. Moreover, he has been staring at the same paper for endless hours. After looking at it for so long, he may overlook something obvious, assuming he has seen everything, missing nothing. A fresh pair of eyes may find such an omission immediately; even someone with little experience can detect a typo or repetition that comprises a mistake.

Mistakes found in the review process of a bid are almost always at least minimally substantial, i.e., over a few hundred dollars, because few estimators spend time appraising work less than that value. The point being that almost any investment in a review process will pay for itself, as every proposal has holes. Sometimes, even a short review process can detect mistakes—all the more reason to invest some time in peer review. Part of the review process must include error reporting, and the editing of such errors. If there are none to report, then something is wrong. Residential projects are complicated, and particularly prone to estimating errors, especially because every residential project, except for developer work, is more or less unique.

The trouble is that the estimator is usually the one most qualified to check for errors; however, if he is the creator, he can't peer review his own work. It is therefore imperative to have on hand someone who has enough knowledge to make the review. In a small company, there simply may not be anyone who can review, and inevitably, the proprietor, or high-level executive must review the proposal. As it is many contractors insist on reviewing the proposal personally. If nothing else, they will give a cursory review. This leaves much to be desired, but it is better than nothing.

Presentation

Once the bid is assembled and reviewed, it is prepared for presentation. Some will do this hastily such as faxing the proposal at the last minute. Others may hand deliver type set pages. At the end of the day, it is the quality of the content of each that will determine its integrity. However, people will partly judge a contractor's acumen by the form that his proposal takes. This being the case there is no reason to preclude an otherwise quality oriented proposal by a poor choice of presentation format. Besides the proposal standing on its own merits as a clear, comprehensive document, it must also appear to be of high quality, as there generally will be no one present to defend it when it is reviewed by the clients.

Written presentations are a weakness for most general contractors for a number of reasons. Oddly enough, this won't matter to many clients, as all they seem to care about in the bid phase is the bottom line. That's unfortunate because the bid phase is the time when their most powerful tools of observation will be needed in order to:

- Judge the content of a given proposal on its own merits
- Make an accurate comparison to other submitted proposals
- Note what qualifications and exclusions are made

All of the above are critical to the contract award process, and will have ramifications for the subsequent phases of the contract.

Rebid and/or Value Engineer

In value engineering the contractor is asked to think of ways to save money without compromising the integrity of the work or design intent. The two most obvious and common responses to value engineering queries are the lowering of prices, or the removal of scope from the contract, neither of which are very imaginative nor constitute value engineering. I believe that once a contractor is asked to value-engineer a project, his motivation begins to nosedive, for experience dictates that the project is underfinanced, overdesigned, and may be a loser. Also, because value engineering and bargain hunting are now commonplace, subcontractors are weary of investing time and money into projects that likely will not turn out for them. They will begin to complain that you are jerking their chain. If a contractor is always asking a subcontractor to reduce his prices, the vendor will soon tire of it and then either begin padding his bids, or seek other, more auspicious accounts. In his mind, he is being asked to provide the same service for less money. Another form of value engineering takes the form of substitutions. The specifications may clearly indicate a given product, or its equivalent. In that case, the contractor should vet his replacement with the architect, as opposed to switching without notification.

One advantage of negotiated bids is the notion that the client can benefit from long running relationships a contractor has with his subcontractors, as the contractor would enjoy leverage with them. If the project is a lock for a contractor, a subcontractor will be more confident in lowering his price a bit, once he is virtually assured the work. Too often, subcontractors are negotiated with before the general contractor issues his proposal. No subcontractor appreciates this; however, many anticipate it, and will accordingly pad their bids. There is no reason a client should be discounted by dint of a contractor's leverage with his own vendors. This is the exclusive right of the contractor. Market valuations should be duly observed in bidding. There is seldom incentive to promise to deliver a contract that is lower than the market rate.

As pertains to rebidding, often a client may request a breakout of trades and scope that can vary in detail from simple to exhaustive. This may technically be a clarification, but it often constitutes rebidding the work in its entirety, or undergoing a tedious deconstruction process. Your experience will dictate how many times you will undertake the breakout exercise for a given prospect. Often, your estimator will have breakout information readily available. At other times, it will be extremely difficult to extrapolate, depending on what is requested. Much of this information the estimator may have to ask the subcontractors for, and they often are reluctant to generate it much for the same reasons you are. The breakout process often seems merely to be an exercise wherein you tip your hand, and for the client to cherry pick the honor cards. Hence, the clarification process is usually related to the value engineering process, and may merely be the architect's way of doing his own value engineering. In exercises of value engineering, remember that the object is to make the job more affordable, not to cut into your profit margin, as it so often does. It does so because value engineered items tend to be the ones with the highest profit margin, as opposed to say labor-intensive tasks, which traditionally don't have a high margin. In drastically value engineered projects, you will find the project has been altered to such a state as to not offer the incentive as it once did. Some call this condition "taking the meat out of the job"; leaving only the bones. At this point, a contractor may decide to increase his percentages, or gracefully decline the next bidding phase.

Often, the value engineering exercise takes place in the form of crude or informal negotiations, across a table, or perhaps over the phone. Such negotiations set the stage for contention, as these off-the-cuff discussions don't always manifest themselves into working directives. For that reason you should insist on written directives for any action modifying the contract documents.

Part of the value engineering exercise may already be incorporated into the project. For example, FBO, or furnished by others—this may be noted in the specifications, or the client may indicate that he has his own supplier or subcontractor for a given scope of work. This arrangement is almost never to your advantage. In procuring his material, you may be liable to absorb costs for:

- Coordinating with the supplier
- Arranging for shipping and delivery (also see below)
- Coordinating the work with other trades: including scheduling, cleaning up after, and isolating work areas

Shipping and Handling the Goods

Including taking delivery, unpacking, inspection, inventorying, repacking, discarding shipping material, site storage, and as necessary, shipping to platers, mill workers, electricians, or other such coordinated trades involved.

Making Arrangements for Missing, Incorrect, Late Delivery, or Damaged Goods

Hopefully, you know early on if there are problems with the client's order. Not having leverage with the vendor, as you would your own vendor, this problem can be a nightmare to remediate.

The idea is that the client believes he will realize cost savings by using his own vendors, thus forgoing your markup, or profit. When you realize that the client wishes to procure his own material, you will want to advise him of the incidental costs that will be involved, as stated above, collectively known as coordination fees. Often, at this time, a client will see to reason. If not, he is in for some headaches as he has effectively just appointed himself cogeneral contractor.

A relative of this tactic is when the client contracts directly with his own subcontractors. This poses an even more difficult scenario. In addition to still having to coordinate their work into yours, you do not have any leverage with them either. Often, they will be the "teacher's pet." As with client-contracted suppliers, you will want to be compensated accordingly to work with these people. If they were your own subcontractors, you would incur general conditions at one rate, whereas, using an unknown quantity, i.e., the client's vendor, you must prorate your general conditions accordingly. Therefore, the client is paying additional below the line costs (general conditions and coordination fees) more than what he would have paid for the general contractor to use his own subcontractors. Moreover, you cannot be liable for the integrity of their product or work, especially if you had no say-so in the qualification process. These conditions can make for a contentious project in more ways than one, and are becoming less commonplace than they used to be.

In the value engineering phase, you may want to consider requalifying your bid, as the terms are likely to have changed. The schedule may have been reduced. Work may have been reduced in scope or taken out altogether. You need to qualify any such circumstances. Optimally, any value engineering measures taken should be reflected somewhere in the contract documents other than only in your proposal; i.e. in a document generated by the architect or the owner. Otherwise, the information can be construed to have emanated in a vacuum.

Revised Presentation

The revised proposal is reissued with savings alternatives incorporated. A company of industry will have thought long and hard about alternatives, and will have other ideas other than knee-jerk discounts and removal of scope. This is a great opportunity for a company to show its stuff. Once the first revised proposal is issued, it is assumed that there will be additional revised proposals. For this reason, never give your bottom-line to soon; always leave room to negotiate.

If the drawings and project documentation have changed, this information must be reflected in your proposal as well as your subcontractors' proposals. Think of a revised proposal as if you were bidding the project anew, for the first time, as opposed to a distillation of its former context. This exercise will force you to reconsider the relevance of the new aspects affecting your approach to the project, a worthwhile undertaking.

Bidding Systems

Contractor proposals come in endless array of forms. They may be composed based on the estimator's takeoffs, subcontractor and vendor bids, or as is often the case of a budget proposal, pulled out of a hat. You may see handwritten one-pagers, bound and collated tomes, verbal quotes, et. al. The form and organization of this information also varies widely. Comparing the varied contractor proposals can be a headache for the client as there is always a good deal of transposing that must first take place.

Traditionally, the proposal is only generated for purposes of acquiring and billing the work. Once the work is awarded, bookkeeping modules are parsed from the proposal information; in other words, double entry exists: estimating, and bookkeeping. Ideally, a system should be implemented, wherein the digital bidding documents are linked to the production and billing documentation. There are commercial computer programs, which offer this grail, and we shall talk about them further in Chap. 6. For now, let us assume there are no such programs. Then the object is to build a coherent system from scratch. There are some advantages to developing your own system:

- You have the ability to tailor it exactly fit your needs.

- It will be adaptable and flexible to changes you may later make; commercial programs tend to be difficult to customize.

- It is cheap: you don't have to pay the hefty licensing, upgrade, and training fees associated with commercial programs.

Assuming that you have a system ready to implement:

- Will it lend itself to integration with project management and billing systems in place, or to be introduced?
- Do you have the resources to implement it?
- Will the system be adaptable to smaller and larger projects and workforces?
- What kind of training will be required for system participants?
- Do you have a "plan B" in the event that system fails?
- Is the system structured such that components (including staff) are replaceable?

Too often contractors blindly roll out their programs with little or no forethought as to the above considerations. This is another reason why the industry is rife with administrative and infrastructure problems.

"0.0 and 1.x Syndrome"

0.0 and 1.x Syndrome refers to the phenomenon of new version[29] releases by software companies; for example, 1.0, 2.0, 3.0. Additionally, the 1.x release of a program will invariably be a beta version. There are many software manufacturers who have no experience in creating programs for the construction industry, or for that matter, any industry. Indeed, the program may be their first endeavor. They will subcontract the code writing, and interface of the program to outside vendors, and then assemble the modules into one unseemly bundle. There are countless such programs in circulation; some of them fly by night, others with more longevity.

Think of buying a new version of software as similar to how a scientist uses guinea pigs. Such software may be touted as cutting edge, featuring countless bells and whistles, all of which render it unwieldy and fraught with bugs. Indeed, these new versions are only beta versions, where in one sense, end users finance all subsequent upgrades necessary to work out the kinks. These programs, often bundled into packages can be costly investments, requiring license fees, and frequent upgrades. Be very selective in buying such software. Fledgling software vendors are ubiquitous at trade shows. The products they sell should be highly scrutinized before you introduce them to your company. The first question asked should be: "May I see the manual?" The answer to this question always generates some highly interesting conundrums.

Three Deal Breakers for Buying Bundled or Comprehensive Programs

- Version 1.0
- No manual, or the manual is not useful
- No demo disk

Also inquire of the customer service/technical support programs, if there are any. Ask about the company's infrastructure. We will further discuss contractors' use of computer software in Chap. 6.

Creating and implementing a coherent bidding system from scratch is a daunting task. For this reason, most companies create as simple a system as possible, changing and updating it frequently. The bidding format, usually a spreadsheet is tied into the proposal, a word-processing generated document. If the contract is secured, this information is then folded into the project management and bookkeeping systems, assuming there are any.

For every contractor in operation, each would seemingly have his own distinctive bidding structure. Some common bidding structures are based on:

- Lump-sum base costs for all trades, with indexed general conditions, profit, and overhead appended
- Percentage only: common for budget and other fee-based projects
- By phase: usually by request of the owner. The reason may have to do with logistics or cash flow, project turnover, et. al.
- By area: also by request of the owner. Painters, mill workers, and carpet layers frequently use this method, but MEP estimators rarely do
- Base costs broken out by trade
- Base costs broken out by trade, area, and by task

This last structure is about as specific as proposals tend to get; with the base costs broken out by trade being the most popular. Such proposals can easily be presented on one page, which surprisingly, many clients and architects prefer to more comprehensive proposals. As I have said, the general requirements often dictate the form the proposal must take. For larger bids, this may be tantamount to "reinventing the wheel"; and for this reason, a contractor may choose to ignore the request for this service, as it can require considerable time and expense. It's as if architects and contractors don't speak the same language, they intuitively see the project two different ways. It is just such discontinuity that plagues architect/contractor relationships—they simply don't think alike.

Whatever bidding system you use, you should think "big picture", in terms of seamlessly integrating this information into your bid presentation, and later, production and bookkeeping departments. That prospect is extremely difficult to realize, and for this reason, at least two systems are utilized for the three tasks, for instance, you may use a spreadsheet for your bidding system, paste it into word processing for presentation, and finally, enter it into an accounts payable/accounts receivable program. If the working contract is an AIA contract, you will need the AIA software to enter billing into a Continuation Sheet provided with an *Application and Certificate for Payment.* Hard copy of this documentation is available for use by contractors without computers, i.e., for manual use, but few contractors are that hard up. To track costs, you will also want to link your payroll into the bookkeeping system. I will later discuss, in Chap. 6, the difficulty of integrating these three related systems.

This mountain of information can be formidable, and resultantly, contractors will only have the wherewithal to implement the minimal requirements. Let me say now, that unless a contractor's work is limited to a few tasks, or repetitive work, it is exigent that at minimum, the person(s) who input and publish this information are computer proficient, and know how to crunch numbers. Manual processing of this type of information is virtually unheard of.

The Construction Specifications Institute

The Construction Specifications Institute (CSI) is a professional organization concerned with the organizational format information used by specifiers. CSI intended to create a system that comprehensively structured every component of any construction project called Masterformat^{TM}. The foundation of the Masterformat^{TM} was a classification system comprising 16 divisions, as follows:

Division 0—Contract

Division 1—General Requirements

Division 2—Sitework

Division 3—Concrete

Division 4—Masonry

Division 5—Metals

Division 6—Woods and Plastics

Division 7—Thermal and Moisture Protection

Division 8—Doors and Windows

Division 9—Finishes

Division 10—Specialties

Division 11—Equipment

Division 12—Furnishings

Division 13—Special Construction

Division 14—Conveying Systems

Division 15—Mechanical

Division 16—Electrical

These divisions were recently expanded to 48 divisions; however, most of these have little to do with residential interiors. Moreover, the surplus information is little inundating. Within each division are subdivisions of all the components, organized by the prefix of the division, followed by three more numbers, for example; 15,700 heating, ventilation, and air conditioning. This standard is widely accepted and seems to be the *lingua franca* of most specifiers, and it should be for general contractors as well for it is an excellent organizational tool for estimators and project managers. Industry software developers also like to use it. Refer to the following example of a CSI division and its subdivisions:

07 50 00 MEMBRANE ROOFING

07 51 00 Built-Up Bituminous Roofing

07 51 13 Built-Up Asphalt Roofing
07 51 13.13 Cold-Applied Built-Up Asphalt Roofing
07 51 16 Built-Up Coal Tar Roofing
07 51 23 Glass Fiber Reinforced Asphalt Emulsion Roofing

07 52 00 Modified Bituminous Membrane Roofing

07 52 13 Atactic Polypropylene Modified Bituminous Membrane Roofing
07 52 16 Styrene-Butadiene-Styrene Modified Bituminous Membrane Roofing
07 52 19 Self-Adhering Modified Bituminous Membrane Roofing

07 53 00 Elastomeric Membrane Roofing

07 53 13 Chlorinated Polyethylene Roofing
07 53 16 Chlorosulfonated-Polyethylene Roofing
07 53 23 Ethylene–Propylene–Diene Monomer Roofing
07 53 29 Polyisobutylene Roofing

07 54 00 Thermoplastic Membrane Roofing

07 54 13 Copolymer Alloy Roofing
07 54 16 Ethylene Interpolymer Roofing
07 54 19 Polyvinyl Chloride Roofing
07 54 23 Thermoplastic Polyolefin Roofing
07 54 26 Nitrile–Butadiene Polymer Roofing

07 55 00 Protected Membrane Roofing

07 55 51 Built-Up Bituminous Protected Membrane Roofing
07 55 52 Modified Bituminous Protected Membrane Roofing
07 55 53 Elastomeric Protected Membrane Roofing
07 55 54 Thermoplastic Protected Membrane Roofing
07 55 56 Fluid-Applied Protected Membrane Roofing
07 55 56.13 Hot-Applied Rubberized Asphalt Protected Membrane Roofing
07 55 63 Vegetated Protected Membrane Roofing

07 56 00 Fluid-Applied Roofing

07 57 00 Coated Foamed Roofing

07 57 13 Sprayed Polyurethane Foam Roofing

07 58 00 Roll Roofing

I have found that using the CSI structure, a companywide system can be implemented that will facilitate integration of estimating, bid presentation, production documentation, and bookkeeping. Not every company or project lends itself to the wholesale use of this system; however, it is considerably adaptable to small and large companies and projects alike.

For the estimator, the CSI structure is a tried and true organizational panacea. You can structure not only your takeoffs, but also your proposal, cost tracking, and bidding systems based on the CSI format. The CSI format is readily available, and should be kept in digital form on your estimator's computer. As he does his takeoffs, he can enter the respective tasks and line items into distinct divisions within a spreadsheet or other bid document. The CSI breaks down each group into a litany of subgroups, which simplifies and organizes data for you as you enter it. For this same reason, some commercial computer programs are, in fact, structured around the CSI format. Working knowledge of the basic divisions of the CSI is essential for using it properly.

The example in Table 2.5 is a proposal format based on the CSI structure. We shall see in Chap. 5 how this structure is readily adaptable for use in future project management and documentation.

The caveat with using the CSI format is that some tasks, for instance, work involving multiple trades, can be difficult to deconstruct into the CSI structure, for example, a brass-plated medicine cabinet, with wood inserts, suspended from the ceiling with backlighting; trades involved: carpenters, architectural metal workers, architectural millworkers, glaziers, and electricians. Also, some of the CSI subgroups seem to cross over into other subgroups, or are too broad. Some divisions and subgroups will never be used. But this is a negligible price to pay for the rewards of being efficient and organized.

Finally, as the CSI is the ubiquitous specifications format, architects and engineers work with it every day, and most are familiar with it. So they are often pleased to see a contractor's proposal in this format.

Cost Tracking

Every company should keep track of its costs. To some, cost tracking is as simple as monitoring the bank account; but that is not cost tracking. Cost tracking often is only calculated at the end of the project: "Did we make or lose money?" However, in order to be in control of costs, one should plan on analytical and frequent tracking. That requires monitoring expenses during the project. This process should be implemented from the inception of the project through the postmortem. It will require coordination between your field managers and bookkeepers, who can monitor progress according to what they observe and enter on to the monthly bill, or continuation sheet, and what is paid out.

The CSI structured takeoffs and proposal your estimator prepares can be readily folded into a cost tracking system, even simply by merely adding a few columns to a spreadsheet. Diligent cost tracking is vital to the financial health of a company—it will monitor profit and loss on a running basis, instead of after the fact, when

TABLE 2.5   CSI Proposal

Trade cost breakdown	5 Floor	6 Floor	Total current
01500 Temperatures	2,500	2,500	5,000
02070 Demolition	7,500	7,500	15,000
02071 Slab cuts	12,500	12,500	25,000
03300 Concrete	15,000	15,000	30,000
03650 Floor leveling	22,400	22,100	44,500
05100 Miscellaneous metals	36,800	29,300	66,100
05500 Architectural metals	N.A.	45,100	45,100
06100 Rough carpentry:			—
subfloors	30,100	36,500	66,600
rough carpentry	76,000	77,500	153,500
06400 Architectural woodworking	825,100	1,552,300	2,377,400
07500 Waterproofing	19,500	13,500	33,000
08100 Hollow metal	3,000	6,000	9,000
08700 Hardware allowance	81,400	58,700	140,100
08800 Glass & mirror	60,900	132,800	193,700
09200 Plaster:			—
veneer plaster	36,400	45,000	81,400
ornamental plaster		5,400	5,400
09250 Drywall	244,900	257,400	502,300
09560 Wood flooring	45,800	56,600	102,400
09600 Marble & stone	275,700	236,900	512,600
09900 Painting	25,000	35,000	60,000
10750 Toilet accessories	7,500	6,200	13,700
11400 Appliances		3,800	3,800
15400 Plumbing:			—
base contract	78,100	53,100	131,200
15450 Plumbing fixtures	54,700	69,000	123,700
15500 Sprinkler	41,000	45,000	86,000
15700 H.V.A.C.:			—
base contract	265,600	405,100	670,700
16000 Electrical:			—
base contract	225,000	153,200	378,200
dimming system	175,000	155,200	330,200
16500 Light fixtures	125,000	162,300	287,300
Trade cost total	2,792,400	3,700,500	6,492,900
Price psf, 3800 sf per floor	735	974	854

it is too late to make adjustments. This information is critical to your bookkeeper, and will help you structure payment schedules on your contracts.

On budget projects, cost-plus, Construction Management, and any other fee-based projects, you will likely be required to track and report to the client cash flow updates, and cost projections. Without a coherent system you will be hard-pressed to accomplish this.

Change Orders

Negotiating change orders

Negotiating and executing change orders are another bane of the building industry, to such an extent that there are entire books and professional level seminars dedicated to the process for everyone from contractors, to lawyers and laypeople. Countless litigation and arbitration processes are necessitated by projects with a high percentage of change orders.

A change order is any written directive by the architect or client that is not a component of the base contract, or modifies the contract documents in some other way. Not to say contractors don't conduct extra work without such a directive, they frequently do; however, they just as frequently are not paid for such unauthorized extras, i.e. informal extra work requests. For this reason, savvy contractors prohibit their workers from conducting such work without proper authorization.

This fact does not go unnoticed by architects and clients, and they will let you know their opinions. They may not agree with or understand you. They may feel that you are inflating your prices even while you have done your best to minimize cost impact. Savvy architects will sometimes insist on the issuance of unit prices as part of your base proposal, to protect against such price fluctuations. The justification of your change orders will be one of the most difficult exercises you will experience on your projects.

The subject of change orders will also be discussed in Chap. 3, as it relates to scheduling, Chap. 4, as it relates to production, Chaps. 5 and 6, as it relates to project and construction management, Chap. 7, as it relates to siege management, and in Chap. 8, as it relates to conflict resolution.

Change orders are necessitated in several ways

- Unforeseen existing conditions: such as bedrock discovered in a crawl space that was to have been excavated assuming only soil was to be removed. Contractors typically, but not always, are not responsible for absorbing the costs of such work; however, if the architect feels the contractor should have known such work was warranted, he may take him to task for it. Even if he doesn't necessarily believe that, he may try to squeeze the contractor to do the work. Hopefully, the contractor has made qualifications not to be responsible for specific existing conditions. Especially, in light of the fact that it's not beyond some architects and clients to hide known defects or liabilities on their project in hope they can stick some poor contractor with it.

    An architect's specifications often feature nebulous language that would seemingly make the contractor accountable for just about any eventuality; however, this language tends to be nebulous, and of dubious legal significance. A basic knowledge of contract law is usually enough to defend against evil-doers, and every contractor should have someone on his staff with such knowledge. Of course, there is no replacement for a good construction lawyer; however, one should only be retained to review the contract.

- Additional scope: the client or architect request extra work, not within the base scope of the contract.

- Deletion of scope: requested by the client or architect. This type of change order has its own special criteria for assessing, which we will discuss below.

- Errors and omissions: these may be the fault of the architect, contractor, or both. It has become so common that architects often have insurance for errors and omissions, as discussed above.

- Tearout and redo: work that has either been installed poorly, or in the wrong location. This work is typically paid for by the contractor, unless it is installed in accordance with the design documents, when the client must pay for it to be done again. For example, the client or architect wishes to have the contractor remove and reinstall work to a new location. They typically do this for aesthetic reasons, or to resolve conflicting program.

Suffice it to say, change order work has its own special criteria for analyzing cost, which we will discuss in detail, below.

Subcontractor change orders

The subcontractors execute the work; they therefore are the impetus for most change order work. In a perfect world, they will issue proposals for this work when they receive an RFP, or request for pricing. This RFP is often a verbal request. It should always be done in writing, so that no one will be laboring under a preconception. The written request should be part of the change order package presented to the client. Not uncommonly, subcontractors will perform change order work without any written directive or consent. At best, they do this as a show of good faith, at worst . . . Even if the work was done in good faith, unauthorized work should be discouraged, as it will have a small chance of being remunerated. By the same token, architects and owners must not be allowed to directly solicit bids, or authorize your subcontractors to do extra work.

Because subcontractor's work can be affected by the work of others, and because their work can affect the work of others, there are often problems between trades created for one reason or another. These problems can create more work, and change orders or back charges are issued. While focusing on the work directly involved with a change, indirect considerations are often overlooked; even though the indirect work may not be explicitly indicated in an RFP, it needs to be done. For example, in order to accommodate a request for an additional light fixture a lighting circuit may become overloaded and require a new feed. The electrician issues a price to run the new circuit, and the general contractor includes cutting and patching expenses. But suppose the tin knocker located a plenum that conflicts with the location of the new light, or obstructs the wire from being fed to it? The contractor is not responsible for moving the duct in question without an authorized change order to cover the cost of the work; however, having already approved the electrical change order, the client won't be too happy to hear that the price is going up again; he may believe he is being taken advantage of. Under these circumstances some architects may state that the price to feed a new circuit to accommodate the outlet should have been inclusive. This, of course, is nonsense; but it is indicative of one way in which change orders often become tortured.

Thus, it is imperative that all work related to a given change order is considered and valuated before a given change order is issued, and especially, before the work is authorized. This should be a mainstay policy for every general contractor, and he should make it his business to advise and remind all of his subcontractors of this policy.

Pricing change orders

The valuation of change orders is an art in itself. At times, methodology may not even resemble the process used to valuate the base contract work. Generally, change orders almost always carry additional costs, which would not have existed had the same work been included in the contract documents. There are several reasons for this:

- A change order may involve tear-out and reinstallation work of areas to facilitate the change order work.

- The change order requires resequencing and time-consuming coordination for the management staff.

- The change order will require additional documentation and processing through the bookkeeping system.

- The change order may cause delays of other work on the project.

- The work involves remobilization such as setting up and breaking down for production. Just like fabricators in the garment industry, piecework always carries a higher unit price than a production run breakout of an item.

Because the majority of change orders are responses to field conditions, and client directives subsequent to mobilization, the project manager or superintendent will be in the best position to valuate them, or at least impart an accurate scope of work to the estimator, who will then draft the change order. For this reason, the estimating and project managers will continue to work closely together to quantify early change order work, until the major change orders are resolved. Because of the nature of change order work, the outcome should always reflect a rate sufficiently higher than that of the base contract. Owners will not empathize, but then they may have their own interests at heart:

> Owners and designers should understand that if they wish to make changes in lump sum contracts as at present, it is reasonable that the owner should pay a premium for them. Otherwise, a so called lump-sum contract is really something else . . .[30]

In other words, they need to learn to appreciate why contractors often lose money on change order costs, and also the notion that it is unfair to aggressively persuade a contractor into such a position.

In addition to direct costs, there are hidden costs to consider when calculating change order costs. One way they can be described is as follows:

Hidden costs are characterized as having two components—impact costs and consequential costs. *Impact costs* are project related and *consequential costs* are nonproject related. The formal definitions of impact and consequential costs are:

1. Impact costs are the indirect effects that changes have on project budgets and schedules as a result of delays, lowered productivity, and material waste.

2. Consequential costs follow as an effect of change order because they are non-project related but can be traced to project change after implementation. Some examples of consequential costs are lost supervision time for another project, resolving, material supply problems on reorder parts, and other problems/costs that are outside the project or only identifiable to a project in hindsight.[31]

Identifying these hidden costs is the first step in understanding how they add up, and is necessary in order to make an accurate claim. The above are not the only hidden costs that exacerbate change order rates. Consider the following:

A contractor installs a $2000 stone floor. Subsequent to the installation, the owner decides that he wishes to change the material. Assuming the material is the same price, he would expect to pay only another $2000, the cost of furnishing and installing the floor. However, the contractor's actual costs do not bear this out:

Original cost	$2000
Tearout cost	600
Reinstallation	2000
Lost productivity[32]	2000
Total cost	$6600
+ Hidden costs	???

In this example, the contractor experiences a loss of about $2600. Even if he were paid the lost $2600, he would at best break-even since these are his costs, not his prospective selling prices.

The nature of change orders

Because change orders involve supplementary efforts, general conditions comprise a much greater component of change orders than they do in base contract work. It is these general conditions that drive the indexed costs of executing change order work. It is not unusual for general conditions to exceed the change order scope of work itself. Think of gas mileage calculations for automobiles—on the open road or highway, a car will travel at x mi/gal, whereas the same distance traveled in city traffic only realizes *.6x* mi/gal. In other words, 40% more effort is exerted to realize the same result. For example, a client may request an additional cabinet to be made and installed. Assuming the selling price of this cabinet was $1000, the client couldn't fathom paying anymore than $1200—tops, with $300 for general conditions and fees, for a total of $1500. Let's run out the costs:

Although the installer only needs three hours to install the cabinet, his men waste a day in transit, moving tools, and going to and from the site. His crew will only get in three productive hours for the whole day. Thus, the subcontractor bills his day rate. The general contractor's superintendent and laborer also have unproductive time:

Delivery charge	$200
Fabrication	500
Installation (day rate, mechanic and helper)	800
Superintendent's time (billable rate, 4 hours)	300
Laborer's time (billable rate, 4 hours)	160
Bookkeeping (change order administration and billing)	
Total	$1960

In the above example, not only does the contractor not realize a profit, he loses money: $460, or almost one-third of the total value of the work.

The notion of conflict over general conditions is a concept that was appreciated early on in contract negotiation:

> The wording of this (general conditions) clause is very important, as in the event of a lawsuit over the contract, the provisions of the general-condition clause are likely to become the basis of over half the arguments in the case.[33]

A project is scheduled to run for 1 year. The general contractor will provide the same team of management and laborers for the duration, billing monthly. Supposing there are many design changes that affect the schedule in such a way as to prolong it an extra three months. Although the scope of work may not have increased, the general contractor still pays his team to maintain the project for the extra duration. Though no fault of his own, the general contractor realizes a 25% increase in these costs (not withstanding indirect costs such as overhead). Feeling sheepish, general contractors are loath to issue change orders for general conditions alone, or with extra general conditions, and tend to absorb these costs. The above was a simple example of calculating lost general conditions. Had it been a construction management project, with billable general conditions, no such calculation would be needed.

However, not all claims for additional general conditions are so simple. Suppose it is not clear who's to blame for a delay, or that several parties are to blame? It then becomes difficult to substantiate your claim. Some project durations are extended as a result of work being added. You may get a reaction from your client when you bill him for extra general conditions because (1) your change orders already have general conditions incorporated into them (although they will not pertain to schedule extensions, or lag in production) and (2) you may be informed by the client that "It's not as if the men were sitting around doing nothing . . ." During the extension; they were on task (being productive, making money). Such contentions can make it difficult for you to negotiate your claim, but that does not mean you are not entitled to one—you may be. Here is one way you can determine if you are:

In the above example, it was simple to multiply the rate of general conditions, as there were no other costs to offset them. Let us say that your weekly general condition rate will remain the same as in the above example. As a rule, we can say that the general conditions are proportionate to the base cost of work. In our example x general conditions are needed to facilitate y in terms of production, with z representing the total contract value. Thus the monthly calculation $x/12 + y/12 = z/12$. But suppose for the additional 3 months, production is only 25% the rate of the base contract rate? Then instead of $x/3 + y/3 = z/3$, $x/3 + y/3 = .25z/3$ (.25z/3 as opposed to $z/3$). That means you are paid for only 25% of the actual extended general conditions. In client extended contracts, you are still entitled to a minimum of the full monthly general condition rate, $x/12$. The following example illustrates the above equation:

For a 12-month project

Base contract:	$800,000
General conditions:	200,000
Total project value	$1,000,000

For a 15-month project (at base contract production rate)

Base Contract:	$800,000
General Conditions:	200,000
Change Orders: *	200,000
General Conditions For change orders: *	50,000
Total project value:	$1,250,000

For a 15-month project (with additional 3 months at the rate of 25%/contract rate of production)

Base Contract:	$800,000
General Conditions:	200,000
Change Orders: *	50,000
General Conditions For change orders: *	12,500
Total project value:	$1,062,500
Difference in contract value:	$187,500
Change orders:	$150,000
General Conditions	37,500
Total	$187,500

*During extension period only

As you can see, with the lower rate of production, you have lost $150,000 in revenue. You cannot bill for this, or write it off as an expense as it is not out of pocket. However, you are entitled to the additional $37,500 in general conditions, of which your profit margin will be nominal. Ideally, you never have to perform this calculation after the fact, i.e. the change order value and general conditions projection are calculated before you agree to undertake the work. In this case, even if you were reimbursed for the general conditions, the offset in revenue makes it hardly worth your while. The precalculation computation is so seldom done that it is virtually unheard of in residential projects. However, research on the subject of loss of productivity due to change orders bear out the facts that although

> . . . there is no correlation between loss of productivity when change order hours are less than 10% of the base contract hours, yet, as change order hours increase as a percentage of the base contract hours, the loss of productivity occurs on a roughly linear basis (Figure 2.3).[34]

As the chart shows, loss of productivity increases with the percentage of change orders.

Type 1. Effects of change order when no other impact factors were present

Type 2. Effects of change order when one other impact factor was present

Type 3. Effects of change order when two other impact factors were present[35]

The consequential loss of productivity by the introduction of substantial (change order >0.1/base contract) change orders is one reason why, by their nature, they will always be more costly to perform than base contract work.

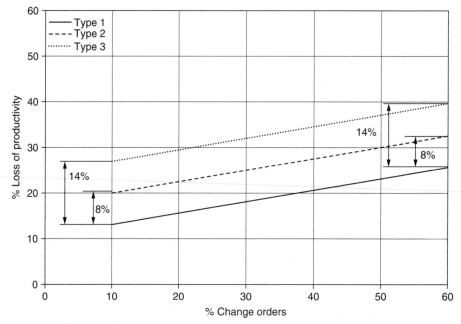

Figure 2.3   Change orders vs. loss of productivity—civil/architectural contracts (types 1, 2, & 3). (*Source*: Based on information from Charles A. Lconard, *The Effects of Change Orders on Productivity*, April 14, 1987.)

Charles A. Leonard,[36] in his Leonard Study, offers a simple equation for calculating such losses:

Total actual man-hours expended on the project
$$- \text{Total actual change order hours}$$
$$= \text{Actual base contract hours}$$
Percent change orders = actual change order hours/actual base contract hours

As indicated above, change orders by their nature carry a higher proportion of general conditions. A general contractor may ask to insert a rider to the contract stipulating that general conditions of change orders will be determined on a case-by-case basis. Otherwise, a separate line item enumerating the extra general conditions may be presented as part of the cost of the change order, as opposed to indexed general conditions. Either way, you are entitled to ask for remuneration of money that you will spend. Regardless, you are not required to do any change order work, if the work should not be profitable—turn it away. This notion is generally a foreign one to most contractors. Additionally, clients do not empathize with additional general conditions for changes, or with the idea that omitted scope does not include a credit for general conditions. This concept is well exemplified in the following statement:

> . . . whereas an addition should be priced so as to add all additional direct and indirect costs to the contract amount (cost job overhead, operating overhead, and profit), an omission should be priced so as to deduct only the direct costs (of labor, materials, and equipment), but not the job overhead and the indirect costs.
> . . . it should be remembered that changes in the work are only made by the owner or his agent, the designer; therefore, in fairness, because any change is usually for the benefit of the owner and is initiated by him or his agent, the contractor should never be put into a position of loss as a result of a change in the work.[37]

On AIA contracts, there is an instrument for change orders, AIA *G701 Change Order*.[38] This is the document the base AIA contracts require for amendments: not only changes affecting the cost of the work, but also for changes to the schedule. It is the contractor's responsibility to generate this document. Typically, a change order will go through several permutations before being ratified. Rather than compose an AIA change order for every version, issue separate proposals until there is a consensus on one, then draft the AIA change order. This will save you time and money.

On some projects, the change order requests are constant. The manpower needed to process every little change order can be debilitating. There is also a greater chance to misplace or forget about smaller change orders, and there is a greater opportunity for holdups. To understand how numerous small change orders can increase overhead consider the following:

A contractor has ten RFPs from his client, each with a negligible value. To complete each AIA form, and circulate it, a clerk needs 1 hour per change order; thus, 10 hours for ten change orders. In some instances, the overhead to produce the change order can exceed the value of the work. If he were to issue one change order including all ten items, he may spend 90 minutes, thus saving 85% of the process period. It is noteworthy that each change order will become a line item on the AIA *G702 Application and Certificate for Payment*, where it must be recorded, and tracked. General contractors seldom bill the client for the time it takes to draft a change order. Thus, an incomplete set of working drawings can portend reams of SKs and RFPs, which will necessitate mountains of change orders. On such projects, you should compute your general conditions with this in mind. Under such circumstances, I have instituted change order processing fees. This is reasonable because if your time was reimbursable, you'd be getting paid. Thus, in the matter of processing client or architect generated change orders, you should also be reimbursed for your time.

Given that, you should set a minimum value for drafted change orders. That doesn't mean you won't do the work if the cost is below the minimum, it means that you will only issue a change order when its components reach a minimum value. The way to assemble such a change order precludes the expectations that every change has its own change order. For smaller, simpler, and less significant change orders it is appropriate to issue one main change order representing the aggregate of a number of small change orders or tickets.

If you have a good relationship with your client, you may suggest that verbal directives for certain types of change orders will be carried out at once. Such work will have a maximum value, and will not be subject to negotiation. In a pinch, this can save processing time that might otherwise cause production delays on the project. The second part of this unofficial directing process is how such a work is billed; it will either be issued as a preapproved AIA change order, or a simple invoice. Although this latter is clearly less work, it can become a red herring for the bookkeeper if it is not kept track of.

On projects that have considerable added and deleted scope, a client will often notice that there is a disproportionate level of change orders to credits. Although this observation may be a moot point, it will generate misgiving on the part of the client, which should be considered natural. It should also induce you to take action to change your client's perception. Some tools you can use to do this:

- Create comprehensive base contract proposals that leave little room for interpretation, and ensuing arguments over responsibility for subsequent works.
- Avoid compound work descriptions in your change orders, or give a level of detail that is clear to the layperson. For example:

The description: "install 50 gal water heater" gives no hint as to the ancillary work necessary to carry out the major task. Instead, for the same line item:

Disconnect and discard existing water heater

Cut and patch masonry for new pipe routing

Replace ball valve

Run new electrical feed

Furnish and install AO Scott 50 gal high-recovery water heater

Although the work involved is the same, the comprehensive description apparently describes something more substantial. This information will be helpful to the client, who otherwise may not understand the process, and how the costs accumulate.

- On addition/subtraction change orders always show the math, especially the credits.

There will always be work you perform that for one reason or another, you do *gratis*. Typically, the client is unaware of this, or if he is, may not appreciate the value of it. One way of demonstrating the value of it, is to document it in a change order or memo showing the value of the work as a charge, with an offsetting credit immediately below (net zero). The caveat here is to be completely sure that said work was not within the scope of your contract.

Additional time

The form AIA *G701 Change Order* includes a line item for that change order's effect on schedule duration, increase or decrease x days. It is a one-liner, found lower on the page, and frequently, architects overlook it only to complain that it was sneaky of the contractor to enter information there without drawing special attention to it—any delay that makes it onto the change order should have been prenegotiated, or at least alluded to. This is one way to secure more time needed to incorporate the additional work into the schedule; however, it does not appear to be the most efficient or appreciated method. Additionally, by merely inserting the information on the AIA form, you in no way indicate that there are up-charges that may be associated with the delay. If there will be expected delays, whether they are related to a change order or not, they should be negotiated prior to issuance of the AIA *G701 Change Order*. The client will want an explanation and the single line item on AIA *G701 Change Order* will not instruct them. Ideally, you have documentation and a tracked schedule (see Chap. 3) to explain how and why the project is delayed, through no fault of your own. If you incur delays of your own doing, you will find yourself very reluctant to draw attention to them, and likely do everything possible to mitigate them before they are noticed or realized. Many contracts now include liquidated damages for delays. Less frequent are incentives for early delivery, as most schedules are constructed merely with *time being of the essence* (as per the contract). The exception is for construction management and budget projects that come in underbudget. Such jobs sometimes do offer incentives.

In addition to advising of a delay on the AIA *G701 Change Order* many contractors fail to realize that they may be absorbing additional general conditions—costs they should be passing on to the client. Even if little or no additional work takes place in a delay window, the general requirements such as field and site management, site mobilization, including protections and cleaning, will still have to be carried out. It is commonplace for projects to slow down to dangerously low levels of production. Besides being late, the general conditions continue to pile up. If a project stops altogether, a general contractor demobilizes it; however, so long as there is enough work for two or more people, general contractors have a habit of manning their projects with in-house field personnel—managers, laborers, and mechanics—regardless of workflow issues. This is a losing proposition for the general contractor, who should address these concerns before they happen, if possible. Even if the long-term effects of work-slowdowns can't be measured, some attempt should be made to appraise them in the present, so as to substantiate future delays, and compensation for them. The following memo illustrates a general contractor's approach to delay notification:

> The last set of drawings issued was 11.19.00. These drawings necessitated some 150 RFIs, 30 RFPs, and 70 SKs, for lack of detail in the bid documents. As such, collectively, they cannot be construed as a working set of drawings. It is noteworthy that no MEPs were ever issued for the project. For these reasons, we have experienced production delays of as much as 75%, and expect the above referenced schedule extensions. We have also had to hire extra personnel, just to coordinate this supplementary information, who have both actually been involved in much D&D and coordination work we seldom do without being remunerated. We were promised a working set of drawings five weeks ago, and as of today, have not received it. This set was to be inclusive of all RFIs, RFPs, and SKs. Without this working set we are forced to build the project out of sequence, and with a surplus of manpower. We have further been asked to issue an expedited schedule, which seems antithetical, as the project is extended, out of sequence, and lacking design information needed to even build the project according to the original working schedule. In addition, our office overhead has probably doubled our budget for much the same reasons as stated above. We have not even calculated this factor, which is very debilitating to the everyday operation of our company. Because of the extra manpower and extended schedule, we are not in a position to contract other work, for lack of resources being tied to this project. Moreover, we have no reference point to gauge when we can free up our manpower.

This is an example of a general notification delay memo. It isn't specific to durations, but it puts the design team on notice.

This same reasoning also dictates why general conditions should be nonrefundable: if the change order is an addition, there will typically be extra forces needed to facilitate the work; however, if the change order is a credit, the infrastructure still must be there to staff the rest of the project, regardless. In theory, this staff will be on hand even when no work is taking place. This notion can be particularly difficult to justify to your client. You will want to make this clear on your proposal.

Making Money by Not Losing Money

Your notion of how you make money will likely not be the same as your client's. Clients who do not understand the construction business will not appreciate how you lose money either. Consider the above examples of lost revenue and general conditions, and the examples of why change orders are more costly than base contract work; the general conditions up charge may be considered to be frivolous by your client, and your change orders as making up for a low bid or price gouging. In either case, it can be extraordinarily difficult to substantiate any sort of up charge extraneous to the base contract, to the uninitiated and experienced alike; whether it is legitimate or not. At the end of the day, you make little profit on your general conditions, and tend to lose money on change orders while at the same time your client feels taken advantage of.

Typically, in a fixed sum contract, your margin on labor will be lower than any other margin, especially materials; perhaps 2 to 5% for labor, and 5 to 20% for materials. Within the window of the contract, material prices tend to be stagnant, while labor rates of production can vary. Projects with a lot of manual work are known as "labor intensive;" the proportion of payroll to materials is higher than it is on more profitable projects. These projects can be volatile. Let us compare two projects of equal value, each which realized a 20% lag in production rate:

Project 1

Proposal: Furnish and install track lighting fixtures as per RCP 1

Estimated cost

Materials	$200,000
Labor	100,000
Markup materials	20,000
Markup labor	2000
	$322,000

Profit = $22,000

Actual cost

Materials	$200,000
Labor	120,000 (lower rate of production realized)
Markup materials	20,000
Markup labor	2000
	$342,000

Profit = $2000

Project 2

Proposal: Furnish and install custom gold plated mortise type lock cylinders and handles

Estimated cost

Materials	$226,000
Labor	50,000
Markup materials	45,200
Markup labor	1000
	$322,200

Profit = $46,200

Actual cost

Materials	$226,000
Labor	60,000 (lower rate of production realized)
Markup materials	45,200
Markup labor	1000
	$332,200

Profit = $36,200

As shown, two projects with the same contract value can have very different profit margins. The obvious factor in the above example is the proportion of materials, which is much higher on Project 2, than on Project 1, which also carry a much higher profit margin than labor. The risk on Project 1 is much higher than that of Project 2 because it is more labor intensive, labor rate is variable; materials are not. Of course, Project 2 appears to have some very costly fixtures. If these were replaced with cheaper fixtures, labor would remain fixed, but profit on materials would go down—the job could become a loser.

Project 2 (value engineered)

Actual cost

Materials	$113,000
Labor	60,000 (lower rate of production realized)
Markup materials	22,600
Markup labor	1000
	$196,600

Profit = $13,600

In this case, even with a slower rate of production, you still realize a decent profit as the project is not labor intensive. However, if you were contracted to use the costlier fixtures, and subsequently the cheaper fixtures were introduced, you should be compensated for the loss of profit, which is $22,600.

Taking the Meat out of the Contract

Clients have an acute awareness of big-ticket items. As part of the value engineering exercise they may simply cutback, delete, or purchase themselves, these big-ticket items, leaving only labor in the contract. This is what I call "taking the meat out of the contract" as there is always room to make cuts on materials, but labor rates and durations are generally fixed, hence, no room to cut. By taking out the most profitable items, they render the contract less appealing by lowering the contractor's margin. Some contractors may take such a contract just to keep cash flowing, or to make payroll during slow times, and there is nothing wrong with that, but if it becomes a habit it will impact significantly.

It is not uncommon for a client to purchase materials or fixtures directly, in hopes that he will forgo your profit on the item. You still will have to do all the receiving, inventory, coordination, and troubleshooting on the order; however, since the fixtures were purchased directly, you are not being compensated for these services. Once the fixtures arrive and these tasks begin, you will realize that you have been had, whether by design or not. It will be awkward to now ask for compensation for these services, as it were after the fact. Many general contractors invoke the same ploy with their subcontractors, who tend to dislike it immensely, as they expect general contractors to know better, which they should. Some projects will have such "value-engineering" built in to the job from the get-go: this will be made clear in the documentation. In this case, simply advise the client of the value of having the general contractor purchase the goods directly, and that alternatively, if he does purchase them directly, he will have to compensate you for the noninstallation related services, or coordination fees. If this is his first time going around the contractor to purchase goods, it will likely be his last, once he finds out the headaches involved with ordering; especially for a layperson. You should also take note of which and how many items are value engineered—what's left out of the project can tell you even more about what remains, as well as the stripe of your client. If the client doesn't aspire to the win/win philosophy, the project may not be for you.

There are other parameters that determine a winning endeavor other than a profit margin. In fact, many projects showing a profit can be considered losers if the clients are unhappy. To be considered a real winner, in addition to turning a decent profit, the clients should show some reasonable measure of satisfaction. An assurance of repeat future business is the highest compliment your client will make, that should be what you aspire toward.

Notes

Key causes of "loser" contracts

- Undervaluation of base contract
- Undervaluation of general conditions
- Aggressive schedules
- Poor cash flow
- Unskilled or inappropriate level production
- Unknown subcontractors and vendors
- Difficult architects and clients
- Lack of leverage in contract

Project checklist: Preconstruction

- Review all design documentation and specifications
- Visit site
- Meet with client
- Quantity takeoffs and bid outline

- Solicit and qualify bids from multiple vendors
- Collect and issue RFIs
- Select bids to sponsor
- Assemble bid
- Qualifications
- Peer review and proofread
- Proposal presentation
- Value engineering
- Reissue proposal
- Negotiate contract

Hallmarks of a winning prospect

- Negotiated bid
- The drawings and specifications are thorough
- The design team is a known quantity
- Familiarity with program
- Adequate schedule
- Reasonable client and architect

Right and wrong ways to make money

Right.   Use your leverage with your vendors and subcontractors to negotiate a little margin; they will be more inclined if they are your regulars and have a working relationship with you.

Wrong.   Don't negotiate just for the sake of making money—if a contractor's price is high, find out why. If you routinely knock your subcontractors down without any knowledge of the value of the work, they will merely pad their bids, or markup their change orders.

.   .   .   .

Right.   Use your expertise and your production team's know-how to expedite and make a project with a tight margin more profitable.

Wrong.   Don't pound the client at the end of the project with inflated or superfluous change orders. The best you'll get is a little more money in your pocket with the knowledge that it wasn't nearly worth the aggravation, loss of a client, or tarnished reputation.

.   .   .   .

Right. In fixed sum contracts, always bid what you believe to be equal or above the fair market value. If you are the beneficiary of a low bid from a hungry contractor, there is no incentive to blindly pass it onto the client. If you did, they would be incredulous and might not believe the gesture is genuine.

Wrong. Don't low-ball a project just to "get your foot in the door." It will set a bad precedent, and the jig will be up once your change orders are issued.

·   ·   ·   ·

Right. Require written authorization of all change orders, whether they are credits, debits, or they do not even affect pricing. Be punctual with your requirements, and don't do extra work without such authorization. If there is a specification or sketches involved, it must be reviewed before you can issue a price.

Wrong. Don't let change orders pile up because you feel that if you didn't do the work without authorization, the schedule would suffer. Don't let any of your workmen including subcontractors engage change order work without authorization.

·   ·   ·   ·

Right. Be punctual and diligent in your applications for payment. If you do not, you are giving your client an excuse to postpone paying you, insisting on a revised application. Sit down with the architect and find common ground before you draft the application, so as to avoid resubmission. And do not forget *lien waivers*; yours, and your subcontractors.

Just as you like to be paid on time, so do your subcontractors. Treat them as you would like to be treated and they will always give you their best. Pay them when you are paid.

Wrong. Do not accept delays of processing of timely and appropriate payment applications. Cash flow is at the heart of your business, and also your subcontractor's and vendor's. The AIA 101 stipulates a 7-day window following an approved *Application for Payment* for the client to issue a check. If your payment is delayed, draw the line quickly, lest this should become a bad habit.

Do not pay your contractors without release of *lien waivers*. Although your client may pay you without *lien waivers*, you must not allow your subcontractors to be paid so.

·   ·   ·   ·

Right. Be honest. Admit mistakes as soon as they happen. Be fair. Put yourself in your client's shoes.

Wrong. Never try to make money which you have not earned: money you can always make back. A bad reputation cannot be salvaged.

Endnotes

1. RS Means, *Means Estimating Handbook*. Subsequent unit prices in this section are quoted from the same.
2. Collier Engineer Co., *A Treatise on Architecture and Building Construction, Volume V* (Scranton: Colliery Engineer Co., 1899) pp. 23–25.
3. See App. A.
4. Nearly 70% of the respondents say they have experienced a decline in the quality of design drawings.
5. Alex Frangos, "Construction Sticker Shock," *Wall Street Journal*, 23 Mar. 2005.
6. FMI/CMAA 2.
7. 100 Acre Wood—a fictitious landscape or habitat from A.A. Milne's *Winnie-the-Pooh*.
8. See Chap. 5.
9. Keith Collier, *Construction Contracts* 2d ed. (New Jersey: Prentice Hall.)
10. See App. A.
11. Joseph A. McManus Jr., "Contractors Amending AIA A201-1997: General Conditions of the Contract for Construction," Glower Jones, ed., *Alternative Clauses to Standard Construction Contracts: AIA Documents A107, A101, A111, and A201* (New York: Aspen, 1998) from Chapter 19. As the title implies, the paper is geared toward the contractor's aspect; however, to a degree, the paper takes into consideration the owner and architects' perspective as well.
12. Indeed, much of the contentious language developed in the AIA document families was inspired by various interest groups, and their respective legal watchdogs that regularly lobbied and petitioned the AIA to accommodate their needs.
13. McManus 529.
14. McManus 499.
15. The first AIA general conditions document was drafted in 1911.
16. Keith Collier, *Construction Contracts*, 2d ed. (New Jersey, Prentice Hall.)
17. Joint Center for Housing Studies of Harvard University, *Measuring the Benefits of Home Remodeling* (2003) p. 8.
18. Ludwig Mies van der Rohe, 1886–1969.
19. Gary S. Berman, *National Conference and Trade Show, San Diego, CA, October 13–15, 2002; The Morphing of The Architect's Role and How it is Affecting the CM* (California: Construction Management Association of America, 2002), p. 4.
20. The term "budget," in this sense of the word, pertains to projects using low quality materials and poorly installed work, usually due to inadequate funds.
21. "Hold" dimensions are issued by the general constructor to the subcontractors in order for the him to receive necessary dimensions for fabrication based on where the constructor believes a given substrate or adjoining component will be installed, i.e., before the preceding work is in place. The dimensions are typically issued in this way so as to gain a leg up on a shortened schedule, especially when the subcontractor doesn't have the luxury of waiting until the predecessor work and/or substrates are in place.
22. Alex Frangos, "Construction Sticker Shock," *Wall Street Journal*, 23 March 2005.
23. Keith Collier, *Construction Contracts*, 2d ed. (New Jersey: Prentice Hall).
24. Hutchings and Kristofferson (2004).
25. *Ibid.*
26. *Ibid.*
27. *Ibid.*
28. *Ibid.*
29. As opposed to update.
30. Keith Collier, *Construction Contracts*, 2d ed. (New Jersey: Prentice Hall, 1979) p. 160.
31. Dennis Doran and Mark W. Bridges, *Guide to Change Order Management, FMI Corporation* (North Carolina: FMI, 2002).
32. Time that could have been spent in doing something else.
33. Colliery, 235.
34. Charles Leonard, *The Effects of Change Order on Productivity* (Apr. 14, 1987).
35. Department of the Army, Office of the Chief of Engineers, *Modification Impact Evaluation Guide* (Washington, D.C., U.S. Army, 1979), pp. 47–9.
36. Charles Leonard, *The Effects of Change Order on Productivity* (Apr. 14, 1987).
37. Collier 159.
38. See App. A.

3

Time

Come and go pervades everything of which we have knowledge, and though great things go more slowly, they are built up of small ones and must fare as that which makes them.

SAMUEL BUTLER

Project scheduling is a difficult and misunderstood component of the construction process, and for that reason it stands out as a problematic issue. The most efficient companies will have a schedule for each of their projects, and will update these schedules every month, whereas the laggards will have only a start and finish date to work with. Simpler projects may not require complex schedules; in fact, they may not require one at all, other than the contract stipulated start and end dates. Even if a schedule is generated, the likelihood of it being utilized in the field is dubious; that is, it may look good on paper . . . If a contractor is proactive and uses a schedule as an effective tool, he stands a better chance of controlling the network logic of his project, and is in a better position to make informed responses to problems. If a contractor's approach to a project is reactive, such that the project itself dictates the program, his schedule will not have been used for its intended purpose.

Because of the diverse nature of residential projects, it is difficult to visualize their progression in such a way as to compose an accurate prospective schedule. This being so, it is nearly impossible to educate most clients about the dynamics of scheduling, the network logic that drives a schedule, and how this information relates to their particular project. Even architects have difficulty comprehending schedules. These smaller projects are strongly driven by the flow (or lack) of information, over which the contractor has little control.[1] In very small projects and those below the radar, the lack of a proper schedule doesn't really matter. But the high-end residential sector is the fastest growing market in construction for the past 10 years (see Foreword). Detailed schedules for high-end projects should be mandatory because they demand the highest tier of service. This being so, the stakes are higher all around, especially for delayed projects, which translates to a risk factor for those companies that do not use proper schedules. The time line allowed for projects has not changed in order to accommodate the increase in complexity, nor the slower rates of production associated with today's more complex building. In fact, an owner's carrying costs often demand a compressed schedule.

The fact of the matter is that productive use of critical path method (CPM)[2] construction schedules is a rarity in the residential sector. Part of the reason is the mutable nature of residential projects—once a project is out of the contractor's control, the schedule, if there was one, is suddenly obsolete. Moreover, the obsolete schedule can't be updated; it is simply discarded and a new schedule is created. Frequently, residential projects seem to take on a life of their own; the pressing needs of the projects determine action, as opposed to the builder being in control. It therefore is not the intention of this chapter merely to advise the reader about the science and practicum of scheduling but to emphasize the unique character of residential construction schedules in particular, and some strategies to consider when planning them.

Companies that effectively use schedules will enjoy a higher rate of success than their competitors. Some of the reasons to use schedules are:

- They enable contractors to compete for projects that require scheduling, and schedule updates. Though few residential contracts require comprehensive schedule updates, companies that issue them should command more respect and should be held in high esteem by their clients.

- Contractors' bid presentations are upgraded in the presence of a good schedule.

- They give contractors the ability to track work, and to forecast future progress.

- They facilitate the means to adjust production levels midstream to accommodate slippages.

- They help project managers to organize complex projects into cohesive structures.

- They provide the means to reorganize and resequence projects without losing network logic.

- They can prevent a project from going out of control.

- They provide valuable analytical insight into the contract administration process.

- They will give contractors some level of comfort in knowing that they are controlling their project, and not vice versa.

- They are an important vehicle of accountability.

While this chapter will emphasize the importance of schedules, particularly tracked schedules, there are a few prerequisites to observe:

- The manipulation of task durations and relationships is central to the scheduling process. Only a seasoned construction professional can really put this information to use by either generating the schedule himself, or by informing the scheduler.

- Even with durations and relationships, if the network logic is not cohesive, the schedule will serve little purpose. Again, a seasoned construction professional should review the network logic as well.
- If the schedule is not "baselined"[3] it can't truly be tracked.

In 1983 those companies that utilized the CPM schedules were late on 27% of their projects, whereas contractors who did not use the CPM were late 44% of the time. Between 1983 and 1995, the percentage of companies that used CPM or a scheduling jumped from 50% to 70%, mostly attributable to the advent of scheduling software. During that time, the rate of projects completed behind schedule decreased from 33% to 22%. The percentage of contractors who did not use scheduling and were late increased from 45% to about 65%. Poor schedules, caused cost overruns 70% of the time, and contract disputes 50% of the time.[4] Although these surveys were not focused on the residential sector, it can be said that use of schedules is considerably lower there, and the consequences exacerbated by this fact.

The implementation of accurate scheduling operations into the high-end residential sector is problematic when compared to other sectors. For this reason, scheduling software is used to a lesser extent—only about 12% of residential contractors use scheduling software while about 73% rely on daily to-do lists.[5] Twelve percent is considerably less than the rest of the industry, which uses such software on between 50 and 70% of the contracts. Larger scale work is more production oriented, simpler, with repetitive tasks, tasks of longer duration and even entire projects nearly identical. Network logic is relatively static. The time line of most projects is a linear projection. Custom and high-end residential projects are seldom built the same way twice. You will find that you will create a template for every new project. The network logic for residential construction tends to be elliptical, as opposed to straight line, more prone to going out of sequence, and more subject to influence by a greater number of interrelated tasks. Simply put, the shortest distance between two points in residential construction is seldom a straight line. A linear network logic approach to residential construction is thought of as the least common denominator for a critical approach to scheduling: it leaves no room for going outside the box, which will inevitably be a necessity.

The nature of proper residential scheduling sets the bar considerably higher for schedulers, in fact, to such an extent that most residential contractors eschew the process altogether. The mistake that many contractors make is to assume that generating and updating schedules is done solely for the client's benefit. Thus, if the contract requirement did not exist, neither would a proper schedule. Generating at least a contract (see further) schedule, indicating start and substantial completion dates is a requirement of any construction project; however, the business of using schedules wasn't necessitated by contractual obligations but by an industry's need to be able to analyze and thus better control its production and resource management techniques. In other words schedules should be central to a general contractor's operations, not just a one-page attachment appended to a contract for its own sake. Otherwise, to some extent, companies are flying by the seat of their pants.

In order for the benefits of a scheduling program to be fully realized, there are two prerequisites:

- The schedules being used must be bona fide tracked schedules created or informed by experienced construction professionals.
- The facilitation of the scheduling program must be companywide and inclusive of all members of a given project. They include: owner, architect, subcontractors, and suppliers.

While there are some talented schedulers, the fruits of their labors are only realized insofar as the job team is willing to make use of them. A topflight scheduler cannot ensure any level of success: it must be a joint effort—joint meaning not just within the builder's organization, but the whole job team: architect and owner. If everyone is not signed up for the schedule, a link in the chain will sooner or later break, and the schedule logic will fall away.

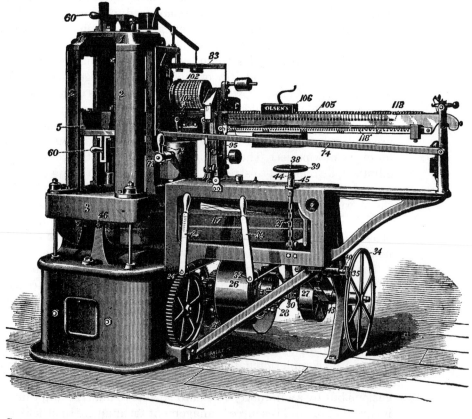

Screw gear.

Critical Path Method

A family of four, on vacation, arrives at an airport gate to check in for a departure. The plane is boarding; however, several anxious prospective passengers are corralled into a bull-pen area to the side. The family is told that their flight was overbooked, and that either someone would have to volunteer to sell the airline the seats back, or the family could take the next flight, 2 hours hence. For this inconvenience the airline would issue four ticket vouchers in the amount of $200 each. Other prospective passengers were offered, and they accepted, these terms. But this family has to make a connecting flight, which, if they agreed to give up their seats, would miss that flight. The next connecting flight is the following morning—16 hours later. These circumstances the family considers untenable. They insist that their seats be returned to them, a request the airline must oblige. While some passengers took the offer without compromising their travel plans, the offer was deemed unacceptable to this family because the delay would upset the *critical path* of their journey, or caused them to miss their deadline. Other obliging passengers critical path remained intact as their travel schedules had *float* time, or a period of extra time between the end of one task and the beginning of the next.

At the heart of a construction schedule is its critical path. CPM is a network logic that will determine what combination of activities will establish the minimal amount of time needed to complete a project. A more comprehensive definition of critical path would be:

> If the time durations of the activities forming a continuous path were to be added for each of the many possible routes through the network, a number of different totals would be obtained. The largest of these totals is the critical or minimum time for overall project completion.
>
> The critical path will be composed of a number of critical activities, which can be defined as activities with zero float, has no spare time, and is; therefore, one of the operations that controls project completion time. For this reason, activities with zero float are called *"critical activities."*[6]

The danger with CPM schedules is that if they are not continually updated, they quickly become obsolete. What happens is that because projects seldom go as planned, the sequence of production will vary from the schedule such that the critical path is subject to change. This is especially true with aggressive schedules, where little float is afforded between tasks. The critical path then becomes a moving target. Such projects are especially difficult to control. A task which once had float may become a critical activity due to delays. If a scheduler doesn't understand the advantages of creating a CPM schedule, chances are that he doesn't understand the CPM. Every schedule has a critical path; however, if it is not a calculated schedule, the critical path will not likely be discernible. Critical paths can be calculated by hand but are most efficiently calculated by means of scheduling software, which will do in a fraction of a second what it might take hours to do by hand.

The CPM is different from other scheduling methods in that it offers the means to adapt, modify, accelerate, or refine activities quickly in such a way that other methods can't. To be more specific, it empowers the project manager with the following information:

1. Concise details regarding the planned sequence of construction operations.
2. A means to predict with reasonable accuracy the time required for overall project completion and the times to reach intermediate construction goals (commonly called *milestones*).
3. Proposed calendar dates at which it is planned that the several activities of the project will be started and finished.
4. Identification of those critical activities whose expedient execution is crucial to timely project completion.
5. A guide for project shortening when the completion date must be advanced.
6. A basis for scheduling subcontractors and material deliveries to the job site.
7. A basis for balanced scheduling of manpower and construction equipment on the project.
8. The rapid evaluation of the time requirements of alternative construction methods.
9. A convenient vehicle for progress reporting, recording, and analysis.
10. A basis for evaluating the time effects of construction changes and delays.[7]

The two most common forms of schedules are the *Gantt* chart, and the *Program Evaluation and Review Technique* (PERT). Both use the critical path method but each calculates it differently. PERT is a diagrammatic sequential flowchart that is widely used for research and development (R&D) projects, where there are many variables and unknowns. R&D projects by their nature have indeterminate ranges for which a PERT chart will calculate an average duration. Gantt charts are essentially bar charts that graphically illustrate the minimum anticipated timeline or progression of a project in a network format. The Gantt chart is more commonly used for projects where there are fewer variables; for example, your average construction project. In fact, it is the rare exception that PERT is used on residential construction projects. Some programs can generate a schedule in both views, Gantt or PERT; however, large schedules with many tasks will become unmanageable in PERT view. The PERT interface illustrates a logic that is easier for laypeople to comprehend, and therefore, can be useful as a presentation tool. Indeed, there is something about the nature of Gantt charts that makes it difficult for people to visualize what is being represented.

A CPM schedule has three basic phases: planning and logistical stage, plotting of the schedule, and monitoring of the schedule. This concept of scheduling a construction project seemingly has endless connotations depending on whom you talk to, and there are countless interpretations of how a schedule should be structured. There are a few basic models or interpretations of the schedule that are most common, each with their own set of criteria and dynamics.

Schedule Formats

The three most common schedule forms used today in construction are:

Contract schedule

Working and reconstructed schedule

Tracked schedule

Contract Schedule

All AIA construction contracts have stipulated start and substantial completion dates. The general requirements of many contracts will also state that a
proper schedule be generated and maintained or kept up-to-date. If not there,
it is referred to in the A201: 3.10. Some will even require that an independent consultant be retained for this purpose, although that is rare on smaller
projects. A general contractor will typically issue a generic schedule for the
project in the bidding stage, and later, if he wins the contract, he may or may
not generate a more specific schedule. Not uncommonly, a contractor will use
the generic schedule simply as a token gesture to meet bidding requirements.
Once the contract is awarded, this schedule is not more fully developed, and
is, in fact, either the working schedule or it is discarded altogether: that means
a schedule meant only for presentation purposes is out of context should it be
used as a schedule proper. Such schedules are routinely generated by people
who either have too little information, or assistant estimators, or have the
information but are unable to organize it into a schedule.

Looking back at the three basic stages of the CPM we can see that the creation of such a schedule ends somewhere after the plotting phase begins; short
of a fully developed schedule, and without a tracking and monitoring phase
other than guessing at the end date.

There are several drawbacks to using a poorly executed schedule:

- You will not be able to incorporate data from earlier versions into a cause and
  effect analysis.

- This simplified schedule will not provide the means to coherently incorporate
  a fine-tuned start and end dates.

- It will not be possible to alter the schedule without redoing it from scratch.

- You cannot take advantage of the analytical and network logic tools for predicting and planning as you can with tracked schedules.

- You will be unable to make comprehensive assessments of the rate of
  progress.

- You will not be able to generate coherent reports from the schedule.

- Your schedule will look unprofessional.

- It will not stand up to scrutiny, especially for litigation.

- You will waste time, or run out of time, trying to make it work.
- Consistent use of inept schedules will handicap you in your efforts to win higher level projects.

Not all contract schedules need be devoid of accurate or comprehensive information. As said, in the bidding phase, the scheduler may not have all the information he needs in order to generate a comprehensive schedule. However, if he has the overall start and end dates, he can determine the critical path and the main divisions of the schedule such that later he need only fill in the blanks.

I recall a 6-month gut project with a schedule that became obsolete within the first week of production. It was an aggressive schedule with little float between tasks. The superintendent duly notified the scheduler of each breached target date. Because the schedule was not CPM based, there was little that could be done to reconfigure the schedule in such a way as to make up for the lost time. However, even if it was a CPM schedule, this project had so little time between tasks that nearly every task became a potential critical task: that is, there was nowhere to make up for the lost time.

Had the scheduler used the CPM, he would have had better control of durations and float times. What he didn't know from experience, he would see in the tight durations and short float times—he would have known that the schedule was overly aggressive, and would have a way to demonstrate this graphically. With such knowledge, perhaps the contractor could have then formed a proactive contingency plan other than a reactive one. Even without a contingency plan, at least with his CPM schedule he could project possible scenarios.

Working and Reconstructed Schedule

Once a contractor is awarded a project, he should begin the task of creating a working schedule. If his contract schedule is an accurate outline, he can use it as his template. In fact, many working schedules are merely contract schedules cum working schedules. Otherwise, if the contract schedule was very basic, he could simply start his working schedule from scratch. This type of working schedule is the most common one used. To paraphrase: using only the contract start and finish dates as parameters, a general contractor will issue a baseline schedule. It typically stops short of a proper tracked schedule, which measures actual dates as compared to target dates, and illustrates them side by side for ready comparison. This basic schedule may get your foot in the door, but it will serve little purpose other than as a general outline; once the actual dates diverge from the target dates, the schedule becomes irrelevant and a new one must be generated.

Therefore, in order to illustrate an updated schedule, a scheduler will typically reenter actual start and finish dates, without showing the baseline, or target schedule. One would have to juxtapose or overlay the original schedule with the updated one in order to compare them. If they are different, the new schedule won't say why, as it is not a true baseline CPM-tracked schedule. Again, the said working schedule, wherein each update is in fact a reconstructed schedule, will suffer some of the same shortcomings as the bare-bones contract schedule.

- You will not be able to incorporate data from earlier versions into a cause- and-effect analysis.
- It will not be possible to alter the schedule without redoing it.
- You cannot take advantage of the analytical and network logic tools for predicting and planning as you can with tracked schedules.
- You will be unable to make comprehensive assessments of the rate of progress.
- You will not be able to generate coherent reports.
- It will not stand up to scrutiny, especially for litigation.

Finally, a working schedule that is reconstructed each time it is updated is no replacement for a tracked schedule.

The industry is used to working with reconstructed schedules, because so few general contractors use tracked schedules. In fact, many don't make the distinction between the two. If you doubt the inferiority of a reconstructed schedule versus a tracked schedule, try bringing the former into courtroom as evidence. In fact, government projects require not only CPM schedules, but also cost-loaded schedules. Consider the following finding:

> Broad generalities and inferences to the effect that the defendant must have caused some delays and damage because the contract took 318 days longer to complete than anticipated are not sufficient . . . Although we do not doubt that plaintiffs and their subcontractors encountered delays and difficulties in proceeding with the plans provided by the defendant, all that plaintiffs have attempted to prove with respect to any of the major claims is the total amount of costs and the total delay experienced on the project. No satisfactory evidence has been presented to differentiate between reasonable and unreasonable government delays, or between delays attributable to defendant and delays unavoidably caused by extraneous circumstances. It is incumbent upon plaintiffs to show the nature and extent of the various delays for which damages are claimed and to connect them to some act of commission or omission on defendant's part . . .[8]

This text discusses some methods of creating accountability for delays, quantification of such delays, and for some preventive measures to help mitigate or lessen the impact of delays in general. However, because these tools are so seldom implemented, or used correctly by general contractors, projects continue to founder on an epidemic scale. Not taking responsibility for a delay doesn't mean the same thing as not being held accountable. Far be from it, owners will continue to seek damages for any delays, and contractors will continue to pay, whether they deserve it or not, often merely because they don't know how to generate and manage schedules. And frequently, the contractor does not deserve the blame—it may be the owner himself, the architect, or both. Either way, only general contractors who have the wherewithal to defend themselves will survive protracted schedule disputes without making some substantial concession.

A common scenario for a delayed job typically has the general contractor toiling away grudgingly under a late schedule, absorbing his losses alone. The client may feel he is entitled to damages from the general contractor due to the delay; however, seldom are they enough to warrant a court claim; the owner will typically want a concession from the general contractor, which he will negotiate with him directly, or withhold from a subsequent payment. The irony is that the general contractor is losing money because of the delay and thus believes he should be compensated. What tends to happen is that it is a tumultuous combination of circumstances from different parties that contribute directly or indirectly to a project's delay. The quantification of blame under these circumstances can be an elusive and fruitless undertaking, especially in hindsight. It therefore, behooves the general contractor to be diligent in documenting delays, and quantifying their effect on the schedule before delays happen, or at least as they are happening—after the fact is often too late. There is nothing that will motivate someone more than informing them that they are in danger of causing a delay, especially if they know they would be held blameworthy.

Tracked Schedule

The dynamics and concept of a tracked schedule must be understood before it can be generated. The mistake most people make is assuming that a tracked schedule only means reissuing a schedule periodically to show projected timelines (see Reconstructed Schedule). In reality, a tracked schedule will illustrate the target early start and finish dates, or baseline, alongside the actual and prospective dates—the projected sequence for the remainder of the project. This information can be critical to any deadline on the project, whether it be related to design or production. The nature of residential construction projects is for them to invariably run "off-schedule" in two ways:

1. The planning and sequence of tasks does not translate to actual conditions, such that it becomes difficult to schedule work ahead of time, and to estimate production rates; in other words, the schedule is not relevant. Production may not necessarily be late but it is out of sequence compared to the schedule.

2. The project is late.

If the schedule is late, it will be difficult to determine the cause and effect relationships of why it is late with any degree of exactitude, and more difficult to make adjustments so as to get the project back on track, if a tracked schedule has not been used. A general contractor will invariably intuit what is late on a project, and maybe even why, but he will be hard put to demonstrate the relationship of a given delay to the whole. A construction manager or scheduler must be able to (a) generate a baseline CPM schedule, and (b) track and update the schedule. This is one of the levels of service that (should) put construction managers a step above their general contractor counterparts. In fact, architects have learned from experience to expect a low level of scheduling service from general contractors, which in turn has become a self-fulfilling prophecy—general contractors have no motivation to generate tracked schedules. Even if they could, they prefer to keep such information proprietary; indeed, only 17.5%[9] of contractors in a study supported the specification of updated schedule requirements, and these were professional schedulers. The good news is that there is plenty of room for general contractors who aspire to deliver a superior product than their competition, part of which entails generating professional schedules.

In the absence of using a bona fide tracked schedule, a schedule that is so outdated and irrelevant must be recreated from scratch to illustrate actual dates. There is an enormous difference in effort required, to recreate a schedule, than there is for software to recalculate a schedule. And the quality of information provided in the latter should always be superior and more comprehensive. Typically, when a project becomes delayed, an architect will insist on an updated schedule as opposed to the general contractor offering it, for which the task may be a challenge, especially if there is no baseline or target dates to compare the actual dates to, save for the contract dates. What he will get is a one-page memo with some target and actual dates on it. This condition tends to occur when (a) the original schedule was neither fully developed, nor tracked, and (b) there is no one, or no program to create a tracked schedule. However, project-scheduling software offers the grail of creating tracked schedules, and we shall see in Scheduling Software, how one program does it. Otherwise, if the project is considered to be on time, the contractor, in all likelihood, will feel no inducement to generate an updated schedule.

Scheduling Software

Scheduling software, when used properly, can be an enormous resource for the industry. In the long view, technology is still relatively new, although the CPM method central to its network logic precedes it by about thirty years.[10] The great advantage to digitally generated schedules is the runtime, or the time it takes to calculate a given schedule, and the ease of printing or plotting it. Once a schedule is generated, it can be reconfigured, reformatted, and recalculated with all logic intact with a few keystrokes, and in a few seconds (a fraction of the time it would take to do manually). Manual schedules serve only as outlines for their more sophisticated digital betters. The exception would be the PERT format, which is nearly equally serviceable manually or digitally. The liquidity and flexibility of scheduling programs is another appeal. For instance, projections of all sorts can be done on the spot with a graphic model generated in a fraction of a second for each model. These projections are critical to the tweaking process as they can graphically represent the effects of one change on the entire network. Finally, the more sophisticated programs generate large format, and handsome graphic representations that would be virtually impossible to create by hand.

There are fair amounts of commercial computer programs available for schedulers and project managers, whether they are construction managers, or are in any other production-related industry. There are also a number of programs that cater specifically to the construction trade. Some of these programs are merely front ends of their betters, while others are too bloated and no good to themselves. Because these programs are so diverse, a project manager moving between companies might have to learn new software for each company. A few general observations can be made file regarding the majority of these programs:

There is no universal platform or file format to which they all conform; each has its own proprietary format; that is, you would need the program in order to open a file created in that environment. The convenient way around this annoying problem is to save the file as a portable document format (pdf), for which you would need a file converter or distiller.[11] Many were designed for project management in general, not specifically construction project managers. Although they all conform to the CPM method, they go their separate ways from there. In some cases, files can be converted from one program to another, but the results can be dubious. I suppose the intent was not to be expeditious to the host program but to make the conversion to a new program more seamless. These programs vary in degree of sophistication; however, the more complicated a program is, the more difficult it is to learn, and the more glitches and restrictions it will have. Some publishers realize this, and offer seminars and training to end users, which is a growing industry in itself. Why would you not refer to the program manual? Actually, you would—the first time you had a question. Subsequent to that, you'll call technical support department, figure it out for yourself, or take a seminar on the subject. This is because most software manuals are written so poorly or are at a loss to illustrate subtleties. After-market program manuals are evidence of the failure of proprietary software manuals to effectively explain their product.

If you only generate contract and reconstructed schedules, scheduling programs are relatively easy to use; however, tracking modules tend to be non-user-friendly. While a seasoned personal computer user can adapt to most software with minimal input from the manual, scheduling programs will even pose a challenge to him. I believe the reason for this is that scheduling software is particularly counterintuitive. For instance, because of the way the program processes data, some actions cannot be undone, rather you have to ditch the working file and start over where you last saved. When trying to troubleshoot a given command, there are so many possible causes that neither the help module, nor the manual can assist. Either of these resources can be subject to great skepticism, as like the software, they are not user-friendly either. This rigidity will necessitate calls to technical support, which can cost time and money. More importantly, the rigidity of the structure of the program leaves surprisingly little room for customization. There is no feeling as helpless as knowing you can't control the program you are using. This fact is enough to convince most general contractors that an investment in these sorts of programs is not worth the money.

One of the difficulties with computerized Gantt (see further) charts is that they tend to contain errors. These errors are nearly always user generated as the Gantt network logic is virtually infallible. Because of the complexity of the system, it is not uncommon that three or four schedules will have to be generated in order to arrive at a single correct one. The more complex a schedule, the more room there is for errors. Even the best schedulers make these mistakes, but they know how to check their work several times—this constant revising comes with the territory, and also applies to schedule updates. Given the exactitude required of scheduling requirements and the rate of errors they are prone to only experienced schedulers should produce them or review another's work.

The investment of time and money spent by companies on acquiring software, training personnel to use it, and maintaining the system for any period of longevity, is relatively small. I have at one time or another had to learn three or four different scheduling programs on my own while working at different companies. Often, only one or two individuals at a company are proficient in using a program, and in fact are the only people using it. Because implementation costs are relatively small, this condition can be considered an underutilization of a resource, even at a small company. However, the biggest obstacle seems to be having someone on staff that can make ample use of it. Employees can waste weeks trying to figure out how a program works, only to generate an inept schedule. General contractors are familiar with this quandary, and tend to have a pessimistic view regarding the production of schedules at their company. However, once it is mastered, the art of scheduling a project takes very little time; even from scratch (without a template). Ironically, the generation of the highly esteemed tracked schedule takes a negligible amount of time, a benefit few contractors are patient enough to realize.

As part of the scheduling program, often additional modules are included such as cost loading and resource tracking. For the purpose of this book, we will not discuss these topics as they relate to software; however, they will be discussed elsewhere. Some publishers have also tried to bundle their scheduling programs with other programs such as project management programs. In theory, these bundles would be a panacea for the digital construction world; however, in practice they tend to be unwieldy, underdeveloped, unprofessional looking, and problematic.

Scheduling software is a small market, not terribly expensive to buy, and I believe that this being the case, development costs are relatively small, compared to what other types of software cost to develop—especially bundled software. After all, the market for scheduling software is tiny when compared with desktop publishing and database programs. Indeed, a company may buy scheduling software for one project manager to create one schedule for one project, only to discard or never use the product again; that is, the product is relatively disposable without experiencing too much loss of investment: it can pay for itself after one or two uses.

However underutilized in the industry, at the end of the day, the degree of efficiency with which a company operates can be partly predicated on the sophistication of its scheduling programs, and how well they are used. There are plenty of firms that get by to varying degrees, without scheduling software; however, think how much more efficient they would be if they used a scheduling program to their advantage. I emphasize the notion that a company should make ample use of a program in order for it to be an efficient resource; the mere fact that a company has the software, and some of the company's employees use it does not necessarily make the company more efficient.

It must also be said that even though the majority of schedulers learn by using the respective scheduling program-user manuals, these schedulers will only access a basic knowledge of scheduling using this method exclusively. These manuals are notoriously poorly written, and don't seem to offer any intuitive insight into the construction process. There are a number of books on the subject, *Construction Project Management*, Clough/Sears, now in its fourth edition is one of the most comprehensive books on the subject of scheduling theory; however, this book doesn't embrace bar charts, mostly PERT; in fact, the term *Gantt chart* doesn't appear in the index. I have to assume the author's reference to the shortcomings of bar charts such as one produced by a spreadsheet does not take into consideration a solid Gantt chart. But the discussion of network logic illustrated is one of the most exhaustive I've seen. Indeed, one should master the science of network logic before becoming a scheduler. Between a good technical book on scheduling, hands-on experience, and a decent scheduling program and manual, a scheduler can develop excellent skills. Finally, a scheduler must have the intuitive insight into the construction process that is absent from software manuals.

Scheduling: Means and Methods

One of the biggest obstacles in creating a computer tracked schedule is finding the resources to implement and maintain it; while one may have computer skills, he may be lacking in building and planning skills, or vice versa. This is a common dilemma and can be somewhat easily remedied if there is a person who is in charge of publishing the schedules. This person can take the target dates from the production team to generate baseline schedules, and then, as he receives updated records from the field, incorporate the new data into an updated schedule. Thus, the creation of the schedule becomes a data entry exercise, which with a little guidance requires little knowledge of construction by the scheduler.

To most contractors, this arrangement more or less would constitute a program or job description that must be created and implemented, an investment only a handful of companies, mostly with large management infrastructures, are willing to make. However, this is a misconception on their part. The problem with implementing a scheduling program isn't a financial one; it is a logistical one as there simply isn't a supply of decent schedulers, especially those who can analyze complex residential projects, such that even if one were desired, the position would be virtually impossible to fill. Not surprisingly, there isn't a great demand for schedulers either, as most contractors don't appreciate the value of a good scheduler. In truth, short of a designated scheduler, project managers generate and maintain their own schedules.

However, the implementation of a scheduling program should not be a great stretch for any decent company, and the return of investment, when it is properly executed, is well worth it. All that's needed are: (a) a computer, (b) the software, (c) the personnel to use the software, and (d) a means of reproduction, such as a large format printer/plotter or a reprographer service. It should be said that such a service must be part of any worthwhile construction management contract. Alternatively, without a scheduling program, it is extremely difficult to calculate and determine the critical path of a project. The benefit of any scheduling program is that the program will do this for you, usually in a fraction of a second. The quality of output of some of this software alone can be a selling point, as output can be managed and customized to deliver magnificent presentations.

Creating a Schedule

There are three phases comprising a proper schedule:

Planning

Plotting

Tracking

Planning

The creation of a schedule begins with the planning stage, the first component being the project start and substantial completion dates. There are two ways to work with overall dates—by using the parameters defined by the bid documents, or as set forth in the contract as hard dates (constrained), or by calculating the schedule at the expected progression rate, and then comparing it to the contract end date (natural). In either case, if there should be a variance (usually too little time), the scheduler can refine the schedule, as we shall see.

Some software features *wizards* or program modules that are available to help organize the basic outline using information that it prompts you for. As you input the information, the software enters the information into a background relational database from which it will generate the components of your schedule. While wizards aren't a bad thing, one should master the mechanics of the logic it uses before becoming overreliant on the wizard. Perhaps, wizards were invented out of the necessity for software developers to render their programs usable to the masses, since using the manual will leave one still wanting information. Like any other software, scheduling software only does what you tell it to. While they have their own organizational logic, there is nothing in them that can be considered intuitive, only the structure needed to generate the critical path of the schedule.

The structure of scheduling software is based on the CPM, as defined previously, which the software will calculate based on the information you input. In the early planning stage, the PERT method can be useful in developing an outline to base a Gantt chart on. There is a fair amount of training needed to generate and use the PERT method; therefore, we will create simple flowcharts, which are the foundation of the PERT method. It is the end user's responsibility to assemble the information logistically, and to format the output or end product so that it is user friendly. A hierarchy of phases, tasks, and subtasks is the most common way to organize a schedule. Later, the information can be temporarily reorganized to represent sorting or filtered information, such as tasks listed in order of chronology, duration, or tasks listed by an activity identification number.

Part of a schedule's planning stage requires verifying start and end dates with resources, vendors, and subcontractors—you wouldn't want to fix a start date of a critical activity only to find out that the resource was unable to meet the requirement. But before checking resources for their availability, you want to roll out your own target dates. If the dates don't coincide with your resources, you'll want to find a way to make it work as opposed to restructuring your schedule around your resource's constraints. For design and development stages, you may be able to, at best, submit the deliverable milestones to the architect for his acceptance. These milestones aren't necessarily indicating how quickly you think he can do his work, they merely advise him of when design information is required in order to facilitate the production schedule. For construction management projects, these due dates are critical, as the work will start before the final drawings are issued. The duplex project model we have discussed had some interesting schedule issues that clarify this point.

The contractor had agreed to an aggressive schedule in order to better position himself toward winning the job. This schedule necessitated expedited design deliverable dates, and shortened submittal and review periods from the architect; however, the architect was never consulted regarding the new dates, nor was he under any obligation to perform thusly. Technically, the project could not finish on time based on this misunderstanding alone. Of course, the irony was that the contractor either never progressed in such a way that the architect's turnaround time ever became an issue, or that the contractor could ill afford even the modest turnaround time that he "allowed" the architect. Therefore, great care should be taken that if you issue deliverable deadlines to a design team, that you will utilize the information substantially when you receive it. Why else press for information that you don't yet need?

We will take a hypothetical construction management project as our starting point for a sample schedule. The project will be for a renovation of a 5000 ft^2 apartment in a prewar apartment building, lasting 16 months in length: 5 months preconstruction and design and development, 10 month's construction, and 1-month closeout. Although it will be a simple project, it should convey most of the information necessary to facilitate a typical 16-month residential schedule, uncompressed through three phases.

Basic Planning Phases Scheduling

Preconstruction

Construction

Closeout

These are the three phases of our construction management model project. All divisions and tasks or activities will fall into one of these three phases. Using this simple foundation will make it easier to build the schedule, and later, to isolate or filter each phase, after the schedule has been created.

Divisions

The divisions of the project will be extrapolated from each phase, by trade, into tasks and subtasks. To begin with, we will start with the preconstruction phase:

Preconstruction

Design and development

Budget

Early submittals and procurement

The initial outline for the three divisions is shown in Table 3.1.

Next, we will define the major tasks of these three divisions. Note: As this is a construction management project, some of the preconstruction tasks will cross over into the production phase. This will be demonstrated further on. The design and development phase main tasks will be defined as follows:

Design and development

Preconstruction

- Survey site
- Probes
- Schematics
- Floor plan: working drawing
- Partition types

TABLE 3.1   Preconstruction Overview

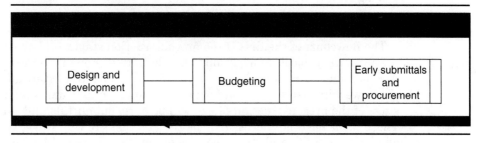

Production

- Section through elevations
- Mechanical electrical and plumbing (MEP) plans
- Reflected ceiling plan

As we shall discuss, the floor plan working drawing and partition types is typically enough to jump-start the production phase.

Budget

- Base building
- General construction
- MEP
- Finishes

As the development of the design drawings takes shape, an estimator can fine-tune his conceptual budget numbers (if he is using them). These numbers, continually updated, will later be used by the project team to monitor past performance and make adjustments for future models. The milestones of a budget may appear as follows:

- Conceptual stage
- Preliminary stage
- Working stage

A construction manager should reissue a budget for each of these stages of development. The owner and architect may show several alternatives to all sorts of designs. This is part of the construction manager's job;[12] however, draw the line at resubmitting a budget every time a minor change is made. The working budget can be locked in at any point as the base contract value, guaranteed maximum price (GMP), or it can remain a working budget. Typically, an owner would like to be locked into a budget and schedule that aren't subject to vacillate too wildly. That all depends on the extent of biddable design documentation and the owner's needs.

Early Submittals and Procurement

- Let base contracts
- Long-lead submittals
- Long-lead orders

The flowchart of the first three preconstruction stages is shown in Table 3.2. As yet, the project information is not definitive enough to inform a schedule. As it becomes more developed, and the information too substantial for the flowchart, we will then fold this information into and create our schedule. The last stage of the preconstruction phase will be early submittals and procurements. These tasks need not necessarily be the last tasks of this stage; typically, they will be done in fits and starts, contingent on the release of design information,

TABLE 3.2   Preconstruction: Expanded View

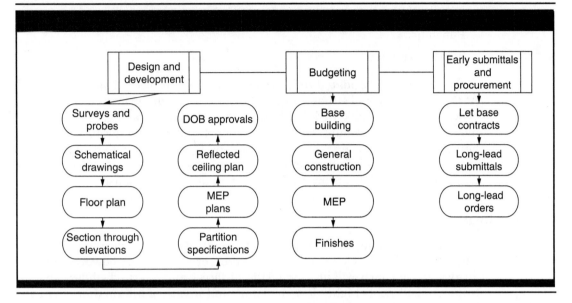

and approval of budgets. It is at this stage that the scheduler must lock-in his suppliers and subcontractors to the target dates. Not uncommonly, the vendor will require at least a *letter of intent* before he is locked-in, if not a deposit; therefore, the scheduler may have to work with hypothetical dates.

The next step will be to develop the construction phase of the schedule. While there is no set model for creating the outline for a production model, I have found that the simpler the structure of the data, the easier it will be to work with. I will use a model that was created for a project similar to our sample.

Construction.   The three basic components to be used for our construction schedule are as follows:

- General construction
- MEPs
- Finishes

As a starting point, three major divisions may be used for the construction phase outline. At a glance, many people would say that we are oversimplifying; however, we shall see that this structure of three divisions will lend itself nicely to our format, and will make the user interface easy to manipulate. From these three divisions, a scheduler can compose and customize his projects any way he likes, while maintaining a central structure to the format—the basic three components will form the foundation of the entire construction- scheduling network.

We can now incorporate the last phase, closeout, into our outline. The closeout phase divisions will be defined as follows.

Closeout

Substantial completion

Punch list

Final completion

The flowchart is updated to incorporate all three project phases (Table 3.3). At this point, we could either continue the flowchart, adding tasks and subtasks, or we could begin our schedule by adding tasks as we go along. As this project has many tasks and subtasks, our flowchart will rapidly become unwieldy; hence, we will now begin our schedule proper. By the same token, had we been entering the above information into the software schedule, the base schedule will already have been formatted or outlined in a general sense.

The Gantt Chart

Gantt charts, invented by Henry Laurence Gantt, 1861–1919, are essentially bar charts that were developed to track the progress of projects; however, a familiarity with bar charts will just scrape the surface. Gantt chart schedules can illustrate a considerably higher level of detail, and wealth of information, than any bar chart schedule, specifically, a means to juxtapose timelines for past, present, and future job performance. They can come in many shapes and forms, and are often convertible (by software) to PERT charts, if that is desired, with network logic intact. Although they are not exclusively used for construction, they lend themselves particularly well to it. The Hoover Dam (1931) was scheduled using a Gantt chart, as were the early arteries of the interstate highway system (1956). Depending on what software is used, the user interface will vary, as will the output; however, network logic should never change, regardless of the platform. Most software will have a resident protocol for setting up each project with an overview, before you enter tasks. These generally consist of the following:

- Title of the project
- Project overview: start (and end date, if known)[13]
- Definition of work-week (5-day, 7-day, 40 h, 60 h, and the like)
- Format, or template, if any
- Others, as required (resources and budget)

From this point, the software wizard may query you for the basic data required to construct a basic schedule; however, the wizard typically finishes its work just after the tasks are entered in the project overview. Short of that, most software offers resident templates. Such templates you will invariably find not to suit your needs, and thus, you will want to generate and tweak some of your own. You can also reuse a custom template that you used on another project, or you can start from scratch. In the outline stage, you will always be able to begin again; therefore, find a structure that you are comfortable with and continue from there.

TABLE 3.3 Full Phase Flowchart

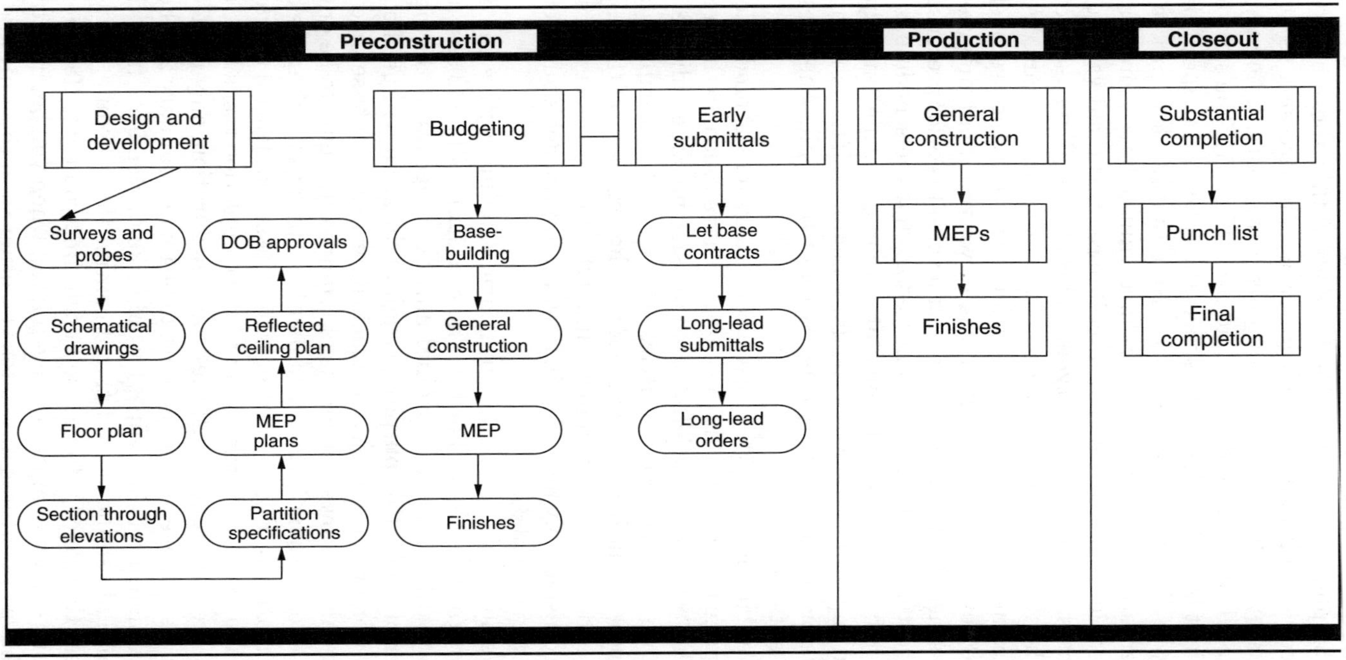

For our project, we will peek in just after we have entered the first phase, divisions, and main tasks. The layout of the chart has been customized so to organize by phases, and then the divisions within those phases. At this time, the scheduler will want to think in terms of progression as he will later organize tasks by early date.[14] The columns, rows, bars, timeline, fonts, and so forth have all been selected by the end user (Fig. 3.1). The software generates a convenient legend in the footer space, the color and shape of the elements make it easy to discern (in a color plot).[15] Note that levels of precedence are defined by indentation and font size. You don't want to have more than five levels, as the schedule will become more difficult to read. The software automatically assigns a font size; however, size, type, and color can all be user defined.

The three phases are now shown in the Gantt chart. We will next take our divisions and assign main tasks for each. Only the preconstruction tasks have been developed to this next level, so we will input them as shown in Fig. 3.2. The schedule now includes the next level of tasks for preconstruction. Notice that the footer section has been omitted so that the schedule is still only one page. It can later be replaced. The ability to make formatting adjustments on the fly is an important proficiency tool for schedulers, if they are going to be able to generate presentation-ready copy. Without this skill, schedules are frequently not presentable.

We shall now input the next level of tasks for the production phase (Table 3.3). To make the schedule fit the page, we have rolled up the preconstruction phase as the "+" signs to the left of each division heading indicate. The closeout phase requires no further task entries. The schedule is complete to this level. For the purpose of this book, we will not add the next level of tasks. Your scheduler now has enough information to do that. Of course, a full rigged schedule would contain considerably more detail; however, this model is sufficient for use in demonstration (Fig. 3.3).

We now have an outline for a basic schedule, with some of the tasks entered in rough chronological order. The next step will be to assign each task a duration. A column named original duration appears at the right of each activity description for this purpose. Original duration will be checked against actual duration once the project is tracked, or has been baselined (see further). Note that only the lowest level tasks require durations to be entered as they are a subset of the next level, the higher level tasks, or roll-up tasks, will be computed automatically. Figure 3.4 illustrates the schedule with the duration of each task entered. Note: Substantial and final completion tasks have duration of zero, as they are milestone tasks; they have no duration, only predecessors and successors. As yet, every task appears to begin on "January 25," because we have not yet assigned relationships. I would like to step back from the schedule at this point and remind myself that I control the schedule, not vice versa. You will repeat this concept to yourself each time you try to decipher the gobbledygook of your early attempts, and even later, when you begin to track your schedule. We have not entered any dates yet, other than the start and finish targets, and we will enter no further dates—the software calculates the dates for you.

Act ID	Activity Description	Orig Dur	Rem Dur	
0001	**Preconstruction**	1 *	1 *	◇▽ Preconstruction
0002	**Design and development**	1	1	Design and development
0003	**Budgeting**	1	1	Budgeting
0004	**Early submittals**	1	1	Early submittals
0005	**Production**	1 *	1 *	◇▽ Production
0006	**General construction**	1	1	General construction
0007	**MEPs**	1	1	MEPs
0008	**Finishes**	1	1	Finishes
0009	**Closeout**	1 *	1 *	◇▽ Closeout
0010	**Substantial completion**	1	1	Substantial completion
0011	**Punch list**	1	1	Punch list
0012	**Final completion**	1	1	Final completion

Timeline: 2005 — JAN (17, 24, 31), FEB (07, 14, 21, 28), MAR (07, 14, 21, 28), APR (04, 11, 18, 25)

Modern Builders Inc.
Sample Residential Project

Start date	01/25/05 2:00 PM
Finish date	01/26/05 1:59 PM
Data date	01/25/05 2:00 PM
Run date	01/25/05 2:00 PM
Page number	1A

© Primavera Systems, Inc.

Legend:
- ◁ Early start point
- ▷ Early finish point
- Early bar
- ▶ Total float point
- Total float bar
- Progress bar
- Critical bar
- Summary bar
- ◀ Progress point
- ◁▷ Critical point
- ◇◇ Summary point
- Start milestone point
- ◇ Finish milestone point

Figure 3.1 Basic divisions.

171

Act ID	Activity Description	2005																
		JAN		FEB				MAR				APR				MAY	
		17	24	31	07	14	21	28	07	14	21	28	04	11	18	25	02
0001	**Preconstruction**		Preconstruction														
0002	**Design and development**		Design and development														
0013	Surveys and probes		Surveys and probes														
0023	Schematical drawings		Schematical drawings														
0033	Floor plan		Floor plan														
0043	Section through elevations		Section thru elevations														
0053	Partition types		Partition types														
0063	MEP plans		MEP plans														
0073	RCP		RCP														
0083	DOB approval		DOB approval														
0003	**Budgeting**		Budgeting														
0014	Base building		Base building														
0024	General construction		General construction														
0034	MEP		MEP														
0044	Finishes		Finishes														
0004	**Early submittals**		Early submittals														
0015	Let base contracts		Let base contracts														
0025	Long-lead submittals		Long-lead submittals														
0035	Long-lead procurements		Long-lead procurements														
0005	**Production**		Production														
0006	**General construction**		General construction														
0007	**MEPs**		MEPs														
0008	**Finishes**		Finishes														
0009	**Closeout**		Closeout														
0010	**Substantial completion**		Substantial completion														
0011	**Punch list**		Punch list														
0012	**Final completion**		Final completion														

Figure 3.2 Preconstruction tasks expanded.

Act ID	Activity Description	Orig Dur	Timeline
0001	**Preconstruction**	1 *	Preconstruction
+0002	**Design and development**	1 *	Design and development
+0003	**Budgeting**	1 *	Budgeting
+0004	**Early submittals**	1 *	Early submittals
0005	**Production**	1 *	Production
0006	**General construction**	1 *	General construction
0017	Demolition	1	Demolition
0027	Layout	1	Layout
0037	Partition framing	1	Partition framing
0047	Door framing	1	Door framing
0057	Ceiling framing	1	Ceiling framing
0007	**MEPs**	1 *	MEPs
0018	Mechanical	1 *	Mechanical
0028	Shop drawings	1	Shop drawings
0038	MEP coordination	1	MEP coordination
0098	Ductwork	1	Ductwork
0108	Equipment	1	Equipment
0118	Grilles and balancing	1	Grilles and balancing
0048	Electrical	1 *	Electrical
0058	Service	1	Service
0128	Field wiring	1	Field wiring
0138	RCP	1	RCP
0068	Low-voltage programs	1	Low-voltage programs
0078	Plumbing	1 *	Plumbing
0088	Sanitary	1	Sanitary
0148	Domestic	1	Domestic
0158	Radiation	1	Radiation
0168	Fixtures	1	Fixtures
0008	**Finishes**	1 *	Finishes
0019	Floors	1	Floors
0029	Walls	1	Walls
0039	Ceilings	1	Ceilings
0009	**Closeout**	1 *	Closeout
0010	**Substantial completion**	1	Substantial completion
0011	**Punch list**	1	Punch list
0012	**Final completion**	1	Final completion

Timeline header: 2005 — JAN 17 24 31 | FEB 07 14 | MAR 07 14 21 28 | APR 04 11 18 25 | MAY 02

Figure 3.3 General construction expanded.

173

Act ID	Activity Description	Orig Dur	Early Start	Gantt
0001	**Preconstruction**	50 *	01/25/05	Preconstruction
0002	**Design and development**	50 *	01/25/05	Design and development
0013	Surveys and probes	5	01/25/05	Surveys and probes
0023	Schematical drawings	30	01/25/05	Schematical drawings
0033	Floor plan	30	01/25/05	Floor plan
0043	Section through elevations	30	01/25/05	Section through elevations
0053	Partition types	50	01/25/05	Partition types
0063	MEP plans	45	01/25/05	MEP plans
0073	RCP	30	01/25/05	RCP
0083	DOB approval	20	01/25/05	DOB approval
0003	**Budgeting**	30 *	01/25/05	budgeting
0014	Base building	10	01/25/05	Base building
0024	General construction	10	01/25/05	General construction
0034	MEP	10	01/25/05	MEP
0044	Finishes	30	01/25/05	Finishes
0004	**Early submittals**	20 *	01/25/05	Early submittals
0015	Let base contracts	15	01/25/05	Let Base contracts
0025	Long-lead submittals	20	01/25/05	Long-lead submittals
0035	Long-lead procurements	20	01/25/05	Long-lead procurements
0005	**Production**	50 *	01/25/05	Production
0006	**General construction**	20 *	01/25/05	General construction
0017	Demolition	5	01/25/05	Demolition
0027	Layout	10	01/25/05	Layout
0037	Partition framing	10	01/25/05	Partition framing
0047	Door framing	10	01/25/05	Door framing
0057	Ceiling framing	20	01/25/05	Ceiling framing
0007	**MEPs**	30 *	01/25/05	MEPs
0018	Mechanical	20 *	01/25/05	Mechanical
0028	Shop drawings	20	01/25/05	Shop drawings
0038	MEP coordination	20	01/25/05	MEP coordination
0098	Ductwork	20	01/25/05	Ductwork
0108	Equipment	10	01/25/05	Equipment
0118	Grilles and balancing	5	01/25/05	Grilles and balancing
0048	**Electrical**	30 *	01/25/05	Electrical
0058	Service	20	01/25/05	Service
0128	Field wiring	30	01/25/05	Field wiring
0138	RCP	30	01/25/05	RCP

Figure 3.4 Tasks with durations.

Act ID	Activity Description	Orig Dur	Early Start	2005 / 2006
0068	Low-voltage programs	30	01/25/05	▨ Low-voltage programs
0078	Plumbing	15 *	01/25/05	▽ Plumbing
0088	Sanitary	10	01/25/05	▨ Sanitary
0148	Domestic	10	01/25/05	▨ Domestic
0158	Radiation	15	01/25/05	▨ Radiation
0168	Fixtures	5	01/25/05	▨ Fixtures
0008	**Finishes**	50 *	01/25/05	▽ Finishes
0019	Floors	50	01/25/05	▨ Floors
0029	Walls	50	01/25/05	▨ Walls
0039	Ceilings	50	01/25/05	▨ Ceilings
0009	**Closeout**	30 *	01/25/05	▽ Closeout
0010	**Substantial completion**	0	01/25/05	◆ Substantial completion
0011	**Punch list**	30	01/25/05	▨ Punch list
0012	**Final completion**	0	01/25/05	◆ Final completion

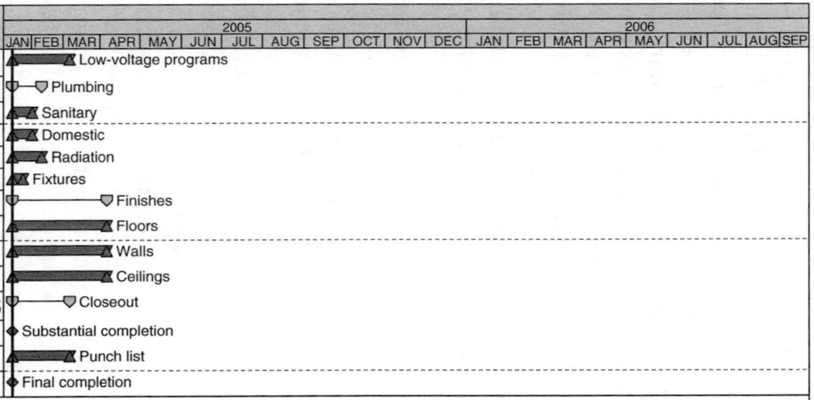

Timeline months header: JAN FEB MAR APR MAY JUN JUL AUG SEP OCT NOV DEC JAN FEB MAR APR MAY JUN JUL AUG SEP

Start date	01/25/05 2:00 PM
Finish date	04/05/05 1:59 PM
Data date	01/25/05 2:00 PM
Run date	01/25/05 3:00 PM
Page number	2A

© Primavera Systems, Inc.

Sample Residential Project

Legend:
- △ Early start point
- ▽ Early finish point
- ▶ Early bar
- Total float point
- Total float bar
- Progress bar
- Critical bar
- Summary bar
- ◀ Progress point
- ◀ Critical point
- ◇ Summary point
- ◇ Start milestone point
- ◆ Finish milestone point

Figure 3.4 (*Continued*)

Otherwise, if you do enter a date, it then becomes a hard-date, or a date that is constrained; it must happen exactly according to the criteria of the constraint, which is immutable. Such hard-dates, if not carefully incorporated into the network logic, can scuttle a schedule's critical path, and make it difficult to analyze. It will also limit your flexibility. What this means is that if you must enter a hard-date then designate a type of constraint to it. Without describing a hard-date with a specific constraint no one will understand the reason for the hard-date given. Later, the program will notify you if you attempt to breach the logic created by the constraint or hard-date. If possible, avoid entering hard-dates with the exception of the overall project start date. If there are hard-date constraints, try to coax the schedule into fitting the criteria without disruption.

Once we have indicated activity relationships, the software will next arrange the tasks in chronological order by date. Except the first and last tasks in a schedule, every task should have at least one predecessor and one successor (except for overall project dates), otherwise, they become isolated or have no relationship to any other task, which would be theoretically impossible had they been part of the critical path. The other exception is known as an independent task, which has no such relationships. These relationships will be refined further along, but for now, we will be concerned with the basic relationships of the predecessor and the successor tasks. Predecessor tasks almost always begin before their successors can begin; however, they can occur virtually[16] simultaneously (see Fig. 3.6). Figure 3.5[17] illustrates these relationships, and their effect on the overall sequencing and duration of the project. The relationships are illustrated by indicator arrows and also in the predecessor and successor columns, which now appear to include respective activity identifications from the first column. Note: We now have prospective early start dates, or the earliest possible start dates for each task, as well as early finish dates, the earliest possible finish date for each task. Now that we have run out of actual dates, we can observe the bar chart representation of our schedule. The software has incorporated the task relationships as we have input, and calculated a sequence.

This level of detail is a common stopping point for many schedulers. However, the schedule is not nearly as useful as it shall soon become. The last two schedule operations require applying constraints and establishing lag times. A constraint is a user-defined fixed date such as start no sooner than, or finish no later than; for example, weather conditions, or a delivery date could constrain a successor task; the former being uncontrollable, and the latter frequently rescheduled to suit. Lag is defined as the amount of time that must pass before a successor task can begin. As it stands now, no task on the model has lag—every task starts immediately following completion of its predecessor. Every scheduler knows that many related tasks overlap; therefore, it is a matter of judgment to assess the amount of the overlap, if the overlap is too aggressive, the men will be fighting for space and speeding up their work. If the overlap is too moderate you will lose the opportunity to save valuable time. A seasoned scheduler will incorporate lags and constraints on the fly, or as he assigns task relationships.

Act ID	Activity Description	Orig Dur	Early Start	Early Finish	Predecessors	Successors	Total Float	Gantt (2005 / 2006 / 2007)
0001	**Preconstruction**	156	01/25/05	08/31/05			84d	Preconstruction
0002	**Design and development**	126 *	01/25/05	07/20/05			39d	Design and development
0013	Surveys and probes	5	01/25/05	02/01/05		0023	0	Surveys and probes
0023	Schematical drawings	15	02/01/05	02/22/05	0013	0014, 0033	0	Schematical drawings
0033	Floor plan	30	02/22/05	04/05/05	0023	0024,	0	Floor plan
0043	Section through elevations	30	04/05/05	05/17/05	0033	0053, 0093	0	Section through elevations
0053	Partition types	10	05/17/05	05/31/05	0043	0024,	0	Partition types
0063	MEP plans	45	04/05/05	06/07/05	0033	0034,	0	MEP plans
0073	RCP	30	06/07/05	07/19/05	0063	0038, 0093	0	RCP
0083	DOB approval	20	06/07/05	07/05/05	0033, 0053,	0017	50d	DOB approval
0093	Working drawings	1	07/19/05	07/20/05	0033, 0043,	0044	0	Working drawings
0003	**Budgeting**	136 *	02/22/05	08/31/05			0	Budgeting
0014	Base building	10	02/22/05	03/08/05	0023	0024	600d	Base building
0024	General construction	10	05/31/05	06/14/05	0014, 0033,	0015, 0034	0	General construction
0034	MEP	10	06/14/05	06/28/05	0024, 0063	0044	16d	MEP
0044	Finishes	30	07/20/05	08/31/05	0034, 0093		0	Finishes
0004	**Early submittals**	55 *	06/14/05	08/30/05			85d	Early submittals
0015	Let base contracts	15	06/14/05	07/05/05	0024	0017,	0	Let base contracts
0025	Long-lead submittals	20	07/05/05	08/02/05	0015	0035	85d	Long-lead submittals
0035	Long-lead procurements	20	08/02/05	08/30/05	0025	0029	85d	Long-lead procurements
0005	**Production**	240	07/05/05	06/06/06			0	Production
0006	**General construction**	95 *	07/05/05	11/15/05			80d	General construction
0017	Demolition	5	07/05/05	07/12/05	0015, 0083	0027	50d	Demolition
0027	Layout	10	07/12/05	07/26/05	0017	0037	50d	Layout
0037	Partition framing	30	07/26/05	09/06/05	0027	0029,	50d	Partition framing
0047	Door framing	20	09/06/05	10/04/05	0037	0057	80d	Door framing
0057	Ceiling framing	30	10/04/05	11/15/05	0047	0039	80d	Ceiling framing
0007	**MEPs**	240 *	07/05/05	06/06/06			0	MEPs
0018	Mechanical	85 *	07/05/05	11/01/05			155d	Mechanical
0028	Shop drawings	20	07/05/05	08/02/05	0015	0038	0	Shop drawings
0038	MEP coordination	30	08/02/05	09/13/05	0028, 0073	0098, 0138,	0	MEP coordination
0098	Ductwork	20	09/13/05	10/11/05	0037, 0038	0039, 0108	105d	Ductwork
0108	Equipment	10	10/11/05	10/25/05	0098	0118	155d	Equipment
0118	Grilles and balancing	5	10/25/05	11/01/05	0108	0010	155d	Grilles and balancing
0048	Electrical	240 *	07/05/05	06/06/06			0	Electrical
0058	Service	20	07/05/05	08/02/05	0015	0128	75d	Service
0128	Field wiring	30	09/06/05	10/18/05	0037, 0058	0029, 0039,	50d	Field wiring

Figure 3.5   Relationships: predecessors and successors.

Act ID	Activity Description	Orig Dur	Early Start	Early Finish	Predecessors	Successors	Total Float
0138	RCP	30	10/18/05	11/29/05	0038, 0128	0068	105d
0178	Fixtures	15	05/16/06	06/06/06	0039, 0128	0010	0
0068	Low-voltage programs	30	11/29/05	01/10/06	0138	0010	105d
0078	Plumbing	230 *	07/05/05	05/23/06			10d
0088	Sanitary	10	07/05/05	07/19/05	0015	0019, 0148	40d
0148	Domestic	10	09/13/05	09/27/05	0038, 0088	0158	0
0158	Radiation	15	09/27/05	10/18/05	0148	0019, 0168	0
0168	Fixtures	5	05/16/06	05/23/06	0019, 0029,	0010	10d
0008	**Finishes**	150 *	10/18/05	05/16/06			0
0019	Floors	50	10/18/05	12/27/05	0088, 0158	0029, 0168	0
0029	Walls	50	12/27/05	03/07/06	0019, 0035,	0039, 0168	0
0039	Ceilings	50	03/07/06	05/16/06	0029, 0057,	0010,	0
0009	**Closeout**	30 *	06/06/06	07/18/06			0
0010	Substantial completion	0	06/06/06		0039, 0068,	0011	0
0011	Punch list	30	06/06/06	07/18/06	0010	0012	0
0012	Final completion	0	07/18/06		0011		0

Sample Residential Project

Start date	01/25/05 2:00 PM
Finish date	07/18/06 1:59 PM
Data date	01/25/05 2:00 PM
Run date	01/25/05 4:00 PM
Page number	2A

© Primavera Systems, Inc.

Legend:
- △ Early start point
- ▷ Early finish point
- ▶ Early bar
- Total float point
- Total float bar
- Progress bar
- Critical bar
- Summary bar
- ◀ Progress point
- ◀▷ Critical point
- ◇ Summary point
- ◆ Start milestone point
- ◆ Finish milestone point

Figure 3.5 (*Continued*)

A lag could exist between the two tasks—plaster walls and paint walls by waiting for the plaster to cure in order to begin painting over it. The following tasks could overlap:

Install ductwork

Frame ceiling

There's no need to wait for all of the ductwork to go in before starting to frame underneath it. So start as soon as possible, perhaps 50% into the installation of the ductwork.

I will not incorporate constraints into our model, yet many schedules will feature them; however, lag and overlap times are a key component to any project. The effect of lag relationships on our schedule is illustrated in Fig. 3.6.[18] A 2-week lag time was entered between 0038 MEP Coordination, and 0098 ductwork to allow for fabrication and delivery to site. An overlap of 1 week was incorporated between 0098 ductwork, and 0057 ceiling framing. This will likely affect the critical path. Linked tasks showing lag will either overlap, or there will be time between the completion of the predecessor, and the commencement of the successor (float). These lags can affect the overall duration. As we enter these lags, we may discover overlooked relationships. For example, the sanitary lines cannot be run before layout is approved; therefore, we will now link them. We can continue to edit the schedule until we save it as a baseline, when it then becomes problematic to edit.[19] As we enter the lags, we must indicate the nature of each lag. If one task can start 10 days after its driving (see further) predecessor starts, then the tasks have a start-to-start lag relationship of 10 days. If a task cannot start until some time after its predecessor is complete, the tasks have a finish-to-start lag relationship. Certain tasks have to start or finish at the same time: they have a start-to-start, or finish-to-finish relationship.

We have entered a finish-to-start lag of 10 days between MEP coordination and ductwork to allow time for the duct to be ordered, fabricated, and delivered.

We have entered a link between ductwork and field wiring, with a start-to-start relationship of 10 days.

The above changes have added 5 days to our production window, which had been 240 work days. We also know that this project, being 16 months in duration, is off that pace by about 3 weeks—the target for substantial completion being the third week of May 2006. We now have to make up for the lost time. Having developed the schedule this far, we can now see the critical path defined by the software as a red bar,[20] and in the float column as a value of zero (excluding roll-up tasks). As expected, the deliverables, MEP coordination, and finishes are driving the project.[21] We can filter these tasks as shown in Fig. 3.7.

This exercise can help tell us where we may be able to save some time. We can now determine which tasks are driving which by reviewing predecessors and successors of these critical tasks.[22] We begin by determining which predecessors are driving critical activities—driving tasks being those predecessor tasks which have the longest duration of other predecessors of the same

Act ID	Activity Description	Orig Dur	Early Start	Early Finish	Predecessors	Successors
0001	**Preconstruction**	**156**	**01/25/05**	**08/31/05**		
0002	**Design and development**	**126 ***	**01/25/05**	**07/20/05**		
0013	Surveys and probes	5	01/25/05	02/01/05		0023
0023	Schematical drawings	15	02/01/05	02/22/05	0013	0014, 0033
0033	Floor plan	30	02/22/05	04/05/05	0023	0024,
0043	Section through elevations	30	04/05/05	05/17/05	0033	0053, 0093
0053	Partition types	10	05/17/05	05/31/05	0043	0024,
0063	MEP plans	45	04/05/05	06/07/05	0033	0034,
0073	RCP	30	06/07/05	07/19/05	0063	0038, 0093
0083	DOB approval	20	06/07/05	07/05/05	0033, 0053,	0017
0093	Working drawings	1	07/19/05	07/20/05	0033, 0043,	0044
0003	**Budgeting**	**136 ***	**02/22/05**	**08/31/05**		
0014	Base building	10	02/22/05	03/08/05	0023	0024
0024	General construction	10	05/31/05	06/14/05	0014, 0033,	0015, 0034
0034	MEP	10	06/14/05	06/28/05	0024, 0063	0044
0044	Finishes	30	07/20/05	08/31/05	0034, 0093	0019,
0004	**Early submittals**	**55 ***	**06/14/05**	**08/30/05**		
0015	Let base contracts	15	06/14/05	07/05/05	0024	0017,
0025	Long-lead submittals	20	07/05/05	08/02/05	0015	0035
0035	Long-lead procurements	20	08/02/05	08/30/05	0025	0029
0005	**Production**	**245 ***	**07/05/05**	**06/13/06**		
0006	**General construction**	**95 ***	**07/05/05**	**11/15/05**		
0017	Demolition	5	07/05/05	07/12/05	0015, 0083	0027
0027	Layout	10	07/12/05	07/26/05	0017	0037,
0037	Partition framing	30	07/26/05	09/06/05	0027	0029,
0047	Door framing	20	09/06/05	10/04/05	0037	0057
0057	Ceiling framing	30	10/04/05	11/15/05	0047	0039
0007	**MEPs**	**245 ***	**07/05/05**	**06/13/06**		
0018	**Mechanical**	**235 ***	**07/05/05**	**05/30/06**		
0028	Shop drawings	20	07/05/05	08/02/05	0015	0038
0038	MEP coordination	30	08/02/05	09/13/05	0028, 0073	0098, 0138,
0098	Ductwork	20	09/27/05	10/25/05	0037, 0038	0039, 0108,
0108	Equipment	10	10/25/05	11/08/05	0098	0118
0118	Grilles and balancing	5	05/23/06	05/30/06	0029, 0039,	0010
0048	**Electrical**	**245 ***	**07/05/05**	**06/13/06**		
0058	Service	20	07/05/05	08/02/05	0015	0128
0128	Field wiring	30	10/11/05	11/22/05	0037, 0058,	0029, 0039,

Figure 3.6 Lags and float.

Act ID	Activity Description	Orig Dur	Early Start	Early Finish	Predecessors	Successors
0138	RCP	30	11/22/05	01/03/06	0038, 0128	0068
0178	Fixtures	15	05/23/06	06/13/06	0039, 0128	0010
0068	Low-voltage programs	30	01/03/06	02/14/06	0138	0010
0078	Plumbing	220 *	07/26/05	05/30/06		
0088	Sanitary	10	07/26/05	08/09/05	0015, 0027	0019, 0148
0148	Domestic	10	09/20/05	10/04/05	0038, 0088	0158
0158	Radiation	15	10/04/05	10/25/05	0027, 0148	0019, 0168
0168	Fixtures	5	05/23/06	05/30/06	0019, 0029,	0010
0008	Finishes	150 *	10/25/05	05/23/06		
0019	Floors	50	10/25/05	01/03/06	0044, 0088,	0029, 0168
0029	Walls	50	01/03/06	03/14/06	0019, 0035,	0039,
0039	Ceilings	50	03/14/06	05/23/06	0029, 0044,	0010,
0009	Closeout	30 *	06/13/06	07/25/06		
0010	Substantial completion	0	06/13/06		0039, 0068,	0011
0011	Punch list	30	06/13/06	07/25/06	0010	0012
0012	Final completion	0	07/25/06		0011	

Start date   01/25/05 2:00 PM
Finish date   07/25/06 1:59 PM
Data date   01/25/05 2:00 PM
Run date   01/25/05 5:00 PM
Page number   2A

© Primavera Systems, Inc.

Sample Residential Project

Legend:
△ Early start point
▽ Early finish point
▷ Early bar
■ Total float point
▶ Total float bar
▷ Progress bar
■ Summary bar
■ Critical bar
— Summary bar
◀ Progress point
◀ Critical point
▷ Summary point
◇ Start milestone point
◆ Finish milestone point

Figure 3.6 (*Continued*)

Act ID	Activity Description	Orig Dur	Early Start	Early Finish	Predecessors	Successors
0013	Surveys and probes	5	01/25/05	02/01/05		0023
0023	Schematical drawings	15	02/01/05	02/22/05	0013	0014, 0033
0033	Floor plan	30	02/22/05	04/05/05	0023	0024,
0043	Section through elevations	30	04/05/05	05/17/05	0033	0053, 0093
0053	Partition types	10	05/17/05	05/31/05	0043	0024,
0024	General construction	10	05/31/05	06/14/05	0014, 0033,	0015, 0034
0015	Let base contracts	15	06/14/05	07/05/05	0024	0017,
0005	**Production**	**245**	**07/05/05**	**06/13/06**		
0007	**MEPs**	**245 ***	**07/05/05**	**06/13/06**		
0028	Shop drawings	20	07/05/05	08/02/05	0015	0038
0038	MEP coordination	30	08/02/05	09/13/05	0028, 0073	0098, 0138,
0048	Electrical	245 *	07/05/05	06/13/06		
0178	Fixtures	15	05/23/06	06/13/06	0039, 0128	0010
0148	Domestic	10	09/20/05	10/04/05	0038, 0088	0158
0158	Radiation	15	10/04/05	10/25/05	0027, 0148	0019, 0168
0008	**Finishes**	**150 ***	**10/25/05**	**05/23/06**		
0019	Floors	50	10/25/05	01/03/06	0044, 0088,	0029, 0168
0029	Walls	50	01/03/06	03/14/06	0019, 0035,	0039,
0039	Ceilings	50	03/14/06	05/23/06	0029, 0044,	0010,
0009	**Closeout**	**30 ***	**06/13/06**	**07/25/06**		
0010	Substantial completion	0	06/13/06		0039, 0068,	0011
0011	Punch list	30	06/13/06	07/25/06	0010	0012
0012	Final completion	0	07/25/06		0011	

Sample Residential Project

Start date	01/25/05 2:00 PM
Finish date	07/25/06 1:59 PM
Data date	01/25/05 2:00 PM
Run date	01/25/05 5:00 PM
Page number	1A

© Primavera Systems, Inc.

Legend:
- ◁ Early start point
- ▽ Early finish point
- ▶ Early bar
- ▷ Total float point
- ▶ Total float bar
- ■ Critical bar
- Summary bar
- ◀ Progress point
- ◀▷ Critical point
- ◇ Summary point
- ◆ Start milestone point
- ◆ Finish milestone point

Figure 3.7 Critical path filter.

successor; the successor begins once the driving task ends, including the lag, if any. In the course of our review, we find that if we sequence carefully, the wall finishes can begin about half way into the floor installations,[23] a significant time savings. After incorporating this change and some others, the schedule is regenerated (Fig. 3.8). We now see that the changes we have made could net a substantial completion date of May 9—almost 3 weeks ahead of schedule. Of course, this is a simplistic schedule; however, the logic will carry through to a schedule of any scope. The ability to perform this action in a keystroke or two becomes no small consideration when compared with doing the work manually.

Plotting the Schedule

Estimating a residential project to finish 3 weeks ahead of schedule sounds too good to be true, and it usually is. You wouldn't want to issue this schedule to your client, a patent oversell. Better to issue the schedule that estimates a 3-week slip. If the project does come in early, you'll be the hero. If you had oversold, and finished 3 weeks early, you would merely be delivering as advertised. Moreover, some contracts offer incentives for finishing early, but these tend to be contracts with liquidated damage clauses for lateness.

However, this compressed schedule will serve some purpose. It is common practice for general contractors to give their subcontractors and vendors an earlier deadline than the schedule actually requires, especially the finish date. The idea is that they will work that much faster to attain this date, and will be less likely to deliver late. In fact, it is such a common practice that subcontractors will ask for the real end date, not the one they were told, as they expect that date to be fictitious. This is a game played in order to keep them on task. If they don't feel pressured by the schedule, they may service other projects when they feel caught up, or not busy enough where they are.

For fixed-sum contracts, there will be less latitude for soft dates, or dates subject to change, as most of the information necessary to create a schedule should be in hand—the contract will require a fixed end date. With construction management contracts, soft dates are often generated for the production phase, until more about the design is known, especially when there is much design and development involved. Nevertheless, soft date or not, you will be called upon to justify your schedule. Gross underestimates especially are not well tolerated without strong justification. A construction manager should publish his schedule assuming the project will proceed according to plan. If it should, the actual progress should not deviate too much from the baseline.

In terms of publishing a schedule, it is usually the general contractor's option to issue updated schedules, unless the project is offtrack, when it may be mandated by the architect or the client. This updated schedule should it be the real deal, will betray the reason for the delay. A general contractor may also consider the information proprietary; he may not want to share the fact that the project may encounter, or has already experienced slip, especially if he thinks he can

Act ID	Activity Description	Orig Dur	Early Start	Early Finish	Predecessors	Successors	
0001	**Preconstruction**	**156**	**01/25/05**	**08/31/05**			Preconstruction
0002	**Design and development**	**126 ***	**01/25/05**	**07/20/05**			Design and development
0013	Surveys and probes	5	01/25/05	02/01/05		0023	Surveys and probes
0023	Schematical drawings	15	02/01/05	02/22/05	0013	0014, 0033	Schematical drawings
0033	Floor plan	30	02/22/05	04/05/05	0023	0024,	Floor plan
0043	Section through elevations	30	04/05/05	05/17/05	0033	0053, 0093	Section through elevations
0053	Partition types	10	05/17/05	05/31/05	0043	0024,	Partition types
0063	MEP plans	45	04/05/05	06/07/05	0033	0034,	MEP plans
0073	RCP	30	06/07/05	07/19/05	0063	0038, 0093	RCP
0083	DOB approval	20	06/07/05	07/05/05	0033, 0053,	0017	DOB approval
0093	Working drawings	1	07/19/05	07/20/05	0033, 0043,	0044	Working drawings
0003	**Budgeting**	**136 ***	**02/22/05**	**08/31/05**			Budgeting
0014	Base building	10	02/22/05	03/08/05	0023	0024	Base building
0024	General construction	10	05/31/05	06/14/05	0014, 0033,	0015, 0034	General construction
0034	MEP	10	06/14/05	06/28/05	0024, 0063	0044	MEP
0044	Finishes	30	07/20/05	08/31/05	0034, 0093	0019,	Finishes
0004	**Early submittals**	**55 ***	**06/14/05**	**08/30/05**			Early submittals
0015	Let base contracts	15	06/14/05	07/05/05	0024	0017,	Let base contracts
0025	Long-lead submittals	20	07/05/05	08/02/05	0015	0035	Long-lead submittals
0035	Long-lead procurements	20	08/02/05	08/30/05	0025	0029	Long-lead procurements
0005	**Production**	**220**	**07/05/05**	**05/09/06**			Production
0006	**General construction**	**80 ***	**07/05/05**	**10/25/05**			General construction
0017	Demolition	5	07/05/05	07/12/05	0015, 0083	0027	Demolition
0027	Layout	10	07/12/05	07/26/05	0017	0037,	Layout
0037	Partition framing	30	07/26/05	09/06/05	0027	0029,	Partition framing
0047	Door framing	20	08/16/05	09/13/05	0037	0057	Door framing
0057	Ceiling framing	30	09/13/05	10/25/05	0047	0039	Ceiling framing
0007	**MEPs**	**220 ***	**07/05/05**	**05/09/06**			MEPs
0018	Mechanical	210	07/05/05	04/25/06			Mechanical
0028	Shop drawings	20	07/05/05	08/02/05	0015	0038	Shop drawings
0038	MEP coordination	30	08/02/05	09/13/05	0028, 0073	0098, 0138,	MEP coordination
0098	Ductwork	20	09/27/05	10/25/05	0037, 0038	0039, 0108,	Ductwork
0108	Equipment	10	10/25/05	11/08/05	0098	0118	Equipment
0118	Grilles and balancing	5	04/18/06	04/25/06	0029, 0039,	0010	Grilles and balancing
0048	**Electrical**	**220 ***	**07/05/05**	**05/09/06**			Electrical
0058	Service	20	07/05/05	08/02/05	0015	0128	Service
0128	Field wiring	30	10/11/05	11/22/05	0037, 0058,	0029, 0039,	Field wiring

Figure 3.8 Schedule revision with resequencing.

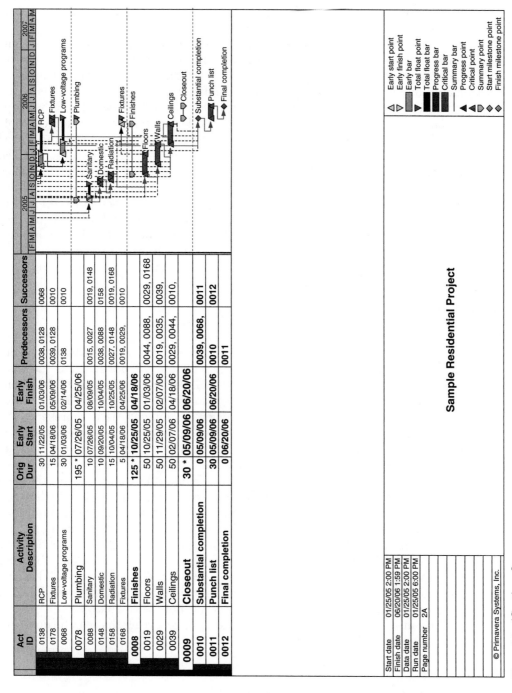

Act ID	Activity Description	Orig Dur	Early Start	Early Finish	Predecessors	Successors
0138	RCP	30	11/22/05	01/03/06	0038, 0128	0068
0178	Fixtures	15	04/18/06	05/09/06	0039, 0128	0010
0068	Low-voltage programs	30	01/03/06	02/14/06	0138	0010
0078	Plumbing	195 *	07/26/05	04/25/06		
0088	Sanitary	10	07/26/05	08/09/05	0015, 0027	0019, 0148
0148	Domestic	10	09/20/05	10/04/05	0038, 0088	0158
0158	Radiation	15	10/04/05	10/25/05	0027, 0148	0019, 0168
0168	Fixtures	5	04/18/06	04/25/06	0019, 0029,	0010
0008	Finishes	125 *	10/25/05	04/18/06		
0019	Floors	50	10/25/05	01/03/06	0044, 0088,	0029, 0168
0029	Walls	50	11/29/05	02/07/06	0019, 0035,	0039,
0039	Ceilings	50	02/07/06	04/18/06	0029, 0044,	0010,
0009	Closeout	30 *	05/09/06	06/20/06		
0010	Substantial completion	0	05/09/06	06/20/06	0039, 0068,	0011
0011	Punch list	30	05/09/06	06/20/06	0010	0012
0012	Final completion	0	06/20/06		0011	

Sample Residential Project

Start date 01/25/05 2:00 PM
Finish date 06/20/06 1:59 PM
Data date 01/25/05 2:00 PM
Run date 01/25/05 6:00 PM
Page number 2A

© Primavera Systems, Inc.

Legend:
- △ Early start point
- ▽ Early finish point
- Early bar
- ▶ Total float point
- Total float bar
- Progress bar
- Critical bar
- Summary bar
- ◀ Progress point
- ◀▷ Critical point
- ◆ Summary point
- ◆ Start milestone point
- ◆ Finish milestone point

Figure 3.8 (*Continued*)

make up for the slip before anyone notices. A construction manager should issue a schedule about once each month. Should there be a slip, or the likelihood of it is imminent; he will need to be able to explain this to the job team in plain terms.

The actual production process of printing or plotting a schedule requires some know-how as other programs, computers, and drivers may have to be coordinated. In fact, to many companies, the obstacle of large format printing is insurmountable. Not uncommonly, because the printing process can be difficult and expensive, a contractor will print the schedule on letter size paper, and then tape all pages together like a patchwork quilt. While that format may be acceptable to the in-house personnel, it should never leave the office. Part of being a good scheduler is finding the wherewithal to publish his work in large format, which reprographers will do for them, provided you send them a workable file type such as a pdf. If your scheduler cannot find the means to produce one-page schedules (oversize), you may want to reconsider the role scheduling software will play in your company. Bar charts are not particularly opulent, and a patchwork bar chart even less so—people simply won't want to look at it. All plots are not equal: some software graphic modules are wholly unpresentable. Output and end product should be a major consideration when investing in any program.

Schedule Tracking

Baseline

So far, we have been able to manipulate each task as much as we want in order to arrive at our final target schedule. This schedule will be known as the *baseline* schedule, to which all actual progress will be measured against. If the software cannot baseline and track the target schedule, the program has dubious value. In theory, the baseline should never be changed, as it represents the target schedule, unless on the rare occasion that the target dates should be changed. However, under such circumstances I would enter the new parameters or target dates as new tasks, or modified tasks, as opposed to changing the existing tasks. In this way the schedule can be changed without altering the original target dates. As I said, once done, going back, or resetting the baseline can be a real chore, and can compromise the logic of the schedule. Some creations will lose their network logic when rebaselined. Once the baseline is set, all future data entries for the tasks shown will appear as actual dates in a new bar below each target bar (Fig. 3.9). The schedule appears with a baseline bar just below the early bar, or the bar we have used so far. This early bar will become the progress bar, once we begin to track the schedule. As yet, the early bar and progress bars are analogous as the project has not yet started.

Without a baseline, there is little tracking or reporting that can be done. An untracked or nonbaseline schedule:

- Is not updatable
- Cannot compare target to actual dates

Act ID	Activity Description	Orig Dur	Rem Dur	Early Start	Early Finish
0001	**Preconstruction**	**156**	**156**	**01/25/05**	**08/31/05**
0002	**Design and development**	**126**	**126**	**01/25/05**	**07/20/05**
0013	Surveys and probes	5	5	01/25/05	02/01/05
0023	Schematical drawings	15	15	02/01/05	02/22/05
0033	Floor plan	30	30	02/22/05	04/05/05
0043	Section through elevations	30	30	04/05/05	05/17/05
0053	Partition types	10	10	05/17/05	05/31/05
0063	MEP plans	45	45	04/05/05	06/07/05
0073	RCP	30	30	06/07/05	07/19/05
0083	DOB approval	20	20	06/07/05	07/05/05
0093	Working drawings	1	1	07/19/05	07/20/05
0003	**Budgeting**	**136**	**136**	**02/22/05**	**08/31/05**
0014	Base building	10	10	02/22/05	03/08/05
0024	General construction	10	10	05/31/05	06/14/05
0034	MEP	10	10	06/14/05	06/28/05
0044	Finishes	30	30	07/20/05	08/31/05
0004	**Early submittals**	**55 ***	**55 ***	**06/14/05**	**08/30/05**
0015	Let base contracts	15	15	06/14/05	07/05/05
0025	Long-lead submittals	20	20	07/05/05	08/02/05
0035	Long-lead procurements	20	20	08/02/05	08/30/05
0005	**Production**	**220**	**220**	**07/05/05**	**05/09/06**
0006	**General construction**	**80 ***	**80 ***	**07/05/05**	**10/25/05**
0017	Demolition	5	5	07/05/05	07/12/05
0027	Layout	10	10	07/12/05	07/26/05
0037	Partition framing	30	30	07/26/05	09/06/05
0047	Door framing	20	20	08/16/05	09/13/05
0057	Ceiling framing	30	30	09/13/05	10/25/05
0007	**MEPs**	**220**	**220**	**07/05/05**	**05/09/06**
0018	Mechanical	210	210	07/05/05	04/25/06
0028	Shop drawings	20	20	07/05/05	08/02/05
0038	MEP coordination	30	30	08/02/05	09/13/05
0098	Ductwork	20	20	09/27/05	10/25/05
0108	Equipment	10	10	10/25/05	11/08/05
0118	Grilles and balancing	5	5	04/18/05	04/25/06
0048	Electrical	220	220	07/05/05	05/09/06
0058	Service	20	20	07/05/05	08/02/05
0128	Field wiring	30	30	10/11/05	11/22/05

Figure 3.9 Schedule with baseline.

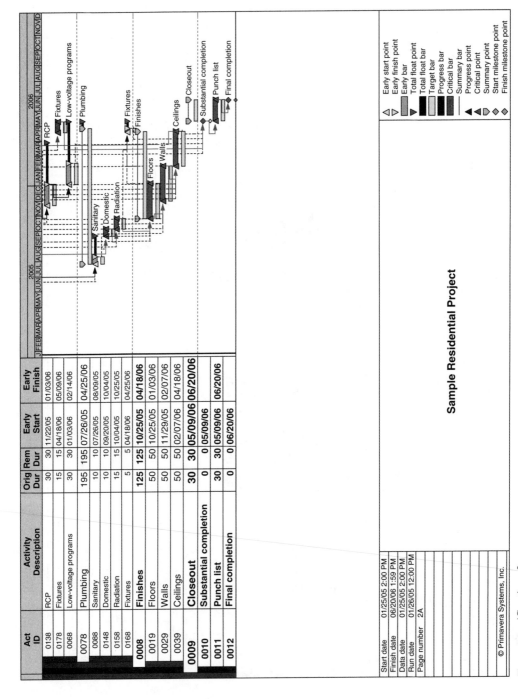

Figure 3.9 (*Continued*)

- Will not generate progress reports or tables
- Are virtually unusable as evidenced in litigation
- Cannot interface with other modules such as resource leveling and cost tracking

Progress Updates

As the project progresses, the scheduler will want to update his information accordingly. Few clients will expect this. They may only require a written or even verbal explanatory update, and then, only to show deviations (specifically, delays). People unfamiliar with scheduling programs will have a hard time understanding a Gantt chart, and for this reason it is good practice to issue annotations with your Gantt chart such as in the following example.

> Pursuant to our meeting, yesterday, and as we have advised in last week's meeting, we are at the business of reconfiguring our working schedule. Herein is information pertaining to that endeavor.
>
> The overall duration has been extended in proportion to the release of the working space. Baseline was predicated on 1.4.02 access. It now stands at >4.22.02. We understand this deficit to be attributable to structural changes involving the core work.

The overall duration needs to be extended further to accommodate the increase in scope, new programs, additional programs not yet identified, and the coordination of any such programs. Chiefly, the effect of the scope of work for electrical distribution will be time: consuming and problematic, especially as each type of signal requires a dedicated pipe. Most piping must be coordinated and installed, prior to heating, ventilation, and air conditioning (HVAC) equipment and distribution systems; otherwise, the program simply will not fit.

The baseline schedule was predicated on having (a) final specifications by the time of mobilization, and (b) the benefit of a preconstruction coordination period as well as a long-lead buyout period. We have availed ourselves somewhat of the former but none of the latter. These are both prerequisites of mobilizing a fast-track project. Durations of certain tasks will be extended for the following reason: additional coordination to make up for periods that were allotted in preconstruction that were not utilized. We must now coordinate during construction, which is more difficult and time-consuming.

> The complexity of the ceiling MEP systems cannot be overemphasized—the coordination of the schematic work, which was targeted to be completed by time of mobilization will require a substantial increase in the coordination period allotted. Some of this slip will be offset by the degree of coordination achieved between now and time of mobilization; however, the increase in complexity of the new scope, and its coordination and integration into the program will effectively increase lags, and decrease overlap; shop drawing preparation, review and release times will also increase to accommodate the added complexity.

The above memorandum pertained to a construction management project that was stalled in the preconstruction phase. It was a complex project with idealistic goals such that any deviation from the program or schedule affecting the critical path required great lengths of explanation. The schedule corresponding to this memo is illustrated in Fig. 3.10. The vertical line in the middle of the timeline represents the data, or the information that was input.

According to this partial schedule, the budget division was on schedule. Moving down the list we see MEP coordination about 5 weeks underway but 8 weeks late. As indicated in the memorandum, the contractor could not gain access to the site as the core work was still underway. Although he was able to establish axes points on 1/05, he was still waiting for the MEP offsets to be completed, which started 5 weeks late, and had an anticipated increase in duration. Activity 0048, offset verification was also to yield critical information for the layout. The slip of this activity was about $5\frac{1}{2}$ months; offsets could not be verified against a layout that couldn't be established. We also see that the construction drawings (CDs) were delivered 8 weeks late: 10/15 . . . 12/17; however, that fact did not yet directly affect the production schedule. Had the core work been done on time, it would have. On the other hand, it created compression for the job team.

The memo attached to the above schedule gives a general sense of this construction manager's analysis of what has transpired, and what he believed would ensue. As it doesn't project too many specific dates, it generated a discussion of the schedule in the general sense. For the client and the architect this package could facilitate the means to correct and minimize delays; however, they did not avail themselves of it. Looking at the same project, 2 months later, the project not only didn't progress it became even more delayed. This second delay was more considerable, and warranted more specific detail:

> . . . regarding your query from yesterday's meeting: you asked for information as to why the lag between the end dates of *0128 HVAC Submittals*, and *0102 Plaster Ceilings* had increased.
>
> Our baseline schedule shows a lag of 54 days, while our working schedule shows a lag of 93 days, a variance of 39 days, based on the following:
>
> We have noted a 20-day increase from start date of 0056 Duct Fabrication, and end date of 0066 Duct Installation.
>
> Contingent on the release of deliverables, and completion of base-building mechanicals, we were to have engaged our MEP coordination, and completed it in an 8-week period. Because this information has not been released, or has been released and changed, we have begun without most of it. Because we will be receiving the required information after mobilization, it will take longer to coordinate it. In effect, we have not gained the leg up we anticipated, because we have not availed ourselves of the preconstruction window. Without this advantage, it will be difficult to achieve an expedited schedule, especially since our original schedule was maximally compressed.

0148: Mechanical Coordination

The duration has increased, because of additional scope, such as perimeter heat piping, dedicated electrical piping for low voltage programs, all of which add a layer

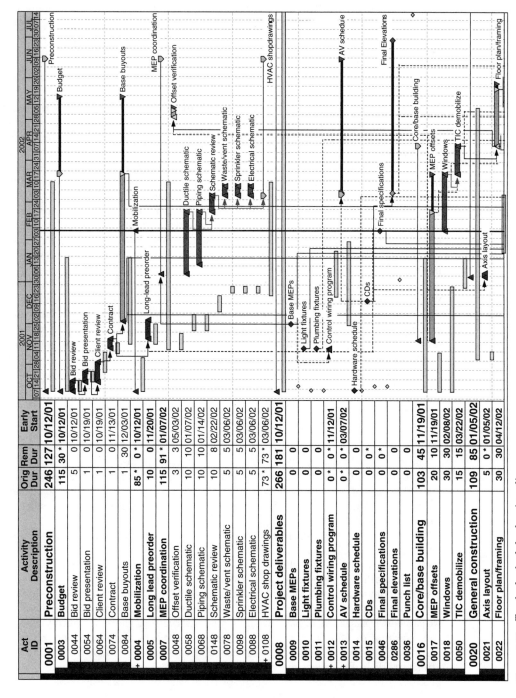

Figure 3.10 Tracked schedule showing slip.

of complexity to fitting our duct and pipe. The raising of ceilings by the design team has also given us less room to maneuver, and more obstructions. Duration has also increased because the scope of work for MEP has increased 15%, chiefly, hot water piping. As it stands now, we will not have 100% coordinated drawings when we expect to begin framing, which was a prerequisite of our original schedule.

0024 MEPS

Most MEPs have increased in scope and complexity; however as yet, only duct and hot water supply/cold water supply pipe fabrication and installation have affected the schedule. We have added extra time for these tasks. Because we will not have precoordinated drawings when we begin work, we will have to coordinate as we are building. This will slow down the framing process; shop drawing process, and fabrication process by increasing lag—less overlap in production. Lags of trades that follow—electrical, plumbing, sprinkler, and gypsum wallboard (GWB), will also be increased. Trade stacking may also become a factor as much of the work is concentrated in small areas. We will also have to wait for the base-building contractors to complete their flue work, and 2-hour enclosures before we begin dimensioning. The anticipated effect will be an unexpedited, or natural production sequence.

Because we do not have all the required deliverables for our coordination period, we know that we will be installing much of the work out of sequence; some work will have to be delayed in order for such work to proceed. Much pipe routing work will take longer and be done later because programs have not been specified; therefore, they cannot go in the initial routing effort, where pipe-rack systems are used. Fortunately, at present, all routing and wiring work is positive-float.

We have noted a 20 day increase from start date of 0052 GWB One Side, and end date of 0072 GWB Ceiling:

A duration increase from 10 to 15 days for 0052 GWB One Side

A duration increase from 10 to 20 days for 002 GWB Two Sides

A duration increase from 15 to 20 days for 0072 GWB Ceiling

The original durations shown are 100% compressed durations, predicated on ideal conditions. Our drywall installers have recalculated their work periods for reasons of increased complexity, and because of obstructions to their ability to operate within the building, such as using the elevators, and more importantly, unexpected congestion on the floors.

Additionally, we feel that more time will be required than originally allotted for GWB finishes, because of the complexity of the work behind the walls; not having a Lutron plan at time of budgeting and baseline scheduling, we expected a typical Lutron installation, which we could quickly drywall over. We now have a multiple interface control system so complex that a systems integrator had to be retained to organize the flowchart of network logic. As we are now more familiar with the plan, we can better assess its impact on real-time construction. There will need to be special coordination efforts between the electricians, and the carpenters and millwork installers, in order to facilitate the location of back boxes, which will be installed after the GWB. We expect more men on the floor, and more time to install in this fashion.

The 12.17.01 electrical additions contribute to the extra GWB effort, especially in the coordination and subsequent closing of the ceilings.

It must also be noted that additional layers of GWB have now been added to the partition types. We have not incorporated the duration of this installation.

It should be said that updated Gantt charts were the primary review documents generating the above information; however, they were actually used as secondary documents in the presentation, because the rest of the job team always found the written updates and job meetings easier to understand. But without the Gantt chart, the schedule analysis could not have been conducted. This distinction reinforces the notion that tracked schedules are primarily meant to be used by contractors for many uses and not just to appease their clients.

This was a difficult project for the construction manager—he had no leverage with the architect, the owner, the owner's representative, or with the base builder. What was to be a 4-month preconstruction window had increased 8 months in length, and counting. However, it appears that he had done due diligence in addressing these matters. He issued monthly updated schedules, with either annotations or presentations, and continued to adjust the budget to reflect the changes in the work. And equally as important, he demonstrated the effects in the present and future of current project conditions, chiefly:

- That he did not have the design drawings necessary to coordinate MEPs within the layout.
- The fact that the base-building work was not progressing as scheduled such that he did not have access to the site for layout and coordination.
- That the scope and complexity of the work had increased significantly.
- That the project could no longer follow the expedited sequencing that was planned.

In the end, the only thing that matters for the client is how he makes productive use of this information. For the contractor, it is a measure of his level of accountability. If action was not taken to remediate schedule problems, the memo may have served the client little purpose.

As this particular project progressed (or didn't), the project team became increasingly nervous. Those in doubt needed to be tutored in comprehending Gantt charts in order to understand the schedule, and even then, were still somewhat hazy—at least they asked. An important lesson was given to one such doubter, who insisted he could shave time off the end date. He was a consulting architect thrust upon the project to help resuscitate it. He challenged the dates of several tasks, which he thought could be started sooner, albeit out of sequence. Being that none of the tasks he referred to were critical activities, and weren't driving critical activities, moving these tasks up had no effect on the schedule other than to force it needlessly out of sequence. The challenge was then put to him by the scheduler that he should be paid $20 for every day he could shorten the schedule. Naturally, he went home empty handed. Although the scheduler was able to illustrate how the project had devolved from a project that was 10 months in length to a 17-month project, the contractor could in no way substantiate how he could have so underestimated the schedule in the first place. In point of fact, the contractor had given the scheduler an 8-month finish date constraint in order to make his proposal sound more appealing, despite the scheduler indicating a minimum 1-year schedule. Unfortunately for the scheduler, it was his task to substantiate the lost time to the client.

The more delayed a project becomes, the more information you will want at your disposal to justify, or explain, the reason(s) for it. The above memorandum referred to a few tasks in a general sense as they related to the onset of fit-out work: the substantial completion date, always a tense topic, was not referred to. Substantial completion related information is germane to the contract, and should have its own forum for discussion. In addition to revised/updated-annotated schedules, additional reporting was warranted such as spreadsheets that would highlight critical path tasks, upcoming and breached deliverable milestones. Some of these types of reports can be generated automatically by the software you use. Again, if you are not tracking your schedule, you will not be able to generate such reports other than very basic information.

We can now present our schedule in the PERT view (Fig. 3.11) as a matter of convenience to our client. The PERT view features a linear flow of logic that most people can readily understand. Again, should a project be complex, and have many tasks, the PERT will begin to resemble a complex tract housing plan or genetic mapping plot.

Change Order Scheduling

Change orders, which by their nature are typically unexpected, can upset the logic and sequencing of a schedule. Depending on when they are introduced, and what effect they have on other tasks, especially critical path tasks, they can render a schedule irrelevant in a hurry.

For example, a 12-month Brownstone project is on schedule. Six months into the project, the contractor has installed all MEPs, has installed substrates on most partitions, and begun closing ceilings. At this time, the architect issues a request for proposals for a humidification system. Had the system been in the contract drawings it would have been incorporated into the MEP phase, while the ceiling was still exposed, and likely not affected the overall project duration. However, since all ductwork has been installed, partitions closed, and ceilings in the process of being closed, the introduction of the system at this time will necessitate significant tear-out work as well as a waiting period for the equipment. The contractor makes all kinds of noise because in order to install this

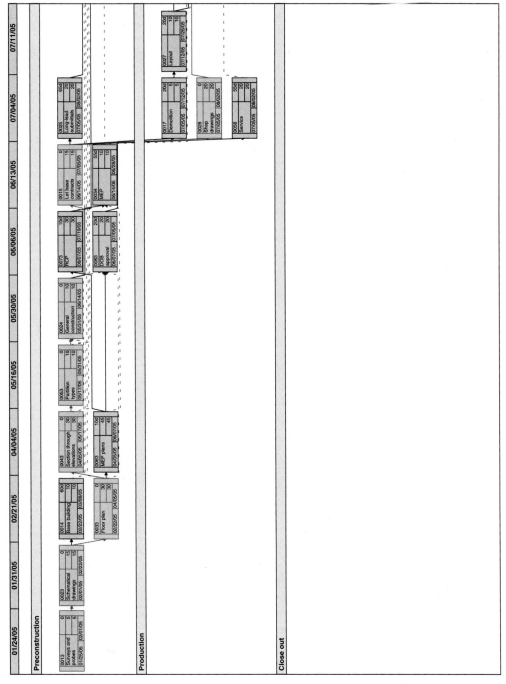

Figure 3.11 PERT chart.

Figure 3.11 (*Continued*)

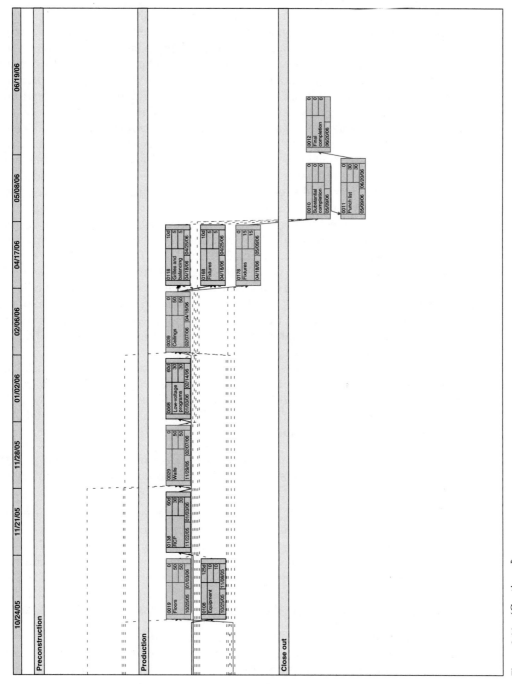

Figure 3.11 (*Continued*)

system he must go backward. The profit he will make from the change could never offset the production lag it will cause. Moreover, the project will lose 4 weeks. Nevertheless, the client is adamant; he wants the system.

The contractor issues a proposal for the work, which includes an up charge for the 4-week delay. He does not factor the production lags as he has no method to quantify them, and thus wouldn't know how to coherently justify this to the client. As expected, the architect wants to negotiate the change order for the system. Having done that, he then challenges the notion that the job will be delayed 4 weeks as a consequence, and is offended that the contractor wants to be paid for what he perceives as idle time. The contractor then explains, as best he can, why the project will be delayed, and why he is asking to be paid for the delay. The architect considers the explanation, and asks to see the schedule. Upon his review, he indicates that if the project was resequenced, and if the system could be delivered sooner, then the delay could be reduced to about 2 weeks. The client may accept the delay but wouldn't dream of bankrolling it; in fact, he would expect a rebate! The contractor regards the architect's resequencing as being hypothetical. Moreover, the logic makes no sense to him, and he disagrees with it. He is disconcerted and anxious that the architect's ideas of resequencing are such that the working schedule would at once be rendered obsolete. He would never agree to discount his price according to that logic. Thus, they are at an impasse. It is not in their best interest to advise the client of the stalemate. They agree on the up charge to install the system with the caveat that the delay will be negotiated after the work is installed. Essentially, they are deferring the confrontation to a later time.

The contractor advises his scheduler that he wants to see the effect of the change order on successor tasks, as well as the overall project duration, represented in an updated schedule. This schedule will later aid them in substantiating the charge for the delay to the client. The scheduler thinks it through and arrives at the following conclusions:

1. The architect's resequencing ideas make no sense, or are not consistent with typical means and methods, and cannot be incorporated into the intended schedule network logic.

2. The resequencing that will be required will slow down production rates for which the respective subcontractors will complain, and likely submit up charges. Additionally, they will bill for "comeback" or remobilization changes. None of this was explained to the architect in the meeting with the contractor. Upon generating the new schedule, he will request a statement of impact from each affected subcontractor as well as any up charges related to the change. He must also notify the architect of these new impending up charges.

Naturally, the prospect of advising the client of these additional charges is unappealing to the contractor. Most contractors would be hard put to quantify or substantiate charges of this nature, and probably wouldn't stomach the architect and client's responses. For these reasons, it is unusual for a contractor to be successful in such an endeavor. Knowing this, they are, more often than not, likely to not speak up.

The contractor has requested an updated schedule from the scheduler. Updated schedules represent progress to date, as measured against baseline tasks. If there are changes to your schedule, how would you represent their effect on other tasks in the updated schedule? There are four methods that come to mind:

1. The change can simply be tracked by measuring the additional duration to affected tasks and overall durations, and subtracting the difference (actual duration—target duration). However, there is a problem with this concept: if the project is delayed, it will be difficult to illustrate that this specific change was the sole cause of the delay, or if it was only a portion, how much? The architect will argue that the project may be delayed for unrelated reasons, and that the project was late regardless of the change order. And this assertion may be hard to refute. At this point, let's refer back to a quote earlier in the text:

   > . . . it should be remembered that changes in the work are only made by the owner or his agent, the designer, therefore, in fairness, because any change is usually for the benefit of the owner and is initiated by him or his agent, the contractor should never be put into a position of loss as a result of a change in the work.[24]

   Thus, there is a basis that the contractor should be reimbursed for changes causing delays on principle alone. Again, if it can't be demonstrated that a particular change caused the delay, he likely won't get paid to finance the delay.

   The baseline can be regenerated with the change as if it were part of the base contract; expected extended durations can be entered, and a new target date established based on these durations. The difficulty with this method is that it can be a considerable undertaking to regenerate the schedule, especially if it is going to be out of sequence.

2. The change can be posted to the schedule as a milestone: as such, one would be able to illustrate graphically when the change was effected, and its relationship to affected task durations, which the scheduler will input as successors. For example, the milestone may be posted on a given date with 30 workdays remaining in a successor task. If the successor task takes 10 working days longer, the progress bar will reflect that. Assuming the progress bar showed that the successor task was on time prior to the introduction of the change, it is almost certain that the change caused the delay. This is not a perfect method for quantifying a claim but it will show real-time comparisons that are part of substantiating such a claim.

3. Perhaps, the most effective method is to incorporate the change, and all successor tasks into the working schedule as independent activities, that is, no relationship to other tasks. This could be posted on a separate schedule, but more effectively, as an inserted subcomponent on to the working schedule. The

successor tasks would be redundant with the baseline tasks; however, the stand-alone group will illustrate its own separate analog to be compared to the overall schedule, and can be baselined and tracked without affecting the overall schedule. For example, the targeted early finish date for a baseline task may have been extended by the change. The cause- and-effect relationship of the delay will be readily discernible in the stand-alone group that has been posted. If the progress bar prior to the change was consistent with the baseline then the delay must have been realized subsequent to the change. The beauty of this method is that it can be incorporated after the fact. In other words, if the claim is challenged, the scheduler can recreate the progress retroactively.

If a contractor is going to actively pursue a substantial claim for delays, and he believes it significant enough that arbitration will be necessary then he must try to present his case as clearly as possible. Without a doubt, the fourth method shown above should prove to be his most compelling evidence.

Notes

The importance of schedules

- They enable you to compete for projects that require scheduling and schedule updates.
- They give you the ability to track work and to forecast future progress.
- They facilitate the means to adjust production levels midstream to accommodate slippages.
- They help to organize complex projects into cohesive structures.
- They provide means to reorganize and resequence projects without losing logic.
- They can prevent project from going out of control.
- They will give you some level of comfort in knowing that you are controlling your project, and not vice versa.
- They are an important vehicle of accountability.

Key obstructions to facilitating a project

- Lack of design information
- Client's inability to make decisions
- Working drawings
- Continually changing program
- Unresolved requests for information
- Inaccessibility to worksite

- Change of project schedule
- Unresolved change orders

Endnotes

1. Compare this circumstance with the role of the construction manager, who can induce the design team to issue required information when it is needed.
2. CPM is a standard method of scheduling network logic.
3. The baseline is the schedule's original target dates to which all actual progress will be tracked.
4. Stephen J. Krone, *Construction Scheduling Specifications, ASC Proceedings of the 32d Annual Conference*, (Texas: Associated Schools of Construction: 1996) pp. 211–212. Only a fraction of the sample group were the general builders.
5. Hutchings and Kristofferson, 2004.
6. Richard H. Clough, Glenn A. Sears, *Construction Project Management*, 3d ed. (New York: John Wiley & Sons Inc., 1991) p. 86.
7. Clough and Sears 18.
8. *Wunderlich Contracting Co. v United States*, 351 F.2d 956 (Ct. Cl. 1965).
9. Krone, 25.
10. The CPM was developed by the DuPont Company in 1957.
11. Adobe Acrobat is one such program.
12. But not the general contractor, whose primary business is not conceptual budgeting.
13. Optimally, you should let the software generate and recalculate the end date as that is what it should do best. You'll have plenty of time later to work back to a target end date.
14. Scheduling terminology, such as early date or original duration varies from program to program.
15. The shortcomings of gray scale herein a case in point.
16. There must be at least a minimum of time to allow for the first task to mobilize.
17. For practical purposes, this schedule was plotted to a width of one page. Hence, a 2-week interval is barely discernible. Schedules should be plotted on a minimum of 24-in. wide paper such that there is more room for graphics and notations. Reprographers offer this service.
18. Here is another instance where wider format would better demonstrate a point.
19. You must then remove the baseline and reestablish it. This is often too much for the software to manage; therefore, it is wise to save a copy of the schedule before resetting the baseline.
20. See Fig. 3.7.
21. This is typical residential remodel projects. In fact, if this is not the case, or float times of these tasks are not minimized, this may signal a mistake in the network logic.
22. Not all the scheduling software offers this information.
23. This particular overlapping should be done with care. If wet plaster will be applied to the walls, there is a good chance that the relative humidity will increase in the space, creating problems with the wood floor installation. Never underestimate the effect water can have on dried wood. This particular overlap example was given because it is a common mistake by general contractors and their schedulers.
24. Collier, 159.

4

Building

This construction is consequently, the prototype of linear expression or, of linear composition. It consists of a square divided into four squares, the most primitive form of the division of a schematic plane.

WASSILY KANDINSKY,
FROM *POINT AND LINE TO PLANE*

At the risk of rendering the above statement out of context, it could refer to the inability of people to "think outside the box." No two projects are alike. Every combination of design, schedule, budget, and production team seems to yield a new experience. The savvy contractor realizes this, and he will form a game plan for each project, based on the unique set of circumstances presented to him. But he is the exception to the rule. Most contractors make the mistake of treating all of their projects more or less the same. I knew a contractor who generated several production schedules with different durations: 3, 6, 9, 12 months, and so on. When a bid went out, the generic schedule corresponding to the contract duration was appended to it. The schedules all had the same trades, scope of work, and sequencing, regardless of the design of the prospective project. If the project was awarded, this document became instantaneously obsolete (not that it was ever relevant)—it was merely a sales tool. At any rate, no architect or client ever scrutinized his schedules enough to realize this, which begs the question: "Why do they bother asking for detailed schedules in the bid documents when all they really want to know is the start and end dates?"

The approach to a given project begins with the first phone call, or meeting, what one might call *intake*. Once a contractor decides to pursue a given project, his work begins. Immediately, several questions should be addressed, which will determine if the project is worth chasing.

Qualification Process

What is the status of the design documents?

The answer to the above question will advise the approach to the budget, schedule, and maybe even the contract structure. If the design documents are 50% complete, will the project go out to bid now, or not until working drawings are complete? If the project will be bid now, there will be a lot of contingencies—for budget and schedule. If the working drawings are biddable, they will be bid in the customary fashion. If they are not biddable—still in development, the project may benefit from a construction management arrangement; however, few residential projects will incorporate one, rather, they will try to build the project piecemeal, negotiating each step of the way. Not uncommonly, schematic drawings are passed off as being "working drawings." This is a semantic quandary, one that signals trouble ahead. Contractors will invariably take on such projects with the mistaken belief that they can be treated like any other job, or that they have a construction management level plan to organize the project, and compensate for informational shortcomings.

What is the budget?

For most budget projects (aggressively cost driven), the working capital will almost never be conveyed to you. The exception would be projects for which there are such meager resources that the architect assumes there is no risk in advertising the information—the tenet being that "No one would ever bid as low as the client's bottom-line." It is almost unthinkable that an architect would divulge the value of a well-endowed budget. The architect knows the budget, as the owner has instructed him to design within certain parameters, or range of cost. But architects are seldom knowledgeable enough, or have the time and resources to figure expected construction costs. Letting the contractor know the budget is considered "tipping one's hand." Wouldn't it be nice to know the budget beforehand? If you did, you would know in advance just how much the inevitable shortfall is. If you knew this, you could disqualify a majority of the budget projects that come across your estimator's desk before you waste time and money bidding them. That would be no small chunk of change, considering an estimator's salary, schedule, blueprint reproduction, and courier expenses. Budget disclosure would be inappropriate in competitively-bid projects; however, it is perfectly reasonable and inevitable for negotiated bids. Inevitable because even negotiated bids are often cost driven to the point where the contractor is left to value engineer significant portions of the work down to the client's budget.

If the project is over budget, there is a strong likelihood that the architect already knows this. He may be bargain hunting. Depending on the shortfall, a general contractor can pass up a project, or offer to value engineer it. However, value engineering services should only be offered once the contract is awarded, or at least a *letter of intent*. You wouldn't want to value engineer a project only to have it awarded to a competitor, or have the architect incorporate your hard-thought ideas to another contractor's proposal. Nonetheless, it is commonplace for bid documents to have a built-in need for value engineering—if information is not complete, the estimator will have to fill in the blanks. This can be thought of as an opportunity to value engineer in order to make a bid more competitive. Additionally, few clients or architects would hesitate to solicit value engineering information from prospective bidders, regardless of their overall bid. This information should be made available to all bidders; however, it seldom is. This is a bit unfair to other bidders, as they are in effect not bidding the same job. Such practice is not permitted in the public sector, and should be discouraged in the private sector as well.

The problem nowadays is that most projects are determined as being over budget in the construction phase, when it is too late to value engineer. Industry protocol dictates that the design intent, no matter how vague, must be incorporated into the drawings in order for a comprehensive bid package to be assembled. The architect will state his fee up front for this service. Subsequently, the construction and furniture, fixtures and equipment (FF&E) budgets are factored according to the remaining funding. Invariably, FF&E are given precedence over construction, especially by the client and interior designers, who have no concern with the cost of building. Residential clients would rather spend money on furnishings than they would, say, on a much needed, but costly infrastructure item such as a booster pump or new piping. Hence, it is no wonder that the construction phase is fated to be over-budget even before the architect takes pencil to paper.

What will be the contract structure?

If the drawings are less than 50% developed, then perhaps the general contractor will suggest a cost-plus fee, or a construction management contract. Many do, even if they are not construction managers. This is an example of the blind leading the blind. The architect should know better than to solicit a hard bid for unbiddable drawings, and a general contractor should not pose as an *ad hoc* construction manager. Such enterprises have dubious prospects. Contractors need to trim the menu of their contract administration requirements, not add to it, as they barely get by with the basics. Any incomplete set of drawings cannot be hard-bid without contingencies. If the drawings are 75% complete, a 25% contingency is a good starting point. If the drawings are 65% completed, then a 35% contingency is appropriate, and so on. Nonetheless, any contingency over 10% will elicit worries from your client, thus few contractors budget contingencies higher than 10%, regardless of missing information. Your estimator must be adept at detecting quantifying such omissions. Depending on the contract vehicle (e.g., AIA 107 or AIA 101), you will be informed as to how to structure your estimate and the bidding process. The contract vehicle is typically indicated in the general requirements section of the specification book. Invariably, it will be stipulated or lump sum, an AIA A101 contract. Even though the contract structure may be indicated, the documentation may not be comprehensive enough to be let as a fixed sum.

Architects will balk at your contingencies, and may even be offended, as a contingency denotes a lack of design information, which the owner likely believes the architect should have provided for his fee. The architect may insist that the information is in the drawings, or the intent of the drawings is sufficient such that a much smaller contingency or none at all is appropriate. The focus is then turned back on the contractor to defend his contention, a dubious undertaking, as the architect has the owner's ear. It may appear that the contractor is trying to take advantage of the owner. Effectively, the contractor may ostracize the architect by explaining himself, at which the architect may try to discredit the contractor. This may sound like childish behavior, but it is not at all uncommon.

What is the schedule?

Like the budget, clients will ask the contractor what the schedule is, even as they have decided this for themselves. The exception is when there is a fixed schedule. If there is a fixed schedule, it generally means it is an aggressive schedule, and you may frequently find a liquidated damages clause in the terms of the contract. For apartment buildings, where other tenants are "affected" by work in their building, the building manager may impose a fixed window or duration for construction; 120 working days is not uncommon, as is the space of time between Memorial Day and Labor Day, when tenants tend to be away in their summer homes. As we discussed in Chap. 3, you will want to have a schedule which is germane to the project, and one with which you can track progress. Additionally, as part of the subcontractor qualification process, you will want to know whether they can commit to your schedule needs. Ideally, this exercise was completed in the bidding stage. A hungry contractor may take on a project with an aggressive schedule whether he thinks he can make deadlines or not; when the time comes to explain delays, he hopes he will have either found excuses, or may not even care. This, of course, is not good business ethics. However, there are countless projects where the contractor takes on accelerated progress work in good faith. When the delays are discovered, he is either thought to be unethical or inexperienced (should have known better); there is no other explanation insofar as the client is concerned.

A contractor I knew was awarded a commercial project in the preconstruction/budget phase. It was awarded based in part on the finish date promised by the contractor, which was always perceived as being unrealistic—so said the scheduler. The contractor felt he had to issue a schedule no longer than the competing bidders', which indicated an unrealistically aggressive duration, or be put out of the running. The contractor was awarded the project based on the accelerated schedule. However, the schedule had design milestones, which needed to be met in order for the work to commence. Being familiar with the architect, the contractor knew it was inevitable that these design deadlines would be breached, and also the workload increased, thereby justifying overall schedule extension. The scheduler dutifully adjusted his schedule each month to show the slip.

What are the qualifications?

What sort of project is it? Does your company have experience with this type of work? And if it is high-end, do you have the resources and managers to produce such work? The erroneous determination of these considerations is at the heart of the majority of project failures; contractors in over their head, and not realizing it. Sometimes, the architect, who signs off on the work, doesn't realize it either. Sometimes the owner doesn't realize it. Often, it becomes apparent that a contractor is unqualified when it is too late. Many contractors function in a state of denial, kidding themselves that they perform above their station, and thus misrepresent themselves in doing so.

I recall one such project. The project was a duplex addition to the top of an old brick building. The architect was qualified, however, stymied by a limited design budget. His drawings, at first glance, looked like any other drawings, however, upon closer inspection, it was evident there were lots of difficult details, knife-edge reveals, and alignments with dissimilar materials, critical offsets and hold dimensions, and other difficult details. To save money, the client contracted the engineers directly. This arrangement effectively put the architect—who being paid only to draft drawings and perform a minimum of contract administration duties would typically manage and coordinate the engineers, out of the loop. The project was undertaken by the contractor, who had no experience with a project of this caliber, who merely wanted to get his foot in the door of where he thought more work was to be had. The prerequisites of winning the contract were to commit to an aggressive schedule, which other bidders could not do, and to issue a low, unrealistic bid. In an instance of unprecedented braggadocio, the contractor insisted on liquidated damages being implemented in the event of delay—a needless oversell. Their bid was indeed unrealistic, yet they were not inclined to realize it. This last fact I relate not to stand on its own demerits, but to exemplify how conditions on some projects may seem downright ridiculous. Thus it seems it's never enough that the project is late, over budget, or below quality standards; there always seems to be some additional unfathomable condition that distinguishes each dysfunctional project. Thus is the singularity of the residential sector.

The project began, and it became apparent from the first day that trouble was ahead—rather than having their own stock of regular contractors, the demolition contractors were sourced from a public directory of subcontractors, or "off the street," as it were. The general contractor had no prior relationship with them, and the only qualification was cost. Large portions of their work were taken out by the estimator in order to keep his target budget. When that became apparent, he tried to get them to do the omitted work for free. The mechanical contractor was also sourced from this same directory, and experienced similar problems; however, he refused to start and man the project without working capital, as he rightly feared not getting paid for his work. When the subcontractors refused to do the omitted work for free, they were either threatened with contract termination, or the superintendent was put upon by the estimator to get the work done "somehow." Not uncommonly, the superintendent saw to the work personally, or with a laborer.

The project was irrevocably cursed when the carpenters appeared. These carpenters did much low-grade commercial work for the general contractor, and agreed to do this project as a favor, since like the contractor they had no experience in this type of work. A successive string of problems was encountered from the get-go, which inhibited any forward motion of the overall project. Since layout and framing were the first major components of the project, the project never got out of first gear. What was put down as floor plate defining the partitions was constantly torn out and rebuilt. In fact, in over 2 month's time not a single element was installed correctly. Besides being unfamiliar with the work, the problems had to do with coordination, sequencing, erroneously installed work, incorrect materials, shortages, understaffing, lack of a foreman, and so on. Without all these problems being addressed, the project was doomed. No corrective measures were ever successfully taken, and thus the project foundered. When the carpenter was taken to task for his inefficiency, he insisted that the superintendent was unreasonable.

Obviously the above problems were not the only ones associated with this project. Mistakes left uncorrected at the onset of a project have a habit of multiplying and exacerbating throughput the remainder of the project. At the end of the day, however, the client was to blame for not taking action when he had been duly advised at such a time when he could have taken action. Poor judgment, and penny-pinching from the start poisoned the well. Although the superintendent and architect were vigilant in warning the client, there was little they could do to control his actions. For this particular project, the general contractor's contract was terminated, and the project was then hastily completed, finally, barely holding any resemblance to the architect's design vision.

Following the qualification survey, your findings will dictate your general approach to each project. Assuming you are awarded the work, you will then develop your staffing requirements according to the given project's needs. These requirements should come as no surprise as you surely will have determined them, considering your fee for general conditions and overhead.

In-house staff

There will be field and office staff needed. The office staff requirements tend not to change, except workloads may vary. Field staff requirements require a bit more consideration. Beginning from the top-down, you must decide on assigning the following.

Project manager. Do the general conditions justify having a project manager? Depending on the type of projects you do, you may have a project manager on some projects, and not on others. Your superintendent may act as project manager. On smaller projects, only a daily or weekly visit from a project manager may be required. Some general requirements will mandate a full-time site superintendent. You will need to assess the overall workload of your project manager and schedule him accordingly, especially if he is managing more than one project. You should have completed this exercise when you quantified your general conditions component of your proposal, as we discussed in Chap. 2.

Regardless of job titles, someone's job description must include processing documentation. Companies that have separate departments for estimating, billing, and production will generate paperwork from their respective offices. Optimally, a project has someone who controls the organization of its documentation. Project managers seem to do this best, as superintendents seldom seem to have the time. Leaving the task of generating important documents to inappropriate level workers is a recipe for disaster. As a result, many companies either poorly document their projects, poorly organize the information, or both. What tends to evolve is a hodgepodge of information; estimating, billing, and production all have different sets of documentation, while the project manager only has what he thinks he needs kept in an overstuffed three-ring binder. Once the integrity of the documentation is compromised, the project becomes vulnerable to mistakes of the sort wholly unrelated to means and methods. If such a project makes it to substantial completion, the closeout stage can be formidable.

Documentation

Being geared toward manufacturing, construction is an industry that does not typically feature people with strong communication skills, of which documentation is a critical component. In fact, a contractor's degree of literacy is often suspect. This is unfortunate, as communication is crucial to the flow of information and accountability. Resultantly, many contractors don't keep adequate or appropriate documentation on their projects. This condition plagues the industry. The residential renovation and remodeling sectors are the most service oriented of all construction sectors; therefore, communication, especially documentation, needs to be brought up a notch above the typical monosyllabic response—the *lingua franca* of the industry. Frequently, inappropriately worded, or poorly written documents are published regarding important issues. When addressing important issues in documentation, you want to ensure that the integrity of your documentation is fit to the purpose. If a project should come to litigation, the illiterate contractor will be hard pressed to produce necessary or adequate documentation to justify his position.

As construction is not the only industry where managers could use an upgrade in literacy, there are ways to improve poor communication, such as seminars, professional guidebooks, and so on. If sensitive documentation is being generated, insist on reviewing it before it is published, especially if you don't have great confidence in the drafter's skills. A well-written document will be recognized as such, and your clients will judge your acumen and integrity by such communications. A company that works in the high-end sector should generate documents no less than equal to the integrity they claim to possess as builders—if they profess to be a high-quality outfit, their documentation should reflect that. It should be professional, accurate, and immaculate. This is especially true for construction managers.

Part of the concept of good documentation policy is to copy concerned parties as required. However, not all documentation is for everyone; discernment should be used. For example, sorting out means and methods with an architect does not require the client's input, and his involvement could be problematic, thus you wouldn't copy him on such matters. Most architects are their client's agent, and as such, insist that you do not correspond directly with their client—only through them. This is reasonable, provided the architect is cooperative. Contractors are clearly at a disadvantage when the architect alone has the client's ear. If the architect will not be induced, or motivated by the contractor to act, a contractor is within his rights to address the client directly. In doing so, the architect invariably will take umbrage for this behavior. Architects take documentation very seriously. Because they don't see that much of it from their contractors, they may sense an air of litigiousness, if you flood them with it. For this reason, you want to simplify and minimize documentation to your architect and client, issuing it only as needed. The exceptions are projects lacking in information. Such projects may be under documented from design through completion. It should be clear early on, if, for whatever reason, the architect is not going to issue the required level of documentation.

There is cause for concern when architects continually don't answer your requests for information or notices of delay. They may not be able to, simply may not want to, or can't be bothered with confrontational issues. This is not unusual. This type of one-way discourse is perceived by many architects as "you covering yourself," a notion of which they are particularly squeamish; however, the content of your documentation is primary—you want to give or receive necessary information, not merely cover yourself as suspicious architects would have it.

Insofar as in-house documentation and proprietary information are concerned, you almost never want to distribute such articles outside your own organization, or even outside your office, for that matter. Failure to scrutinize what documentation is sent to whom can lead to all sorts of trouble. For example, I recall a meeting where a change order was being negotiated. The contractor had presented his defense, and the meeting was adjourned in contemplation of a resolution. However, the contractor had inadvertently left on the meeting table for the client to find, estimating spreadsheets and other proprietary documents relating to this change order that were quite inconsistent with the contractor's presentation. Needless to say, the contractor's negotiating position was compromised.

Most complex projects are driven by the flow of information between the design and production team, and the production process. Requests for information (RFIs) that are not processed in a timely manner need to be reissued, sometimes with a delay notification. For whatever reason, should information not be forthcoming, this fact should be documented. However, any documentation must not be considered an end in itself. Too many managers fail to take appropriate action when their documentation is ignored. If all repeated attempts to solicit information from the design team fail, it is time to force the issue, for example, call a meeting for the purpose of resolving the issue. The point is that nearly all documentation requires follow-up.

Most general contractors are not crack documenters. This is good news for architects, who seem to shun putting things in writing. They are also wont to complain that you are overdocumenting, and may even be threatened by it, as they may consider it litigious. That complaint should generally be taken as a compliment, although it never is intended to be. Regardless of the negotiated level of documentation, there are some standard documents that are mandatory.

Application for payment

American Institute of Architects (AIA) publishes *G702 Application and Certificate for Payment*, and its accompanying worksheet *G703 Continuation Sheet for G702.*[1] It is a standard form for contracts in the industry, and the person in charge of billing should be literate in utilizing the system, which can be purchased as loose hard copy, or as a software, from the AIA. The G703 is structured with a schedule of values column, which the general contractor bills against each month. The progress is indexed by percentage, and the respective value of each line item is calculated. A retainer, usually 10%, is withheld, payable upon final completion, and the payment application is then notarized and issued. Depending on the architect, a good deal of negotiation can go into determining the value of each payment. If this is the case, the calculations should be a joint venture between the architect and the contractor, who won't necessarily get larger payments, but he will have his application approved sooner and hopefully be paid soon.

Short of the AIA documents, there must be some written accounting form to serve the same purpose. Verbal requests are not acceptable. The *Application for Payment* process will be discussed further in Chap. 6.

Acknowledgment of request for pricing/change in the work

Not only does an acknowledgment of request for pricing/change in the work confirm a change in the work, but in case your client didn't think it did, may acknowledge that you are treating the directive or found condition as an extra. Your proposal for the referenced changes should follow under separate cover. For projects that began with incomplete drawings, you will find yourself writing these notices quite often. A sample notification for an unforeseen condition or implied addition may be written as follows:

> Please be advised that the existing 4" sanitary line is oxidized and eroded to the point of needing replacement some thirty-feet past the tie-in point indicated. Kindly issue a sketch and RFP to remediate this condition.

Often a change in the work is discovered in a more subtle fashion:

> Pursuant to your red-lines of our sheet-metal shop drawings, kindly issue a specification, control wiring diagram, sketch, and RFP for the duct smoke detector that has been added to the return plenum from the kitchen.

There are other approaches and nuances you should be aware of, as these notifications can be sensitive issues:

> Please find enclosed a draft change order for the additional duct smoke detector you have detailed in shop drawing M16. As per our contract, we are not authorized to furnish and install this work without a signed change order.

Drawing and SK log

A sketch (SK) log should be kept and updated with each new SK issue, to reflect any approved design changes on the project. It should be circulated on a regular basis. This record is critical to the project, as it represents amendments to contract-design documents. Unlike SK logs, which are constantly updated, drawing logs should be complete no later than 25% into the construction phase. Otherwise, the design process begins to disrupt production sequencing. Of course, architects know this, and have a habit of issuing basic drawings in the form of sketches. By their nature, SKs should only clarify design intent, not provide it as drawings proper do. Too often, the flow of design information is not continuous, and not everyone has up-to-date or the same set of design documentation. This is often a problem at the administrative level, or with office help, whose responsibility it frequently is to see that any such information is distributed. Because many contractors delegate drawing distribution as an administrative level task, they don't monitor and track these transmittals as they do for things like payments and change orders. Sometimes a sketch or specification is hand-delivered in the field to the superintendent or project manager, who then files it away without copying anyone. Lack of proper documentation distribution is a dereliction of duty. The degree of mishap caused by poor documentation habits cannot be underestimated.

A sample-drawing log is given below (Table 4.1)

TABLE 4.1   Drawing Distribution Log

Drawing	Title	Issued
A000	Cover Sheet	4.15.02
A0001	General Notes	9.28.01
A002	Partition Types	4.15.02
A101	Construction Plans: 51 Floor	4.8.02
A102	Construction Plans: 52 Floor	4.15.02
A110	Power and Audio/Visual Plan—Legend	4.15.02
A111	Power and Audio/Visual Plan—51 Floor	4.15.02
A112	Power and Audio/Visual Plan—52 Floor	4.15.02
A121	Flooring Plan—51 Floor	4.8.02
A122	Flooring Plan—52 Floor	4.15.02
A123	Floor Details	12.17.01
A124	Floor Details	12.17.01
A125	Floor Details	12.17.01
A126	Floor Details	9.28.01
A201	Reflected Ceiling Plan—51 Floor	4.15.02
A202	Reflected Ceiling Plan—52 Floor	4.5.02
A203	Ceiling Details	4.15.02
A204	Ceiling Details	4.15.02
A500	Interior Elevations Finish Legend	4.15.02
A501	Interior Elevations—Elevator Lobby	4.15.02
A502	Interior Elevations E. Corr 5102; W. Corr. 5112	4.15.02
A503	Interior Elevations Ent. Hall St. 5103; Powder Room 5105; Dressing Room 5107	4.15.02
A504	Interior Elevations Living Room St. 5104	4.15.02
A505	Interior Elevations Bedroom Suite 5108	4.15.02
A506	Interior Elevations Bath1 5109; WC 5110; Shower 5111	4.15.02
A507	Interior Elevations Ent Hall St. 2, 5113; Powder Room 5115; Dressing Room 5116	4.15.02

TABLE 4.1 Drawing Distribution Log (*Continued*)

Drawing	Title	Issued
A508	Interior Elevations Living Room St. 2, 5114	4.15.02
A509	Interior Elevations Bedroom St. 2, 5117	4.15.02
A510	Interior Elevations Bath 2, 5118; WC 5119; Shower 5120	4.15.02
A520	Interior Elevations 52 Elevator Lobby 5201	4.15.02
A521	Interior Elevations 52 W. Corr. 5202	4.15.02
A522	Interior Elevations 52 Powder Room 5205; Office 5203	4.15.02
A523	Interior Elevations 52 Living Room 5204	4.15.02
A524	Interior Elevations 52 Library/Bedroom 5206	4.15.02
A525	Interior Elevations E. Corr. 5207	4.15.02
A526	Interior Elevations 52 Dressing Room 5208; Dressing Room 2, 5211	4.15.02
A527	Interior Elevations 52 Bath1, 5209; Bath2, 5212	4.15.02
A528	Interior Elevations 52 Spa 5210	4.15.02
A529	Interior Elevations 52 Bedroom 5213	4.15.02
A530	Interior Elevations 52 Pantry 5215	4.15.02
A600	Sections—Wall Finishes	12.17.01
A601	Sections—Window Conditions 51	12.17.01
A602	Sections—Window Conditions 52	12.17.01
A603	Sections—	9.28.01
A604	Sections—Built-in Millwork	9.28.01
A700	Door Schedules	12.17.01
A701	Door Types	12.17.01
A702	Door Jamb Details 51	9.28.01
A703	Door Details—Base	12.17.01
A704	Door Details	12.17.01
A705	Jamb Details	12.17.01
A706	Jamb Details	12.17.01
A801	Vanity Details	9.28.01
A802	Vanity Details	9.28.01
A803	Vanity Details	9.28.01
A804	Vanity Details	12.17.01
A805	Bath Tub Details	12.17.01

It was composed of a spreadsheet with several workbooks for each trade, and a summary sheet (shown). The summary sheet shows the working drawings, and the workbooks for each trade (not shown). Track the issues of the drawings through all their versions and permutations (Table 4.2). Make it a habit of keeping your own logs, and comparing them with the architects.

Some architects are very informal when implementing changes. They may draw up a rendering on a napkin or whisper in a mechanic's ear, neither of which is acceptable practice. This habit can also be inspired by the client, who feels he isn't obligated to document his requests in writing. Insist on written formal directives for any design information imparted by the architect before you agree to accommodate them. This is another requirement that some architects will balk at, however, good architects should do this without being asked. It can become difficult for them too, as a client may make many changes, which would require the architect to draft more design documentation for additional services for which he won't be paid. He shouldn't have to work for free any more than

TABLE 4.2 Amended Drawing Log

		Drawing Distribution	3/1/2006							
Drawing	Title	Issued	Rev	Rev	Rev	Rev	Rev	Rev	Rev	Rev
M1	Title Sheet, Abbreviations, and Symbols	9.28.01	11.30.01					4.5.02		
M2										
M3A	51 Floor HVAC Demolition Plan	9.28.01	11.30.01	12.10.01						
M3B	51 Floor HVAC New Work Plan	9.28.01	11.30.01	12.10.01		1.30.02		4.5.02		
M3C	51 Radiant Floor Heating							4.5.02		
M4A	52 Floor HVAC Demolition Plan	9.28.01	11.30.01	12.10.01						
M4B	52 Floor HVAC New Work Plan	9.28.01	11.30.01	12.10.01			2.19.02	4.5.02		
M4C	52 Radiant Floor Heating							4.5.02		
M5	53 Floor HVAC Demolition Plan	9.28.01	11.30.01							
M6	53 Floor HVAC New Work Plan	9.28.01	11.30.01				2.19.02			
M7	Detail Sheet	9.28.01	11.30.01				2.19.02			
M8	Schedule Sheet	9.28.01	11.30.01				2.19.02			
M9	Building Section Sheet 1	9.28.01	11.30.01				2.19.02			
M10	Building Section Sheet 2	9.28.01	11.30.01							
M11	Specification Sheet 1	9.28.01	11.30.01	12.10.01			2.19.02			
M12	Specification Sheet 2	9.28.01	11.30.01	12.10.01			2.19.02			
M13	Specification Sheet 3	9.28.01	11.30.01							
M13A	Specification Sheet 4	9.28.01	11.30.01				2.19.02			
M14	51, 52, 53 Senercomm Wiring Diagram & Specs.	9.28.01	11.30.01		12.17.01		2.19.02	4.5.02	5.17.02	6.05.02
M15	Riser Diagram 1	9.28.01	11.30.01							
M16	Riser Diagram 2	9.28.01	11.30.01							

you should have to undertake unofficial directives. If the architect only verbally requests extra work, you run the risk of not getting paid for it. Some grafter architects realize that contractors have great difficulty in getting paid for undocumented extras, and deliberately ask for extras off the record in hopes of getting work done for free.

Meeting minutes

Meeting minutes are one of the most useful, yet, underutilized management tools available to the industry. They are critical for tracking information on a project, and also a contactor's accountability. The minutes should also identify unresolved issues, set target dates for their resolution, and assign a responsible party for each task. Because so many issues may get resolved in job meetings, it is critical to document each one accurately. Copies of the minutes should be distributed to all subcontractors whose business has been discussed in a given meeting, whether they were present at the meeting or not. Otherwise, these people may be unaware of developments that concern them directly, especially if they are only represented in the minutes.

A meeting minute's format includes the following:

- Cover page: indicating when and where the meeting took place, and who attended
- Separate sections for each trade
- Tasks sorted into sections with target dates, and responsible parties
- Old minutes, or open items from earlier meetings. Old minutes should be revisited each subsequent meeting until they are closed

The taking of meeting minutes by a general contractor has different ramifications, than the minutes of the construction manager, as we shall see in the next chapter. As the construction manager may be concerned with building, he also happens to be the agent of the client. That is one reason why it is somewhat a conflict of interests when the construction manager is also the constructor. This being so, general contractors tend to reflect their own interests in their versions of meeting minutes, sometimes to the extent that the architect insists on generating his own minutes. Because the minutes become project documentation, what they say, and how people respond to them can sometimes be construed as provocative. The meeting forum is a convenient place for a general contractor to attempt to resolve issues, since the architect, and often the client will be present; hence, many decisions are made there. Therefore, one should be mindful of the content of the minutes and the way in which they are presented. While this sounds general and simplistic, it is no easy undertaking. Judging from the quality of minutes that are routinely taken, there is considerable room for improvement. On the one hand, verbatim accountings and stenographers are unwarranted, yet selective and interpretive minutes don't always present things the way everyone expected.

Request for information log

Requests for information (RFIs) are always done in writing; it must be said, for it is so common for verbal directives and other pertinent information to flow freely between the architect and the production team, or the owner and the production team. Enforce strict adherence to this rule, and make it clear that no RFI is considered closed without a written directive, even if you have to write it yourself. Each RFI should be entered into a log, and kept open until it is answered satisfactorily. The log should be brought to weekly job meetings for review (Table 4.3).

Notice the contents of the "Refer To" column of Table 4.3; they are digital file names and locations that contain the RFI information. Additionally, they can function as embedded hyperlinks to the respective files, that is, by clicking a mouse on the hyperlink, the referenced file will open (assuming it is on your hard drive, and correctly linked).

As I said, a contractor should issue as many necessary RFIs in the bidding stage as possible. Sometimes this isn't possible, especially when someone happens upon a condition during the production phase. There are a few reasons why getting RFIs out early is so important:

- The processing of RFIs during production can slow the pace of the work, or even stop the flow of work altogether.

- RFIs frequently require new or revised design documents, which often generate change orders. Waiting for both to happen can slow down the project.

- Unresolved issues, whatever stage they are in, make it difficult to create a coherent schedule, or to track one.

- By failing to address an RFI at the earliest possible time, a contractor can assume ownership of the work by what the architect may construe as an oversight on the contractor's part, that is, if he could have known, then he should have known. Architects typically make such a stipulation part of their general requirements, because such oversights can become problematic to resolve.

By clarifying in the bidding stage, the estimator has more complete information at his disposal in order to make an accurate estimate. In addition to the information requested, the contractor should indicate a date by which the said information must be furnished, just as he would stipulate a change order.

Submittal cover/submittal log

It is amazing how much protocol goes by the wayside regarding the business of issuing submittals and approvals. Often, only a passing comment or nod of the head from an architect is sufficient approval for a general contractor. On the other hand, the manner in which many submittals are presented by a general contractor can be so informal and unprofessional, that there is no sound basis for the architect to approve or reject.

Slow processing of submittals is often the biggest cause of administrative delays that can affect a project. Those who know this are vigilant in making their submittals as early as possible, and being aggressive in following up on them. They

TABLE 4.3   RFI Log with Hyperlinks

RFI Log

RFI #	Date	To	DWG	Description	Refer to	Directive
12.12.01.01	12.12.01	ENG	M14	Re control wiring diagram; E52-1 fan	..\MEP\12.12.01.01.doc	M14, 12.17
12.12.01.02	12.12.01	ARCH	P50D	Advise on TIC Demo schedule	..\MEP\12.12.01.02.doc	no response
12.17.01.01	12.17.01	ARCH	N/A	Laundry Chute	..\MEP\12.17.01.01 Laundry Chute.doc	Referred to TIC. See ENG comments: OPEN
12.18.01.01	12.18.01	ARCH	N/A	Lighting Fixture Mock Ups	..\Arch\12.18.01.01 Fixture Mock-Ups.doc	CLOSED
12.27.01.01	12.27.01	ARCH	GEN	Axis Line Reference Points	..\Arch\12.27.01.01 Axis line ref points.doc	CLOSED
12.27.01.02	12.27.01	ARCH	AV52	52 Floor AV Schematic; 51/52 Signal	..\Arch\12.27.01.02 52 Floor AV Schematic.doc	CLOSED
1.02.02.01	1.02.02	ARCH	A500	Wood Floor Mock Ups	..\Arch\1.02.02.01 Wood Floor Mock Ups.doc	CLOSED
1.08.02.01	1.08.02	ARCH	A121/2	Wood Floor Spec	..\Arch\1.07.02.01 Wood Floor Designation.doc	CLOSED
1.25.02.01	1.25.02	ARCH	A201	Ceiling height conflict	..\Arch\1.25.02 elec riser.doc	CLOSED
1.25.02.01	1.25.02	ARCH	A126	Wood Floor Substrate	..\Arch\1.25.02.01 sub floor.doc	CLOSED
1.28.02.01	1.28.02	ENG	P51/52	Plumbing Offsets	..\MEP\1.28.02 Plumbing off sets.doc	CLOSED
1.30.02.01	1.30.02	ARCH	Spec	Switch Plate Schedule	..\Arch\1.30.02 SWPL Finishes.doc	
2.04.02.01	2.04.02	ENG	N/A	Base Building Programs	..\Arch\2.4.02.01 Base Building.doc	
2.13.02.01	2.13.02	ENG		Motorized Mirror Panels	..\MEP\2.13.02.01 Motorized Panels.doc	
2.13.02.02	2.13.02	ENG		Electrical Distribution	..\MEP\2.13.02.02 EC spec.doc	CLOSED
2.14.02.01	2.14.02	ENG	*P	Fan Coil Drainage Systems	..\MEP\2.14.02.01 FDs.doc	CLOSED: drains to risers
2.14.02.02	2.14.02	ARCH	E	Additional Lutron Points	..\MEP\2.14.02.02 Additional Lutron Points.doc	

(*Continued*)

217

TABLE 4.3   RFI Log with Hyperlinks (Continued)

RFI Log

RFI #	Date	To	DWG	Description	Refer to	Directive
2.14.02.03	2.14.02	ARCH	M4B	In-floor Baffles and Grilles	..\Arch\2.14.02.03.doc	CLOSED
2.19.02.0	2.19.02	ENG	M14	Siemens	..\MEP\2.19.02 Siemens Schematic.doc	CLOSED
2.26.02.01	2.26.02	ENG		Service Hall Make-up Air	..\MEP\2.26.02 Air For Service Corridors.doc	CLOSED
2.28.02.01	2.28.02	ARCH	16500	Revised Lighting Fixture Schedule	..\Arch\2.28.02.01 Revised Fixture Schedule.doc	CLOSED
3.05.02.01	3.05.02	ARCH	N/A	WP Details at Exterior Walls at Elec. Panels	..\Arch\3.05.02.01 WP detail.doc	CLOSED
3.06.02.01	3.06.02	ARCH	N/A	Future LV/Control Programs	..\Arch\3.06.02.01 PTP LV.doc	
3.07.02.01	3.07.02	ARCH	A201/2	Access Doors for Riser Valves	..\Arch\3.07.02.01 Access Doors reopened.doc	REOPENED
3.13.02.01	3.13.02	ARCH	M6	SW 10 Taps on 53	..\MEP\3.13.02.01 53 Risers.doc	CLOSED
4.16.02.01	4.16.02	ARCH	Spec.	Electrical Fixture Specifications	..\Arch\4.16.02.01 Light Fixtures.doc	CLOSED
4.17.02.01	4.17.02	ARCH	E12	Dimming Zones	..\MEP\4.17.02.01 Dimming Zones.doc	CLOSED
4.18.02.01	4.18.02	ARCH	Spec.	SIS Adhesive	..\Arch\4.18.02.01 SIS adhesive.doc	
4.18.02.02	4.18.02	ARCH	Spec.	Type C Fixture	..\Arch\4.18.02.02 Type C Fixture.doc	CLOSED
4.24.02.01	4.24.02	ARCH	Spec.	Electrical Fixture Specifications	..\Arch\4.24.02.01 Light Fixture Sched..doc	CLOSED
5.03.02.01	5.03.02	ARCH	A101/2	Attic Stock Window Location Details	..\Arch\5.3.02.01 attic stock window wall detail.doc	
5.15.02.01	5.15.02	ARCH	M14	Sensors/Siemens RFI#1	..\MEP\5.15.02.01 Sensor Cuts.doc	
5.23.02.02	5.23.02	ARCH	E2	Electrical, Misc.	..\MEP\5.23.02.01 Electrical Misc..doc	
5.23.02.02	5.23.03	ARCH	M3C/M4C	Radiant Heat Zones Wiring	..\MEP\5.23.02.02 Radiant heat wiring.doc	
5.28.02.01	5.28.02	ARCH	M7	Fire Smoke Dampers	..\MEP\5.28.02.01 Damper SOO.doc	

also know which to prioritize, and which will be the most difficult. The contract documents should indicate the processing period for submittals. For an average project, 20 days should be the limit an architect deliberates over a submittal; and that would be for the more complex details. Twenty days is industry standard. If there is to be a resubmittal, either the window for the original submittal, or the window for the resubmittal should be about 10 days. Many architects will chafe at foreshortened review periods; however, if the client is driving an aggressive schedule, the contractor must push in this way. For submittals that also must be approved by an engineer, you may allow an extra 10 days. When there is a submittal involving both architect and engineer, it is good practice to copy each party, and request that they review the submittal simultaneously, rather than wait for sequential review. Architects tend to choose to not honor this request, as they will want to review the engineer's comments before they issue their own. Otherwise, it seems like double work to them. While that remains a moot point, projects with aggressive schedules should incorporate reduced review times for the design team, as the schedule will not afford a generous review period. Architects generally are not compensated to expedite submittal reviews, and don't appreciate the pressure. Once they know a project is to be expedited, they should realize that submittal review periods may be shortened, yet very often they do not make any adjustments to their approach. Contractors must go on record as having advised the architect as to expedited reviews, or else the architects can't be expected to comply.

When a project schedule is aggressive or accelerated, a general contractor should take an aggressive approach to the resubmittal process by insisting on working meetings with the design team and detailer (draftsperson) in order to iron out kinks, as opposed to a casual sequester. Again, architects are loath to sign-up for this exercise; as such meetings will be time consuming, especially if the submittal is not far along in development; indeed, their time is frequently wasted by incomplete and erroneous submittals. Additionally, by the time working meetings are requested, the architect's typically meager contract administration budget for the construction phase has long been exhausted. However, if their original designs are well developed, so should the corresponding submittal, which would have been scrutinized by the project manager before he passed it along to the design team. Otherwise, a working meeting could waste time.

Every presentation made to the architect for approval should include a submittal cover page that (a) identifies the contents enclosed, and (b) includes an area for signature and comment. This information is entered into a submittal log (Table 4.4), which will track the status of each submittal as it goes back and forth between the architect and the contractor.

The sequence of facilitating submittals is as follows:

- Create cover template for project
- Create log for project
- Create submittal requirement list. The architect should also indicate required submittals in his project manual
- Generate target submittal and response deadlines for each submittal
- Review procedure with architect, subcontractors, and in-house production team

TABLE 4.4 Submittal Log

Shop Drawing and Sample Record

Project:	Residence, 123 Main	Spec: Lighting
Trade:	Electric	Section#: 16500
Vendor:	XYZ	

Contractor	Modern Builders Inc.
Architect	
Engineer	
Designer	

Received	Drawing/sample#	Title	Sample	# Received	TO Date sent	Date R't'd	Approved	App. as noted	Revise/resubmit	Rejected	Contractor	Owner	Field	File
5.2.02	1 FA: Nulux			8	5.2.02									
5.2.02	2 FA1: Nulux			8	5.2.02									
5.2.02	3 FC: Starfire XF			8	5.2.02									
5.2.02	4 FK: Bartco BL250-32,40			8	5.2.02	5.23.02		X						
5.2.02	5 FL: CSL ST27W			8	5.2.02	5.23.02		X						
5.2.02	6 FQ1: Belfer 7215WH			8	5.2.02	5.23.02				X				
5.2.02	7 FQ2: ELP175THWW			8	5.2.02	5.23.02			X					
5.2.02	8 FAF: Bega 2022			8	5.2.02	5.23.02		X						
5.2.02	9 FAG: Tokistar			8	5.2.02	5.23.02		X						
5.2.02	10 FAJ: Kert Versen H7816WH			8	5.2.02	5.23.02				X				
5.2.02	11 FAP: CJ Lighting 1850 T8			8	5.2.02	5.23.02		X						
5.2.02	12 FAT: Mercury 35E-2-32-OCT9A-ELB-XXX-20GA			8	5.2.02									

Submittal process general approach

- Time and date stamp incoming submittals, enter into log
- Review submittal for compliance. If it meets criteria, go to next step. Otherwise, return to subcontractor for revision
- Create submittal cover and transmittal letter
- Issue at least four copies to design team
- Record transaction into log
- Confirm receipt
- Copy project manager or superintendent
- Follow up architect for status: advise of possible delays, if necessary

Upon receipt of architect's review:

- Stamp and enter into log
- Confirm stamp or signature (status)
- Make copies and redistribute as necessary
- If rejected or to be resubmitted, repeat general approach
- If approved, distribute to production team, and archive into files

In the absence of a submittal cover with an area for sign-off, there are some acceptable alternatives one can use, shown below; however, because they are the exceptions, and won't conform to your general approach, should be your first choice. You should also amend your contract to indicate any arrangement deviating from the contract requirements, as it will likely require formal procedures.

Alternative submittal approval methods

- For on-site installations, the architect's signature or initials on the product itself are sufficient.
- Confirmation letter of a verbal approval: this letter should indicate that should the disposition be other than "approved," it must be administered in writing.
- Audio/video recording of a verbal approval.
- A line item in the meeting minutes.
- E-mail confirmation.[2]

While there is no set format for submittal covers, there must be consistency with the format you use, such as the Construction Specifications Institute (CSI) index; you should submit every submittal in the same format, and establish a consistent numbering system for the purpose of tracking. Thus consider the relation of the submittal cover to the submittal log, of which it is a subcomponent. Additionally, be sure that *at least four copies* are issued to the architect.

A word to the wise.   With the onslaught of litigation against design professionals, many have become leery of stamping or signing submittals from general contractors. This practice seems to have become so commonplace that many general contractors don't bother waiting for signatures or stamps of approval from an architect. This effectively puts the contractor at risk, should there be future problems regarding the work. No more should you process unsigned or unstamped submittals, than you would an unsigned change order. If you make submittals without a cover page, you will not likely receive a formal sign-off or approval. Every submittal should have a cover, be tracked and entered into a log, and provide a space for comments and stamps or signatures. Also, beware of nebulous stamps, such as "reviewed" or "no exception taken," which in themselves are no true indication of approval or rejection, regardless of how many times they are mistaken for one. Only "approved," "approved as noted," and "furnish as corrected" are acceptable. The architect's stamp and his initial or signature should also be part of the sign-off.

Change orders/change order log

The organization and tracking of a project ridden with change orders can be a formidable undertaking, especially if there is constant haggling and negotiating. Sooner or later production logistics will be affected. In some cases, unresolved change orders can be such an inhibition to progress that a contractor feels he has no choice but to finally execute the work without authorization and move on. In fact, the architect and owner may insist on it, despite that not being their prerogative. In either case, the work is done without proper authorization or integration into the contract.

A change order log should be kept, and updated at least weekly with new change orders, dispositions on existing change orders, and reissued change orders (Table 4.5). Just like the RFI log, if the change order log has a lot of unfinished business, it should be reviewed each week until closure can be reached. The rest of the job team might tire of this exercise, but it has to be done. Deadlines should be issued for pending change orders, indicating when the delay will begin to affect other tasks, and possibly, price guaranty duration. The change order log has breakouts for all the subcomponents of each change order, a status for each, and completion percentages to bill against. The actual documents can be hyper linked for quick access.

Change orders can go through several permutations before they are approved. For that reason, we have said that an AIA *G701 Change Order* should only be drafted when approval is imminent. It's up to the general contractor what format will best suit the change order log; however, there is some basic information, aside from the obvious that should appear in all change order logs, chiefly, status, issue, and response dates, which can sometimes be more important than the cost:

- Copy of working change order and its backup
- Initialization date—from, RFP or notice of conditions
- Status

TABLE 4.5   Change Order Log

AIA#	CO#	Sub 1	Date sub	Date app	Trade	Vendor	Description	Base	GC	Fee	Total	Comp.	Amount due
	1R1	3.8.00	3.14.z00	3.29.00	Tile		Revised tile schedule	$ 6,056	$ 606	$ 666	$ 7,328	50%	$ 3,664
	2R2	3.8.00	4.3.00	4.4.00	Arch. Mill.		JMCO 7-10	$ 7,975	$ 798	$ 1,075	$ 9,848	50%	$ 4,924
	3R1	3.8.00	4.7.00		Plumbing		Floor drain, hose bibb	$ 3,453	$ 345	$ 380	$ 4,178		
	4		VOID		Glazing		Change to Starfire at skylight						
	5R2	3.9.00	3.29.00	3.31.00	Doors		Change to door schedule	$ 7,500	$ 750	$ 825	$ 9,075	50%	$ 4,538
	6		3.10.00		Carpentry		Batt insulation	$ 2,125	$ 213	$ 234	$ 2,571		
	7R2	3.10.00	3.13.00	3.14.00	Carpentry		Rem. Ply. replace w/Q deck	$ 1,959	$ 196	$ 215	$ 2,370	50%	$ 1,185
	8		3.10.00	3.14.00	Arch. Mill.		JM CO: cabinet and sill	$ 2,900	$ 290	$ 319	$ 3,509	50%	$ 1,755
	9R2	3.31.00	3.31.00	4.13.00	HVAC		Various	$ 6,659	$ 666	$ 732	$ 8,057	50%	$ 4,029
	10R1		3.28.00		Arch. Mill./Carp.		Shoe cabinet and framing	$ 26,325	$ 2,633	$ 2,896	$ 31,853		
	11		4.3.00		Structural		Designs, extras	$ 9,370	$ 937	$ 1,031	$ 11,338		
	12R1	4.3.00	4.7.00		Fireplace		Fireplace hearth extension	$ 8,508	$ 851	$ 936	$ 10,295		
	13		4.3.00		Plumbing		Runtals	$ 5,567	$ 557	$ 612	$ 6,736		
	14R1		—		FAI louvre								
	15R1		4.10.00	4.13.00	HVAC		Humidification	$ 9,000	$ 900	$ 990	$ 10,890	50%	$ 5,445
	16R1		4.6.00	4.6.00	Arch. Mill.		Walnut upgrade	$ 11,280	$ 1,128	$ 1,241	$ 13,649	50%	$ 6,824
	17R1	4.6.00			Elec. Fx		Actual fixtures	$ 18,287	$ 1,829	$ 2,012	$ 22,127		
	18	—			Metal		Upgrade canopies						
	19		4.11.00		Carpentry		Various	$ 2,860	$ 286	$ 315	$ 3,461		
	20		4.12.00		Hardware		F/I Butler	$ 12,742	$ 1,274	$ 1,402	$ 15,418		
	21		4.12.00		Skylight		Two skylights, glazed and flashed	$ 7,320	$ 732	$ 805	$ 8,857		
	22		4.12.00		Security		Security and coordination	$ 4,744	$ 474	$ 522	$ 5,740		
	23				Electrical		Revised electric budget	$ 7,450	$ 745	$ 820	$ 9,015		
	24		4.14.00		Arch. Mill.		Per SK 58.1	$ 1,650	$ 165	$ 182	$ 1,997		
											$ —		
											$ —		
											$ —		
			Total					$163,730	$14,989	$16,685	$157,285		$32,363

- Date of issuance to client
- Date received with disposition from client
- Subsequent reissue dates
- Subsequent return dates

Schedule updates. You should track your schedule and update it at least once a month, if for no other reason than for your own peace of mind. A client may also request an updated schedule, especially if the project is off track. If you do issue an updated schedule, you should either make a presentation of it to the architect, where you can explain the logic and answer questions, or you should include annotated notes. Clients are not in the business of learning how to read schedules, and they shouldn't have to be. In most contracts, there is no schedule update requirement, or if there is, it is loosely enforced. Moreover, contractors don't generally issue updated schedules to their architects, just new milestone dates. In the event of a delay, a memo or "notice of delay" should be issued to the architect stating:

- The nature of the delay
- The cause for the delay
- The anticipated duration of the delay
- The effect the delay will have on present and near-future operations
- The anticipated effect the delay will have on the overall project duration and budget

Why is it so important to document every little delay? Because the aggregate of small delays can add up to one big substantial delay. The contractor who documents each delay will be in a better position to explain the sequence of events leading to the overall delay, whereas the contractor who doesn't keep track will be at a loss to retroactively justify how and why a given project will be delayed. Moreover, he did not duly notify his client of such delays as they were realized. Documenting each delay is a tedious job, and each instance has the potential of infuriating the architect and client. In some cases, a contractor feels it is not in his best interests to rock the boat in this way, which is perfectly understandable. However, this doesn't mean that you forgo the requirement of documenting each delay; only that you don't share all of this information with the architect. In that case, delays are documented, but the architect is not duly notified. Thus, a compromise is warranted. For example, a 1-year project may have recorded 75 delays varying in duration from 1 to 20 days. So as not to besiege the architect with 75 notice-of-delay memos, a contractor may decide to notify the architect of only those delays that are 5 days or more in length. Should he be pressed to justify the remaining delays, he will produce his records. Scheduling update memos are discussed at length in Chaps. 3 and 5. Note that all delays are not treated equally—a task may be delayed, and delay other work without upsetting the substantial completion date. This would be considered a passive delay, whereas a delay affecting the overall project deadline would be more serious.

Discrepancies in Design Documents with Existing Conditions

Notification of unforeseen existing condition

- Behind closed walls, existing conditions often don't meet people's expectations.
- Architects don't always accurately show the relation of a new program to existing conditions.

The above two considerations should always necessitate a notification to the architect—it is so written in most contracts, or found in the project manual general requirements. The timing of such notifications can be critical. If a contractor notifies an architect of a critical design conflict, 6 months into the project, such as adjusted overall dimensions, it becomes a moot point that the architect may have made a mistake. The larger issue is that it took too long for the contractor to discover it. By not issuing timely notification, the architect may have missed the window of opportunity to make the necessary design adjustments to obviate the delay. The failure or poor timing of such notifications can effectively pass responsibility onto the contractor.

Documentation referencing any of the above should not offend the eye of your architect. Such documents are standard protocol, and should be issued regardless of the response they get. Of course, if an architect responds defensively to your documentation, you will want to do your best to explain that you are merely doing your job. Such a notification needn't advise of an impending change order; this should be done separately.

Production Department Job Descriptions

Job descriptions are essential to facilitate positions at all levels—no employee should be without one. With a job description, not only does everyone know their own and each other's work, but also the opportunity for oversights and redundancies is kept to a minimum. Additional job descriptions are discussed in Chaps. 2, 5, and 6.

Project manager sample job description

Title: Project Manager

Report To: GM

Objectives

Administration and implementation of jobs as follows:

Preconstruction

- Plan and prepare project Gantt chart with deliverable milestones
- Plan and prepare bill of assemblies
- Prepare job directory

- Prepare project manuals
- Meet with staff to coordinate buyouts
- Plan and begin mechanical electrical and plumbing (MEP) schematic process
- Plan for long-lead items and purchase orders (POs)
- Ensure that all insurance certificates are issued correctly and are up-to-date
- Coordinate with building management start-up
- Coordinate start-up with staff and subcontractors

Construction

- Mobilize project
- Track project progress and update schedule
- Maintain and track drawing, shop drawing, sample and submittal, and RFI logs weekly
- Manage office job folders and files
- Attend job meetings weekly, and record and issue minutes
- Coordinate special production meetings as necessary
- Maintain ultimate responsibility for schedule, budget, and quality control
- Issue and track change orders
- Track general conditions and budgets, or allowances
- Document any modifications or consequential information
- Process continuation sheets, monitoring progress
- Notify of check requests
- Solicit and process waivers
- Generate and implement punch list

Closeout

- Execute punch list
- Arrange for sign-offs
- Issue warranty/manual package to client
- Arrange for end-user demonstrations
- Demobilize job
- Closeout job with architect: accounts receivable (AR)
- Closeout job with vendors: accounts payable (AP)
- Closeout job file—prepare for archiving
- Issue postmortem analysis
- Arrange house-warming package

The failure of project managers to produce their paperwork will make their job more difficult, but it will make the general manager's job impossible, as he is reliant on this documentation to command the big picture. In the absence of it, he must solicit and search for the information piecemeal. An informed general manager requires some basic documentation:

Weekly

Progress report

Meeting minutes

Change order log

Submittal log

Monthly

The profit and loss report (P&L) for each project

Updated schedule

While this list includes only five items, the project manager and general manager who subscribe to and enforce this concept are the exceptions. For the most part, management documentation goes unrecorded, unpublished, or done incorrectly. Project administration is done on an as-needed basis—when someone asks for, or the situation demands. One of the companies referred to in Chap. 1 suffered from just such a calamity. The general manager asked for the above documentation from three different project managers. Over a period of 8 months, out of a minimum requirement of 168 required documents, he received none. Is it any wonder this company could not put work in place?

Superintendent sample job description.   Except for small projects, and projects that don't require constant supervision, every residential project should have a full-time field superintendent. Many residential projects have superintendents, but only on a part-time basis—an unacceptable arrangement. As I said, it is not unusual for the superintendent to become the *de facto* project manager. This arrangement tends to be happenstance; however, it may also be calculated by savvy contractors who know that their superintendent can handle the responsibilities of both, but regrettably, it tends to be a matter of cost cutting by the contractor—their budget may typically not afford a decent project manager. This will be the downfall of many a project, and will also compromise the integrity of a company in the long run. On more complex projects, without the necessary management team in place, you will find yourself "flying by the seat of your pants."

Of the aforementioned duplex project, the contractor did have the cognizance to hire an experienced site supervisor, however, the rest of his staff, being unknowledgeable and uncooperative, handicapped the supervisor. The infrastructure and systems of the contractor's company were substandard or nascent at best. To their credit, there were members of this company who were leery of the project; however, they were in no position to ameliorate the situation either. In other words, this project was not adequately qualified by the general contractor. Worse, denial inhibited him from taking corrective measures, and the project went the rout of dysfunction and litigation. The advice given to the client was, "Either find a new general contractor, or sell the apartment." The point is that although a project may have a first-rate superintendent or project manager, if he doesn't receive the necessary support from his company, he will fail his mission.

The following tasks are germane to the superintendent's job description. Some of them may be shared or done by the project manager.

Preconstruction

1. Review design documentation and contract documents
2. Review job book with project manager
3. Review schedule
4. Meet with subcontractors
5. Arrange for mobilization: crew, tools, and equipment
6. Coordinate site logistics: storage, office, staging areas, refuse, protections, and the like

Construction

1. Provide access to site
2. Closeout site daily: clean, sweep, rubbish removal, shut-offs, locks, and the like
3. Generate daily reports
4. Manage time sheets
5. Coordinate deliveries: store and inventory on-site material, tools, and machinery
6. Protect finished work
7. Attend job meetings
8. Interface with project manager
9. Coordinate trades
10. Review shop drawings
11. Maintain drawing log
12. Process RFIs
13. Manage HAZMAT book and safety programs

Closeout

1. Demobilize site: tools and materials
2. Check all equipment, devices, and fixtures for safe and correct operation
3. Install new filters on any equipment, such as an air handler that has been running during construction process. Some equipment should be serviced, depending on exposure

4. Issue as-builts

5. Issue valve and shut-off locations to client (Table 4.6)

6. Secure and organize company files

7. Final cleaning

8. Walk through with client, architect, and project manager

9. Meetings with factory commissioning: training and installations

Laborers.   An overlooked and undervalued asset, laborers are important to any project. They are the general contractor's foot soldiers, and will be responsible for a large portion of the general conditions. The trick is to have the right number of laborers on the project, and to be diligent in facilitating them. Too few laborers,

TABLE 4.6   Control and Shut-off Directory

Room	Type	Location
Bath 1	Whirlpool motor	Lower right corner, tub skirt
Bedroom 1	Exhaust fan	Above dresser
	PTAC access	SW corner
	ACU 2 access	SE corner (service by removing flooring)
Bath 2	CW/HW riser valves	SW corner, below WC
Bedroom 2	PTAC access	SW corner
	ACU 1 access	NW corner (service by removing flooring)
Kitchen	Gas valve	Lower right cabinet, below range
	Motorized WD valves	Behind cabinet at overhang counter
	WD overflow sensor/reset	Inside lower cabinet at overhang counter
	Ice maker line angle stop	Below sink
	Motorized radiator valve	Behind sink
	CW/HW riser valves	Lower left range cabinet
Mech. Closet	AHU 2 access	
	CP1 access	
Living Room	Motorized radiator valve	Radiator enclosure
	Gas valve	In-floor, opposite fireplace
	PTAC access	NE corner
Dressing Room	CP 2, 3	Interior AP NE corner
	Humidifier access	AP NE corner
	AHU1 motor	AP N ceiling
	AHU 1 filter and coil	AP S ceiling
	Humidifier wand	AP N ceiling
	Exhaust fan	AP N ceiling
	Humidifier CW supply	AP N ceiling, E face of column
Family Room	Motorized valve	Radiator enclosure
Master Bedroom	PTAC access	E wall
	CW/HW riser valves	Interior AP column
Master Bath	Boiler unit	Behind center bay of vanity
	In-floor heating T'stat	Righ center bay of vanity

All appliances and plumbing fixtures provided with angle stop valves
All radiators provided with shut-off valves

and you are understaffed; you don't have the man power to do what you need. The site will get messy and disorderly, safety may be compromised, and the integrity of the project will suffer. Too many laborers will tend to decrease their output to fit the workload. Naturally, overstaffing is a waste of resources.

It should be said that many construction workers, especially laborers, are by and large either uneducated, illegal aliens, or non-English speaking. Some of them will appear to be rough around the edges, making some people uncomfortable. This is not meant as a criticism, however, it must be understood that residential clients can be squeamish of the types of individuals you bring into their home, especially if they are storing their furnishings, or the project remains partly furnished during construction. High-end residential construction mandates that all workers observe an acceptable level of comportment, therefore, be wise in selecting workers for your projects. There is a special vernacular that applies to high-end construction in particular, and your men must be fluent in it.

General approach and milestones: anatomy of production.   Every project has a critical path, as was discussed in Chap. 3. For a typical residential project, some of the major production milestones might look like this:

- Layout approval
- MEP coordination
- Layout (plan) 100%
- MEP at partitions 100%
- Close walls (white box[3] part 1)
- MEP at ceilings 100%
- Close ceilings (white box part 2)
- Substantial completion
- Punch list
- Completion

These are the larger tasks, which are driven by all the smaller ones. The commencement of each is contingent upon completion of its predecessor. Some of these milestones tend to correspond with what we regard as critical path tasks, discussed in Chap. 3. When the project is discussed in broad terms, these milestones will be continually referenced, as they should be. If your payment schedule is milestone based, it will likely be an analog of the above sequence. The life of a project through its main phases can be conceived as an allegory of *The Divine Comedy* without the fulfillment of paradise (completion and final payment), whereas the build-out is an allusion to the *Inferno*, and substantial completion is an endless *Purgatorio*.

Mobilization.   Once the staff needed to implement your project is activated, you are ready to start your project. Many like to hit the ground running, a show of zeal;

however, this effort shouldn't preclude deliberate action. High-end residential work has its own set of criteria for mobilization, which will differ considerably from other types of work. This will bc evident when you bring in salty tradesmen who work in other more vigorous sectors, who aren't used to the kid-glove approach. The following is a mobilization checklist for the average project:

- Review project and strategy with all production team members.
- Secure necessary permits and perforated set (stamped set of drawings).
- Notify building owner (if necessary), and/or client of intent to mobilize site.
- Photograph and document existing conditions of site and adjacent tenants/owners as required. Also notify them in writing of intent to start, with contact telephone numbers.
- Circulate personnel information to design team and owner.
- Prepare lists of materials and tools necessary to mobilize the site.
- Issue fire extinguishers, and first-aid kits.
- Issue site documentation: drawings, HAZMAT books, employment law required documentation, and safety tools—signs, markers, caution tape, and the like.
- Arrange for production team to man site.

Predemolition

On just about any project, save for condo conversions and new space, tear-out and demolition of existing conditions will be required to facilitate the new design. Before demolition begins in earnest, in addition to mobilization tasks, the following must take place before ground is broken.

Protections. Safeguards against property damage and personal injury must be taken before any work begins. Some projects require extensive protections, such as building lobbies with ornate finishes. These protections are a common place for contractors to cut costs, as they are labor intensive. For high-end residential, skimping on protections would be an unconscionable circumstance; high-end clients take it for granted that you will effect comprehensive protections. These protections should be done neatly, be changed when damaged or soiled, and care should be taken into consideration regarding the surface area beneath and also that the protection is both appropriate and adequate. You will repeat this process later, after you have installed your own work that needs protection. Projects where some existing spaces are to remain as-is, or that have owner furnishings stored on-site, require a higher level of protection vigilance. Surprisingly, it may seem simpler or cheaper to include an area for construction than to exclude it. The respective tradesmen and personnel should be consulted as to the correct protection material, as some materials are reactive or can damage certain types of surfaces when they come into contact with them, for instance, certain types of tape adhered to different finished wood floors and stone.

Inspection.   The production team, seeing the site for the first time, must conduct its own thorough investigation to familiarize themselves with site conditions, and report any discrepancies, or other problems. They may look through a different lens than your estimator and sales people, and thus have valuable insights. Knowing that disconnects and temps are prerequisites to demolition, they will want to locate all shut-off valves, and verify that all valves are holding.

At this time, they should also consider logistics, such as the following:

- Locations of temporary service tie-ins
- Key distribution and site security
- Safety program
- Emergency contact information
- Shipping and receiving areas
- Staging areas: shanties, tool sheds, refuse, and materials
- Employee changing, personal storage, eating, and washing areas
- Location of site office
- Location of meeting area

Disconnects and temporary facilities.   MEP disconnects are a prerequisite to demolition and removals. This work must be left to the respective trades. Do not let anyone conduct demolition where there are live electrical or plumbing lines. Remember, demolition teams tend to be unskilled laborers, and they may not be aware of these precautions. In apartment buildings, building shut-downs are often required to open and isolate a line. These shutdowns often must be coordinated in advance. Additionally, you may need to have respective standby mechanics on-site during the demolition process. In some jurisdictions, this is a requirement. Once disconnects have been done, temporary MEPs must be installed for practical purposes, and per Occupational Safety & Health Administration (OSHA). These typically are electrical receptacles, lighting, running water, and heating. Some buildings may require a temporary sprinkler loop.

Often, in older buildings, there are existing plumbing or heating branch valves not holding or missing altogether. These should have been identified in a predemolition meeting with your plumber or mechanic, and the building must arrange to shut off the line at the closest valve, usually in the basement. Before the shutdown takes place and disconnects begin, notify the client that this would be an ideal time to install new valves as necessary, as waiting will be more costly and require another shutdown.

Demolition and removals

After MEP disconnects are inspected, valves and plugs tested, temps are in place, the demolition is ready to begin. Depending on the scope of the work, sequencing may vary. A typical residential demolition process may look something like this:

- Protections
- Salvage: any material to be saved is removed and stored
- Drain down and MEP fixture removal
- Strip-out: refers to the removal of finishes, such as built-in cabinetry, doors, wall tile or paneling, and the like
- Substrate removal: ceilings, especially drop-ceilings are first removed, then wall finishes
- Partitions (nonload bearing) and framing
- Floor finishes and substrates

The superintendent has a special responsibility in the demolition process, which can't be passed off to a foreman. For his part, he must debrief the demolition team foreman, and walk the job with him. He must be aware of removal sequencing, such that he knows where he must be at a given time. Much demolition is known as *selective*, or those removals which are partial, dimensioned, or need to have a hard boundary to adjoining components. The superintendent will indicate with broad marker or spray paint any such areas. Some selective demolition is better suited to a skilled carpenter. Have the estimator break this work out from the demolition contractor's scope of work, and reassign it as required. In other words, a skilled mechanic may be called upon to do more complicated removals. If the estimator doesn't highlight sensitive areas, the superintendent must still be diligent in scoping out any possibilities.

The demolition process can be vigorous and, at times, dangerous—sometimes the site may resemble a war zone. Removal contractors tend to be unskilled. The superintendent must manage the process, with special attention to safety—particularly means and methods used for removal, sensitive areas such as MEP risers and valves, and work to remain. The debris should be removed off site as it is stripped out. The demolition phase is notorious for occurrences of damage and accidents, which is why you should take extra pains to hire qualified people to do it. Additionally, insist that helmets, gloves, hearing protection, work boots, and goggles are worn by all demolition personnel, as required (by OSHA). In some apartments and other buildings, demolition is prohibited during business hours. Often there is a short window of operation, which adds to the already hectic pace.

Inspection.   Subsequent to demolition and removals, all MEP valves and plugs must be inspected again after the lines are reloaded to verify that they are holding; this inspection includes new valves and plugs, existing valves and plugs, and preexisting[4] valves and plugs. Typically, temporary lighting must be restrung after the initial demolition as it is generally tacked along a ceiling, which is later to be removed. At this time, you should conduct a survey of newly exposed and preexisting conditions, and advise the architect as to types and locations. As I have said, it is stated in some general requirements that the contractor is responsible for preexisting conditions. This isn't really fair, and technically, is not legally enforceable. Even after postdemolition inspection, a contractor should not be held responsible for unknown preexisting conditions, assuming that such knowledge was not reasonably evident. As part of the survey process, it is the architect's responsibility to probe and investigate conditions that could affect the design before he issues the working drawings. Too often, this is left to the contractor. If the contractor misses something, he may even be asked to take responsibility for an omission. However, if a contractor is aware, and does not inform the client of such a condition, the circumstances change dramatically. For this reason the architect should either conduct his own inspection, or accompany the general contractor on his, thereby taking some ownership of the responsibility for preexisting conditions.

The purpose of the postdemolition inspection is for the architect to note any glaring design discrepancies, and for him to then make the changes in the design documents. A more complete survey will be taken in the layout phase. But for the contractor, the inspection is also conducted in order to confirm what, if any damage was done in the demolition process. It is not unusual for a pipe to loosen or rupture during the vigorous demolition period, only to burst weeks later, or for a rotten steel beam to be unexcavated. Detailed reports should indicate the root cause of any damages; for example, if a joint is found to be leaking after demolition, it may also have leaked before demolition, or been in such a state that it was predisposed to leaking, once exposed to disturbance, no matter how mild. Frequently, general contractors are blamed and assigned responsibility for preexisting conditions of which they had no control over.

Postdemolition inspection checklist

- Violations: code, building department, and fire department
- Live lines entering space with no local shut-off
- Disconnect live lines feeding other apartment units
- Preexisting exposed MEP conditions that are no longer safe and/or code compliant
- Rupture of in-slab or in-wall piping
- ACM (asbestos containing material) installations
- Inspect neighboring apartments for damage, especially below the site
- Preexisting structural damage: rotten steel, concrete, and the like
- Evidence of past leaks or breaches from water or sanitary lines
- Any unforeseen conditions not consistent with the design plan

Any of the above must be reported to the architect as soon as possible.

Axes lines and benchmarks.   Following the demolition, the architect may ask for a survey of existing conditions, as he may not have been able to order one with the existing work still in place. Such a survey can range from an informal walk-through, to a full-blown scaled drawing, which is then compared to the prospective design. This latter can be time consuming and costly, however, contractors are seldom asked to do it. Such a survey would, among other things, indicate square, level, and plumb of the existing walls, however, the chief concern will be with overall dimensions—that the new program will fit the space. Based on these findings, a reference point will be designated, such as a long wall or a course of brickwork, or the architect may be asked to furnish reference points, as well as benchmarks (for elevation), if he has not done so already. The line or plane of these reference points will be projected to determine the boundaries of the layout. All installations will be referenced from these points. It is therefore important to also have a written record of the benchmarks, such as on the as-builts, as they will eventually be covered up by the program. A sample request to an architect for approval of reference points is provided:

> Pursuant to our discussion, yesterday, we shall move ahead, this Saturday, 1.5, with striking axes lines as follows:
> We will find the center points between east and west shear walls. From there, we will offset four right angles to form a square about the core wall. We will also lay radials perpendicular to center axes points to check alignment of MOs, and poured concrete. We are expecting you to inspect these axes, particularly their relationship to pre-existing walls, Monday morning. Pending your approval, we can proceed sketching the following day.
> If there are discrepancies, which there likely will be, we can hopefully make them up in the perimeter framing, without compromising the integrity of the layout. Such modifications need not be done now, but should be decided before we lay-out, no sooner than the second week of February.
> To clarify, all future layouts will be struck from central axes, as opposed to simple off-set dimensions from existing structure, as they appear. Only in this manner, can we deliver a truly symmetrical layout.

The x and y axes points should be struck with an indelible marker or scored, and then sealed in, with lacquer. The z-axes should be struck to define a constant datum for elevation. These axes lines should be checked, and double-checked, as they will dictate the final footprint of the entire project. They should be maintained so that they are always highly visible. A sketch referencing the location of these points should also be made in the event that they are defaced or lost, such that they can accurately be reestablished.

For high-end projects, the tolerance, or degree of differential allowable is at a minimum. One-eighth inch variance in 8 ft of a level plane, such as a floor or ceiling is typical. Architectural mill workers and metal workers in the high-end sector work with $\frac{1}{64}$ in., as their machinery is that accurate. Consider this when your axes lines and benchmarks are to be struck—was a chalk line used to demark the axes lines? Chalk lines tend to deflect when you snap them. Additionally, the width of the chalk line form one side to the other may vary up to $\frac{3}{16}$ in. Thus, the laser level has virtually all but replaced chalk line axes lay-outs. Assuming it is calibrated correctly, the laser level can project within a tiny fraction of an inch over a few hundred yards or more, however, many laser projections are merely overstruck with a chalk line, which somewhat defeats the purpose of the laser. Many laser beams cast a beam spread as much as $\frac{1}{4}$ in. Depending on where the beam is marked, and if it is calibrated correctly, you may or may not end up with an accurate line. In lieu of a chalk line, a jet line, a spool of twine about as thick as a piece of thread can be used. This method is also useful to offset other elements of the work, such as a soffit or floor leveling. Short of a jet-line, a taut chalk line or string held tight to the floor can be painted over, such that the area below the string is rendered as negative space once the string is removed; some of the paint can rub off, however, the line cannot.

One layout method used (and abused) is the Pythagorean theory, or as layout carpenters like to say, 3/4/5—the relationship of the base, leg, and hypotenuse of a right triangle. The application of this theory in the field is often used to establish the x/y axes. Typically, the three corners are located, and a line is struck at a right angle to the existing line. Because it tends to be done at relatively close range, there is a huge margin for error in projecting the line to greater lengths. For example, a triangle $\frac{1}{8}$ in. out of square from a 3 ft base, to a 4 ft leg, projected to 100 ft, will yield a line about 1 ft out of square. One-eighth inch can be lost in the width of a pencil mark, chalk line, or incorrect demarcation. Thus, more and more contractors are hedging their bets with laser instrumentation, even though they too can vary in accuracy. Nonetheless, the 3/4/5 method is handy for projects such as laying out floor tile in small rooms, such as bathrooms.

Benchmarks refer to fixed elevation points for which the height of all installations will be referenced. In existing structures, there is typically a fair amount of variation in existing conditions, specifically the floor, of which its highest point will determine the benchmark. Once the benchmark is struck, the offset to the preexisting ceiling is measured to ensure that the program will fit as designed. In many cases, floor leveling or chopping is required in order to achieve clearances. In others, the architect may lower the ceiling height to accommodate program above the ceiling, which they are invariably loath to do. If the ceiling is squeezed, or not lowered to allow more working room, it becomes that much more difficult for the contractor to coordinate and fit his infrastructure. For example, at first appearance, the raising of a ceiling height has little ramifications for the carpenters and drywallers, yet it may make life difficult for the MEP trades, that is, it may create more work for them. We discussed just such a project in Chap. 3. If it should, they are entitled to an upcharge or even schedule extension. This is a difficult concept to explain to a client, and for this reason, it is uncommon that upcharges or extensions are awarded for such changes. Nevertheless, they must be presented for discussion. If an extra or extension is not granted, the contractors should be given the consideration that goes along with making a generous concession without being reciprocated, especially when the project is large and complicated—such a concession would be considerable. Of course, this discussion assumes that a contractor not only identifies the specific nature of the problem of squeezing his space, but also can quantify it into days and dollars; no small undertaking.

Once axes lines and benchmarks are struck, another level of scrutiny of existing conditions takes place, and the architect again should be advised of any known deviations. A layout mechanic or the architect will first check the space against overall design dimensions,[5] and then proceed to check the partitions within.

Layout

Now that reference points have been established, your production team is ready to begin layout. At this time, consider who will be your point man in the field—whether it is a superintendent, working foreman, or other. If possible, you want this individual to remain on the project through its completion. Too often, contractors juggle supervisors according to their needs on other projects. This point person, you hope, will be a walking repository of the project's history, which sees the project through, from start to finish.

The on-site production coordinator will retain a remarkable amount of knowledge about the project in his head—knowledge that may exist nowhere else. This can be a problem if this person is taken off the project or otherwise becomes absent. The duplex project we discussed above had just such a problem. Because the drawings were not fully developed, and dimensions, especially overalls, required verification, a great amount of design information was processed by the production supervisor. However, because the carpenters were unskilled, the information was never implemented. Much of the information had to do with discrepancies in layout, which were negotiated verbally with the architect, who because of his small commission, was not going to generate clarifying sketches. On a difficult project, such as this one, the project could not be built correctly without this information. The supervisor left the project, and the company was hard-pressed to make any sense at all of the project's progress, or where it needed to go.

Once discrepancies have been negotiated, the layout team will then demarcate the rough framing of walls, which they will back out from finish dimensions. This is a critical component of the layout process, and should be done by the lead mechanic and superintendent. The layout may be struck in chalk, or defined by floor plate, which is tacked in for this purpose. Once the layout is down, critical dimensions, and dimensions, which are not negotiable, are verified with any discrepancies being reported back to the architect. Examples are the location of a toilet drain, the location of a riser offset, structural framing which might interfere with the new program, and so on. For this exercise, the respective tradesmen should be consulted for their input, especially those who require strict tolerances. Once verified, the architect should be called in to inspect the layout.

General construction

For the purposes of this book, general construction includes all infrastructures: demolition, structural framing, concrete, substrates, rough carpentry, and partition framing. All subsequent work, MEPs, finishes, and closeout, will be addressed elsewhere further along in this chapter.

The general construction sequencing of a project should involve little guesswork. It should be planned well in advance, and have tolerance for surprises.

The order of installations has everything to do with the expedience of the project. Think in terms of "putting the horse before the cart." As discussed in Chap. 3, most tasks are dependent on other tasks being completed before them, and have successor tasks following them. For example, you wouldn't pour a concrete floor before the waste pipe was installed, or close a wall with gypsum board before the electrician ran wires to all backboxes.

Let us consider a typical high-end gut project. It may be an apartment with new MEP, partitions, and finishes. Based on your layout lines, you will frame most of the walls. Most of the MEPs will end up above the drop ceiling. The infrastructure portion of the project is thus conceived from the top down: ductile piping, vent lines, electrical conduit, and then light fixtures. Although the light fixtures are last to be installed, they tend to take precedence over other programs whenever there is a conflict—a pipe or duct will be moved so as not to affect the lighting layout. Wouldn't it be nice to know there was a conflict before you had the offending work installed? That is why coordination drawings, as discussed, should be used. The responsibility for conflicts is a gray area in high-end residential; it isn't always clear who's responsible for a given conflict. The high-end contractor is expected to anticipate any glaring conflict early in the game, before tear-out of new work is necessitated by the conflict; being a highly skilled contractor, he should know better. Even if he is more vigilant in detecting conflicts, the architect and engineer still need to do their job, and resolve potential conflicts before the drawings go out to bid. The degree to which they are willing to do this varies a great deal, but in general, they do not seem to regularly coordinate overlays to any significant extent. Nowhere are conflicts more prevalent than in the MEP fit-outs. More importantly, MEP conflicts tend to be more expensive to correct than say a carpentry layout conflict.

MEP coordination.   By its nature, the schematic phase of MEP coordination must be done before the project can be accurately framed. Schematics may include single-line drawings, flow charts, and other graphical tools. Subsequent to coordinated schematics, shop drawings are issued for approval, and lastly, a sketcher will take field dimensions. The sequential installation of the coordinated work must be observed. If it is not, there will be conflicts and mistakes. This process is considered part of the means and methods of most residential installations, which are unique, in that no other building construction so regularly compresses allotted space and area for infrastructure. This is because of the high value of usable rental space and real estate. Not uncommonly, an architect may even ask that a beam be cut and reinforced so that a duct may pass through, so as not to affect the ceiling height. For example, a retail outlet store may have as much as 20% excess free space above the ceiling to adjust routing of the MEP programs, that is, the location of components is not so critical, as there is extra room. Ceiling space in large retail stores generally does not encroach on the program beneath. The same cannot be said for residential work, where components must be reinstalled if they are not positioned correctly, as they will invariably conflict with other programs. Moreover, most residential buildings skimp on ceiling heights, so to maximize the number of units. How much space are we talking about? Suffice it to say that a contractor's request to lower a

120 in. above finished floor (AFF) ceiling to 119 in. would seldom be entertained by an architect. The 1 in. could affect MEP installations considerably. If there were only 24 in. clearance above the ceiling, 1 in. would be a little over 4% of the available space. It may not sound like much, but it is when you consider everything that must fit in this 24 in. For example, a $^{10}/_{24}$ duct (10 in. high), a 3 in. waste line, a 7 in. high light fixture, and 2 in. of armored cable routing would leave only 2 in. clearance. Assuming the components (including ceiling framing and underside of slab clearance) have $^{1}/_{2}$ in. between them, there would be $-^{1}/_{2}$ in. clearance, that is, the program is $^{1}/_{2}$ in. too deep.

Architectural drawings are detailed by architects. If there is an engineer on the project, he will likely handle the MEP details, delegating MEP to his respective engineers. He should then issue stamped drawings. In some cases, the architect will generate the MEP drawings, and the engineer of record will stamp them. The problem is architects don't know nearly as much about engineering as an engineer, and engineers tend to know little about residential construction period. At minimum, the architect and engineer should overlay each other's work before they get too deep into their designs. Sometimes, an interior designer is the MEP draftsperson, with an architect of record only, and the likelihood then is that the level of MEP design coordination will be even lower than usual—sometimes nonexistent. This is true especially if the project is not to be filed. Therefore, whether they are designing and detailing, or reviewing shop drawings, neither the engineer nor the architect consistently takes into consideration the integration or coordination of each other's designs in more than a cursory fashion. This is generally left to the installers to figure out. Qualified architects designing high-end projects should be expected to do more in the way of coordination, and some do, however, they are the exception.

It is a moot point that the coordination should be done before the working drawings are released. For large projects, such as warehouses and schools, where the volume of space allows for large tolerances for MEP installations, the engineer and architect can more or less precoordinate the work. For such projects, there may only be one MEP coordination meeting or none at all. In residential spaces, where space is at a premium, ceilings and walls (collectively called *the envelope*) are always pushed out to allow for more usable space. The tolerances can become so small that only field dimensions can give accurate locations for work. These field dimensions are the upshot of the MEP coordination process, and on residential projects should be done by the subcontractors, as no one is in a better position to do it. Architects and interior designers have come to expect this service, and because they expect it, they tend to detail and coordinate even less than they ordinarily would (which is little to begin with).[6] General contractors realize that in effect, they are doing other's work for them, and I expect they index the cost of their work accordingly.

MEPs are tricky for high-end residential installations. High-end projects happen in expensive neighborhoods, where space is at a premium. They therefore tend to maximize floor and ceiling heights, squeezing infrastructure for living space. Frequently the infrastructure is more complex, involving additional program needing more space. Additionally, the exposed detailing or finishes of

MEPs can be integral to the overall designs. For high-end projects, these installations use high quality materials, and require accurate installations. Some examples are the following.

Mechanical

- Flow-bar diffusers and tapeable or flangeless grilles
- Complex zoning and individual comfort controls
- Remote control valves
- Remote sensors
- Air-flow modeling
- Air-treatment systems
- Humidification systems
- Direct digital controls (DDC)
- Custom fireplaces
- Custom gas fixtures

Electrical

- Tape-in fixtures with large framing kits
- Projection fixtures
- Custom fixtures
- Backlighting, cove lighting, and up-lighting
- Dimming systems
- Touch screen interfaces
- System integration
- Custom device plates/engraving
- Extra electrical metallic tubing (EMT) piping distribution (for low voltage)
- Audio/visual programs
- IT programs

Plumbing

- Control alignment to data, for example, centering valve on tile grout line
- Fountains, flowing water designs
- Steam rooms
- Saunas
- Pools
- Back flush wall-mount toilets
- Custom fixtures/plating
- Custom tubs, sinks, and shower enclosures

This usable space maximizing effort has the effect of compressing infrastructure and reducing clearances, making it more difficult to install, and easier to make mistakes. Therefore, the MEP coordination stage is vital on such projects.

The MEP coordination process should involve a series of meetings and shared schematics with all affected trades, and should also involve the architects and engineers, that is, the design team is more active in the coordination process, having to do more than simply review shop drawings, which is all they are traditionally expected to do—they will help coordinate. And so they should, as they are in control of all design directives that will affect MEP coordination. A Mylar or other transparent overwritable medium is used to schematize the heating, ventilation and air conditioning (HVAC) contractor's work. The placement of his work is determined by finished dimensions. Once his schematic is approved, he will field measure, and generate a shop drawing, which he will submit for approval to the design team. Once approved, his shop drawings are overlain on top of the reflected ceiling (RCP) drawing, which should show all light fixtures, air supply and returns, sprinkler heads, and any other ceiling program. Then the remaining trades—electrician and plumber—will sketch their program, which is also integrated into the overlays.

As important as it is, this coordination process is seldom done with diligence, and most times, not at all—even in the high-end residential sector. This fact is to blame for an enormous amount of time and money being wasted for tear-outs and redos on projects everywhere. There are a few reasons I suspect are to blame for this ignorance.

First, we must exclude all contractors who either don't know any better or would be unaffected, even if they did utilize MEP coordination drawings.

- There is no one team member who has the required knowledge of all trades affected, who can spearhead the mission.
- One or more of the subcontractors either are unwilling, or are unqualified to produce a working document.
- There is no budget provided for, to provide a decent coordination process.
- There is no time allotted in the schedule to mount a coordination effort.
- The project design or criteria keeps changing.

This last circumstance is one bane of the industry. Indecisiveness and capriciousness by the owner or design team wreak havoc on the MEP coordination stage. Drawings have to constantly be revised, often with an upcharge from the subcontractor, or restocking fee from a supplier.

Because the HVAC work takes up the most volume, and is tightest to the ceiling, thus installed early, and because his components are so large, this contractor has the least latitude to relocate his work. Therefore, he would seem to be the most qualified candidate to lead the coordination effort. The coordination effort is no small task. It requires resources, and a leader with know-how and patience to handle the other trades, and program considerations; he must know much

TABLE 4.7   MEP Coordination Matrix

	Coordinate	Trade	PreReq	Duration	Status
001	Working Drawings	PMA			
002	Core: Offsets	Base			75%
003	Core: SW Pipe	Base	002		100%
004	Core: Duct	Base	002		100%
005	Core: Flue	Base	002		
006	Core: Plumber	Base	002		75%
007	Core: Fire Rating	Base	002	30	0%
008	Backgrounds	HVAC	Bid Set		100%
009	Control Lines	Carpentry	001*	2	n/a
010	Schematics: Pipe	HVAC	008	10	75%
011	Schematics: Ductile	HVAC	009; 010	10	
012	Schematics: Pipe	Electrical	008	5	
013	Schematic Review	HVAC	012	10	
014	Shop Drawings	All	006	20	

*also floor access

more than simply his own work; he must know everyone else's. Assuming he is given accurate and timely schematics from the respective trades, he will coordinate the MEP shop drawing process. Table 4.7 represents a schedule update showing the relationship of a base-building contractor's MEP work with the interior contractor's fit-out.

The project superintendent should have knowledge of the base MEP schematic and program regardless of an MEP coordinator, as he will be cosupervising installations along with the mechanic's foreman. One thing he can and should do is to have the schematic transposed onto the floor layout; at least light fixtures and ductwork. These references will be very useful to all trades, who might otherwise be unaware of adjoining a program to be installed. Such layout references are almost always struck on the floor, as it is much easier to transpose lines to a flat surface, than to a ceiling, which may have interruptions, such as beams, unevenness, or other obstacles; the mechanics can plumb upward from the lines on the floor in order to transfer them to the ceiling. Subsequent to installation, the superintendent should verify that installations are correct. Even if the MEP coordinator is top-flight, there is no guaranty that his installers will be as effective. It is in the undertaking of these tasks—MEP coordination and verification, which superintendents are so prone to underperform. There are two reasons for this (1) they simply don't have the know-how, and (2) they don't have the time. Both of these shortcomings can be remediated, thus it can be said that there is no excuse for them. There are a number of ways in which they fail to do their job:

- They neglect to verify that work is consistent with the approved shop drawings, and specifically location in plan and elevation.

- Even if they do verify locations, they take it for granted that subsequent installations will therefore also be accurate. Once the ductwork is installed, there is an excellent opportunity to verify the entire coordination process, as there is now a physical reference point. This opportunity is seldom taken or is not taken soon enough.

■ They lcave the business of means and methods to the trades. They may do this out of laziness, or simply because they simply don't understand the process well enough to make a credible assessment.

Often, mechanics have to make adjustments in the field, which diverge from the approved shop drawings. Superintendents often do not red-line such installation adjustments in the shop drawings, or record them in the as-builts. They may not even be aware, as the mechanic's may not have told them, and also because they have not verified locations.

Systems Integration

As we saw in Chap. 2, high-end residential projects are becoming more complex everyday. Not uncommonly, a residence may have some or all of the following signal systems to control:

■ Dimming

■ Window treatments (shades, blinds, curtains and the like)

■ Audio/visual (AV) systems

■ Security

■ Telephone

■ Information and technology (IT) systems

■ Climate controls

Each system will require its own set of (primary) controls. Many designs now require that control wires are routed within EMT conduit, or a plastic equivalent. Such piping is costly, time consuming, and should be included in the MEP coordination process, although a shop drawing proper is generally not required. This is sometimes considered or referred to as *wire management*. With the advent of technology, more and more clients are demanding that the controls and equipment of these systems be integrated, or consolidated into a single platform, for ease of use, and for a higher level of control. In order to do this, someone familiar with all of the systems must be consulted to furnish an interface, wiring diagram, user's manual, warrantor, and end-user training program. This person is known as a *systems integrator*. Before he does, it must be ascertained in the design stage that the systems can be integrated. For example, do they follow the same protocol or can they talk to each other? For many manufacturers, they consider the code used in their software control packages to be proprietary—they fear a conflict of interest in making their product compatible with other manufacturers' product. Resultantly, many systems don't talk to each other—they can't be integrated. You can always tell a project that lacked a systems integrator; secondary controls remain idle, and are not terminated or connected to the main interface. Dreaded single-pole switches, intended as backup controls, are now the primary means of control. For example, a computer control interface may have been specified to control AV, dimming, window treatments, mechanical and security systems, yet it only really can control the dimming system and window treatments.

There is no one systems integrator that will be familiar with every system on the market; however, some of the more popular systems are being specified repetitively, and thus, system integrators are more familiar with them, and are able to integrate them into one interface; hence the term *systems integration*. Some manufacturers are now at the business of rolling out preintegrated programs, for example, a dimming system manufacturer also sells a window treatment program, which is already integrated into its control interface. One of the advantages of such programs is that they will carry a warranty, whereas a systems integrator isn't in the business of issuing warranties. In either case, systems integration is a nascent industry. Frequent underutilization by the end-user, and substandard support services are just a few of the obstacles to the expansion of this industry. Without the preintegration of these systems by the design team, the project can become difficult to coordinate, and impossible to integrate. The less integration there is, the more stand-alone systems there will be. Stand-alone systems control no other, and are controlled by no other interface than their own. On the whole, a grouping of complex stand-alone system controls will not be user-friendly. If the RS232 protocol is used, they only then need the software to facilitate the integration of the systems. Indeed, software developers are hard at the task of developing whole-house control systems, but there doesn't yet seem to be one that takes into consideration the idea of flexibility, that is, there are great limitations on what types of equipment they can control. For more information on the RS232 protocol, refer to App. D.

Ordinarily, the MEP engineers will specify the requirements of their control systems; however, they stop short of point-to-point (PTP) wiring diagrams, manufacturer specification, and systems integration, save, for example, crossovers of duct sensors with the fire prevention and warning system, which must be filed. The respective vendors will also provide varying degrees of support for their own controls. Again, this effort may not take into account integration with other systems. The implementation of a systems integrator should be done before the system controls are specified. He can tell you what will work and what will not, before the fact, as opposed to after the fact.

System integration refers to the large picture of controls for a given project, which are now often integrated in addition to stand-alone. Moreover, these individual systems are becoming more sophisticated. Problems will arise with different interfaces as well. A systems integrator will do the following:

■ Consult with each vendor so as to determine the critical path to integrating their respective systems into the main interface (assuming that the systems are compatible).

- Compose a flow chart of how each control component relates to the whole system, which will have a main interface, such as a Crestron touch screen with a graphic user interface (GUI), and/or hand-held remote infra-red/radio-frequency (IR/RF) devices.

- Provide PTP wiring diagrams and sequence of operations for each system.

- Provide a user-interface compatible with all the systems, or as many as possible.

- Get the system on-line.

- Troubleshoot the system.

Because having too many controls for each system can be complicated for the end-user, and a headache for the designer, consolidation (assuming it works) has many benefits. On the downside, no system interface "talks to" or will control every system out there. The RS232 interface, however, is one of the most versatile available, and will likely be the most universal, however, there are others available.

Think of the problem as being similar to the way in which PCs and Macintosh computers needed (and still need) to be integrated. Nevertheless, there will inevitably be things to consider:

- That many components of designer systems will remain stand-alone; will not be controllable by secondary interface.

- That all of the systems will have to retain their proprietary control functions.

- That although a system claims to be RS232 compatible, often such is not the case. For other protocols, a converter (to RS232) may be utilized, but these tend to be unreliable.

- That there will always be troubleshooting, end-user training, platform customization, and maintenance issues associated with an integrated system

- That each system component will dictate which other equipment is compatible with its infrastructure. Often, these will be proprietary and thus your choices will be limited. Manufacturers often do this by design—what incentive would they have to integrate competitors' systems?

The notion that a systems integrator is needed to coordinate complex programs is not yet catching on[7] the way say local area network (LAN) administrators did years ago; however, the need for them is there. There are not a lot of systems integrators in business, and most of them probably shouldn't be. Worse, are the people who profess expertise outside their realm, such as an audio/video consultant posing as a systems integrator. Like anyone else, the systems integrator should be sourced through a professional organization, such as the CSIA. Often, the myriad of systems cannot be integrated, and the interface is abandoned save for a few basic functions—a costly error, especially after all the PTP wiring has been run and terminated.

Most recently, many companies are approaching the systems from the controls side (as opposed to the equipment side). They offer solutions that are governed by the controlling interface and software program; however, this practice will likely have the effect of narrowing choices of equipment specification. Still yet other companies are approaching the problem from the distribution side, that is, PTP wiring, which can be a problem to install into a furnished space. By using transmitters and signals they hope to eradicate the problem and expense of wire distribution. This is a nascent industry as well, and so far, products look pretty flat. One thing is for sure—the more platforms there are rolled out, the messier it will become to make sense of it all. If there were some sound universal standards, such as was RS232; there wouldn't be such a need for systems integrators.

MEP Coordination Process

- Confirm riser and valve locations (for hydrostatic systems)
- Duct and/or pipe and equipment schematics[8]
- Overlay reflected ceiling plan (RCP): light fixtures and the like
- Ductile shop drawings
- Waste and vent shop drawings
- The EMT distribution shop drawings[9]
- Fire control system shop drawings as required
- Overlay integration and coordination

Rough-in and framing inspections

Like layout, framing inspections as they relate to the architectural design, are performed by project architects. The framing inspection generally does not take into consideration the rest of the program, which has to be inspected separately. Frequently, oversights are made because no one coordinated the actual layout to the RCP and the MEP programs. This is not the responsibility of the architect—it is the general contractor's. I have heard it said often that if an architect approves a submittal, or passes an inspection, that he does assume responsibility for inherent errors in such submittals. However, if the architect did not integrate and coordinate the design, as he should, he may be liable for the mistake. In either case, do not expect the client to empathize with you. You should approach all your work with the intent of satisfying or exceeding industry standards, regardless of an architect's scrutiny.

The same holds true for rough-in inspections, such as the location of electrical back-boxes, light fixture housings, plumbing controls, waste lines, and so on. Although an architect approves the location, his assumption is that it is dimensionally correct. Because the general contractor is responsible for locating all program in the field, most architects don't even bother inspecting rough-ins, or finish dimensions for that matter, unless they should offend their eye; if he doesn't notice a conflict in the rough-in stage he likely will in the finish stage, at which time remedial work must take place at the general contractor's expense. A general contractor's field personnel must therefore have working knowledge of all installations, their rough-ins, and substrates, such that they can ensure the integrity of the installations; this cannot be left up to sub contractors.

White Box

White box refers to a project in the state of having all walls and ceilings closed and spackled. At this point in time, there can be no doubt that all walls and ceilings are ready for finishes, and all built-ins (cabinetry, doors, and metalwork) can be dimensioned. However, white box is somewhat an idealistic concept. If every project waited until all walls and ceilings were spackled before fabricating dimensions were taken, no project would ever finish on time. The first level eschewed is the state of closed ceilings. With so much program going in, the ceilings are always the last to be closed, often, not soon enough. Dimensions are commonly taken without the ceilings closed. To go one better, some projects are dimensioned without even the walls closed; layout lines may indicate where the finished walls occur, or guaranteed or hold, dimensions are invoked, wherein the contractor assures a finish point to later be built up to. This method requires the most exacting level of fabrication and installation. Optimally, one would wait for substrates to measure from; however, aggressive schedules and budgets seldom afford this luxury.

Shop Drawings and Dimensions

As I have said, ideally, dimensions are taken after substrates are installed—but what about shop drawings? On fast-paced projects, the finish trades shop drawings should, if possible, start no later than once the framing is approved. In some cases, especially with stand-alone pieces, shop drawings can be rendered before the project even begins. Some detailers do not prefer to work this way, because they feel they are doing double work. However, in high-end residential, there should be at least two preproduction stages—shop drawing and dimensioning. For MEP trades, schematics are often done before shop drawings. The advantage of this sequence is that the design intent of the shop drawings can be approved by the design team without exact or final dimensions. This may enable the contractor to order his material in advance.

If guaranteed and hold dimensions are invoked, there will be more pressure, and less room for mistakes by the framers and carpenters. Technically, I consider held and guaranteed dimensions to be out-of-sequence operations, however, strong contractors and mill workers will have less difficulty with this arrangement than will most. For the uninitiated, hold dimensions can be a nightmare.

The difference between the submittal requirements (usually found in the *Specifications Book*) for a high-end residential project and an average project

TABLE 4.8   Required Submittals Worksheet

Section	Description	Submittal	Shop drawing	Mock-up	Sample	Control sample or SK	Issued
05500	Metal Fabrications	x	x				
05700	Ornamental Metalwork	x	x		x		
	Toned bronze, sheet						
	Polished silver, plating						
	Light Box (baths)	x	x	x	x		
06100	Rough Carpentry	x					
06400	Architectural Millwork	x	x	x	x	x	
	Veneer						
	Cerused Oak				x		
	Fiddleback Anigre				x		
	Lacewood				x		
	Paint Grade				x		
	Sycamore				x		
	Solid				x		
	Cerused Oak				x		
	Fiddleback Anigre				x		
	Lacewood				x		
	Paint Grade				x		
	Sycamore				x		
	Finishes	x		x	x	x	
	LQ1, Brugier			x	x		
	Wood Ceiling	x	x	x			
	Wood access door			x			
	Blind access panel			x			
	Curtain Pocket (12/6 AFF)			x			
	Hardware						
	5	x					
	6	x					
	Plating				x		
07210	Building Insulation		Not required				
07900	Joint Sealants		Not required				
08000	Door Hardware	x	x		x		
	5						
	6						
08110	Steel Frames	x	x				
08210	Custom Wood Doors	x	x		x		
	5						
	6						

is significant. A sample submittal requirement sheet is shown in Table 4.8. In addition to there being extra submittals, there are submittals for things that are routinely procured or installed without a submittal on less sophisticated projects, such as a mechanic's shop drawings or appliance *cuts*. Even if the specification seems cut-and-dried, if there is a submittal requirement it must be met. Even if there isn't, it can be a good idea to make an extra submittal. Chances are there was an error or omission that the architect would have otherwise been unaware of.

Finishes

Wood, stone, metal, glass, and paint

Exotic and elegant finish materials are the trappings of a high-end project, and should always command special attention. The tolerances on true high-end work typically do not allow for joints, which must be caulked, or joints wider than $\frac{1}{16}$ in. Joints over $\frac{3}{64}$ in. in stone, metal, or wood (other than paint grade) are outright unacceptable, regardless if this is spelled out in the spec book or not. The use of wood fillers in joints other than flooring is unacceptable.

With unforgiving material, such as glass or granite, subcontractors like to leave a little wiggle-room to fit their work. The concept of *wiggle-room* is antithetical to high-end installations. Although the general requirements may state the tolerance one way, you likely will want to exceed it. I will mention just a few for the purposes of evincing the mind-set that should be utilized in executing quality work, and what obstacles may be encountered. Even these small mentions, if observed, can go a long way in improving quality control.

Wood. Wood will shrink and swell with changes in humidity and temperature, which means filled joints are prone to crack, sometimes while you are still on the job. As part of your warranty, you should service your clients by touching up these joints once or twice a year. If there is no humidification system, the likelihood of cracking will increase especially, should the relative humidity drop below 25%. At the other extreme, swelling will occur when the humidity level is above 55%. Ranges below 20% and above 80% are almost guaranteed to cause problems.[10] When wood absorbs moisture, it also tends to stain. The American Woodworking Institute issued a warning in 2003 regarding the specification, installation, and maintenance of wood installations:

> Responsibility for dimensional change problems in wood products resulting from improper design rests with the designer/architect/specifier
> Responsibility for dimensional change problems in wood products resulting from improper relative humidity during the storage and installation rests with the general contractor
> Responsibility for dimensional change problems in wood products resulting from humidity extremes after occupancy rests with engineering and maintenance[11]

Like any other high-quality installation, a quality product demands a quality fabricator and installer. Some of the attributes of inferior work are readily noticeable:

- *Scribes*: Narrow spacers contoured or contrived to fit between separate installations, so to close a gap. New work must be straight—an existing adjoining surface should be made straight to meet it. If the existing element is known to be out of level or plumb, the architect may or may not have directed it to be remediated. In either case, the contractor must point out the discrepancy as early as possible. Remedial work, such as corrective skim coating might be ordered. Depending on the case and severity, the contractor may be entitled to an extra

- *Fillers*: All should be avoided; wood plugs may be acceptable on things like dimensional lumber—stairs, doors, and the like, but the architect must approve. Joinery techniques, adhesives, and blind fastenings make just about any assembly potentially free of fillers
- *Exposed fasteners*: Blind fastening, pocket fastening, spline joints, gluing are all acceptable substitutes to an exposed screw or filled countersunk screw
- Chip-out, or tear-out happens during the fabrication process when an incorrect or dull saw blade is used, inferior equipment is used, or there is poor machining technique
- Caulking of joints
- Tooling marks, such as saw or jointer/planer blade marks
- *Uneven finishing*: Alligatoring, orange peeling,[12] bubbles, and so on

Identifying high-quality wood installations

- Blind-fastening methods
- Absence of noticeable joints, delaminating, or tear-out
- Stable substrates: especially for oversized products
- Consistent veneer patterns
- Evenly spaced drawers and doors with $\frac{1}{32}$ in. gaps
- Heavy-duty functional hardware
- Accurate mortising for hinges and other hardware— $\frac{1}{32}$ in. gaps
- Installations plumb, level, coplanar, and aligned correctly to adjoining work
- Quirk details at joints
- Back veneering (to prevent warping)
- Evenly applied and cured high-volume-low-pressure (HVLP) finishes

While good wood workers will surely shine once their work is installed; the integrity of their shop drawings can be an excellent bellwether of things to come.

Veneer selection.   Veneer is specified when there is either short supply of wide solid material, or a certain grain pattern or character is desired. Often, only veneer is offered, as the trees are not wide enough to yield solid stock, or the species has been overforested to the extent that no old-growth trees are available. Veneer species go in and out of vogue rather quickly, according to availability, and are often dictated by media hype. Often, the overspecification of a "hot" veneer will vanquish the supply, much the way as it did recently with anigre, and then wenge. Design professionals often have no idea of the physical characteristics of a given species other than what they saw in a magazine. They may not be aware of the special procurement process for veneers. It is an ethical responsibility of the general contractor to inform his architect of the process (assuming he is familiar with it). If he is not, his mill worker must be, and should advise him. The submittal process for veneer work can be considerably more involved than it is for just about any other material, especially for high-end installations. The submittal process may include some or all of the following:

- Sampling from veneer house
- Visit to veneer house to select books, or flitches produced from individual trees
- Sequencing or *book-matching* of the veneer patterns
- Blueprinting of flitches (designate locations in elevation)
- Substrate submittal
- Joint sample; especially corners
- Edge and profile samples
- Stain sample
- Finish sample
- Mock-ups

Informed architects will be familiar with this process, and may even issue specifications, such as sheen value—a measure of reflectivity for applied finishes. As always, a control sample should be issued from the architect to the fabricator. Otherwise, a lot of energy can be wasted in second-guessing.

Stone.   For those who can afford it, exotic and dimensional stone has become very fashionable. It is a challenge for most stone installers to fabricate and install their work within high-tolerance guidelines. Uneven and oversized grouted joints are epidemic. High quality stone fabrication and installation is a dying art. The management of the stone procurement, fabrication, and installation process requires a few basic understandings.

Procurement.   The architect should provide a control sample to match, or introduce the supplier of the stone. If it is a patterned or venous stone, the architect or client should select specific slabs by visiting the yard, or looking at digital photos. He should then blueprint, and/or specify sections and orientations of the selected slabs.

Stone suppliers like to pretend that they are the exclusive suppliers of different species. To obfuscate this ruse, they conjure up code names, such that no other supplier could recognize the species without having seen it. Though they do this in order not to lose out to other suppliers, they can create havoc in the marketplace by confusing information regarding price, characteristics, and availability, especially when legitimate species are confused with incorrect classifications.

More and more stone is being imported on a per order basis, an arrangement that can create delays. Overseas stock presents an inhibition to visiting the site; slabs must otherwise be selected from photographs, which is not the most effective method. Typically, an overseas dimensional stone order is processed as follows:

- Once the material is located an order is placed.
- If it is already quarried, it will then be cut to size.
- Material trucked to port.
- Material loaded to freighter for overseas trip (1–3 weeks).
- Order arrives in customs, where release times can be indeterminate.
- Material shipped to site; typically sidewalk delivery, that is, a crew has to unload it.
- Quantities checked and inventoried; damaged or broken material discarded.

Stone is porous, and therefore is sensitive to shock and vibration—some more than others. For example, limestone is very prone to fracturing, as compared to most granite. By the time it gets to the site or shop from overseas, it has been moved so many times that it's a wonder it isn't all broken.

Fabrication.   Many of the tools available to the stone fabricator are of extremely high quality, and will yield a superior product, assuming the operator is qualified. However, not all fabricators have high quality tools, or craftsmen. By the time an inferior piece of stone gets to the site, the stone contractor is not likely to reject it especially, if it came from his shop. Typical fabrication problems attributable to poor quality machinery and workmanship are:

- Fractures
- Stains
- Chip out of edges
- Uneven finishing
- Uneven or large joints
- Inaccurate transposition of template
- Poor line quality, especially for profiles

Few of the above are really controllable by the general contractor, with the exception of templating. Templating refers to the task of creating an exact one-dimensional representation of the footprint and boundaries of a proposed piece of stone, glass, and the like. Often, the subcontractor does his own templating; however, invariably such templates are inaccurate, or provide too much tolerance, so as to make the fabrication and installation process simpler. Given that, many general contractors generate their own templates created by carpenters, who frequently have better layout and template rendering skills than stone setters.

Installation.   High quality stone may arrive at the site, be templated correctly, and things may still not go according to plan. If the stone is matching the template, which is accurate—that helps. However, there are still things that can go wrong from there.

- Installation not level and plumb
- Installation not aligned to adjoining work correctly
- Poorly executed or incorrect grout color and line
- Uneven finish or tinting from the sealing process
- Damage to unprotected installations
- Insufficient grounds provided by general contractor

Limestone.   Limestone has become extremely fashionable for some time now. The best features warm sandy tones and consistent color areas devoid of interruption that seems to lend it particularly well to the *Zeitgeist* designer vocabulary of off-white palates. A common bane of the industry is the overspecification of limestone, and the use of certain limestone in wet areas. There are hundreds of limestones in the market, each with their own properties and characteristics. Unfortunately, they all (especially imports) don't undergo an American Society for Testing and Materials (ASTM) process to determine their viability for given applications. There are a lot of considerations to observe before working with limestone.

Low-density limestone is very porous—it will absorb water, stains, and dirt more readily than denser limestone. Portland-based cements will often permanently stain limestone, thus it must be used in conjunction with, or be replaced by a latex-based cement. Limestone will not always hold a hard edge adequately, or edges will be subject to chipping. Slabs will be prone to fracturing. All limestone is subject to these shortcomings to some degree. If it must be used, deliberate testing should have been done to guarantee that the material is suited to a given application.

Given these limitations, certain limestone should not be used in kitchens and bathrooms where it will be exposed to water, stains, or chemical cleaning products, and it should not be used in high traffic areas. Regrettably, it is ubiquitous in these places. A good stone fabricator should be familiar with the limestone that he has been asked to install. He should be able to advise you as to the characteristics of a given stone. If he can't, then certainly the supplier can. These limitations should be translated into qualifications in your contract, for example:

> Please be advised that our fabricator has informed us that limestone sample 'A' is not recommended for wet-area applications. We therefore cannot warranty the installation against staining, calcification, or any other chemical reactions commonly associated with reactions to impurities in the water supply and various cleaning products.

The intention of this qualification is meant to indemnify a contractor against future claims that may require costly tear-out and replacement. Not all stone fabricators or suppliers will advise that limestone may be a problem. You therefore must discuss warranty matters with them prior to letting their contract. If they will not warranty the stone, you must make this clear to the client.

Metal. Architectural metalwork in interior construction details is becoming more fashionable than ever, although for residential projects it tends to be piecework, which always carries a higher unit price than production work. It is also very expensive because the material is costly, labor intensive to finish, and extra time has to be allowed to achieve aggressive tolerances. There seem to be only a handful of metalworkers around who (a) can be bothered to do piecework, and (b) can produce quality piecework. Another problem is the tendency of metal fabricators to not install their own work. Additionally, designers and architects don't seem to have a good understanding of the dynamics of metallurgy and metal fabrication, enough to generate comprehensive design documents. Frequently specifications are loose for:

- Proper alloy
- Grade
- Form
- Joining method
- Weld types
- Engineering and design
- Dressing
- Tolerances
- Finishing
- Fastening
- Structural support methods

Consequently, specification is left to the metal fabricator. However, to match a control sample is another thing altogether. I recall a specification which called for "metal 1: bronze cap," and "bronze laminate." What was actually desired was 0.375 in. brass 260 (alloy) plate, oxidized and unsealed, to match a control sample that had no oxidation recipe; or didn't include a specification for the chemical agent and exposure process. Because of the loose specification, months of sampling and refinishing were added to the process. A lot of time could have been saved, had the provider of the sample issued the specification.

If the specifications and design documentation are adequate, there still is the problem of producing quality. It is touch-and-go with small shops doing piecework; skilled fabricators are very hard to find. The biggest problem outside of skill level is that metalworkers don't spend enough time on the finishing and preparation process because they are either impatient, aren't given the time by their supervisor, or are unable to correct a piece's shortcomings, such as burns, nicks, scratches, unsightly welds, and grinder marks. Some of the more common problems with producing quality architectural metalwork are:

- Prohibitive lead times
- Malformed material: bent, wracked, crooked, and the like
- Frequently off the template
- Poor welding or bolting technique
- Substandard dressing (preparation of material)
- Substandard machining
- Poor-quality finishing
- Lack of uniformity in directional finish
- Lines in nondirectional finish
- Damage in shipping
- Low-quality installation—in fact few shops offer installation as part of their package
- Insufficient level of integration with adjoining work
- Insufficient level of coordination with coproducers; such as a glazier or millworker, whom they may need to interface with to produce a piece
- Insufficient grounds provided by general contractor

A relative of the above hazards applies to the project turnover. Metals are especially sensitive and quick to react with cleaning solutions containing acids. Many callbacks and refabrications could easily have been avoided, if only the end-user had been advised of suitable cleaning products. A general contractor should always make a *care and maintenance manual* part of the turnover package. The same holds true for architectural wood and stone.

Plating.   After-market (postmanufacturing) plating has become a four-letter word to metal-fabricators. Many of them begrudgingly agree to do it, but will not guaranty the work. It is usually something they parse out to another shop— an electroplater, for example. There are few metal shops that would want to plate, even if they could. The reason for this is the poor quality and longevity of most piecework plating processes. The plating process could be immaculate, only to then ultimately fail (discolor or delaminate) down the road because the product wasn't prepared correctly, or because it was cleaned and maintained improperly by the client. If the metal isn't in top condition plate-ready when it gets to the plater, it will not get any better, regardless of the quality of the plating process. The fabrication and plating preparation process of metal piecework yields notoriously unsatisfactory results. For some goods there is a finish on the material that must be stripped in order to apply the new finish.

Additionally, the plating will tend to get worn off outside edges and protrusions. This characteristic is especially troublesome to Modernist designers, who fancy sharp linear lines. The tendency of the plating material to delaminate is also a constant concern.

Many high-end fixtures come in a variety of finishes and plating. This plating is done at the manufacturing level, as opposed to the after-market level, and generally yields an acceptable product, as the larger machinery tends to be superior. However, there are no standards of finish; one company's satin nickel finish may resemble brushed stainless, and another's brushed chrome. Often these elements are juxtaposed. The architect might then insist on one or the other being refinished. Insofar as plumbing fixtures are concerned, replating is a dubious enterprise, for example, a lavatory set will have to be disassembled and internal parts—washers and bushings set aside, before it can be sent to the plater. Most plumbing fixtures are plated by the manufacturer before they are packaged and would have to be stripped in order to be replated. Stripping and replating the moving parts of plumbing fixtures is problematic, and often voids the warranty of the fixture.

Glass.   High-end residential architectural glass (nonfenestration) installations are as worrisome as any other unforgiving material. The latest fashion has been to use designer glass that may be patterned, curved, stained, diffused, sandblasted, fritted, contoured, etched, and so on. Many of these glasses are nonstructural being used in structural and safety applications, and then require a laminate interlayer between two sheets in order to conform to building codes, thus adding another step to the fabrication process. Architectural glass fabrication and installation has similar challenges to that of architectural metalwork:

- Breakage
- Frequently off the template
- Overground edges and corners
- Mottling
- Air entrapped or soiled interlayer
- Inexactitude in fabricating radii
- Damage in shipping
- Damage in installation
- Large joints
- Inconsistent or overapplication of caulking
- Failure to integrate with adjoining work
- Insufficient grounds provided by general contractor
- Overstressed or undergasketed installations

In addition to the above, many professional organizations offer guidelines and standards for various materials. It would behoove one to be familiar with this information before specifying or fabricating the material; however, architects and general contractors invariably leave this up to the subcontractors, or merely reference the guidelines without describing them in their specifications.

Paint. Painting is another quandary for general contractors, especially high-end residential. The nuances of a good paint project are hard to visualize for many people—general contractors included. By its nature, the quality of a good paint job is subjective. Designers tend to select colors, base composition, and may include some standards in their specifications. However, this information is difficult to translate. Because painting is one of the last tasks on the project, the specifications for it, especially colors, often aren't fully developed until late in the project. Allowances or budgets for painting are commonplace; yet, its difficult to be accurate. Consider three projects: two with fixed prices, and one with a budget.

One fixed price project had a fairly well-developed specification when the contract was let. It was to be a first-rate paint job, and the contractor priced it accordingly. Because some of the prep work and built-up plaster (by others) were substandard, the painter ended up doing a huge amount of corrective work. Additionally, many rooms were painted three times. Regardless of this extraneous work, the painter asked for little or nothing in the way of upcharges. From experience, he had expected a fair amount of extraneous work, and allowed for it in his base proposal; what a relief it was not to hear him complain every time he had to repaint a room.

Another project was a budget (underendowed) job—a townhouse that had only an allowance for painting. Despite the project being continually value engineered, when it came time to select paint colors, the architect issued a three-page specification, with about 30 designer colors; he was after a sort of gingerbread house effect. The contractor nearly doubled his price when he saw this, which of course led to endless haggling. The question had to be raised; if the architect and owner were bent on trimming down the budget, why would they request a top tier paint job that they could never pay for? There is no acceptable answer to that question.

The third, and for lack of a better word, *silliest* paint job I recall was a two-bedroom apartment in a prewar building. The walls were plastered over metal lath, and were in poor condition. The moldings, which were everywhere, were ancient, and had so many layers of paint slathered on them that their profiles were completely indistinguishable. Moreover, they were installed poorly, and had nothing to recommend them. The painters scraped and sanded these profiles with an archaeologist's precision, but it soon became apparent that the owner expected to see raw wood beneath the layers of paint. It would have been faster and less expensive to replace them. The painters then came and did a "customary" amount of preparation work, after which the owner insisted was not enough. The contractor doubled his preparation efforts, a good faith gesture wherein he lost money, and then proceeded to prime and topcoat. Still, the owner whined that the work, especially the trims, was not satisfactory. Yet again, the contractor stepped up his efforts, not realizing that his efforts to appease the client were futile. Clearly, this client was completely clueless as to the value of a construction dollar, and to the obvious drawbacks to painting old beat-up apartments. Consequently, he refused to pay the contractor on the principle that the job didn't look new. The contractor was to be blamed in that he wasn't specific enough in his proposal to the client; this client took undue advantage.

The moral of these three examples is the following: whether the painting is specified, or not, the general contractor, if he is not dead certain of the scope of work, should partner with the architect to negotiate the value of the painting contract; even if this means sharing the subcontractor's proposals. The fact is, anyone can hold a brush in his hand but to turn out quality product requires a lot of skill—more than most bring to the table. Apparently, the product would be vastly improved if painters were more meticulous and didn't try to rush their work. Painting is labor-intensive and takes time; it's more than just slapping paint on the wall. For this reason, paint jobs are notoriously substandard. It doesn't help that good painters are hard to find.

Even people who are willing to pay for a top-notch paint job may have difficulty finding a qualified painter. Often a painter will have to paint a room five times before a color is approved. This phenomenon has been more or less resolved by a tacit understanding by "those in the know". The criteria for finish standards in true high-end work is pretty close to perfection. Areas may have to be repainted several times to accommodate changes in the work and tweaking. If there is a complaint, it will be heard and the offending area redone—no questions asked. This is why top quality paint jobs are expensive. There is a dearth of top-notch painters in the market. If you are going to sell a client a paint job for a high-end project, you will have to avail yourself of one of them.

High-end paint jobs may cost as much as double or triple the cost of an average paint job. Subcontractor bids will often reflect this disparity. Clients sometimes make the mistake of thinking that the painting scope of work is a windfall for the contractor—it rarely is. In fact, many general contractors will choose not to do the painting on a project if given the choice, because the paltry margin on a typical paint job is seldom worth the headache.

Substantial Completion

Substantial completion is a critical milestone for any construction project. It represents the satisfaction or completion of all critical path tasks to that point. Substantial completion is almost always tied to the last substantial progress payment. The state constituting substantial completion on a project seems to no longer have a fixed definition, or its proper definition has become diluted over the years. The AIA definition doesn't shed a lot of light on it either:

> Substantial Completion is the stage in the progress of the Work when the Work or designated portion thereof is sufficiently complete in accordance with the Contract Documents so that the Owner can occupy or utilize the Work for its intended purpose. (A201: 9.8.1)

For general purposes, substantial completion is the level of completion on the project that the client can make substantial use of the space, or when he can move in without being disturbed by the execution of the remaining work. Because some clients don't choose to or can't wait, these requirements may not be wholly enforced, or partially waived. If they are, the clause should be modified in the contract documents according to agreement. The A201: 9.8.1, stated earlier, seems to leave open an avenue for various interpretations of substantial completion, suggesting that modification of the meaning of the term is commonplace, which it is.

Regardless of whether or not a state of substantial completion is designated, there is a minimum of requirements:

- An enclosed space, impervious to the elements: walls, roof, windows, exterior doors, and so on
- Plumbing and electrical service
- Plumbing fixtures
- Electrical switches and outlets
- Heating and ventilation
- Satisfaction of all fire code requirements: smoke detectors, fire alarms, and the like
- Lighting
- Locksets on all doors
- Finished floors
- A functioning kitchen
- A functioning bathroom
- Bedrooms to sleep in and closets to store clothes in
- Temporary Certificate of Occupancy (TCO)[13]

These basic requirements may seem obvious; however, it is not uncommon that even they are subject to compromise. However, the local governing authorities will not likely issue a TCO without satisfaction of these basic requirements. The AIA publishes G704 *Certificate of Substantial Completion*; however, this is a tedious, contractor-unfriendly, and unnecessary document that is too stringent to meet the needs of an average project and I do not advocate its use. Moreover, I have never seen it used in the residential sector. Most projects will incorporate a milestone of substantial completion into the progress payment section of their contract, a strategy which makes issuance of a certificate a moot point.

Punch List

A punch list refers to the final touches a contractor will put on a project. Each item on it should be substantially complete, only requiring minor adjustments. As this work is now incorporated into the base contact, it is subject to the same criteria. A significant change order added to a contract late in the production stage can delay substantial completion status, and progress payments tied to its issuance. Often, this is an unfortunate and also unfair circumstance for the general contractor, who may have otherwise completed the project. For this reason, I believe that the practice of withholding a progress payment because of unfinished change order, work should be examined and negotiated in such a way that all parties are treated fairly. By the same token, final payment should always be indexed by the value of the remaining outstanding scope of work.

The object of an efficient punch list is to minimize it, with short-term duration tasks, mostly cosmetic in nature. A good schedule executed in a timely fashion will help to ensure that the punch list is kept to a minimum. Also, a preliminary punch list can be drafted, which should also help keep the final punch list small. If the architect issues a punch list before you have compiled your own, then you know you are late in preparing yours.

Good practice states that the punch list is not appended to more than once. Often punch lists are constantly revised, with new items being continually added. Theoretically, the list may never end. Punch lists which are issued too soon are subject to this phenomenon; the project should be substantially complete before a punch list is issued. This topic will be discussed further in Chap. 8.

Final Completion

Final completion requirements may include the following:

- Completion of punch list
- Release of lien waivers for 100% of the contract value
- Sign-offs for all controlled inspections
- Temporary or permanent certificate of occupancy

The client is entitled to withhold a retainer pending closure of any of the above requirements; however, the TCO is not normally tied to a contract requirement. Ten-percent retainer is a common rate of withholding. This 10% is notoriously the most difficult payment to reconcile on your project. It often becomes evident that the retainer is disproportionate to the value of outstanding items. It is good practice to require that the retainer is indexed in the same way as the base contract work was. This requirement should be discussed during the contract negotiation stage. One can easily valuate tangible line items; however, sign-offs and such have a nebulous value, which is hard to pin down; they would have to be negotiated.

"Tricks of the Trade"

Some tricks are helpful hints to be more efficient, while others are designed just to get over. This latter is a concern for general contractors. Of course, the litany of ruses and shenanigans are too numerous to mention here; however, a good place to start would be to identify certain obvious general behaviors and approaches I associate with poor means and methods, so to set the tone for high-end residential projects. I use the term "obvious," because much cheating tends to be done surreptitiously, or under the eye of a "green" superintendent. A superintendent should be as knowledgeable in the wrong way of doing things, as much as he is in the correct way. While some of these means and methods may be commonplace even tolerated on simpler projects, they are unacceptable on any high-end project.

Unauthorized installations

Substitutes and nonsubmitted scope: labor or materials. Where prevailing wage laws are in force, the contract will usually indicate it. In such cases, it is illegal practice to use replacements. Within unions, there are clear-cut divisions of "A" and "B" localities. As I have said, some contractors have priced their labor according to one criterion, only to substitute inferior labor. Established relationships with your subcontractors will generally help to eradicate this behavior; however, if you have negotiated too heavily with them, they may invoke their replacement tactic. In any case, union residential interior fit-outs have been the exception, as they seldom claim such work. For residential building, unions generally stick to developer work and start to demobilize after the core and shell-work is complete.

More commonly, substituting cheaper materials for more expensive ones called for in the specifications without architect approval is not contract-compliant behavior, as we shall see in Chap. 8. Even if there is a submittal process for a given material, you have to police your vendors to make sure they are delivering what was purchased and approved. This awareness is part of a good quality control program.

Some subcontractors install their work, or procure their material before or without an approved submittal, often with disastrous results. If they do, they are completely liable for any inconsistencies with the contract documents, and the installation may still be subject to rejection by the architect. Thus, the general contractor may be protected from footing the bill for the rework, but chances are the mistakes complicated other work and trades. I recall a HVAC contractor working on a tricky project with low ceilings, with beams and other obstructions. His work would require a lot of coordination. Surprisingly, he refused to produce shop drawings for his ductwork. Consequently, his work had to be refabricated, torn out, relocated, and necessitated complicated routing for other trades. Had he issued shop drawings, most of these conflicts never would have arisen. Had he been a finisher or mill worker, his mistakes would not affect subsequent trades. But as a duct installer, almost all-succeeding work was predicated on the correct placement of his work.

Finally, the specifications and general requirements, will state means and methods. These means and methods sometimes will take a back seat to (a) the shortest distance between two points and (b) the preferred method of the subcontractor, neither of which is necessarily consistent with common practice or the contract requirements. A typical example would be cutting corners on plywood subfloor nailing patterns, using fewer nails than needed. Or perhaps, using watered-down concrete. Some can be plain dangerous, such as the aforementioned watered-down concrete, or poorly executed welds. Therefore, subcontractor means and methods must be under constant scrutiny by the contractor. The architect may also observe, but he is not liable for them as is the contractor.

Pace

For the most part, a knee-jerk reaction to falling behind schedule or the realization that the labor for a given project was underbid is to accelerate production rates. Contractors and clients love to see work go up fast; but that does not make it a good thing. The faster the pace is, the more the likelihood of mistakes. Quality also decreases when pace increases. Your production supervisor should know what the natural pace of an installation is; however, there are those who work more slowly, or more quickly than the average. The trick is to gauge whether the level of workmanship is commensurate with the pace of the work at hand. Those who work slower tend to make fewer mistakes, but you want to know if they are merely slow, cautious, or if they simply may lack skills. Otherwise, some mechanics feel the need to speed up to keep pace with the rest of production, or to impress their boss.

Inevitably, projects with aggressive schedules tend to have work piled up toward the last minute. This is where compromises are made between quality and delays. It is a foregone conclusion that your client will not empathize with your dilemma, and thus the decision is made for you—they want both on time and top quality. This circumstance will be discussed further, in Chaps. 6 and 7. Often, even though the overall schedule may be unaffected, subcontractors may underman, or accelerate the production of their crews because they are losing money on a project. This type of behavior must also be kept under close watch. For example, coordination might require that mechanics spend a good deal of time sitting around, waiting for adjoining work to be installed. This is a commonplace necessity of sequencing on residential projects; however, if the men are not consistently on task, the contractor may pull them off the job, regardless of foreknowledge, only to return when they can be on task 100% of the time. While this may be more equitable to him, it botches the coordination of other related trades and forces the project out of sequence. The arrangement may make sense to the subcontractor, but it won't for you, or your other trades. High-end subcontractors come to expect phased installations, and the better ones will gauge their labor costs accordingly.

Therefore, the general contractor must indicate each subcontractor's position on the project schedule. These dates should be part of the general contractor-subcontractor agreement, thus leaving no opportunity for the subcontractor to screw up. Good subcontractors understand the stop-and-go sequencing of residential projects, and will coordinate their work according to the project's needs; not their own.

Poor workmanship

Some mechanics adopt the bad habit of cutting corners because they are lazy, inexperienced, or want to show a higher production rate. It is your field supervisor's responsibility to monitor their work habits so to identify such antics. Otherwise, because of the shortage and cost of skilled labor, the industry is inundated with incompetent workers. They are discharged for subpar performance from projects on a routine basis at an alarming rate. You would think that in the high-end sector that termination for poor performance was rare, but it is actually more commonplace than in other sectors of construction, because standards are higher.

Levels

There are many tools mechanics use every day, and it would be impossible to discuss them all here, however, one tool deserves critical consideration; bubble type levels have their place on a job site, but their use is limited. Once a benchmark is established, the level can be used to work within a small or local area. Too often the level takes the place of the benchmark, or the proper tool, a laser plumb or plumb bob, such as when a carpenter holds his small level parallel to a stud in order to align a plumb 10 ft space between floor and ceiling, or when a long line is projected from a short level. These methods have a negligible degree of exactitude and have no place in high-end installations. Accuracy between different levels can vary widely; in fact, some levels read differently when you flip them over. For these reasons, it is good practice to forbid them during the layout process.

Sequencing

Sequencing refers to the order in which things take place. There is the customary or natural order, and there is out of order or out of sequence. Somewhere in the middle is room for ingenuity and tweaking, wherein task durations can be shortened. This strategy we discussed in Chap. 3. Subcontractors champing at the bit are always a threat to cause the project to get snarled. They will want to get as much work done, as fast as they can, so that they can get paid as soon as possible, without regard for your fragile logistics, or other trades. A project out of sequence generally causes more problems than its worth; it tends to cause logistical snafus (see Chap. 7). Usually, a decision is made to reposition certain tasks in front of their predecessors, that is, out of sequence. However, there are times when one can do this without affecting logistics. For example, you may reposition a task because you discover a way around having to wait for its predecessor to be complete, as your scheduler may have thought. This is called *overlapping*, and is part of a skillful manager's tool kit. Critical tasks cannot be overlapped, nor can driving tasks.

Lag and overlapping.   As we have discussed in Chap. 3, overlapping refers to the practice of beginning a task before the completion of its predecessor(s). Lag is the amount of time between two tasks, or downtime between the end of one, and start of another. Increased overlapping or decreased lags tend to happen when a project is behind schedule, or when a contractor believes there is an opportunity to increase profit by expediting the schedule. Many tasks can be overlapped with their successor tasks at least to some extent. Your schedule should reflect this. Some tasks lend themselves well to it, some do not. For example:

Drywall installation tasks can be effectively overlapped. The sequence of a drywall installation is as follows:

- Install gypsum board
- Install beads
- Spackle screw heads and paper tape seams (first coat)
- Second coat
- Light/full sand
- Third coat (if necessary, then full sand)
- Polish coat

If the areas being completed are large enough, each crew can move through each stage of the installation without interruption—one on the heels of another. If the project is or must be done piecemeal, this process is less effective. Some contractors would schedule the drywall tapers as areas are closed. Residential projects tend not to lend themselves well to overlapped painting, as they do taping. Areas on residential interiors get released piecemeal. Each room always seems to have one or two things missing that are needed in order to paint, making full closure of the space untenable. Despite popular opinion, painted walls don't get touched-up, they get repainted in their entirety. Thus, four or five seemingly minor glitches can multiply work exponentially for the painter; all the more reason not to lay down final topcoats until a room is otherwise complete. When projects are squeezed toward the end, the general contractor will call in the painter once 25% of the space is free, because waiting for full closure would extend the schedule. Painters do not like to work this way because their rate of production nose-dives, and invariably, each room is painted two or three times because subsequent work damages the previous paint application. This is one reason why painting prices are becoming prohibitive, especially in high-end work, where eggshell, and oil-based paints raise the bar.

Some other projects and tasks do not lend themselves well to overlapping:

- Concrete and plaster surfaces must be 100% cured before they can be top-coated
- So does a polyurethane coated floor; there is no opportunity for overlapping here
- Closing walls and ceilings before MEP infrastructures are installed
- Shipping finished products to the site before they have cured

An example of a project for which both substitute materials and overlapping yielded disastrous results are related as follows:

A new high-rise was in the process of being erected. The concrete decks were installed, and no sooner had the concrete dried, then it was stripped of forms and the next floor was formed, poured, stripped, and so on. Controlled inspections of concrete generally require compression tests withstanding 3000-psi compression, after 29 days curing time. For whatever reason, the contractor chose not to wait for the test results, and proceeded to aggressively overlap production—erecting floors above. After an early result showed that a few of the lower floors failed the compression test, the project had to be redirected to costly tear out and reinstallation of the substandard decks a few floors down from the present floor.

For interiors, ductwork almost always is installed before any other ceiling program. However, it isn't necessary for all the ductwork to be installed before the next trade follows. Work may be released in parcels, such as, one area at a time. Generally, an aggressive scheduler will know up front what the lagging and overlapping tasks are, however, the production team will advise as to when to release each trade, as it happens on each particular project—this is overlap. Typically, much to the chagrin of the field personnel, upper management often makes the call to overlap tasks too aggressively. Technically speaking, they are rendering the project out of sequence.

The misuse of overlapping and sequencing methods is to blame for the demise of many projects. Resequencing should be done scientifically, with input from all concerned parties. If not everyone is apprised of a project resequencing, the effort can be rendered futile. For example, a contractor picking up extra time may be unable to avail himself of it only because he didn't run the plan by one of the affected tradesmen.

Too often, accelerating methods are a rash attempt to triage a late project's delays. Having your eyes and ears open, and schedule tracking should reduce the need to employ such tactics. As I said, acceleration tends to happen when either the workload is increased, or when the contractor has underestimated his production capabilities. The former may merit a schedule extension from the client, and if so, an increase in general conditions, however unfair, extensions are routinely not granted.

Some of the consequences of out of sequence and improperly overlapping tasks on a project are as follows:

- *Trade stacking*: The compression of man power, or too many people working on top of each other, is a classic out-of-sequence condition. Mistakes will be made, and conditions can become unpleasant and stressful; this arrangement has no empathy for the sensitivities of human nature.

- *Variably partially completed work*: When areas are in different degrees of completion, where men must constantly remobilize in each area according to the project's needs, or as a given area becomes available. This will stretch out task durations, and increase labor costs.

- Delay of the commencement of successor tasks due to their predecessors not being complete. If work were allowed to progress at a natural rate, this would not be a factor.

- Tear-out and corrective work.

- Finishes being installed while rough work and substrates in other areas are not complete; if components are ready, subcontractors will be anxious to get them out of their shop, and to the project. The general contractor will also expect their work to be shipped as soon as possible, even if it means the work must be stored on the site, and be subject to damages. One reason they may do this is so that they can bill the client for the work as being stored on-site. Another is the belief that even if the work is not ready to be installed, the client may not realize it, and may be left with a false sense of progress by the presence of the material.

When a project goes out of sequence, it becomes difficult to track the schedule using any scientific method. Thus, companies that tend to build out of sequence have little use for real schedules.

Increase man power and expediting.   Antithetical to an unhealthy pace imposed on a project, there are ways to increase rates of production without sacrificing quality and logistics. Often, a project may only need more men, or men sooner in order to keep the schedule moving. If this arrangement is not available for the asking, there are always incentives. You must weigh the concessions you intend to make against the pay-offs. Undermanned projects are frequently the fault of a subcontractor, such projects serve as examples of where incentives would not be appropriate because the subcontractor is evidently not fulfilling his contractual obligation. On the other hand, it is all too common that a subcontractor is delayed by the general contractor or other trades in such a way that his other projects become jeopardized; thus, he would be within his rights to postpone the delayed project, and take on other work. General contractors should be wary of using small contractors in busy times, or contractors with whom they have little leverage. Often, in such cases, these subcontractors can't afford to be put off. If the scheduler is aware of this, he should make it clear to the production team that a given subcontractor's work may not be rescheduled. Otherwise, a subcontractor with more resources and flexibility should be considered.

A general contractor often finds that his subcontractors are not manning a project adequately, and insists that additional man power be added to make up for the lost productivity. The subcontractor may have to take men from other projects (even for the same general contractor) to do this, and those jobs will now suffer from being undermanned. If he has to take men from another job, he will likely want to get it over with quickly. What tends to happen is that instead of implementing a larger crew over a short period of a week or so, an even larger crew is sent in for just 1 or 2 days for a frenetic crash, which is just fine with most contractors who are happy to see the extra men. However, this arrangement can do more harm than good:

■ The sudden unexpected increase in man power can set the project out of sequence by displacing the everyday workers to accommodate the increased crew. Their work now falls behind or slows down.

■ The superintendent becomes distracted from his daily routine by the change of pace. Moreover, with the glut of bodies, he can't be everywhere he has to be, thus work goes unsupervised.

■ The larger crew is there for only a short time. They will work faster, making more mistakes and will be more difficult to supervise.

The general contractor may not be in a position to insist that the increased man power be spread out over 7 days instead of 2, because his schedule may not allow for that. Had he addressed the production slowdown earlier, chances are he would not be in this position. This is no small problem for the residential sector, which is by and large serviced by small subcontractors, who don't have the infrastructure of larger companies to mobilize men when they need them.

Red labeling.   Red labeling refers to expediting, or speeding up delivery of materials or other goods. It is often necessary to invoke this strategy when a project is late, or has an aggressive schedule. It is also used often on fast-track projects. Optimally, you will know up front if you need to red label deliveries, so that you can charge accordingly, as you can be sure your vendors will.

One downside of red labeling is that it notoriously shortens or omits the submittal process, thus creating greater margins for error. Therefore, all team members, especially the design team, must be on board for an accelerated review process. Red labeling is not helpful with complicated submittals, such as:

Ductwork

Cabinetry

Dimming systems

Wood flooring

Plaster and cementitious finishes

You should know the delivery schedule of all your goods, particularly long lead items, when you are composing your proposal. Then, you will not be unpleasantly surprised by missed deadlines due to delivery lags. You should also be knowledgeable in typical delivery dates and durations, as you may be asked to be flexible on projects where all the specifications are not available.

Coming up short in a shortage.   During shortages, it can be difficult to get materials to the site. The effect of material shortages on a project is not wholly the responsibility of the general contractor; however, not to be aware of, or to fail to strategize for a shortage is irresponsible. Material shortages affect companies differently. Larger companies tend to know sooner than the smaller ones, and are better prepared to plan. They can order early, or stockpile. When push comes to shove, suppliers tend to service their larger accounts before their smaller ones—invariably residential builders. It helps to have a regular vendor with whom you have a good relationship. If he cares about your account, he will warn you of impending shortages. If you place small orders among several suppliers, it's unlikely they will make a courtesy call advising you of a shortage.

If it can be demonstrated that there was a material shortage of which a general contractor should have been aware of, and failed to act, he can be held liable, should this fact exacerbate the delay. Had he addressed it sooner, perhaps a substitution could have been made. Estimators and buyers must keep abreast of market supply for products needed for their projects. This sort of diligence can help to avoid being caught in a shortage.

Notes

Project checklist: Preconstruction

- Long lead submittals
- Schedule
- Permitting

Project checklist: Predemolition

- Walk-throughs with subcontractors
- Protections
- Effect safety program
- Arrange for shutdowns; check valves and breakers
- Arrange for temporary services

Project checklist: Mobilization

- Review project and strategy with all production team members
- Secure necessary permits and perforated set (stamped set of drawings)

- Notify building owner and/or client of intent to mobilize site
- Photograph and document existing conditions of site, and adjacent tenants/ owners as required
- Notify owner and building owner or managing agent in writing of intent to start, with contact telephone numbers
- Circulate personnel information to design team and owner
- Prepare lists of materials and tools necessary to mobilize the site
- Issue fire extinguishers and first-aid kits
- Issue site documentation: drawings, HAZMAT books, employment law required documentation, and safety tools: signs, markers, caution tape, and the like
- Arrange for production team to man the site

Project checklist: Production

- Layout approval
- MEP coordination
- MEP at partitions 100%
- Close walls (white box part 1)
- MEP at ceilings 100%
- Close ceilings (white box part 2)

Project checklist: Closeout

- Substantial completion
- Punch list
- Client turnover
- Completion

Endnotes

1. See App. A.
2. For a project that has solid digital accountability, e-mail is a tremendous facilitator that obviates the need for time-consuming paperwork. The submittal itself can be e-mailed, or it can be hand-delivered or faxed, with an e-mail approval from the architect. For web-based management, this can be a very effective method. However, when shop drawings with red lines and comments are involved, e-mail is not sufficient protocol.
3. The term *white box* refers to the nondescript appearance of an interior project when all walls and ceilings are closed and spackled, and finishes are then able to be applied. Few contractors wait until the entire space is a white box, as their schedules seldom afford them this luxury. Typically, they begin finishes whenever and wherever they can.
4. Preexisting refers to what was installed before the existing installation. These valves sometimes are found only subsequent to demolition and removals.

5. Just who is responsible for undertaking this procedure is a great bone of contention between architects and contractors.
6. 60% of the FMI/Construction Managers Association of America (CMAA) survey respondents indicated that having subs complete the design increases miscommunication and delays, whereas 63% agreed that the quality of design documents has declined to the point where subcontractors, such as electrical and mechanical, are actually completing the design through the shop drawing (FMI/CMAA) pp. 7.
7. According to the Control Systems Integration Association (CSIA), about 9–10% annually for North America, although these firms by and large are concerned with large-scale plants and manufacturing operations. However, as of March 2002, only 10% (140) of about 1200 systems integrators are CSIA certified.
8. There is a great distinction between schematics and shop drawings. Some trades will use schematics for coordination purposes before they issue shop drawings; others won't.
9. Depending on scope and complexity, these drawings may need a higher priority.
10. American Woodworking Institute, *AWI/AWMAC—8th Edition Quality Standards*, 2003.
11. *Ibid.*
12. *Alligatoring* and *orange peeling* are two terms used to describe the texture of poorly applied spray finish coats.
13. Temporary C of O, or *Certificate of Occupancy,* generally not the responsibility of the contractor.

Residential Construction Management

*From Colonial times until around 1850, clients and
builders designed almost all houses in America.
Architects had to create their profession against the
odds. They had to persuade their countrymen that
important distinctions existed between the art of
designing and the act of building. Once architects
had made some headway with their case, many
builders without formal training began describing
themselves as architects, too. Doubtless many more
declared, as Thompson[1] did, that trained architects
were merely superfluous beings.*

*Between 1830 and the Civil War, architects
published scores of pattern and style books. At one
point or another, most of those volumes argue that
an architect offers the client protection from the
builder. The case is often founded on social class,
the architect being the client's ally by virtue of
education and breeding. The argument plays upon
the suspiciousness of clients about builders, a
wariness that seems to have been around for so
long that it probably deserves to be called natural.*

*"There is a glaring want of truthfulness
sometimes practiced in this country by ignorant
builders, that deserves condemnation at all times,"
wrote Andrew Jackson Downing in 1850, in one of
his very popular style books. In this case,
"truthfulness" meant right-minded aesthetic
sensibility. Competing with builders for the
patronage of people with the money to build, in an
age of emerging specialization, architects staked a
claim on taste. Pattern and style book writers
defined taste in many ways, but ultimately it
seems to have been simply something a trained
architect had and a builder didn't. And while
clients usually were described as having taste,
most needed architects to find their way to it. An
architect could protect clients from themselves as
well as ignorant builders.*

TRACY KIDDER, FROM *HOUSE*[2]

The above text illustrates two perceptions held by many American architects of builders that date back to the mid-nineteenth century, namely, a presumed class superiority assumed by architects over builders which dictated a natural alliance of the architect with the client, and an avowed distrust of builders by architects, which they impressed upon their clients. This was a telling statement, for remnants of this adversarial relationship still exist today. The natural suspiciousness of builders by clients is still pervasive. Resultantly, architects have happily assumed the position of client's advocate. This "us against them" relationship predisposes project teams to conflicts for which there is no intermediary. Today's construction manager (CM) can fill that role; while at the same time contribute significantly to the contract administration process.

Traditional residential contractual arrangements almost never include a CM. I suppose most people, especially architects, don't feel the need for one. For the most part, it is true that most residential projects have no such need; however, for more complex and high-end projects, a CM will facilitate a project more effectively than your average contractor. Typically, between the owner, architect, and general contractor, the consensus is that the project has all the brainpower it needs. What's more, adding another layer of management can be construed as adding a middleman, who will inevitably take from their market share. The architect and the general contractor might chafe at the prospect of incorporating a CM into their project, feeling that their ability to manage the project is being called into question, that they will have to answer to the CM, and that they will cede some portion of their fee to help finance the CM—all true. Yet, if residential projects don't need CMs, then why do the vast majority of them suffer from mismanagement and logistical failure?

Construction management contracts have been around for about 45 years. They are generally geared to commercial, governmental, institutional, or other volume-oriented projects. For this reason, this type of contract has been used only sporadically in the residential sector. As Gary Berman put it to me, "Who in their right mind would sign such a contract for building a residence?" Well put—sort of like dropping a nuclear bomb on Hackensack. Being used so infrequently, it is misunderstood, and when invoked, misused by residential contractors. Part of this problem can be attributed to there being no set criteria for residential construction management. Hence, it has been left up to the industry to form an *ad hoc* definition. The reason for there being no set criteria for the residential industry is that there was never a constituency, or a large enough one, that insisted on the creation of such criteria, as might be set forth in contract documents.

To some, a CM merely goes about his business as he normally would for any general contracting project, and happily collects his percentage at the end of each month. This is the lowest functioning form of a CM, and it is a jaundiced manifestation. Nonetheless, these arrangements are commonplace. Every other general contractor seems to fancy himself *as a construction manager*, a term which to them, is redundant with the term *general contractor*. This practice is dishonest, and unbecoming to the industry. Because so many contractors are poor managers, any one who endeavors to upgrade the level of customary management may consider himself a CM, but design professionals and others will not, as exemplified by the following statement: "One reason for the advent of construction management was the increase of poor management by many general contractors."[3] This statement, at least 18 years old, still rings true. Many of these general contractors likely sold CM services, for which they underdelivered, that is, misrepresented themselves.

A CM is typically contracted for projects that may have several general contractors, or other projects that are large and complex. He is the one who will make it all work and fit together. His relationship with the rest of the project team was illustrated in Figs. 2.1d and e (Chap. 2). Compare this arrangement with that of a standard general contractor–owner relationship, Figs. 2.1a, b, and c.

For the high-end residential sector, the traditional role of the CM must be a distillation from its traditional meaning, especially in his preconstruction role, facilitating the design team. Some of the traditional CM services that are seldom performed by residential CMs are:

- Land acquisition
- Feasibility study
- Property closing services
- Financing
- Lease negotiation
- Loan arrangement
- Selection and control of design team
- Cash flow management (to a lesser degree)

These tasks are not germane to a CM for most residential projects. Residential architects will have less experience with CMs and may be leery of them. Because the CM's role must be diluted in the smaller residential market, the exact definition of his responsibilities is somewhat inscrutable. Construction management firms lend themselves better to large projects. Their area of expertise on the subject is considerably wider than their cousins involved in residential projects. On the other hand, CMs outside the high-end residential sector typically don't have a clue as to that sector's needs. Strong residential contractors have a leg up on the larger CMs in that they have expertise in their niche. This author will argue that:

- There is a need for CMs in the residential sector, especially high-end.
- The implementation of construction management contracts into the high-end residential sector would net at least the same rate of return on investment as it does in any other building sector.
- The integrity and efficiency of CMs now in the residential sector could vastly be improved.

- The role of the residential CM requires clarification, as it varies from the traditional role.

Another misperception is that a cost-plus fee contract would be better let as a construction management contract, because they are so closely related. This idea has gained a fair amount of acceptance, one reason being that the term "cost-plus fee," does not have a lot of allure for a prospective client, whereas, "CM" serves as a ready-made euphemism. However, as I have said, this notion is also a misnomer, as will be demonstrated later.

On the whole, construction management contracts have little appeal to most clients in the residential sector. One reason for this lack of popularity is that there is a requisite leap of faith that the client must make in entering into such a contract, a stretch that few residential clients are able to justify or even give fair consideration out of ignorance more than anything else. Additionally, being unfamiliar with the mechanics and risks associated with CM contracts doesn't improve his aspect. One of their chief misgivings is that by ceding so much control to his CM, the client exposes himself to being cheated, as ultimately, the CM is scrutinized on an honor system basis only. Under this arrangement, a CM could conceivably manipulate to his own advantage in any number of ways, without fear of discovery. Because of the propensity of this sort of mismanagement, architects may be apprehensive of the CM arrangement. This is where the lines become blurred between the term cost-plus fee and construction management contract. A CM in an *advisory* role can somewhat dispel a client's fears of being cheated, as his vested interest is considerably less than it would be were he the CM and constructor. Additionally, residential clients tend not to appreciate the value of what a CM brings to the table; not being a developer, retailer, or other entity experienced with construction management, they simply can't appreciate it as other builders do. They also don't grasp the concept that they have responsibility in the contract and that they aren't merely spectators.

Despite market perception, there are some very strong incentives for residential clients to direct a project into a construction management contract arrangement. Some of the more savvy players, especially constant builders, are realizing the advantages construction management contracts have over standard agreements, and the appeal is beginning to spread, at least for some of the larger projects. As high-end residential spending now comprises such a vast majority of the home building sector, construction management can no longer be ignored. If they observe nothing else that can be said, the client will hear and appreciate the concept of 100% return on investment that a CM should be able to yield. And lastly, there is incentive for an architect and general contractor to enter into the construction management arrangement, as they stand to gain by the higher level of efficacy, just like the client. The CM advisor, as a disinterested party, can be extremely industrious at working out disagreements and contract disputes, only without the yelling and screaming.

Other causes that argue for an increase in construction management contracts are as follows:

1. The inability of some designers to estimate and control construction costs during the design phase, with many budgets consequently bid at amounts much higher than owners' budgets

2. The lack of practical construction experience of some designers and their consultants, resulting in impractical and expensive design details, ill-made contracts, extensive change orders, and disagreements on the job site

3. The general inflexibility of the lump-sum contract with a general contractor leading a team of subcontractors

4. The traditional sequence of (a) complete design, (b) bidding, and (c) production, that prolongs a project's time, and therefore, enlarges its financing costs[4]

Because a CM is best utilized at the conception stage of the project, he can begin his work early. He can advise the design team and owner of helpful value engineering techniques in terms of constructability during design and development. However, his work stops short of reviewing design documents for integrity, or compliance to the owner's program—a service only a licensed architect should provide.

Once the design is ratified, he can spearhead the creation of a production budget. After the design and budget are prepared, the bid packages can be assembled. From this point in time, a construction management contract timeline takes a different path than the average contract, as shown in Fig. 5.1. This graph shows a 15% reduction in the timeline between a traditional and construction-managed project. A residential remodel project would sequence differently, and wouldn't include the structural work; however, the fifty-week timeline is an excellent benchmark.

As illustrated, because the CM is involved in the preconstruction process, the job team is able to start production earlier, or when not all of the design is finalized; somewhat like a fast-track project. As building proceeds, the design team continues to work at the next level of detail, so to keep the project on task. So long as the design and production teams continue to produce at acceptable rates, the project will be delivered much sooner than had production begun only after final designs were drafted. If the project is delivered sooner, the client's carrying costs during the overall design and construction period will be less, and the project will be less subject to material and labor price fluctuations.

In terms of the production phase of a project, a CM should finish the same scope of work faster than the average general contractor. This is because he has the advantage of the planning and foresight of the preconstruction phase. He can conduct much of his problem solving and troubleshooting before the work starts, instead of while the work is taking place, or after the fact. More importantly,

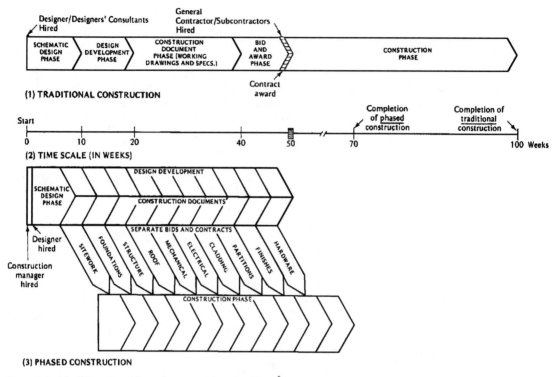

Figure 5.1 Traditional vs. phased construction timelines.[5]

he can address requests for information (RFIs) that will lead to critical information that otherwise might slow or arrest the progress of the work. This being so, an effective CM as constructor, should always outperform a general contractor *sans* CM. Some general contractors realize this and have made adjustments to make up for the deficit; they add the term *Construction Managers* to their business card and letterhead. The irony is that most traditional competitively bid working drawings are only about 50 to 75% developed at the beginning of production—borderline bid drawings.[6] In other words, many fixed-sum contracts begin without full designs, much like their construction management counterparts, except that they do not benefit from the preconstruction phase; problems are solved in the field, and on task. Merely because they are processing design information midproject, they believe they are functioning as CM.

Another incentive to use a CM is less tangible. It holds that a project led by an efficient CM will run more smoothly, and will yield a superior process than that of a general contractor of equal skill. Even if their end products are indistinguishable from one another, the construction management contract should still prove to be a more efficient structure. Once the production phase begins, the CM may stay on as advisor, take on the project as constructor, or move on. Architects and general contractors are only too familiar with dysfunctional projects, and it is easier for them to brush off bad experiences, but for many owners, the project is a one-time experience. If it goes badly, it can seemingly take years off a client's longevity, as the client will not be inured to the slings and arrows of construction purgatory. The cost of the CM to the client could easily be offset by the prospect of callbacks and psychotherapy bills.

When a client uses a CM he has a strong entity representing his interests, he will also realize intangible gains during the contract that will later translate into equity. The advantage will be no more evident than in the matter of managing the flow of information, and conflict resolution, two areas where losses often originate. Without the CM as intermediary, the intricacies of managing a difficult project are left to the caprices of the architect and contractor, who often will waste time arguing, instead of solving problems; the CM may act as arbitrator, thereby keeping conflicts from sidetracking production. If the CM is the constructor, he may not act as an arbiter, but the nature of his former proactive role should lead to a more expedient conflict resolution process.

Much of what is said about these incentives can be considered theoretical; however, there is one considerable incentive that should be realized. Using an efficient CM should generally net at least 100% return on investment, especially if some of the CM's fees are offset by the absence of a general contractor, and by reduction of an architect's fees, as a proactive CM assumes some of their workload. However, try convincing an architect of this—dead issue. Even without a concession from the architect, if the CM's fee is 5%, it is likely the client will reap 100% rate of interest, and the architect will be empowered to perform more tasks closer to his area of expertise—design, as opposed to management.

Owner's Responsibilities in Construction Management Contracts

Clients don't really believe they have a workload, or responsibility in the process, as they feel that a customer, by his nature, has no such obligations. This is a misconception that you will want to refute early on in the negotiating process. Let them know that the opposite is true, that they are part of the team, play a central role in the decision-making process, and that nonperformance on their end of the contract can be as detrimental to the project as anyone else's shortcomings. Construction management does not denote a turn-key process. The Construction Management Association of America (CMAA) A-1 contract format includes a section[7] that outlines the owner's responsibilities. Constant builders and some who commission larger projects are well familiar with the process. I believe residential owners stand to gain a lot of experience from their perceptions.

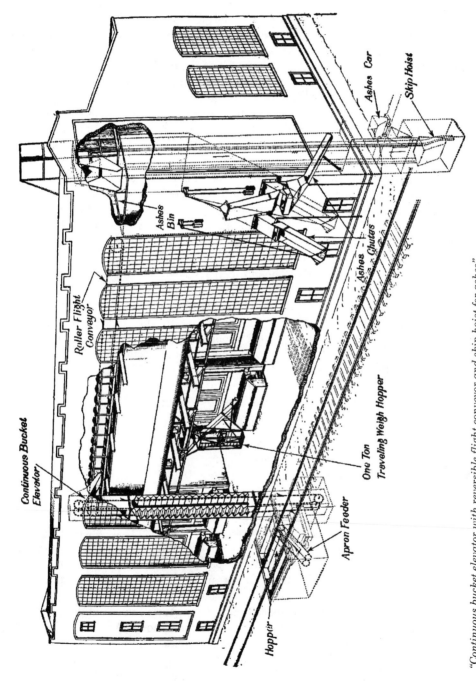

"Continuous bucket elevator with reversible flight conveyor and skip hoist for ashes"
The pivoted bucket carrier shown is designed to handle both coal and ashes. At the time, 1917, maintenance costs for one type of pivoted bucket carrier were calculated at $0.0036 per ton of coal handled. Harding and Willard, *Mechanical Equipment of Buildings, Vol II: Power Plants and Refrigeration* (New York: John Wiley & Sons, 1918)

Since many general contractors and architects often do the least they can do management and documentation-wise to get by, they should be only too happy that someone else would be willing to do these things for them. The CMAA advises us of the following basic advantages to the client of the CM arrangement:

- Enhanced control of the scope of work
- Optimal project/program scheduling options
- Best use of individual team member's expertise
- Maximum avoidance of delays, changes, and claims
- Enhanced design and construction quality
- Optimum flexibility in contracting/procurement options[8]

To general contractors, the term construction management is synonymous with what a general contractor should and could do, if he were paid a little more money; the only difference being that an extra fee is apportioned to the CM. General contractors should:

- Provide timely and accurate documentation
- Issue and manage schedules, with reports and updates
- Manage and coordinate the subcontracting trades
- Be more diligent in realizing and responding to clients' needs
- Work more fluidly with the design industry

They should not require additional remuneration to perform these tasks. General contractors could:

- Provide timely and accurate documentation.
- Issue and manage schedules, with reports and updates
- Manage and coordinate the subcontracting trades
- Be more diligent in realizing and responding to clients' needs
- Work more fluidly with the design industry

The above redundancy is by design; most general contractors believe that what they perceive as construction management level services, are different from standard general contracting level services, while they are not. The missing elements are simply services they do not provide as general contractors. In truth, they are misrepresenting themselves by claiming to be CMs.

The perception exists because general contractors seem to do so little in the way of management that any extension of their basic service they construe as a construction management provision. As a response, it appears that architects and designers are becoming less inclined to go the extra yard, as they sense an overarching feeling of self-centeredness from the building industry, which translates to fewer services provided to them by general contractors, and more conflict between architects and contractors. In the end, the client loses, as he frequently is being underserviced by both architect and contractor alike. There needs to be a back to grassroots type movement to motivate industry professionals to perform according to their discipline and not the minimal requirements of it. From there, then consider the role of a CM proper.

Construction Management Contract Structures

There are a number of CM contract vehicles available. There are three main providers of these documents—the American Institute of Architects (AIA), CMAA, and Associated General Contractors of America (AGC). The AGC models will not be considered in this text, as they don't seem to be as popular as the CMAA and AIA documents; moreover, the AGC does not seem to even acknowledge the existence of the residential construction sector.[9]

The AIA CM series contract documents seem to be somewhat vague in their definition of the CM's role, whereas the CMAA contract documents are comprehensive and specific, which makes sense; the CMAA's bailiwick is construction management, and the AIA's architecture. In either case, neither organization's instruments were intended to be used for residential contracts. Architects are loath to sign CMAA documents and CMs cannot make ample use of the AIA's construction management contract language. Accordingly, an owner might have to contract the architect with an AIA contract and his CM with a CMAA contract.

Some architects believe that CMs encroach on their livelihood, by offering services they normally provide, or *would* normally provide. I emphasize the word "would" because it implies that if such services were warranted, they would fall within the architect's area of expertise. In fact, the AIA even offers a document, the B144, to contract them for such services:

> B144^{TM}ARCH-CM-1993 Standard Form of Amendment to the Agreement Between Owner and Architect Where the Architect Provides Construction Management Services as an Adviser to the Owner
> B144^{TM}ARCH-CM-1993 is an amendment to B141^{TM}-1997 for use in circumstances where the architect agrees to provide the owner with a package of construction management services to expand upon, blend with, and supplement the architect's design and construction administration services described in B141^{TM}.[10]

Although some architects may know something about construction management that does not make them CMs. Moreover, the idea of involving an outside entity to monitor their work and their projects must seem odious to them. It is a moot point whether or not their objection is valid regarding small projects, but it is outright unacceptable regarding larger, more complex projects, where architects often falter under the impetus of a more stringent contract administrative workload.

The CMAA has been exemplary in its defining role as a construction management professional organization since 1981. While this accolade is a bit reductive, it helps understand that there are several vehicles available to facilitate a construction management project. As I have said, a typical contractual arrangement would consist of the architect–owner agreement using an AIA instrument, and the owner–CM of CMAA. The downside of there being multiple contract formats is that there is a lot of crossover in defining responsibility, especially between architects and CMs, and alternatively, there are tasks that will slip through the cracks, as it may not be clear whose responsibility they are. Oddly enough, the implication of undefined scope would essentially require that the owner provide the service for himself. Additionally, the AIA and CMAA contracts go so far as to state responsibilities that other parties will not perform. This problem is the source of endless conflicts. An example would be where the AIA owner–architect agreement indicates that administration of the trade contracts is not the CM's duty, whereas the CMAA owner–CM agreement states that contract administration is a shared duty between the architect and CM. This conflict would infer a struggle for control.

There are two types of contractual arrangements between CM and owner provided by the AIA—contracts where CM is also constructor and contracts where he is only an advisor.[11]

American Institute of Architects (AIA) construction manager agreements

A101™CMa-1992 Standard Form of Agreement Between Owner and Contractor where the basis of payment is a Stipulated Sum, Construction Manager-Adviser Edition

A101™CMa-1992 is a standard form of agreement between owner and contractor for use on projects where the basis of payment is a stipulated sum (fixed price), and where, in addition to the contractor and the architect, a construction manager assists the owner in an advisory capacity during design and construction. The document has been prepared for use with A201™CMa-1992, *General Conditions of the Contract for Construction, Construction Manager-Adviser Edition.* This integrated set of documents is appropriate for use on projects where the Construction Manager only serves in the capacity of an adviser to the owner, rather than as constructor (the latter relationship being represented in documents A121™, CMc-1991 and A131™CMc-1991.) A101™ CMa-1992 is suitable for projects where the cost of construction has been predetermined, either by bidding or by negotiation.

A121™CMc-2003 Standard Form of Agreement Between Owner and Construction Manager Where the Construction Manager is also the Constructor (AGC Document 565) This document represents the collaborative efforts of The American Institute of Architects and The Associated General Contractors of America. AIA designates this document as A121™CMc-1991. It is intended for use on projects where a construction manager, in addition to serving as adviser to the owner, assumes financial responsibility for construction of the project. The construction manager provides the owner with a guaranteed maximum price proposal, which the owner may accept, reject, or negotiate. Upon the owner's acceptance of the proposal by execution of an amendment, the construction manager becomes contractually bound to provide labor and materials for the project. The document divides the construction manager's services into two phases: the preconstruction phase and the construction phase, portions of which may proceed concurrently in order to fast track the process. A121™CMc is coordinated for use with A201™-1997, *General Conditions of the*

Contract for Construction, and B151™-1997, *Standard Form of Agreement Between Owner and Architect*. Check Section 9 of B511™-2001, *Guide to Amendments to Owner-Architect Agreement* for clarification.

This latter arrangement (A121) can be structured as follows: The CM acts as advisor, or agency to the owner in the preconstruction phase. Once the scope of work is more fully developed, he may become the constructor (at risk). Risk has a lot to do with contractual positions, and how the contract is structured. This dynamic can partially be exemplified as follows:

Parties who bear the risk in an endeavor are due their rights to control their destiny. The greater the risk profile, the greater the need to control. Loss or perceived loss of control leads to fear of a negative outcome. This fear leads to an assertion of the right to control, resulting in frequent disputes. Therefore, the key to successful management of the construction process is the placement of risk in the hands of those who are best equipped to manage it.[12]

I would go one better and apply the above statement to any construction contract relationship.

A201™CMa-1992 General Conditions of the Contract for Construction, Construction Manager-Adviser Edition
A201™CMa-1992 is an adaptation of A201™-1997 and was developed for use in projects where a fourth player, a construction manager, has been added to the team of owner, architect, and contractor. Under A201™CMa, the construction manager serves as an independent adviser to the owner, who enters into multiple contracts with prime trade contractors. A major difference between A201™ and A201™CMa is evident in Article 2, *Administration of the Contract*. A201™CMa, Article 2 sets forth the construction phase duties and responsibilities of both the architect and the construction manager-adviser.
Caution: It is important that A201™CMa not be used in combination with agreements where the construction manager takes on the role of constructor, gives the owner a guaranteed maximum price, or contracts directly with those who supply labor and materials for the project.[13]

The AIA documents for CM contracts are somewhat limiting in their scope and breadth in terms of describing services, especially when compared to the CMAA documents. Any CM worth his salt would not likely offer an AIA CM agreement as a contractual instrument.

The CMAA furnishes CM contract documents as well, which are geared toward the CM, and more importantly, the client, but finally, they more clearly and comprehensively define the CM's role than the AIA format does. They were revised in 2005.

Construction Management Association of America (CMAA) document family

The CMAA contract document family is specifically designed for CMs. However, the average construction management project is quite large and complex. The level and scope of services it describes would be exorbitant and unnecessary for the residential sector. As it stands, the CMAA membership does not have a great demand for a revised or abbreviated construction management contract, such as would befit the residential sector, because not a lot of bona fide CMs work this sector. As we have discussed, I believe the implementation of construction management proper could be a great boon to the residential sector, such that perhaps, one day, the CMAA will draft a contract specifically for that purpose. In the meantime, the CMAA A-1 can be amended to serve this purpose well enough. Unlike most documents requiring amending, the CMAA documents are overqualified for the residential sector, as opposed to lacking in terms and conditions like so many of their competitors.

The revised CMAA A-1 takes into consideration some past shortcomings, and incorporates new language to more clearly define each contract party's responsibilities.

CMAA Document A-1 Standard Form of Agreement Between *Owner and Construction Manager* (Construction Manager as Owner's Agent)[14]

The A-1 is the primary CMAA construction management–owner contract designated for use by the CMAA. Alternatively, the AIA offers the above referenced forms. However, the 2005 A-1 has been updated to include a comprehensive list of services to be provided by the construction manager, as well as the owner's responsibilities. This document spells out the CM's responsibilities better than any other CM–owner contract format available. Even with the understanding that the A-1, like any other contract, is chiefly intended for major construction projects and with some deletions and amendments, it could be used for the smaller projects of the residential sector.

Other published standard CMAA forms compatible with these construction management agreements are:

CMAA Document A-2 Standard Form of Contract Between *Owner and Contractor*

This document is very contractor oriented. It is also a bit simplistic. This traditional contract structure is really not the bailiwick of the CMAA. Few architects or owners would sign it, and few contractors offer it.

CMAA Document A-3 General Conditions of the Construction Contract Between *Owner and Contractor*
Interestingly enough, the A-3 is nearly as long as its counterpart, the AIA 201 (38 pp.); it is 37 pages in length. The closest AIA counterpart to the A-3 is AIA A201 CMa; however, the AIA advises, mentioned before in the chapter, that the A201 CMa should not be used in conjunction on contracts where the construction manager is also constructor. I suppose an AIA A201 CMc could theoretically someday serve that purpose. In the meantime, the standard A201 will continue to be used. The A-3 is meant to be used in conjunction with the A-1 or A-2.

CMAA Document A-4 Standard Form of Agreement Between *Owner and Designer*

The CMAA A-4 is not widely used. The closest AIA instrument to the CMAA contract is the AIA B141/CMa owner–architect agreement, because it is relatively well coordinated with the (CMAA) CM agreements. Whether it is better coordinated with the CMAA owner–construction manager contract is a moot point, as architects will not likely sign this document; they will insist on an AIA contract. However, it does serve a valuable purpose to owners by defining what the architect's scope of work should include as a counterpart to the CM's scope of work defined in the CMAA A-1.

Additionally, the CMAA offers a construction management guaranteed maximum price (GMP) contract:

> **CMAA Document GMP-2** Standard Form of Contract Between *Construction Manager and Contractor*
>
> **CMAA Document GMP-3** General Conditions of the *Construction Contract; Construction Manager-Contractor* Contract

However, a CM can work simply in an advisory role, for an owner engaged in just about any contractual arrangement with a general contractor. This can be defined as "pure agency," which can be folded into a variety of arrangements depending on the owner's needs, and how much risk he feels must be saddled with the CM. Some of them would seemingly suit certain residential projects nicely.

Pure agency construction management with general contracting and hourly CM fee. The CM works for the owner, managing a general contractor or several contractors. The CM works on an hourly basis, applying the hours needed for the level of service required. He typically works against a budget for his fees. The CM is responsible on a professional services basis to provide advice, guidance, and counsel to the owner within the current standard of care for construction management practice.

The CM essentially has no cost risk, and gets paid for every hour he works at a rate that covers his direct costs, overhead and agreed-to profit. The owner maintains full responsibility for the execution of the project, with the exception of any problems caused by the CM's negligence. The CM's performance risk is one of negligence, and should be covered by professional liability insurance.

The cost of the CM is offset by savings generated through cost and schedule management, value engineering, and helping the owner with good management practices throughout the planning, and design and construction of the project.

Pure agency CM with general contracting and a lump-sum CM fee. This is essentially the same as the preceding subhead, with one exception; rather than getting paid for every hour he works, the CM has a lump-sum fee for defined services for the duration of the project. This places the CM at cost risk for his fee but no more. The owner benefits, as the CM has a contractual cap on fees, based on a defined scope of services. But the CM may be tempted to provide less service than what was contracted for to increase profits. This requires some diligence on the part of the owner, similar to what the owner would apply in managing his architect under a lump-sum fee arrangement.

Pure agency CM with phased construction.   In this scenario the owner bids the work to multiple contractors to meet a tight schedule. Site work will be bid before the building design is complete, and foundations may be bid before the building interior design is finished. There can be up to five or more separate construction contracts such as site work, site utilities, foundations, base building, and interiors.

The CM takes on more risk and responsibility. The CM defines the interfaces between contractors and manages and coordinates the individual contractors to meet the owner's cost, schedule, and quality requirements. This additional responsibility brings some added risk to the CM due to his coordination of separate contractors working on the same building. Poor coordination can cause delays and claims. But this is performance risk tied to delivery of professional management services. It does not place the CM at additional conflict of interest with the owner, as the individual contractors are still responsible for the execution of the construction.

The CM's contractual responsibility to the owner remains in the agency category. While the increased responsibilities place greater duties upon the CM, the CM still serves as an agent to the owner and is on the owner's side of the table. If the project is delayed because of the CM's negligence in coordinating contractors, the owner would have a claim against the CM.

Pure agency CM – multiprime with a "soft" cost guarantee.   This is the same approach as the preceding subsection, with one additional wrinkle. The CM guarantees, by contract, that if the bids come in over budget, the CM will go through the repackaging and rebidding process to get the job within budget at no expense to the owner. Also, the CM either agrees to pay for redesign costs or the CM and the architect share in the expense of redesign and rebidding.

The CM is still in a pure agency relationship, but its risk has been increased and tied directly to performance at one of the most visible times in the design and construction process—the bid opening. The CM is still in a professional services relationship with the owner and subject to performing to a standard of care. But the guarantee of bidding within budget provides added hard measurable criteria and an associated remedy to evaluate a critical component of the CM's performance, and very little potential for conflict of interest has been added.[15]

Regardless of the number of CM contracts available, the total scope of work (which would be tedious to enumerate) required by each party is never adequately defined. This adds a third layer of complexity to the architect–CM relationship. Architects and CMs are only too familiar with this problem, as recent survey demonstrated:

A single simple question was opposed to each: In construction today, what gaps, duplication of services, or conflicts exist between the architect and CM (serving as an agent of the owner)? In other words, where do you find either CM disputes with the architect, or vice versa, on who should perform certain services on the project?

The following is a list of the scope items generated from the survey. For each item listed, the contract agreements of AIA, CMAA, and AGC were examined.

Determination if the work performed by trade contractors is in accordance with the contract agreements

Administration of the trade contracts

Production of record documents (as-builts)

Services during the bid (procurement) phase

Changes in the work during the construction phase

Contractor pay applications

Verification of field conditions

Substitution by trade contractors

Sequencing or phasing the work of trade contractors

Requests for information or clarification

Value engineering trade proposals

Claims by trade contractors[16]

Division of Labor

Many architects complain that CMs are cutting into their market share by effectively providing client representation through their construction management services that they themselves would normally provide. This is utter nonsense. The CM is needed on complex projects to not only control the other contractors but also to facilitate the design team. Naturally, architects are loath to be controlled by outside parties, who they perceive as not knowing their business, architecture and engineering, as well as they do. Moreover, they are used to controlling the contractor, not being controlled by him. However, this perception misses the point of the necessity of a CM. No one will argue that on certain projects, there is a need for controls on overall production; however, controlling the design team is less popular with architects for the reasons I gave above, especially in residential and remodeling, where architects are more hands-on in regards to the contract administration process. The industry needs to understand when and why a CM is needed, and what the inherent advantages there are for all parties. Facilitating is the preferable operative term for CM/architect relationships. AIA uses the term *assist*. While both are vague terms, a clear cut description of services provided by the CM should clear any haziness.

Resultantly, many contractors are asked by architects to provide CM level or type services without either party being aware of it. This being so, much of the industry is unaware of what a CM really should do. However, many contractors and architects knowingly engage in this level of service. Why do they do this? Although there isn't always a need or resources to hire a CM, there will always be a level of service required above and beyond the scope of the general contractor and architect. Because this level of service is typically not remunerated and is taken for granted, there is less incentive for owners to pay extra for such services. In the end, everyone gets sold short—the owner often does not get the level of services he needs, and the architect and contractor perform the bare minimum of construction management services gratis. Because they perform them for free, they do them as quickly and cheaply as possible. At the end of the day, the client is done a disservice. Despite these perceptions, there are some set protocols in publication that help to clarify the CM's role. The following is one synopsis of the full complement of a CM's preconstruction tasks. From a synopsis such as this one, the owner and CM can form a distillation of services that should be incorporated into the scope of work according to each project's needs, which are as follows:

Preconstruction Construction Management Services

Review and evaluate owner's proposed procurement methods[17]

Recommend method of selecting contractors

Establish bidding schedules

Recommend breakdown of bid packages to be let

Prepare forms of contracts and proposals

Preparation of construction contracts

Preparation of general conditions

Preparation of supplemental conditions

Preparation of special conditions

Preparation of instruction to bidders

Preparation of invitation to bidders

Preparation of summary of work

Preparation of the bid form

Preparation or collection of the payment, performance, and bid

Bond forms

Preparation or collection of the noncollusion certificate

Reproduction of bid package documents

Conduct a campaign to increase bidder interest in the project

Prepare and place notices and advertisements to solicit bids

Prepare addenda

Review addenda

Reproduce and distribute addenda

Maintain a log of bidders

Expedite delivery of bid documents to bidders

Organize and conduct prebid meetings

Administer the bid clarification process and coordinate responses to bidders

Prepare responses to requested clarifications during bid phase

Evaluate requests for substitutions during bid phase

Organize and conduct bid openings

Receive, evaluate, and analyze bids for responsiveness and price

Conduct postbid conferences

Notify bidders of bid results

Negotiate with bidders

Assist in contractor selection

Organize and conduct preaward meetings

Attend preaward meeting

Assembly, delivery, and execution of contract documents

Prepare prequalification criteria for bidders and prequalify bidders

Prepare design documents for alternative bids

Distribution of bid documents

Assist[18] in the award of contracts

Approve subcontractors and suppliers

Prepare summary of negotiations document

Issue Notice to Award[19]

The above list may seem exorbitant, but for a large scale, full-rigged construction management project, it is not unreasonable. The scope and budget of most residential projects won't necessitate all of these tasks, and the breadth of each task will be considerably less than a large project, as we shall see later in the text. However, the regimen of CM preconstruction services will convey the intent of involvement that is expected from him. It is interesting that although the CMAA A-1 specifies owner responsibilities, it does not refer to the architect's responsibilities. These are treated in the CMAA A-4, which as I have said, few architect's would agree to sign. In lieu of this, architects will elect for an AIA document, which may not be coordinated with the CMAA contract, thus creating the possibility for redundancy, and omitted scope.

It is clear why a complex project may need an overarching controller, the CM, one who manages production and schedule in the large scheme of things. Contractors and architects alike understand this although neither seems genuinely happy under the arrangement; the architect to a lesser extent, as it is the exception that a CM will have any real control over him, especially in the residential sector. The reason for this is as follows: when an owner decides to build his project, he typically begins with the design. He will set a budget, and the conscionable architect will try to design within that budget. If the owner does not already have a contractor in mind, he will ask the architect to recommend one. If the architect has a good following, he will either nominate a few bidders to a bid list, or he may recommend a negotiated contract with a given contractor. In either case, the architect will almost never recommend a CM for a residential project. The downside of not involving a CM in the design process is that he cannot advise on constructability or value engineering matters. Even if he is retained only for the production phase, it will be a little too late for him to have an impact on these issues.

Yet, there are incentives for an architect to actually be the one to suggest a CM, if only they'd realize them. Good architects have a good understanding of preconstruction design services, as about 85% their fee will be allotted to it for a traditional contract arrangement (fixed sum). They will generally perform this service at a profit although this fact has no bearing on their end product. Thus, 15% of their fee is allocated, or rather remaindered, to the construction phase. It's only a matter of time before the architect begins to lose money in the construction phase. In the construction phase, they have contract management responsibilities, which as I have said, are typically 15% of their overall fee. In order to be more competitive, architects cut back on their already meager contract management budget. This practice is a key determinant in the fate of many projects. Architects do not prioritize contract management services, and the project management component of these services is rarely their strong suit. They may even appoint lower-level staff to the task, such as interns or assistants. In other words, once working drawings are issued, the architect really doesn't expect to be doing a whole lot more. He figures that once the project is in the construction phase, the contractor will assume total responsibility.

The CM will be better suited to managing what the architect typically overburdens himself with, such as troubleshooting and constructability issues, or negotiating change orders, and the fee allotted to the CM would be well worth the percentage. On the project, the CM can do the "dirty work"; fighting the nasty battles with the production team while the architect sits out as spectator. In fact, some owners may even contribute toward financing this additional (for the residential CM) level of management, as it is provided in traditional construction management agreements, if it can be demonstrated how helpful it would be.

To further understand what a CM does, or can do for the residential sector, it is helpful to differentiate between what a general contractor does and does not do. The best field of observation for this demonstration is the project life cycle, discussed in the following.

Residential Construction Management Project Life cycle

Preconstruction phase

Preconstruction services provided by a CM may include, but are not limited to the following, in chronological order.

Feasibility study. The residential CM should assess if the client's budget is consistent with the intended design concept before working drawings have been developed. Sketches and schematics will suffice this purpose. A design consultant or an architect may be utilized; in fact, he is typically hired by the client before the CM. It has not been the bailiwick of residential CMs to advise the client on the selection of a design team; however, a good CM should be able to. Subsequent to the finding of the feasibility study, the client will decide whether or not to proceed with the project.

Additionally, the CM can determine if there are any other obstacles to the project, such as local zoning laws, planning boards and landmarks or neighborhood committees; however, this is typically not the role of the residential CM, but of the architect. Zoning laws tend to be immutable, therefore predictable; however, local authorities may present extreme obstacles, such as waiting periods, submittals, and any other exercise they deem fit that may make the timeline of a project unfeasible. They can scuttle a project before it begins, or worse, in the middle of the project. Often their objections are completely unreasonable. I offer the following observation:

In New York City, in addition to the Department of Buildings, the Landmarks Preservation Committee (LPC) has overarching authority in the approval of construction for buildings and districts designated as "landmarks."[20] The LPC was formed as a response to ruthless urban renewal and development, of which, the destruction of the classic original Pennsylvania Station, in New York, stands out. While it is a well-intended entity, I have noted certain restrictions placed on building that makes little or no sense. For example, the area comprising the West Village is classified as a landmark district. This being so, blanket restrictions apply to the renovation of buildings in this area. Most noteworthy is the restriction on building frontages, which states that they may not be altered. Many older residential buildings in this area, eighteenth to early twentieth century are grumpy old walk-ups, seemingly ready to implode, with little aesthetic appeal. They may have originally been carriage houses, tenements, or other downscale edifices, as opposed to seven-figure handyman specials. The value of the property is in the land, not the building, which may be considered a liability. This is because it is cheaper to construct a new building than it is to prop up and retrofit the structure of an old poorly built tenement, just to preserve the frontage, which must invariably be underpinned because the foundation is shot. Not to say there are not lovely architectural gems in this area; however, they tend to be the exception.

To minimize the element of such surprises, a code consultant may also be retained. He will assist in filing the project, and also advise on what local laws are applicable. In extreme circumstances, legal counsel may be warranted. If it should come to litigation in order to facilitate the project, the client may now draw the line, and scuttle the project, as such litigation is frequently a losing prospect.

The CM should also advise the client of his estimate of the overall duration of the project. The specificity of this finding can be critical to the client—often clients are moving out of one home into another. In order to do that, they generally will need to sell their old home. They will need to know when to sell, and when the move-in dates will be for their new home, and for the buyer of their old home. If a gross error in time approximation is made, the sale may fall through, or they may have to sell despite their new home not being finished. That is why the generation of estimated overall schedule durations is done in the planning or feasibility stage. Some loan agencies require, and some clients will ask for, a cash-flow projection. Once the budget is approved and a schedule drafted, it shouldn't be difficult to generate a projection. A sample projection is shown in Table 5.1.

Selection of design team. As stated above, the design team—at least the architect is typically preselected by the client. The design team, which will be selected and led by the architect, will generally include the following members:

- Project architect
- Mechanical electrical and plumbing (MEP) engineers, and structural engineer, if required
- Interior designer; the architect often takes on the interior design
- Consultants

The difference in a construction management agreement is that the CM can bring subcontractors and vendors in during the design process. These people can play an important role in working with the design team. They can present options, value engineer, and take the lead in the design, especially in MEP, as many of these subcontractors have engineers on their staff. In the high-end sector, you will often find that the talented MEP subcontractors who build these projects can be more helpful than most engineers. If the subcontractors are offering their help, it will likely be a much more economical venture than to hire consultants, that is, they will perform these services gratis with the promise of being awarded the work.

Creation of timeline or schedule for project. We discussed in Chap. 3 what a typical full phase construction management project looks like on paper. The overall duration will already have been assessed in the feasibility study. The timeline creation phase will assess the durations of the three main phases of the project, and designate milestones for critical tasks.

The scheduler must be accurate in phasing and sequencing a project to include basic deliverables to be received subsequent to site mobilization. He must have a sense of not only the production windows but also of how long it will take the architect to generate approved drawings. The architect must ratify the timeline. The owner can then hedge his bets accordingly. A deliverable timeline schedule issued to an architect from a CM might look something like Table 5.2.

Preconstruction design phase. The CM should be an integral part of the design process, offering his expertise on building and constructability issues as necessary. He should draft a schedule of design deliverable milestones, and administrate it as necessary. The design process should progress as follows.

TABLE 5.1 Cost Projection

	Scope of work						Cost projection					
		July	August	September	October	November	December	January	February	March	April	Total
1	Demolition	$42,410										$42,410
2	Site work		$1,883	$1,883	$1,883							$5,650
3	Structural steel		$18,625	$18,625	$18,625	$18,625						$74,500
4	Concrete				$47,402	$47,402						$94,804
5	Masonry				$30,326	$30,326	$30,326					$90,977
6	Rough carpentry/GWB			$38,633	$38,633	$38,633	$38,633					$154,532
7	Thermal and moisture					$5,461	$5,461					$10,921
8	Millwork/finish carpentry		$58,990		$58,990		$58,990				$58,990	$235,960
9	Stairs/fences				$15,829		$15,829		$15,829		$15,829	$63,315
10	Doors and windows											$ —
	Wood doors and frames			$22,875					$22,875			$45,750
	Wood windows			$15,375			$15,375					$30,750
	Steel doors/windows			$26,387		$26,387		$26,387				$79,160
	Window treatments							$4,500		$4,500		$9,000
11	Hardware			$17,003			$8,502		$8,502			$34,006
12	Finishes/painting						$32,746	$32,746	$32,746			$98,237
13	Stone & tile			$68,229				$34,115			$34,115	$136,458
14	Wood flooring				$19,002		$8,313		$8,313		$11,876	$47,505
15	Electrical & lighting											$ —
	Panels/service upgrades		$5,000								$5,000	$10,000
	Wiring and devices		$15,331			$15,331		$15,331			$15,331	$61,324
	Light fixtures		$29,178							$29,178		$58,356
	Lite touch system		$16,210							$16,210		$32,420

16 Plumbing											$ —
Roughing		$16,439			$16,439		$16,439			$16,439	$65,756
Fixtures and fittings		$15,000							$15,000		$30,000
17 Appliances						$9,641			$9,641		$19,281
18 HVAC		$32,857			$32,857		$32,857			$32,857	$131,427
19 Protection/sidewalk bridge	$17,500										$17,500
20 Shower enclosures								$5,775		$5,775	$11,550
21 Glass and mirror						$3,750			$3,750		$7,500
22 Accessories installation									$2,500		$2,500
23 Awning					$1,050				$1,050		$2,100
24 Metal fabrications					$10,980				$10,980		$21,960
Subtotal	$59,910	$209,513	$209,010	$230,690	$243,490	$227,564	$162,374	$94,039	$92,809	$196,211	$1,725,609
Contractor fees											
9 General conditions	5,392	21,856	18,811	20,762	21,914	20,481	14,614	9,264	9,248	17,659	160,000
2 Insurance, bonds, Permits	1,306	4,627	4,556	5,029	5,308	4,961	3,540	2,066	2,045	4,277	37,712
10 Overhead & profit	$6,661	$23,600	$23,238	$25,648	$27,071	$25,301	$18,053	$10,537	$10,410	$21,815	$192,332
Monthly total	$73,269	$259,596	$255,615	$282,129	$297,783	$278,306	$198,580	$115,906	$114,512	$239,962	$2,115,653

TABLE 5.2   Deliverables Timeline

Deliverables	Schematic	Wiring diagram
Lutron	11.30.01	1.23.02
AV	11.30.01	1.30.02
Senercomm	12.21.01	1.23.02
Security	11.30.01	1.30.02
Tel./comm./data programs	11.30.01	1.30.02
Motorized shades	11.30.01	1.30.02
Submittals	Review	Release
HVAC shop drawings	12.10.01	12.21.01
Sprinkler shop drawings	2.13.02	3.06.02
MEP coordinated	2.18.02	3.15.02
Wall covering	12.10.01	12.21.01
Architectural millwork[1]	3.01.02	4.15.02

[1]Veneers approved by 12.21.01.

Site survey   Plot actual overall existing dimensions and site conditions, including status of infrastructure, MEPs, structure, and any possible limitations, such as building rules, that are typically indicated in the "alteration agreement," if it is an apartment building. The alteration agreement is a document that a cooperative uses to convey its rules and regulations for construction projects in its building. The client must sign this document before construction begins. Likewise, condominiums generally have their own set of building work rules. Be leery of bidding postdeveloper work, as these contractors have a tendency to prolong their stay in hopes that they can contract fit-out work for themselves.

Architects will sometimes conduct their own site survey in order to generate reference points for the new program, or at least to define overall dimensions. In the absence of an architect's survey, a licensed surveyor can be retained to conduct the survey with the architect advising him of what is to be referenced. Overall dimensions should be verified by the general contractor regardless of surveys. Feasibility of the intended program can again be considered at this point in time.

Design and development management

Design and development (D&D) is the preconstruction stage where progress sets of design drawings leading up to the bid and construction sets of drawings are issued. Not unusually, D&D items encroach on the production phase, especially when they amend or add to the scope of work. A good CM will see to it that D&D is kept to a minimum in the production phase. D&D progresses as follows:

- Concept
- Budget
- Value engineer as necessary
- Schematics

- Coordination with engineers and consultants
- Plans
- Elevations
- Sections
- Specifications
- Clarifications/ sketches (SKs)

Architects have a protocol for their various drawing issues:

Preliminary.   These may be used for budgeting but not for accurate bidding. Often designated "Not for construction."

Bid set.   These are used for bidding the work, and usually serve as base contract documents; however, they are likely to be superseded and thus are also often designated "Not for construction."

Working drawings.   Working drawings are meant to be the build set; however, shop drawings, reissues, and sketches will amend these as well.

Final set.   I saw some drawings stamped thus once or twice. Otherwise, they are seldom designated as such.

Sketches.   Meant to be supplementary, they often show designs that should have been in the bid set. Technically, they reflect latent D&D.

On a construction management project, construction may begin as early as the release of the preliminary set, subject to permit issuance. Most municipalities require stamped sets of architectural and engineer drawings. Often, this set of drawings is schematic in nature, a rendering showing minimal detail but enough for permit approval. These drawings may only schematically resemble the final working drawings or end product, however, they are only intended to impart as much information as necessary to start the approval process and get the project moving. On highly detailed projects, it is not uncommon for an interior designer to render the drawings, and then have the drawings stamped by an architect who has no other association with the project; he is merely the architect of record, and is generally paid a fee for his stamp, as he assumes liability by putting his name on the drawings. Subcontractors do something similar to this when they file their project under the license of another contractor; however, unlike the surrogate architect of record arrangement, it is illegal for them to do so.

It should be said that in the construction management model, the work may begin when the design is only half finalized, as we have illustrated in Chap. 3, and later in this chapter, as opposed to the full set required by a lump sum competitively bid contract. At some point before working drawings are released, the project team may want to bring in consultants to advise them on certain aspects of the project. While this can be helpful, it often suffices that respective vendors and subcontractors, who will be part of the project, give their input to design and development, thus obviating the need for costly consultations. Of course, the tacit understanding of a vendor or subcontractor's input is that their services will be used on the project. Otherwise, they should be paid for their time. This arrangement is popular under the negotiated bid model.

The CM's expertise during the design stage is predicated on his ability to advise the client and his architect as to constructability issues, how certain design elements may affect the schedule, value-engineering issues, and in selecting some of the equipment or material. To do this effectively, the design team should be in lockstep with the CM. For example, before a costly heating system is considered, the CM should be contacted to advise the design team as to constructability, schedule issues, and budget options. In the event that the system should not fit into the program, the design team will have wasted little time and effort. Had they not asked the CM beforehand, they may have wasted valuable resources developing a program which had no chance of being used from the start.

Selection of bidders and bid solicitation

Once the team is confident that there is sufficient information to begin the project in earnest, a bid field is created, and bid packages are assembled and issued to the respective bidders. For each major trade, clients will want to see comparison spreadsheets showing three or four bidders. In order to do this, there must be a coherent scope of work for each of the respective trades. This can be tricky if the work is only half developed—the bidders may not want or be able to bid the work in a comprehensive fashion.

Whether budgets are to be solicited, or fixed prices, the CM will indicate the structure that each bid form shall take, such that he and others can make ready comparisons. For example, if two heating, ventilation, and air conditioning (HVAC) contractors bid the same project, they may have arrived at their budgeted costs differently, and reflected that in their presentations. Because the bids were not presented according to the same criteria, one of them, or both, may have to go back and conduct time-consuming breakouts to fit the bidding requirements of which they should have been advised of earlier.

Some subcontracts will be let early so that the team can avail themselves of a subcontractor's preconstruction input. There are many subcontractors who can be very helpful in assisting the design team, or they may design themselves. This is especially true in residential work, where the scope is smaller and more localized. If they are MEP subcontractors, chances are they will give valuable advice as to how to instruct the engineers to proceed. Otherwise, a lot of clock time can be wasted by consulting engineers, especially those without a design directive. Whether they advise the engineers early or not, they will always need to embellish and refine the design information the engineers detail through submittals and shop drawings; engineers tend to show a program in schematic only. Some engineers will resent the fact that the subcontractor's input took precedence in the D&D process. Such types will require monitoring as they can respond reactively.

Bid qualification

The art of bid qualification for the CM as advisor is different than it is for the general contractor. For one, because the CM is the agent of the client, none of the bidders' proposals can be considered proprietary. All bids are shown in accordance with an open-book review. For example, if a contractor saves 10% on a line item of a lump-sum contract, he will merely pocket the difference, whereas if a CM saves 10%, the savings go directly to the client, who sometimes may offer incentives for such a result.

Once all the bids are received, they are qualified and compared to each other, and to the working budget. They are then presented to the client with a recommendation to either select a given bidder, or to value engineer the project back within the budget. Sometimes the subcontractor is selected, and then asked to value engineer, as that exercise is best done with the understanding that a contract is imminent. Subcontractors are leery of dispensing such information without at least a *letter of intent*; as such generosity may have been taken advantage of in the past. However, by the time a consulting subcontractor issues his proposal, the qualification is a formality, as he should be in the position of making a negotiated bid, that is, without competition.

Once all the parties necessary to begin the work are contracted, and permits granted, the project may be mobilized. For residential projects the first contracts will be:

- Any remedial or abatement work
- Temporary site facilities
- MEP (at least for disconnects and temporary services)
- Demolition

These programs will be enough to get the project started without prematurely locking in other subcontracts. The demolition process will likely yield new information for the design team to process, and for the CM to incorporate into the scope of work.

Subcontracts

Finally, the CM will present to the client bid spreadsheets representing all proposals considered for the work. At this time he should also have recommendations to award the work. Once agreed, the subcontracts can be negotiated, and drafted. In the capacity of advisor, the contracts will be between the owner and the subcontractor, and the CM will issue and administrate these contracts. Otherwise, the CM (as constructor) will contract with the subcontractors directly.

For a residential general contractor, the subcontractor's proposal or a work authorization as contractual instrument is common practice for smaller contracts as opposed to the issuance of a full blown AIA A401 subcontract that will also include by reference the AIA 201, which is overkill for the purpose, especially if the contractual parties have a long-standing relationship; however, for the CM, the owner may be contracting the subcontractors directly. In that case, abbreviated form contracts are available. One such would be the AIA A107, discussed in Chap. 2.

In 2003, The American Subcontractors Association of America signed a partnering agreement with the CMAA. This was a significant step in the advancement of the business of construction management for the industry. While the existence of this agreement signifies little for the residential industry in the present, in the future the concept of partnering with CMs will hopefully trickle down to subcontractors in the residential sector.

Stalled Projects

Full-phase construction management projects often founder in the design phase. There is an incentive to facilitate and resolve these issues for the CM, as he isn't making any money sitting around. His fee typically becomes substantial when production begins, especially if it is indexed to the value of work installed, having a project manager do no more than issue memos, attend meetings, draft schedules, and reissue budgets is not how a CM makes money. He makes money in terms of managing or putting work in place—the aggregate of all work they have built, or managed the building of. Architects use this same gauge to measure their volume. However, if the CM has no leverage with the design team, he can only make suggestions and cannot otherwise induce them. If the design team was preselected, he very likely won't have leverage. Thus, a CM can suffer from the lack of design information in much the same way as general contractors do.

Like the tracked sample project in Chap. 3, not everything always goes according to plan. For that project, the CM had to continually notify the client of delays, rebudget the scope of work, and track the flow of design information, which was not forthcoming, and constantly in flux. Had the project been in the construction phase, the general contractor likely would have demobilized his forces until such time as there was enough information to move forward in a substantial manner. I emphasize the term "substantial" because so many contractors make the mistake of staying on task even though the effort is half-cocked due to a dearth of information. However, the CM's job should be to facilitate the job team to get the project back on track. For the given sample project, design criteria were client driven and therefore the CM also tried to motivate the client by applying to him directly.

> A list of client-driven decisions affecting milestones for the project that we hope to have resolved by the end of the client's next visit, week after next, is given in the following. By next week, we will have composed as much material as possible for the client's use in making these decisions.
>
> 1. Client milestones
>
> Base budget approval
> 100 at the rate of window treatment and controls package
> User interface directive

TABLE 5.3 Deliverables Sequenced with Tasks

Deliverable	Working	Projected	Affected
RCP	2.22.02	3.15.02	0148, 0066, 0076, 0127
Lutron schematic	2.22.02	3.22.02	0148, 0237
DDC schematic	2.22.02	4.22.02	0148, 0267
User interface schematic	N/A	3.29.02	0148, 0097
Window treatment controls	2.22.02	3.22.02	0148, 0207, 0217
Data IT schematic	2.22.02	4.22.02	0148, 0197
AV	2.22.02	4.22.02	0148, 0177

User interface with BMS related systems: floor radiant, fin tube, and humidity.

2. Other milestones

Award subcontracts to MEP and then architectural contractors

Award contract to AV and telephone vendors

Finalize RCP and lighting fixture schedule

Finalize finish schedule

Detail of control submittals, particularly millwork

Additionally, he mapped out deliverable milestones for the client to help concentrate his efforts according to time criteria dictated by the project schedule (Table 5.3). This table also refers to the activities delayed by the respective deliverable.

Construction Management Documentation

The minimum acceptable level, quality, and nature of a CM's documentation will mirror that which a diligent general contractor should provide. Otherwise, a CM will generate far and away much more documentation. It should be said that insofar as pertains to documentation, quality trumps quantity. In other words, it shouldn't be created for its own sake. Furthermore, architects have a general antipathy for overdocumenting general contractors.

Design team management documentation by contractors is exclusive to construction management contracts. In the preconstruction services list mentioned earlier in the chapter, I have underlined those services that a general contractor also performs; however, these tasks he does for himself, not the client. Therefore, the information remains the same, the only difference being that some of the information is proprietary for the general contractor; there is no proprietary information for the CM, as he is acting for the client.

The dynamics of sharing certain information on a construction management project have different parameters than they do on traditional contracts, for instance, information exchanged between the architect and contractor. We have said before that it is generally poor practice to involve the client in matters that don't concern him, especially those that should be worked out by the architect or contractor. An owner will likely see considerably more documentation from his CM than he would from a general contractor. This can change the way contractual parties communicate, especially if the CM is in charge of the design team although that arrangement is rare in the residential sector. Consider the following example:

Three general contractors were asked to make a presentation to an architect for consideration of the award of a residential contract. The architect agreed to sponsor one of them. The contract, a stipulated sum, was let to this general contractor before the design documentation was complete. As the project progressed, the designer established a pattern of negligence in not furnishing the missing design information, some of which was client driven. The contractor diligently notified the designer of all approaching and missed deadlines. These notices, sent only to the designer over a period of 10 weeks or so, amounted to a stack of single page memos 3/4 in. in thickness.

It soon became evident to the client that the project was stalled. Not being satisfied with the designer's response as to why, he asked the general contractor directly. The general contractor was reluctant; however, he was forced to admit that he had issued documentation to the designer regarding the matter; he then had no choice but to copy the client. Twenty-four hours later, the designer's contract was terminated; however, the general contractor remained.

Under these circumstances, this general contractor felt he had acted reasonably; he was reluctant to hang the designer out to dry by forcing issues, or notifying the client, especially since he felt indebted to him for awarding him the work. In the end, he had no choice. Had this been a construction management contract, this scenario would have never taken place.

Residential Construction Management Project Life cycle

Production phase

The difference between the mobilization of a construction management project and that of a standard contract are virtually indistinguishable. It is only when the design documents are perused that it becomes evident that the standard contract project has more fully developed design documentation. Assuming the balance of the design is forthcoming in keeping with the scheduler's milestones, the CM should take no longer than the general contractor in completing the work. In fact, with the advantage of his preconstruction foresight he will have a leg up on the general contractor.

The sequence of installations should be no different than that which was illustrated in Chap. 4.

- Layout approval
- MEP coordination
- MEP fabrication and installation
- Close walls (white box part 1)

- Close ceilings (white box part 2)
- Substantial completion
- Punch list
- Completion

Although the production paths are the same, there are many nuances between the general approach a CM and a general contractor can take, for complex projects a CM should yield a superior result through the following:

Rate of production

The CM will monitor the progress of a project as will the general contractor; however, a CM should provide more detailed, more accurate, and more frequent schedule updates. Consider the occasion of a delay on a project with a CM and general contractor—a general contractor will be loath to announce the fact that he is late; he may try to mask this fact and quietly make up the lost time, if possible. The CM will address the delay at once. If it is appropriate, he will notify the client. In either case, if he is diligent and honest, he will document the delay, and begin discussing taking a course of action. If the general contractor does not have an acceptable plan, the CM should form one for him. Without the CM the general contractor is left to his own wiles to mitigate a delay, and will typically act in his own best interests, which don't necessarily coincide with the clients. For example, the project may need more men; however, the general contractor prefers to keep his men on another project. Under the watchful eye of a CM, the general contractor will be notified in writing of the delay, and thus will be compelled by him to take action.

Quality controls

The CM will perform periodical inspections, as needed, on the site conditions and installations. For high-quality residential projects his vigilance will be acute, as the bar is set considerably higher than any other market niche. Depending on the integrity of the general contractor, his involvement in quality control can vary. This is not to say that the design team is not considered, indeed, they have the final say in such matters; however, they will scrutinize less frequently, and will be chiefly concerned with end product, whereas the CM will judge the work on a more comprehensive basis: since the CM is the expert in all facets of construction, not just finishes, he will check quality earlier, more frequently, and more completely than an architect has time to, or cares to. Indeed, few architects pay much attention to what goes on behind the walls. It is this additional layer of scrutiny that should yield a superior installation when compared to traditional contracts. Moreover, the CM will flag conditions that he knows will yield a given poor result before it has a chance to establish itself. This sort of preemptive foresight is one of the strengths of a strong CM.

Quality control is generally considered a measure of production acumen and prowess; however, the CM will extend these criteria to other concerns as well, such as:

- The quality and accuracy of documentation, and the timeliness of the issuance of documentation
- The integrity of site conditions: cleanliness, safety, and organization
- The organization and structure of job meetings
- The consideration and negotiation of change orders and progress payments

These extra levels of service are another example of how a construction management arrangement can step up the overall level of integrity for a project.

Production management structure

On the surface, a construction management project may look identical to a general contracting project. There will be similar hierarchies of staff members, the same subcontractors working away, and similar administrative programs. However, on a construction management project, there should be notable differences specifically within the role of the CM as compared to a project manager.

General Conditions on Construction Management Projects

A CM's project should have a more comprehensive general conditions program than that of the general contractor. General contractors are notorious for skimping on general conditions, providing only the bare minimum, and often, less than that; however, this is a common practice, and acceptable to a degree. If general contractors went overboard with general conditions on their projects they would cease to be competitive. A construction management–led project should never provide less than the bare minimum of requirements. The bare minimum rule should only be invoked for cash-strapped projects. By the same token, cash-strapped projects don't lend themselves well to the construction management structure.

The CMs should always endeavor to provide a superior level of service than the average general contractor as they are the specialists. When a general contractor outshines the CM, it is time for reevaluation of theCM's role. When a CM figures for the project's general conditions, he should begin with the notion of ideal or optimal provisions, and should the budget be a factor, work his way backward. Because he was involved in the project from the start, he should have found the equity to finance the required level of general conditions.

Site conditions

The worksite will always be adequately staffed with the appropriate level of manpower: laborers, mechanics, and always a superintendent or foreman on hand. This team will maintain the integrity of the site, keeping it broom swept everyday, removing refuse regularly, ensuring safety provisions, such as protections, temporary installations, and signage are up to snuff. Tools and materials will have specific staging areas, and the site in general will be efficiently organized. Each trade will also need to be designated an area to "shanty" in.

Sounds unreasonable? For any serious general contractor these should be basic provisions; however, because the concept of general conditions has become so diluted within the industry, these requirements are seldom met, and are often considered as supplemental by general contractors.

Bookkeeping

Like basic site conditions, a CM's bookkeeping necessarily not only provided for on a higher tier of service, but has different ramifications. A general contractor only needs to be concerned with accounts payable and receivable, and payroll. A CM's bookkeeper will still process accounts payable /accounts receivable (AP/AR) and payroll, but he must also present this information to the client in an open-book fashion. He will generate at least twice as much paper as the general contractor's bookkeeper as he is the client's agent.

Cost tracking

A good general contractor will track costs. He will generally do this in two ways: work with hard numbers and percentages, and keep tabs of cash flow on the project to meet his target profit margin. A CM's accounting must go much further. To begin, he will generate a budget range as part of his feasibility study. Subsequently, a working budget will be ratified. He will then prepare a cost projection. For each subcontract he will present to the client actual costs as compared with the budget. Each month he will update his budget comparisons and cost projections, and present them to his client for review.

When the project comes in underbudget, everybody is happy; in fact, some contracts offer incentives to the CM. However, like any other contract, if additional time and monies are needed, the contractor will have a lot of explaining to do. The tracked project shown in Table 3.10, was just such a project. While there were budget concerns, the bigger concern was the extended schedule, because the project was a commercial space that lost revenue for every day the schedule was extended. The contractor had promised a 7-month schedule based on ideal conditions—prompt turnover by the core-work contractor, and working drawings, neither of which deadlines was achieved. As a result, the contractor issued a new schedule with a 4 1/2-month extension, nearly an increase of 2/3, and issued a new general conditions projection. Needless to say, the contractor knew the client would never take the news sitting down. In order to make a more palatable presentation to the client, the contractor issued the following spreadsheet and annotated memo:

> Please find attached a spreadsheet of a current general conditions projection model for the above referenced project, with a copy of our June 2001, general conditions projection. The following are comments for your use in understanding the criteria which generated these projections:

(a) May, 2001 General Conditions Projection

This model illustrates a seven month project, to include four-weeks of Pre-construction, and twenty-four weeks of production. This was predicated on a mid-October turnaround, and the issuance of the May 28, 2001, drawing set. This schedule was designed to incorporate MEP, and most other coordination, on-the-fly, as opposed to having a typical *nonproduction submittal/coordination period*. At this time, the scope of work was less complex, and presumed a less sophisticated MEP design than what is now the working program, hence, the on-the-fly method. The schedule was based on a fast-track model, with 100% CDs, of an average degree of difficulty.

(b) October, 2001 General Conditions Projection

This model illustrates an eleven and a half month project, to include ten-weeks of preconstruction, and thirty-six to forty-weeks of production. This was premised on a January 1, 2002, TIC turnaround, and the September 28, 2001, drawing set. This schedule takes into account the more complex MEP design program, based on our sense of it, although it is not 100%. As such, it must avail itself of a non-production submittal/coordination period of eight or so weeks. It is necessary that the MEP CDs are 100% prior to commencement of the coordination.

The change in perceptions of the project is based on information we have analyzed from the new design documents; our discussions in meetings with the job team; discussions with vendors who are familiar with the project, and who may have worked on the 32d floor; and observations taken from our walk-thrus on the 32d floor.

We highlight the following criteria as determining factors in schedule extension:

1. The scope and nature of control packages for AV, lighting, shades, environmental, and the integration of these controls. The R&D of this package is ongoing, and the final design remains to be considered. Whatever it is, a sufficient learning curve must be afforded, as the program will be fully customized. Many of the vendors are rolling out new programs exclusively for this project.
2. The effect of the above on the architectural millwork package on the 32d floor was considerable, such that production times had to be moved back to negotiate the location and founding of cut-outs for custom Lutron back-boxes. In fact, we assumed in large part that we could fabricate most of the millwork using 'hold' dimensions, which of course, is not now tenable.
3. The overall degree of complexity, especially, in custom or specialty finishes; all meticulous and time-consuming installations.
4. The increase in scope of work as drawn, which is considerable.
5. The debilitating effect of current events (9/11) on mobilization of construction projects in the tri-state area. Tightened security, antiterrorist measures, and other war-time programs are having a general slow-down effect on shipments, and on deliveries.

It must be noted, that the schedule still remains an aggressive one, with virtually no float, i.e. any slip runs high risk of delays. That is the essence of an aggressive schedule. Once the schedule is finalized, we will issue *deadline* and *no-float summary* reports. One advantage that this particular project features is that *once production begins*, the schedule, as it now stands, allows healthy submittal review windows, without sacrificing production. This arrangement is critical to the success of our project.

Schedule tracking

A CM's scheduling requirements are more stringent than the general contractor's. Even if a general contractor issues an updated schedule, it is unlikely it will be a tracked or baselined schedule, or that he will offer the constructive analytical input of a CM. The feedback he will issue should be more insightful and specific, like the sample in Chap. 3. If a CM's general conditions are reimbursable, as they often are, a late project can end up costing the client money by extending these general conditions.

Closeout

A CM will have a lot more work to do in closing out a project than his general contractor counterpart. His tasks may include, but are not limited to:

- Issuing guarantees and warranties
- Issuing of operation manuals, instruction manuals for equipment
- Maintenance schedule
- Keying schedule
- Factory training, when necessary
- Lien waivers
- Issuance of as-built drawings
- Spare parts and attic stock
- Terminating temporary services
- Preparing punch list with architect
- Closing out subcontractors and vendors with final payments
- Controlled inspection and required sign-offs

Although general contractors should perform most, if not all, of the above tasks, they tend to get lazy or sloppy. Not uncommonly, the closeout phase of a project is so difficult for a contractor that he may pull out, thus forgoing final payment rather than toil with what may seem to him an endless and thankless process. CMs do not have this luxury; however, there should be no incentive for a CM not to finish the project.

The Consummate CM

There are so many tasks that a CM must do or facilitate others to do on a project that he seemingly often runs the risk of becoming unorganized, and less efficient, under the pressure of the work load and complexity of coordination. This is especially true when he is managing multiple projects, and is common at smaller companies, where everyone seems to be spread too thin. There always seems to be too much to do, and at the end of the day, things get left undone.

This theory crosses over into more complex tasks that the CM must do: such as organizing documentation, keeping correspondence up to date and general macromanagement of his project. The harried CM is indeed an afflictive disorder, which will compound itself if not kept in check. Assuming the obvious that more manpower will not be deployed to assist the CM, he must somehow find a way to prioritize his responsibilities, and get the job done.

We will discuss some concepts below, which are intended to streamline the CM's quotidian, and make him more effective in the long run, by establishing some strategies.

Never lose sight of the big picture

Like the misguided single proprietor, it seems only too easy to get caught in the micromanagement mode. Once there, it is easy to lose sight of the big picture, or how smaller factors must be considered in terms of their relationship to the whole. For some CMs, this disoriented state is indicative of their career track, and likely there will be no self-corrective action taken. For the savvy CM, a little alarm will go off inside his head that presages each problem before it happens.

Know your place in the big picture

The ever important yet overburdened CM can easily lose sight of his objective. As he is accountable overall, he will sometimes try to "wear all the hats," or do the job of several people. He will be compelled to take on any number of tasks that would otherwise be more appropriately delegated to others. Finally, he is his own worst enemy because he saddles himself with too much responsibility. To keep this from happening, he must have a full sense of the big picture, and what his ultimate role is, before he dives headlong into a project. Once he has this parameter in mind, he must consistently refer back to it as the project becomes more complicated. Often, he will find that his heading is off course, and must make adjustments. The act of delegating and parsing out workload will be the first adjustment he will make.

An important part of defining one's role is predicated on understanding what the architect and general contractor's role (if there is one) is. Additionally, the efforts of all job team members, subcontractors and consultants alike, inform this equation.

Orchestrate a game plan

As the CM is accountable for the entire project, it is up to him to delegate and assign resources. It is in this exercise that each team member will be advised of his respective responsibilities. The most difficult will be tasks that involve coordination with other team members. He should think of his team as if it were an orchestra, and he the conductor. Each player has his role and script, and should not diverge from his purpose. These team members should have clear directions on what their specific responsibilities are.

Follow-up and unfinished business

Nowhere are more efforts wasted than in the follow-up process, or lack of one. In general, people don't like to repeat themselves. They tend to perform their portion of the work and pass it on to the next person, and hope that it comes back to them finished. I suppose they feel that they cover more ground that way. When they delegate tasks, they consider the directive an end in of itself, that is, once having made the directive, they consider that a *fait accompli,* or not to require any further action on their part. In reality, there is no closure, and the unfinished business will later resurface as a problem. Sometimes this is because they are lazy, or because they feel they have no more time to commit to the task— as in football, hand the ball off to the halfback and hope he makes a first down (quarterbacks seldom block). Any task that requires further action should be followed up on until it is complete, lest it become unfinished business.

Unfinished business can be a dangerous element for a project. The longer issues go unresolved, the more they tend to become exacerbated. Typical pieces of unfinished business or responsibilities that require aggressive follow-through may be as follows:

Notification of delay. When a delay is encountered or expected a contractor typically notifies the architect of the delay and receives either no response, or comment. The contractor has issued the memo, and feels his duty has ended there. That may or may not be so, but it in either case it doesn't indemnify the contractor from being blamed. However, unresolved delays can become a critical piece of unfinished business as the end date is often affected. A small matter tends to go unresolved, but pretty soon, all the small problems add up into one long dirty laundry list. Short of forcing the issue, many contractors merely serve delay notices merely as a matter of record, having no expectation of significant action being taken by the architect. This they come to know from past experience.

Unapproved change orders. Some change orders can dramatically affect budget and schedule. At times, the negotiation of change orders takes so long that it begins to affect the project adversely. By the time it is ratified or rejected its impact may take on new dimensions such as delaying other work, complicating coordination, or forcing successor work out of sequence. Rather than negotiate unapproved change orders, or delay work until they are processed, contractors have the habit of completing the work under protest, hoping to get paid for it later. This they do because the effects of a delayed change order can be more troublesome and costly than the change order itself. For small change orders this might be acceptable; however, not if it means setting a bad precedent such as getting only partial or no payment for such efforts.

RFIs. Unresolved requests for information will often hamper the flow of production. If the contractor doesn't have much needed information, the project can be delayed or forced out of sequence. Often, an RFI requires action on the part of the client such as selection of material, or the placement of a wall or fixture. If a client is indecisive, the flow of information to the contractor closes, and he is left without answers. Contractors and architects may be leery of pushing the client to a decision for fear that this may be perceived as being too aggressive. However, in their minds, they have done diligence merely by asking the client once or twice. Once the unresolved matter is left to sit, it then becomes unfinished business.

Inevitably, push will come to shove, and the client will unhappily be put on the hot seat, forced to make a decision. Whether he decides or not, he will wonder why it came to this. He will not want to hear that it is his own fault, that he was duly notified. It is important to be persistent in resolving open issues, while at the same time being diplomatic, especially when the client is directly involved. Architect driven RFIs should never cause delays without the architect assuming responsibility. Architects are responsible for delivering a complete design package that will facilitate the contract schedule. By and large, RFIs generally refer to information that should have already been issued. Change order work requiring RFIs can be exceptions; however, they can be just as troublesome as any other RFI. Thus the change order review process and untimely issuance of information are two of the most common client side driven factors creating delays on residential projects. The project manager must be unrelenting in his attempts for closure of these kinds of problems. That means full answers to each RFI as opposed to piecemeal and tentative directives.

Get the job done

Simple enough concept; however, the rate of failure for construction and project managers is exceedingly high. When one interviews for a position, inquiring about the work hours, he is often told, "Whatever it takes to get the job done." Thus many managers are putting in 50- to 60-hour work weeks as they feel they must work more hours to be more effective. In theory, a project manager could keep busy 100 hours every week, should the workload be there. As we know, productivity and quality decrease with the increase of workload, so more hours won't necessarily help. I once had a project manager under my supervision who consistently worked 60-hour work weeks. He was run-ragged. No one asked him to do this. When I looked at his rate of production, I could understand why he did it. He wasn't increasing his efficiency at all; he was merely treading water, and affecting a martyr image. He had next to nothing to show in terms of progress on the few small projects he was running. In fact, they were languishing disasters. Others seemed to think his habits exhibited a positive work ethic merely because he worked so many hours and they never factored in the results of his futile efforts. What did he do all day? I have no idea but I do recall him generating reams of spreadsheets with such titles as "Spreadsheet Log of Active Spreadsheets," or "Spreadsheets Tracking Distribution of Spreadsheets." Being so taxed with "workload" when he was directed to other, more meaningful tasks, he didn't have the time to do them.

Ironically, his counterpart, another project manager, was a production wizard with a nose for the critical path; however, he could not generate a single document for his projects. I have never advocated 50- and 60-hour workweeks as a standard. I also notice that experienced people can be twice as effective as their green counterparts, thus achieving the same production rates as their colleagues in half the time.

Finally, the consummate CM has an innate sense of what to do and when to do it. This is his intuition—his most valuable asset. Because he is constantly reevaluating his projects and the role he plays in each of them, he is planning ahead so as not to later get caught behind. He will know when it is time to be aggressive, and when it is time to be diplomatic. He will have appropriate relationships with his project team such that as project leader he can facilitate them efficiently. His responses to problems may not always be cause- and-effect based, or deductively reasoned. They are hatched from his general sense of what is the best plan for the project. And this sense should be intuitive, and reliable.

Notes

Summary of construction management preconstruction life cycle

- Feasibility study
- Election of design team
- Creation of timeline or schedule for project
- Site survey
- Design and development
- Selection of bidders and bid solicitation
- Bid qualification
- Subcontracts

Consummate CM's production philosophy

- Never lose sight of the big picture
- Know your place in the big picture
- Orchestrate a game plan
- Follow-up and unfinished business
- Get the job done

Code of Professional Ethics for the Construction Manager[21]

Since 1982, the Construction Management Association of America (CMAA) has taken a leadership role in regard to critical issues impacting the CM industry, including the setting of ethical standards of practice for the Professional Construction Manager.

The Board of Directors of CMAA have adopted the following *Code of Professional Ethics of the Construction Manager* and recommend that it be accepted and supported by the CM industry and the membership of the CMAA as a guide to the execution of the individual CM's professional duties.

Corporate and individual practitioner members of Construction Management Association of America make a commitment to conduct themselves and their practice in accordance with the Code of Professional Ethics of the Construction Manager. As a professional engaged in the business of providing construction management services, and as a member of the CM profession, I agree to conduct myself in my business in accordance with the following:

1. **Client Service.**   I will serve my clients with honesty, integrity, candor, and objectivity. I will provide my services with competence, using reasonable care, skill, and diligence consistent with the interests of my client and the applicable standard of care.

2. **Representation of Qualifications.**   I will only accept assignments for which I am qualified by my education, training, professional experience, and technical competence, and I will assign staff to projects in accordance with their qualifications and commensurate with the services to be provided.

3. **Standards of Practice.**   I will furnish my services in a manner consistent with the established and accepted standards of the profession and with the laws and regulations which govern its practice.

4. **Fair Competition.**   I will build my professional reputation on the basis of my direct experience and service provided, and I will compete fairly and respectfully with my professional colleagues.

5. **Conflicts of Interest.**   I will seek to avoid any and all conflicts of interest and will immediately acknowledge any influences and offer to withdraw from any assignment when any actual conflict exists which may impair my objectivity or integrity in the service of my clients.

6. **Fair Compensation.**   I will negotiate fairly and openly with my clients in establishing a basis for compensation, and I will charge fees and expenses that are reasonable and commensurate with the services to be provided and the responsibilities and risks to be assumed.

7. **Release of Information.**   I will release public statements that are truthful and objective, and I will keep information and records confidential when appropriate and protect the proprietary interests of my clients and professional colleagues.

8. **Public Welfare.**   I will not participate in any racial, sexual, or political discrimination related to any assignment I may undertake. I will avoid any conduct that would be considered unethical or will interfere or conflict with any laws, statutes or regulations, and I will uphold the safety, health, and welfare of the public in the performance of my professional duties.

9. **Professional Development.**   I will continue to develop my professional knowledge and competency as a practitioner, and I will contribute to the advancement of CM practice as a profession by fostering research and education and through the encouragement of subordinates and fellow practitioners.

10. **Integrity of the Profession.**   I will avoid actions which promote my own self-interest at the expense of the profession, and I will uphold the standards of the construction management profession with honor and dignity.

Endnotes

1. A nineteenth century carpenter seeking damages against a nonpaying client.
2. Tracy Kidder, *House* (New York: Houghton Mifflin, 1999) pp. 180–181.
3. Collier, p. 43.
4. *ibid.*
5. Keith Collier, *Construction Contracts*, 2d ed. (New Jersey: Prentice Hall, 1979).
6. Nearly 50% of the FMI/CMAA survey respondents indicated that construction documents issued at the beginning of construction were "sufficient with significant information needed" FMI/CMAA 8. In other words, although they could start building, the documents were still substantially incomplete.
7. Appendix B, Article 7.
8. Construction Management Association of America, *An Owner's Guide to Construction Management* (2002).
9. This fact is regardless of the fact that the AIA crossreferences the AGC documents in their synopsis.
10. Standard AIA Owner-Architect Agreement.
11. At the time of writing, the AIA indicated that the CMa series is undergoing revision.
12. *Ibid.* This CMAA statement pertains to construction management contracts in particular.
13. Statement by AIA.
14. See Appendix B.
15. Chuck Kluenker, *Risk v. Conflict of Interest—What Every Owner Should Consider When Using Construction Management, CMe Journal*, (2002) pp. 4–10.
16. Berman, 15–16.
17. Underline denotes tasks also done by general contractors (also, see under Construction Management Documentation).
18. Author's quotes. Berman states that the term "assist" used in CMAA contracts, lends itself to interpretation, whereas the term "shall" is more succinct. For litigation, the term assist can become problematic. The CMAA seems to have duly noted this conundrum, and made the necessary adjustments in its 2005 edition. The word assist no longer is referred to the construction manager–designer relationship; however, it is used to describe the owner–construction manager relationship.
19. Berman, pp. 20–21.
20. The LPC has its own rubric for what constitutes a landmark building, and it is not necessarily consistent with any other working concept I have seen.
21. http://cmaa.net.org/ethics.php

6

Operations

*There is no idleness by which we are so easily
seduced as that which dignifies itself by the
appearance of business.*
DR. JOHNSON, FROM *THE IDLER*

The average residential general contracting management structure reminds
me of an assemblage I once saw at the Stedelijk Museum in Amsterdam. It
may have been one of Moholy-Nagy's early works: this particular creation was,
unlike his motorized *Licht-Raum Modulator*, evidently a complicated contrap-
tion that made a cacophony of noise and frenetic motion, but served absolutely
no purpose other than to convey the artist's statement, which may have been a
pun on technology. As a metaphor for business operation, the assembly would
constitute anathema; running in place, yet it is just such ineptitude of organization that characterizes many of today's general contractor infrastructures
and systems that inadvertently exist for their own sake.

A construction business is much the same as any business in that it too must
have a basic structure in order to function. These structures vary considerably,
from company to company, especially in the construction sector, and also may
change when a business expands or downsizes. If the owner of the company is
not well-versed in business administration, doesn't otherwise have a natural
knack for management, nor has anyone on his staff that does, his company will
be disorganized. One would think such disorganization could quickly imperil the
livelihood of any company; however, it would appear that some level of disorganization is the rule, not the exception for most organizations. Unfortunately,
protocols are loosely defined in the construction industry, and it is thus particularly prone to dysfunction. There are a number of reasons for this:

- Personnel is not comprehensive enough to facilitate thorough job descriptions and training—loosely defined systems, inconsistent procedures, and
  poor work habits preclude healthy infrastructure

- Low priority of business administration
- Turnover is so high that setting up companywide systems is implausible
- There is no industrywide standard for job descriptions, management structures, and office infrastructures that can be readily duplicated or adhered to
- Formal education curriculums are no better at refining the loosely defined protocol of standard procedure of which there is no consensus

The structure of a company should be a direct response that is relative to what the company does or will do, how many employees will be needed, how large an office will be needed, and what systems will be utilized. Many small companies will hire personnel as work comes through the door, only to lay them off once things cool down. Either they simply don't make value investments in personnel, or they can't afford to keep them on payroll unless they are 100% on task, that is, they can't bankroll downtime. This condition makes it very hard to develop a cohesive staff structure, or implement systems, as there is a lack of personnel continuity. A resourceful company will find a way to make productive use of its personnel even when they are between projects.

In residential construction many mid-level and upper-management level practitioners are clearly underqualified for their position. They persist for three reasons: (1) there is a short supply of talented and qualified individuals in this sector; (2) salaries can be competitive or prohibitive, such that a qualified individual cannot be retained by a company with a low salary cap; and (3) drawn by the lure of high salaries, there are enormous number of underqualified individuals saturating the market.

It is hard to tell just how many people to keep on payroll, and it can be a real dilemma when your higher paid people are idle. A good planner, and one who has a keen eye for the market and what his share of it is likely to be, is in a relatively good position to gauge his staffing needs ahead of time, as opposed to the reactive response of a contractor who only hires on an as-needed basis. If you could book your projects about 12 months ahead of time, you would be in a better position to strategize for lulls in the market. Although they are limited, there are a number of things management level personnel can do when they are not on task, assuming they have the capability.

- Source new work
- Train new personnel
- Perfect and troubleshoot existing systems
- Develop new systems
- Organize stored information
- Assist on other projects
- Take their vacation
- Attend training seminars

Small Company Infrastructure

Ideally, as a small business owner, you will set up a basic nucleus of a structure, which you can embellish slowly as it grows. Some companies get by with only the following:

- Owner
- Bookkeeper
- Superintendent
- Laborers

__a skeleton crew, with little structure. However, the above does not constitute the foundation of a well-oiled machine, which at minimum should consist of the following:

- Owner
- Bookkeeper
- Superintendent
- Project manager
- Administrator
- Driver
- Laborer(s)
- Mechanic/foreman

This is the essential infrastructure. Of course, the mere presence of all these individuals in no way guarantees a working structure. Short of that, personnel will have to assume multiple job titles. Under such conditions, it is difficult for people to be efficient; they will be overworked, and likely be frustrated. Few entities will open their doors with all of the above staffing without adequate cash flow, and will subsist on the skeleton crew as described. They will not make the investment in personnel until revenue begins to flow. They feel that they can't afford to put their capital at risk, or they simply may not have any capital. While forms of infrastructure may vary from business to business, they coincide with four basic company needs or departments.

- Executive
- Sales
- Administration
- Production

If your company is growing, your staff should be more active or on-task. However, there will be downturns in the market, and for those times you must consider what you will do with your prospectively idle workers. The trick is to incorporate a structure, which is durable and flexible, in that, is readily adapted to growth, downsizing, and system implementation. If people say about someone "What would we do without so and so . . .?" you want to have a ready answer. In other words, your business is structured such that it will not fall apart if one or two individuals suddenly disappear. For small companies this dilemma is a persistent problem—if there are five employees, and one should leave, the company may effectively find itself at a 20% man power shortage. An example of constructive downsizing would be to combine closely related job descriptions such as superintendent/project manager, bookkeeper/office manager, or estimator project manager; however, do not let this be the rule. If you must keep payroll down for a time so be it, but when things improve, you must upgrade your staff quotient to a proper complement. If you are in the high-end sector, you won't make it by skimping on management.

For each position in your organization, you will want to have a specific job description that will make it clear to them and their teammates where their responsibilities begin and end. When new hires join the team, they will follow the same script. A sample project manager job description is provided below:

Job Title:

Project Manager

Report To:

GM

Objectives:

Administration and implementation of projects as follows:

Preconstruction

Plan and prepare *bill of assemblies*

Prepare job directory

Prepare project manuals

Meet with estimator to coordinate base POs

Coordinate submittals for long-lead items

Ensure that all insurance certificates are issued, up-to-date, and correct

Coordinate start-up with building management

Coordinate start-up with staff and subcontractors

Construction

Mobilize project

Track project progress and update schedule

Maintain and track drawings, shop drawings, sample, and submittal logs weekly

Maintain office job folders and files

Attend job meetings weekly and take and publish minutes

Maintain ultimate responsibility for schedule, budget, and quality control

Issue and track change orders

Track general conditions, and budgets or allowances

Document any modifications or consequential information

Process applications for payment

Notification of check requests

Closeout

Facilitate punch list

Arrange for sign-offs

Issue warranty manual package to client

Arrange for end-user demonstrations

Demobilize job

Closeout job with architect—accounts receivable (AR)

Closeout job with vendors—accounts payable (AP)

Closeout job files

Issue postmortem report

Arrange house-warming package

Prepare job documentation and maintenance packages for long- and short-term storage

The above sample job description comprises of basic project manager responsibilities, some of which can be parsed out to other staff, such as superintendents. Part of the epidemic of poor project administration is the failure to acknowledge and perform these tasks. Depending on a given company and its needs, a project manager's job description may include more or less responsibility, and may change from project to project. However, the above job description is lacking in two critical elements:

Division of responsibilities between project manager and superintendent

Definition of coordination with other staff

Although the project manager is aware of all his duties, if his efforts are not methodically coordinated with his colleagues, he will operate in a vacuum. For example, sometimes he may copy accounts payable with work authorizations, other times he won't. If his tasks aren't regimented, his performance will be subject to flaws. The same rules of management coordination holds true for any project team. Project team coordination will be different for every project, contingent on the nature of the project, and the project team. Therefore, a systematic approach should be taken for each new venture to ensure that the needs of a given project will be adequately met.

Before venturing into the morass of middle mismanagement, keep in mind the following maxim:

> *So much of what we call management consists in making it difficult for people to work.* Peter F. Drucker

Mr. Drucker has certainly seen his share of discombobulated management structures, and clearly finds that they often are their own worst enemy. The more managers try to improve things, the harder it becomes for others to do their job. There are a number of reasons for this, and they are not very pretty. Some of them are

- General business administration ignorance
- Conservatism
- Stupidity
- Rigidity
- Thirst for power and control
- Competitiveness
- Sabotage
- Self-aggrandizement

The above circumstances sound rather harsh, but this description is commensurate with the malignancy that incompetent or malevolent managers subject their people to. The degree to which managers can render their charges insignificant or discontent cannot be underestimated, and as illustrated above, is affected by idiosyncrasies both personal and professional. A poorly managed company is like a ship with an impending mutiny. A company lacking in management is like a ship without a captain—the men have no bearings, and no one to guide them to their destination. They risk the peril of foundering, or even perishing. In either case, worker output will be retarded by poor management techniques. The latter four behaviors refer to the inherent narcissism and greed of aspiring executives and company heads whose only concern is moving up the food chain, even at others' expense. Oddly enough, the fact that personality has little to do directly with operations does not mitigate the level of damage such behavior can cause companywide; thus, my continual allusion of mismanagement to cancerous growths.

Construction Staff Structures

Construction staffing consists of three structures: executive, field, and office. Some will only function in one realm, the office or the job site, while others will vacillate between the job site and office. For example, some companies with larger projects requiring a full-time project manager maintain a site office for him, as well as an administrative assistant, but this is the exception—a full-time superintendent, and part-time project manager being the norm. Even if he is needed full-time, the project manager is typically so burdened with other projects and chores that he can't devote sufficient attention to any of his jobs.

Although job descriptions at various companies are doggedly inscrutable, they can be categorized in a general sense.

Executive

Principals

Boss: He may or may not be on the payroll, and his involvement in the day-to-day operations is variable. In general, he should not be involved with low-level tasks, only executive tasks such as managing cash flow, negotiating contracts, managing hires and terminations, interfacing with accounting, seeing to clients' needs, and sales work. It isn't hard to judge the integrity of the company by gauging the stripe of the owner and what role he plays in the company (see Chap. 8, and Chap. 1).

If there is more than one owner, say a partner, a whole other set of dynamics comes into play that must be considered; the roles of each partner must be immutable as any measure of inconsistency on their part will be magnified exponentially down the staff hierarchy. Since each partner virtually has complete control, they must continually coordinate efforts so as not to repeat each other, and to stay on the same page. There were three or four partners managing our duplex project, each moving in a different direction, and no one apprised or aware of another's actions. This condition manifested itself as an egregious deconstruction of reason, as there was no connectivity or synthesis whatsoever. Such a dynamic is more prevalent at large corporations with bloated bureaucracies. When a small to midsize contractor's upper-management strata begins to resemble a lumbering multinational corporation, the entertainment and futility of purpose begins in earnest.

General manager

The general manager is the overlord of the day-to-day operations: production and administration, and as such is accountable for the entire team performance as a whole. He answers to the owner and will share in some of the executive level tasks that the owner could also do. He has authority over all the staff, but in order to be effective, he will work mostly with project managers and superintendents, facilitating their production teams down the line. He will also direct bookkeeping operations, and may have an office manager to oversee administrative tasks. Thus, the general manager should be the most important employee in the staff structure. Sadly, not enough companies have a general manager proper—his job description is diluted, and then variously distributed to middle management, and quite often, the owner of the company; in either case, falling far short of the mark. On the other hand, there is a dearth of capable individuals available to fill the position of *residential construction general manager*.

Additionally, being the right hand of the company owner, the general manager may handle tasks that the owner would normally handle, such as client management, contract negotiations, and the hiring and terminating of staff. This includes fielding complaints, handling emergencies, and running the company for the owner in general. The office manager can see to the administrative side of things, while the general manager facilitates production through his project managers, and they through their superintendents. Other than this basic job description the general manager's role remains somewhat inscrutable. If it had to be described in one sentence, it would read: "Whatever it takes to get the job done,"[1] which, when taken literally, renders a formal job description superfluous.

A good general manager facilitates the company's principals by minimizing the number of responsibilities that fall into their bailiwick, which enables them to focus on top priorities. The general manager should be able to do almost anything they do, and facilitate everything that they should not be doing. Thus is the general manager's role a holistic one that relies on considerable intuition. Few individuals fit these criteria—some more than others, however, for many, their superhuman efforts take a considerable toll on their psychophysiological well-being—the job takes years off their life. It is the fortunate general manager who has a strong team working for him. If he does, he can depend on them to tell him what they need, as opposed to vice versa—he is there to facilitate their job, not second-guess it. If he needs to be telling his managers what they should be doing, then it is likely that they don't have a full comprehension of their job description.

Recruitment and Interviews

When they need warm bodies, most companies will run a "help-wanted" advertisement to source their middle management team. Depending on their budget, they will establish salary ranges. Applicants are asked to state their salary requirements up-front, a habit I've always regarded as a bit gauche; if a candidate is the "real deal," he will prove well worth a generous salary because (a) good people are hard to find, and (b) strong people yield healthful, tangible results. If salary requirements seem too high, they will set a candidate's resume aside without an interview. If it is in their range, and they do offer the position, they will likely chisel down the applicant anywhere from 5% to 20% of the asking price. I consider this a preemptive show of disingenuousness and bad faith: how much do they care about cultivating their people if the first question they ask them is to take a salary cut? Answer: not much. The chief consideration in new hires is "what can they do for us now, how quickly can they get it done before we discharge them, and for how little will they do it?" They hire and then discharge their people in the same way as they might buy equipment for each project; like a dispensable commodity. While this position would seemingly represent their most pressing and self-centered needs of cash flow, it does little to add to a company's infrastructural growth. Perhaps this happens because companies don't believe in investing in people. They would invest in tools or office equipment as they consider them to be assets. Evidently they don't consider people as assets, or if they do—disposable assets. Additionally, by keeping tenures short-term, they hope to keep their unemployment insurance rate low by discharging employees before they are eligible for benefits, and keep them off of any in-house benefit plan such as health insurance. If salary cap is an encumbrance to pay the asking price of a person you really want on your team, share this fact with them, and let them know that as things improve, so shall their pay stub.

Companies with high turnover sometimes source their managers through agencies. Perhaps they've had their fill of interviews, or maybe they don't want to advertise publicly, where their reputation for high turnover may become evident. Companies that run a want advertisement for the same position 15 times a year obviously don't get "it." Obviously they don't keep running the advertisement because they are fruitful and multiplying, and thus need 15 new project managers . . . . Agency hires tend to have short longevity, and are paid as little as possible for a career position, or a decent salary for a temporary commission. For many companies this is just fine, as they have no interest in personnel development, and enjoy the discounted salary requirements they stipulate with the personnel agencies. They hire personnel for each project through an agency, and gleefully discharge them as soon as possible. They don't lose money in retraining people because they offer no training, or as little as possible. Many agencies work with the same general contractors for years, burning through armies of applicants. The agencies reap the steady flow of finder's fees, and their clients avail themselves of an endless supply of warm bodies. Yet it can be awkward for a contractor to introduce a newly hired manager to a client—no client wants their project to be the proving ground for an aspiring manager. They want a tried and true person; one who has been with the company. For this reason, contractors are loath to advertise the fact to the client that the manager is a new hire, or worse that they can't keep quality people for prolonged employment. It is a dubious sign denoting instability.

If contractors' projects are cost-driven, they will seek candidates with lower salary requirements. If their clients' projects are a negotiated bid, or well-financed, they should be more liberal with the salaries they offer, as they don't want to skimp on a well-endowed project. However, out of force of old habits, many companies will continue to bottom feed the labor force, even for complicated and high-end projects for which they are wholly unsuited. In other words, although high-end companies promise more qualified personnel, they aren't necessarily willing to pay their salaries, and thus, often have underqualified personnel, who are paid less. This practice may have begun with the inception of the company's tacit mission statement, or it may be a necessity of chronic meager general conditions.

A simple brief discussion or synopsis of a resume will sometimes betray an applicant's shortcomings, or marquee any special talents, the former being the norm. After you've seen enough resumes, you soon become fluent in quickly translating the signals that resumes will inadvertently transmit. For example, it's not unusual to set aside 90 out of 100 management resumes in a few hours of cursory review time. Reviewing thousands of resumes from upper-management applicants asking for large salaries I've been awestruck by how pathetic many of them are—poorly written, typos, unorganized, and often wholly inappropriate, it's absurd to think that people with such resumes deign to apply for a position for which their resume doesn't even begin to substantiate. Such is the state of the estimator and middle- and upper-management talent pool. If salaries were offered based on the quality of their resumes, most middle managers would be earning only a fraction of prevailing wages.

Perhaps shortcomings are part of the criteria, as real talent gets paid real money, which many employers aren't in a position to offer—they don't mind using the lowest qualified individuals. Instead of discarding all of the under-qualified applicants, the legitimate candidates are eliminated, as companies can't afford to pay them, as if to say that by being legitimate, they are overqualified. Additionally, experience tells contractors that people tend to overassess their talent on their resumes, or misrepresent their skill levels and knowledge—they've been burned before. Of course, the market is almost entirely cost-driven, thus, companies are always bargain hunting the employees either to maximize margins, or minimize payroll. This approach tends to sell the industry short by sponsoring underpaid and underqualified managers to facilitate high-end construction projects. Everyone shares the blame in this circumstance, including clients who are too aggressive with their budgets, and refuse to compromise as they want to "have their cake and eat it too." Contractors promise to deliver top-quality on cash-strapped projects with underqualified personnel, and architects continue to design overbudget, and withhold critical design information.

Interviewing is a necessary and resource-consuming evil. Nowhere is it more difficult than in assessing the aptitude of middle management and estimators. It is an inexact business to be sure. Every company seems to subscribe to a different curriculum; however, there are some old hackneyed schools that most adhere to. These would include the interviews that begin with the enticement "So tell me about yourself." The interviewee does most of the talking, and the interviewer observes, taking in the tawdry details, feigning genuine interest. In fact, the whole interview may resemble an exercise in affectation—indirect biopic incisions into the applicant's true nature, and enthusiastic hyperbole regarding his own abilities from the applicant. The result is an oil and water coagulation that leaves both parties where they started—knowing little or nothing as to the true nature of each other, each with something to hide from the other. Employers don't really care about what the applicant says: the interview exercise only serves as a litmus test for them to gauge aptitude and appropriateness. Some employers still issue dreaded commercial work application forms; completely inappropriate for applicants who have or should have a resume. Another form of passive interview is probably the most common form wherein dialectic takes place. There is discussion of the interviewee's aptitudes as described on his resume, and then a brief smoke-blowing presentation of the company's prowess. The interviewer will inquire as to why the applicant left his former company(ies). This type of interview is passive because other than this interview, there will likely be no further measure of the interviewee's acumen before he is either hired or rejected, save for verifying references. This leaves the interviewing company in the position of having no benchmark to judge the applicant's ability other than what he says he can do, and his resume, which is a very subjective perception; not particularly useful. The upshot phase of the interview is always an interesting phenomenon. It's almost a relief to hear someone say "We don't think we're a good match"—directness is typically supplanted by some sort of obliquity, in keeping with the company's image: such as "We'll call you." Suffice it to say, most companies are still stuck in the twentieth century when it comes to interviewing prospective employees.

Companies typically make their decisions based on this single interview. A follow-up interview almost surely results in a job offer. The employer will keep a close watch on their new hire, expecting to gain more insight into his abilities. This constitutes their new employee quality control program. Unfortunately, this process may take a few months to play out, in which a lot of time and money can be wasted. The rapid and high rate of turnover of such hires points to either a flaw in the process, or a dearth of experienced personnel. In fact, both are to blame. On the other hand, an employee's longevity at a company isn't necessarily an accurate barometer of his or his employer's acumen.

I recall a very odd interview, in Boston, some years ago. The company had an impressive history, and their present portfolio suggested complex and aggressively scheduled projects completed on time and within budget. They wanted to open a New York satellite office and needed personnel. Visiting Boston by way of New York, from a construction person's aspect, one can't help be reminded of the never ending saga of that city's "Big Dig"[2] fiasco, as the project is literally ubiquitous in that city, and it is hard to lose this association. Not a day seems to go by without *The Boston Globe* exposing some new flaw or defect in the project. Although the Big Dig is a transportation infrastructure overhaul project costing over 14 Billion dollars, it bears some striking resemblances to its distant cousins in the residential sector: overbudget, off schedule, and mismanaged.

Although this was an old company, they seemed to have realized the shortcomings of the traditional interview process, and had constructed their own:

> Prior to the interview the applicant was sent a questionnaire of the sort you find in self-help books and grocery store check out lanes, albeit, a step-up—a contrivance borne of a new-age corporate hiring consulting firm. This same company would measure the applicant's responses from a socio-psychological standpoint, that is, there was no consideration of the specific nuances of the particular occupation. The questions were well written and relevant to therapeutic endeavors; however, there was an uneasy quality of a tacit smug psychobabble about them; there were no "right" answers, only those that were designed to betray personal characteristics about the applicant. You couldn't say what you mean, only indicate the closest approximation offered from a list of what they assumed you meant. Based on their

findings, you might be rated anywhere from a passive to an aggressive type. If you were a take charge, no-nonsense type, you would answer aggressively, and probably be considered "inappropriate for their needs," as this particular company smacked of touchy-feely-ness.

The company had its own building on a pleasant side street. The offices were bright and cheery. On many of the walls were large banners and posters with "smiley" faces promoting brotherhood and benevolence, or some postmodern jargon to lively up the inhabitants. The interview consisted of a group of short meetings between each member of one of the divisions and the applicant, wherein the applicant would do all the talking, as the interviewers looked on, or rather observed. Some of the interviewers were lower management—below the applicant's prospective position, and likely his future underlings. As such, many of their inquiries were inappropriate to a prospective superior; however, although there was a staff hierarchy, this company eschewed the food-chain protocol and fostered what I call the *immaculate teamwork* ethic, a fictitious politically correct work environment where everyone works together in perfect harmony and equality, and lives happily ever after. The applicant's qualifications were beyond reproach, and he thought he interviewed well, despite having a fierce respiratory flu. Some weeks later, not having heard from the prospect, the applicant called their human resource department to follow-up on the interview. What he was told was that he would not be considered for the position because there was (ahem) "a lack of chemistry . . ." Further inquiry solicited the response that the questionnaire pointed to some disturbing perceptions, chiefly that the applicant was a take-charge, no nonsense type individual—virtues antithetical to the company's ethic. These were the only criteria used to discern the applicant's suitability for the position.

This company's interview process personified a new-fangled flaw in the integrity of the art of the interview. It didn't fail in the traditional sense but it served no purpose in the practical sense—it merely found a new way to arrive at the same flawed conclusion. What it has in common with the traditional interview is that neither seems to take an accurate measure of the applicant's practical abilities. This wastefulness is totally unnecessary. Would it not be simpler to hearken back to simpler days? Observe the following discourse:

Foreman: "So, have you done a lot of structural work?"

Applicant: "I framed houses in San Diego for 6 years."

Foreman: "O.K., set up with that crew on that section there, and we'll talk at the end of the day."

Elapsed time: 60 seconds.

At the end of the day, the man was either offered wages, or turned away, based on his work quality and output.

Things could never be that simple today, especially for a position as subtle as management; however, they could and should be simpler, and they should return to the true measure of ability, for which there is no replacement other than demonstration. Residential middle managers and estimators should also pass a simple test before a prolonged interview process takes place. Using such a test as a prerequisite, perhaps 80% of nonproductive interview time could be reconnoitered by turning away unsuitable prospects. That is no small chunk of time, considering the hours companies must put into the recruitment process.

The simple but telling preinterview process enfolds as follows: subsequent to a brief screening that prequalifies an individual and goes through some introductory formalities, the applicant is given a set of drawings; either the drawings for the project he would be placed on, or a similar one. He is asked to review the drawings, and to be prepared to discuss them in a general sense, 15 or 30 minutes hence. He reviews the drawings, writes down some notes, and then discusses his findings with the interviewer, who will also have prepared general questions pertaining to the drawings for the applicant to answer. Depending on the quality of this discussion, the applicant may or may not be further considered for the position. You might say that a lot is missing from this preinterview; however, this test is simply a prerequisite to the interview proper. If this hurdle is cleared, it is then appropriate to discuss further details about the applicant and the interviewer; otherwise, there is no point other than being gracious. The reason for this brief pulse taking is that an overwhelming majority of middle-management interviewees in the residential sector are unqualified to perform their function, and misrepresent themselves as being suited to the task. This notion advised by judging the gauge of managers at work, and considering the rate of discarded resumes in proportion to every hireling. Misrepresentation should be easily discernable to the trained eye in the prequalification interview process. This rubric is the same one that applies to any ability—a musician, a bricklayer, or an automechanic. It speaks volumes over the applicant's resume, which may give a skewed or fictitious representation.

Administrative

Office manager

Essentially, the office manager is the person responsible for the oversight of the distribution of information and documentation between company personnel and outside entities. The flow of information and documentation are key components to project management; hence the importance of an efficient office manager cannot be understated. Typically, for smaller companies that need someone to coordinate office traffic, an administrative level worker functions as the *de facto* office manager. Without proper training, this is usually a futile effort. Fail as they may, contractors still try to get by without an office manager. General managers and office managers are unusual job titles because they facilitate others; that is, their tangible output is hard to measure. If a contractor can't readily assess the value of a person's work output in dollars and cents, then the concept of paying them money to do their job strikes them as counterintuitive. The problem isn't only the failure of contractors to appreciate what competent departmental managers could do for them, but it is also the failure to recognize what is missing from their present arrangement.

An office manager is not exigent, especially to a small firm; however, if the office is busy, this person will help keep it all together, and improve the company's performance. They will facilitate secretaries, interns, shipping and receiving, and bookkeepers with their jobs. They can be the point person for directing all upper-level administrative tasks. Busy offices without office managers can easily become disorganized. Upper-level management will have to go through people individually to see to their needs, and there will be no one accountable for the big picture. It helps if the office manager has a construction background.

The office manager may also see to the following:

- That the office is opened and closed everyday
- That servers, telephone systems, fax machines, and alarms are all operable as necessary
- That the office is staffed with all necessary supplies
- Oversee telephone and message management
- Monitor information technology (IT) systems and interface with local area network (LAN) personnel
- See that new hires are adequately trained

The above job description also applies to site offices, which will have similar needs, although on a smaller, local scale.

In the absence of certain administrative personnel, the office manager may also take on the following responsibilities:

- Payroll reporting and distribution
- Answering telephones
- Generating project correspondence
- Courier management
- Scheduling meetings for sales and executives
- Preparation of AIA *G702 Application and Certificate for Payment* and AIA *G703 Continuation Sheet for G702*
- Preparation of AIA *G701 Change Order*
- Drawing of contracts
- Bookkeeping: AP/AR
- Handling of in-house labor problems and emergencies
- Arranging for special events
- Dispatching driver, laborers, and other field personnel
- Ordering material

- Generating purchase orders or subcontracts
- Managing reprographic services
- Processing complaints and other PR-related issues
- Coordinating marketing and advertising

Most of which should not be part of their job description, and the more of this they do, the more quickly they will burn out. This laundry list is no small undertaking, and not infrequently office managers are saddled with some or all of these responsibilities. The proper and appropriate workloads and tasks delegated to office personnel must be coordinated and properly allocated in order for these people to function effectively. If the office managers are debilitated, how can they facilitate people working under them, or enable their superiors?

The Office Paperwork Conundrum

Inbox

The exception is the office where paperwork is truly organized and information readily accessible. Every company seemingly has its own methods, or sometimes none, or no recognizable method. Implementing a distribution system to 100% efficiency is untenable. Eighty percent would be a good score, with about 50% the average. If you figure that most projects require about 80% efficiency, then indeed, most companies perform well below the mark. Typically, documents are not distributed to all the required parties, and a link in the information chain is broken, thus causing a breach in the system. Ironically, many people get multiple copies of the same document, and no copies of other documents. Finally, even when documents are circulated, crucial follow-up is lacking to the point where it no longer matters who reads what and when.

Contractors sometimes get the urge to implement comprehensive and foolproof systems, as a panacea for all their administrative woes. Perhaps some of them would be useful; however, most either fail entirely, or go along half cocked because:

- The system is too rigid and complicated to begin with
- The system simply isn't viable
- There is no one to administrate, oversee, or monitor the system
- The system isn't fully integrated into the company and all its employees, or not, everyone chooses to use it
- The connection between the field and office is not fluid

This last condition is particularly problematic. For instance, if the main office receives a document intended for a field person, it may languish in their in-box until they come to the office and happen upon it. Distribution of documentation is a classic shortcoming of the average management team. One of the difficulties with efficiently distributing paperwork is that the task is often delegated to an administrative level person, who may not get the job done for any number of reasons. On the other hand, middle managers are often the culprit, as they are often the direct recipients of much documentation that never gets properly distributed—they assume that such responsibilities only pertain to administrative level personnel.

While there is no system that fits everyone's needs, the same criteria of any other system, for example, general estimating systems discussed in Chap. 2 are applicable to documentation management:

- You have the ability to tailor it to fit your needs: Many computer programs promise to deliver this need right out of the box, or else promise flexibility; however, when it comes the time to customize or tweak the program, the program is invariably unable to accommodate them.

- It is inexpensive: You don't have to pay the hefty licensing, upgrade, and training fees associated with commercial programs.

Before implementing a new system, you must consider the following:

- What is the basis of your assumption that the system is useful and will be successful?

- Will it lend itself to integration with project management and billing systems already in place, or to be introduced?

- Do you have the staff to implement it?

- Will the system be readily adaptable to change and customization?

- What kind of training will be required for end users?

- Do you have a "plan B" in the event that the system fails?

- Is the system structured such that the components (including staff) are replaceable?

Regrettably, few contractors take the time to weigh these considerations. Necessity becomes the mother of rash invention, that is, systems are created to prop up, or better manage the detritus of a failing system; thus, treating the symptom and not the disease. They should realize that it is sometimes easier to start over than to try to repair something that isn't worth fixing. I recall an interesting contrivance.

Realizing the need to upgrade the accessibility and storage of documentation, an executive at a midsize company decreed the following edict: he directed that a master binder be created for each project. This binder would be managed and maintained by him alone, something like a rabbi and his Torah. No one could remove any document except for the purpose of reproduction. The program was put in place. After a few weeks, documents continued to be haphazardly distributed to team members, and more often not distributed at all, even to the main recipient, just as they had always been. The said master binder's existence could never be verified; however, no one dared raise the question. They merely continued to scramble for the paperwork they required. The executive's instincts were correct—organize and control, but their manifestation jaundiced. Furthermore, there was no follow-up—there was only the edict, which was an end in itself. The tendency to create solutions, but never implement them constitutes a death knell for any system. Contractors' bookcases are full of barely used training manuals and computer programs. It is the responsibility of executive-level management not only to create the necessary systems, but also to see that they are actually implemented, and to assign someone to administrate them. Master document binders should be kept in the main office for every project. This doesn't mean that every document associated with a given project be kept there, only those relevant should be. At the end of the project, the superintendent and project manager can add their binders to the office collection, which should yield a comprehensive account of any project, contingent upon the quality of the content and the organization of the documents. This documentation should then be compiled and archived. Companies will certainly be eager to pack up a complete project, but few will organize or correctly archive it. Perhaps it can't be organized, or there may be not enough time allotted to the task. Too often, contractors rush through the closeout stage in order to put a project behind them, and hit the ground running for the next endeavor. Whatever the case, the files are hastily thrown into a shallow grave, hopefully to never be reopened.

Short of reinventing the wheel through micromanagement, a few simple considerations may be all that's needed to enhance or replace a dysfunctional system of organization. To begin with, start with a fail-safe distribution system. Any distribution system should have a vehicle for indicating what goes to whom, including intraoffice, and for incoming paperwork; for instance, the distribution spreadsheet as shown in Table 6.1.

Paperwork to be copied to more than one person could receive a simple matrix form, a rubber stamp impression (Table 6.2), with everyone's initials; perfect for

TABLE 6.1   Documentation Distribution

Information Tracking and Distribution System: Intraoffice							
Item	Log	OFF, MGR	AP/AR	DG	PM	SUPER	GM
Proposal				X			X
Purchase order		X			X	X(no$$$)	Sign
Signed purchase order	X		X				
Change order, with back-up	X	X		X			
Signed change order	X		X	X	X	X(no$$$)	
RFI	X			As needed	X	X	
Specification					X	X	
Job memo/correspondence				X	X	X	As needed
Minutes				X	X	X	As needed
Request for PO		X					
Check request			X				

TABLE 6.2 Distribution Stamp

Joe	√
Patti	
Tom	√
Rich	√
Bob	
Therese	
Lloyd	√
Field	√
File	√

a small office, as there may not be more than 9 or 10 names. If a check appears in the box next to a person's initials, they are to be copied. Notations can be entered, such as *"NO$"* denoting "no dollar amounts," when paperwork is to be issued to the field,[3] and *"SIGN"* for paperwork requiring a signature.

In addition to distribution to required parties, the documentation in this system should go into a central file or database. A relational database can be a great asset when it is used to its potential. Digital document retrieval will always trump manual retrieval. Team members can retrieve documents from the company network or Web site. While the main office has its own systems, field offices may have a completely different system, as the main office system may not be practical in the field. Project managers in the field often have their own personal organization systems that require another level of sorting or parsing. Thus, the two must be considered separately. With all this sorting and transposing, things get lost. Most offices prefer sectioned binders; however, few can control and maintain organization of their documentation in this manner. Years ago, a contractor had one of the most simplistic systems I had seen. Although, it was not the most organized or regimented system, it turned out to be one of the most effective. Documentation was sorted according to its basic content. Depending on its nature, it would be designated a color that corresponds to one of four color folders:

- *Red*: Proposals (base and change order) and takeoffs, subcontractor and vendor material purchase orders

- *Yellow*: In/out correspondence, notes, memos, requests for information (RFIs)

- *Blue*: Control documents, such as permits and sign-offs, approvals, sketches and specifications

- *Green*: Contracts and executed change orders

For the main office, this simple system has its merits. Green and blue folders pertained mostly to the prime contract, and were easy to control. Red and yellow folders were organized by the trade and team members. All information was kept in lateral files. Documents were sorted by date in their respective folders. Once the project was complete, the files went into storage. The field personnel kept their files however they wished.

The interesting thing was that this system could be somewhat unorganized and still be useful—if the paperwork was not sorted by date, at least it appeared in the right project file, and correct color folder; hence, it was always accessible at some level; in a pinch, there was a catchall folder for every type of document. At best, the folders could be sorted into subsets that offered a higher level of organization. Thus, a system need not be large and complex to be effective—large and complex systems generally yield a greater degree of user-unfriendliness, and a lesser rate of utilization—more trouble than their worth.

Outbox

In addition to a system for managing received documentation, there must be a correlative system for managing outgoing documentation. Too much correspondence is merely sent off to its recipient and at once forgotten, as if the act of sending it were an end in itself. Like control documentation, outgoing correspondence should not only be filed internally as well but it should also require receipt confirmation and follow-up.

Consider the odyssey of an average correspondence from an architect to a contractor:

> Please be advised that the in-line exhaust fan has been relocated to the position shown in the attached sketch. It has also been changed to a smaller unit as per the attached cut-sheet. Note, that the access panel must be relocated accordingly.

The memo and its sketch may be copied to the project manager, who copies this to his superintendent, who in turn copies it to the mechanical vendor. At best, the fan is relocated, as is its access panel. This level of distribution may seem acceptable to most; however, even a seemingly small issue can generate multiple questions that may never be addressed:

Was the memo copied to the electrician, carpenter and mechanic alike? Was receipt of same confirmed? Did everyone get all the page attachments?

Are the project manager and superintendent advised as to who was copied on the memo?

Was a statement of impact received from the electrician, mechanic, and carpenter?

Was the original fan purchased or installed already? If so, there will be a charge to uninstall and restock it?

Was a request for submittal solicited to the mechanic?

Is there a revised control-wiring diagram associated with the new fan?

Do the engineer's equipment schedule and load calculations need to be modified to show the change?

Was the architect asked to issue a request for proposal (RFP), or notified of an up charge for the change?

Are there any RFIs generated by this memo?

Will the schedule or sequencing be affected by this change?

As you can see, a relatively minor or simple change can seem miniscule in proportion to the amount of time and effort spent correctly incorporating it into the project, yet consider how much trouble could be raised if these questions were not taken into account? In the above example, improperly integrating the new fan into the project could cause problems for countless successor tasks. Changes that have few or no successor tasks are less likely to cause disturbances. Typically, full notification and documentation requirements are not met, as few contractors are willing to invest much time on what they perceive as small matters; time for which they will likely not be remunerated. Your managers must understand the dynamics of information management and processing, as well as interrelationship between team members, such that they understand what documentation must be shared with whom, regardless of the general condition budget.

The Paperless Office

The modern superintendent and project manager need not have so much paper on their hands as they are wont to have; it is cumbersome to organize, a pain to store or carry around, and either gets lost or can't be readily found. I knew a project manager who was lauded for his work ethic because he toted stacks of binders with him to every job meeting. However, upon being asked to produce a given document, after much rifling, it became evident that he was generally incapable of finding anything. Rather, he was more in the habit of asking others for copies of what he could not locate. He had so much paper that he couldn't really be sure what he had and what he was missing. Managers should be able to reduce their hard-copy load significantly with a simple laptop computer, and considerably more so with an Internet connection. Any document created on a computer is digitalized, and stored as bits of information. In theory, it needn't ever be printed to be referred to. A manager can carry with him on digital media nearly every document on a given project, save for those with stamps and signatures, and oversize hand-rendered drawings (which, in a pinch, could be scanned). In fact, he could carry with him all digital documentation for all of his projects on one hard drive or even *data stick*. Architects often prefer e-mailing correspondence, which makes storing and archiving that much simpler. Even computer aided design (CAD) files can now be converted to readable files without *AutoCAD* software by using a special converter. Like any other archiving, the digital information must be organized. The disk operating system (DOS) file directory tree format that is the same format for Windows, only with a graphical user interface (GUI), lends itself well to this method, as it is based on a directory and subdirectory trees. It is worthwhile to create a directory template and use it as a basis for all projects. An example is given below:

Drive://Project Name/

Administration/
  Daily Reports
  Notices: changes, delays, shutdowns.
  Progress photographs
  Petty-cash statements
  Accident reports

Contract Documents/
  Contract/
    Base Contract
    Change Orders/
      Approved
      Pending
      Rejected
  Drawings/
    Architect
    Engineer
    Specifications
    Sketches (SKs)
  Insurance certificates
  Payment Applications
    In/
    Out/
    Lien waivers
  Subcontracts and Purchase Orders

Control/
  Inspections
  Permits
  Releases

Correspondence/
  Owner
  Architect
  Engineer
  Subcontractors
  Others

Cost Analysis/
  Cash flow Projection
  Estimates
    Base Proposal
    Budgets
  General Conditions Projections
  Profit and Overhead

Minutes/
Agendas
Minutes

Notes/
Memos
Project Directory
To-do Lists

RFIs/
Closed
Log
Pending
Responses

Schedules/
Baseline
Current
Look-aheads (short-term schedules)
Superceded

Submittals/
Covers
Log
Specifications

Files will be stored in their respective folders and will be automatically sorted chronologically for easy reference. The form in which a project directory tree may vary from project to project, and according to personal preference such a method should be more efficient, flexible, and user-friendly than just any hard-copy storage system in use today, and will be the choice of the future. Just how far in the future digital archiving will happen at the middle management level is an open question, as all managers would need computer training and the equipment to implement any such system.

It is a satisfying and empowering feeling to have the entire project available at your fingertips. All data are readily accessible. When a document is required for presentation, there is no frantic rifling through messy dog-eared documents. The document is secured in a few mouse clicks. Begin digital archiving for some of the simpler documents—such as spreadsheets and word processing documents. Later, when you get a good feel for it, you can add more complex files, such as digital photos, digital videos, CAD files, portable document format (PDFs), scans, and even audio files.

Project Manager

Every project needs a project manager, or at least some individual to perform the tasks that are typically his responsibility. Like any other specialist, good residential project managers are hard to find, especially high-end practitioners.

I believe that there are enough mechanics out there who aspire to be superintendents, who might later step up as project managers. I would prefer such an individual to the typical construction management or engineering degree-wielding graduate—these individuals tend to have little hands-on know-how, the kind that makes a successful manager. The "men" (workers) know this, they can smell a manager's lack of hands-on experience a mile away. Unfortunately, this has created an unhealthy stereotype among them that all middle managers, especially project managers, are lacking in practical building knowledge:

A superintendent on a project was overseeing two carpenters in the construction of a curved wall. One of the carpenters, a new hire, who was already showing signs of discontent, took issue with one of the superintendent's directives regarding his means and methods in constructing the wall. The carpenter refused to fit the work accordingly and commented that he felt the superintendent was not qualified to direct him thus, as superintendents, typically learn everything they know at school, and have no construction experience. The superintendent explained to the carpenter that, in fact, he had come up through the ranks; started out with a shovel and pickax, and furthermore, had no right to make such an assumption. The point was not well taken and the superintendent had to instruct the carpenter to collect his tools and quit the site immediately. Thus, not only are there sometimes stereotypes between management and mechanics but also envy and hostility.

A project manager's skills should include the ability to facilitate or do himself, any of the superintendent's tasks, as he may become a *de facto* superintendent. He must understand the superintendent's job if he is to effectively manage him. To do that, he should really have experience as a superintendent. Additionally, it helps if he has some business background, and estimating skills, as he must understand and facilitate the bookkeeper and estimator's job. Today's top-level project manager will also be able to act as a construction manager, a job description we will explore further along in this chapter.

Project managers are answerable to the company owner, and/or the general manager, if there is one. They are largely responsible for the production of their respective projects, and for the majority of the paperwork and documentation that facilitates contract management. Production work they facilitate through superintendents, or directly through their workmen. Their administrative work typically involves interfacing with just about every office staff level—bookkeeping, estimating, and clerical personnel.

Project managers who spend time in the office do their paperwork, make phone calls, and meet with their colleagues there. Some project managers spend more time than others in the office, depending on how much they are needed in the field, and how busy the company is. Compare this to a project manager at a large company who may spend all of his time at a site office, or to a project manager who also doubles as a superintendent on smaller jobs, spending most of his time in the field. The former will be administrative oriented and the latter concentrated on production.

Sounding.
After the site for the building has been defi-
nitely determined, soundings should be made
to form the basis of an estimate of the quantity of rock to be excavated. In a case of this
kind, when soundings of a moderate depth
are to be made, a long steel crowbar and a
heavy striking hammer are generally employed
for the purpose, as shown. The bar should be
driven at intervals of 10 ft each way and down
to the depth required for the excavation, or
until it strikes solid rock, as the case may
be. *A Treatise on Architecture and Building
Construction, Vol. V* (Scranton: The Colliery
Engineer Co., 1899).

There are lots of gray areas in terms of where a superintendent's work stops,
and a project manager's begins. The work distribution can vary from job to job,
and has a lot to do with the ability of the staff, and size and complexity of each
project. The allocation of tasks for each project should be determined at the start;
otherwise, there is greater chance for omitted and repetitive tasks—some superintendents and project managers will do each other's work, in addition to their
own, while some will do neither.

Estimator

Estimating should be a separate department from administration and production. Estimators work with the owner, or head salesperson, in generating proposals to clients and architects. They will also have a fair amount of involvement
with the project manager, especially with change orders or postmobilization
buyouts. Sometimes they will interface with bookkeeping in order to help
manage billing. There are different methods of estimating, and different sets of
skills required for an estimator depending on what system is used, which we
discussed in Chap. 2.

For construction management projects, the estimator will work more directly
with the client and architect to create budgets, and value engineer, especially
in the preconstruction phase. To facilitate this interaction, your estimator should

have at least some of the necessary people skills unique to this endeavor: patience, agreeableness, salesmanship, and a special intuition for negotiating problems and working things out. This is because the residential sector frequently involves the unique factor of uninformed inexperienced clientele, who require special guidance. The advantage of the construction management/client relationship is that all information is transparent—there are no hidden agendas or proprietary hang-ups to interfere with synergy.

In the beginning, a general contractor may do all his own estimating. Subsequently, he takes on an estimator, whom he will keep on a short leash—the owner will want to thoroughly evaluate each proposal. Because a project manager will often engage contractors in postmobilization buyouts, he too should have a background in estimating. A company's owner or controller, if there is one, should review all proposals issued for approval, save for the smallest irrelevant ones. He should also keep apprised of market values for all the work he sells. These are long-term processes for which the owner must be diligent, or rely on others as best he can.

The issuance of bid packages can be a daunting task, for which bigger companies may hire a *clerk of the works*, who will manage the flow of copied and distributed project information: blueprints, specifications, and so forth. Short of a clerk of the works, the estimating team, or administrative staff typically distributes the information. In the case of the latter, extra care should be taken that the job is done thoroughly, as failure to issue complete bid packages is the bane of the estimator; administrative level staff seldom has a comprehensive understanding of the process sufficient to manage it alone.

A sample estimator job description is presented in Chap. 4.

Bookkeeping and Accounting

Bookkeeping generally refers to accounts payable and receivable. Other fiduciary matters should be handled by others (see later in the chapter). The bookkeeper should work closely with the project manager and general manager to track cash flow on all projects. He will also work with the estimator. Most prime contracts will use the AIA form, which is available in digital format from the AIA. The AIA *G702 Application and Certificate for Payment*, and accompanying worksheet AIA *G703 Continuation Sheet for G702* is part and parcel of the contract facilitating process, and this should also be done using AIA's software. To do it manually will waste time and invariably result in mistakes.

The integrity of your accounting department is crucial to your company's financial constitution. Even a company with decent cash flow can have bookkeeping problems if staff and systems are not up to the task. A certified public accountant for a small company will function as an advisor, and may file their income taxes. A bookkeeper will handle the day-to-day AP/AR, and report to the accountant at regular intervals, as well as at the annual report meetings. This duty can be extremely painstaking. Keeping it all together can be a real challenge. For this reason, a personal computer (PC) accounting program must be used. We will talk about such programs and how they relate to other programs further along in this chapter.

Payroll can also be tedious and painstaking; thankfully, there are a number of services who will do this for you. Do yourself a favor and avail yourself of one of these services. Doing it in-house is seldom worth the effort. These services will also file W2s as well.

Administrative Support Staff and Interns

Good administrative support staff tends to be overworked, overlooked, and underpaid—the more they are given to do, the more difficult they are to keep track of and to follow up on. There is rapid turnover of such hires because there is seldom a condition of mutual admiration between an overbearing employer, and an underperforming underpaid minion. They tend to be entry-level, and not have a lot of skills, specifically, in the field of construction; nonetheless, they are frequently saddled with tasks that are clearly out of their bailiwick, and invariably given too much to do. No wonder they disappoint. Some may be paid well, yet have a poor work ethic and still not be motivated.

It is the office manager who must ensure that the support staff is not unduly taxed, or given inappropriate level work to do. Unfortunately, many contractors do not have an office manager, or they have someone who is underqualified toiling at the position. A company that has well-rounded office personnel will not need to assign high-level tasks to its support staff. Even so, the practice of following up on their work is even more important, especially if they are preparing memos and issuing documentation, which is mostly what they are asked to do. There are many dangers to be wary of concerning administrative staff that can be a cause for great concern. For one, the presumption tends to be that, whatever they are doing, it is an *administrative level task* or low priority. Hence they aren't monitored very closely. As we shall see, this presumption can be problematic. In general, there is a tendency of support personnel not to followup on tasks. Perhaps people feel that they will be perceived as doing more, if they routinely perform the minimum, and quickly move on to the next task. This habit can be attributed to inexperience, lack of discipline, attitude, or inefficiency. Managers should be wary of this tendency and should take the necessary precautions to prevent oversights. If they are wise, they will teach people to take their own initiative in such matters.

Architecture and engineering students often wish to embellish their education with a brief internship, and sometimes, working at a construction company can appeal to them as giving them a rare look at the industry's means and methods—one they won't get in an architect's CAD galley. Interns are often an overlooked asset, and are not infrequently relegated to the go-fer job description. They are subject to receive directives from just about anybody, when optimally they are given a single mentor who manages their quotidian; takes them on as a protégé. Misuse of interns wastes an energetic and motivated resource, one who is paid little, yet will typically work hard; he is there because he wants to be there, not because he has to be. Surprisingly, one encounters them rarely in the construction industry. Placement offices at colleges, universities, and other schools will post job offerings that many students are eager to entertain for even the experience alone. If only haggard long-term employees showed a fraction of the interest and energy that young vibrant interns bring with them . . .

But more importantly interning aspiring architects and engineers could take their experiences in the construction industry into their mature careers. It would be to everyone's benefit if more did so, and used such knowledge as a way to bridge some of the gaps between the design and building industries.

Sample Intern Job Description
Title:
Intern
Report To:
Office Manager and Estimator
Objectives:
 Cover phones, fax, and 2/Way radio as necessary
 Prepare Fedex Airbills and arrange messenger service for estimating department
 Compile copies and collations
 Assist estimating department in follow-ups and bidding processes
 Assist in distribution of incoming faxes and interoffice communications
 Run special missions

Common Administrative Problems

Typos in correspondence top my list; not the stray comma type that bedevils our single proprietor (see Chap. 7): mistakes with spelling people's names, errors with numbers, and poor execution in general can cause all sorts of problems. Typos are the sort of mistake that bedevils the managers because they could always have been detected with a simple proofread. A manager will always have enough trouble on his plate with mistakes that he could not prevent. Suffice it to say, he shouldn't have to deal with easily preventable problems.

Administrative level personnel should not be in the business of generating dates or numbers; for example, pricing or scheduling information. Other things to watch out for are the following:

- Failure to complete or follow-up tasks, such as issuing documentation to required parties, and confirming receipt of same.
- Absentmindedness and forgetfulness: if overburdened as they so often are, they may simply forget what they have to do, or how to do it.

These are only two types of common problems associated with administrative tasks; however, the gravity of problems generated from them can be staggering.

Despite their high maintenance, many interns and apprentices are an overlooked asset that not enough companies appreciate or cultivate. They tend to be young, full of energy, and eager to learn, especially those who are attending college, who can be very thorough and organized; just as they must be in their studies. Colleges and universities have job placement offices and bulletin boards where you might find such people. Nevertheless, they should be kept on the same short leash as any other administrative staff.

Production

Superintendent

The production team lightning rod is known as the project superintendent, or project supervisor. He is the liaison between the project manager and the workmen, as well as his company and the project subcontractors and vendors. He will likely interface with the architect a great deal, and he will assist in project management administration to varying degrees.

Many superintendents come up through the ranks, and have manual skills, thus they often assist in production. They are known as working superintendents. Generally, a working superintendent does not belong to a complex high-end project because his management contribution will not be his top priority—building will be. Not to say he may not ply his skills from time to time, especially on smaller projects. In fact, he should be somewhat of an authority on production methods, and able to produce, demonstrate, or facilitate all scope of work on his project. Although he is more or less a middle manager, the superintendent has one of the most difficult and volatile jobs in the industry. On smaller projects, he may be called upon to do a project manager's work as well, and vice versa; this former condition is obviously more problematic than the latter as it requires him to step up.

Like his immediate superior—the project manager, good superintendents are scarce in the residential sector. They are so scarce that nowadays it's not unusual for them to be compensated higher than a project manager. Many come up through the ranks, as we have said, and the production skills they may bring with them can be extremely useful. Yet many people who work up to the position don't necessarily receive the proper management training; in fact, they may be oblivious to the management skills that are required. This is no fault of their own, and points to a lack of effort by the industry to properly train such individuals that was discussed briefly in Chap. 1.

Just as many superintendents are prematurely promoted to project manager; many foremen and leadmen are promoted to superintendent, not because they have learned the skills necessary to do the job but because there is no one else to do it. These superintendents must sink or swim, and learn on the job (assuming they will be taught). A common arrangement is for an ex-lead-mechanic cum superintendent, to be appointed the position, even before he has mastered his former station. When he is called upon to perform tasks beyond his capabilities, his superior steps in and takes up the slack. Not only does this arrangement do a disservice to the aspiring worker, but it does not give clients a fair deal insofar as what the general requirements of their contract are. Not unlikely a contractor is paying a lead mechanic acting as superintendent carpenter's wages, and charging the client for this individual as if he were a bona fide superintendent.

Mechanics/Laborers/Drivers

The workman would appear to have the most humble position in production, especially the laborer. This does not mean he is not important or doesn't make valuable contributions. Like a superintendent or project manager, there is a dearth of skilled mechanics in the high-end sector. A general contractor's mechanics must be skilled in the same way a subcontractor's mechanics are skilled—commensurate with the level of work they are performing. Because of the skilled labor shortage, skilled carpenters and general construction personnel are generally subcontracted, with the general contractor's mechanics or laborers performing only rough work. It's easier for a subcontractor to build a team of specialists in his trade than it is for the general contractor. A skilled carpenter may become a *lead carpenter*, who may later aspire to become a superintendent. One must be careful not to saddle them with such responsibility before their time. Frequently, they have no way of knowing that they are in too deep too soon, making the transition from production to management.

No one do I find more diverse and interesting than laborers. It is a true wonderment to see them work, to talk to them, and to learn about their diverse cultures. I, myself, started my career as such a one. But the real value of a laborer to his company must be assessed in how much work he produces, and how well he does it. Some of the work output of these men is truly amazing. Often, these individuals aspire to a higher station, and will work harder to learn more skills. They also will "get around" more than anyone on the project, and will be able to report valuable information that might otherwise fall below the radar, such as a mechanic cutting corners, or a client on the warpath. So, there are a number of good reasons to keep these men equally as happy as any other staff. When they are happy, they tend to be fiercely loyal—a quality that can't be overvalued.

It can be tricky to assess such an individual's value up front, as having little or no skills; they may have no work background. Having no work background may inhibit examination of their work history. They may be "off the street," be rough around the edges, or even have a criminal history. For this latter, you should always check, as the information is readily available. Indeed, a number of statistics put the cost of company theft at an average of 11% annually. Otherwise, you have only your intuition to go on in deciding whether to trust them or not. Many speak little or no English, which can create a barrier. They are typically paid only a little more than minimum wage, and are quick to leave for better climes, given the opportunity. Your high-end clients will become nervous of those whose actions make them uncomfortable, and you must also take this into consideration by making it clear to them that your high-end residential project requires a higher level of comportment and etiquette than does the average commercial project.

Finally, no company is complete without a driver. Even for a small firm, the driver will be furiously busy, running from job to job, to the lumber store, and back and forth from the office. The alternative to the driver is a courier service, or a combination of the two. For a busy company it's almost always more equitable to use an in-house driver than courier services. Ideally, your driver has some mechanical skills and understands construction. If he doesn't at least understand the work his company does, he should not be the driver, as there will be a disconnection between him and the tradesmen.

I knew a contractor who seemed to have created a strategy to counter the negative effects of turnaround. Whether he did so by design or not, I can't be sure, but he did manage, and still does, to function reasonably well, albeit with extra efforts. The structure of his company was thus—he had a general manager who facilitated four or five project managers, and several superintendents. There was an estimator, and a bookkeeping department, and some basic administrative office help.

What struck me as unorthodox in the company's structure was this—each project manager would start out each job with all the available project documentation, including a schedule and general construction and mechanical, electrical and plumbing (MEP) buyouts. However, from that point, he would then take on almost all of the responsibility for the project, with his job team, interfacing with the general manager and bookkeeper only as necessary. The project managers seemed to be talented, and the owner had to be confident in their abilities in order to give them so much independence.

It was interesting to observe this contractor's operation over the years because his infrastructure was so simple, it was easily adaptable to market conditions, slow and busy. If a project manager or superintendent had to be laid off, it had little or no impact on the company's infrastructure. On the downside, companywide use of systems was impossible. Each division had its own systems, and each project manager had his. Accordingly, organizing paperwork and closing out projects was next to impossible, and double entry and repetitiveness were common. Problem projects were treated symptomatically, which led to a lot of regression back to the root, and general inefficiency in the long scheme of things. However, because this contractor did deliver quality work, he was able to offset, or finance his company's handicaps with profit, which tended to be liberal. On the other hand, there was little or no opportunity for individual growth at this company. The only measure of growth that mattered was the annual revenue.

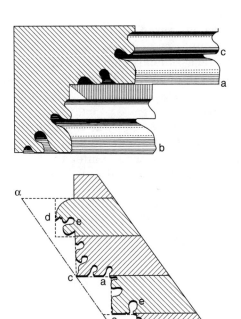

Plaster molding
*A Treatise on Architecture and
Building Construction, Vol. V*
(Scranton: The Colliery Engineer
Co., 1899).

Now that we have reviewed some of the basis job descriptions, I will go into further detalis of specific tasks and responsibilities.

Project Manager Level Tasks

A project manager's responsibilities should begin in the preconstruction phase, or before the project starts. His level of involvement in this stage and subsequent stages will depend on the project. A construction management contract will modify a project manager's responsibilities accordingly.

Preconstruction Phase Tasks

Issue project book to superintendent

Refine the schedule

Visit the site/survey the site

Preconstruction meetings with vendors and subcontractors RFIs

Assist with buyouts

Long-lead submittals

Depending on when a project manager joins the project team, and his abilities, his preconstruction responsibilities will vary. For the average fixed-sum project the project manager should assemble a "job book," or "hand-off package," well before the project is set to begin. There can be an enormous amount of documentation for some projects. The more there is, the more important it is for this information to be organized.

I have seen many jobs never get out of the gate due to poor hand-off practices. Optimally, you would want your project manager to have all the relevant documentation before building begins, as opposed to after the fact, when he will have to backpedal to locate it, process it piecemeal and always wonder and hope he has it all.

A proper job book and hand-off package should contain all of the following elements:

- Working drawings
- Specification book
- Permits
- Client information
- Contact list: design team, production team, and vendors
- Copy of base contract and payment requisitions
- Submittals and logs to date
- Copy of all subcontracts and insurance certificates
- HAZMAT book
- Copy of alteration agreement (for Condos and Co-ops)
- Project schedule (he or his superintendent should generate this, and may have done so already to accompany the bid package to the architect)

All of the above are distributed in the preconstruction phase. With this information the superintendent can now help his project manager to facilitate the work. Once the hand-off book is issued, the superintendent and project manager should begin creating templates for the project documentation.

Refining the Schedule

Now that a start and finish date have been established, the scheduler can take the schedule issued with the company's proposal, and enter hard dates for it. Schedules issued with proposals tend to have general information which, should the contractor win the project, he will later refine with greater detail, as we discussed in Chap. 3. He can now set the "baseline" that the schedule will be tracked against. Most general contractors stop short somewhere between the schedule issued with the proposal, and a more refined schedule. Highly detailed coherent schedules are the exception with a critical path method (CPM) tracked updating system in place virtually unheard of: if a schedule must be updated, it is typically redone from scratch.

A contractor I knew had an interesting method for generating schedules required for bid submittals: he kept on hand generic schedules, which were formatted into 3-month increments, and would issue a copy in accordance with each bid package based on the expected duration, regardless of the scope of work. Subsequent to this issue, the schedule was discarded. What was even sillier than this behavior is that he couldn't see why this practice was irresponsible. The point is that this contractor's flagrant negligence of a key component of logistics is commonplace, to such an extent that many architects hardly even expect a working schedule any more.

The reason for industrywide incompetence in schedule development is that in order to create such a schedule one has to be fairly fluent in some scheduling program, and also know construction—particularly his project. Many scheduling programs are not user-friendly, and resultantly, few people take the time to make the most out of them; it seems easier to start from scratch each time an update is required then to learn how to use the update module, but in the long run, this is not so. A new schedule each month constitutes an updated schedule; however, in creating a new version for each update there is no progress tracking, or record, of how the schedule progressed from its last permutation. There are people who having learned scheduling programs would be decent schedulers, but they tend not to have the practical building knowledge to create usefully detailed schedules and networks with complex sequencing, that is, they are strictly office staff, or fresh out of management school. As an alternative, one person may be adept at the computer program, and another at scheduling; between them they could create a workable schedule. Whoever does the data entry must query the superintendent as to remaining durations and any delays during the production phase of the project.

Assuming the schedule is to be refined, the project manager will need additional information from his subcontractors and vendors, and perhaps his superintendent. He will verify task durations and delivery dates with his resources, and fold these into the general game plan until he has a schedule that works. This will be the baseline schedule that he will compare to actual progress, each month. If there are critical dates, such as those defined by long-lead items, these must be guaranteed by each respective resource.

Site Visits/Surveys

Assist with buyouts

Before a contract is signed, the site game plan should be well developed. Having familiarized himself with the project and its documentation the project manager will know a fair amount about the site. The estimator will have debriefed him on all buyouts to date, and all subsequent buyouts. The next step is to meet with his superintendent, and the subcontractors who will be building the project.

In his meeting with his superintendent the project manager will now:

- Issue project job package
- Review the schedule
- Review mobilization plan
- Review project team membership: design team, vendors, subcontractors, and in-house personnel
- Discuss production strategy
- Review distribution of responsibilities

In issuing project documentation, the project manager should go through the material with his superintendent, as opposed to simply dropping it in his lap, as so many project managers are wont to do. The superintendent will likely now have questions, and will have more questions after he reviews the material more closely.

After reviewing his job book or project manual, interfacing with resources and the design team, and refining the schedule, the project manager is now in a good position to assist in buying out the project, if it has not been already. Even if he isn't buying out the project, the project manager should have the same level of familiarity with the scope of work as the estimator as pertains to costs. Typically, the basic trades and the largest scopes of work are already contracted before the project mobilizes.[4] The remaining trades may then be bought out by the estimating department, project manager, or both. Often, a good deal of the work requires further investigation by the contractor and his subcontractors, and the project manager may need RFIs answered before he can let out the subcontracts. Some of these subcontractors may already have their contract, while others will need to visit the site, ask questions, and resubmit their proposals with finer detail, or submit their first proposal.

The project manager will now be able to solicit some required submittal information from the respective subcontractors, and present these submittals for approval by the architect. Other submittals will follow subsequent to the site meetings.

Preconstruction Meetings

An often overlooked necessity of project coordination is the preconstruction meeting that should take place between the superintendent, project manager, and various trades. Typically, a subcontractor waits until his check arrives to ask when he needs to start. He is given a date, and may not be heard from until that date. Thus, there is often little precoordination taking place on residential projects.

Each subcontractor should be debriefed separately and then in a group with related trades. For example, all MEP trades should meet together; the carpenter and millworker; the door fabricator and the hardware supplier. Otherwise, coordination must either be done on the fly, with little time afforded, or the superintendent or project manager must do their coordination for them. While the contractor's people oversee the coordination process, they shouldn't be defining it without the involved tradesmen's input. This is a time-consuming and exacting process. Better to leave it to the respective tradesmen to coordinate as they see fit, and let them present their plan for approval. This should yield a better result, and save much wasted effort by the contractor.

Long-Lead Submittals

The first submittals will be (1) long-lead items, (2) large infrastructure, especially MEP, and any building components not requiring dimensioning for approval; and (3) any other immutable specification such as hardware, which may not be subject to change. With early approval of the long-lead items a contractor can release the purchase orders that are most time sensitive. MEP fixtures and equipment also tend to have lead times, thus it is a good idea to submit them early for approval. Finally, as a rule, any specification or work not subject to change should be submitted in the preconstruction phase if possible simply because one can submit them. In other words, submit what you can as soon as you can. There will be plenty of submittals to present and track in the production phase of the project, so why not minimize the workload?

The project manager must first make a list of items that will require long-lead times. He may have to call vendors and others to find out but should know from experience.

There can be notoriously long submittal delivery periods for the following materials:

- Light and plumbing fixtures (many manufacturers close for the summer)
- Overseas deliveries: these can also get sequestered in customs
- MEP control packages
- Certain heating, ventilation, and air conditioning (HVAC) equipment
- Touch screen interfaces
- Exotic veneers, wood flooring, and stone (subject to shortage)
- Doors
- Custom architectural glass
- Custom glazing
- Custom architectural millwork
- Custom architectural metalwork
- Custom hardware and plating
- Shower enclosures (from the time they can be dimensioned)
- Linear diffusers and flow bars (from the time they are dimensioned 5 to 8 weeks)

Samples and submittals for the above materials should be generated as early as possible. It will help to create a schedule to track these items in particular.

The design and development (D&D) period for the following typically requires an early start:

- Dimming systems
- Reflected Ceiling Plans (design deliverable)
- MEP coordination (will facilitate release of shop drawings)
- Door schedule
- Finish schedule
- Hardware schedule
- Audio/video systems

Ordinarily D&D should not fall inside the production phase, except construction management projects; however, architects know the base work can begin regardless, and the above information furnished later. They also are increasingly dependent on subcontractors and vendors to provide them with the specifications, which they normally do in the submittal process. While it is OK to wait for certain specifications and shop drawings, all basic programs should be fully developed before production begins, if they are to be correctly coordinated and integrated into the overall program. Additionally, many of the busier vendors and scarce specialty vendors will need to be locked in to a production schedule early. This information should be realized when creating the project schedule, keeping in mind that schedule slip could create delays if a given vendor is not locked in.

Production Phase Tasks

Levels of service at different companies are so diverse that even simple management technique becomes a free-for-all. Fortunately, there are some protocols in the industry, and individual project general requirements to guide people. Even so, these guidelines are routinely ignored. Any decent company will have basic guidelines for project administration; however, the integrity of their administration will only be as good as their management staff.

Below are discussed some of the primary production phase administrative tasks which a project manager should be responsible for.

Submittals

Job meetings

Cost tracking

Schedule tracking (discussed in Chap. 3)

Applications for payment

Change orders

Submittals

Depending on the project and contractor, either the project manager or the superintendent will facilitate the submittal process. The critical path and long-lead submittals should take precedence over any other submittal, as they are the most time-sensitive. Assuming all submittals that could be done in preconstruction have been done, there are many submittals that will be dependent on further information, such as adjoining work, RFI directives, and dimensioning. This information will be furnished either by the design team or by other subcontractors and vendors. Some examples would be as follows:

- Sheet metal (ductile) shop drawings
- Domestic and sanitary piping details
- Point-to-point wiring diagrams
- Door schedule
- Architectural finish shop drawings and samples, such as stone, millwork, metals, and glazing
- Wall, floor, and ceiling topical finishes: paint, plaster, et al.

The protocol for issuing and reissuing submittals is as follows:

- Create a prioritized list and schedule of all submittals. Request same from architect, and compare with the in-house list
- Solicit submittals and samples from respective vendors
- Upon receipt of submittals, enter each into submittal log
- Review each submittal for compliance
- Issue submittal to architect
- Upon receipt of disposition of submittal from architect enter information into submittal log
- Release or resubmit the submittal as per architect's directive
- Copy concerned parties and confirm receipt
- Issue drawings to superintendent
- Archive for future reference

The tendency of many managers is to merely pass on, or rubber stamp, submittals from their subcontractors and vendors to the design team without really reviewing them: perhaps he doesn't feel he has the time, or he may not be familiar enough with the work to review the submittal. He also assumes that it is the architect's responsibility to review the submittal, therefore, it doesn't matter what he thinks. In either case, this is unfortunate, and often leads to trouble, especially if the architect only gives the same level of scrutiny as the negligent manager. When the submittal turns out to be inaccurate, the architect will say that the general contractor is responsible for the integrity of the submittal (true), whereas the general contractor will say that since the architect approved the submittal, the mistake is his responsibility (true or false). The A201 dispenses with this misunderstanding nicely:

> By approving and submitting shop drawings, Product Data, Samples and similar submittals, the Contractor represents that the contractor has determined and verified materials, field measurements and field construction criteria related thereto, or will do so, and has checked and coordinated the information contained . . . (3.12.6).

and

> The contractor shall not be relieved of responsibilities for errors or omissions in shop drawings, Product Data, Samples, or similar submittals by the Architect's approval thereof (3.12.8),

finally,

> The architect will review . . . but only for the limited purpose of checking for conformance . . . in the design documents . . . Review of such submittals is not conducted for the purpose of determining the accuracy and completeness of other details, such as dimensions and quantities . . . all of which remain the responsibility of the contractor . . . (4.2.7)

It is unreasonable, as the phrase "only for limited purpose of checking for conformance" must be considered exculpatory for the architect. If only more general contractors paid heed to the A201, submittals would be much less of an encumbrance than they normally are. The fact of the matter is that under certain circumstances, both parties are negligent in their work. For example, an interior designer was foolish enough to specify a hot-water radiator for use in a multiple dwelling high-pressure steam building. A cut was submitted and approved by the designer. Not to be outdone, the plumber ordered the equipment approved by the designer, and showed up with copper tubing to install it.

Weekly job meetings

The method of conducting meetings seemingly is never the same for two different companies, and often can vary from project to project within one company. It is important to establish your own protocol for your company and to stick to it. If everyone at your company sticks to the same format, then you will find it much easier to disseminate and organize such information than if it came in several different formats. This is important as the flow of information and the quality of it are such critical aspects to facilitating a project. Otherwise, the opportunity for errors and omissions can quickly increase. Many architects will insist that they generate the minutes, or they may publish their own in-house minutes, when they are unhappy with the contractor's minutes. They typically complain that the contractor's version is biased. For this reason, a contractor can incorporate language such as the following to facilitate responses to the minutes from the architect, or other team members:

These minutes reflect Modern Builder's Inc. understanding of the issues, questions and decisions from the above noted meeting. Any discrepancies or disagreements with these minutes should be made in writing and issued to Modern Builder's Inc. within three-days of receipt of minutes, or minutes will me assumed to be accurate. Any corrections will be updated in the next set of minutes and duly noted.

In the amended minutes, corrections and additions can be italicized for easy identification.

The form of minutes can resemble anything from a stenographer's verbatim manuscript, to an informal, loosely written memo. These forms would represent two extremes, neither of which is appropriate. Rather, a distillation of relevant information should be pursued for the sake of brevity and expedience. Some managers prefer to take notes as they chair the job meeting, while others appoint an administrator to the task. In the former, I have found that there isn't enough time for one person to chair the meeting, and at the same time take comprehensive minutes. Typically, both, the caliber of the meeting and the minutes are compromised. In order to make good notes, the minutes' taker must either pause the meeting, or take notes while people are still talking. For the latter, unless the recorder is a seasoned professional, there may be errors and omissions, or vagaries. One possible system used works as follows:

The meeting is conducted as usual. The proceedings are recorded on an audiotape. Some notes are written as the meeting takes place; however, the bulk of the minutes will be input after the meeting, when the recording is reviewed. In this way, there should be no question as to veracity of the proceedings, and no excuse for incorrectly recorded minutes. The minutes will be more comprehensive than they would have had they merely been hastily scribbled down; the minute's taker can pick and choose which and exactly how much information he will enter. More importantly, the recording can be archived for future reference. Some architects may be put off by the tape recorder; regarding it as suggestively litigious. Merely point out that the recording is only used to expedite the rendering of the proceedings into minutes. The recording is your prerogative.

To avoid the typical shortcoming of meetings and minutes, it helps to understand the nature of poorly executed meetings and minutes. Some of the attributes of poorly executed meetings and minutes are as follows:

- *Lack of follow-up on old business*: The item is revisited each week in the meeting, with little or no action taken between meetings. The issue is never forced.

- *Failure to have all concerned parties present*: Notable absences are the engineers; on residential projects, the engineering fee on residential projects typically isn't generous enough to have the engineer come to each meeting, in fact, they will balk at coming to any meeting; however, the respective engineers should be present at MEP related meetings. The architect will generally advise that the engineer is reluctant to appear, and he likely will not unless you insist. If he does come, be careful to expedite his business, as he will be sensitive to having been summoned; his time is valuable, and he bills by the hour; he will want to get in, and get out. If you do not, he may come once, never to return.

- *Poorly worded meeting minutes*: A lack of clarity can render minutes partially or entirely worthless. If you think people who lack clarity in their verbal discourse are ineffective, you can only imagine how challenged they are when it comes to written communications.

- *Loosely run meetings*: When unorganized, a meeting can lose the attention of its participants, and bleed time off the clock. A structured agenda with relevant topics will help keep the meeting on task. It is up to the meeting chair to keep all members on task, not to allow digressions, and to prevent extraneous issues from being presented in the course of other topics. A special discussion time can be set aside for issues not in the agenda. Preferably, at the end of the meeting.

- *Items that aren't designated resources (team members) and finish dates tend to be overlooked*: No one is ever assigned responsibility, thus an issue founders. Issues that require joint responsibilities are especially prone to "no accountability oversight." This often can be blamed on the contractor's passivity; a fear of pressuring responsible parties—especially the owner and design team, into doing their job.

- *Inappropriate or superfluous material*: Too many meetings waste time on issues that aren't germane to the meeting, such that important issues may not be discussed for lack of time. It is up to the agenda drafter to avoid presenting such issues for discussion. First and foremost of irrelevant issues are design issues. Any such issue should be held in a separate meeting solely for that purpose. Design issues are routinely trotted out in the middle of job meetings, usually by the design team or owner, and are one of the leading causes of distracting and setting job meetings off course. For example, the agendum may read as "confirm location of thermostat." The response sought may be as simple as a follow-up sketch from the design team. But a different scenario may unfold.

The owner, upon consideration of the thermostat location, decides that he wants to think it through with the architect. No sooner does he advise the architect that the owner and architect rise and leave the meeting, and begin walking the site, discussing the location of the thermostat. Before this is allowed to happen, the meeting chair must insist that the discussion may not take place during the course of the meeting, as it will disrupt the meeting, and scuttle the agenda.

First, you should establish ground rules that can make your meetings run more efficiently:

- The meeting will have a chairperson who will conduct the business, and introduce topics from the agenda.

- The meeting shall follow an agenda: divergences from it are generally discouraged.

- Discussions of issues outside the agenda must wait until the meeting is done before they can be discussed.

- Private discussions are generally discouraged.

- Interruptions (cell phone calls, et al.) will not be permitted unless they are an emergency.

- Time frames should be established for each topic. When the allotted time is spent, the group moves on to the next topic.

With a room full of people, it isn't hard to have the meeting degenerate into a free-for-all of side discussions. A project for which I chaired the weekly meetings had a tendency to degenerate in this fashion, such that people would filter out, thinking the meeting must be over. It became necessary to reel everyone back into the fold before the meeting could continue. I recorded these meetings. At such times when the meeting came apart I would, in a very blatant fashion, turn off my recorder, indicating that the extraneous matters at hand were (1) not germane to the agenda, and (2) would not be entered into the minutes as a matter of record. This discouraged people only a little from the problem behavior.

The conducting of job meetings and the directives generated in them are one of the main arteries of information for a project. This is especially so when the architect and owner are both present; the contractor or the architect can force the issue by putting each other on the spot in front of the client. This is a good thing. Therefore, meetings should require special considerations regarding format, organization, and content, especially meetings with the design team and client. Following is a step-by-step process for facilitating a project meeting with the architect:

Establish a set time for the meeting, and durations for each topic or discussion

Generate an agenda

Publish meeting minutes

Follow-up in subsequent agendas

Meeting times

Find out when it is most convenient for your architect and/or client to make a set weekly meeting time. Make it clear and exigent that the meeting time must be adhered to each week. Changes to the meeting time will disrupt the project. Some days and times should be avoided. These are as following:

- End of the workday, especially Fridays. These are times when people are tired and would rather not sit in a meeting. More than likely, their mind is somewhere else. Typically, the minutes won't be recorded until after the weekend, an interval that can lead to some difficult recollection exercises for the minute's taker. A recording of the minutes makes this an irrelevant issue.

- Lunchtime, unless lunch is provided. Few people enjoy sitting around a meeting on an empty stomach at the time of day when they are usually eating.

However, it is impossible for the chair of the meeting to lead the discussions, take the minutes, and eat at the same time.

■ Eves before holidays.

■ Early mornings: clients may insist on meetings before their workday; however, architects tend to be late risers. Especially avoid Monday mornings; most people use this time to get back on track, and to reinvigorate themselves. This is a very busy time of the week.

■ When noisy or dusty work must be done. Meetings should always be scheduled around the work, not vice versa.

Time will often have to be set aside for part-time meeting participants, such as a vendor with a presentation, or subcontractor who needs to review a small matter. They need not attend the entire meeting—waiting for their issue to come up. They should be given an appointed time for their business. It is good practice to bring in other production team members to a meeting. If they have issues, they can be discussed with the team as a group, rather than individually.

Agendas

Agendas should be distributed to all parties at least 48 hours before a meeting is conducted so that participants will have enough time to prepare. Agenda items should also be solicited from participants before the agenda is circulated, so that if others have business, it will be added to the agenda; that is, even though it's your meeting, you are not the only one with an agenda. Make a deadline for outside agenda such that you have a window to incorporate additional items into the main agenda.

As the agenda is discussed in the meeting, minutes are taken and published in *minutes of the meeting*, which are distributed to all attendant parties, and should be copied to subcontractors, present or no, especially when there are particular items concerning them. When doing so, either highlight for them items relevant to their work, or issue to them only such material, as they will not want to be bothered with perusing the entire document for a few small sentences. If you are expecting a subcontractor to be "duly notified" in this manner, you absolutely must confirm that he has received and acknowledged the information; otherwise, consider it as a passive communication—one likely to be overlooked.

The components of a meeting agenda are (1) introduction, (2) agenda items (3) old business, (4) new business, and closing. Observe the following example:

Meeting Agenda

Introduction
  Schedule update
  Progress report
  Report on heat gain submittal

Advise status of millwork D&D
Discuss mechanical control program
Review structural loads
Advice on window treatment controls
Advice on dimming schedule
Advise on single-line service diagram
Sixty-minute break for lunch
Discuss schedule: baseline adjustment pending
Advise on blind mock-up progress
Discuss window treatment motor routing
Review open item worksheet
Advise on base buyout status
Discuss site access
Deliverable status
Submittal status
RFI review
Old business
New business

Summary
Adjourn

You will note that "new business" is scheduled next to last. New business refers to any item foreign to the agenda that someone wishes to present. There is a reason why I put new business at the end of the meeting; peoples' attention spans dwindle as the meeting wears on, especially if they have their own agenda, which may include getting out as soon as possible. They may ask if their new business can be moved up in the meeting; again, so that they can leave as soon as possible. If new business is at the top of the agenda, members will tend to present their business, and tune out for the rest of the meeting, or may even get up and leave. If new business is at the end, they must keep attendant until such time as new business is presented. You'd be amazed at how attentive a captive audience can be.

Other key agenda components that should be reviewed and discussed every weekly meeting are as follows:

- Schedule update

- Progress report

- Submittal status

- Deliverables status

- RFI review

This may look and seem like a lot of work to do every week, but you will find it to be an effective tool of accountability, one that is comprehensive, and does not leave a lot of room for interpretation. After a time, you will master the art of consolidating and organizing project information, and making the best use of your meeting time as possible. In the long run, this perseverance will be rewarded with time saved for all team members. Many contractors will consider such comprehensive meetings inappropriate for their projects because of the level of administration established by their architects; if an architect does not observe the industry protocols and standards that have been established by the contractor and tracked in the minutes, the minutes will have less relevance than they would with a coordinated project. For example, if the paper trail is all one-sided—contractor to architect, written follow-ups, responses, and directives from the architect will be missing. Their absence precludes the efficacy of the minutes, and their intended purpose is to facilitate joint project administration with the architect.

There is at least one major discussion which is the responsibility of the general contractor to lead: *schedule update*. In addition to dispensing this information, notice that without this agendum, most of the discussion is focused on the architect. You want to avoid focusing too much attention on one party, as it tends to put one on the defensive. Always be sure to give the impression that you are "sharing the load," and that you subscribe to the teamwork ethic. You are not putting undue pressure on the design team, while at the same time not taking responsibility for your share. There should be parity in the focus of the discussions.

In the above agenda format, each line item contains a reference to the nature of the business for the specific item. At the end of each will be the initials of the party who will take action. A basic set of operators introducing each line item will be established and adhered to the duration of the project: report, advise, discuss, and review.

Report: Someone is going to issue new information to the job team.

For example: Timeless Mechanical (TM) to issue heat gain values.

Advise: Someone is to indicate the status of a certain issue.

For example: J. Smith to give progress update of single line drawing of additional service leg.

Discuss: A new and/or unresolved issue is to be discussed collectively.

For example: MBI (a fictitious company) requests that millwork design drawings be more fully developed before a bid is solicited.

Review: Information that has already been presented will be discussed collectively.

For example: Team to validate structural loads for wide flange beam schedule.

We will look at two different ways the above items may be interpreted into meeting minutes, further ahead in the chapter.

Publishing the minutes

Meeting minutes are recorded as a matter of facilitating your project. They are typically a general requirement of your contract. They also play a key role in your accountability during and after the project. But they can also serve as a vehicle to circulate information on a group scale as opposed to individually.

The integrity of meeting minutes will be proportionate to the analytical and communicative skills of the person who generates them and his understanding of the project. Seldom does an efficiently run project not have concise meeting minutes, and likewise, failing projects invariably have insignificant meeting minutes. However, concise minutes in no way guarantee any result but they will maximize the potential for resolution, and due diligence will have been done insofar as facilitation goes. There are some basic rules to follow in the generation and facilitation of meeting minutes:

- Avoid litigious language.
- Avoid the recording of important issues as an end in itself. Merely addressing an issue in the meeting is not a sufficient vehicle for communicating important or complex issues. Always issue follow-up documentation for such issues.
- By the same token, the weekly job meeting should not serve as a catchall for every outstanding issue but only critical issues, those which require face-to-face interaction, and those which require the presence of several parties, for example, owner, architect, contractor, and subcontractor.
- Publish the minutes in a user-friendly format, and highlight standout information.
- Try to be concise and succinct. Long, wordy meeting minutes tend not to be read very thoroughly.
- Remove resolved issues from the minutes.
- Exclude superfluous references.

> For example: JR issued shop drawings for the second floor rear elevations, and first floor plan. He needs to speak with the engineer to confirm the detail; however, the engineer is on vacation until next Saturday: architect to advise.

At a glance, this wordy description might strike one as comprehensive and informative, merely because of its length and degree of detail, when in fact, it says very little. When recording your minutes, always try to do more with less—get to the point and avoid extraneous details. Remember, you are not a court stenographer. Consider the following rendering of the above item from the previous example.

> MBI issues JR partial shop drawings for engineer approval.

The rest of the information, although relevant, does not belong in the minutes; it can be facilitated accordingly, independent of the minutes. It also contains some informal material that is superfluous, and inappropriate to the minute's format.

Now let's look at how minutes could generate from the hypothetical agenda we set forth above. Examples both comprehensive and inefficient respectively follow the items:

Example 1
Report
HVAC 14.2 Timeless mechanical issues spreadsheet of heat gain trials at second floor. Rooms 201, 204, and 205 are subject to overheating: TM to meet with engineers to specify smaller coil. GM 4/26
Mechanical electrical and plumbing Jeff issues heat loads to architect.

Example 2
Advise
ELECTRICAL 14.4 J. Smith indicates that engineer has not returned shop drawings of service run. Architect to ask engineer to expedite same. SB 4/19
J. Smith still needs approved drawings.

Example 3
Discuss
MBI indicates that there is insufficient level of detail in the following drawings:
Door schedule A6.1.1
Finish schedule A7.2
Details to library A5.4–9
Cove molding profiles A6.2.4
ARCHITECTURAL MILLWORK 14.5 Architect issue SKs 18–21, Details of Library
Millwork 14.5: Architect issues clarification SKs.

Example 4
Review
STRUCTURE 14.4: Architect presents engineer's comments regarding load calculations. Pending vendor resubmittal, engineer to respecify beam #s 3, 7, and 9, and column #s 1 and 3 SB/DF 4/19
Steel: Engineer's comments on beam schedule reviewed. He said that if the detailer wanted to meet him before next meeting, then they could go over some of the loads.

Some of the differences between useful, somewhat useful, and useless can be divulged from the four comparisons above. The former examples feature effective communications indicating:

Item description, which is clear and to the point

Party responsible for generating or facilitating a resolution

Target date

Clear designation of a reference number for each item

Conversely, the last examples given above demonstrate inherent flaws in each item:

- Example one clearly represents underreporting, or not giving enough information. This lack of clarity will likely slow the resolution path of the item. Not that it is incorrect, it is merely vague to the point where it only accomplishes the bare minimum—scrapes the surface.

- Example two is also vague, but additionally, once it gets incorporated into the minutes, it won't be clear what agendum it refers to, as it has no reference number.

- Example three warranted much more information. Later, it will become difficult to determine what the architect issued, and what he didn't issue.

- Example four is vague, and includes some unprofessional extraneous material.

- Ultimately all four latter examples fail to meet the requirements set forth in the former examples.

In addition to relating the minutes in a cohesive fashion, equally important is the organization of this information. Many meetings are conducted with great care, only to become insignificant because of the disorganization in the minutes format. Like any other meeting business, find a format that works and stick to it. Consider the following format created for a residential project:

General categories

General

Design and development

General construction

MEP

Finishes

Subcategories

General
  Schedule update
  Site conditions

Design and development
  RFIs
  RFPs
  Deliverables (from design team)

General construction
  Carpentry
  Masonry
  Structural steel
  Concrete

MEP
  Mechanical HVAC
  Electrical
  Plumbing
  Sprinkler

Finishes
  Glazing
  Stone
  Millwork
  Doors

Wood flooring
Paint
Plaster
Carpet

On more complex projects, these subcategories can also be exploded, for example:

Mechanical/HVAC
  Equipment
  MEP Coordination
  Air distribution
  Water distribution (hot water supply (HWS)/return cold water supply (CWS)/return)
  Grilles
  Finishes (grilles and diffusers)
  Controls and control wiring diagram

Some of these subcategories may interrelate with other categories, such as *controls,* and especially *MEP Coordination,* which likely will include the electrician and plumber. In that case you then want to cross-refer the line item, for example:

Controls 14.2 Control Specialists advises using 16/6 shielded wire for all thermostat connections *(see Electrical 14.5)*

Since there is something here for both contractors, we include it in both of their subcategories.

Structure the information you record so that it readily can facilitate other departments. For instance, the estimator can inaugurate the general approach to a project. The scheduler will then use the estimator's logic and format to generate a production schedule. The combination of scheduling and estimating information can then be folded into the minute's format. When this information is considered together, which it will be continually, it will have a more fluid dynamic. If these three tasks were done independently, with no consideration for their counterparts, there would be little interrelational content—the stuff that productive meetings are made of. Thus, each party is prioritizing his own agenda without regard for the project's needs—stand-alone as opposed to network. It then will take more resources for the general contractor to disseminate such information, and especially to present it to the architect and owner.

Old minutes

Meeting items that are introduced as being new business should be recorded in the next issue of published minutes. Some of these items may be resolved at or by the time they are represented in the subsequent meeting, while others will require further discussion. These items, should they go unresolved by the time of the meeting following first publication, will appear as "old minutes," or unresolved items on subsequent minute's issuances. They should remain in that category until such time as they are resolved. Some agendum, when couched incorrectly, may be too complicated for such an approach. The comment, "MBI requests details of all millwork sections from architect," is asking too much all at once. The information will likely come piecemeal; moreover, the millworker's detailer will generate much of this information himself. Such a request could remain old business for months to come. A more intuitive approach would be

> MBI requests all available details for millwork sections, and a schedule for issuance of open items.

You are asking for the same thing; however, you have structured the requirement such that it is more comprehensive, without getting too specific. It also addresses the need to break the information out into subcategories. This item is a good example of an issue that requires aggressive follow-up outside the meeting forum. By the same token, it is too broad and critical a topic to relegate to only job meeting discussions.

Having old minutes constantly resurface in your bailiwick is egg on someone's face. Thus, requirements set forth in the minutes should be structured such that they can be readily facilitated, so that they need not reappear as old business for time eternal. For example, if the item "MBI requests details of all millwork sections from architect" should constantly reappear as old minutes, it is no wonder, since this is a long-term undertaking, incapable of immediate or short shrift resolution. Thus, it is fated to the long-term old minutes. The fact that it reemerges every week as a moot point merely rubs the architect's nose in it. It does nothing to help facilitate the architect. It merely points out the fact that he has not submitted the information. The comment "MBI requests all available details for millwork sections, and a schedule for issuance of open items" is helpful in that it breaks out the information needed, and provides a structure for it. By breaking the larger tasks into smaller subsets you are making the approach to resolution simpler. For the time being, you are only requesting a schedule for the information, not the information itself.

Old minutes can read like a list of unfinished business. People will read the item and then ask who's accountable for closure. If it is a broad general requirement, such as the example above, the architect will feel put on the spot every time it is revisited. For this reason, one must be conscientious in terms of how new business requiring action is presented in the meeting and incorporated into the minutes. It will only be a matter of time before old minutes become burning issues. An item may no longer have any more float time before it is resolved, at which time a response must be given, or there will be a delay. Old minutes are good reminders to everyone that something has gone unresolved. Inattention to them over a long period can result in the issue becoming an emergency. Had the item only appeared in a brief memo or RFI, it may have been long forgotten. Thus, use your discretion in what business you aspire to deal with in or outside the weekly meeting forum.

Cost tracking

The project manager, with the help of the estimator, should be responsible for tracking costs on his project. Generally, he will create a buy-out sheet that shows the contract line item values, and the actual buyouts. However, this is not cost tracking. Resultantly, few general contractors really track their costs, save for an end of the year Profit and Loss statement, or a brief look at the monthly bank statement. Cost tracking should include all outlays from the general contractor, including payroll, general conditions, insurance, and any overhead. Much of this information the project manager has no access to. The people that would have access to it likely will not receive the backup they need from the project manager in order to complete the exercise.

Hence, when projects hemorrhage cash little by little, it isn't until much later that the general contractor realizes the condition. Had he known sooner, he could have at least tried to make the necessary adjustments to stem the outflow. Short of this, seasoned project managers have a nose for negative cash flow conditions—you might call it intuition. Indeed, seasoned veterans can take a measure of the prevailing sentiments on most projects merely after a brief overview, and make a fairly educated guess as to whether the project is a winner or loser. Some project managers are perfectly able to track costs, but they may not have the extra time it takes, or the cooperation of the rest of their colleagues responsible for generating the information they need. On the other hand, some project managers who can do the math may not have the intuitive skills to isolate the problem. For this reason, cost tracking should be a joint venture between the project manager, superintendent, estimator, and the bookkeeping department. If possible, the design team should be consulted as well. Ideally, a general manager will be responsible for managing overall production, billing, and cash flow for the entire company.

Contrast this tentative approach with the project manager's cost tracking responsibilities on a construction management project in Chap. 5. Ironically, it would appear that contractors only go the extra mile when they are paid for it, even though the effort is usually in their best interests.

Application for payment

AIA *G702 Application and Certificate for Payment*, and its accompanying worksheet AIA *G703 Continuation Sheet for G702*, are the instruments for which the majority of construction contracts will stipulate that contractors use to apply for contract progress payments. It is generally the project manager's responsibility to generate these documents; however, many project managers simply can't. Resultantly, this task is frequently done by bookkeeping. As we will discuss in Chap. 8, the value of each *Certificate for Payment* must be ratified by the architect before he presents it to his client. The approval process generally involves negotiating with the architect over completion percentages, or work in place that will determine the certificate value. In addition to work in place, the *Continuation Sheet* includes a space for the value of "materials stored." The document is noteworthy for what it does not include—a provision for application for deposit payments other than the initial payment. For example, significant midproject equipment and material purchases often are floated by the general contractor, and only billed when the material is on-site.

Most contracts will stipulate a deposit payment for materials only (labor not subject to deposits), which will subsequently be credited to the first *Certificate for Payment*. This deposit can be anywhere from 5% to 25% of the total value of the contract. This structure or payment schedule frequently leaves the contractor short of cash to facilitate the project, especially on high-end projects where often the proportional value of equipment and materials to labor is considerably higher than most other construction projects.

For example, consider a project having custom made mortise locks and handles, compared to a project with standard off-the-rack medium grade hardware. The custom hardware has a material value of 75% of the whole, whereas the standard hardware only 15%. If 10% is the rate of deposit, the contractor will have to fork over the remaining 40% (assuming 50% deposit) required for deposit by the vendor—an obvious and possibly considerable shortfall. The above circumstance will likely apply to other trades. This inequity can be avoided. Instead of carrying fixed percentages for deposits across the board, actual values of required deposits should be negotiated and incorporated into the owner's payment schedule based on a schedule of purchases: why bill for a deposit in January for a payment not required for another 6 months? If a purchase is anticipated, the billing statement just prior to the purchase should include the deposit for the materials. Consider the following example in which projects of the same value have very different cash flow dynamics:

> *Project A*, and *B*, each have a value of $1,000,000. Both contracts stipulate a 10% deposit, or $100,000. Project A, an average project, requires $200,000 for materials. The vendors for this project require deposits valued at 20%, or $40,000. For this project, the 10% contract deposit will net a surplus of $60,000—idle capital from the owner's standpoint.
>
> *Project B* has many custom and exotic specifications; $300,000 is the value of materials. Because many of the materials are special order, some of the vendors require up to 50% deposits. The vendors for this project require deposits valued at 30%, or $90,000. For this project, the 10% contract deposit will net a surplus of only $10,000.

Both projects realize a surplus in the required deposit calculation; however, consider what happens subsequent to the deposit payment; the second *Certificate for Payment* will index the deposit, as well as the first payment cycle, 10% for retainage. For Project B, this would be $10,000, or 100% of the working capital left on his project.

Once material orders are released, vendors will typically require 100% payment. Depending on payment windows, these monies must be paid anywhere from 0 to net 60 days, with net 45 days being about average. The *Certificate for Payment* does not provide a vehicle for prepayment for the balance of materials; therefore, the contractor must often put his own money up-front to get material to the site [cash on delivery (COD) material]. For small companies with limited cash flow this can be a challenge.

The A201 also has a provision that could affect a contractor's position regarding progress payments:

> The Architect may also withhold a *Certificate for Payment* or, because of subsequently discovered evidence, may nullify the whole or part of a *Certificate for Payment* previously issued, to such extent as may be necessary in the Architect's opinion to protect the Owner from loss for which the Contractor is responsible, including loss resulting from acts and omissions described in Section 3.3.2 because of:
>
> 1. Defective work not remedied;
> 2. Third party claims filed or reasonable evidence indicating probable filing of such claims . . .;
> 3. Failure of the Contractor to make payments properly to Subcontractors or for labor, materials or equipment;
> 4. Reasonable evidence that the Work will not be completed for the unpaid balance of the Contract Sum;
> 5. Damage to the Owner or another contractor;
> 6. Reasonable evidence that the Work will not be completed within the Contract Time, and that the unpaid balance would not be adequate to cover actual or liquidated damages for the anticipated delay; or
> 7. Persistent failure to carry out the Work in accordance with the Contract (9.5.1.1-5).

The above language seems to leave itself open to interpretation, such that it could be abused. While sounding succinct, it is nebulous. The nullification of previously issued *Certificates for Payment* is especially striking, and I consider it a show of poor faith. Like many other A201 provisions, this is another red-herring that is best left in the water, and my experience is that such contractual rights are rarely exercised. Still, it is unsettling to have such language in one's contract, even if it is rarely employed.

Change orders

The science of estimating and negotiating change orders can be substantial; in fact whole books are devoted to the subject. We have treated the topic extensively, in Chap. 2, and will continue the discussion here, as it pertains particularly to the project manager's job description. AIA *G701 Change Order* is the instrument for which the majority of construction contracts will stipulate that contractors use to apply for changes in the work. It is cross-referenced in the AIA billing documentation as well. Each approved change order will then be appended to the AIA *G702 Application and Certificate for Payment*, and its accompanying worksheet AIA *G703 Continuation Sheet for G702*.

To understand the project manager's aspect regarding change orders, it should be understood that in addition to a given change order, the project manager has responsibilities toward the following parties in order to facilitate his change order(s):

Architect

Owner

General manager

Superintendent

Resource (in-house or vendor or subcontractor)

Architect

The architect will be the first point of contact for submitting a change order. The project manager may notify him of a change in the work in writing, requesting an RFP, or the architect may have already issued an RFP. If the value of the work is not known, it is then either calculated or a subbid is solicited. Once having submitted the change order, the architect must either approve or reject it. The AIA 101 should stipulate a processing time that indicates how long the architect can take to deliberate on a change order, but it does not. If a disruptive change order is deliberated for too long, it can cause other work to fall out-of-sequence. If there is no timetable provision for processing, the project manager can advise that the change order work in question will have a given effect on the schedule, which accomplishes the same thing. Having the clause in the contract goes one better.

On the other hand, if a change order requiring immediate action should be deliberated, the architect can issue a nebulous document known as a *Construction Change Directive* (A202:7.3), upon which the contractor must perform the work, although he may do so under protest; however, I have never seen one used. This will be discussed further in Chap. 8.

Owner

Once the architect has approved a change order, it should be a formality for the client to approve it; however, such isn't always the case. When an owner habitually rejects architect approved change orders, there is a clear breakdown in the level of authority vested in the architect by the owner. If this nonsense should continue, it will only be a matter of time before the contractor objects, or even stops work. This is indeed an awkward circumstance, one that should necessitate a meeting to reestablish the lines of communication and authority; a contractor should not appeal to the owner when there is an architect acting as his agent, as he does in AIA contracts.

Change orders can be problematic, as we shall see in Chap. 8. You must set guidelines to negotiate with architects and clients for when they contest change orders. In broad terms, expect almost every change order to be contested. Quite often, especially with architect's *errors and omissions*, the architect will be loath to approve your change order, as it may implicate them as being the impetus for the change. This, most frequently will result in your having to appeal to the client directly, which is invariably a futile effort; even if he does approve the change order, he will do so begrudgingly, with the impression that the discontinuity between you and the architect is costing him money.

General Manager

Upon an approved change order, the project manager will advise his general manager, or other immediate superior, of the approval, and issue original copies to be stored with the original contract. The change order is then incorporated into the contract, and billing system. If the project manager is not making headway with a complex or sensitive change order, he can call in the "big-gun," the GM, to induce some closure. Some general contractors use such a two-pronged approach as a means to work the client to their advantage from different angles. This is an effective strategy, especially when negotiations are headed for an impasse. It is a direct relative of the good cop/bad cop dynamic discussed in Chap. 8.

Superintendent

Once a change order is ratified by all parties, the project manager will set it in motion by notifying his superintendent, who is aware that the change order was pending. The superintendent will make the necessary adjustments to site conditions and the project schedule to accommodate the new work. Without such authorization from his superior, he should take no action whatsoever. One of the most aggravating things a superintendent can do to offend the general contractor is to take direction directly from the owner or architect; especially to do extra work. The tendency is, for larger and more complex change orders, for some contractors to do all the leg work or preparation in advance for a pending change order, with the assumption that it will likely be approved. The architect and owner might even insist on such preparation. This, of course, runs counter to the protocol of taking no action without an approved change order. Should it not be approved, enormous amounts of time and energy can be wasted in the preparation process, such as delaying other work that otherwise would have taken place. Regrettably, large and costly change orders typically are set aside or rejected; that is, seldom approved, or approved in a timely fashion.

In some cases, a superintendent will advise his project manager that a pending change order might render certain work superfluous—said work being torn out should the change order be approved. This too should be brought to the architect's attention. Nevertheless, the work in question should continue until such time (if and when) the architect issues a (rare) stop work order. Some requested changes can be so complicated that your superintendent will tell you that there is no way to quantify the amount of work it will take to facilitate it. This sort of change order is an indication of inadequate design planning; anything that could change the scope of the work and schedule so dramatically should be incorporated into the working drawings and base contract, or not at all. Not all architects appreciate this notion, and will continue to make their design changes regardless. There is little you can do to change their mind, especially if the change is requested by the client, which is usually the case; you can only go about your business. For overly complicated change orders, you may want to insist on a cost-plus fee arrangement, as that will be the only way you can broker yourself a fair deal.

Resources (In-House, Vendors and Subcontractors)

Once a change order is approved, it needs to be incorporated into the scope of work at the site, and if necessary, the schedule will require adjustment. In many cases, a deposit may be required for materials. It is up to the contractor if he will proceed without the deposit, or wait until the next payment application to proceed. If it is the latter, he should make this clear to the architect. It is not unreasonable to ask for a deposit on change order material if there isn't time to wait for the next billing cycle.

For labor-intensive change orders, especially in-house labor, it is easy to get cracking right away on the new work. Others, vendors and subcontractors, will want a signed proposal or other such work authorization, which they should have.

Construction Managed Project Management

While the project manager's role in construction management projects was discussed in Chap. 5, a general overview of his responsibilities is necessary to set the criteria for his objective. The project manager's responsibilities are generally the same for any type of contract: construction manager or a fixed-sum contract; however, the degree, nature, and timing of his efforts have much different ramifications, especially in the preconstruction phase. He will perform the same preconstruction tasks, with some additional responsibilities, and some other tasks unique to the construction management contract. For this discussion, we shall assume that the project is a construction management project, with the construction manager acting as constructor (AIA *A131CMc Owner Construction Manager Agreement Form—CM Constructor*), that is, not simply as his agent, for which AIA *A101CMa Owner-Contractor Agreement Form—CM Adviser* is used by most architects, as opposed to by other publishers, for example, Construction Management Association of America (CMAA).

Degree and Nature of Involvement

A construction managing project manager will likely be much more immersed in his project than his general contracting counterpart. For one thing, he doesn't have the kind of constraints that tend to make the general contractor's project manager less vital. The tacit understanding is that the construction manager will do a more thorough job, and represent the owner's best interests at the same time.

When a project manager performs under a construction management arrangement, his relationship with the architect and the client is meant to be devoid of the constraints of adversity, which are so common in traditional contracts. In a sense, the project manager is working for his own boss, and at the same time, for the client. This relationship would constitute a conflict of interest for your average general contractor. It must be said that some architects will try to saddle the construction manager with his own agenda, which may include covering for him, as he realizes the implications of the construction manager's position, and ability to absorb any sort of problem that may arise. For this reason, it is important to adhere to the structure of the contract, which must define each party's responsibilities. Alternatively, loosely defined contracts can easily be abused. In the end, a construction manager will make the architect's job much easier; not only by doing a better job himself, but also by helping the architect coordinate his work, which is in everyone's best interests.

By his nature, a residential construction manager gets involved as early as possible in a project. An average starting point would be when the design is in the schematic stage, or preliminary drawings have been issued for budgetary purposes. This is when he can do some of his most worthwhile work— pre-coordination of the design and production of the project. This differs from the traditional role of the construction manager, who often is involved before a property is purchased, or the design team is even appointed.

Construction Managing Project Manager's Preconstruction Phase Tasks

The construction manager/project manager has a specific role in facilitating a construction management contract. We discussed several typical construction manager preconstruction responsibilities in Chap. 5. They were as follows:

Feasibility study

Selection of design team

Design and development management

Creation of timeline or schedule for project

Site visits/surveys

Preconstruction meetings

Assist with buyouts

The feasibility study, selection of design team, and D&D management tasks are strictly construction management duties. Ideally, your project manager is a construction manager. He is experienced in, and well suited to the tasks above, as opposed to other staff members, who would not be involved in building and managing the project, should it be realized. If the project manager is spearheading the preconstruction effort, no one will be in a better position than he to facilitate the project when it goes into production. However, finding such an individual who can meet the criteria necessary to perform these functions within the residential sector is an elusive task. In his place, several individuals may join forces to accomplish these early tasks.

Feasibility study

A project manager can work with his estimator, subcontractors, and perhaps independent consultants to ascertain if a given program can be implemented for a client's space. This type of feasibility is an offshoot of a traditional feasibility study, which would be more concerned with financial considerations, such as return of investment, real estate conditions, marketing analysis, or retail market calculations.

However, for a residential construction manager feasibility study takes on added dimensions; traditionally, the design team creates a design to fit within a working budget. This is a difficult process to be left to the architect, especially with custom and high-end residential, where it is difficult to gauge costs. Nowhere does the construction manager earn his keep more than in this undertaking. If he feels that the concept for a program will be overbudget, he can do himself, the architect, and the client a favor by demonstrating this fact, and what alternatives there are so that the project will be realized instead of scuttled.

Selection of design team

Although, the project manager may have some input, the design team for residential projects will generally be selected by the client, and/or by the general contractor. In most cases, the client has already hired the design team. A general contractor with strong design profession relationships is in a good position to recommend an architect, who can then recruit the engineers and other designers. In that event, the contractor would have considerably more leverage with the architect and his design team than if the client had his own team; however, construction manager nominated design teams are the exception, not the rule. In a sense, a construction manager's lack of leverage with the design team runs counter to the concept of construction management, as he has to go through the client when he needs added leverage. The design-build industry touts the panacea of design and construction under one roof; however, only about 1% of all architects work at design-build firms—a fraction of them would be residential specialists.

Design and development management

Once the design team is selected, the project manager should draw up an outline for a preconstruction schedule, to include design team deliverables (drawings, specifications, details, and the like), and milestone dates. These dates will be determined by what the project manager believes they need to be, in order to make the schedule work. Once the outline is done, the project manager will meet with the architect to determine if the dates are tenable for him. Once the dates are agreed upon, the project manager can publish the preconstruction schedule to incorporate them. The project manager will then track the progress of the deliverables through the duration of the design phase. Tracking will include more than entering target and actual dates; it will include frequent progress checks, advisories for upcoming deadlines, and for breached deadlines. This is a level of management that is exclusive to the construction management approach; it would not be a priority for a general contractor, who typically would simply track the deliverables without managing them, advising of breached deadlines only.

Refine the schedule

The difference in the creation of a schedule for a construction management project as opposed to more traditional projects is that the initial schedule will include at least a good portion of the preconstruction phase, especially D&D. Refining a construction management project's schedule is typically done in the preconstruction phase, as that is when the whole picture can be visualized. If nothing else, it will be tracked and updated. It should also be understood that the integrity of a construction manager's schedule should generally eclipse that of your average contractor, for the construction manager is the avowed expert. We discussed in Chap. 3 what a construction manager's schedule should look like.

Like the working budget of a construction manager's project, the creation of the schedule is also done in tandem with the design team. The difference is that in a fixed-sum arrangement, the logic determining the schedule is proprietary. Consider two different approaches to the same project.

According to a construction manager, a given project has a production window of 16 months. However, a general contractor estimating the same schedule believes he can win the project by issuing a 12-month schedule. The construction manager, if he is worth his salt, has estimated an average schedule, whereas the general contractor, whether he indicates it or not, has produced an expedited schedule. Now let's assume that the contract value was the same for both of them. That being the case, if the construction manager is accurate, it follows that the general contractor purports to build the project 25% faster than his estimate of 16 months, with no expediting fees. Giving the construction manager the benefit of doubt, the general contractor cannot deliver as advertised; the construction manager should be awarded the work based on a 16-month schedule, or a 12-month schedule to include expediting costs. If not, the general contractor's schedule, being in question, should be analyzed for veracity. The scheduler must nevertheless be in a position to generate a schedule for either circumstance, whether he is constructor or the general contractor. Sad to say, an overselling contractor is too often embraced by a giddy owner, who doesn't realize what is in store for him. Even if he does, he mistakenly assumes that the upshot of any delays or production problems will be borne by the contractor. Not so—all must suffer into the truth together.

If the schedules should be examined, the general contractor may be hard put to justify his claim that he can work faster at a natural pace, and may even have no incentive. The construction manager will do his work and show his methods out in the open if necessary, at times coordinating with the design team; for he has nothing to hide. If the general contractor is awarded the contract, he will be in an even more difficult position when he has to justify slip in the schedule.

During the design phase, the construction manager will track the architect's deliverables. Many of the deliverables are slated for the production phase; this, of course, is one of the advantages of construction management projects; the overlap of the design phase into the production phase nets an overall schedule shorter in length than a traditional project. Construction managers must be careful to ensure that the requisite design information is available at the start of the production phase. They must not begin the work based on loose assertions by the design team that missing or late information will be forthcoming. Either it will not, it will be late, or it will come in the form of despised hastily rendered SKs.

Visit the site/survey the site

For a construction manager, again, a higher level of performance applies to visiting the site and surveying it. These tasks fall under the project manger's job description. The design team will likely request probes and sometimes surveys[5] before they detail the project, and the construction manager will be at their disposal to facilitate this work. In terms of surveys, a high degree of detail and accuracy must be accomplished as the survey will dictate the design parameters, not just the builder's benchmarks. Therefore, a survey from a general contractor is for one purpose, and of considerably less detail than the construction manager's, which is for another. Additionally, the construction manager may hire an outside surveyor to generate a survey with such a high level of detail.

Preconstruction meetings with vendors and subcontractors; RFIs

The preconstruction phase of a project is when a construction manager can avail himself of early access to the project by meeting with his subcontractors and vendors. In addition to discussing schedule and scope, they may at this time make predesign observations that will influence the working drawings and scope of work. Such early efforts can be very worthwhile, whether the contract is construction management, or traditional.

A contractor I knew was working on the demolition phase of an old townhouse. As part of the site survey and application for building permit, the architect ordered an asbestos investigation, which consisted of minimal sampling, and yielded a certificate that indicated that the project was a minimal abatement project—to wit, a small amount of pipe lagging (jacket insulation). The abatement process would be relatively insignificant in cost, $8,500 or so, and under less scrutiny from monitoring agencies. Subsequent to demolition, an abater was asked to price the work. This abater conducted his own sampling before issuing a proposal. His sampling of untested elements such as the composition of substrates, indicated that there was considerably more abatement necessary to remediate the project; the first survey had not even tested the content of the plaster walls and ceilings, which were saturated with friable asbestos containing material. This was the restoration project turned away by this same contractor, referred to in Chap. 2—*The One that Got Away*. The cost of the added abatement was over $100,000, and delayed the rest of the work by months. No wonder the contractor sensed something amiss—his premonitions were dead-on.

Had the contract been let as a construction management agreement, the contractor would have had the presence of mind to order a more substantial asbestos investigation before he created a budget for the remedial work. Why was a "drive-by" inspection done? Probably either because the architect didn't budget for a comprehensive inspection, only wanted the inspection in order to get the certificate, or both. In either case, a gross disservice was done to the owner.

Following early meetings with subcontractors and vendors, the design team can incorporate their comments into the design documentation; in fact, they may even generate the material. Once progress sets are published, these same subcontractors and vendors can comment and issue RFIs pertaining to these, and each subsequent set of drawings. Again, the project manager acting as construction manager will facilitate this process, creating a log, and distribution cycle, that always will include follow-up. This level of involvement between subcontractors and vendors, and the design team, is more or less exclusive to construction management projects, or high-level service general contractors.

Assist with buyouts

Having been integral to the design and budgeting processes, the project manager should now be in as good position as his estimator to buyout the project. Depending on who created the budget, the project manager and estimator will now meet with the respective subcontractors and vendors to negotiate contract values. By this time, many of these people have invested time and effort into the design phase, and should already have received a *letter of intent*. Without this letter of intent, many contractors will only go so far.

The project manager will help create a spreadsheet of subcontractor's and vendor's bids for presentation to the architect. He will have reviewed each bid, and will have in mind his selection, of which he will advise the architect. Once agreed, the subcontracts will be drawn and sent to the architect and owner for signature. The contracts will then be entered into the bookkeeping system. When the project manager is involved with the buyouts, he will then be in a better position to negotiate subsequent change orders. This is so for a few reasons:

- Many negotiations and arrangements made between the project manager and subcontractors and vendors regarding base contracts will later become relevant when changes to the work are directed.

- It is hoped that a rapport is struck, and the basis for a contractual financial relationship established, such that there are mutual understandings between the project manager and his respective resources. Again, future negotiations will ensue that much more quickly if there already exists such an understanding.

- It is critical for a project manager, especially a construction manager, to have a comprehensive understanding of the contract finances, as he is effectively the owner's representative. For traditional stipulated-sum contracts, this service is the responsibility of the architect; however, few architects seem to have more than a basic and generalized understanding and control of project finances.

Construction Managing Project Manager's Production Phase Tasks

Like preconstruction tasks, a construction manager's production phase responsibilities will also differ from the traditional project manager. Again, he is not constrained by a general contractor who is constantly trying to minimize general conditions. Basically, the construction manager will go the extra yard without checking his watch every 5 minutes; he will do whatever it takes as opposed to whatever the general contractor's budget allows.

Submittals

A construction manager should devote as much time as it takes to ensure that coherent submittals are issued, and to make comprehensive reviews of their content before they are presented to the design team for approval. This may make each submittal take longer to be presented to the design team; however, the quality and integrity of the submittal will be higher, and the number of resubmittals fewer. Errors and omissions can be addressed without wasting calendar days, and the architect's time. Moreover, although the design team may approve a submittal, there is no guaranty that errors and omissions have not been made. Despite popular belief, the contractor is responsible for the work regardless of design team approval. In the long run, the construction manager's submittal process will be quicker and more efficient than the typical general contractor's, resulting in faster processing from the design team, and more rapid integration of the approval into the project. He will also issue as many submittals as possible within the preconstruction window, especially those that represent long-lead items.

Job meetings

Weekly job meetings should take on another complexion in construction management projects. As we have demonstrated the interrelationships of the contractual parties should be nonadversarial. In fact, concepts such as *team*, and *partnering* should come to mind. Without this inhibition, discussions will flow more smoothly, and decisions will be arrived at sooner.

Without the constraint of a limiting or insufficient general conditions budget, the construction manager can feel comfortable scheduling other meetings as necessary to facilitate the project, as opposed with doing as little as possible. This includes meetings with consultants who might not otherwise be involved with the project, or would have been less involved, and meetings with subcontractors and vendors who would not ordinarily have the opportunity. If a general contractor is squeezed, so will be his subcontractors. He won't want to schedule special meetings any more than they will.

Applications for payment

The ratification process for each payment application should be a more fluid and expeditious process than on traditional projects, where haggling is commonplace. Whether the client writes the checks, or the construction manager does, there should never be cash-flow problems. In either case, the client should be responsible for the working capital on his project. A construction manager should use his cash-flow projection to estimate when specific funds will be needed. That being the case, the construction manager need not have to negotiate every line item on the *continuation sheet*, and wait forever for his check, as many general contractors do; especially if he functions only in the advisory role—architects shouldn't be in the business of second guessing the construction manager who is now the owner's agent. With no cash-flow problems, everybody gets paid on time.

To the construction manager's AIA *G702/3 Application and Certificate for Payment and Continuation Sheet* will be appended a lot of backup, such as invoices, receipts, bills of laden, and payroll records that a general contractor would consider proprietary. This information helps expedite the process, and also helps the owner to track expenses. It is also conducive to the concept of open-book and transparent bookkeeping; a feature of the construction management contractual arrangement.

Cost tracking

Tracking finances on a construction management project is a more sophisticated undertaking than it is for a general contractor. For one thing, a general contractor doesn't have to track costs—at least for the client, whereas a construction manager must as part of his contractual responsibilities. Just like the general contractor, cost tracking will likely be a joint venture between himself and the bookkeeping department.

The project manager should generate a cost projection for the project to give the client an idea of how much cash he will need, and when he will need it. If a bank loan is involved, he will use this information to apply for financing and requisition funding. This cost projection will serve as the baseline for the financial position of the contract for the duration. Monthly financial statements illustrating the status of the cost projection should be executed and presented to the client.

Much of a construction manager's cost-tracking reports will use backup information submitted with his AIA *G702/3 Application and Certificate for Payment and Continuation Sheet*, although the G702/3 is a billing instrument, not a cost-tracking worksheet. Construction management projects often do not have fixed budgets and some even have no budget at all until the construction manager submits one. Once approved, the budgeted values become targets that the project manager will compare to actual expenditures each month. It is in this endeavor that a construction manager shows his true acumen. If he has strong control of the project, and has generated accurate information, then the variance between target and actual costs will be small. If there is a considerable shortfall due to estimating oversight, the construction manager will have to answer for it. However, a good construction manager will (a) anticipate the shortfalls before they are realized, (b) will be able to explain the cause for the shortfall, and (c) likely will correctly attribute it to a condition for which his company cannot be considered at fault, such as a *bona fide* extra or unforeseen condition. If he can't, he will do everything in his power to find a work-around, or minimize the impact.

Change orders

Changes in the work, especially additions, take on a whole other dynamic in construction management contracts. We have treated the subject extensively in Chap. 2, and found that it can be a complicated process, often leading to conflict, as we shall discuss in Chap. 8.

Most work orders and subcontracts will be drafted after the prime contract is signed as working drawings typically won't be in hand at that time. Once cohesive bid packages are put together, they can go out to bid. There will be less likelihood for change orders, as the construction manager will have made certain that the RFPs are comprehensive. Had the contract been a standard fixed sum, most of the subcontracts would have been drafted right after the prime contract was awarded, regardless of the status of the design documents. Subsequent work orders in the fixed-sum contract are treated as change orders.

Just as in any other contract, the change order can be necessitated by the same factors as discussed in Chap. 2:

- Additional scope
- Deletion of scope
- Errors and omissions
- Tear-out and redo
- Delays

However, client mandated additions or deletion of scope should necessitate a construction manager's change order but not errors or omissions, and tear-out and redo work. The reason for this thinking is that in the construction management preconstruction phase, due diligence should have considerably limited the chances of mistakes in the design. If such a mistake should be realized, the architect and construction manager will be called upon to answer for it. It follows that in the production phase additions and deletions will also be minimized, for the client has had plenty of time to make up his mind. Insofar as remedial tear-out and redo work, the respective subcontractors must be held accountable just as they would in any other contract.

A big incentive for hiring a construction manager is that he will control costs better than a general contractor. As general contractors become more notorious for indexing rates higher for their change orders, many architects should begin directing their loosely designed projects to construction managers, who have no incentive to inflate or propagate change orders. Without such an incentive, the negotiation process, if there is one, will proceed quicker, and with less *agita*.

Conflict Resolution

The art of conflict resolution is treated at length in Chap. 8. Insofar as the construction manager is concerned, his project should have a minimum of conflict between the contractual parties, as they are all "on the same team." Most of the conflicts should be limited to discussions between the construction manager and his subcontractors and vendors. Of course, this isn't always the case, especially when the construction manager is only in the advisory role, and must deal with the general contractor.

Not to say there is no opportunity for conflict between the contractual parties. If the construction manager is not adept in his work, he too can lead the project into turmoil and incur the wrath of the client. Because the construction manager is the expert, he should experience less conflict than his general contractor counterpart, even when given more opportunities to do so.

Superintendent

The project superintendent or supervisor is the on-site representative for the general contractor, or construction manager as constructor. Although he is not the highest-ranking manager at his firm, his role is no less important than his immediate superior—his project manager. On smaller projects, a superintendent may also act as project manager. For this job description, we will assume that all trades are subcontracted, that is, the only in-house labor provided for are general conditions.

The superintendent should be a full-time presence for any residential project. The exception would be occasions such as when only painters or wood floor finishers are on the site, or any other self-sufficient task is underway. Too many contractors compromise on what they believe to be self-sufficient tasks, leaving the site without critical support. They do this in order to service another project with the same superintendent. Perhaps this is why the general requirements of many contracts mandate a full-time superintendent.

The superintendent is chiefly responsible for on-site production, and managing the site conditions in general. For this reason, he should only be required to do as little paperwork as possible; every time he has to draft a document, his attention is drawn away from his chief responsibility: production. As we shall see, there is little time to sit behind a desk; if there is time then something is amiss. The superintendent should be on task most of the time, but certainly not all of the time. What little paperwork he should do is considered in-house record keeping as opposed to official job documentation.

Most project managers prefer that all directives from the owner or architect to the general contractor be referred to them. For one reason, the general contractor's chain of command is structured thus; for another, it shouldn't be a superintendent's responsibility to facilitate such directives; and last, many superintendents aren't trained to correctly manage such matters; that is, the project manager's job. However, architects are wont to issue all sorts of directives to mechanics, superintendents, or anyone who'll listen. While this text does not condone such behavior, the A201 gives the architect or owner the choice:

> The superintendent shall represent the contractor, and communications given to the superintendent shall be as binding as if given to the contractor. (A201:3.9.1)

As I said earlier, I don't approve of this sort of structure. It is a mistake to stipulate it as a contractual requirement.

A superintendent's base job description should be same for any residential project; regardless of the contract structure. It should include the following:

Housekeeping

- Provide access to the site for all trades and deliveries. Secure site after each workday
- Post all required and up-to-date permits
- Create an area for a site office with provisions to exhibit drawings and storage for other project documentation
- Ensure that any necessary protections are in place, and are replaced as necessary
- Keep on hand all necessary tools and materials required by the general contractor to do his work
- Maintain organization of shanties and staging areas for tradesmen and materials, as well as an area for meetings
- Maintain a clean site, including staging areas leading to the site
- Maintain a safe site, and provide safety protections as necessary: barriers, caution tape, adequate ventilation, signage, smoke detectors, alarms, and so forth
- Keep a HAZMAT book with data sheets for any material fitting the criteria: volatile organic compounds (VOC) et al.
- Ensure that all MEP shutoffs are functioning, and that all branch valves are holding pressure

- Provide fire extinguishers and ensure they are fully charged
- Provide first aid kits and eyewash stations as necessary
- Post emergency telephone numbers
- Ensure that temporary services, lighting, power, telephone, heat, ventilation, water (potable and sanitary), toilet, and protection from the elements are maintained throughout the duration of the project. If necessary, maintain a fax line and Internet connection
- Monitor any job conditions relating to neighbors, or landlords
- Supervise conduct of workmen, and ensure that they conform to behavioral criteria[6]

Record Keeping

- Maintain as-built set of drawings
- Generate and circulate daily reports
- Take progress photographs, and maintain a log of same
- Publish "look-ahead" schedules at regular intervals, for example, 2 weeks
- Generate RFIs to project manager
- Keep time sheets for employees
- Maintain a shipping and receiving log
- Sign off each general contractor delivery, and archive bills of laden
- Maintain a drawing log
- Generate accident reports as necessary

Production

Basic and daily tasks

- Ensure that all trades are represented with the appropriate crews and equipment; chase down negligent or absentee tradesmen
- Coordinate demarcations of axis lines, reference lines, benchmarks, and layout marks: ensure that these lines are maintained for as long as necessary[7]
- Arrange for sign-offs of same from design team
- Manage manual labor to create routing for installations through existing structure
- Provide access to areas of the site as needed by tradesmen to work
- Manage day-to-day and short-term production scheduling of trades
- Maintain organization of on-site material, fixtures, and tools

- Monitor production to ensure that workmen are conducting their work in a safe manner, and using OSHA equipment as required

Complex tasks

- Coordinate sequencing of installations, and ensure that sequence of installations is consistent with schedule
- Issue progress information and data to scheduler in order for updated schedules to be facilitated
- MEP coordination (see Chap. 4)
- Manage medium- and long-term production scheduling of trades
- Follow up on in-house and subcontractor and vendor orders, especially long-lead items
- Coordinate and review shop drawings

Quality control

- Ensure that installations are code compliant, consistent with drawings and specifications, especially tolerances, and are executed with a level of integrity consistent with the project mission
- Inspect material delivered to site; reject as necessary
- Protect work as it is completed from being damaged or moved
- Maintain site conditions that will ensure a stable atmosphere and environment for all installations
- Monitor means and methods of production staff
- Arrange for design team sign-offs
- Inspect and reinspect installed work to ensure that it has not moved or been damaged

Superintendent/Project Manager

A very talented superintendent can also perform project manager level tasks. As I said above, on some smaller projects, a superintendent can also be the acting project manager. In that case, he must do any number of tasks in addition to those stated above. It is highly unlikely that a superintendent can perform his quotidian as well as all of the project manager's tasks. For this reason, it makes more sense that in the event that only one individual will act as both project manager and superintendent, that person should be a project manager acting as a superintendent as opposed to the reverse; the distinction being that the project manager has to perform tasks of a lower order than he is accustomed to, as opposed to stepping up to a higher level. Whatever the case, this individual can expect long hard hours in order to consolidate his company's payroll.

Superintendent/Project Manager Task Prioritization

First-priority superintendent tasks (acting project manager)

When a project manager is also acting superintendent and vice versa, essentially one person is doing the job of two people. Depending on the scope and complexity of the project, tasks will have to be prioritized in such a way that the most important tasks will be done, and the least important tasks are to be compromised or dropped altogether. In all likelihood, the superintendent level tasks will be superseded by higher-level tasks. The record-keeping tasks are the first to go. Companies can get away with this since a typical contract insists on a full-time superintendent, and does not make stipulations regarding the project manager; however, the idea is wholly unacceptable for construction management contracts.

While this book does not advocate the practice, it sometimes is a matter of survival that dictates multiple job descriptions. If such is the case, a company must cover for what the superintendent is unable to accomplish. Short of that, we can begin to cherry-pick priority tasks from the superintendent's job description that when combined with the prioritized project manager level tasks given under "Minimum Project Coordination" are the possible scenarios for this combination of job descriptions.

Minimum Project Coordination

Housekeeping tasks (see previously)

All housekeeping tasks are required and are not negotiable

Record keeping

- Maintain as-built set of drawings
- Generate RFIs to project manager
- Maintain a drawing log
- Generate accident reports as necessary

Production

- Coordinate demarcations of axis lines, reference lines, benchmarks, and layout marks: ensure that these lines are maintained for as long as necessary
- Arrange for sign-offs of same from design team
- Manage manual labor to create routing for installations through existing structure
- Coordinate access to areas of the site as needed by tradesmen to work

- Manage day-to-day and short-term production scheduling of trades
- Coordinate sequencing of installations
- MEP coordination (see Chap. 4)
- Follow up on in-house and subcontractor and vendor orders, especially long-lead items
- Ensure that installations are consistent with drawings
- Ensure that installations are code compliant, consistent with drawing and specifications, especially tolerances, and are executed with a level of integrity consistent with the project mission
- Protect work as it is completed from being damaged or moved
- Maintain site conditions that will ensure a stable atmosphere and environment for all installations

Some tasks omitted from this list still have to be done; however, it would be redundant if they were seen to at the execution level, as opposed to the review level, such as means and methods, a requirement that ideally should not need review. Therefore, the base level of execution and vigilance will have to be stepped up a notch, so that the project manager is not buried with quality control issues. Other tasks from the above list can be allocated to others, such as office personnel, or laborers, in order to relieve the project manager of some of his workload. Examples of such tasks would be the following:

- Follow up on in-house and subcontractor and vendor orders; especially long-lead items
- Maintain site conditions that will ensure a stable atmosphere and environment for all installations
- Protect work as it is completed from being damaged or moved
- Coordinate access to areas of the site as needed by tradesmen to work
- Arrange for sign-offs from design team

First Priority Project Manager Tasks (Acting Superintendent)

The following tasks combined with the above job description of abbreviated superintendent acting as project manager can be offered as a possible response to limited personnel conditions:

- Process RFPs and generate AIA *G701 Change Orders*
- Generate agendas, chair the meetings, and distribute meeting minutes
- Coordinate and manage submittals and shop-drawing log
- Coordinate and manage RFIs and RFI log

■ Generate AIA *G702/3 Application and Certificate for Payment and Continuation Sheet*

Additionally, this hybrid operator should do whatever else he has time for. If he does all these things, he likely will have time for nothing else. His performance must be monitored and constantly reassessed for its level of efficiency, as it can be subject to oversights given the increased workload.

Modern Interface and Information Technology

Before discussing the rewards of developments in information technology for the construction industry, the entire discussion should be prefaced with some observations that are indirectly related to it:

■ Information technology is no panacea; in itself, it doesn't guarantee performance enhancement.

■ Overreliance on information technology is increasingly deemphasizing the human element, particularly reasoning and common sense. That is not a good thing. Computers are merely facilitators of the end user—they only do what they are told. If there is a mistake, it is likely that the end user was the originator. The quality of data output (PC) is directly proportional to the quality of data input (end user).

■ Despite the ubiquitous presence of state-of-the-art hardware and software, it is evident that the full benefits of these developments are underutilized in the construction industry. One reason for this is that the construction industry, especially the private sector, spends precious little on training and education.

■ The increasing role that information technology plays in everyday company operations inevitably diminishes attention paid to manual operations, in some cases, phasing them out altogether.

■ Information technology does not necessarily increase the level of accuracy of a company's documentation stream; in fact, the rate of checks and balances allotted to such information tends to decrease in proportion to the number of computer generated documents; the assumption being that computers are less prone to error.

For most of the construction industry, up to the late twentieth century, interfacing has changed little for most, while a few have made great strides. The innovations began in earnest in the 1990s with the advent of computer networks, and ultimately, the Internet. Wireless and broadband communications continue to develop, making interfacing possible almost anywhere. Much interface still takes place over the telephone, and most documentation is still hard copy. A lot of what could be done digitally is still done manually. Does this mean technology has improved the quality of communication? Not necessarily. It merely provides the means to facilitate more expedient communication. However, for those who master the art, there are considerable advantages. These advantages will continue to play out in the emerging innovations of Web site based project management, and Web site conferencing Internet service providers (ISPs).

Like any new market phenomenon, there is a discernible lag in the effect of digital technology on today's construction industry. Like the initial reaction to new alternative materials, and green building, the industry is slow to change. However, larger companies that do not change with the times inevitably will become obsolete much in the same way auto and steel production have moved overseas. Smaller companies will find the industry more competitive, and may not survive either, but then small companies will always come and go ceaselessly. The construction workforce has never been, and will never be as technology savvy as say media industries; however, the more computer oriented the construction industry becomes, the more efficient it will become.

For some, this will mean loss of jobs—as workers' output increases, the number of workers needed to generate the same work output will decrease. This tenet alone will inspire objections, especially from organized labor, which has a general antipathy for those who will most benefit from progress—management. One key operating concept of the digital world is that it facilitates multitasking. Multitasking is another concept antithetical to the work ethic of organized labor where everyone must do only their own share of allocated work; therefore, it only there takes place, if at all, at the management level. Thus, organized labor may be the last to adapt to new developments in technologies. Business owners are not stupid, and they understand the value of multitasking; however, inevitably their knee jerk response to the windfall in output is to offset it by unduly burdening few with the work of many—mindless downsizing.

Despite technological advances, there will always be laggards, for a number of reasons, especially among the less educated, and companies with little resource. Many construction workers are transient, moving on frequently, not taking the time or caring to make an investment, and likewise, their employers have no interest in developing their skills. Construction companies also tend to be ephemeral; not around long enough to develop a coherent infrastructure or development and human resource programs. Not to say that they will become obsolete, as builders are the lifeblood of the construction industry. But the larger conglomerates, with hefty payrolls and layers of management, will go the way of the dinosaur, because the only way they will be able to sustain is by entitlement contracts, and resting on their laurels. But even so, they will cede significant market share to leaner and meaner competition.

Changes in technology, such as mobile telephone networks have greatly improved the platform for communications to such an extent that some feel obviates the need for further improvements—it only postpones it. From the telephone came the pager, which begat the cell phone, which merged with Web access, and wireless IT. Technology will continue to develop at a rapid pace and the construction industry will continue to lag. Understanding this conundrum (and accepting it) is the key to the negotiation of what compromises and adjustments will be necessary to keep the industry healthy as it changes, that is, recognition of the special relationship between management, and the workers, which is becoming more complex with developing technologies. Like the disparity of wealth in the United States, we must be careful not to ostracize those who do not participate in adapting to new technologies, and don't need to. With that in mind, it must be said that digital communication evinces a challenge to the community; the ability to discern when to use different types of communication and technologies, be it fax, e-mail, face-to-face, or otherwise.

Personal computers, LANs, and the Internet are emerging factors in the increased productivity rate of construction companies. E-mail alone is a huge enhancement, as are Web sites. But their implementation alone does not mean that they necessarily make a company or individual more efficient. Why not? Because the systems are only as relevant as the information generated by and through them. What good is a big expensive LAN, when it may be underutilized, or filled with superfluous data? Like the implementation of PCs in schools, greatly lauded by the technology companies, one wonders who was the most to benefit by their implementation—the students or the sponsoring manufacturers.

Despite innovations in digital publishing, much of the industry is still tethered to the hard copy. Legal instruments must necessarily be executed on paper, though this is changing by way of digital signatures. Design documents not created in CAD can be scanned or copied, but they are still, by and large, analog creations. Until such time as more workers in the field work with computers, blueprints will always be needed in the field. Moreover, it is not practical for say a steam fitter, or ductile sketcher to generate CAD drawings. But it is practical to scan their mechanical drawings, and post them to an interactive Web site. This translation of analog to digital is one of the key connections between old, and new, school operations.

The transmission of CAD files over the Internet sounds ideal; however, because of the structural complexity of CAD files, they are particularly vulnerable to corruption and omissions, such as dropped "layers." Architects know this, and are reluctant to email CAD files save for record. In fact, there are still holdouts in the architectural community who refuse to use CAD. For many of them, the need for CAD is not exigent. They will argue that your average Bachelor of Architecture (BArch) graduate of today wouldn't know a drafting table from a ping-pong table—they cease to be drafters, only CAD operators. However, some of these skeptics simply don't have or know how to use CAD. The architectural educators anticipated this, and now, CAD training is required for virtually all BArch students, who are the fodder of future architect firms. Alas, similar foresight was not envisioned for the construction industry—schools leave their charges woefully unprepared.

Like the average mechanic, your typical engineer will also be reluctant to absorb the new wave of technology. The engineering industry is characteristically old school. This is understandable, as it is more scientific than architecture; more involved with formulas and information that is immutable. Some are daunted by the digital age, or simply threatened by their own inevitable obscurity. They will never be as productive as their peers who maximize their efficacy through computers. Why are these people not empowered, as are many modern engineers and mechanics? Because their education was behind the times; they are still immersed in the old ways of the predigital world. This instinct of self-preservation may be the weak link in the digitally enlightened design team chain. But it is changing, wherein more engineers are using CAD. These engineers will continue to gain market share.

Because CAD was a relatively precocious digital innovation; PCs are an integral part of most architectural firms' infrastructures. Digital technology is becoming the *lingua franca* for the design community (not including engineers and detailers), and it behooves the building community to follow suit. But be wary, because digital technology morphs at such a rapid pace, one has to be prudent in scrutinizing the needful from the superfluous. Nowhere is this more evident than in the glut of software being generated for the industry. The development of construction industry software invariably seems to be going in reverse; endeavoring to accommodate what the industry dictates as its past needs; this is a triage approach. Since the industry does not intuitively know how software should be modeled, the software is forever trying to catch up with the industry. This is regressive behavior; as technology should advance industry, not play catch up to it. It's like a patient telling his dentist where he should drill.

At closer inspection, the software geared toward contractors comes in two forms: front-end programs, which tend to be of dubious value, and beefier stand-alone programs, which typically are consolidated into bundles. The two big modules are accounting, and project management, including job billing. It is the interaction of these two that is the crux of managing cash flow. The challenge in the past has always been continuity and cooperation between the two, or inter-operability.[8] This has historically been difficult because in the past, separate programs were required of each; hence, a new regard for the term "*double entry accounting.*" There are now programs that promise the grail of module integration under one program; however, in effect, this code is in its infancy, and proves relentlessly inefficient. It is feared we will be using double entry accounting for some time, or the deficient programs, which tout single entry, but really are no more efficient than the former. The general accounting software available is so superior to any construction project management software that bookkeepers would be foolish to abandon their tried and true programs for an unproven program. Moreover, the infrastructure of project management programs tend to be rigid, not allowing customization or tweaking; hence, upgrades and new versions are frequent, as are training seminars and costly licensing fees. Data output tends to be crude and unprofessional looking. Finally, the bundled programs tend to be too bloated for their own good, having too many unique component modules, and bells and whistles. If, as is often the case, the modules are designed by separate code writers, the bundle will be even more subject to inefficiency: "too many cooks . . ." The percentage of capital invested by the construction industry that goes into fixing bugs and improving substandard code by software publishers is not a good return of investment; software should be more sophisticated, and up to snuff with the software of other industries—let the software industry bankroll their own development innuendoes.

Nevertheless, project collaboration and communication at larger companies, who are software publisher's prime end-user group, that is, nonresidential, requires a software interface. The industry has to make-do with what is available. Such software has been around for the past 5 years or so, and has taken quite a foothold in the industry in that short time. Almost 30%[9] of the FMI/CMAA owners surveyed indicated that they use such software. Still, about 19% regard collaboration software as being too complicated.[10] This fact will not go unnoticed by software developers, and they will surely begin to step-up the quality and integrity of their products in the near future. But for now, one of the biggest impediments to wider use of project collaboration software is the limitation of interoperability with other programs. Sixty percent of the FMI/CMAA respondents indicated dissatisfaction with their vendor's approach to interoperability. While they are efficient at churning out their own code, they do little to make it more accessible to other programs.

In 10 years, much of what is said here regarding technology will be obsolete; such is the nature of modern technology. However, the majority of the construction industry geared software will continue to lag behind. Perhaps the new glut of college level programs will begin to empower this community. This remains to be seen. What will not change; however, is the need for practical knowledge—there is no replacement for good field experience; working the tools. This knowledge will never be attained from behind a desk. It is also through this knowledge that one can connect with field personnel on a professional, and most importantly, personal level; a vital key to successful professional relationships with the workforce. And no matter what technology is available, it will only be as useful as its end user makes it.

Web-Based Project Management

A handful of ISPs now offer *web-based collaboration* platforms for the construction industry. They are more commonly used in larger, more complex projects. A recent example would be the Orange County Sanitation District's 20-year, 146 project $2.5-billion system overhaul; however, the appeal is quickly spreading to smaller companies and projects. Still, about only 19% of surveyed contractors use such platforms, and few of them were residential builders. Of these, only firms with at least $100 million in yearly revenue showed significant usage; however, this number is expected to grow rapidly. The incentive to use more effective management tools may be influenced by owner-side dissatisfaction with current management practices. In a survey, 80% of the owners believed project collaboration software would be an enhancement.[11] One of the things they have to offer is wide area network (WAN) access to all site members—wherever they are, so long as they have an Internet connection. For large and lengthy projects the payoff can be substantial; much information that would normally require a site visit can be sent via FTP (for uploading files) to the Web site, saving time and the need to travel to and from the site. If the team members are spread around the world, the allure is even more apparent. These platforms vary in degree of user-friendliness and requisite skills, and for today's market that is a big consideration, for as we have said, the industry is slow to change and adapt to new structures.

The way such platforms work is as follows: the general contractor or construction manager arranges with the ISP to use the platform for a fee based on duration, and storage space on their servers. A site is then set up for the organization, where a uniform resource locator (URL) for the project will be created. The site administrator, ideally the project manager, will then select the team members who will have access to the site, and he will assign levels of access to certain folders and files that he has uploaded to the site. One way this works is that the selected member receives an e-mail indicating that he has now a participant to the site. A URL contained in the e-mail will direct him to the ISP, where he will download any necessary software, and another URL for the particular project. Certain members will have "uploading" privileges via FTP, for example, the architect may upload SKs and specifications. Financial information will typically have limited access.

The files will be stored in a directory, with folders structured just as any MAC, DOS, or Windows-based OS, using the windows GUI—it will be familiar to most end users. Users with "read" privileges can then access unlocked job files from any Internet portal. Users with "editing" privileges can make changes to a file, and save it as a new file. The original version remains in tact. Whenever a file is uploaded or edited, the administrator is notified via e-mail, and subsequently, additional team members as necessary.

Although the greatest return of investment for using such a service is highest on larger jobs, with many team members, small companies and small projects can be facilitated just as effectively. There are some other incentives to use the service:

- It provides an all-in-one "clearinghouse" or interface for the entire project, and tracks every change or addition of information to the site.
- A company can manage several projects through one Web site.
- Progress photos, samples, and site conditions can be viewed on the site: a client or design team member out of his office can keep tabs on daily project developments.
- Owners and vendors can track, and comment on, the status of RFIs and submittals.
- Team members can access PDFs of updated schedules.
- Webcams can be installed that will offer real-time digital snapshots of site conditions and progress.

Many of the ISPs now feature live Web-conferencing, where the administrator can present information on his screen using the GUI of the platform, which will also appear on all meeting attendee's screens, much like a live presentation, only with two-way dialoguing. Videoconferencing will also soon be available.

Notes

Project hand-off package checklist

- Working drawings (including SKs)
- Specification book
- Permits
- Client information
- Contact list: design team, production team, and vendors
- Copy of base contract
- Copy of all subcontracts and insurance certificates
- Copy of alteration agreement (for Condos and Coops)
- Project schedule

Submittal checklist

- Create a prioritized list and schedule of all submittals
- Solicit submittals and samples from respective vendors
- Upon receipt of submittals, enter each into submittal log
- Review each submittal for compliance
- Issue submittal to architect
- Upon receipt of disposition of submittal from architect enter information into a submittal log
- Release or resubmit the submittal as per architect's directive

Endnotes

1. This mantra is apt for the general manager; however, it is often used out of context—as a sometime superintendent and project manager, I recall hearing this same parable uttered at several companies, which I took as an ill portent.
2. Big Dig is the Central Artery Project in Boston, which has relocated 7.5 mi of Interstate 93 underground, and extended Interstate 90. When finished, it will be the most expensive highway project in U.S. history. However, it will also be known as one of the most notorious projects in history. At present, the project is running about $10 billion overbudget; originally estimated at about $4 billion, it is now up to $14.6 billion. It was to be finished in 1994, a 4-or 5-year project now in its 17th year. Recent cracks and leaking have been detected, and some blame them on a design flaw involving the walls-ceilings joint. A recent leak backed up traffic 10 mi on the Massachusetts Turnpike. The Governor of Massachusetts, Mitt Romney, has recently asked for the removal of the MTA Chairman Matthew J. Amorello from his project oversight post. The State Attorney's office has opened fraud investigations of the project's contractors, who among other things, failed to include the 19,600 seats Fleet Arena in its design drawings and budget.

According to the *Boston Globe*, this and other construction-management mistakes cost the project about $1.1 billion in cost overruns. For further reading refer to *The Boston Globe's* coverage of Big Dig, specifically Raphael Lewis's excellent pieces.

3. As a rule, contractors consider any document with dollar amounts to be proprietary, and thus, do not wish to maintain such documents where they could be seen by others—in the field.

4. A construction management project is often the exception.

5. Nowadays, architects don't allocate enough resources for a proper survey. In lieu of a surveyor, an intern or low-level functionary may be given the task. In either case: sure to disappoint.

6. This is a nebulous undertaking but necessary for companies who prioritize their image.

7. This task is typically the bailiwick of the lead-carpenter; however, because the axes lines are used by all the trades for reference, it is the superintendent who should have the ultimate responsibility for their integrity.

8. *Interoperability*: The dynamic interchange of data between platforms and software applications. This is no small matter. The NIST (National Institute of Standards and Technology) has reported (NIST GCR-04-867, August 2004) that, "inadequate interoperability" cost the "U.S. capital facilities industry" $15.8 billion per year.

9. FMI/CMAA 14.

10. FMI/CMAA 15

11. Construction Financial Management Association 2004, *Information and Technology Survey of General, Highway, and Specialty Contractors.*

Crisis and Siege Management

*Once a change of direction has begun, even though
it's the wrong one, it still tends to clothe itself as
thoroughly in the appurtenances of rightness as if
it had been a natural all along.*
F. SCOTT FITZGERALD, FROM *THE CRACK UP*

As F. Scott observed, all sorts of mistakes are made without the least notice of those affected by them. However, it isn't the ability of calamity to disguise itself, but the inability of people to recognize it in its many subtle forms. Because people are so slow to identify the root cause of their problems, the fight to prevent projects from going out of control is often a losing battle. While most projects have problems, not all of those are out of control. Out-of-control projects require much more constructive intervention than an average bear can bring to the table. Frequently, they will degenerate into a state of anarchy, such that the project no longer bears any resemblance to its intended purpose: a fast-tracked high-end residential penthouse could quickly become a leaky-roofed hodge-podge of tarpaulins, tear-out work, half-done installations that are 50% behind schedule, and a general contractor that is ready to walk.

Certain residential projects will be predisposed to problems and conflict. These types include, but are not limited to:

- Underbid projects
- Underfinanced projects
- Understaffed or inappropriately staffed projects
- Underdesigned projects
- Union projects
- Aggressively scheduled projects
- Overdesigned and projects with customizations
- Projects in Co-op buildings

- Projects subject to committee or agency inspection and compliance
- Projects with difficult architects and clients
- Changeable design projects

Many of the listed projects are architect-and-owner–driven problems, but the general contractor himself may be the driving force. Regardless of who is on the spot, there is almost always enough blame to be distributed to all the contractual parties. Denial will also be evident, proportional to the amount of blame. Sometimes a client and an architect can influence a contractor to underbid a project. Technically, that's not their problem. But in reality "stripped-down" projects hold the promise of disappointment for all parties, and a client may be the one left holding the bag on an underbid project. While it is true that some contractors will underperform, regardless of how well compensated they are, underfinancing creates unnecessary obstacles for companies that otherwise would perform satisfactorily. This fact saddles at least some of the blame on the owner side. As stewards of their work, and as their clients' agent, it is up to architects to ensure that there is budget ample enough to build a given project. Unfortunately, there is no consensus on just what that means. Moreover, it is likely to be different for every project. This is a task that a construction manager should be able to do. If nothing else, they can advise as to what degree a given contractor should be chiseled down, as negotiation will be a prerequisite to signing a contract.

Predisposed problem projects will start off on a bad foot and stay there, as if they were fated to do so. It is a rare exception for a failing project to fully recover from substantial built-in obstacles to achieve success; think of a horse with a slow jump out of the gate, all at once out of the race. One would assume that any project rescued from failure must have involved replacing the contractor and/or the architect. Other projects fall into panic mode, somewhere between halfway to three-quarters of the way into production, when it is problematic to replace the contractor. Late job-team restructuring on a project seldom seems plausible, because they typically involve transition downtime and additional expense. Nevertheless, clients who try to ride it out with a failing contractor end up kicking themselves for not having made changes, or made them sooner.

It's interesting enough to observe the approach of different contractors to various projects, but it is downright fascinating to watch them try to recover from a debilitating set of circumstances, in an effort to regain control. The following approaches are typical:

- "Bomb" the job (with man power) in the "eleventh hour."
- Invoke overtime work shifts.
- Red-label (expedite) deliveries.
- Harass and pester the subcontractors to step up their operation, which usually means that their other jobs will suffer, as they demobilize them in order

to service the siege project. Often, these other jobs are from the same contractor, who then becomes guilty of spreading his resources too thin.

■ Send in upper management to the site to induce crashing.

The above methods typically net "a day late, and a dollar short." No one in their right mind would plan (*proactive*) to manage a project utilizing the siege approach, save for projects that require a lot of compression. Thus the above methods are considered *reactive* responses. The chief difference between proactive and reactive responses is that the former is a premeditated rational response to maintain control, whereas the latter is a rash, often emotional response to regain control.

All contractors will experience states of emergency on at least a few projects in their careers; however, only those with constructive responses to the pressure will be able to control the inevitable fall out from such endeavors. You might call it "damage control." While some companies have the infrastructure to bomb jobs when they need to, this method is a poor return on investment, and will take its toll in the long run if it becomes standard practice; no one can afford to pull out all the stops on every project. Moreover, complex residential construction doesn't lend itself well to expediting. It isn't enough to live to tell about surviving a tragic project, especially at an exorbitant cost. That would be a Pyrrhic victory. Only those who can do it without a great sacrifice are worthy of praise. I would use as metaphor of the 2004 United States invasion of Iraq, and the ensuing effort to rid that country of terrorists. There, an ill-conceived concept led to egregious overspending, protracted length of occupation, and poor results in general.

Many clients insist on expedited schedules, despite their high rate of failure, because they are likely unaware of the nature and frequency of such failures. Often, they will bring their idea of a schedule to the bargaining table, at the time it is negotiated with the contractor. Why a contractor would accept terms of an overly aggressive schedule without a generous incentive is beyond me. Nevertheless, they are falling all over themselves everywhere, trying to do just that, often charging less money to build a project more quickly. They are underpaid because they frequently underestimate the cost impact of acceleration and overtime. The reasons why clients insist on expedited schedules are not so cryptic:

■ The carrying costs of two dwellings—present and future—are too substantial for the client to bear for any extended period of time.

■ A client's lease may be expiring, or the buyer of his existing home may have to withdraw due to his own time constraints. Not uncommonly, a seller will hold up in a hotel room between the time he vacates his former residence, and takes occupancy of his new home, which is a costly and inconvenient arrangement.

■ The design phase has been extended such that the production phase must be shortened in order to finish on time. Planned or not, this is the fate of too many projects, and cause for concern.

■ General naiveté regarding the nature of expedited schedules.

- A Co-op alteration agreement may stipulate a fixed construction period that is untenable; this condition is commonplace in metropolitan areas. Typical durations are 120 days, 6 months, and the period of time between Memorial Day and Labor Day, when other tenants tend to be away on summer vacation.

- They simply "want what they want; when they want it," the credo of the "entitled," but disillusioned patron.

Again, had a savvy construction manager been part of the planning team, the likelihood of some of these problems would be significantly decreased.

Once a schedule is approved and incorporated into the contract, any delays, accelerations, must be accounted for. If there is a delay, a contractor will hopefully make the adjustment to overcome it. If a client insists on an expedited schedule after the contract is signed, a negotiation for the cost of this service should take place, as it has not yet been taken into consideration. The calculation of the costs of acceleration, like any other cost, should be done scientifically. This is one of the most difficult calculations for an estimator to make, as it involves complex indirect costs.

The antithesis of a project under siege is a "controlled desperate project." That may sound like an oxymoron, but it makes sense whether the siege approach is controlled, or not. A siege managed project is still in a state of desperation; only it is more so when it is out of control. Even a war zone can be under control, despite appearing random. The manager of this undertaking requires high-level organizational skills, patience, and discipline. At times, he will resemble a military commander on the battlefield. This is a very special person indeed, and he is the exception to what most managers bring to the table. Given that, few projects operating under a state of siege are controlled. Out of control projects may or may not be completed, but such endeavors will always be tortuous, and yield dubious results. There are great incentives not to deliberately take an overaggressively scheduled and/or out of sequence project:

- Such projects require control and coordination that is typically lacking from the average contractor's staff members, even on a seemingly healthy budget.

- The return on investment for the contractor is seldom worth the effort.

- Mistakes are more frequent, and quality is compromised more than usual.

- Production rates decrease, even if the project finish date is reached sooner, just because extra men are on the project doesn't mean that they are more productive, in fact, the opposite tends to be the case.

- Creeping burnout, affecting the general contractor and his relationship to his staff, subcontractors, architect, and especially the client, is seldom worth the incentive offered, if any, to expedite a project.

Because out-of-sequence and accelerated projects are so difficult to control or manage, expedited schedules should be the choice of last resort. Many times, the impetus for dysfunction is out of the contractor's control. Once it dawns on the contractor that the project schedule is in jeopardy, it is his responsibility to notify the architect. He should not delay in his notification, as things can deteriorate rapidly, especially on a short schedule. If he is not timely, he may end up taking responsibility for some or all of the delays, merely by not reporting. When a contract is signed, the start and end dates are fixed. Architects and clients have expectations, and they will be upset when these expectations are not met. It is the general contractor's responsibility to be timely and *coherent* in notifying the architect of any condition that could or has already affected the schedule. This text has shown examples of notifications that distinguish between what is coherent, and what is not, in Chap. 3, and elsewhere. Many times, there are built-in challenges that are likely to complicate a project, yet the contractor is too slow to realize them. Typically, a contractor will be taken to task for those that were considered avoidable by the client and architect. He may not be liable, but if the oversight was egregious, he will be considered either ignorant, or duplicitous; that is, he should have known better, or he did know better, but kept quiet about it, the latter being perceived as an accessory to the act.

Contingent on their relationship with the architect, contractors will approach each project differently. For example, if an architect has sponsored a general contractor to build his client's project, and the architect should then miss important deadlines, the contractor may feel sheepish about issuing documentation that could incriminate the architect in front of the client, biting the hand that feeds him. While that is a sensible observation, the tenor of the client-architect relationship should not govern either's actions. There are ways to get the information across without antagonizing. If an architect has sponsored a contractor, there should theoretically be less conflict, and more trust in their relationship, such that they can talk to each other; hence, it should be easier to resolve conflicts. The flow of information has the same relevance, regardless of the contractor's relationship with the architect. To appreciate that, consider the average problem project: the architect and contractor are adversarial, their discussions are tense and defensive, and resultantly, little gets resolved through verbal negotiation. At times, relationships become so strained, they resemble bad marriages crying out for divorce.

There are two chief components of managing out-of-sequence or expedited projects: client and architect management, and the project itself. If either objective is lacking, the project will be subject to all sorts of calamity.

Triage

The wild things roared their terrible roars and gnashed their terrible teeth and rolled their terrible eyes and showed their terrible claws but Max stepped into his private boat and waved good-bye.

MAURICE SENDAK, FROM
WHERE THE WILD THINGS ARE

Before a dysfunctional project can make a comeback, the entire project team must be involved in the process. Otherwise, the team has a missing link in its chain: think of a football offensive lineman missing his blocking assignment, leading to a quarterback sack. The architect and general contractor no doubt have "been there" before. This doesn't connote that they are therefore seasoned problem solvers, but they will be less surprised than the owner, this likely being his first experience. It's hard enough for industry professionals to negotiate problem projects, but owners typically have little stomach for it, as they don't understand the process, and will likely be anxious or angry as pertains to what they do not understand. Therefore, the general contractor and architect must take the lead in reigning in the client to a more agreeable attitude, even if it requires an encounter group or two. A big component of client management is enlightenment, or the education of the client. Problem solving with clients on residential projects tends to be idiosyncratic, dependant on the client's personality. Any given discussion must be couched from three different perspectives: architect to client, architect to contractor, and contractor to client. All feature a distinctive dynamic that must be observed. A contractor should be able to demonstrate his point of view effectively to a layperson or professional, as should an architect. It is in the disregard for these rules or sensitivities that so many project teams do not experience the healthy synergy needed to establish sound communications and positive rapports.

Being the client or patron, the owner often feels that he must be mollified for the transgression of a breached finish date. After all, he feels—it's his money, he's calling the shots. This is the first client misconception that needs be finessed, for fear it will continue to rear its ugly head in the form of disrespect and animosity. Clients who believe they have no other obligation other than to sit and watch their projects get built are typical. Their aloof attitude and self-alienation can instigate all sorts of problems. Even before the first conflict arises, you should have a pretty good idea of how your client will respond to conflict. You must have a game plan ready to invoke for clients who become upset. A client can become a determinant of the spin put on his anger by the manner in which he couches it. That is, it's not just the nature of the problem, but how the client conveys it that can influence the contractor's response.

Passive responses

On a costly project, with a lot of money at risk, the client isn't likely to take bad news sitting down. That is his prerogative; however, he must defer to his architect and general contractor for direction when it comes to getting the project back on track. This requires composure that few first-time and one-time builders (most residential clients) have. Rather than look to their team for help, they seek to punish them for their transgressions. Therefore, it helps if it can be demonstrated that the client shares responsibility for the problem, as well as founding its resolution. This is an important component of the team ethic. A passive response to conflict from your client is a welcome circumstance. If he has been involved in the process from the beginning, and has a comprehensive understanding of the project gained through his architect and contractor's input, he will be less anxious, and more easily induced to be reasonable, and to contribute to solving problems, rather than exacerbate them. Of course, if the problems are clearly attributed to poor service, he would be well within his rights to become hostile and less likely to see to reason (if any can be demonstrated).

Aggressive response

These are the table thumpers—they jump and scream, pound their fists, write nasty memos, call their lawyers, and foment a contagion of hysteria. They will be comforted only when everyone has subscribed to the same hysteria, or thought like them, which is extremely unlikely to happen. The priority is then no longer addressing the problem generating the anger, but first dealing with the anger itself. Anger, which is present in so many responses to conflict, is perhaps the most ubiquitous inhibition to constructive problem solving in any relationship—personal or professional. It is human nature to believe that once the problem is resolved, the client will be happy again; however, that maxim tends to be inconsistent. You don't want to encourage the protocol wherein the client screams, and you don the kneepads. Once the client sees this as an effective method, he will attempt to solve all his problems in this manner, and expect you to act accordingly; he's simply vying for control. You must try to make the client understand that aggression is not constructive. They will seldom listen to this sagacity; however, the point will be heard, if not well taken. At the very least, you make it clear that the level of response has bearing neither on the nature or gravity of the problem at hand, nor on its resolution.

You can't control how clients will react to conflict; however, you are in command of your own reactions, which although should not be predicated on your client's reactions, must be taken into consideration. Lacking in character, many general contractors don't have the backbone to negotiate a client's outbursts other than reactively; they become unglued, and irrational themselves, perhaps yelling and throwing tantrums. In part, they do this as a show of control (to mask the circumstance of loss of control), especially if the client is watching. But such histrionics are merely a ruse to conceal inaction. They must believe that since the client reacts a certain way, the client will expect the same approach from the contractor on his end. Thus acting as he does, they have fulfilled the client's wishes. While this may be true, it is not a constructive approach to conflict resolution, nor does it serve any other legitimate purpose.

So commonplace are such upsets that over time they have a decreasing impact on problem solving; they can generate such a level of discomfort that civil and productive discourse becomes untenable. Having seen my share of outbursts, I have only rarely seen a useful solution generated by an angry response. Upsets used to be novel forms of entertainment, but after seeing so many, they become tedious. It is a waste of time to approach a problem thus; after all, such responses should not really be considered as "approaches," merely reactions. After the reaction, an approach can then be entertained. Nevertheless, clients will continue to have upsets, and a good general contractor will have strategies in place to tone things down, as we shall discuss in Chap. 8. Just as importantly, he will invoke his own anger management program as necessary.

Identifying Dysfunctional Projects

Delays have dangerous ends.
WILLIAM SHAKESPEARE,
FROM *KING HENRY VI, PART I*

Before a project should become expedited or rendered out-of-sequence to make up for lost time, there must be an understanding between the contractual parties that:

1. The acceleration is necessary in order to meet the finish deadline.

2. The sequence of events that led to this condition has been identified.

3. There is an agreement or an understanding as to what *caused* the sequence of events, and who is responsible for them.

4. Measures will be taken to stop or minimize further delays.

5. The financing of this acceleration must be quantified, and assigned.

The list represents a comprehensive approach; in all likelihood only points 1 and 3 are addressed, with 3 being a moot point. It follows that the road to salvation for lost projects is an unchartered one, with little accountability. Again, a construction manager should see that the full menu 1 through 5 were part of the remediation process. He would ensure the undertaking was not half cocked, like it so often is; a typical general contractor doesn't command or exert that level of control.

It should never come as a surprise to anyone that a project has suddenly become accelerated. Many memos and schedule updates should foretell the slip of successor tasks, long before they cause real-time delays. Of course, this is seldom the case. Many contractors realize delays too late, underestimate their magnitude, or fail to realize all the consequences. It can dawn on them all of a sudden. Having missed the opportunity to preplan for a delay due to their own ignorance, they have precluded their own credibility; any solution they offer will be subject to scrutiny. The client and architect will perceive almost any delay as a contractor oversight, and typically become alarmed. If delays have not been adequately tracked and documented, which is usually the case, then there really isn't anything worth negotiating; the contractor should cover it and keep quiet. Unfortunately for them, even though they realize they are not to blame for delays, they are hard-pressed to demonstrate why, and thus must absorb them.

In many cases, a fickle client, who can't make up his mind or keeps changing it, is to blame for delays. This is a residential construction phenomenon. Next to getting married, a large upgrade on their home is the second biggest financial decision a couple will make in their life, and they are prone to deliberate every decision, no matter how insignificant, with equal consideration. Therefore, there is a tremendous amount of attendant anxiety and attention deficit that they bring to the project. A contractor needs to be aware of his client's anxiety, and do his best to prevent it from metastasizing into the project. Unchecked, a client's anxiety can itself completely derail an otherwise healthy project. It is relatively easy to identify nervous clients, especially if you work with them all the time. Identify them early in the process, and then work on a solution. Savvy contractors will be proactive in this endeavor—they will invoke a client management program designed to put him more at ease, or deflect negative energy away from themselves.

Delays tend to affect the general contractor more than they do the architect, regardless of who is to blame for them. It is the responsibility of the contractor to describe and attribute the delay, and architects can be wily and cunning in their ability to deflect blame. I believe this to be true in part because architects tend to be more educated than contractors. The contractor will hemorrhage cash on a delayed project, and has an incentive to move the project along. It typically doesn't matter to the architect when the job gets finished, until he starts to worry if he is going to get his final payment or not. Often, the contractor will notify the architect of a delay, in hope that he can resolve it, or at least rationalize it to the client. If the architect is blameful, he may be reluctant to notify the client of delays, as they may be drawing attention to his own negligence. Often they say nothing to the client, in effect forcing the contractor to be the bearer of bad news. This is often merely a setup, wherein the architect hopes to be exonerated by the contractor's inability to deflect blame from himself. Thus, the contractor is put on the spot to account for the delays. In that case, the contractor must inform the client, and if he implicates the architect, he does so at his own peril. If the delay is a moot point, which it so often appears to be, the client will invariably side with his peer, the architect. The contractor's alleged aggression may be used as a cover by the architect for their own ineptitude. These are merely strategies used to deflect blame from oneself, or redirect toward others. Contractors and architects may feel reluctant to be too aggressive in driving the client to make decisions; however, as the contractor begins to lose time and money, they soon get up the nerve—after all, telling a client that his slow decision making is threatening the project is constructive input, and in his best interests. He may then undergo the thankless task of convincing the client to bankroll the compression necessary to get the project back on track. He won't ask the architect: whoever heard of an architect getting back-charged for contributing to delays on a residential project?

Some contractors will call in the troops without warning or fanfare; often, this is not necessarily a bad thing, especially if it was premeditated, or invoked in a moment of prescience. They realize the project will be late, and that they can improve their performance with more man power. They may feel that they can finance the undertaking without bothering the client with a long drawn-out negotiation. Many high-end residential general contractors work this way, as they expect that there will be delays, they factor this risk into the budget. They realize that your average high-end client would never tolerate a discussion for consideration of a change order to finance delays, even if he were all or partly to blame for them. It is hoped by the contractor that the client does not realize or mind that he has made adjustments to the production process in order to make up for lost time.

Whatever the case, the general contractor must be vigilant in documenting every delay and its effect on the schedule. This does not mean that he distributes all this information to the job team, as some of it is likely proprietary; however, the upshot of it must be conveyed to all concerned parties. As we learned in Chap. 3, it is difficult to project the effect an early delay may have on the overall schedule without a tracked schedule, and sometimes even with a tracked schedule. For that reason, contractors will merely document a delay, without recalculating prospective finish dates, or they may arrive at these dates speculatively. Should there be arbitration regarding losses due to delay(s), it will be difficult to establish the cause and effect relationship necessary to accurately attribute accountability. As we discussed in Chap. 5, a construction manager advisor's position regarding delays is much more proactive than that of the general contractor. Although an advising construction manager is less at risk in his delay management, he will still make decisions considering the interests of all parties, that is, it isn't a one-way street. General contractors stand to learn a lot from construction managers' delay management techniques.

As I mentioned earlier, without a tracked schedule, one can only speculate as to the overall effect of an early delay; especially on a complex schedule. Therefore, the quality of documentation the general contractor issues is relative to the integrity of his schedule. Any decent construction manager should maintain a tracked schedule, and thus be able to make comprehensive assessments of delays. The difference in quality is readily apparent. Consider these two notifications—first, a typical brief from a general contractor, and second, a notification from a construction manager:

> Pursuant to our memo of February 11, we are still not in receipt of the reflected ceiling plan for the above referenced project. We expect the absence of this information to negatively affect the finish date.

While the above example does document that information has not been issued, it fails to convey other critical information:

- The original target date for the information
- The effect of the delay on current operations
- The effect of the delay on the overall schedule
- The revised early finish date for affected tasks
- The reason (if known) for the delay
- Suggestion of an avenue of approach to solve the problem

Absence of the above information qualifies the notification as virtually irrelevant.

Although the general contractor is not obligated to furnish the above information (likely he doesn't have it all anyway), it would be in his best interest to do so, especially if he is not blameful. A contractor may continue his diligent, but terse notification process for the duration of the project, and he may believe he has done his best to report delays; however, because his documentation is lacking in specifics, he will be hard put to attribute future delays to it with any degree of exactitude. The reason for this is because the delay and its effect on successor tasks, especially substantial completion, are never isolated in his memos; there will be other instances of delays on the project that will compound this and other delays, such that it will become impossible to isolate the effect of, or quantify any one of them. Again, this dilemma could preclude his arbitration position, should it come to that.

A more comprehensive notification might read something like the example below, from a construction manager to an owner's representative, regarding slip in the preconstruction phase:

> The purpose of this meeting is to illustrate how actual task durations have changed, and why they have changed, since our first schedule issuance. For reference, please see attached memo of 3.26.02, and Gantt chart of 3.28.02 (Table 3.10):
>
> *0001: Preconstruction*
> A chief reason for extended duration requirements on this project is the fact that our Premobilization milestones have not been met. These are: *(0148) MEP Coordination, Project Deliverables (0008)* including, but not limited by, final elevations, specs, mechanical electrical and plumbing (MEP) schematics, fixture schedules, final elevations, and low voltage programs. They also include *Base Buy-outs (0084)*. To date, no subcontract has been let. Many of the subcontractors required for coordination have not been retained, and only HVAC submittals have been processed.
> Contingent on the release of deliverables, and completion of base building mechanicals, we were to have engaged our MEP Coordination, and completed it in an eight-week period. Because this information has not been released, or has been released and changed, we have begun without most of it. Because we will be receiving the required information after mobilization, it will take longer to coordinate it. In effect, we have not gained the leg up we anticipated, because we have not availed ourselves of the Preconstruction window. Without this advantage, it will be difficult to achieve an expedited schedule, especially since our original schedule was maximally compressed.
>
> *0148: Mechanical Coordination*
> The duration has increased, because of the nonsequential release (or non-release) of the floors, and also, because of additional scope, such as perimeter heat piping, dedicated piping for low voltage programs, all of which add a layer of complexity to fitting our duct and pipe. The raising of ceilings by the design team has also resulted in less room to operate, and more obstructions to negotiate. Duration has also increased because scope of work for MEP has increased 15%, chiefly, hot water piping. As it stands now, we will not have 100% coordinated drawings when we begin framing, which was a prerequisite of our original schedule.
> Additionally, we do not have a working RCP and plan drawings.

0024: MEPS

Most MEP has increased in scope and complexity, however, only duct and SW pipe fabrication and installation have affected the schedule. We have added extra time for these tasks. Because we will not have pre-coordinated drawings when we begin work, we will have to coordinate as we are building. This will slow down the framing process, shop drawing process, and fabrication process by increasing lag: less overlap in production. Lags of trades that follow; electrical, plumbing, and sprinkler, will also be increased. Trade stacking may also become a factor, as much of the work is concentrated in small areas. We also will have to wait for the base building contractor to complete their flue work, and two-hour enclosures before we begin dimensioning. The anticipated effect will be a nonexpedited, or natural production sequence.

Because we do not have all required deliverables for our coordination period, we know that we will be installing much of the work out of sequence: some work will have to be delayed in order for such work to proceed. Much pipe routing work will take longer and be done later, because programs have not been specified, therefore, they cannot go in the initial routing effort, where pipe-rack systems are used. Fortunately, at present, all routing and wiring work is positive-float.

0033 Wood

Our original schedule allowed for a 4-month production/installation window. All bidders now have indicated 6-month windows. The 4-month window was predicated on the Preconstruction milestones being met (see above), which would expedite the production process.

As you can see, this is a comprehensive document that accurately demonstrates cause-and-effect relationships for the delays. The memo makes it clear that delays were expected by the contractor due to the fact that:

- He was missing important deliverables.
- He could not gain access to the site to render his MEP schematics.
- The scope, nature, and complexity of the work were enhanced by additions and changes to the design.
- The delay in the preconstruction phase would preclude the planned sequencing of the project.

The contractor was able to issue such specific information because he maintained a tracked schedule of the project, which he continually referred to, as well as written updates to the job team explaining milestones and slips. This enabled him to report on the project in real time, and projected time. Although the construction manager could have factored the delay into the overall duration of the project, it was not exigent that he did so; moreover, he lacked the data to make an accurate projection of this date. It is impossible to make an accurate production schedule with a vague or incomplete set of drawings. Without final designs, he rightly concentrated on the preconstruction phase, and its general anticipated effect on the production phase. Not uncommonly, clients will ask for revised completion dates based on present designs. The correct response to the query is to request the date that working drawings will be issued. After such time, the schedule can be calculated.

Foundation.
A trick practiced by some builders, to be guarded against, is this: where the cellar excavation is cut in rock it often happens that the rock when it shows a good vertical face is not excavated far enough to admit of the foundation wall being built to its full thickness; the rock is faced, as it were, instead, and unless the superintendent has been fortunate to discover it in time, no indication of the sham work will appear unless perhaps at some future time when it may fall away below the top of the rock, due to the action of water keeping it constantly saturated, or due to a great superimposed weight; the wall may fall away gradually or collapse suddenly to the possible risk of human life, and damage to the building. *A Treatise on Architecture and Building Construction, Volume V* (Scranton: The Colliery Engineer Co., 1899).

Managing Dysfunctional Projects

> *Art is the triumph over chaos.*
>
> JOHN CHEEVER

Siege responses to predisposed dysfunctional projects

Underbid and underfinanced projects.   These projects are "losers" from the start; however, this fact is only alluded to in hushed tones, for if it was known to be "bad," no one would be foolish enough to undertake such an endeavor. For some contractors, such jobs are their bread and butter—the only work they can get. Sometimes these contractors are referred to as "bottom feeders." For every loser project, there will be five or ten subcontractors going along for the ride. Why is this relevant to you? Because you must be on your guard to avoid such liabilities.

You would ask yourself, "How do these contractors survive?" There are a few ways they do, and this information can help you to identify and avoid getting mixed up in such business:

A contractor I knew had plenty of work. Trouble was he couldn't build a straw out of it. For one thing, he typically didn't have adequate design information for his projects, and he was afraid of ostracizing his architects by being more aggressive in requesting information. His projects languished and lost money. Naturally, he was terrified at the prospect of asking the client for more funds to cover the delays. The subcontractors who invariably took his projects at a low margin, were often asked to give back at the end of the project to make it more profitable or less of a disaster for the general contractor. Many of them agreed to this arrangement, with the promise of future work that was touted as a prospective windfall. If the subcontractor hung around long enough, he might see a profitable project with this contractor, but certainly never enough to offset his losses on the other projects. In this way, unscrupulous general contractors can indefinitely string along their subcontractors who can't afford to leave them. The irony was that this particular contractor took on these projects under similar overtures from the project architect, and was also abused in this fashion.

If you know your business, you will generally take low-margin projects knowingly only with some other incentive then profit, such as the promise of future work. Be careful not to rush through such projects so to reconnoiter costs, especially if the project is introductory, or being done as a courtesy; that would be a show of ingratitude and disingenuousness. Remember, your objective was not to make a large profit. Although your mission as a successful contractor is to minimize your diet of unprofitable projects, you may find yourself inadvertently with a financially challenged project. Contractors respond to this threat by engaging siege operations. Sometimes, this is a necessity, but more often, it is not. One thing is for certain, if the panic button is pushed, everyone need not panic, but form a single line and calmly . . . , that is, out of chaos, make order. Most people don't have the bandwidth or the stomach to make order from chaos: they invariably become unglued, or simply don't have what it takes to cope. The notion brings to mind Robert Shaw's role, and the scene in *Jaws*, where the shark rams the side of the boat; the ship's hull is splitting and splintering, the boat is rocking, water is rushing in, the boat seems like it may disintegrate at any moment, and the shark is marauding. The crew, Richard Dreyfuss, and Roy Scheider, are falling all over themselves in a state of panic. Scheider gropes for his .38. As Quint (Shaw) gathers some gear, he notices in his peripheral vision that a kerosene lamp has been upended; the kerosene spilling out, igniting, and threatening to spread throughout the cabin. Without turning his head, he calmly calls to Scheider something like "put that out for me, will you Chief." He was personifying the quality of composure under duress—an elusive ability necessary to control dicey circumstances.

There are unhealthy and healthy responses to pressure, and constructive and destructive responses. Having the right staff in control of your siege operations is critical to effective reconnaissance. I specifically use the term *reconnaissance* because like the term *siege*, it is also a military term that refers to the inspection of conditions for the presence of enemies after a battle—a metaphor for *damage control* in the world of construction. Managers will acknowledge the need for siege responses, but few have the chops to facilitate effective action. To demonstrate some of the fickle responses that contractors are prone to use, I will further extend the military metaphor.

The first US-Iraqi war, also known as Desert Storm, lends itself particularly well to this exercise. On the Iraqi side, the military was undermanned, undertrained, and without modern weapons, and intelligence technology. Their forces were being pummeled by an enemy whom they could not see, and whose location could not even be determined. When the Americans reconnoitered their targets, they found their enemy's position and equipment abandoned. The vehicles were haphazardly facing every conceivable direction, with their gun turrets aimed in futility at an invisible adversary. The Iraqis didn't have a clue. This was a typical battlefield scenario. Nevertheless, the Iraqi government continued to report that the enemy was nearly vanquished, and that victory was imminent. On the American side, there were some interesting parallels to the Iraqis. Although the American forces were completely dominant on the battlefield, their overall intention was obfuscated by smoke and mirror propaganda, such as the efficiency reports of the Patriot missiles. More importantly, the mission was abruptly declared successful. As everyone knows, the American government, for its own reasons, stopped well short of its advertised cause, leaving the job largely unfinished.

Construction companies resemble such bumbling military commands in the way that:

They focus on the wrong priorities at the wrong time, thus wasting time, resources, and falling short of their goal.

They don't coordinate their efforts.

They don't finish the job.

They skew the results of their efforts to suit their needs.

Unhealthy responses to underbid projects

No sooner does it dawn on a contractor that they have taken on a losing proposition that they take action to minimize their losses. This will necessitate an immediate change in plans—a divergence from the intended general approach. On the other hand, some contractor's standard *modus operandi* mirrors that of a contractor trying to offset losses. Such contractors seemingly are operating at a loss on every project. Their damage control strategy may include the following:

- Insist that the project subcontractors discount the cost of their work, or find the lowest bid possible.
- Rush the work.

- Look for ways to cut corners such as substitutions of cheaper labor and materials.

- Minimize in-house costs, specifically, general conditions—laborers, site managers, and the like, by understaffing and underservicing the project.

- Plan ahead for opportunities to inflate change order costs to offset their losses.

- Look for opportunities to blame the architect, or deflect blame away from themselves.

- Request schedule extensions.

Obviously, you're not going to win any friends this way; your subcontractors will not want to work for you, and the architect will not be putting you on his bid list any time again soon. For example, take the duplex model we have been using: this project was terribly underbid, as one would expect, none of the contractor's regular subcontractors would go near it. Likewise, the contractor was reluctant to sully his relationships with his regular subcontractors on a loser project. Having no resources, the contractor solicited his vendors "cold," or without qualification, from the Blue Book,[1] as they cared not what the outcome of such prospective relationships with strangers would be. They felt a sense of comfort in the mistaken assumption of their own anonymity in dealing with unknowns; if it turned out to be a money maker, so much the better, if it was a loser (for the subcontractor), as expected, they were using bridges once, and then burning them behind. Imagine trying to build the project with these vendors! Many of those who showed were either hungry, so incompetent that they couldn't find other work, or were his regular hacks doing the contractor a favor by helping him out of a jam. The wiser of the newly sourced subcontractors took the precaution of insisting on an aggressive payment schedule, as they had no level of established trust with the general contractor.

Alternatively, you must enact more constructive measures to navigate your underfinanced projects. If nothing else, define the mistake and make this information a consideration for all future bids, so as not to repeat the mistake.

Constructive responses to underbid projects

Bite the bullet. Taking your lumps won't save any money, but then again, you won't have compromised your integrity by spreading the wealth, or insisting that others suffer in your place or along with you. However, once a problem is recognized, you then put in place aggressive remediation and monitoring programs to ensure that the project is managed in such a way as to focus on mitigating further losses. This attitude will save face with your resources; subcontractors and vendors, who otherwise would not appreciate absorbing your losses, and with the architect, who would only resent the notion that you are stewing over the fact that you underbid the project. They will perceive your actions as a show of inexperience, and will be wary of your cost-cutting strategies, such as those mentioned above, and of you padding your change orders. If a project has an unexpected low profit-margin, or is a loser, take your medicine like an adult. Others will respect you for it. What you might make up in wheeling and dealing, you will lose in reputation. Remember: it's your problem, don't make it someone else's.

In the event that a project is seriously underbid, a general contractor simply cannot execute it, and may try to get out of it. From the client and architect perspective, a walk-off general contractor isn't a good scenario; however, alternatively, to keep him on task may be more problematic than terminating his contract. What's worse than losing a contractor one month into the project, is losing him when he's well into the infrastructure phase. The longer he is on-task, the more damage will be done, and the more difficult it will be to transition to a new contractor. If he intends to leave, you can assume that most of his work will be torn out or redone, creating double work for the next contractor. This phenomenon has created a cottage industry in itself.

Hopefully, the high level of scrutiny you now focus on your troublesome project will prove to be a positive exercise, where you will use your knowledge to your advantage in executing future work. On the underbid project you will conduct your own value engineering, similar to that which you might do to reduce the contract value. However, in this instance, you are tweaking to save your own skin. For some contractors, to value engineer the project without compromising its integrity is the equivalent of reinventing the wheel, and they invariably fall back on bad habits. Their first attempt at value engineering is to remove scope. Such behavior betrays an ignorance of the difference between cost engineering and value engineering.

Underdesigned Projects

Although underdesigned projects are the rule rather than the exception, they are surprisingly commonplace on high-end commissions. You would expect that a project with a generous budget would yield sophisticated design documents. Although the integrity of a high-end architect's designs are generally above average, there always seems to be a lot of open-endedness; unfinished details. Perhaps this is true because such projects are more complicated. What often happens is that many interior designers, who excel in interior details, don't have the architectural know-how to finish working drawings: the requests for information (RFIs) for architectural details come pouring in; many architects, whose milieu is architectural with some engineering, don't normally go to the level of detail that designers do. There are a number of other reasons for this, some of which we discussed in Chap. 2. To reiterate, and additionally clarify, consider the following:

- Insufficient design window (Chap. 2)
- Insufficient design budget (Chap. 2)
- Underqualified design team (Chap. 2)
- Indecisiveness on the part of the design team and/or client

- Inaccessibility to required design information, such as field measurements referenced from work not yet (or not able to be) installed
- Insufficient shop drawings and submittal coordination and approval process
- Lack of coordination between trades

The degree of design detail for high-end residential projects needs to be high. Many design packages are released for production without such details, with the promise of the remaining details to follow in forthcoming sketches and clarifications. Although this may sound reasonable, it can be a problem, because the full design package is rarely issued in a timely fashion. I recall a project that was underdesigned. Not only did it require clarifications, but it also lacked components that were still in development. Over a period of 12 months, some three-hundred crudely drawn sketches were generated, piecemeal; many revised several times, half of them as response to the contractor's RFIs, and the remaining, extraneous details and changes by the design team. To obtain some of the details was like squeezing water from a stone, and resultantly, areas of the work sat idle for long periods. To keep the job moving, the contractor became proactive and began doing some of the design work himself, an effort that yielded dubious results.[2] The inadequate flow of information caused the project schedule to double in duration, without even changing the design intent. Nevertheless, although the majority of the working drawings were done in freehand sketches (SKs) the architect was confident he had delivered a comprehensive design package. He had, in fact, delivered a more or less comprehensive design package; however, had he issued it once, as working drawings, the project would have been built faster, and cost less. Moreover, there is an enormous difference between building a project from sketches as opposed to blueprints.

Some shrewd designers will deliberately not provide details, and will hold that these details should be addressed by the respective draftsmen, in their shop drawings, and the contractor in his means and methods. They will allude to this notion in their general requirements. The AIA 201 also can be interpreted by architects as saddling the contractor with some of the design responsibilities when it suits them. While draftsmen must show details, they are not designers. This problem is somewhat of a grey area, because many draftsmen don't show an adequate level of detail in their shop drawings. Conflicts in the design coordination process can be expected, but on a poorly executed project, they will be exacerbated, causing mistakes and delays. This phenomenon is one way design teams cut corners to save money, or overcome design budget shortfalls or low-balled design commissions. Such drawings are readily recognizable for their schematic features, and stark lack of detail.

There will always be a high degree of coordination between trades. Much of this coordination is part of the means and methods of the overall project execution, and often the design team will leave this entirely to the contractor. On more complicated projects this is an ill-advised approach. The contractor and his subcontractors need to coordinate more closely with the design team than they would on an average project. Often, this rule is not observed, and a great deal of coordination falls between the cracks. Perhaps, half of such coordination is the responsibility of the design team, the other half belonging to the contractor. If both sides of the project team did their homework, there would be fewer grey areas to argue over whose responsibility a given task was. The idea of partnering with an architect and a contractor to build a project is a positive one, and should always be considered, whenever possible. By really working together, all parties are subject to a better experience. Unfortunately, architects, in seeking to further indemnify themselves, are reluctant to help coordinate a contractor's installations.

As we discussed in Chap. 2, your estimator's review of the design documentation should give you an idea of the level of detail that exists. From this information, you will adjust your budget and schedule accordingly, and calculate a risk factor, as discussed in Chaps. 2 and 3. You will often find that in order to take on a project without all the details, you will either need to pad your bid, provide generous budgets for unspecified items, extend the schedule duration, or any combination of the three, none of which is good news for your client. If drawings are vague and underdeveloped, a contractor must realize this in the bidding stage. If he does not, he may later be held responsible for executing the intent of the drawings, which likely is much more than he bargained for. Many architects incorporate nebulous language into their boilerplate general requirements that intends to saddle the contractor with the responsibility for just about anything that could go wrong on a project. For example:

> Minor details not usually shown or specified but necessary for proper construction of any part of the work shall be included as if they were indicated on the drawing.

Or,

> The contractor shall visit the site and inform himself fully of all conditions and limitations that will affect his work. The contractor will include in his contract a sum to cover all work called for in, or reasonably inferable from the drawings including any labor, materials, and means of construction necessary for a complete installation. The submission of a proposal will be construed as evidence that such an examination has been made. Later claims for all labor, equipment, and materials required for difficulties encountered, which could have been foreseen, had an examination been made, will not be recognized.

Such language is among the first exceptions I denote in my qualifications. A construction manager must identify any underdesigned elements in his constructability analysis, an exercise every general contractor should also invoke. However, it is the architect's responsibility to inform a contractor that certain information is missing, and that an allowance should be indicated for any such work. To knowingly not advise the contractor of omissions and hidden scope is either a deceitful practice, or the attribute of an incompetent designer. In either case, it is a shame to see a general contractor take the fall for a bad architect. To avoid omissions in their design packages, architects will argue that intent or inference is enough to substantiate the existence of a given design. What they may qualify as intent can be anywhere from a single line on the drawings to a tiny note in the side bar. Thus, the omission may be construed as being 90%, as compared to 100%—by definition, not an omission. Of course, this thinking is convoluted and an exercise in semantics, but it is commonplace.

Some projects are put out to bid for a fixed fee, long before the drawings are ready. It is just as foolish to try to bid such projects as a fixed sum, as it is for the architect to call them "working drawings." Underdeveloped design documents can inspire some dubious expectations:

- That you will have to negotiate every future allowance and change order without the leverage you had when negotiating the main contract
- That you will be unable to project a production schedule without working drawings, running the risk of financing a delayed project
- That the design and development (D&D) process will encroach on meetings, production, and inhibit progress
- That you will spend extra overhead and general conditions acting as a construction manager without being compensated for the service

There is nothing wrong with passing up a project; however, business owners invariably see a passed project as a missed opportunity, or are concerned about losing clients. One option available to the general contractor with the wherewithal to do so is to suggest that the contract would be viable only if it should be let as a construction management project. A small company I knew took on a lot of hand-holding projects with new architects who needed their guidance, but also promised more work. The owner rightly recognized the need to get involved in the planning process, and was sometimes successful. However, where he failed, was in his inability to incorporate a coherent construction management program to facilitate these projects, and to be remunerated for his services, which were inconsistent and undefined.

If a project is underdesigned due to indecisiveness on the part of client, this may be an indication of things to come. One such project we will discuss later in the Dog and Pony Show section. Because this particular project had the promise of such a high contract value, the contractor felt he had no choice but to accommodate any request, no matter how unreasonable. Considering the budget, you could almost empathize with him; however, he was willing to a fault. It is noteworthy that the design process of this project lagged for so long that three things happened: (1) the program, which was at the time relevant to the client's family situation, needed to be changed; a child who was to live in the space was now of college age, and moving out; (2) the client had lost interest in the project, could no longer make decisions concerning the design, and was weary of the process; and (3) the value of the real estate had appreciated in value such that the owner could not pass up the opportunity to put the space back on the market, thus obviating the need for the contractor. The contract was terminated after a brief mediation process, part of which included a grant of one-quarter of a million dollars in the mechanical subcontractor's coordination fees: he had never actually installed a single piece of work. The remaining compensation barely covered the contractor's overhead. In other words, this project was too good to be true.

Aggressively Scheduled Projects

We will discuss below projects that suddenly are stepped up to an unnatural pace as a response to production delays or any other impetus. Many projects have an accelerated pace built into the schedule from the beginning. For some projects, this is called fast-tracking, which we briefly discussed in Chap. 2; however, for the residential sector, this is a misnomer. Residential projects don't lend themselves to fast-tracking. If they should resemble a fast-track project, it is likely because the schedule forced it to be so. Projects with a built-in accelerated schedule require a special approach. They all have in common the tenet that all parties must be signed up for the regimen. If not, there is a weak link, or inherent flaw that will inevitably complicate or even scotch the mission. The coordination between owner, architect, and contractor for fast-track projects must be lockstep.

Compressed schedule

By definition, any schedule that aspires to be completed sooner than the contract schedule states is a compressed schedule in that it shortens the duration of its tasks. This is also known as an "expedited" schedule. Any schedule that aspires to be completed sooner than industry standards or a natural progression would dictate it as a compressed schedule. The difference between the two is as follows:

- An expedited or compressed schedule incorporated into the project subsequent to the ratification of the contract is a legitimate change order.

- A schedule that has been underestimated and must be stepped up to make the due date is the responsibility of the contractor. It may be compressed in order to make up for lost time, but it is not expedited. It is merely accelerated in order to get back on track.

As we discussed in Chap. 3, compressed schedules reduce float times to a minimum; in other words, there is little or no downtime between predecessor and successor tasks. Additionally, lag times will be shortened, and overlapping increased. If an opening is found, it is quickly filled with delayed tasks. Projects with such a schedule might resemble anthills. This notion in itself is not a bad thing; in fact, if the project is compressed, it should resemble an anthill. If you know anthills, you know that the worker ants toil diligently, 24/7, in a highly ordered fashion. It is something to marvel at. For the ants, this is natural. Obviously, this pace is unnatural for humans, and is subject to high rates of failure. As a project team aspires toward this ideal, a high degree of organization is required. Hence, the general in the war zone image evoked earlier.

For an average meat-and-potatoes project, the team leader might only function as a straw-boss; cracking the whip so to maximize production out of his workers. On more complicated residential projects, especially high-end, this approach is not helpful; quality work cannot be rushed. The process is a bit more complicated, and requires a specialist-led team to take on the task. Because this notion is routinely flouted, rushed projects tend to look the same, whether they were known to be rushed projects, or if the crunch was thrust upon them mid-production. To account for this deficit, a general contractor may send a project manager to the site, or may himself go, for as short a period as he deems necessary. The assumption being that the higher quotient at the management level will up the production quantity and quality. The presence of additional management to the job site also serves to show the client that the problem is being taken seriously.

There are two approaches to compressing a project—scientific and arbitrary. Inability to accurately define the cost and impact of compression will generate an arbitrary approach. Compressing a project without any methodology other than stepping up production is a process that is impossible to quantify. On the other hand, scientific methods to compression require a lot of analytical skill, and experience with similar projects. For a cost-plus fee project, merely keeping track of payroll will yield most of the information needed to quantify additional costs. For fixed sum projects, the process is more complicated.

Ideally, to accurately quantify a compressed schedule you would want the following information at your disposal:

- Original task durations
- Expected task durations
- Expected additional overtime employee hours
- Cost of expedited (red-label) deliveries
- Expected additional general conditions to manage the compression
- Effect of loss of productivity due to decreased overtime production rates
- Effect of loss of productivity due to trade stacking or congestion
- Effect of redo work due to increased margin for error

The first four items can be estimated, more or less, methodically, such that a cost or range can be generated. The next four items require a more in-depth analysis, to an extent far beyond most estimators' capabilities. Thus, somewhere in between is perhaps what can be considered an acceptable assessment of the effects of compression on a given project.

Additional man-hours can be calculated with a reasonable degree of accuracy. The remaining factors must be estimated. Simple calculations for a compressed project can be generated. Assume that the project is a 1-year project that is to be compressed to 9 months, at a rate of 25% compression. The project value is $1,000,000. Calculation would formulate as shown in Table 7.1.

TABLE 7.1   Compression Valuation, Simple Method

Initial project value	$1,000,000
Labor component	$250,000
25% addition for compression of labor	$62,500
Total	$1,312,500

Table 7.1 is the simpler method; however, it doesn't take into consideration the intangibles as does Table 7.2. The net difference is about 10%. The opportunity for oversight using the simpler method is considerable. While Table 7.2 is not ideal, it can serve as a good starting point for negotiating an upcharge, or it can be offered as a budget to be later clarified. If nothing else, it will help substantiate your claim to the client.

Latently Dysfunctional Projects

These are projects where although the project may or may not have been predisposed to delays, it was not realized until some time into the production schedule that the project was in peril, at which time a response was then implemented. This condition would seemingly describe the majority of construction projects. If a project is known to be a challenge from the start—aggressive schedule and budget, more contractors are going to be put off by this fact, and will either bid it artificially high, or decline to bid altogether. More often than not, a job that is predisposed to delays will find a willing victim who either doesn't grasp the potential delays, or believes that his bid is generous enough to accommodate delays. Otherwise, owners would have to wise up and either reissue more complete bid packages, or scuttle their projects altogether; options seldom taken.

A seasoned contractor will intuit the likelihood of an ill-conceived project in the bidding stage. At this time, there is still room to negotiate, and to find a way

TABLE 7.2   Compression Valuation, Complex Method

Initial project value	$1,000,000
Labor component	$250,000
25% addition for compression of labor	$62,500
Productivity losses (15%)	$9,375
Overtime (.5 × 20% employee hours	$6,250
General conditions	$60,000
(12 weeks at $5,000/week)	
Overhead and insurance (12%)	$46,575
Cost of expedited (red-label) deliveries	$2,500
Profit (5%)	$21,860
Total	$1,459,060

to make the project work, or to pass it up. The contractor can issue a report with what he believes are factors that will likely cause delays, and a statement of impact of this report: typically, an expediting charge. It is the contractor who is caught unawares of such circumstances who will be subject to the most abuse; if the chief project components—schedule and design—have changed little from the bidding phase, he will likely weather the storm of delays alone, as the opportunity to speak up has long passed. Thus, foresight must be considered one of the most important analytical skills in the industry.

Responses

Acceleration

Speeding up production is a knee-jerk response to correcting a late project. When pace is stepped up without any forethought, it is a mindless undertaking. Invariably, when fallout occurs, the project manager or superintendent is blamed; however; he will likely attribute blame to the workmen or subcontractors and vendors. Having seen this dilemma before, the men who have been on the project recognize this exercise in futility and will laugh amongst themselves at the contractor who didn't see the writing on the wall until it was too late. They think that they can afford to laugh, because the contractor always foots the bill, but they will experience unrelenting pressure from the production manager in order to minimize losses, that is, they will work much harder to earn the same dollar. While it is plain as the nose on your face to them, it would have been a great stretch for the contractor to be on the same page.

As much as project managers and superintendents are blamed for delays, it is rare that they are the sole cause or party accountable. General contractors may go through armies of project managers and superintendents without ever looking past these people to find underlying causes for their difficulties. In this respect they are unable to learn from their mistakes. Any decent superintendent will advise his project manager of delays affecting the schedule. A diligent superintendent will advise continually, even if no action is taken. Why a company would ignore such warnings is a mystery; however, it is a ubiquitous circumstance. On some level, upper management, or the owner, must heed the warning. Perhaps this is that quirk of human nature, known as denial. Inevitably, a big push is invoked in the eleventh hour, and the accumulation of all advisories and warnings comes to a head. Perhaps having all their problems in front of them at once is the only way that some managers can negotiate through them, hence, the last minute anarchy. Think of this habit as the accrual method of problem solving. The intent is to allow all problems to accumulate, and then deal with them all at once so as to minimize the duration of the process, and make it a simpler process by consolidating the work. This is an ineffective method, and puts undue pressure and responsibility on the production team, who will invariably take the blame when the project falters. If problems were addressed when they were identified, there would be no backlog of obstacles to finish a project, and most siege operations could be avoided or minimized.

A project, which has been accurately scheduled and built in accordance with that schedule, may become delayed for reasons not related to production; more often than not, a lack of design information. In such cases, the client may ask that the pace be accelerated so to put the project back on track. The assumption is that if a project is moving below the average pace, acceleration should be applied to bring the work back to a natural progression. This is not *compression*; it is *correction*. If the project was moving along at a natural pace, and subsequently accelerated, this condition is considered compression. Compression always involves additional contractor resources, and it should be priced accordingly. Some of the problems associated with compression are:

- Decrease in worker output rates
- Increase in general conditions—supervision, laborers, and the like
- Incorporation of overtime pay scales
- Lowering of quality standards
- Tendency to make more mistakes
- Trade stacking
- Displacement of trades
- Higher rate of accidents

Everyone feels the need to accelerate a delayed project, as the need has been made exigent by the general contractor and his managers. There is no mistaking this phenomenon, even to the layperson. I recall two such expedited projects treated differently:

The first project was for an upscale art gallery. It had an aggressive schedule from the beginning, which was exacerbated by remedial work, and the fact that the client moved up the finish date 3 weeks or so during the winter holiday season, compressing duration about 20%. The reception area was about 25 ft wide, 18 ft deep, with 12 ft high ceilings. There was a grid of 36 or so flangeless light fixtures (tapeable), which had to align perfectly on three planes, sheetrocked, and then plastered. In this room at a given time there might be anywhere from six to eight electricians, three carpenters, two laborers, one super, three storefront mechanics, and three moving scissor jacks, each carrying two plasterers. I suppose the intent was to allow for zero downtime between trade sequencing. In addition to the crowding factor of 23 men in one room, all were working at a frenetic pace. The scissor jacks were constantly lurching backwards and forwards in quick sudden motions. Not unsurprisingly, a laborer became pinned between a scissor jack and a wall. Additionally, the light fixtures were repeatedly installed incorrectly, with the sheetrock over them. The sheetrock had to be removed, the lights realigned, and the sheetrock reapplied three times. In many cases the framing had to be redone to accept the fixture mounting kits.

The second project also had the writing on the wall. It was a retail project, also with an aggressive schedule, but in addition, this project lacked an experienced design team. The drawings went the route of amateur designers working with an architect of record. The store's existing fixtures (product display, vitrines, and the like) were to be modified, with many additional new fixtures. The contractor, lacking in resources, sourced the wood and metal store fixture house cold (without referral) on the Internet. It was based in Oklahoma, the project being in New York City. Though there were signs, it did not become completely evident until too late, that the fixture house was having production problems. Instead of staging several partial deliveries to accommodate fast-track sequencing, everything was sent in two huge deliveries, both past the deadline, with one being at the last minute, when the store's warehouse had already shipped its product to the site, and they had staff ready to place the product into built-in displays that were as yet still sitting on a truck. The installation was really something to see. It went late into the morning, two nights in a row. As soon as a piece was unwrapped and installed, the goods were immediately hung or folded into them. Most of the metal work was sent out to be stripped and refinished, as it did not pass muster.

It was noteworthy that in the course of the siege the general contractor seemed intent on focusing on menial details, as opposed to real problems—an eccentricity of the affected single proprietor. His neurotic state precluded his ability to make important decisions. This was relevant because he had assured the client that there would be no problem making the deadline, and that he had built many such jobs before. It is interesting to compare the approach to these projects. On both projects, it was known that the schedule was aggressive from the start. Only on the gallery project did the end-date get moved up. The gallery project management realized what needed to be done, and although it wasn't pretty, got the job done. This was because they had good resources, an experienced general contractor, and a strong design team. The retail project, however, did get completed, but it had so many flaws, it could not be closed out. The biggest problem had to do with using an unknown subcontractor, with whom the general contractor had no leverage, for the most critical work. The contractor lost money installing unauthorized change orders, and was promised another project by the designer to make up the loss. The offsetting project, having the same inexperienced project team, and difficult client was also a loser.

Another common oversight affecting schedules is the effect of change orders on the sequencing and overall duration. Change orders, when they add scope to the project, will often necessitate compression. The point is, they add up. One large change order may be easy to handle, but when there are multiple small change orders, they will likely upset sequencing, and extend the duration of the project by increasing coordination needs, in addition to more scope. A client may reluctantly concede extra time to a contractor to accommodate one or two large change orders; however, when multiple small change orders are executed over 3 or 4 months, impact evaluation becomes difficult. It is impossible to demonstrate the cause and effect relationships of multiple small change orders to the big picture with any acceptable degree of accuracy. However, if one takes the aggregate of all change orders in relation to the contract value, an estimate can at least begin to be assembled. A study comments on the nature of quantifying the effect of several small change orders:

> When the changes are small in scope and few in number the impact is real, but relatively minor. The change may or may not affect the critical path, and even when it does, the fundamental logic of the work remains in tact. With respect to loss of productivity, the major effect is loss of momentum, loss of efficiency, and extended overhead associated with administration of changes and other aspects of the work.
>
> When there are multiple changes on a project and they act in sequence or concurrently, there is a compounding effect—this is the most damaging consequence for a project and the most difficult to understand and manage. The net effect of the individual changes is greater than the sum of the individual parts. Only may there be increase in cost and time required that the project logic may have to be redone.[3]

The concept of "the net effect of the individual changes is greater than the sum of the individual parts" is seldom appreciated by the client, thus clients are reluctant to agree to pay a prorate fee for change order work.

It is reductive thinking that adding more man-hours will simply yield more production. The *quantity* of production may increase, but the *rate* of production will go down. To be sure, quantifying the effect of increased man power is an unexacting business. Production rates decrease with the increase of hours, or overtime, as shown in Table 7.3[4] in one sense, defeating the objective of the initiative.

Several studies demonstrate that productivity is decreased by 10% beginning with the first 50-h workweek. According to the above referred study, after 12 workweeks, productivity will have dropped 35%. The effect of the decrease in production rates translates to lost dollars. Table 7.4[5] illustrates how costs are affected by the additional overtime and loss in production.

If the project is a union job, costs will increase even more, such that incorporating overtime becomes increasingly untenable, except for the most aggressive projects. However, should a project come to litigation, neither of these methods will prove sufficient to substantiate the award of damages. In fact, contract lawyers and their clients who utilize various models to quantify these damages are also routinely not accepted by the courts, who regard such information as speculative:

> It is a rare case where loss of productivity can be proven by books and records; almost always, it has to be proven by the opinions of expert witnesses. However, the mere expression of an estimate as to the amount of productivity loss by an expert witness with nothing to support it will not establish the fundamental fact of resultant injury, nor provide a sufficient basis for making a reasonably correct approximation of damages.[6]

In the above referenced decision, the contractor was awarded damages, but considerably less than he had litigated for. An earlier decision dispensed information that should be helpful to contractors in substantiating their claims:

TABLE 7.3   Cumulative Effect of Overtime on Productivity

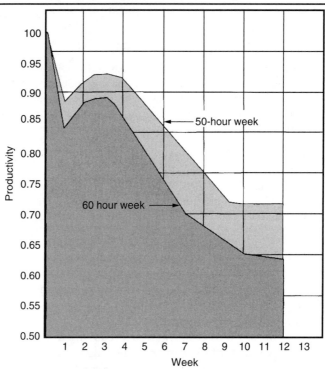

Table 7.3 represents the reduction in productivity, normally experienced on projects operated on a basis of 50 hours per week and 60 hours per week. The data for these curves is from project operations in an area of tranquil labor relations and with excellent field management direction. The measure of productivity is a comparison of actual work hours expended for preplanned operations with a fixed standard base of calculated work hour requirements called a "bogey." These observations are on a weekly basis, with all completed work recorded from physical count or measurement and the work hours expended, obtained from actual payroll hours. The curves reflect the averages of many observations.

A claimant need not prove his damages with absolute certainty or mathematical exactitude . . . It is sufficient if he furnishes the court with a reasonable basis for his computation, even though the result is only approximate . . . Yet this leniency as to the actual mechanics of the computation does not relieve the contactor of his essential burden of establishing the fundamental facts of liability, causation, and resultant injury.[7]

As these court findings demonstrate, litigation will likely yield less than hoped for; therefore, it should be a priority to settle such matters before they become liabilities, which is no simple task, as most projects can't come to a screeching halt to allow for prolonged negotiations. If a project needs to be compressed or accelerated, time will be a critical factor that is nonnegotiable for most owners.

TABLE 7.4   Relationship of Hours Worked: Productivity and Costs

1	2	3	4	5	6	7	8
	Productivity Rate		Actual Hour Output for 50-hr. Week	Hour Gain Over 40-hr. Week	Hour Loss Due to Productivity Drop	Premium Hours	Hour Cost of Overtime Operation (at 2X)
50-Hour Overtime Work Weeks	40-Hr. Week	50-Hr. Week					
0-1-2	1.00	.926	46.3	6.3	3.7	10.0	13.7
2-3-4		.90	45.0	5.0	5.0	10.0	15.0
4-5-6		.87	43.5	3.5	6.5	10.0	16.5
6-7-8		.80	40.0	0.0	10.0	10.0	20.0
8-9-10		.752	37.6	-2.4	12.4	10.0	22.4
>10		.750	37.5	-2.5	12.5	10.0	22.5

Table 7.4 shows the effect of reduced efficiency of a 50-hour week and the premium cost of overtime. When a job is scheduled for 50 hours per week, there is a reduction in productivity for the total 50 hours—not just for 10 hours of overtime. Column 3 reflects an interpretation of the productivity rate from Table 7.3 for the periods shown in Column 1. Column 4 reflects the return in productive work for 50 hours of scheduled operations, due to the reduction in productivity. Column 5 shows the productive effort gained for the week over 40 hours due to the overtime hours worked. Column 8 shows the cost of this gain. It is interesting to note that after working overtime for six to eight weeks, labor cost is inflated by 50 percent with the productive returns no greater than would be accomplished on a 40-hour week. Records indicate that continuous overtime operations beyond eight weeks results in an actual productive return of less work accomplishment than a regular 40-hour week.

Select Out-of-Sequence Tasks

It isn't hard to pinpoint the reason(s) for a delayed project. It's usually pretty obvious. Assigning blame and responsibility is another matter, which will be discussed in the next chapter. The trick is to address delays before they happen, not after they have compounded one another beyond recognition. Even the most inexperienced contractors have a nose for delayed critical activities, or those that will truly delay a schedule. Should a project become late they will fix their attention on the most at risk critical activity, and the tasks driving that activity, and focus their efforts there. At this point, the schedule is not necessarily delayed, but it is at risk of becoming out-of-sequence, and being so, subject to additional problems. Chances are other work on the site has proceeded without stopping to wait for the delayed task to catch up. The best managers have a prevention program, which may con-sist merely of a little foresight; most delays would be avoidable with only a little extra effort in the planning stage—"an ounce of prevention is worth a pound of cure." Without a schedule it will be difficult to tell exactly what effect the shift of focus will have on other trades, or on the overall scheme. Even with a schedule, working with an out-of-sequence project poses several prob-lems. Some familiar examples:

- Extra work is created to facilitate mobilization, breakdown, and remobilization.
- Task times are reduced in deference to the accommodation of out-of-sequence tasks.
- Lead and review times are shortened.
- Trades become uncoordinated.
- Design team tasks are forced out-of-sequence.
- Walls and ceilings are closed in before all the MEP program is installed.
- Finishes completed or engaged while rough work is still being done.
- Material and equipment on site too early, which must constantly be restored, and be subject to damage.
- Trim kits for wall and ceiling mounted fixtures installed before paint.

Any or all of the above may be caused by the general contractor trying to reach milestones before their time, for which he hopes he can bill the client.

There are some basic reasons why a project goes out of sequence, other than ordinary delays; these are deliberate actions taken by the contractor:

- To evince the appearance of having reached a certain level of progress, especially to make a deadline.
- To try to mitigate delays of noncritical activities in the mistaken belief that they affect the schedule.
- To prioritize scope of work with the most value, so to bill against it.
- To be unwilling to wait for delayed work to catch up.

However, a shrewd general contractor can take a project out-of-sequence without it becoming a free-for-all. If it is done methodically, and with a tracked schedule, he will have more control in implementing changes and monitoring their effect. This is a deliberate undertaking, as opposed to the typical mindless response. A responsible contractor will understand the effect the out-of-sequence tasks will have on the rest of the project, as opposed to the tasks being done in a vacuum, on their own timeline, and without predecessors and successors, network logic. Architects and clients will not respond positively to a project that a contractor takes out of sequence on his own initiative, especially when he is making up for time that he himself lost, and when the project appears to be going out of control. To the trained eye, there is no hiding the fact that the project is not progressing according to the schedule. If a project should be taken out of sequence, this condition should be pointed out to the architect before it is begun. Otherwise, it appears that the general contractor has something to hide, and is covering up for his own mistakes before they are noticed.

A contractor may feel the need to feign a higher level of progress, or rate of production in the same way that a *dog-and-pony* show does, especially if he is behind. He may have walls closed temporarily until they are seen by the client; once the client leaves, the wall coverings are removed, and the work behind continues. He may have finishes installed even though the project is not ready for them; the client may then think the project is more developed than it really is. When a project is out of sequence, it becomes difficult to gauge remaining durations of tasks still in progress, as logistics become staggered. A contractor may then use this explanation as an excuse for not having a hard or tracked schedule, especially if he feels he is not fully to blame for delays. A proper schedule then becomes impossible to generate. However, he may truly believe that he is accelerating progress by pushing ahead other tasks.

Dog and Pony Show

As the term denotes, *dog and pony (D&P) shows* are an attempt to evoke the appearance that great progress is being made. This exercise may be ordered by the contractor when he feels the project is going too slowly, and the need to conceal this fact. Any task, whether relevant, in or out of sequence, will be considered as a showpiece for the client to convince him that he is either on schedule, or at least trying his hardest; as if to say "it is not for lack of effort that the project is off schedule." The contractor may have a sense of what his client will perceive as progress, and he will set store by this idea. Typically, clients consider finishes as progress; they don't really understand the progression of infrastructure; hence, many contractors rush the finishes to their late projects to mollify their clients.

A project that was 3 years in the making was sitting idle for lack of final design. Nevertheless, the contractor did not want the client to arrive at the weekly job meeting only to see no new progress. A hastily held meeting was convened by the contractor out of which came the following dictum: the superintendent was to notify the sheet metal contractor that, for the sake of appearances, he must have a truck load of duct work on the site by the next day, regardless of whether or not it was to be used on this project. This exercise was for the purpose of impressing the client. The subcontractor was notified, and indicated that he could not accommodate the directive, as sheet metal workers make work for specific projects, and never have spare truckloads of duct sitting around. The manager who ordered the exercise was beside himself, because he was hard put to contrive another scheme. Ironically, had the material been delivered, no one from the client's side was there to see it, as they canceled the meeting. In the D&P show, unnecessary level of man power may be implemented to give the appearance of accelerated progress and a sense of urgency and good faith by the contractor. This ploy is merely a common ruse. The client sees the wealth of man power on the site, and assumes a big push is being made. However, just like taking the project out of sequence, a contractor himself may be convinced that simply adding man power to the project will accelerate its production. If nothing else, it will at least resemble a busy project.

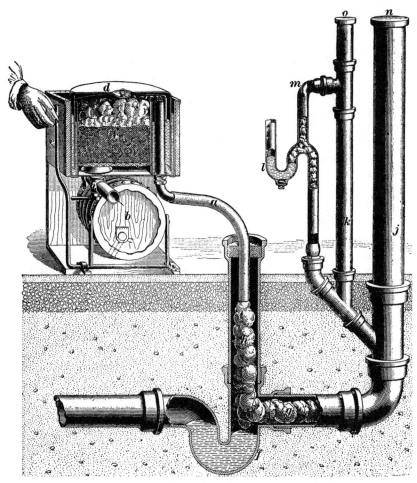

Smoke test.
A modern smoke machine, which is commonly used for testing plumbing is shown in Fig. 58. The fuel in *C*, being ignited at the bottom, burns upwards, and the air supplies the oxygen necessary for a slow and incomplete combustion of the mass. Smoke, consequently, is given off from the surface of the fuel (which is generally old, greasy cotton waste gathered as scrap from the pipe vise) and is forced down through the hose a into the drainage system. *A Treatise on Architecture and Building Construction, Volume IV* (Scranton: The Colliery Engineer Co., 1899).

Effect on Morale

A little push at the end of a project is typical. However, pervasive pressure will start to wear on people's nerves, just as the micromanager does. The project begins to resemble or become an unhappy one, where team members start to feel they have no control of their work, and they lose faith in the project team. This fact will not escape the client's notice, will likely rub off on him, and pretty soon, everyone is unhappy. Naturally, when people are unhappy in their work, they tend not to perform to their top capability. In addition to a project being delayed, if it is then accelerated and taken out of sequence, the ensuing pressure on the job team can be formidable.

For those affected by pressure giving way to poor morale, corrective measures should be taken, as you want people to be happy in their work. This could mean anything from buying lunch every Friday, a short pep talk, or a more wholesale adjustment that legitimately reduces stress loads. Ideally, a small raise is a good incentive; however, small increment raises often do more harm than good. If you're going to give a raise, make it reasonably significant. Regrettably, many projects involve more investment of stress than they do of physical labor. There is no reason for this; however, you must plan for it. Regrettably, few general contractors provide any measure of comfort for their distressed workers, who will eventually succumb to burnout. They are expected to sink or swim: dysfunctional projects tend to be the rule, not the exception.

Other than work-load pressure, never underestimate the effect that a nervous supervisor, or micromanaging general contractor can have on morale. Just about any project under siege will feature such a stressed-out individual. Needless to say, supervisors who are continually stressed are a chronic inhibition to worker contentment. In fact, more work relationships are probably terminated due to this disharmony, than they are due to overwork complaints. Most men are not afraid of a little hard work; however, if they are repeatedly exposed to someone whose behavior they find objectionable, it is only a matter of time before their performance begins to founder, or they up and leave.

Poor morale stands out, and is readily discernible in the workers' faces and mannerisms, as it is in the work itself. There's nothing the men like to do better than to sit around complaining to one another about the project, and their employer or supervisor. If you ask them, they will likely tell you that all of the contractor's projects resemble this one. You can take that with a grain of salt, as the worker no doubt contributed to the demise of past projects, but the comment regarding the nature of past projects is likely to be accurate. When you observe that complaining and mockery are a daily topic of conversation among the men, understand that these attitudes don't emerge from a vacuum. They are the result of prolonged negative experiences. On a stressed-out project, anxiety is understandable. If the men arrive at the site with this attitude at day one, or succumb to it in the early phase of a project, take this as an ill portent. They are merely waiting for the other shoe to drop. Thus, if possible, endeavor to take a measure of the prevailing wind on a project as you pass through it. Projects wear their heart on their sleeve, and you will take note of it.

If only clients understood this simple psychology, for they often are the source of this angst, which filters down through the project team. This will be discussed in the next chapter as well.

The Single Proprietor Syndrome

This discussion takes place in this section of the text because it is a variant of the topic "crisis and siege management." Projects will always have problems, be high pressure, and can at times, resemble a war zone. Generally, there is cause and effect reasoning invoked to warrant emergency level operations; however, for some, it can be part of one's quotidian; that is, for some managers, it is their *modus operandi*, and they could not function otherwise. To wit, we discuss the small company single proprietor general contractor. As of 1997, there were 57,400 self-employed general contractors, and 141,200 specialty contractors[8] (Table 8.1.) What you can say about them can be applied to almost any industry, not just construction. However, because high-end residential construction is so complex, high stress, and requires so many different ingredients, individuals and subcontractors, and the like, I believe that there is a proclivity to dysfunction when one person asserts too much control, or fails to relinquish it when he should. Managing and building construction projects is a team process, not a monarchy.

Small contractors will micromanage out of habit, or out of necessity. Companies that are too small to maintain a management infrastructure often feature such an individual at the controls. Not to say that all contractors who also act as general managers are unsuccessful; however, it is a rare individual who can function effectively in this dual capacity. Chances are the company's growth will be limited and that may be alright, depending on where the company sets its sights. The challenge is for companies that aspire to a higher level, to adapt from a classic small micromanaged company, to a small version of a "corporate" environment, or one with more than one level of management structure.

The relative to the flawed single proprietor is his avatar—the general manager or senior project manager. If the owner is a nervous Nellie, he will instill his anxiety in his right-hand man, who must fulfill his vision for him. It's easy for a company owner to do this: by constantly raising the bar on "acceptable performance," success will always be unattainable, thus his men will toil endlessly in a Sisyphusian exercise. Even if there is no cause for siege, the affected manager will create the semblance of one. It then no longer matters to people if there is a need for hysteria or not; they are signed up, regardless. Such a general manager must sink or swim according to the prevailing currents of the contractor's whims and caprices. Having little real independence, this arrangement precludes a general manager's fulfillment of his potential (assuming he has any).

No one person can build and manage an entire project. It takes diverse individuals, with different abilities. Nevertheless, there are those out there who can't help but micromanage their projects, refusing to cede control. There are many different reasons for this, and they all have in common the attribute of dysfunction. Some of the more common reasons are as follows:

The general contractor has weak resources, and must 'wear all the hats.' A contractor often knows his team is weak, and fears that when things get overlooked, no one else will pick up the slack. Having a small infrastructure, many single proprietors do not have adequate management on the project, and try to get by with the bare minimum—say a working foreman, while they themselves take on the upper management responsibilities. And there they inevitably find themselves, on the job-site, exactly where they do not belong. Sooner or later, they are overwhelmed, and the stress of the arrangement takes its toll on people's nerves. Some owners will never relinquish control to another, preferring to go down with the ship after toiling years at the helm. This is understandable with small specialty contractors, but in order to survive general contractors need more wherewithal to build their projects.

Many contractors operate outside of their element by taking on work for which they are not prepared to adequately service. If an architect and owner conduct a thorough qualification process, this condition will come as no surprise. Nonetheless, many clients contract with tiny general contractors because their project is cost driven, even though they realize that small contractors often have infrastructural shortcomings. Failing to make the adjustment for using a nonresourceful general contractor, clients get what they pay for. Companies with low overhead, like single proprietorships, are the go-to guys for such projects. Before getting caught in a similar trap, be meticulous and conscientious by ensuring that you are prepared, and have the means, to execute your projects properly. Remember that most quality-oriented residential projects go bad because the contractor was incompetent in one way or another, and could not control the project's fate.

The work is going slowly or is poorly executed. A general contractor may not have the patience or the confidence in his production team's ability to perform. Not being able to think of a legitimate triage program to implement, he feels he must "take the bull by the horns," and the siege approach is engaged. It will not be a happy time for anyone to watch a company owner go through the throes and transmogrifications of an angry, nervous, and baleful micromanager, for it is never pretty. I offer the following recollection of just such an individual:

> He could be described as intense and impassioned, to a fault. In fact, this was his general approach, regardless of context. When he became impassioned (hysterical) he became unglued; at such times he raised his voice, shouting and waiving his arms; his eyes popped out of his head. He repeated himself endlessly, as if repetition could in effect directly induce action. He assaulted his team with sharp, often inappropriate verbal attacks, and pointed accusatory, trapping questions. This individual's behavior precluded his efficiency. His people were not afraid or in awe of him: they only resented him all the more. For this reason, only new hires would agree to work under his authority. Subsequent to that experience, they would never agree to work with him again.

This neurotic individual precluded his efficacy by his poor approach. He was incapable of stating his purpose intelligibly. His message rarely got through because of his inability to transmit it appropriately; however, this doesn't necessarily mean he should be dismissed out of hand. Part of the reason he responded so vehemently could be blamed on latent reactions to years of bad experiences. He was confounded by, and rightly so, the lack of industry and sense of urgency by managers who had worked under him. He had experienced such frustration in his years of that he expected it to continue on all future projects. His case is not uncommon, and is indicative of the communication void between executive level managers and their underlings.

To production members, this atmosphere can resemble a harsh dictator-ship, where one person wields all authority, and insists on monitoring every task, no matter how trivial. Acceleration and out of sequence are the order of the day, and the workers will surely resent it. After all, it probably isn't their fault, the job is late, so why should they be the ones put upon? And they will not abide by such an arrangement; they will shirk their duty or leave at the first opportunity.

Architects and clients will often be mistakenly impressed or distracted by apparent focused and intense efforts. So long as they respond in this way, managers will continue to stage their D&P shows for their clients, much to the chagrin of their personnel. It's bad enough for a project to warrant such atten-tion; however, should it be necessary, a middle manager must be implemented, not the company owner. A company owner micromanaging a work-site is a *bona fide* red flag, if he pays inordinate attention to one project, he's probably neglecting some other need.

The general contractor does not trust his people. He may be loath to admit this to anyone, including himself. He feels he must follow through every prob-lem and approve every step of the process no matter how small or insignificant. This behavior I regard as neurotic, as do I consider the notion that some con-tractors keep workers they don't really approve of around merely as conven-ient scapegoats. Such a person can exacerbate an already problematic project, and also adversely affect morale, as well as professional relationships with other team members. However neurotic, this fear does not evolve in a vacuum. Years of experience with problem individuals will make contractors wary. Because the man power supply side of the industry is so challenged, there may be millions of such individuals. Chronic disappointment makes it hard for some to reestablish a benchmark for acceptable performance criteria—soon a con-tractor will trust no one.

A small-time contractor was running his project manager ragged. He was renovating a crumbling nineteenth century merchant's brownstone in Brooklyn, New York, at the time, for an incompetent homunculus of an architect who con-tinually whined his dissatisfaction in a stringent high-pitch tone. Indeed, the building was in imminent danger of collapse; however, he was oblivious to this fact. Although it was touted as a high-end project, most of the mechanics on the project were non or semiskilled, seldom bathed, and may not have been legal. The company owner had halitosis and was given to anxiety attacks. Although it was a small project, he paged the project manager about 20 times each day just to see what he was doing at the time. Nevertheless, the project manager had to make do. The project manager began identifying some structural prob-lems. A three-storey load-bearing brick wall showed excessive unnatural crack-ing, and the project manager wished to point this fact out to the engineer. After a brief inspection, the engineer ordered crack chasing, or filling of the cracks with grout, a purely cosmetic band-aid approach to a solution. Upon this directive, the project manager fearing safety, refused to enter the building, and would not let the men enter the building until they temporarily shored some of the girders.

Subsequent to that, the project manager indicated that an exterior brick wall supporting one end of the roof was failing; there was little or no mortar left in the brick joints, such that the bricks could all easily be removed by hand. A door needed to be put at this wall; however, no work could continue until an engineer looked at it, and issued a structural detail for repairs—the detail did not involve rocket science. Days went by without the engineer being summoned until the project manager could wait no longer. After some minor shoring, which he did, he could continue the work; however, remedial and change order work would be warranted. No sooner had the first brick been removed from this wall that the architect tried to assign ownership of any and all remedial structural work to the contractor under the tenet that "you touch it, you own it." The owner of the company was petrified by this insinuation and figured judgment day had come. Dripping with sweat and his whole body shaking, he came to the sight and confronted the project manager. In this condition, the owner could not be as reasonable as he may have liked to be, and he became unglued. The project manager did not entertain the discussion and calmly resigned at once.

If a contractor has people working for him who he does not trust, he should do both parties a favor and discharge them, as they are unlikely to leave of their own will until things completely fall apart. Too often such relationships are left to fester, with the contractor continually distrustful of his workers' performances, and an evident mutual feeling of resentment. I marvel at the longevity of some workmen who do nothing but complain about their position, but do nothing to change it, and the employers who allow these soured relationships to languish.

Nature of the Afflicted

Most contractors start out small, and in the beginning, must necessarily over-involve themselves in the day-to-day operations. However, as the company grows, so should they, weaning themselves from activities better delegated to others. Very often the weaning process never takes place, especially if there is no growth, or growth is slow. Invariably this condition will stunt the growth of the company.

The affected single proprietor is not a happy person. He will tend to make those around him edgy and nervous, save for those who must suck up to him. As his condition worsens, he will further immerse himself in his neurosis. At times, he may resemble an insane person. I recall one such character, a contractor whom I worked for reviewed a worksheet of a multiple page spreadsheet, which was just sent to a client. He was absolutely beside himself with the fact that the documents were issued with an inadvertent comma somewhere in the middle of one of the pages, an otherwise blank section. He characterized the mistake by saying people would assume his company was ignorant. While I am a strong advocate of proofreading, I do draw the line at such anality. This same contractor would, as he should, visit a project that was in the feverish closing stage, where the site was extremely congested with men working on critical path tasks; however, his focus was fixated on insignificant work, such as a power outlet that was awaiting substrate in order to be installed, not on things that mattered. Clearly, he was at a loss to prioritize. He did nothing to help the job along when it could have made a difference—too little, too late. Thus, we are talking about *distraction* and errancy of purpose that neurotic managers experience in their relentless pursuit of some as yet undefined ideal, that drives them off-task in the most unsuspecting ways.

The neurotic general contractor is anxious and insecure regarding his own ability to perform, and is terrified of the consequences of failure. This response may be disproportionate to reality. While this may sound like psychobabble—not the stuff of a technical book, it is not. It is a serious business that requires attention, as it is an inhibition to sound judgment. Some people simply don't have the chops; professionally or emotionally, to command a complex construction project. After a while, the response no longer needs an impetus, but has become ingrained into the general contractor's methodology. If left unchecked, the situation will only get worse. Some proprietors will carry on halfcocked for their entire careers. The direction for resolution is simple: find a suitable general manager, seek assistance in working on management skills as well as emotional health, or both. Though the direction for the solution is clear and simple, the undertaking is evidently a formidable task.

Thus, the reason for including discussion of this phenomenon in this chapter is that it belongs here, for all the trappings of the micromanaging owner create the appearance and condition of siege and crisis. The point is, this is wholly unnecessary, in fact, it should be the approach of last resort. Nonetheless, it is commonplace, and deserves our serious consideration. The behavior and actions of an unfettered neurotic dictator can cause a project to resemble a state of desperation, and often, can be a self-fulfilling prophecy. I began this discussion with the single proprietor because he is the one in the best position to control the problems that frequently cause projects to fall into disarray, if, for no other reason, because he is often the instigator of these problems. But he himself must be reasonable and knowledgeable if he is to be effective at a very difficult process—siege management. If he is not, he will preclude all attempts to take corrective measures.

Multiple Project Management and the Harried General Manager

The general manager or production manager is typically the right-hand man of the single proprietor. This is typically a thankless task, prone to long frustrating hours of problem solving, and putting out "fires." It will take years off a person's life. General managers tend to focus on production and contract related issues, and often are devoid of administrative skills. Not that they should be doing paperwork, but that they should attach as much significance to the contract documents as they do the work. At small companies, this person is typically spread so thin that his efficiency is precluded. Often, he has no one to delegate tasks to, and spends an inordinate amount of time doing things that are better suited to administrative or low-level managers. Very small companies often have no sound middle management structure. They may have a general manager trying to manage the work of four project managers, with only a few superintendents to assist him. This indeed is an unwholesome company structure. Just like the misguided single proprietor, look for this person to exhibit the same troublesome characteristics. No doubt his boss's responses rub off on him the same way he drives his men up the wall. Nevertheless, companies with multiple projects need a general manager or senior project manager. He is the one who should make it all come together in the big picture. It is the responsibility of the executive level managers or owner of the company to empower him, and more importantly, ensure that he is happy in his work. If he is unhappy, not only will he do a poor job, but his sentiments will poison the well water for all those beneath him.

A general manager, I knew, a Yale graduate, was extremely talented; however, his approach to facilitating others was so vehement and noxious that he undermined his own efforts. I recall him saying that he felt that I didn't exude or have a sense of urgency regarding a tough project. I replied that I did appreciate the project's needs as much as he did, but we differed in our approaches. He was compelled to yelling and screaming to inspire others, where I felt that cooler heads would prevail, achieving the same ends in a calm manner. As it turned out, his out-of-proportion impassioned approach to this project was the same for any project. He had only one gear, and that was overdrive.

Other Siege Conditions

Tear-out

Tear-out refers to work that has to be redone, having been rejected by the architect, client, or by the contractor. A qualified high-end contractor will generally notice work that is substandard or incorrect before it is completed, and will direct that the work be remediated. In some cases, it isn't the workmanship but the material that is rejected, which may or may not be the responsibility of the contractor. It is an embarrassment to have work rejected, especially when one should have known better.

There are two responses to remediating rejected work: Crack the whip, apologize profusely, and cause general mayhem, so to instill unfettered motivation in the offending party, such that their response is extreme. This may merely be a show put on for the benefit of the client, to acknowledge the grave nature of the offense, and a hypercritical response to it, which is often only affectation. The work will be torn out and reinstalled double time. The emergency approach to remediation does not lend itself well to high-end installations. Observe this tenet, and impress it upon your subcontractors, as they will often rush through work being redone.

Take the rejection as part of the process; regardless of its implications, the approach to remediation will have no effect on what has already been done. Therefore, it serves no purpose to take egregious action. The pace of the corrective work should be expedited without once again compromising quality. Instruct the subcontractor in private. They likely will be unhappy at the prospect of redoing the work—a sentiment best kept under wraps, that is, avoid exposing this to the client if possible.

Nagging neighbors

Nagging neighbors can be a vast understatement for what can sometimes be described as hysterical or militant behavior. They are an ever-present concern on multiple dwelling projects, and can potentially thwart your mission. A general contractor has little control over neighbors' reactions, but he must do diligence in minimizing the likelihood of offense. Complaints regarding noise, dirt, dust, fumes, vibration, hours of operation, decorum, and a host of other trespasses come with the territory, especially in apartment buildings, where everyone lives closely together. These are "quality of life complaints," and are mostly indigenous to urban residential areas. Businesses and commercial concerns are much less squeamish, and won't make nearly as much trouble. They respect the need to conduct business, and generally can empathize. Complaints may or may not be legitimate. Suffice it to say, as part of a high-end project delivery, legitimate complaints should be the exception, as top contractors are extra careful not to make easily avoidable mistakes that could sully their image.

Sometimes complaints are addressed to the client, sometimes to the contractor, and sometimes to a building manager. Other times, police or building inspectors are summoned. As long as you go about your business in accordance with the contract, the alteration agreement—if there is one, do your best to mollify complainants and keep your nose clean with officials you won't have too many worries. However, if you do give someone looking for a reason to shut your job down, they will find it. Many contractors are unscrupulous in their operations and their trespasses are the cause for most complaints. However, there will always be a smattering of neurotics, hysterics, malcontents, and jealous types who feel their quality of life is being threatened by a project. They will complain more vehemently than a rational person. They can become obsessed with the idea of shutting the project down. Theirs is an obsessively self-righteous moral crusade. While their complaint may or may not have merit, their behavior should not be taken seriously or personally. The exception is when they become militant:

A tenant living below a project in an apartment building was disenchanted with the din of construction above. While the owner had every right to conduct his project, she felt the work was an egregious trespass of her personal space. She complained to no avail to every agency she could think of. When these efforts failed, she took measures into her own hands. When a scaffold was erected and fastened to the building, she produced a hammer with which she attempted to bang loose the scaffold bracing from the third storey fire escape. When protective netting was applied around the scaffold she viciously slashed through it with a box knife. When these efforts failed to stop the work, she forced her way into the site and insisted that work stop. She tried to physically bar workers from entering the building, in one instance, sandwiching a worker's thigh between a door leaf and frame. While she was good for laughs, she had to be taken seriously because she was putting the men in danger. When all attempts at mollification failed, the owner paid her $10,000 to keep quiet. Such a tenant in a high-rent Co-op can perhaps persuade the Co-op board to shut the project down, based on their complaints. Co-op boards have their own sovereign bylaws—some of them overly stringent, sort of like a mini-dictatorship. Under the banner of these bylaws, they can wield ultimate power over all contractors who enter their building, without fear of retribution. Some of these Co-ops are so malevolent that they make doing work in the building next to impossible. Savvy contractors know these buildings and tend to avoid them, or charge a premium to work in them.

The other menace to be vigilant of is the freeload grifter; a neighbor who frivolously claims that damages have been to his property as a result of your nearby or adjacent construction operations. Typically, they are nickel and dimers, who just want to get a little something for nothing. They generally don't ask for too much, as a large claim might substantiate a proper investigation by an insurance adjuster that might evidence a fraud. If a complaint is made, it should be investigated by the contractor, who having diligently photographed the neighbor's property, can attest to the veracity of the complaint. If it is legitimate, he should offer to repair it, free of charge. He might even make a new friend or prospective client in this way. If he or his insurance company is refused access to verify the damage, one can be almost certain the complaint was baseless. In such instances, a letter from their attorney will follow the complaint.

Punch-out list

Punch-out or punch list should refer to minor tweaking to work that is already installed, or work that has a very short installation window. A more formal definition states that "the word *punch list* should be reserved for a list of items of work that have actually been performed, but require some *small* degree of adjustment or correction in order to meet the standard of quality specified in a contract."[9] Contractors are aware of these connotations, yet continually allow the meaning of the term punch list to degenerate. Thus, punch lists seem to be getting longer and longer. Perhaps this is because project durations keep getting shorter. Punch lists often have work on them that should have been complete, or more advanced before they became a legitimate punch list item. If the duration between substantial completion and final completion exceeds 30 days, the punch list almost surely includes base-contract work. There is often a great amount of pressure to complete the list, which can be daunting. It is approached from a siege mentality, and that is why it is included in this chapter. It was discussed in the form of a natural progression in Chap. 4, as were strategies to keep the list as short as possible. Often, a client is in the process of moving in, or is already moved in, before the punch list is complete. Worse, he may not be able to move in until the list is complete.

In defense of beleaguered contractors, many punch lists are ridden with so much change order work that is in various stages of completion, that theoretically, the project could go on forever. As long as the punch list thrives, the contractor won't receive his final payment. Technically speaking, if a schedule extension was not requested for such work, a contractor has himself to blame. But schedule extensions are virtually unheard of for residential projects. Even if the situation warrants, contractors feel that it would be a waste of time to bother asking. Nevertheless, there are some strategies to control the effect of change order work on punch lists, as well as ways to get final payment sooner:

If change order work is likely to cause the schedule to be extended, make this fact known to the owner. He won't grant a schedule extension, but you can insist that payment for *punch-list change order work* is separate from the *base-contract punch-list,* i.e., the change order punch list must not affect base-contract progress payments.

If a schedule extension is necessary to accommodate change order work, but not granted, it follows that compression will be necessary to fit the work into the schedule. In that case, an expediting charge should be negotiated.

When the contract is negotiated, insist that a clause is included which states that retainage must be indexed to the value of the remaining work to be completed.

In any case, the above terms must be negotiated at the time when the change order is requested. It is futile to negotiate after the fact.

Punch-list tasks sometimes have an inordinately high proportion of general conditions to facilitate the change work, which is one incentive to minimize changes in the work. Think of it this way: if you were asked to fabricate ten doorjambs of equal dimensions, you would set up a system of production, and move onto the business of making them. The set-up and mobilization cost for the production system will remain the same, no matter how many jambs you fabricate; however, it would not be worth your while to set up such systems in order to fabricate one additional doorjamb. If it were a change order, you would want to pass on the set-up costs of the second production run (one jamb) to the client.

Out-of-sequence, delayed, and other dysfunctional projects will typically have a large punch list, including tasks that should have been done as part of the base contract. Because they were set aside in order for prioritized tasks to take place, they will later resurface as punch list tasks that have to be revisited. Other tasks that frequently appear on punch lists that shouldn't are:

- Change order tasks that could not have been completed within the production schedule. Not uncommonly, a contractor has done his best to minimize the punch list only to have it sabotaged by a smattering of late-issue change orders. Payment for such work should not fall under the same criteria as base contract work.

- Work that has been signed off on (approved).

- Any work driving substantial completion.

- Work other than cosmetic, remedial, adjusting, monitoring, and the like.

- Work that is less than 90% complete. Any such work is considered unfinished, as opposed to needing a minor adjustment.

Punch-list work is often done haphazardly, with little planning, and the handicap of working in less than ideal conditions. Because the work is so problematic, a project manager should have a strategy to minimize the size and difficulty of the punch list before it is issued. The project manager should generate the punch list before the architect issues his own, and issue it to the architect for comment, who can then either embellish it, or create his own. By generating his own punch list, the project manager stays one step ahead of the game, instead of waiting in dread anticipation of an architect's punch list that he may be embarrassed by. There are some general strategies that a project manager can invoke to keep his punch lists to a minimum:

- Create a bill of assemblies, or checklist of tasks, that keeps track of which work is complete, and which isn't. The tasks are crossed out as they are completed. If the estimator has bid the work in this way, the project manager can utilize the same worksheet or spreadsheet.

- Emphasize to the production team the notion that installations must be 100% before the work will be approved.

- Start the list early, beginning with unfinished tasks, although they wouldn't be considered punch-list tasks, they are the most subject to remaining incomplete.

- Hold a meeting with the architect for the purposes of forming a joint approach to the creation of the punch list. This will reduce the potential for future argument over its composition.

- Require that a final punch list be issued by a certain date, after which additional entries for approved work are not allowable. There's nothing more contemptible than a punch list that won't die. According to what some architects and clients believe is legitimate punch list execution, theoretically the punch list would never be completed, and accordingly, the contractor would never receive final payment.

One small company's solution to maintenance and punch-list work was as follows:

The company, like many others, was trying to streamline its approach to servicing maintenance and punch-list operations, which were creating a logistics nightmare, and costing them money. Realizing that certain tasks required only one or two individuals to perform, they wondered: "wouldn't it be nice to consolidate such tasks in one department or individual?" Of course, one person can't do everything, but they did have an individual who went from job to job in order to either complete or facilitate these operations. He was more or less a jack-of-all-trades; at least insofar as fine finish work was concerned, and he was therefore able to complete a good deal of problematic scope. He would travel from job to job, bringing with him the tools and materials that he would need. For work he couldn't do himself, or needed a particular subcontractor, he would coordinate that work as well.

As yet, our discussion of siege operations has focused on projects where the siege operations are the general *modus operandi* of many builders. Given that, most contractors would seemingly have their hands full. We must now consider incidental and specific crises—the kind that put life and limb at peril, and drive lawsuits and insurance premiums to record highs. A company on the ropes may be ill-prepared to handle such incidents.

Emergencies

Construction projects are a key contributor to the overall number of work related injuries. This fact is reflected in the skyrocketing rate of worker's compensation insurance rates. Many claims happen on the job, for example, a fall from a ladder, or a laceration. While these may sound like minor instances, one has to be prepared for them, and also for more serious occasions. Of course, safety should be the first priority of any project. Nevertheless, accidents happen. A strong team leader must be prepared to meet the challenge of dealing with accidents, and many other problems, such as worker comportment, theft, and conflict. A good measure of mettle is an important asset for a team leader, as is the ability to stay calm under duress.

In addition to an efficient safety plan, there are a host of other crises to be ready for. A 1996 survey of heavy-highway contractors shows some interesting results, although some of the crises mentioned were germane only to that type of work (italicized). The nature of these crises, in order of frequency, was:

1. On-the-job accident requiring hospitalization
2. *Damage to utility lines*
3. Contractual disputes with client resulting in litigation
4. Equipment failure
5. On-the-job-fatality
6. *Highway accident*
7. Theft/embezzlement
8. Noise/dust pollution
9. Sexual harassment
10. Labor strike/work stoppage
11. Complaints to the media
12. Fire explosion
13. Community/environmental protests
14. Environmental violations
15. Structural/subsidence collapse
16. Merger/acquisition

17. Workforce violence

18. Serious cash-flow problems

19. Sabotage

20. Loss of key supplier

21. Bomb threats

22. Loss of bonding capability

23. Owner or key employee dies

24. Scandal involving top management

25. Sexual discrimination

26. Long-term structural problems

27. Bid-rigging accusations[10]

The contractors surveyed indicated that they experienced about five such crises over the past 3-year period. Although 41% responded that they had in place a crisis management program, 59% felt that their ability to handle a crisis was "good to excellent."[11] Such is the fallacy of the industry's self-examination. The propensity of such crises has a negative effect on contractors' bottom-line, employee productivity, and reputation, such that 67% employ a fulltime safety manager. It is rare for any residential contractor not working on a large scale to have a safety manager.

As claims against contractors continue to increase, the costs to the industry will also escalate. However, there is incentive for any party to the contract to minimize workplace liabilities; not only can lawsuits be brought against owners by construction workers injured on the job, but courts are beginning to allow for owners to sue their architects for contract and common-law indemnification in such instances.[12]

Notes

Preventable problem projects

- Underbid projects
- Underfinanced projects
- Understaffed or inappropriately staffed projects
- Underdesigned projects
- Union projects
- Aggressively scheduled projects
- Overdesigned and projects with customizations
- Projects with difficult architects and clients
- Changeable design projects

Endnotes

1. *The Blue Book of Building and Construction* is an annual national, regional, and local directory of contractors and suppliers.
2. In fact, a contractor can expose himself to liabilities for which his insurer will not indemnify him, especially, as regards MEPs, which require filed design documents and controlled sign-offs.
3. Westin T. Hester, John A. Kuprenas, & P.C. Chang, *Construction Changes and Change Orders: Their Magnitude and Impact*, Construction Industry Institute Source Document 66, 35 (Oct. 1991).
4. The Business Roundtable, Scheduled Overtime Effect on Overtime Projects: Report C2 (1980) 10.
5. *ibid* 12.
6. Luria Bros, & Co. v. United States, 369 F.2d 701 (Ct. Cl. 1966).
7. Wunderlich Contracting Co. v. United States, 351 F.2d 956 (Ct. Cl. 1965).
8. Joint Center for Housing Studies of Harvard University, *Remodeling Homes for Changing Households* (2001) 16.
9. Andrew M. Civitello, Jr., *Complete Contracting: A–Z Guide to Controlling Projects* (New York: McGraw-Hill: 1997) 283.
10. Janine Reid, "Research Shows Increase in Crisis Planning," *Construction Business Review*, 2002.
11. *ibid*.
12. Deyo v. County of Broome, 638 NYS 2d 802 (A.D. 1996).

Resolving Conflicts: The Art of Negotiation and Survival

There are four types of players:
Those who play the game,
Those who know the game, but don't know the
score,
Those who think they know the game,
And those who don't want to know the game or the
score.[1]

The context of the above quote refers to some basic ethical positions that can be taken by industry professionals in regards to negotiating in the long and short term. The first three terms require no comment other than they appear to be unacceptable. It follows that the last term would be the ethical antithesis to the first three, which it is. Although you want to have a respectable code of ethics, you won't survive if you don't "play the game," because playing the game is a requisite of working in the construction industry.

How do I define playing the game? By adopting some strategies to maneuver an enigmatic and confounding system that doesn't respond to value structures, which is as follows:

Right and wrong. The meaning of right and wrong doesn't have the same ramifications in resolving conflict in the construction industry, as it does in personal relationships. You can lead an ethical existence by strictly adhering to a positive value system, but this attribute is almost irrelevant in the construction industry, and will not yield the same measure of excess; chiefly, because the industry has no concern with ethics, only with getting things done.

Observe quid pro quo as a fundamental negotiating tool. Give and take has everything to do with maintaining a level of parity in contractual as well as personal relationships.

Offer solutions, not problems. If you don't have a solution, don't address the problem without having at least a sense of direction where the solution may lie. The exceptions are problems that you are directly responsible for. For example, if you identify a problem and relate it to the responsible party, then you have done your job. You may follow up on the problem as well. However, if the problem is not addressed by the responsible party, you probably don't want to force the issue, as this seldom induces action, and more often than not, tends to make people feel pressured. You want to be proactive, but not at the cost of ostracizing yourself. In other words, don't try to solve other people's problems for them unless they ask you to, and know when to back off pursuing an issue, especially a volatile one.

Don't become involved in negotiations for which you are not in a position to offer terms. Negotiation is treacherous terrain, and best left to those directly accountable.

Learn to appreciate the nuances of industry relationships. There are subtleties that you must be aware of for each relationship on each project, and they will always be variable. General protocols therefore must not be used as knee-jerk solutions. For example:

A mechanic was underperforming on a project. He issued no duct shop drawings, undermanned the site, and the quality of his work was substandard. On several occasions, the superintendent notified his project manager of the problem, which was affecting other elements of the project. Despite his warnings, no action was taken. The superintendent knew that this particular contractor was a favorite of the general contractor, and for that reason, stopped shy of being more directly aggressive in confronting the contractor, such as he might be for a contractor held in less esteem; problems with the same ramifications are treated differently dependant on the parties involved. He pulled his punches because he sensed that the general contractor would resent him leaning on a pet contractor, even if that seemed to be the right thing to do. Although the contractor should have been given an ultimatum, he was not, and the superintendent could only stand by and watch, helplessly.

Another common example is the architect who isn't issuing design documentation according to the general contractor's needs. The superintendent will want to be aggressive in requesting information from an unresponsive architect; however, the general contractor would regard this position as self-defeating in the long run: if he ostracizes the architect on this project with forceful requests for information, he may jeopardize his relationship with the architect, who may be a source of work he is loath to part with. The superintendent would be doing his job; however, his goals are different than his boss'—he wants to build the project. His boss wants to build the project, and remain in good standing with his architect. Therein a conflict of interest for the diligent superintendent: his hands are tied.

The art of being wise is the art of knowing what to overlook.
      WILLIAM JAMES

Despite what some people might think, building isn't the crux of residential construction problems: conflict is. If there were no conflicts building would move right along, virtually unimpeded; theoretically. Conflicts, by their nature, impede the flow of work. Indeed, time on-task can seem small compared to the time spent arguing and debating. Conflicts have such a debilitating effect on the industry as a whole that extensive arbitration clauses are now built in to the AIA contracts. The Empire State Building was built in 18 months. That same project built today might take 4 or 5 years, so to allow time for resolving conflicts and processing information. At the center of most disputes is money; however, personal conflict plays a surprisingly important and underestimated role. Regardless, only fiduciary conflicts are relevant to the contract. There are endless manifestations of money disputes:

- Late payments
- Underpayments
- Overcharges
- Undervaluation
- Negative cash flow
- Schedule delays
- Overhead
- Liquidated damages
- General conditions
- Contingencies
- Fees

The list goes on . . .

The list of particular factors driving these conflicts is exponential; however, with a little forethought many of them can be avoided. Understanding the nature of the different kinds of disputes, and having a plan to negotiate or obviate the need for them is also crucial. Savvy contractors will have a conflict prevention program in place: they will be fluent in the language of negotiation, and generally will avoid the mistakes that their lesser competitors make. This does not mean having an attorney on the payroll or retainer; however, some companies are so trouble prone that they keep their attorney fairly busy. Others will plunge headlong into the project without any consideration of or preparation for conflict: either overly optimistic, or ignorant of the nature of the business.

There are an infinite number of potential conflicts that are likely to arise on your projects. Some of them you can control; others, you cannot. However, there are steps you can take to minimize the most common and debilitating problems: be clear and comprehensive in your proposal; define what you are building and how long it will take you to do it in such a way as to leave no room for interpretation. By the same token, be specific in indicating what work is *not* included in your proposal. This process starts at the bidding stage as we discussed in Chap. 2. It is helpful to identify issues that have potential to become troublesome, and to clarify them with your client even if they are already mentioned in your proposal. With due diligence, this alone will constitute a substantial measure of prevention.

The same holds true with your subcontractors, even more so: the subcontracts are merely extensions of the prime contract.[2] The difference is that the prime contract is all-inclusive for the project. If a subcontractor has made an error or omission, he may be liable to the contractor; however, ultimately, the prime contractor is liable to the client for the whole project, and all subcontractors referenced in "the work." Just as your due diligence with the prime contract will pay off, so it shall with your subcontracts. If your estimator has done a thorough qualification process, and conducted a comprehensive bid, this will have been done for you.

No matter how proactive you are, you will still experience your share of conflicts with some or all of the project team members, and ancillary personnel. In addition to the client, design team, and subcontractors, you may have to deal with building managers, building architects and engineers, building superintendents, business managers, public agency inspectors, and many others. Any one of them can create problems for the project, such as shutting the project down, issuing summons for violations, mandating tear-out work, picketing the job, and so forth. For every project you must be aware of all the people connected with it, and establish a protocol for interacting with each of them. You must also plan for unexpected interferences, such as a visit from a business manager, or Occupational Safety and Health Administration (OSHA) inspector.

Common sense dictates that it would be unwise to point out to a client everything that could possibly go wrong on a project, for fear this might betray a lack of confidence, pessimism, or prelude to explaining away future ineptitudes. In theory it is sound prevention, but in practice, it will only prove unsettling for the client. However, the alternative, saying nothing, is less appealing, especially when it can be demonstrated that a given conflict could have been avoided had it been discussed sooner. For example, there is a big difference between a conflict which you identified as a potential problem, than there is for a conflict which you should have identified as a potential problem, or should have known better. At least in the former circumstance you identified the potential conflict early on, and were on the look out for it. Regardless of whether they want to hear it or not, go on record. Don't call a war-room meeting: simply issue the list to the architect each month as a matter of record, and highlight any item that needs to be discussed. This sort of diligence is standard for the efficient construction manager, and it should be for general contractors as well.

Not surprisingly, clients are often to blame for driving and perpetuating conflicts. The understanding of this concept is the key to prevention programs. The early implementation of a strategy begins with establishing a positive relationship with the job team; specifically, the architect, subcontractors, and the owner, as they will be the source of most conflicts. It is important to involve the client and architect early in your prevention plan, *before* bad things happen, not *after*, when they will not want to hear it; again, be proactive instead of reactive.

Although we will discuss avoiding conflict, a conflict prevention program pertains to the job team as a whole. The plan should provide as follows:

- Identify existing program conflicts
- Identify known *potential* program conflicts
- Identify potential schedule conflicts: your schedule will report this for you starting with critical tasks, down through tasks with minimum float
- Identify *possible*[3] conflicts
- Define the process by which potential or actual conflicts are identified, or how one party will advise the rest of the job team. For example, memos may be standardized or job meeting time set aside
- Identify a procedure for addressing potential conflicts: it should include the means to assign accountability, target date for resolution, and follow-up measures

Having a conflict prevention plan in place won't keep people from getting overly anxious when conflicts do arise, but it should decrease the incidence of conflict, precoordinate responses to conflicts, and result in a more controlled approach to remediation. In addition to these benefits a conflict prevention program:

- Should result in team members being more prepared to resolve conflicts that do arise
- Should encourage a team approach to resolving conflicts, as opposed to self-preservation tactics
- Should result in fewer siege operations
- Should improve your approach to managing projects, and your clientele's opinion of your approach
- Should decrease the likelihood of ugly surprises, and the lesser appealing responses to them

The majority of the remainder of conflicts not directly related to money is performance, behavior, and innuendo related. It seems ludicrous that conditions having nothing to do with the work or the contract could wreak such havoc upon a project, yet, this not only happens, but it does so on a large scale. This tenet requires investigation:

Performance. Residential owners and architects will be hypersensitive to how you and your team perform your role, as they will use this information to help form their perception of you and your company. If you allow it, the focus can be drawn away from *what* you do, to *how* you do it. In your client's eyes, their perception of your performance will influence and often jaundice the outcome—your work will cease to be judged on its own merits. If you meet the contract requirements of what you must do, your client's perception of how you do it should not matter.

I remember when I was a carpenter how I diligently plied my trade. I only desired a day's work for a day's wages. What frustrated me was the fact that it seemed that it was never enough that I only do my job; there were always supplementary demands put upon me for which I was not compensated: things such as tolerating abusive behavior, language, and criticism, and sucking up to people, which had nothing to do with my performance. I began to see this phenomenon affect colleagues, and I watched their uncomfortable responses. I wondered, and I still do to this day: when did the aggregate of a worker's output become predicated on matters unrelated to the work itself that is, when did the measure of production verge away from discernible quantity and quality to subjective perceptions complicated by innuendo?

And it is so in the relationship of the residential contractor to owner—it is not enough that the contractor merely perform his duties to be successful, but he must satisfy demands and requirements unnecessarily thrust upon him, often which have nothing to do with the work. Not to realize and accommodate this phenomenon is to guaranty that you will be frustrated and disappointed. Residential clients tend to be oblivious to the need for, and benefit of, mutual respect, often assuming the role of master and commander. This attitude betrays an unwillingness to "play ball," and eventually may draw out sensitivity on the contractor's part, as he may feel disrespected. It would be interesting to graph responses over the course of a project; invariably, mutual opinions would depreciate considerably over time, depending on how the project is doing. Residential projects can resemble bad marriages—they start out with the best intentions, but invariably go downhill from there. The process can be an allegorical *cinema verite* for the owner: the setting is his home, he is the parent, and you are the reactive, troubled adolescent . . . —this path continues to uncharted territory best left as such. One must hold the expectation of conflict as being inevitable, and plan for it as best he can. You won't stop it from happening, but then you won't be caught unawares.

Behavior. Furthering the marriage metaphor, over time, your client will begin to respond to you according to their perception of your behavior. Think of the aphorism "the honeymoon is over"—just like newlyweds, you and your client may get on each others' nerves. Hostility and resentment may be manifested as predicates of future responses, that is, people's feelings may skew their good reason—steer them in the wrong direction, or make it impossible for them to reasonably assess your performance.

Innuendo. In this sense, innuendo refers to any extraneous behavior or response, especially those irrelevant to the project. People will get angry, hurt, frustrated, and a host of other maladies over the course of a project.

These are natural responses to stress. However, as anxiety increases, inappropriate responses begin to surface. These are innuendo. Such responses can truly resemble madness. Any unglued individual is subject to these responses, however, only those without discipline will succumb to them.

In addition to practical business experience, and a conflict prevention program it helps to have a basic understanding of human nature and especially behavioral *responses under duress*, in order to facilitate your client management program, which should commence with your first interview with the client.

Sizing Up Process

"First impressions are everything." While this is a simplistic observation, it does expose a common flaw of human nature. What also can be gleaned from the implications of this statement is that human behavior and responses tend to be unpredictable and often irrational. The first glimpse of you and first words out of your mouth in the presence of your client will be scrutinized more acutely than any other interaction you will have with your client, whether he realizes it or not. This first interaction will likely be your introduction to the client, your first meeting with him. The remainder of the meeting will also be a highly scrutinized performance.

By the same token, you will be sizing up your prospective client. Just as it is for him, this first meeting will be very telling for you. You will want to be keenly aware of his responses and mannerisms, and especially aware of your own. If you are a sharp observer, you will note important features, such as what the client's priorities are, what he likes and doesn't like, what his general disposition is, and so forth. This information can be very useful to you throughout the contract process. Just as I have said "no two projects are exactly alike," the same holds true for each client. Of course, you and your client will be on your best behavior for the occasion, and a lot of the over gratuitousness will quickly dissipate over time. Use your good sense in sorting out what is sincere and what is affectation. And be careful not to be over gratuitous yourself, lest you should be considered a phony. Remember, it is OK for the client to put on airs, but you will be suspect if you do so yourself.

Just as in any working relationship, if the respective parties like each other on a personal level, things will go more smoothly—conflicts will be easier to resolve. However, sometimes, dislike cannot be helped. It may be based on a subconscious or other uncontrollable level. These natural responses often surface upon first sight. There is not much you can do to alter this. Dislike, if it is evident, tends to increase with time, if not checked. However, you or your client may not like each other—the feeling is mutual. It's not the end of the world, but this condition will be a strong determinant governing your interaction with the client, and *vice versa*. Whatever the case, you must make a conscious effort to bring about whatever level of approval is possible, even if it means appointing another individual to interface with the client.

Common Ground

Like men and women, it seems as if contractors and clients are from different planets—they couldn't be more different. This is true especially in residential construction, where, unlike many other construction sectors, clients tend to be uneducated in the field. Smart clients realize this dichotomy, and take pains to bridge the gap by either educating themselves, or bonding with the contractor, because they understand that having some rapport with their contractor can make things go more smoothly. Nowhere does the language barrier become more apparent than in the negotiating and conflict resolution process. Seldom will both parties walk away from the bargaining table feeling satisfied. However, a little empathy and understanding can make a lot of headway in closing communication barriers. I recall a trip to France some years ago. We planned to stop in Rouens for two nights. After the first day we realized that we had seen all we wanted to, and decided to move on after just one night. However, having reserved a room for two nights, the hotel owner insisted he was within his rights to charge us for both nights, whether we stayed or not. He was as obstinate in his position, as we were determined to get our money back. I decided to negotiate on his terms. Using my limited French vocabulary, I quickly paraphrased to him what the problem was, and that if he was agreeable we would split the difference with him. He immediately changed his tune, almost became pleasant, and made the concession.

Client Psychology

December 1
Glory be! Bill Cole says the bank and its lawyers
are almost ready for the closing. I suppose this
means we're going to get our money at last. We're
pretty far behind with all of Mr. Retch's
requisitions and I certainly hope it's going to
improve his disposition when this money business
gets cleared up. All Jim has to do now, apparently,
is give the title lawyers $500 "in escrow" in case
anything goes wrong with those beastly "waivers
of lien" from those filthy subcontractors. Jim
turned purple at the idea of giving Barratry,
Lynch another $500, but there was nothing for
him to do but write out a check just the same. Five
toilets arrived today and they're lying all around
the field. They look unspeakably vulgar.
    Eric Hodgins,' from Mr. Blandings
        Builds His Dream House

One of the most difficult assignments for the residential general contractor is client maintenance, or keeping the client happy. There is a whole set of dynamics at work that must be observed. As I have said, seldom does it suffice to merely "do a good job." Sometimes, the caliber of the general contractor's relationship with the client is not even connected to the success of the project. The project may be very successful, yet because the client does not get on well with the general contractor; it would appear, at least on a personal level, that the project is dysfunctional. It's no small wonder clients bring their reservations to the project considering the industry's well-tarnished image. Nowadays, contractors have to live down the reputation of their predecessors before they can gain the trust of their clients. Contractors are presumed guilty until proven innocent.

I recall a project where the architect was sponsoring one of the general contractors bidding the project; in fact, he wanted him in the worst way, because he felt that the favored contractor was ill suited to the project. Although his contractor's bid and schedule were acceptable, the contractor eventually lost the project—he lost it because of his personality and inability to relate to the client during preconstruction meetings. Indeed, this contractor ostracized the client by fixating on what was not included in his budget. Moreover, the client simply didn't like him.

Oddly enough, a contractor may have a positive relationship with the owner, even though he is otherwise unsuccessful on the project. The architect may find the contractor and his works objectionable, yet the client is smitten with his contractor, regardless. This is a conundrum that states that, at times, the rapport of the client and general contractor is not necessarily proportionate to the general health of the project, and *vice versa*. On the other hand, some clients and architects affect admiration merely to string along a failing contractor until such time as it is convenient for them to terminate him. For example, when all the labor intensive and nonfinish type work is complete, or when the client is sufficiently ahead in the payment schedule. Although the architect may have high standards, often clients can be mollified with a modest concession from the contractor when the architect begins his whining. Conversely, it may not be enough that you only do a good job. Some people will never be happy with you no matter how well you do, and you can then only perform your work to the best of your capabilities. Even if the job looks great, don't expect to be called back for more work, but don't be disappointed—they are doing you a favor. Malcontents make for poor accounts. They simply lack a sensible rubric with which to measure your or anyone else's performance.

Residential clients are notorious for being unknowledgeable in the design and construction process, and typically are not willing pupils, as they fear information may be dispensed according to an agenda. In this way, they are very unlike the rest of the demand-side of the sector, who tend to be more educated in the business: investors, developers and retailers; those who the text has referred to as "constant builders." These people are less prone to the same hypersensitivities and anxieties of their lay counterparts—their skin is thicker. Understand that the residential construction process "hits close to home" in every sense of the word. Residential clients become more emotional than other industry clients. This is because they have a lot of personal investment in their project, which is typically their home. There are a host of services and general conditions related provisions, which you will find are endemic only to residential construction.

You will experience more direct interaction with your residential clients—they will require coddling, and handholding. You will feel induced to mollify them at the slightest show of discomfort. They will need to feel more comfortable in their relationship with you, because they are insecure about the whole process. Your relationship will become more than professional; it will become personal. If you are not prepared to negotiate this fact you will find yourself in trouble. They will expect provisions that are not typical of other sectors, for example, they may insist on an inordinately high level of cleanliness and order about the site. They may want to see fifteen different paint colors that more or less look the same. They may not allow smoking, and sometimes, not allow eating. They may be squeamish of swearing, radio playing, and some of your workers' conduct. The attack can be two-pronged when a husband and wife seem to disagree on everything, which is quite often.

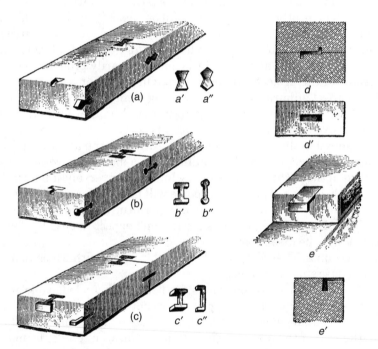

Dowels joggles cramps
The methods of tying or linking stones together by means of stone or metal are various, and as an adjunct to, or sometimes even in the absence of mortar, have been practiced for ages. Theoretically, blocks of stone used in the construction of buildings should, when their beds are level and their faces vertical, preserve their position, from the fact of superposition in obedience to the simple laws of gravitation, without a binding medium between them, such as mortar or mechanical devices. In Fig. 18 several forms of cramps are shown: *a'*, *a"* represent cramps which are made of a tough stone, and at *b*, *c*, *d*, and *e*, the forms shown are usually made of metal, and for this reason, they are not made as large as stone cramps. At *d* and *e* are shown how the stones are cut to receive the cramp.
A Treatise on Architecture and Building Construction, Vol. V (Scranton: The Colliery Engineer Co., 1899).

Some projects require that you work while the owner is still living in the space, or has furnishings stored in the working space. Working alongside the clients as they try to live in the space is extremely problematic, and should only be recommended when both the client and the contractor are familiar and experienced with such arrangements. The worst-case scenario is when the client moves in before the project is complete. It may happen at the most critical time of the project, that is, closeout, and can make life difficult. If the client has furnishings on the site, they must be protected from damage. They will be hypersensitive to the treatment of their property, and will deem any trespass of it as a personal affront. If a client has no other choice but to congest the space, then there isn't much you can do about it; however, the line should be drawn when performance is compromised due to owner created congestion. Often, personal effects are stored in boxes and such until the project is completed. The contractor may become a *de facto* moving company—moving boxes and furnishings from room to room so to free up work areas. This sort of undertaking can complicate logistics and use up a surprising chunk of clocktime. If the client insists on congesting the site with stored property, or moving in early, he should be encouraged to do so only as a last resort. As part of the contract requirement he must provide access to the work site; if he is to blame for site congestion, he owns the liability of not providing ample access.

Clients will show their discomfort in a variety of ways, the most common being anger. Anger is something many people use as a leverage tool, and in managing their anxiety, or situations that are generating anxiety, that is, it can be thought of as a "security operation," where anger is the antidote to anxiety.

> This comes about because anger is much more pleasant to experience than anxiety. The brute facts are that it is much more comfortable to feel angry than anxious. Admitting that neither is too delightful, there is everything in favor of anger. Anger . . . often makes things worse in the long run, but there is a curious feeling of power when one is angry. In other words, the expressive pattern of anger tends to drive things away. Not only is anxiety thus avoided, but the initial index of its presence fades from observation . . . [4]

This means that the condition which generated the anxiety becomes obfuscated by the presence of anger, which now becomes the working problem. However, if you can subdue the angry party into rationality, it will quickly become apparent that their hostility was subsidizing their point of view. Without hostility, their contentions suddenly become unconvincing. Unfortunately, this is invariably a futile and thankless task—few irate clients can see to reason.

There are three critical observations of hostile behavior that affect client-contractor relations, all of which Harry Sullivan alludes to above:

- That there is some degree of pleasure to be gained by an angry response
- That the pleasurable angry response drives away an unpleasant feeling—anxiety
- That the feeling of power experienced through the angry response brings with it a feeling of being able to control a situation

This last consideration may be deliberate—a client believes a show of anger will influence others to rollover. When you think about it, an infant uses the same methodology. However, although you must be on your guard for an angry client, you must be equally vigilant in controlling your own responses; for although you are more experienced in your work than your client, you are subject to the same frailties of human nature.

The worst thing you can do is to respond in kind to hostile behavior. Such a response plays into the whole manipulative scheme of distracting attention away from the real issues, and will undermine your arguments. For example, if the client can draw you out into a hostile argument, he can then demonstrate that you are "unreasonable" by example of your behavior. If you can be perceived as unreasonable, your credibility can then become suspect. There is also tacit understanding that you work *for* the client, as opposed to the intended *quid pro quo* dynamic of a mutual contract, wherein rights are distributed equitably. This is a handicap that contractors have willingly carried on since time eternal. It is an extension of the hackneyed adage "the customer is always right." Although the client may be unconscious of his methodology, he is no less forceful in his vying for control. Understanding these emotional responses and forming constructive strategies to negotiate them will make you a more successful client manager.

You cannot treat your residential clients as you would your commercial clients. Underestimating a residential client's personal investment in a project is a common pitfall for contractors, and frequently leads to conflict. If residential work is your bread and butter, you will have an advantage over a competitor who specializes in another sector, who may be trying to cross over. These cross-over contractors don't understand the real nuances of servicing residential clients. Unfortunately, this lack of understanding in no way inhibits their attempts to pursue work out of their element.

Account Manager: Good Cop/Bad Cop

Because your rapport with the client is critical, in addition to doing a good job, you hope to stay on good terms. Often doing a good job isn't enough, especially if it is late, and overbudget. To get along as a general contractor, you should have an ability to get on with people in general, especially in business relationships, where things tend to get dicey. It helps to be affable; in fact, some get pretty far on charisma alone; however, this tends to be a temporary circumstance, especially if things don't pan out. There must be someone involved on the project that will serve as the "account manager"—the person who will massage the client whenever necessary. This person will have the people skills necessary to command this post. As a rule, this person will be the designated "good cop"—the one who is of an agreeable demeanor, and not prone to disputes. He will make the decisions of when to assuage the client, and he will offer any concessions. If the client chooses not to deal with him, he will have to deal with the bad cop— the uncompromising one, with only the company's best interests at heart. This dynamic is worth exploring.

There will always be someone deemed the "bad cop"—the one who raises contentious issues, or sits in the hot seat. His bias will be decidedly procontractor. This is a requirement of the management structure, for no contractor can be effective by being exclusively passive and accommodating. Needless to say, the bad cop tends to be unpopular with the client; however, this is not necessarily a bad thing. Many general contractors approve of this method, because they can saddle this person with the responsibility for any number of calamities. Often, the bad cop is scapegoated. This may work as follows: a general contractor must deal with many contentious and sensitive issues in order to navigate a project. The production of a project is its lifeline. In order for the project to move, someone must be an aggressor who forces solutions to problematic issues, and urges unpopular decision making. If one is not already in place, he who chooses to accept the privilege will become the *de facto* bad cop. By and large, he tends to be the superintendent, or site supervisor, for he is the one on the front who needs answers, and will push for them. In fact, his job depends on it, and his boss knows it. He may be pushing the design team for answers, or harrying subcontractors to man the job. He is the lightning rod on the project, and lives and dies by the rate and quality of production. As this is his *raison d'etre*, he often is held accountable for just about *anything* that could go wrong. This being so, there is considerable turnaround in this job description. I know of a smallish company, thirty men or so, with a few projects running regularly, who ran a want ad for a superintendent almost every Sunday for 3 or 4 years. Project managers had longevity at this company because they were able to toady up to their superiors and clients, and saddle their superintendents with blame for any failure. Building, however, connoted a foreign concept.

"Bad cop" may sound like a nebulous job description, but his is in fact a more productive job than the good cop, who in addition to requiring "people skills," (in this case, shorthand for "sucking up") will often find himself compromising his company's interests in order to satisfy the client. Indeed, the bad cop can get much accomplished by forcing issues, whereas the good cop can only play the sap. In the end, if the client is unhappy, he will come to the good cop with grievances who will make the concessions. He must keep the client relatively content, or else things can deteriorate rapidly, as the client may feel he has no one to go to, save for his architect. In the end, the good cop is always the hero. The good cop/bad cop strategy works well when it is deliberate and meticulous. If they act independent of one another, they tend to cancel each other out. For example, a superintendent may refuse a client's requests to do a little extra work, which the client believes is of little value. The client is angered by what he perceives as niggardliness. The issue can die there, with both the superintendent and client angry with each other. However, suppose the project manager (good cop) is apprised of the situation. He senses a great opportunity, as the client has asked for extra work. Since it is a minor change, he decides on the following: on his next change order, the client's request appears as a line item with a value of $1000. Directly below the line item appears a "courtesy" credit of $1000, which offsets the change order. He has accomplished the following:

- Demonstrated goodwill
- He has shown the client that he supports his superintendent's position, that is, that the work is a legitimate extra
- He has illustrated the good cop/bad cop dynamic that the client now knows he must observe in order to negotiate the project; he will now play according to the script

If a client has a large personal investment in the project, he may require extra coddling, which is never easy. The likelihood of a positive client/general contractor relationship tends to be pretty small, and clients don't realize the incentive to change that. The exception is with negotiated bid projects. Thus, clients prefer to have their architects represent them. The architect becomes the client's avatar—the one whom the contractor must keep happy. The client's level of contentment is proportional to the architect's level of contentment only until the architect's performance can be qualified, at which time he also becomes vulnerable to scrutiny. However, because he is not the client, he will not be treated with the same level of gratuity by the general contractor. And so, typically the client is removed somewhat from the action, and a member of the design team represents his best interests. This arrangement makes it more difficult for the contractor to appease the client, as there is no longer a direct link. If the problem is generated from the design team side, it will be tough for the contractor to "work his client" as he is insulated by his agent, who is protecting *his* own interests. As we saw in Chap. 5, this is where a construction manager can work his magic.

A typical good cop/bad cop structure features an upper management staff member or owner in the good cop seat, and the superintendent (or project manager) as the bad cop. It may be inevitable that the client feels he can make no headway with the bad cop, a fact which may actually be testament to the superintendent's acumen: many clients will try to work the contractor's people; give them instruction and ask them favors. When the client hits a wall, he will start to hold the bad cop in low esteem, and will likely make this fact known to the contractor. If the good cop/bad cop scenario was instituted by design, he will play along with it; if not, he will come down on his superintendent, who likely was just doing his job.

Too often, the owner of a small company will act both as the beneficent account manager, and as the person who makes unpopular decisions. In other words, he is both good cop and bad cop simultaneously. This is not good practice. There should always be at least one other person who can intercede as negotiator, should the point man hit a wall. Many contractors are aware of this predicament, but don't have the ability to remediate it. The good news for them is: at least they are aware of the problem. Refer to some of the company staff structures we discussed in Chap. 4 for more on who would be the best person in your company for the job.

It would seem that the account manager has a conflict of interest by his very definition, he must make both the client and the contractor happy. How does he accomplish this if in order to make one party happy, he must do so at the expense of the other? For example, an unpopular change order, difficult to substantiate and justify, must be discounted, or set aside altogether in order to make the client happy. This concession is given at the expense of the contractor. How can a win-win scenario emanate from such a seemingly one-sided or biased process? The answer is, to achieve a balance of satisfaction for *both* parties. The two contracting parties will seldom be happy *at the same time*, but in the end, you want them close to a mutual sense of satisfaction with the *overall* project negotiations. This is done by (a) whenever possible, solving issues in a way that satisfies all parties, or (b) satisfying one party at a time; for instance, making a concession to the owner on one issue, and finding for the contractor on the next. The account manager is an arbitrator who should negotiate accordingly to bring about this sense of parity. However, in the long scheme of things, group satisfaction is the aggregate of all negotiations that will determine each party's level of contentment. The account manager will keep a running tab of these negotiations, and will indeed, take a continuous reading of the prevailing winds. Again, the account manager must have the necessary intuition to act correctly, including the appreciation of the concept that many clients believe it is not in their best interests to ever show a sign of being placated.

In order to be an effective account manger, it would appear that a degree in psychology is required. While a degree in psychology is not required, a basic understanding of human nature will help guide you. Ignorance of human nature or a lack of people skills will disqualify a candidate.

Clients and Their Discontents

"The customer is always right"

Not true—even when this dubious adage was hatched. It betrays an over willingness to appease the client at any cost, whenever he complains, and will quickly debilitate a company's negotiating position. This reductive philosophy holds that if the client is unhappy, you must do whatever you can do to satisfy him, or else the project is a failure. Surprisingly, many contractors still subscribe to this overly simplistic business ethic. Many clients continue to believe that they are calling the shots merely because they are footing the bill, and because it is convenient for them to do so. This belief betrays their ignorance of their responsibilities in the contract.

However, the task of reeducating your client that he is not always right requires a great deal of finesse. This mission can be carried out by your account manager, and a *"plan B,"* such as another company representative, should be waiting in the wings, as he always should be during negotiating periods. Be careful when juggling account managers and negotiators, lest the client should feel there is a lack of continuity in your company's structure. There should never be multiple negotiators. There should always be an ultimate go-to person for the client. Never let the client lose sight of this person, and give him constant reminders that this person is there for him. A company I knew had several executive level managers with a share in their company. It was anybody's guess which one would show up at the job meeting. Naturally, none of them had full knowledge of the project. The client thought it was ridiculous.

"I am unhappy with . . ."

Complaints are typical for any project. Naturally, people's tolerance will vary. The most intolerant are those that are done a disservice, or those that believe they are being done a disservice. Many of these are clients who don't understand the value of what they have purchased, and feel they are being cheated. They are seldom shy about telling you this. There are some shrewd clients who complain continually, not because they are always dissatisfied, but because they are manipulative. They feel that the unhappier they appear to the contractor, the more he will do to ingratiate himself. Then there are clients who complain continually merely because it is their nature—these are the malcontents. This type of client is the most difficult to control, as his complaints are often generated from an emotional standpoint, as opposed to a rational one. The gravity of a minor situation can quickly escalate into calamity. The worst client is the chronic complainer, who chooses yelling and screaming to get his point across. He may himself be a businessman who has a history of success in subjugating his minions through intimidation.

On a more primal or subconscious level, because it is human nature to be distrustful when money is involved, there is a dynamic at work where if one party appears to be happy, the other party assumes that he is happy at his expense. That is why some clients always behave as if they are unhappy. They may believe that if they appear happy to the contractor, he might think that his client is getting too good a deal, and will soon make adjustments to compensate for this presumed deficit. Contractors in general are only too aware of this, and not unusually will feign sheepishness when they negotiate. For example, a contractor may appear to begrudgingly concede a discount to his client, when in fact his starting price was padded in anticipation of a negotiation session. At the end of the day, his client believes he has saved some money, and the contractor reaps a windfall. This may appear on the surface to be win-win, but clearly it is not. The best contract participants will subscribe to a true win-win philosophy; however, they are the exception, because (a) people don't trust one another, or (b) they can't see past their own interests, even though keeping their partner content *is* in their best interests. There are many who would willingly embrace the win-win philosophy, but either they can't navigate its subtle currents, or find a willing partner, that is, an owner and contractor who genuinely want each other to be content.

"Why am I paying extra for that?"

Some clients are convinced that because they have paid a certain sum of money, that in their estimation, these monies should include everything and anything. Nowhere is this more true than in the high-end residential market, where $/square foot prices are highest. For example, a client may have signed a 3-million dollar contract to renovate a three-bedroom home, with an exclusive job team. He may even be willing to pay a premium in the false hope that if he does, he won't have to pay out extra—sort of like an all inclusive vacation. Because he considers the project exclusive, he expects a turnkey delivery with no snags, and no change orders. It can be difficult, at times, to keep a straight face when the client announces his disappointment and what his expectations were. This is the reason why it is important to be extra specific in defining the scope of work in the contract documents—define what is included, and especially, what is not. Anything left open to interpretation is subject to become a liability to the contractor. The client must be educated early on that his contract is not all-inclusive *before* the contract is signed. Not to prime him for change orders, but to inform him of the specific content of his contract. This nuance should also be made clear to the client. A precontract signing scope review is the perfect forum for this. Such meetings can dispel any presumptions for all parties concerned.

"Construction is an industry prone to dishonesty and corruption"

There are many reasons why customers think contractors are crooks, some of them legitimate. They may have had bad experiences, or they may remember all the corrupt union officials and building inspectors who frequent our correctional institutions. In fact, mutual distrust among the industry's participants is rampant. Whatever the case, the industry is endlessly trying to live down its reputation, as it is obviously bad for business. However, the construction sector is no more prone to dishonesty than any other for-profit industry. Suffice it to say, you would like to establish and maintain the client's trust. This is truly a thankless and often untenable aspiration. So elusive is being considered trustworthy that many no longer care, as they feel there is little they can do to change this perception. Truth be told, some clients are more untrustworthy and dishonest than the most hardened con artists. Be vigilant of actions that can be perceived as suspicious, as your client will be on the lookout for them. Often contractors inadvertently send out suspicious signals, such as when they don't calculate their math correctly, or otherwise make a mistake in their favor. Obviously, only you can control this with your own informational quality control program.

"The contractor is out to hose me"

For whatever reason, there may be lots of change orders on a project. They may arise because of errors and omissions by the design team, contractor, or both. If you have discounted your contract value as part of your negotiation, your client will be sensitive to the change order process, as he may believe you are compensating for what you lost at the bargaining table. This is a ubiquitous assumption held by many clients. Some perceive this behavior as lowballing, which we discussed in Chap. 2. To avoid this, you must be careful to be specific in defining your scope of work, and your qualifications in your contract. And of course, work hard to let your client understand that you are honest and well intended. For example, if he contests the cost of a given change order; treat him to a special screening of your proprietary backup, which should allay his suspicions;[5] that is, show him the math.

In many cases, abundant change orders may be unavoidable, as the job may have been awarded before the design documents were complete. Thus, every modification to the contract documents necessitates that a change order be generated. Ironically, the change order tends to be where contractors lose money, not make it. To convince a client of this notion is next to impossible. If you know that a contract structure will generate many modifications (change orders) make certain to point this out to your client before the contract is ratified. An excellent alternative would be to allow a contingency for unspecified scope, or build the project cost-plus or as a construction manager.

The Stress and Patience Accounts

I also like to compare construction contractual relationships with marital contracts. There is the honeymoon, the marriage, and quite frequently, a divorce. It is the divorce that you seek to avoid, because of the financial ramifications. You don't want to be put in a position where you will likely lose revenue *and* face; rather you want return business from the architect, and referrals from the client. There is a general barometer of the quality of rapport on projects that can be sensed intuitively, and by correspondences and interactions with your client. It is a subtle instinct—think of Captain Ahab sensing the presence of a whale from miles away, just as a ship's dog can portend the approach to a savage inhabited island. This barometer can be thought of as a savings account, which can either increase, or become insolvent depending on what is put in and withdrawn from it. Assuming that no project is without a substantial amount of stress, there must also be a relatively healthy supply of patience at the start of a project. Patience and stress have an inverse relationship—as one increases, the other decreases. Think of these offsetting concepts as "stress and patience accounts."

In the beginning, there is only the attendant stress and patience that each party brings with him to the table. Throughout the course of the project, the level of stress will vary. The descent can start from the beginning, which it often does, or it can engage when the project becomes late and/or overbudget. Even a successful project often experiences stress in the beginning, but this is more a factor of nervousness than anything else. It may even increase regardless of project health; however, when the end is in sight, things can start looking once again rosy. Such is human nature that the stress response may not be rational; however, it must be considered a natural phenomenon: in other words—it must sometimes be taken with a grain of salt.

You must keep frequent tabs on the level of stress and patience prevalent on your project. Should the stress account increase to the point where patience is bankrupt, you may find yourself working for a very unhappy client. An unhappy client soon becomes an irrational client, one who may not want to play ball; at this time you will then have even less recourse. By monitoring levels of client satisfaction, you can hope to make whatever adjustments you deem necessary to eradicate conditions, and avoid meltdown. Just like a nasty divorce, things can get ugly in the fallout stage. Do everything within your power to avoid this, for the health of the particular project, future commissions, and your own equanimity.

Avoiding Conflict

In order to check the onslaught of conflicts, it is important to understand the issues that are driving and perpetuating them; a problem that is solvable should eventually be resolved. It is the problems that won't go away, and those that we can't control that we worry about. If a project is fraught with *elliptical* problems, it is sooner or later likely to become dysfunctional, as malingering problems are the hallmark of poor relations: a sign of unwillingness to cooperate and negotiate. Elliptical problems are a phenomenon that states that certain problems are *by someone's* design, not resolvable: that one will always return to the starting point—the invocation of the problem. The designer of the problem has an agenda for maintaining a perceived level of dissatisfaction. The most convenient problem raised is the indication that someone simply does not like or resents another, such that their differences are irreconcilable. Elliptical problems have no resolution, or so many possible resolutions that it is impossible to discern a satisfactory one. Perhaps the intention of raising such a problem isn't in hopes of resolving it, but to create a vehicle for unrest; it is their way of either making another's life more difficult, or driving the perception that others are making his life more difficult. If the problem were resolvable, its creator will have failed his purpose. It is therefore important to understand the mechanics behind some of the forces that drive clients' responses. To begin to incorporate a constructive conflict avoidance program, it is necessary to remove the obstructions.

Know thyself[6]

First and foremost in the avoidance of conflict is the area where you have the most control—your own involvement. It's always easier to find fault and to criticize others; however, self-examination for most, remains uncharted territory. We discussed some of the more positive characteristics of self-awareness in Chap. 1. In addition to your self-awareness, you will need interpersonal skills. Your success in mitigating conflict is predicated on your ability to:

- Build a level of confidence and trust in your clients
- Establish mutual levels of respect with contractual parties
- Solve problems
- Plan ahead
- Negotiate with difficult people

These are all elusive attributes of character. It is a rare individual indeed who exemplifies these virtues, even less so in the construction industry. I suppose such standouts aspire to more hospitable occupations. This absence of character in the members of the industry translates to an unhealthy level of discomfort for the demand side, such that many stereotypes persist. Some of the more common stereotypes of members of the construction industry held by clients are as follows:

- They lack formal education
- They lack integrity and honesty
- They are disrespectful
- They can be hostile and unreasonable
- They are déclassé
- They are only out for themselves

Most importantly, the client can't identify with you as a peer, as he does his trusted architect. Although these stereotypes are about as much use as any other prejudice, people in the industry do precious little to alter these presumptions. Even though many architects and clients fit these same stereotypes, they are seldom accused of or asked to defend them, and are never held to the same level of scrutiny as the lowly builder. Some of these stereotypes of contractors are embraced by design professionals, as these same ideas were what nineteenth century architects argued separated themselves from the builders from whom they were seeking to siphon market share. These presumptions create barriers which inhibit constructive interactions, especially when things become stressed, such that the great majority of conflicts require twice or thrice the effort to settle, all because of personal innuendo. Without such innuendo, only the conflict would remain, and only a solution to the original problem would be needed. Quite often the secondary problems generated by the inability to get along eclipse the urgency of the original matter. As I said, this is just fine for some people: an architect may feel threatened by a diligent manager who eventually will likely expose his shortcomings. It would be easier to draw out the manager into secondary arguments rather than run the risk of being discovered as being blameful. If and when the manager becomes angry enough, the architect will point this out, and ideally for him, force the owner to choose sides between the architect and manager: a no-brainer: the contractor can easily find another manager, but changing architects can be a major undertaking.

By being conscientious, deliberate, and smart, you will keep yourself out of hot water. There will be enough problems beyond your control to negotiate, without having to worry about unnecessary problems you bring on yourself. If only keeping one's nose clean were as simple as heeding a little advice. An owner can get away with as much as he likes, whereas a contractor seemingly has no slack. Architects tend to stay out of hot water because they generally have the owner's ear, and because they are well protected by the AIA contract structure. Even if your performance is impeccable, there will always be conflicts. You can't erad-icate them; you can only hope to minimize the frequency of them.

Don't take it personally

It's easy to fall into the trap of resenting a client for his abusive treatment of you. Many clients deserve it, but such hostility will only make matters worse. While it may be true that a client has a special place in his heart for you, and he manifests his anger and fashions it in the form of a personal affront, the truth is that he would likely behave this way regardless of who you were, or if it were another general contractor; this is his *modus operandi* for negotiating his anx-iety. If you should take his abuse personally, you would likely reciprocate such behavior in-kind, as is human nature. But remember: "violence begets violence," and the deconstruction of reason.

It is unfortunate that people lose objectivity when negotiating difficult issues or with difficult people. Such behavior betrays a lack of confidence in their prin-ciples and convictions, or indicates a lack of discipline and maturity. Negotiating with the world for such people is an exercise in militant diplomacy. Such people are often insecure, and quite often narcissistic. They can truly menace the health of your project, and quality of life. Neurasthenic considerations aside, it is helpful to realize not only why some people may act this way, but why *you* may act this way. The manner in which you negotiate conflict will greatly influ-ence the way your colleagues and clients perceive your behavior and relate to you. Regardless of your objective approach to a conflict, if you preclude your good reasoning with nastiness or malevolence your good reasoning will not be heard without reservation: some bad news is more palatable if it is packaged in attrac-tive wrapping. It's not only what's being said, but also *how* it is being said.

De-escalate the provocative issues

Defuse situations that are likely to raise the most turmoil. The importance of creating a calm and reasonable environment or forum for resolving disputes cannot be overemphasized; when people are upset and angry, they tend to be less reasonable. There is little to be accomplished when one or more of the par-ticipants are unglued. If the situation can't be toned down, then save the dis-cussion for a more appropriate opportunity. Some de-escalating tools at your disposal could be: postponing the discussion, or discussing the issue one-on-one; perhaps over coffee or lunch.

It is easy for a hot topic to degenerate into a free-for-all shouting match, or hostile interaction. Such responses can only generate more animosity. As we know, it is easier for some people to negotiate this way than to be reasonable, especially when they know they're wrong. Others will take advantage of a degen-erating conflict negotiating process by egging on—the fighting soon obfuscates the original issue. They hope that if you are perceived as unreasonable in your arguing, than your credibility becomes subject. If you are in the right, you should not allow this to happen. Nonetheless, there is no positive outcome to virulent discourse, or if there is, it seldom is worth the effort. Understand that everyone is subject to being under stress, especially on a difficult project. It isn't sufficient that you only be vigilant in managing known stressors—you must be prepared for any situation that rears its head. As part of this vigilance, you will have a basic procedure for:

- De-escalating tense situations and reestablishing rationality and civility
- Defusing difficult situations, and implementing an exit strategy
- Providing a future means of negotiating or settlement

Get along

Establishing a good rapport is the best prevention of conflict mechanism at your disposal. As we have said, a person should be designated; someone with social skills, who will be the contact person for the client, that is, the public relations (PR) person. A common mistake, whether inadvertent or not, is to appoint a person who is not able to connect with people. Often, it happens because this nuance is never considered, and either the point person is a *de facto* nominee, or there is no one to take on the responsibility of massaging the client. At very small firms, this condition is hard to control. A good P.R. person is an attribute of a comprehensive service-oriented company; in other words, the exception to the rule. If you have a good P.R. person, consider yourself above the fray.

If the anointed contact person is not on good terms with the client, then an alternate should be chosen. Basic human nature dictates that a team that does not play well together will not conduct business well together. No matter how well you do your job, if you are not well liked, you are always playing with two strikes against you.

Another consideration is the fact that although you may do your best to avoid directly instigating conflict, you will find that there will always be conflict induced indirectly, or through actions of which you were unaware of. Some of these you can control through your own personal discipline, others you can't. You must be on the lookout for the possibility of such dangerous undercurrents, as they can breach the surface and make you your own worst enemy.

Finally, cut your client a little slack—it's probably his first time on a construction project; sort of like a first date, and he is likely riddled with anxiety. You should be less anxious than he, and you should expect him to be uneasy. As part of your mission, strive to be less reactive to your client, and more empathetic.

Accentuate the positive

It's an old expression that smacks of affectation; however, when employed as a business philosophy, it can be a quite formidable neutralizer to the ubiquitous ethos of discontentment in the marketplace. People are prone to be discontent—according to Freud, it is in their nature. For some, the discontentment is merely latent infantility. But more often than not, they are insecure about the decisions they have made, and will have to make regarding their project. Thus, even before they begin construction on their home, they may have a bone to pick with you. If you belong to the same club—that of the glass always being half empty, you will likely be at odds with your client, as "misery loves company." Moreover, the discontent can sense their fellow sufferers from far away—it won't take long for things to become unpleasant. They will sense a vehicle and repository for their anxiety in you, and draw you into their world of conflict by depositing their conflict there. Naturally, the phenomenon occurs in degrees, and so should your response to counteract it. Learn to judge fairly and accurately assess your client's complaints.

By concentrating on the positive aspects of a project or just being positive in general, you can emphasize a "feel good sensation." It won't be particularly contagious, so you must do your best to see that the effort is genuine, and consistent. Otherwise, it will wither just as quickly as it came on. People need such reassurance to make them feel better and more confident about their project. Some clients are extremely high maintenance in this regard, and no matter how well the project is going, they will suffer if you do not put them at ease. Even if you don't, they may appreciate the fact that you are trying. More importantly, the happier a client is, the less there will be incidence of conflict. And think how much more unhappy they would feel if they felt your negativity.

Conflicts of Perception

Thus far we have discussed psychological influences that can affect the level of conflict on a project, all of which often have nothing to do with the work directly. The nature of practical conflicts is just as far reaching. A good transition point from what could be termed *subjective conflict*, to what could be termed *objective conflict*, would be the discussion of conflicts of perception, which often involves objectivity and subjectivity. The most common conflicts of perception reside in the interpretation of the contract documents; by and large, the design documentation—drawings and specifications. Common misinterpretations and grey areas are discovered regarding:

- Quantities
- Quality requirements
- Boilerplate general requirements
- Management and coordination activities
- Contradictions

Quantities

If your estimator and your subcontractors have both done the math, the likelihood of scope oversight should be small, as checks and balances are part of the qualification and buyout processes. Errors and omissions by your subcontractors must be reconnoitered and folded back into your subcontractor's scope of work. Mistakes by your own estimating department are your responsibility. In either case, the general contractor is responsible for the missing scope.

Design professionals also make errors and omissions, to such extent that they purchase special insurance to protect themselves from them. Yet it is a rare event that a design professional needs to refer a contractor's errors and omissions (E/O) claim to his insurance company. This is not why they purchase the insurance; however, the cost to the industry for these kinds of E/Os may very well substantiate a need for such provisions. Typically, if a contractor believes an architect made a mistake or omission on his design documents, such that substantiates extra costs, he will point this out to the architect, as he would like a requests for proposals (RFP). Architects are loath to issue such RFPs for their errors and omissions, as in so doing they advertise their errors and omissions to the client. Rather, they would try to defend the accusation tooth and nail, which they are incredibly industrious at, before they would concede capital to finance their own mistakes. This means, that by hook or crook, they will find a way to induce the contractor to do the work, while at the same time having him hide or eat the cost of it. The trouble is that contractors will be loath to negotiate after having to justify a change order for an architect who should have known better. Thus, change order negotiation typically reaches an impasse. Contractors will not expect an RFP for an architect's error or omission; however, it is their contractual responsibility to point out what they believe constitutes either one.

When an impasse is reached regarding an E/O, the contractor must decide whether or not he will pursue the claim further, as there are reasons "for" and "against" such action. Assuming the contractor has not as yet notified the owner of the claim, if he were to pursue it, client notification would be the logical next step. Before he issues his claim, there are some considerations:

■ Is the claim worth pursuing? Does the value of the claim justify the possibly ostracizing and incurring the wrath of the architect, and very likely the client?

■ Is the claim easily demonstrable or will there be a prolonged debate over responsibility, which could easily stalemate?

Often it is necessary to take a step back and consider the big picture; a rancorous debate regarding a claim might guaranty that not only will the architect pay you back in-kind for the gesture on the project, but you will likely be removed from his bid list. A contractor may not want to rock the boat—high-end projects carry the tacit implication that what the architect doesn't detail, the contractor will cover for him using his liberal contract endowment. While this is sometimes true, many architects take advantage of the practice by showing less and less. No high-end contractor ever wants to be regarded as a "nickel and dimer," a *déclassé* moniker, not endemic to the lofty high-end sector. Of course, for negotiated bids, a contractor will almost never hang an architect out to dry.

Quality requirements

Much endproduct is scrutinized on the basis of one or two people's subjectivity, which may not necessarily take into consideration what the design documents direct; hence, quality conflicts are very common. There are some obvious tools to monitor quality, such as the specifications; however, for custom manufactured goods, which are commonplace on high-end residential construction, there is no replacement for a control sample. A control sample is a specific design-team generated object that is representative of what the client expects for you to deliver to him. If you are using material that is exotic, or expensive to fabricate, a control sample from the design team should be mandatory. Quality should only rarely come into question on high-end projects; it is taken for granted that high-end contractors are handsomely paid to produce the highest level of quality possible. Part of the premiums paid for such a level of service should obviate any chance of the conflicts associated with tight budgets, especially quality issues. As we discussed in Chap. 2, quality control problems should be identified at the middle management level, that is, before the client or architect notices; "high-end contractors are supposedly incapable of delivering poor quality" is the assumption. Mistakes are made, but quality contractors are quick to eradicate such problems. Nevertheless, this idealism is not representative of reality. Clients and contractors will argue endlessly over quality, even on high-end projects. More often than not, a general contractor fighting to justify substandard quality, by that distinction alone, fails the criteria test for high-end residential construction.

Change orders

Just as you will find yourself substantiating quality, you will also be asked to justify what you perceive as change orders. Architects are squeamish of change orders that are generated without a request for pricing (which they seldom will issue), that is, they dislike and don't expect unsolicited up-charges. A contractor might otherwise issue a change order based on unforeseen conditions, or what he believes constitutes extra work. He genuinely believes the work is extraneous to the contract documents through his interpretation of them. Architects resent such change orders because they have difficulty justifying them to their client, who expects a turnkey design package devoid of extras attributed to errors or omissions. This being so, they are loath to approve change orders based solely on a contractor's interpretation of design documents, no matter how ambiguous they are.

However, if a change order is ratified by the architect, there still is the task of selling it to the client. If it can be perceived as an architect error and omission, the architect will leave this charge to the contractor. Invariably, the contractor will be hard put to drive his point through to the client as aggressively as he did with the architect, as he will be leery of the client's negative responses, which have a greater import than the architect's.

In terms of evident progress, distinctive contract parties will often see the project differently. This fact has a direct bearing on the negotiation of progress payments. When it comes to agreeing on completion percentages, it is as if everyone speaks a different language. To you, the project may seem 50% done, however, to some clients, the cup is half empty—50% not done. An owner unfamiliar with the construction process will often have a jaundiced view of what he perceives as progress. He may scratch his head at how long the mechanical electrical and plumbing (MEP) infrastructure is taking, only to stand in awe of the sheetrock installation, which will cover a lot of ground in a short time, yet could not have begun before the MEP roughs were completed. He may also see that although the project is half over, only 30% has been billed, because the finishes have not yet been released. If he thinks production is off, he may or may not say so. If he does speak up, you should be eloquent in explaining to him why things appear as they do. However, ultimately you will plead your case to the architect, the owner's agent who will review your *Application for Payment*, of which he has the final say-so. Although architects have a more comprehensive sense of progress than their clients, they can be equally as parsimonious. What's more, they have an imperative to maintain the client's financial leverage over the contractor throughout the life of the contract.

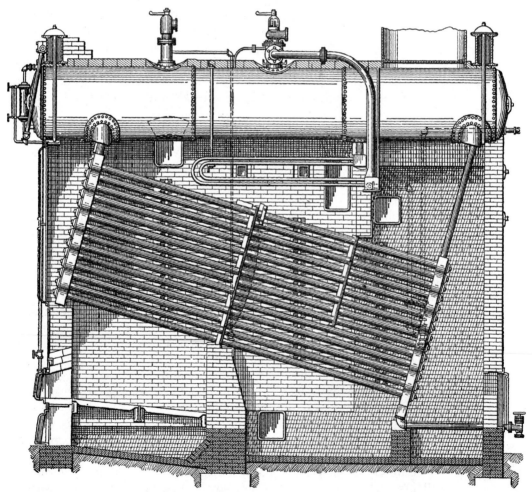

Wrought Steel Inclined Header, Longitudinal Drum Babcock & Wilcox Boiler Equipped With Babcock & Wilcox Superheater
Harding and Willard, *Mechanical Equipment of Buildings, Vol II: Power Plants and Refrigeration,* (New York: John Wiley & Sons, 1918).

Boilerplate requirements

Boilerplate notes are catchall notations found in the drawings or specifications that are meant to be applied to every sort of project. Sometimes they exist only because they were a vestige from a former project. On the whole, they are included as contract language to cover any variety of circumstances for which the architect feels he could possibly be liable for—that is, they are exculpatory in nature—think "disclaimer" and "indemnification." Therefore, they are not drafted for one project as they should be, but for general use, regardless of their relevance.

Boilerplate language is readily discernible by virtue of its blunt, didactic, and legalistic pretensions, and overgeneralizing irrelevance. If one were so inclined to take it verbatim, it would be in his best interest to strike such language from the contract. Like many of the curious AIA A201 provisions, architects seldom refer to boilerplate language; however, if their back is up against the wall, they may invoke it as cover. When a specification book is prefaced by a considerable tome of boilerplate language, this may be an indication of an insecure architect, or one that is too familiar with litigation. I have seen contractors insist that such general requirements be set aside altogether, and I have just as often seen them thrown into the trash without being opened. If you are not comfortable with the boilerplate language, don't agree to it. However, be politic in doing so. Don't refer to the exception in your bid proposal, which could be considered preemptive, but do raise the issue should your proposal be considered for contract negotiation.

Management and coordination

Remember what we discussed regarding the realization that sometimes it's not enough to simply do your job well? Part of a manager's thankless quotidian often involves stomaching the onslaught of owner or architect directives or requests for provisions, or changes in services, that he is not able or willing to make. Clients and architects will engage in the micromanagement of your organization, not only to a degree that is extremely objectionable, but out of accordance with the contract requirements which state:

> The Contractor shall be solely responsible and have control over construction means, methods, techniques, sequences and procedures, and for coordinating all portions of the Work under the Contract, unless the Contract Documents give other specific instructions . . . (A201:3.3.1),

and,

> The Architect will neither have control over, or charge of, nor be responsible for, the construction means, methods, techniques, sequences and procedures, or for the safety precautions and programs in connection with the Work, since these are solely the Contractor's rights . . . (A201:4.2.2).

Such language (when invoked) should protect contractors from meddlesome owners and architects. Owners are often given carte blanche to get involved as much as they like; this by dint of the tacit apotheosis of the client so common in high-end contractual relationships. Toleration of meddling is so common-place it would seem that contractors are wholly unaware of the contractual language regulating such behavior.

However, one must be wary when referring to regulatory contract language as the basis for a complaint or argument, because such gestures are invariably considered litigious and even hostile. This is unfortunate, as often, a contractor has no other means to protect himself from incursions by controlling clients and architects.

Typical Conflicts

Design team conflicts

Conflicts with the design team start early and end late in the timeline of a project. They start before the client gets too involved, because most architects are the owner's agent, and almost, if not all early communication is done directly with them, with the client as spectator, or excluded entirely. Arguments with the design team are commonplace. There are many reasons for this. The interpretation of design documentation is a leading cause. Errors and omissions are also regular problems. The manner in which you deal with conflicts with the design team can have a great influence or can be a key determinant on your current project, and can affect future relationships. If you get on so poorly that you don't care how they feel, or if you have a future with them, then you don't need to be so deliberate in your dealings; however, even if you will never see them again, consider even a poor working relationship an opportunity to learn something.

The first conflicts will likely be over how the intent of the drawings is interpreted. Errors and omissions will appear as the subcontractors are awarded their contracts. The intent of drawings is debated endlessly in litigation proceedings. As a contractor, your awareness of the quality and relevance of the drawings is key to the negotiation process. If all drawings were done thoroughly, there would not be so many arguments over design intent; however, architects, sometimes deliberately, and other times unintentionally, incorporate nebulous material into the design package. Sometimes through their detailing, other times through language. Some terminology to look out for:

- General contractor to coordinate
- As required
- As needed
- As indicated
- As shown
- Typical (TYP)
- See structural (or other) drawings
- See specs
- Verify in field (V.I.F)

These terms merely relate information by inference, which is never a substitute for the direct reference of information—a general contractor may or may not get the message. However, the contractor cannot be held responsible for omissions of inferred scopes of work. Although he is not responsible for such work, he must be vigilant of it, and must point it out to the architect. Architects use these notes as shorthand for work that they have not detailed, otherwise, there would be no need to infer it. As part of the errors and omissions review that your estimator conducts, he should highlight and review any such references, issue requests for information (RFIs), or make provisions in the proposal as required.

To indemnify themselves against contractor claims, architect's general requirements frequently invoke exculpatory clauses, such as those requiring the contractor to visit the site, read the plans, and insist that in doing so, they assume responsibility for any and all possible scope of work. In a critical 1918 Supreme Court decision that generated *The Spearin Doctrine*,[7] such language was put to the test in a claim of a contractor against the government. The court held that "an owner providing such plans and specifications also impliedly warrants the accuracy and adequacy of those plans and specifications," and "that the responsibility of the owner is not overcome by the usual clauses contained in construction contracts."[8]

> Simply put, contractual language obliging the contractor to examine the site did not impose upon the contractor the further duty of making a diligent inquiry into local conditions to confirm whether the owner's representations in the plans and specifications were accurate. The contractor was also not obligated to second-guess the adequacy of the plans and specifications to accomplish the purpose of the project.[9]

The Spearin Doctrine has vast implications for the industry, as conflicts regarding responsibility for contract work are debated endlessly. In fact, the Colorado Supreme Court recently expressly acknowledged and cited the 1918 case, in their finding for a contractor.[10] If contractors and design professionals were more familiar with the Supreme Court's findings, perhaps there would be fewer arguments.

There are several types of design team/contractor relationships that exist, and each dictates a special set of parameters for conflict resolution. The nature of a contractor's relationship with the architect can influence their respective approaches to the project.

Design team sponsored contractors and negotiated bids. Under this arrangement, the understanding is that the design team and contractor have a preestablished relationship since the design team is sponsoring the contractor. When conflicts arise, they are handled more diplomatically by each party than they would be on a typical contract. The contractor may be sheepish in pointing out errors and omissions since he may feel guilty—"biting the hand that feeds him." In negotiated bid contracts an architect will be very resentful of a contractor who he perceives is making him look bad in front of the client, or is contentious since he believes the contractor is indebted to him for awarding him the work. Instead, conflict resolution takes place in private, away from the client. In this way, problems can be resolved and the client is insulated from an often contentious process, one that he should not be involved in any way. This isn't a bad method for conflict resolution on any project; there is almost no incentive to air out differences in front of a client, regardless of the contract type, unless it is at the expense of the other party, which is of course, spiteful and unnecessary. Nevertheless, architects and contractors go toe-to-toe every day; often right in front of their clients. This often happens when they can no longer work things out between each other—a communication breakdown.

For example, suppose a design omission is discovered by the contractor. He can either generate a memo and/or change order to the architect and client or he can present it only to the architect in private, in hopes that there is a way to resolve it without hanging anyone out to dry. Architects will appreciate the latter method and general contractors do as well. Needlessly involving clients in technical matters can bring more contention into the negotiation process.

However, projects will continue to be awarded to contractors other than those preferred by the architect. Architects have preferred contractors who are loyal, reluctant to embarrass them with petty change orders and will routinely cover their architect's errors and omissions. Thus, an architect may be resentful of his contractor not being awarded the project and anxious of his new relationship with the selected contractor.

New relationships.   Few people would hire a contractor no one has heard of; yet, it is interesting how many contractors are vetted on the most superficial level. A client will generally ask his architect to form a bidding field of appropriate contractors. If he does not have resources, he will be hard pressed to do this, and thus his level of scrutiny may be handicapped when he does select bidders. By the same token, contractors hungry for work don't question where the work comes from and often find out it is an unsatisfactory source.

In either case, it can be difficult and contentious for an architect and contractor who have little or no prior working relationship to negotiate and resolve conflicts. In the end, the client will be done a disservice. Since all relationships must start somewhere, architects and contractors who are new to each other should take the extra time to become better acquainted with each other's means and methods, likes and dislikes, such that they arrive at a healthy mutual understanding and respect for each other. Most importantly, they should establish a means for negotiating conflicts. While this approach is good strategy, it is exceptionally difficult to accomplish, as its success is wholly contingent on human nature.

A client and architect team without a past history is subject to the same understanding. If they are out of sync with each other the contractor will be the odd man out. Client–architect disagreements are more common when the two don't know each other well and more difficult to resolve. Typical conflicts are:

- Degree of detail in the design documents (usually pointed out by the contractor)
- Areas of work not taken for by either general contractor or architect
- Expectation of construction management services without a construction manager
- Inability to please; especially both a husband and wife
- Indecisiveness on the clients' part
- Delays of deliverables

Owner elected contractor/subcontractor.   The architect may feel like the odd man out when the owner nominates his own contractor, as he feels the contractor will have the client's ear. He will not have as much leverage when negotiating with the contractor as he would have had he nominated the contractor. A similar dynamic comes into play between the owner and general contractor when the owner brings in his own subcontractor(s), which they offer to do.

Some of the tacit understandings owner-sponsored subcontractors bring to the table can be problematic. For one thing, their experience with other general contractors is the traditional arrangement, where they are subjects of the general contractor. Some of them have grown weary of this arrangement and take the opportunity of working for an owner directly to flout their new found independence—they feel liberated. This is nothing new and general contractors are wise to this response. Many will often rightly demand remuneration for coordinating an owner-sponsored subcontractor's work, just as they would, had they subcontracted them directly. They generally don't appreciate having an unknown quantity, especially one whom they have no leverage with, working on their project. Whether the owner sponsored subcontractor is working for the general contractor or the client, his working relationship with the general contractor is subject to conflict.

I recall an individual who exemplified the prototype of the scorned and baleful subcontractor. Unfortunately, he was as unreliable and incompetent as he was disagreeable.

He was an electrician, whom the owner was long acquainted with. This electrician made it clear to the general contractor early on that he was uncooperative; in fact, he required the contractor to cooperate with him. If 15 out of 16 rooms were ready for him to work in, he would insist that he had to work in the only room not ready for him. If the general contractor was working in one room, it was always the room that the electrician insisted he had to work in. If all the material was procured by the general contractor for the electrician, save for one item, it was that item that he must have and could work on no other task. Naturally, these objections all arose *after* the fact. However, as he related to the owner, it was the general contractor who was to blame for being uncooperative. To the general contractor, this became a moot point when the electrician's errors and omissions became painfully apparent; nevertheless, the owner continued to worship this electrician. While the electrician was responsible for his own work, he caused considerable coordination problems which affected the rest of the project.

In such instances, a knowledgeable general contractor will assert himself accordingly. If the subcontractor is a plumber or electrician, a general contractor may become even more leery. Once an MEP contractor files a job, or begins a job, it becomes difficult to terminate and replace him, should that be desired. The termination part is not difficult, however, few contractors will want to pull a permit on a job that was begun by another mechanic, under another permit (the removed permit should first be closed or signed off).

Often, owners are unaware of their responsibility regarding use of their own contractors. The A201 informs them accordingly:

> The Owner shall provide for coordination of the activities of the Owner's own forces and of each separate contractor with the Work of the Contractor, who shall cooperate with them (6.1.3).

Yet,

> The Contractor . . . shall connect and coordinate the Contractor's construction and operations with their Owner's forces as required by the construction documents (6.2.1).

How would an owner of a residence provide coordination? He wouldn't. He would expect the general contractor to do it for free, which many do as a courtesy. The above articles seemingly represent a contradiction, making the assignment of coordination unclear. The real surprise for the owner is when he finds out that his own forces have made errors or omissions—had they worked for the general contractor, the general contractor would be liable. When they are the owner's own forces, the owner is responsible, as he has assumed the same rights as his general contractor would have. This is a fair arrangement, one that architects should advise their clients accordingly. However, A201 accords the owner's subcontractors relatively easy means for claims against the general contractor:

> The Owner shall be reimbursed by the Contractor for costs incurred by the Owner which are payable to a separate contractor because of delays, improperly timed activities or defective construction of the Contractor (6.2.3).

The substantiation of any such claim is purely up to the subcontractor. This condition suggests even less of an incentive for a general contractor to work with an owner's own forces. Another troublesome provision for owner's forces refers to cutting and patching:

> The Owner and each separate contractor shall have the same responsibilities for cutting and patching as are described for the Contractor in Section 3.14 (6.2.5).

Few subcontractors do their own cutting and patching. Accordingly, a general contractor will provide cutting and patching for his subcontractors. If he doesn't speak up, he will provide this service *gratis* for the owner's subcontractors. In short, an owner using his own forces is usually a losing proposition for a general contractor. Like the electrician described above, these subcontractors are seldom worth the trouble.

Construction manager/design team conflicts

As the construction manager typically has no contractual relationship with the design team, conflicts are treated differently. Refer to Chap. 5 for discussion on this topic.

Subcontractor or vendor conflicts.

Just as you wouldn't expect an architect to hire a contractor he has never heard of, a contractor should not hire a subcontractor or vendor whom he has never heard of; however, it is common practice to do so. Here are some of the reasons:

- There may be specialty work that he has no resource for.
- He may not be able to find a low enough price.
- He can't populate a bid field.
- The subcontractor may be prenominated by the architect or client (see above).
- He simply may not have an appropriate level subcontractor for the project.
- The job may not appeal to his regular stable of resources.
- He may not have the requisite experience to facilitate the work.
- He may not feel like putting forth the effort of sourcing out a small or problematic scope of work.

In any case, there are obvious disadvantages to entering into contracts with virtual strangers, such as a lack of leverage in negotiating and the risk of using an unknown quantity. You should never contract a vendor sight unseen. If nothing else, ask for references and see some examples of his work. You might want to check if consumer complaints are filed against the company or if the owner has any past legal history or judgments against him. The handicap of not having a working relationship with a contract party is a common cause of conflict. Just as you approach a new architect or client with caution, so should you your subcontractors.

On the other hand, you will establish seemingly healthful relationships with subcontractors, only to have a falling-out with them somewhere down the line. Regardless of your history with them—it's over. Only the divorce proceedings need to take place. A fair number of such relationships sour and go bad in the middle of a project—the subcontractor may bail out, leaving the general contractor to his own devices. A general contractor will likely give his regular subcontractors a little more leeway than he does others who he does not have history with. Sometimes, too much leeway is given, such that a subcontractor can do as he wishes, even at the expense of others. Regardless of history with a subcontractor, all should be held to the same standard of performance.

Fiduciary conflicts.   Arguments over money are more ubiquitous and more serious than any other problems we have discussed. Typical fighting over money fixates on progress payments, change orders, delays, and quality control.

Progress payments. The discussion of payments is indigenous to the section dealing with contract negotiation; however, because there are so many problems related to financial relationships in construction contracts, I locate the discussion here—in the discussion of conflicts.

We discussed what sort of problems arise on a project with poor cash flow in Chap. 2, specifically, losses of time and money. To control this problem, contractors need to create cost projections for their projects and structure the progress payment section of their contract accordingly. If they are being paid on time, yet still don't have enough cash to run the project, they either generated an inaccurate cost projection, had no cost projection, or were aware of the limitation as a requirement of winning the contract, yet took the project anyway. As it is, architects and clients will expect to negotiate the progress payment section of their contract to their own advantage—whoever has control of the cash controls the project. The AIA contract and *Application for Payment* are structured in such a way as to leave ample funds for the owner to finish the project should the general contractor leave or be terminated.

Progress payments are defined by milestones, and/or work in place in stipulated sum contracts. In fee-base contracts, payments tend to be monthly. Progress payments are a boilerplate component of the AIA 101 contract. As such, architects will consider your Application for Payment against what the contract progress payment clause says. The way it usually works, a contractor will send his Application for Payment, along with the required *continuation sheet*, to the architect for his review. More often than not, the application is rejected by the architect. This may be for a number of reasons: the contractor may be overbilling so to gain the monetary advantage on the project; the architect may be disapproving so to yield more control to his client; or the architect may be stalling for more time.

In either case, a negotiation is conducted, wherein a new application is issued by the contractor and reconsidered by the architect. This practice is so common that contractors are prone to inflate their assessments of progress with the expectation of the negotiation exercise. Rather, applications for payment should be prepared in tandem with the architect, such that once the application is notarized, it has already been approved by the design team or owner's agent. In the end, everyone is happy with the payment amount and the contractor is paid in a more timely fashion.

Article 5.1.3 of the AIA 101 provides an instrument for processing payments to the general contractor, will stipulate when payment applications are due, and when payments are due. Thirty days can be thought of as an average interval between payment approval and payment issuance. Not uncommonly, this wait period is less than the time it takes to generate an application of payment that the architect will approve. Even so, if a payment is late by a week or two, what recourse does the contractor have? Of course he can take action, but this will be considered to be antagonizing. Besides, it's not the end of the world. Contractors know this and are loath to rock the boat too aggressively when they are not paid on time. There is some sagacity to that notion; however, beware—once you accept a late payment without comment, you are setting the precedent for all future payments.

Change orders. As we discussed in Chap. 2, change orders are a notorious bane of the industry; however, not just for clients and architects, as they would have it, but for the general contractor. Outside of delays, change orders are perhaps the greatest source of conflict on residential construction projects. Despite misconceptions, (honest) general contractors do not have a high profit margin, or one greater than the base contract, for change orders. This is, in part, because subcontractors experience and pass on the prorated costs of change order work to the general contractor—the change order is high even before the general contractor attaches his fees.

From what we discussed in Chap. 2, it follows that although change orders are generally troublesome and problematic, they should not be a source of endless conflict between the general contractor, architect, and owner. This concept flies in the face of the reality that few general contractors manage their change order work without such conflicts—they need not.

If the processing and management of change orders is done efficiently by the general contractor, he can substantially lower the rate of incidence of conflict. To demonstrate this technique, we must explore the nature of conflict regarding change orders, the typical response to them and the consequences of those responses, and finally, the techniques that can be used to obviate such conflicts. Essentially, there are two basic arguments regarding change orders—responsibility and cost.

Conflict 1. Whose responsibility is the change order? The cost may or may not be determined. If the cost isn't substantial, the owner or general contractor may concede it. As a rule, it is a good investment for a general contractor to concede a small change order, as he will likely reap some return on investment, even if it is merely acknowledged as only a good faith gesture. Often, it isn't clear who is accountable for a given change order. This can complicate matters even before an RFP is issued (an RFP connotes the solicitation of a price as an extra).

Response: Assuming no party takes responsibility, it now becomes a conflict, with all parties drawing a line in the sand. Having no set process or methodology for conflict resolution, the problem persists. If the conflict is not resolved, other work may be delayed. Sooner or later, negotiation is forced, or the general contractor decides he must do the work without authorization, for fear of the delay effect on other scope. He even may do this without furnishing a price for the work. At worst, he should furnish a price, and conduct the work "under protest." In the meantime, an architect reserves the option to issue the loathed *Construction Change Directive*, as we shall see below. Nonremuneration for the change order by the client may inspire a claim by the general contractor.

Technique: There is no such thing as a change order for which no one is responsible. Someone is *always* responsible or accountable; the irony is that in residential contracts change order work is initiated, more often than not, by the owner. However, the general contractor and architect may be loath to point this out, especially if they feel they can saddle their each other with the responsibility for it. Determine responsibility before any directive is authorized. With good contract documentation this should not be tantamount to reinventing the wheel. Owners, architects, and general contractors need to be reasonable in order for this process to work.

Conflict 2. The price is unreasonable. Responsibility has been assigned; however, the price being unacceptable is now the problem.

Response: Typically a negotiation takes place. Depending on how and when negotiation follows will dictate when the work will actually take place. Owners do not understand the logic behind the valuation of change orders. Some architects understand; however, they may not agree with the methodology. Unfortunately, the methods with which many general contractors manage and control change order costs do not offer a ready explanation, or one at all, for how they arrived at a given cost. In fact, for some, there are no methods.

Technique: As we said in Chap. 2, no contractor should be forced into the position where he is apt to lose money on a change order. Using the preventive measures of estimating, a general contractor can assess *known* risks, and point out to his client where change orders are likely to occur *before* they happen. He can also do this in a general way, especially for projects with incomplete designs, where he can provide a contingency as part of the base contract for undefined scopes of work. While a general contractor should be able to demonstrate why his change order may be prorated, or why he is charging higher for the same work included in the base contract, he isn't *obligated* to.[11] Finally, the ball is in the client's court—just as he did with the base contract, he can take it or leave it. However, few contractors will take this route if the work must be done, is holding up other work, or for fear they will antagonize their client.

The A201 has some interesting articles in it pertaining to change orders, some of which are antithetical to common practice. For one, in the absence of agreement on a change order the owner may issue a *Construction Change Directive* (7.3). Whether the general contractor agrees with the terms set forth by the architect—adjustments to contract sum and/or time, he is required to proceed with the work (7.3.4). Furthermore:

> If the Contractor does not respond promptly or disagrees with the method for adjustment in the Contract Sum, the method and the adjustment shall be determined by the Architect . . . (7.3.6).

For which the Architect can insist on an accounting (7.3.6.1-5). The same holds true for credits due the owner. Indeed, these are nebulous terms, and I can't recall them ever being enforced on a residential project. The A201 also gives architects further latitude in what it terms *Minor Changes in the Work* (7.4), as defined by the architect as not affecting the contract sum or contract time (7.4).

Claims

The A201 contains language meant to facilitate the process of claims by the owner or contractor. There are three types:

- Claims for additional costs (over contract sum)
- Claims for additional time
- Injury or damage to person or property

Any such claim:

> Must be initiated within twenty-one days after occurrence of the event giving rise to such claim, or within 21 days after claimant first recognizes the condition . . . (4.3.2).

Unfortunately, for the contractor:

> Pending final resolution of a claim . . . the contractor shall proceed diligently with performance of the Contract, and the Owner shall continue to make payments . . . (4.3.3).

The architect reviews and will determine whether a claim is legitimate or not. This isn't particularly good news for contractors, especially if the claim refers to a liability on the part of the architect, wherein the architect would have a conflict of interest in such matters. Any dispute of an architect's determination must be referred to mediation or arbitration.

Final payments

One of the most elusive grails in the construction industry, most any contractor will tell you, is final payment. Effectively, if you have finished your work and not been paid, and the client is not motivated to pay you, you likely have either played all your cards or ceded too much financial control to him. Final payments are the hardest dollars you will ever earn. If you have performed your contract 100% you should be paid 100%. However, some clients seemingly feel no incentive to pay you 100%; they may offer you a fraction of what you are owed. Needless to say, such clients you don't need, however, they will invariably find you. If a client is late[12] with a progress payment on the project, you can always advise that you will demobilize the project until it is adequately financed as per the contract. If then, as there is no more work to postpone on the project, such as when it is complete, what recourse do you have? You still have avenues of litigation mentioned above but equally as effective, you may choose to delay issuance of control documents, such as sign-offs and inspection certificates required by local jurisdictions. Without these, a certificate of occupancy cannot be generated. Without a certificate of occupancy, the title to the property cannot be transferred.

However, general contractors are often themselves to blame for unfinished work for which they are not paid. Sometimes it is clear what the specific reason for nonpayment is, sometimes it is complicated. On successful projects final payment is generally not an issue. As it were, few contractors seemingly cruise along through a project right up to the finish without incident that would jeop-ardize their final payment—there are simply too many things that can go wrong and at least one always seems to.

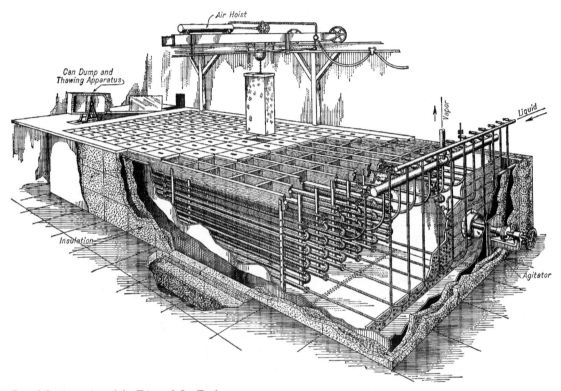

Detail Construction of the Triumph Ice Tank
In this system, the condensed exhaust steam from the main engine and auxiliaries, purified by reboiling and fil-tering, is generally frozen in galvanized sheet-steel cans immersed in a brilia tank, the brine being agitated by a propeller wheel and cooled by direct expansion piping placed in the tank. A standard sized block may measure 11in. × 22in. × 44in., and weigh three-hundred pounds
Harding and Willard, *Mechanical Equipment of Buildings, Vol II: Power Plants and Refrigeration*, (New York: John Wiley & Sons, 1918)

Litigation

Avoiding litigation

The prohibitive cost of litigation is a great incentive to keep matters out of court. For this reason, arbitration is a common solution to contracts destined for litigation. You'll never get all your money back in arbitration but it usually beats the return of investment for litigating. Litigation should be a last resort, such as when a client refuses to pony up or there are damages involved. Even winning litigation can be a Pyrrhic victory, where compensation is made years after it was earned, if at all. Even so, the arbitration can be a time-consuming and costly process. The American Institute of Architects (AIA) restructured its A201 to require a mediation period for contractual conflicts so to lower the incidence of litigation:

> Any claim arising out of or related to the Contract, except Claims relating to aesthetic effect and except those waived . . . (shall) be subject to mediation as a condition precedent to arbitration . . . (4.5.1)

Strive to achieve a win-win situation and make this philosophy clear to all parties concerned. If people feel you are at least somewhat empathetic they will be more likely to be reasonable and negotiable. To avoid litigation, you must first limit the impetus for it, which is conflict.

When Projects Go South

This text repeatedly states that the majority of residential construction projects are unhappy ones. Inevitably, there is some misery afforded at least one party of the contract. On some projects, everyone is unhappy. Then there are projects where the level of misery becomes untenable. The point where this becomes evident is the turning point of the project, or when it goes "south" or "bad." It is at this time that you need to consider an exit strategy. Ideally, you saw the writing on the wall and you have made accommodations for this condition. At worst, you were blindsided and have no idea what to do. You stay on task and see what happens. That would constitute the "worst case scenario."

Last Resort

Hopefully, this day never comes; however, invariably it seems to rear its head. "Last resort" typically means contract termination and/or litigation. There are different avenues of litigation and a host of vehicles at your disposable; but beware, the client will have his lawyers. As most construction contractual complaints occur over nonpayment by the client, the simplest, yet most effective tool, in most jurisdictions is the mechanic's lien. A mechanic's lien is a claim of unpaid assets on a property for which you have made physical improvements, hence, this type of lien is generally for the construction industry. Your subcontractors will be familiar with the lien process and you should expect them to lien the property of a nonpaying client just as you do. In fact, if you don't pay your subcontractors they will lien the property, making it difficult for you to get paid until you pay them.

The lien will be appended to the title of said property and must be satisfied before the title can be transferred to another party. If the client does not satisfy the lien through payment or bond, you may then foreclose the lien—demanding payment. The beauty of the mechanic's lien is that you no longer need to spend hours doing paperwork or paying a lawyer to prepare and serve it; there are now clearing houses that will do this for you for a very reasonable fee. As banks finance most mortgages, the mortgagor's bank will receive a copy of the lien and will be none too happy to have one of their interests at risk. As with any legal action, be extra diligent in providing accurate information and having correct documentation to support your argument, which can be nullified if either is found wanting. Finally, neither you nor your client *really* wants to fight— settlement is always the better way.

There are a variety of outcomes of untenably dysfunctional projects. Here are three of the most common.

Contract terminated by owner for lack of performance by contractor

Typically, by the time a contractor is officially terminated, he has either left the project by his own volition or he has been asked to leave. A nonperforming contractor often will leave before he is asked. This happens on underbid projects and projects where the contractor finds he is in over his head, like the duplex project we have discussed. He may need to leave because the project is late, quality issues, or both. Not uncommonly, a nonperforming contractor doesn't have the good sense to opt out of a project when he first realizes he can't build it. The conditions on the project become exacerbated until such time as action becomes exigent.

This text states that contractors who can't cut the high-end residential sector mustard are an epidemic. This being so, termination of their contracts is commonplace. It doesn't help matters that it is with great difficulty, and often more capital, that the owner must pick up after a discharged contractor. This is truly a disincentive, such that some owners will keep a failing contractor on so to avoid it—settling with less, rather than go the alternate route. That's purely a judgment call on their part, which has everything to do with the *status quo* of the project and the client's priorities.

Generally, the owner can terminate the contract for cause:

- Inadequate level staffing or skill of staff
- Failure to pay subcontractors
- Failure to perform according to contract
- Failure to observe local laws, codes, jurisdictions, and so forth

In order to finish the work:

> If the unpaid balance of the Contract Sum exceeds costs of finishing the Work, including compensation for the Architect's services and expenses made necessary thereby, and other damages incurred by the Owner and not expressly waived, such excess shall be paid to the Contractor.

We can fairly speculate that the number of such conditions does not appear to be ubiquitous. Yet,

> If such costs and damages exceed the unpaid balance, the Contractor shall pay the difference to the Owner (A201:14.2.4).

What's good for the goose is not good for the gander—neither instance is likely to be a slam-dunk. If a party feels shortchanged, there will be ample incentive for arbitration or litigation.

The unfair fact of the matter is that the owner doesn't need a specific reason to terminate a contractor:

> The Owner may, at any time, terminate the Contract for the Owner's convenience and without cause (A201:14.4.1),

However,

> In case of termination for the Owner's convenience, the contractor shall be entitled to receive payment for Work executed, and costs incurred by reason of such termination, along with *reasonable*[13] overhead and profit on the Work not executed (14.4.3).

A contractor should not take too much solace in this condition. Trying to get money from an owner who has terminated your contract will generally yield a poor return on investment, especially if it is up to others to quantify what is meant by the word "reasonable." If an owner feels that for whatever reason, he doesn't like the contractor, he feels the contract value is inflated or just on a whim—he can terminate the contract for convenience.

Contractor litigation for nonpayment by owner

The client and his design team may not agree with the amount of money you are invoicing for services rendered, especially for change order work as the base contract sum is a *fait accompli*. If you feel that nonpayment is becoming a pattern, you may have no choice but to demobilize the project, at least until payments are up to date. Demobilization on account of nonpayment is considered "one foot out the door," and one step closer to terminating the project. Termination will require litigation, which typically is settled out of court with an arbitrator. The client will undoubtedly have a counterclaim, as he invariably will see things differently.

The A201 provides for termination of contract by contractor:

- If through no fault of his own (or his subcontractors) the work should stop for a period longer than 30 days
- If a Certificate of Payment has not been issued, has been held without comment, or has been approved, but payments not made according to contract

Although most projects won't completely come to a halt, especially for longer than 30 days, rates of production or percentage of time on-task can dwindle to the point where the contractor loses money as a direct result of lost production.

The A201 describes the given protocol for properly terminating any AIA contract using the A201 general conditions—there is no alternative. Assuming the contractor is within his rights, he may:

> . . . recover from the Owner payment for Work executed and for proven loss with respect to materials, equipment, tools, and construction equipment and machinery, including *reasonable* overhead, profit, and damages (14.1.3).

Again, the use of the term "reasonable" regarding the amounts of money due a contractor strike one as being particularly nebulous. In other words, if an owner terminates the contract for convenience, at best, the contractor may receive some small token gesture representing a fraction of the remaining value of profit and overhead remaining on the contract, or if the contractor terminates for good reason, the contractor will at best, be reimbursed for work in place, and any other tangible assets now intrinsic to the part of the work executed, that is, no compensation for overhead or other intangibles. The contractor does not have the luxury of terminating for convenience.

If it hasn't happened already, it will happen to you; a customer simply doesn't want to pay his bill, for lack of a better term—a freeloader or deadbeat, or someone who merely wants to get something for nothing. The writing is usually on the wall regarding such characters; however, chronic scammers are known to perpetrate regularly. They may string along a contractor to the end, while never having any intent of paying him his last payment, with the idea in mind that the project will be nearly done and that with a fraction of the money he begrudged his contractor, he can bankroll completion by another contractor. Clients regularly do background checks on contractors—should this work both ways? This is taking unfair advantage as contractors invariably have the weaker cash position with their projects.

Project abandonment/firing of contractor

Some projects become so unbearable to a contractor that he feels induced to all at once walk off the project. You probably have seen many such projects, having been asked to pick up the pieces or clean up after them. In fact, you may have felt like walking away from a project yourself. Abandoning a project is generally considered irresponsible. The contractor who leaves a project has no prospect of being further remunerated short of litigation. Since there is no provision for project abandonment in most contracts, this action can be considered a breach of contract. Anyone who ditches a project should consider his financial and legal position, and obligation regarding the project, before he decides to leave. No doubt you have seen your share of subcontractors and employees get up and walk out, however, they have less at stake. There may come a time when you encounter a project which becomes completely untenable.

Just as project abandonment is considered preemptive, so is its antithesis, firing or lockout by the owner. This is not the same circumstance as contract termination by the client, as discussed above. Without legal contractual procedure, firing and lockout are also considered rash and irresponsible actions. The difference is there is a tacit understanding that the contractor is working for the owner, that is, the contractor can't fire the client. In truth, the contractor is working *with* the owner, however, only when the owner is meeting the terms of his part of the contract, that is, contracts are a two-way street, not a one-way, such as in a traditional employee–employer relationship. It is much less scandalous for an owner to fire his contractor than for the contractor to walk off—the contractor has his reputation to consider. Whether the contractor leaves of his own volition or is forced off a project, invariably, he will always be considered the aggressive party, or the one who forces the issue. What drives this perception is the industry's reputation—that it is for the most part, corrupt and incompetent. The *post mortem* will judge the validity of this perception as it scrutinizes the behavior of all contract parties. The conclusion will find for or against either party, but it can never attribute blame to the entire industry.

We discussed in Chaps. 2 and 4 some of the various ways in which a project becomes dysfunctional. We also looked at some tools to control these problems and also how to avoid them. Nevertheless, you will encounter numerous conflicts on all of your projects. To be an effective manager you must have people who are experienced, and have the wherewithal to solve problems early, before they become unmanageable.

Conflict Resolution

Whenever you're in conflict with someone, there is one factor that can make the difference between damaging your relationship and deepening it. That factor is attitude.

WILLIAM JAMES

Effectively, understanding and resolving conflicts in construction contracts is an art that requires much skill. Many contractors, architects, and especially clients, are nearly completely clueless as to how to go about resolving conflicts in a constructive fashion; yelling, screaming, and nasty letters seem to be the most common methods used. Perhaps this is why arbitrators are so busy playing marriage counselor. Arbitration should be invoked to negotiate a settlement; however, it should be the contractor's last choice; he would rather resolve disagreements and put them behind, where they can no longer threaten or hang over his head. The manner in which he negotiates conflicts will determine how efficient he will be at this task and whose interests he has in mind (should be everybody's). In order to be an effective facilitator of conflict resolution, you should have the following skills.

Strong communication: an ability to demonstrate facts in an objective fashion

This includes the people skills required to deal with those who may be angry, and their sometimes irrational and hostile responses. This is one of the most elusive skills in any business relationship, just as it is in personal relationships. Only people of character will have the wherewithal to cope with difficult situations. They must be disciplined, patient, and know their business.

Some people, though they are completely in the right, preclude their success by the manner in which they present themselves. If they take a contentious path, they clearly are either expecting resistance or have a chip on their shoulder. The discussion can quickly degenerate away from the issue and diverge into matters less relevant. Objective and simple presentation of the facts is all that is required. The contractor must control the protocol of such discussions, such that they keep to the issues, rather than let them get away, and to keep extraneous or irrelevant issues from obfuscating the original one.

Willingness and ability to negotiate: a firm, but reasonable sense of fairness

Some of the negotiating skills required to be a good deal closer we discussed in Chap. 2, however a different set of negotiating skills is required for conflict resolution. First of all, understand that you are not out to affix blame to a party; you are out to negotiate a solution, regardless of the blameful party. You often will find yourself being blamed. This mere condition is enough to put most people on the defensive and render them prone to contentiousness. Again, the emphasis is on solutions, not on who is blameful—even when you're under the gun. Although you may be right, this condition doesn't necessarily dictate the course of action, that is, in of itself, righteousness alone will not solve the problem. Before you consider your own position, first put yourself in the other person's shoes. Then you can form a plan that will take into consideration the whole picture, hopefully, generating the win-win scenario you set store by.

Of course, the architect and client must be signed up for the negotiating process. It should be expected on any project and the general contractor should have a protocol at the ready to implement. This protocol focuses on:

- Identifying the issue
- Solving the issue
  - Identify steps to resolution
  - Attribute responsibility
- De-escalating conflicts
- Preventive strategies

Too often the process of negotiating issues, especially relating to money, becomes a contentious free-for-all. A lot of yelling and arguing must take place until some one backs down enough or the issue remains unresolved, as no one wants to touch it.

Full knowledge of contract documents: know your business

Should it become apparent that you believe or impart inaccurate information, your credibility, as well as your negotiating position can be compromised.

Without knowledge, you cannot speak with conviction. And if you speak without conviction you will lose respect and trust. As there are often several representatives speaking for one contractor, these spokesmen should also speak only from an informed standpoint. If they cannot, they should be forbidden to discuss important matters with the clients.

If you know what you're talking about, you will have a command of conveying this sense to others, such that they will listen and be less inclined to take issue, whereas if you don't really know, your credibility will be quickly and perhaps permanently undermined and your negotiating position will be gone with it.

Familiarity with all circumstances affecting the conflict(s)

Have all your facts straight. Talk to all parties involved as their perspective will inform your decision on what action to take. Conduct a team meeting with project members from your company. Deliberate on the matter over at least a short period of time, especially if it is a sensitive issue. If it is a matter involving the client, apply to the architect for his opinion of how to best arrive at a resolution. There is no improvement upon presenting an argument with a built-in solution; people don't like questions—they want answers.

Basic knowledge of contract law

A basic knowledge of construction law will help you determine when it is time to become litigious, and it will also help guide you away from litigation, which should be your goal. You don't want to invoke your knowledge of contract law prematurely. Even when conflicts arise, keep this knowledge to yourself and use it to help guide you. Your client will be less than impressed to hear you discuss contract law. If the project does head for litigation, you will want a good construction lawyer.

Know how to choose your battles

You are not going to win every argument. In fact, you will probably lose most of them, and at times, this is a good thing. By backing down from a stand-off you are, in effect, making a concession, and thereby in a sense, gaining some leverage for future negotiation. Besides, not every claim is worth pursuing. You may have a record of one win and 12 losses; however, the one win can make the twelve losses seem insignificant. Scrutinize your position before entering into an argument, and endeavor to sort out which battles are worth fighting and which are not. You will have plenty of opportunity. Respect and understand the concept of *quid pro quo*. It states that:

■ Even if you think you're always right, don't be—being wrong every so often beats always being right.

- Negotiating is a two-way street—if your counterpart continually gets no reward for his negotiating efforts, he is likely to sooner or later shun the process as being a poor investment of his time

The client and architect's response can provide a benchmark for where you draw the line. If they are squeamish of conflict, you will likely be more tolerant of their minor trespasses. However, if they begin to cite the project documentation, such as A201, you must be prepared for their obstinacy. You need to decide if a given claim is worth pursuing or if it should be set aside.

Documentation for Accountability

The paper trail on your projects is the key vehicle for tracking information, but equally important, documentation is crucial to accountability on your project. You will use documentation to track information to and from the architect and client, as well as other job team members. Documentation is also critical to conflict resolution as it should reflect the sequence of events and flow of information on your project, which you will find yourself answering for frequently. Some of the most important documentation to maintain, in terms of accountability are:

- Tracked schedule
- Meeting minutes
- Applications for Payment and Continuation Sheets
- Change order log
- Submittal log
- RFI log
- Drawing and sketches (SK) log
- Notifications, advisories, and other contract related correspondence

All of the above should be maintained for use in backing up your historical position on the project. Additionally, you should have progress photographs or video footage documenting the sequence and real-time of the work.

In terms of conflict resolution, you may find yourself notifying the architect in writing of problems such as design discrepancies. Many architects will be put on the defensive by such correspondences and may retaliate as if they were enjoined in a paper-war. When at all possible, work out conflicts on a verbal basis, documenting only the directive—no one wants to see a slew of dirty laundry. If it works, you and your architect will work very well together. Take the following example.

It is the early stage of a project, just after demolition. As yet, there is no enmity between the contractual parties. An architect's drawing shows a 4 in. waste connection to a riser, located in a wet-wall. However, subsequent to demolition, it becomes evident that the riser is in an adjacent false column, 15 ft away from where it is shown on the drawings. Evidently, the architect overlaid his design drawings over an old drawing set the client gave him from some years ago without verifying the information. Not so smart, but not uncommon. Resultantly, the plumber is asking for an extra to do the work. The contractor has a few options open to him.

Figure a way for the plumber to do the work for free or find some other way to offset the mistake. This option is for contractors who are either scared to confront their architect or don't want to ruffle any feathers—both passive nonindustrious positions. The work may be done without any conflict but the transference of the conflict will soon take on a life of its own.

Bring up the conflict as a topic of discussion in the next job meeting. This could subject the architect to embarrassment and to the wrath of the client. The architect will not appreciate this. An item is not an issue until it becomes one. If you and your architect can find a solution, the item will never become an issue. If together you cannot resolve the conflict, then you have an issue. An example would be an impasse over who was to pay for extra work.

Notify the architect in writing of the conflict. That's a start, however, do not yet advise the client of the conflict. What purpose would that serve? In of itself, it merely documents the conflict, which is OK; however, without the intention of proactive follow-up on the contractor's part, it has the effect of "dropping the problem in the architect's lap." Moreover, once documented, the architect may sense that you are concerned with indemnifying yourself. Such a notification should include a phrase such as: "our project manager will try to reach you by telephone regarding this item," or "please advise as to when we can schedule a meeting to resolve this issue."

Now, consider a hypothetical response by the contractor—the misplaced riser was detected on a Monday morning. Understanding that the contractor–architect relationship was still relatively casual and unceremonious, he would like to keep it that way for as long as possible before the inevitable meltdown. The superintendent advises his project manager of the problem and that he wants to try to work it out with the architect before making an issue of it. The project manager advises the architect in a telephone call that same morning indicating the problem and offering the opportunity to resolve it before it becomes an issue. In order to take advantage of this offer, the meeting must happen by the end of the next day, or work will be delayed. The architect appreciates this and agrees to a meeting the next day. The next day, the superintendent, architect, and project manager are on site to discuss the problem. The architect, being reasonable, acknowledges the conflict and asks for suggestions. As yet, no one has pointed any fingers. The plumber advises that if there is sufficient pitch, he can reach the actual location of the riser; however, it is going to be an extra. The architect requests a price from the plumber; however, the superintendent interjects that the RFP must go through the general contractor's office.

Once the RFP is processed by the general contractor, a draft change order is prepared and the project manager discusses it with the architect. Before he does, the project manager prepares his responses to the architect's likely questions; if the architect is agreeable to the price, the project manager may release the work to the plumber, even without a signed change order. If the architect is hesitant, he will indicate that he cannot authorize the work. As it turns out, the architect realizes his error; however, he is not in a position to ask the client to finance his oversight. The project manager senses the architect's willingness to be reasonable and negotiate and offers to haggle with the plumber. Upon request, the plumber discounts his price 10%; however, this is not enough to make the problem go away. The project manager then begins to peruse the drawings to look for a way to offset the cost of the plumber's work. He will look at plumbing scope first. As there were a lot of plumbing allowances, perhaps he will find something. He sees that one of the existing set of riser valves to be replaced as part of the work was recently installed and therefore, will not need replacement. He tells his plumber that he is willing to trade the credit of the valves for the 15 ft addition of the waste line. The plumber considers this for a moment. At the general contractor's request, he already had reduced his bid to a very tight number. And now that demolition is done, he sees a tougher job than he expected. He is beginning to feel taken advantage of. He indicates to the project manager that he is willing to take another 10% off the price, however, he won't be happy about it. The project manager decides not to pursue the credit for the valves, as the plumber has not acknowledged it, and it will likely cause an argument over a moot point, which he does not want.

The project manager now has a real problem—he has to make a decision that his boss, the architect, the plumber, and his superintendent can all live with. The change amounts to about $800. He doesn't feel comfortable negotiating further with one of his trusty plumbers and would rather not sully the relationship with the architect over a negligible sum. He doesn't want to hold up the job and wants his boss to come out ahead. Considering all the pros and cons, he makes his decision.

He telephones the architect to advise him that he is going to make what he feels is a good-faith gesture—his company will pay for the relocated waste pipe. Additionally, he points out the perfectly good set of riser valves that need not be replaced. He explains why he thinks a credit should not be pursued for the reasons given above. Upon hearing this, the architect is more than content. He asks that the contractor authorize the work and indicate the relocation in his as-builts. He telephones his plumber to advise him that the work is released and that, he will request only the first 10% discount. He also tells him that the cost is out-of-pocket for the general contractor. The project manager figures that everyone will be happy except his boss, who just lost $800. The boss reacts with anger at the loss; however, in an ideal world, once his project manager points out that the reasons that he thinks this is a good investment, the boss begins to come around and agree with him. Now, everyone is happy and the client was never troubled.

Of course, every problem will require a unique solution. The above illustration isn't intended to provide a solution for a particular problem, but to show that conflict resolution is often less about dollars and cents, than it is about good sense. Some things, such as an architect's trust, a subcontractor's appreciation, cannot be measured in terms of currency—there are often other incentives, much more valuable. To realize these incentives often requires thinking outside the box. If nothing else, before firing off that change order or advisory, at least consider all options open to a win-win scenario.

Above all, if you keep accurate documentation, you will find it much easier to justify your position when negotiating and you will realize better returns on your investments in the project. More importantly, should a project become dysfunctional and lean toward litigation, your diligent documentation will discourage claims against your company. In a pinch, you will find yourself settling out of court, thus avoiding prohibitive legal fees. Alternatively, if you do not document well and a project should become litigious, the client's legal representative will enjoy easy pickings.

Notes

Basic conflict avoidance measures

- Know thyself
- De-escalate provocative issues
- Don't take it personally
- Get along
- Accentuate the positive

Tools for conflict resolution

- Strong communication: an ability to demonstrate facts in an objective fashion
- Willingness and ability to negotiate: a firm, but reasonable sense of fairness
- Full knowledge of contract documents: know your business
- Familiarity with all circumstances affecting the conflict(s)
- Basic knowledge of contract law
- Know how to choose your battles
- Documentation for Accountability

Documentation for accountability

- Tracked schedule
- Release of lien waivers
- Meeting minutes
- Applications for Payment and Continuation Sheets
- Change order log
- Submittal log
- RFI log
- Drawing and SK log
- Notifications, advisories, and other contract-related correspondence

SAMPLE MECHANIC'S LIEN: New York State

Prepared by, recording requested by and

return to:

Name:

Company:

Address:

City:

State: Zip:

Phone:

Fax:

----------------------Above this Line for Official Use Only---

----

Notice of Lien–Corporation

(N.Y. Lien Law § 9)

COMES NOW, _____, as a representative of

_____ a _____ corporation which has provided labor or

materials for the improvement of the property located at and described as

_____

_____, and would

provide notice of the following:

1.   The undersigned lien claimant, _____, may be reached at the following mailing address, _____

_____, or, if applicable, through the undersigned's attorney of record,

_____, whose address is

_____.

2.   On information and belief the undersigned would state that the above described property is owned by _____, whose interest in the property, if known, is that of

_____.

3.   The undersigned provided the following labor and/or materials at the following agreed price, or value thereof, under an agreement with _____.

Labor / Material Provided   *Agreed Price or Value*

_____

_____

4.   The amount currently unpaid to the undersigned for said labor and/or materials is

$_____.

5.   Said labor and materials were first provided on the ____ day of _____, 20____, and were last provided on the _____ day of _____, 20____.

           This the ___ day of _____, 20____.

I, _____, do hereby swear or affirm that the matters alleged and things contained in the above Notice of Lien are true and correct to the best of my knowledge, information, and belief.

_____

Affiant

_____

Title

_____

Corporation

STATE OF NEW YORK

COUNTY OF _____

On the _____ day of _____ in the year _____ before me personally came _____ to me known, who, being by me duly sworn, did depose and say that he/she/they reside(s) in _____ (if the place of residence is in a city, include the street and street number, if any, thereof); that he/she/they is (are) the

_____ (president or other officer or director or attorney in fact duly appointed) of the _____ (name of corporation), the corporation described in and which executed the above instrument; and that he/she/they signed his/her/their name(s) thereto by authority of the board of directors of said corporation.

_____

Notary Public

Printed Name: _____

Endnotes

1. Author's quote.
2. In most contracts, CM as advisor being an exception.
3. The distinction between *potential* and *possible* conflicts is that potential conflicts are those tasks inherent to the project program that are likely to cause problems whereas, possible conflicts are those that are unrelated to the work itself, such as delays in deliverables, or production. These possible conflicts need not be iterated, only referred to as a group, and addressed

as they surface. To draw attention to them preemptively is not necessary nor is it a vote of confidence. An exception to this rule is the *liquidated damages* clause.

4. Harry Stack Sulllivan, *The Psychiatric Interview*. New York, W.W. Norton & Company, Inc., 1970; p. 119.
5. Somewhat. Some contractors will ask their subcontractors to generate documents with inflated costs solely for this purpose.
6. "He hath not learnt the first precept of philosophy, which is Know thyself; for whilst he braggeth and boasteth that he can discern the least mote in the eye of another, he is not able to see the huge block that puts out the sight of both his eyes." Francois Rabelais (1483–1553), from *Gargantua and Pantagruel*, Chap. 3, XXV.
7. See App. E. There are exceptions to the *Spearin Doctrine*, such as obvious defects, or any condition the contractor would have previous knowledge of. Note, these comments are of a general nature and are not meant to be substituted for professional advice in specific situations.
8. Thomas C. Clark, *Suitability of Plans and Specs*, Rocky Mountain Construction, 2005.
9. *Ibid.*
10. *BRW Inc. v Dufficy & Sons Inc.*, 99 P.3d 66 (Colo. 2004).
11. As will be discussed, the A201, 7.3.6 would seemingly give the architect the right to either determine the costs or demand an accounting of a disputed change order; however, this is a tenuous right seldom invoked.
12. This is a provision to be negotiated and entered into the AIA contract. The AIA 201 stipulates a 7-day grace period hence of the authorization date (A101:5.1.3).
13. All italics in A201 citations are author's. The inference of suggesting that the term "reasonable," under these circumstances, can be adequately quantified is, of course, absurd.

Afterword

So it was a fitting irony that one of my last commissions prior to submitting this manuscript inspired what I believe to be an ideal exemplum of life imitating art. The firm in question consisting of two low-functioning primitives—a tiny father and son entity, personifies in a grotesque sort of way the essence of nearly every contractor shortcoming investigated in the text, a culmination of several key negative aspects of the residential construction industry that we have discussed.

I shall spend a little extra effort in conveying the visual and physical aspects of this company, as this shall convey the full experience necessary to put it into context. In short this company might be described as what I would call "a condition of timeless surreal intellectual and social degeneration." Said proprietors could best be described as resembling in form and manner Tweedledum and Tweedledee: two three-hundred pound simpletons. If they weren't so egregiously pathetic they would be contemptible, but that is a moot point.

The company occupied about 400 square feet of an inner compartment of a large prewar office building. It had a small entry room, about 7 by 10 ft in area, where two greasy Barcelona knock-off chairs served as hospitality. Two oxidizing chrome plated perforated-steel models of neo-Modern skyscrapers adorned a festering chrome and glass coffee table. The montage perhaps harkened to the inscrutably vapid early 1980s hey-day of this company, yet the clocks there had stopped.

The main office space was about 250 square feet. It had three 8×8 cubicles, and two desks at either end, opposite the cubicles. As many as six people might work here, but no more than that. It was virtually windowless, save for a shard of light coming through a grime clotted windowpane. To say the space was unbecoming or grimy would be to do disservice to its comic integrity. Upon entering the office one was assailed with a stench that most closely resembles a recently vacated sick bed of a long convalescing invalid, or the sluice of an ancient shower trap, with hints of cheap booze and stale cigarettes. The carpeting may have contributed to the stench, as it had considerable staining all about. All equipment—computers, telephones, file cabinets—were covered with a pervasive soot-laden layer of grease. An overburdened bookshelf sported 20-year old publications and catalogs—a hallmark of the devolving general contractor. The space was dimly lit with sickly fluorescents, and had no fresh air, save for an occasional puff from a sash-mounted air conditioner. It had not been freshly painted for many years.

The Past

Senior, as we shall call him, had recently been summoned from a gluttonous retirement to prop up the son's (*Junior's*) remnants of the near-dead company, which he had successfully neglected to the point of abandonment. His persona was a combination of a witless Falstaff and lower order primate. *Senior's* mental acuity was continually brought into question due to his unpredictable and foolish behavior, and his atrocious decision making. He was stubborn, misinformed, and refused to listen to anyone. This behavior was virtually constant, without cessation. Despite these shortcomings, he smugly and arrogantly wielded his purported wisdom as leader of the company. Even after years of failure and countless bankruptcies, he fancied himself a champion of the industry. Although he could count (he could not spell or write legibly) he had no reference for measuring the value of a construction dollar. His conceptual budgets were underestimated a staggering average of 50% to 300%. He was so technologically challenged that he couldn't even use a calculator or check his voice-mail.

As it is with some, his relationships in his personal life may have been different; however, his acumen for managing professional relationships was incredibly flawed. There was virtually no synergy between him and any person he associated with professionally. It did not help that he was alternately belligerent, inconsiderate, rancorous, and insolent in his comportment. He had frequent infantile temper tantrums, at which he required scolding like a child. His chief elemental fault was the inability to achieve closure on even the most mundane tasks. The result was that he ordered the same tasks done repeatedly, only to never see them through, or that he never did what he needed to do. Thus, he was virtually incapable of generating any finished product. He epitomized inaction. Although his desks were relatively neat, with orderly stacks of paper, he was incapable of generating a simple directive thereof without a gargantuan effort. It should be said that he was typically unable to locate any specific given document from these stacks; however, few of these documents were up-to-date or relevant anyway.

Today

Junior was another specimen who insisted on garnering either your pity or contempt or both. He was the acting president of the company, but only in name. Although he spent much time in his cubicle, most of this time was spent in

Internet chat rooms. His job description consisted of signing checks; he did nothing else. His cubicle was remarkable. There were a desk and long table, both littered with enormous mounds of loose papers, stationery, mail, and garbage. Where the carpet appeared between mountains of paper, Coca Cola stains were prevalent. These he drank warm, from the can, with reckless abandon. He also kept a stockpile of syringes in his cubicle.

In fairness, this individual apparently suffered from some "social condition" that consumed his ability to execute tasks other than eating, sleeping, and those stated earlier. It would appear that he was cursed with being the unfortunate offspring of a polluted genetic pool, that is, his father, and for this reason should not be considered entirely blameful for his predicament.

Like his father, he was devoid of professional social skills; however, he didn't allow himself to unravel into a snit the way his father did, he would merely withdraw and hide. On the rare occasion that he did speak or issue a directive, it was either an inappropriate or irrelevant gesture. When he spoke, his voice trembled and cackled and his narrow beady eyes sparkled and darted. This had the effect of leaving one disconcerted.

It was disenchanting to relate to them when together. They exuded a jaundiced unsavory dynamic and energy that projected and fouled any semblance of ambient positivity or pleasantry, such as any person needs in order to thrive. That is, it was so pervasive that it could readily be innately or intuitively sensed. This sensation I often compared to a worker at a toxic waste clean-up project.

The Future

What I have described earlier is no less than a spectacular aberrancy of human condition. The import of this observation is that it follows that although these two creatures are remarkable; they are merely exaggerated prototypes of a rampant circumstance. That is to say, not only are there implications regarding such behavior professionally, and within the residential construction sector, but also socioeconomically, as they, and their countless partners in crime function within that realm. As such, they and their ilk must be considered as nefarious menacing elements that must be extirpated from any consequential position of influence.

Eradicate

By educating industry players, architects, owners, and contractors, we can collectively begin to phase out such entities through disuse, litigation, and degeneration. Only by ridding the industry of these negative elements can we significantly upgrade, and ensure a better future for the evergrowing, critical, residential construction industry of tomorrow.

Endnote

1. *From Planet of the Apes*, by Pierre Boulle.

American Institute of Architects (AIA) Documents

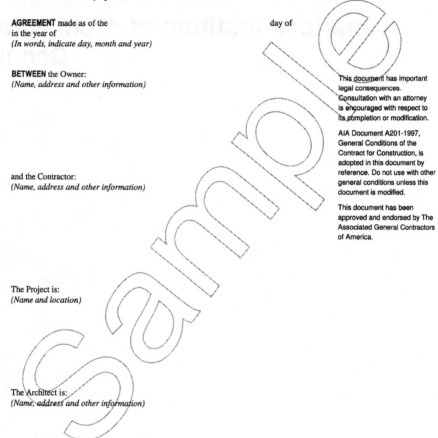

▓AIA® Document A101™ – 1997

Standard Form of Agreement Between Owner and Contractor
where the basis of payment is a STIPULATED SUM

AGREEMENT made as of the   day of
in the year of
(In words, indicate day, month and year)

BETWEEN the Owner:
(Name, address and other information)

This document has important
legal consequences.
Consultation with an attorney
is encouraged with respect to
its completion or modification.

AIA Document A201-1997,
General Conditions of the
Contract for Construction, is
adopted in this document by
reference. Do not use with other
general conditions unless this
document is modified.

This document has been
approved and endorsed by The
Associated General Contractors
of America.

and the Contractor:
(Name, address and other information)

The Project is:
(Name and location)

The Architect is:
(Name, address and other information)

The Owner and Contractor agree as follows.

ARTICLE 1 THE CONTRACT DOCUMENTS
The Contract Documents consist of this Agreement, Conditions of the Contract (General, Supplementary and other Conditions), Drawings, Specifications, Addenda issued prior to execution of this Agreement, other documents listed in this Agreement and Modifications issued after execution of this Agreement; these form the Contract, and are as fully a part of the Contract as if attached to this Agreement or repeated herein. The Contract represents the entire and integrated agreement between the parties hereto and supersedes prior negotiations, representations or agreements, either written or oral. An enumeration of the Contract Documents, other than Modifications, appears in Article 8.

ARTICLE 2 THE WORK OF THIS CONTRACT
The Contractor shall fully execute the Work described in the Contract Documents, except to the extent specifically indicated in the Contract Documents to be the responsibility of others.

ARTICLE 3 DATE OF COMMENCEMENT AND SUBSTANTIAL COMPLETION
§ 3.1 The date of commencement of the Work shall be the date of this Agreement unless a different date is stated below or provision is made for the date to be fixed in a notice to proceed issued by the Owner.
(Insert the date of commencement if it differs from the date of this Agreement or, if applicable, state that the date will be fixed in a notice to proceed.)

If, prior to the commencement of the Work, the Owner requires time to file mortgages, mechanic's liens and other security interests, the Owner's time requirement shall be as follows:

§ 3.2 The Contract Time shall be measured from the date of commencement.

§ 3.3 The Contractor shall achieve Substantial Completion of the entire Work not later than   days from the date of commencement, or as follows:
(Insert number of calendar days. Alternatively, a calendar date may be used when coordinated with the date of commencement. Unless stated elsewhere in the Contract Documents, insert any requirements for earlier Substantial Completion of certain portions of the Work.)

, subject to adjustments of this Contract Time as provided in the Contract Documents.
(Insert provisions, if any, for liquidated damages relating to failure to complete on time or for bonus payments for early completion of the Work.)

ARTICLE 4 CONTRACT SUM
§ 4.1 The Owner shall pay the Contractor the Contract Sum in current funds for the Contractor's performance of the Contract. The Contract Sum shall be   Dollars
($), subject to additions and deductions as provided in the Contract Documents.

§ 4.2 The Contract Sum is based upon the following alternates, if any, which are described in the Contract Documents and are hereby accepted by the Owner:

(State the numbers or other identification of accepted alternates. If decisions on other alternates are to be made by the Owner subsequent to the execution of this Agreement, attach a schedule of such other alternates showing the amount for each and the date when that amount expires)

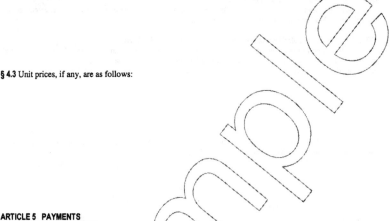

§ 4.3 Unit prices, if any, are as follows:

ARTICLE 5   PAYMENTS
§ 5.1 PROGRESS PAYMENTS
§ 5.1.1 Based upon Applications for Payment submitted to the Architect by the Contractor and Certificates for Payment issued by the Architect, the Owner shall make progress payments on account of the Contract Sum to the Contractor as provided below and elsewhere in the Contract Documents.

§ 5.1.2 The period covered by each Application for Payment shall be one calendar month ending on the last day of the month, or as follows:

§ 5.1.3 Provided that an Application for Payment is received by the Architect not later than the day of a month, the Owner shall make payment to the Contractor not later than the   day of the   month. If an Application for Payment is received by the Architect after the application date fixed above, payment shall be made by the Owner not later than   (   ) days after the Architect receives the Application for Payment.

§ 5.1.4 Each Application for Payment shall be based on the most recent schedule of values submitted by the Contractor in accordance with the Contract Documents. The schedule of values shall allocate the entire Contract Sum among the various portions of the Work. The schedule of values shall be prepared in such form and supported by such data to substantiate its accuracy as the Architect may require. This schedule, unless objected to by the Architect, shall be used as a basis for reviewing the Contractor's Applications for Payment.

§ 5.1.5 Applications for Payment shall indicate the percentage of completion of each portion of the Work as of the end of the period covered by the Application for Payment.

§ 5.1.6 Subject to other provisions of the Contract Documents, the amount of each progress payment shall be computed as follows:

.1   Take that portion of the Contract Sum properly allocable to completed Work as determined by multiplying the percentage completion of each portion of the Work by the share of the Contract Sum allocated to that portion of the Work in the schedule of values, less retainage of   percent (%). Pending final determination of cost to the Owner of changes in the Work, amounts not in dispute shall be included as provided in Section 7.3.8 of AIA Document A201-1997;

.2   Add that portion of the Contract Sum properly allocable to materials and equipment delivered and suitably stored at the site for subsequent incorporation in the completed construction (or, if approved in advance by the Owner, suitably stored off the site at a location agreed upon in writing), less retainage of percent (%);

.3   Subtract the aggregate of previous payments made by the Owner; and

.4   Subtract amounts, if any, for which the Architect has withheld or nullified a Certificate for Payment as provided in Section 9.5 of AIA Document A201-1997.

§ 5.1.7 The progress payment amount determined in accordance with Section 5.1.6 shall be further modified under the following circumstances:

.1   Add, upon Substantial Completion of the Work, a sum sufficient to increase the total payments to the full amount of the Contract Sum, less such amounts as the Architect shall determine for incomplete Work, retainage applicable to such work and unsettled claims; and
(Section 9.8.5 of AIA Document A201-1997 requires release of applicable retainage upon Substantial Completion of Work with consent of surety, if any.)

.2   Add, if final completion of the Work is thereafter materially delayed through no fault of the Contractor, any additional amounts payable in accordance with Section 9.10.3 of AIA Document A201-1997.

§ 5.1.8 Reduction or limitation of retainage, if any, shall be as follows:
(If it is intended, prior to Substantial Completion of the entire Work, to reduce or limit the retainage resulting from the percentages inserted in Sections 5.1.6.1 and 5.1.6.2 above, and this is not explained elsewhere in the Contract Documents, insert here provisions for such reduction or limitation.)

§ 5.1.9 Except with the Owner's prior approval, the Contractor shall not make advance payments to suppliers for materials or equipment which have not been delivered and stored at the site.

§ 5.2 FINAL PAYMENT
§ 5.2.1 Final payment, constituting the entire unpaid balance of the Contract Sum, shall be made by the Owner to the Contractor when:

.1   the Contractor has fully performed the Contract except for the Contractor's responsibility to correct Work as provided in Section 12.2.2 of AIA Document A201-1997, and to satisfy other requirements, if any, which extend beyond final payment; and

.2   a final Certificate for Payment has been issued by the Architect.

§ 5.2.2 The Owner's final payment to the Contractor shall be made no later than 30 days after the issuance of the Architect's final Certificate for Payment, or as follows:

ARTICLE 6   TERMINATION OR SUSPENSION

§ 6.1 The Contract may be terminated by the Owner or the Contractor as provided in Article 14 of AIA Document A201-1997.

§ 6.2 The Work may be suspended by the Owner as provided in Article 14 of AIA Document A201-1997.

ARTICLE 7   MISCELLANEOUS PROVISIONS

§ 7.1 Where reference is made in this Agreement to a provision of AIA Document A201-1997 or another Contract Document, the reference refers to that provision as amended or supplemented by other provisions of the Contract Documents.

§ 7.2 Payments due and unpaid under the Contract shall bear interest from the date payment is due at the rate stated below, or in the absence thereof, at the legal rate prevailing from time to time at the place where the Project is located.
(Insert rate of interest agreed upon, if any.)

(Usury laws and requirements under the Federal Truth in Lending Act, similar state and local consumer credit laws and other regulations at the Owner's and Contractor's principal places of business, the location of the Project and elsewhere may affect the validity of this provision. Legal advice should be obtained with respect to deletions or modifications, and also regarding requirements such as written disclosures or waivers.)

§ 7.3 The Owner's representative is:
(Name, address and other information)

§ 7.4 The Contractor's representative is:
(Name, address and other information)

§ 7.5 Neither the Owner's nor the Contractor's representative shall be changed without ten days written notice to the other party.

§ 7.6 Other provisions:

ARTICLE 8 ENUMERATION OF CONTRACT DOCUMENTS

§ 8.1 The Contract Documents, except for Modifications issued after execution of this Agreement, are enumerated as follows:

§ 8.1.1 The Agreement is this executed 1997 edition of the Standard Form of Agreement Between Owner and Contractor, AIA Document A101-1997.

§ 8.1.2 The General Conditions are the 1997 edition of the General Conditions of the Contract for Construction, AIA Document A201-1997.

§ 8.1.3 The Supplementary and other Conditions of the Contract are those contained in the Project Manual dated   , and are as follows

Document	Title	Pages

§ 8.1.4 The Specifications are those contained in the Project Manual dated as in Section 8.1.3, and are as follows:
(Either list the Specifications here or refer to an exhibit attached to this Agreement.)

Section	Title	Pages

§ 8.1.5 The Drawings are as follows, and are dated   unless a different date is shown below:
(Either list the Drawings here or refer to an exhibit attached to this Agreement.)

Number	Title	Date

§ 8.1.6 The Addenda, if any, are as follows:

Number	Date	Pages

Portions of Addenda relating to bidding requirements are not part of the Contract Documents unless the bidding requirements are also enumerated in this Article 8.

§ 8.1.7 Other documents, if any, forming part of the Contract Documents are as follows:
(List here any additional documents that are intended to form part of the Contract Documents. AIA Document A201-1997 provides that bidding requirements such as advertisement or invitation to bid, Instructions to Bidders, sample forms and the Contractor's bid are not part of the Contract Documents unless enumerated in this Agreement. They should be listed here only if intended to be part of the Contract Documents.)

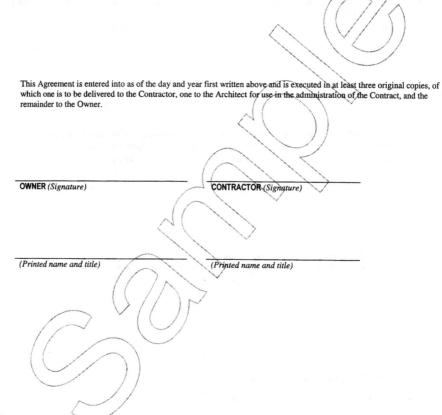

This Agreement is entered into as of the day and year first written above and is executed in at least three original copies, of which one is to be delivered to the Contractor, one to the Architect for use in the administration of the Contract, and the remainder to the Owner.

_____
OWNER *(Signature)*

_____
(Printed name and title)

_____
CONTRACTOR *(Signature)*

_____
(Printed name and title)

The American Institute of Architects is pleased to provide this sample copy of an AIA Contract Document for educational purposes. Created with the consensus of contractors, attorneys, architects and engineers, the AIA Contract Documents represent over 110 years of legal precedent.

2000 EDITION

AIA DOCUMENT | G701-2000

Change Order
(Instructions on reverse side)

PROJECT:
(Name and address)

CHANGE ORDER NUMBER:

DATE:

ARCHITECT'S PROJECT NUMBER:

CONTRACT DATE:

CONTRACT FOR:

OWNER ☐
ARCHITECT ☐
CONTRACTOR ☐
FIELD ☐
OTHER ☐

TO CONTRACTOR:
(Name and address)

THE CONTRACT IS CHANGED AS FOLLOWS:
(Include, where applicable, any undisputed amount attributable to previously executed Construction Change Directives.)

The original (Contract Sum) (Guaranteed Maximum Price) was $ _____

The net change by previously authorized Change Orders $ _____

The (Contract Sum) (Guaranteed Maximum Price) prior to this Change Order was $ _____

The (Contract Sum) (Guaranteed Maximum Price) will be (increased) (decreased)

   (unchanged) by this Change Order in the amount of $ _____

The new (Contract Sum) (Guaranteed Maximum Price) including this Change Order will be $ _____

The Contract Time will be (increased) (decreased) (unchanged) by _____ (   ) days.

The date of Substantial Completion as of the date of this Change Order therefore is _____

NOTE: This Change Order does not include changes in the Contract Sum, Contract Time or Guaranteed Maximum Price which have been authorized by Construction Change Directive for which the cost or time are in dispute as described in Subparagraph 7.3.8 of AIA Document A201.

Not valid until signed by the Architect, Contractor and Owner.

ARCHITECT *(Typed name)*	CONTRACTOR *(Typed name)*	OWNER *(Typed name)*
(Signature)	*(Signature)*	*(Signature)*
BY	BY	BY
DATE	DATE	DATE

©2000 AIA®
AIA DOCUMENT G701-2000
CHANGE ORDER

The American Institute
of Architects
1735 New York Avenue, N.W.
Washington, D.C. 20006-5292

AIA® Document G702™ – 1992

Application and Certificate for Payment

TO OWNER:

PROJECT:

APPLICATION NO:

PERIOD TO:

CONTRACT FOR:

FROM CONTRACTOR:

CONTRACT DATE:

VIA ARCHITECT:

PROJECT NOS:

Distribution to:

- ☐ OWNER
- ☐ ARCHITECT
- ☐ CONTRACTOR
- ☐ FIELD
- ☐ OTHER

CONTRACTOR'S APPLICATION FOR PAYMENT

Application is made for payment, as shown below, in connection with the Contract.
Continuation Sheet, AIA Document G703, is attached.

1. ORIGINAL CONTRACT SUM	$
2. Net change by Change Orders	$
3. CONTRACT SUM TO DATE (Line 1 ± 2)	$
4. TOTAL COMPLETED & STORED TO DATE (Column G on G703)	$

5. RETAINAGE:

a. _____ % of Completed Work
(Column D + E on G703) .... $

b. _____ % of Stored Material
(Column F on G703) .... $

Total Retainage (Lines 5a + 5b or Total in Column I of G703) .... $

6. TOTAL EARNED LESS RETAINAGE	$
(Line 4 Less Line 5 Total)	
7. LESS PREVIOUS CERTIFICATES FOR PAYMENT	$
(Line 6 from prior Certificate)	
8. CURRENT PAYMENT DUE	$
9. BALANCE TO FINISH, INCLUDING RETAINAGE	$
(Line 3 less Line 6)	

CHANGE ORDER SUMMARY	ADDITIONS	DEDUCTIONS
Total changes approved in previous months by Owner	$	$
Total approved this Month	$	$
TOTALS	$	$
NET CHANGES by Change Order		

The undersigned Contractor certifies that to the best of the Contractor's knowledge, information and belief the Work covered by this Application for Payment has been completed in accordance with the Contract Documents, that all amounts have been paid by the Contractor for Work for which previous Certificates for Payment were issued and payments received from the Owner, and that current payment shown herein is now due.

CONTRACTOR:

By: _____ Date: _____

State of:
County of:
Subscribed and sworn to before
me this _____ day of _____
Notary Public:
My Commission expires:

ARCHITECT'S CERTIFICATE FOR PAYMENT

In accordance with the Contract Documents, based on on-site observations and the data comprising this application, the Architect certifies to the Owner that to the best of the Architect's knowledge, information and belief the Work has progressed as indicated, the quality of the Work is in accordance with the Contract Documents, and the Contractor is entitled to payment of the AMOUNT CERTIFIED.

AMOUNT CERTIFIED .... $ _____

(Attach explanation if amount certified differs from the amount applied. Initial all figures on this Application and on the Continuation Sheet that are changed to conform with the amount certified.)

ARCHITECT:

By: _____ Date: _____

This Certificate is not negotiable. The AMOUNT CERTIFIED is payable only to the Contractor named herein. Issuance, payment and acceptance of payment are without prejudice to any rights of the Owner or Contractor under this Contract

AIA® Document G703™ – 1992

Continuation Sheet

AIA Document G702, APPLICATION AND CERTIFICATION FOR PAYMENT,
containing Contractor's signed certification is attached.
In tabulations below, amounts are stated to the nearest dollar.
Use Column I on Contracts where variable retainage for line items may apply.

APPLICATION NO:
APPLICATION DATE:
PERIOD TO:
ARCHITECT'S PROJECT NO:

A	B	C	D	E	F	G	H	I
			WORK COMPLETED					
ITEM NO.	DESCRIPTION OF WORK	SCHEDULED VALUE	FROM PREVIOUS APPLICATION (D + E)	THIS PERIOD	MATERIALS PRESENTLY STORED (NOT IN D OR E)	TOTAL COMPLETED AND STORED TO DATE (D+E+F)	BALANCE TO FINISH (C - G) % (G ÷ C)	RETAINAGE (IF VARIABLE RATE)

CAUTION: You should sign an original AIA Contract Document, on which this text appears in RED. An original assures that changes will not be obscured.

Construction Management Association of America (CMAA) Documents

CMAA

CMAA Document A-1 (2005 Edition)

Contract

THE CONSTRUCTION MANAGEMENT ASSOCIATION OF AMERICA, INC.

CMAA Document A-1 (2005 Edition)

Standard Form of Agreement Between
OWNER AND CONSTRUCTION MANAGER
(Construction Manager as Owner's Agent)

This document is to be used in connection with the Standard Form of Contract Between Owner and Contractor (CMAA Document A-2), the General Conditions of the Construction Contract (CMAA Document A-3), and the Standard Form of Agreement Between Owner and Designer (CMAA Document A-4), all being 2005 editions.

CONSULTATION WITH AN ATTORNEY IS RECOMMENDED WHENEVER THIS DOCUMENT IS USED.

AGREEMENT
Made this _____ day of _____ in the year of Two Thousand and
_____

BETWEEN The Owner:

and the Construction Manager, (hereinafter, referred to as the "CM"):

For services in connection with the Project known as:

hereinafter called the "Project," as further described in Article 2:

The Owner and CM, in consideration of their mutual covenants herein agree as set forth below:

Construction Management Association of America
7918 Jones Branch Drive · Suite 540 · McLean, VA 22102-3307 · 703/356-2622 · Fax 703/356-6388 · www.cmaanet.org

CMAA Document A-1 (2005 Edition)

TABLE OF CONTENTS

Article:

CMAA Document A-1 (2005 Edition)

ARTICLE 1
RELATIONSHIP OF THE PARTIES

1.1 Owner and Construction Manager

1.1.1 Relationship: The CM shall be the Owner's principal agent in providing the CM's services described in this Agreement. The CM and the Owner shall perform as stated in this Agreement. Nothing in this Agreement shall be construed to mean that the CM is a fiduciary of the Owner.

1.1.2 Standard of Care: The CM covenants with the Owner to furnish its services hereunder properly, in accordance with the standards of its profession, and in accordance with federal, state and local laws and regulations specifically applicable to the performance of the services hereunder which are in effect on the date of this Agreement first written above.

1.2 Owner and Designer

1.2.1 Owner-Designer Agreement: The Owner shall enter into a separate agreement, the "Owner-Designer Agreement", with one or more Designers to provide for the design of the Project and certain design-related services during the Construction Phase of the Project. The Project is defined in Article 2 of this Agreement.

1.2.2 Changes: The Owner shall not modify the Agreement between the Owner and Designer in any way that is prejudicial to the CM. If the Owner terminates the Designer's services, a substitute acceptable to the CM shall be appointed.

1.3 Owner and Contractors

1.3.1 Construction Contract: The Owner shall enter into a separate contract with one or more Contractors for the construction of the Project (hereinafter referred to as the "Contract"). The Contractor shall perform the Work, which shall consist of furnishing all labor, materials, tools, equipment, supplies, services, supervision, and perform all operations as required by the Contract Documents.

1.3.2 Form of Contract: Unless otherwise specified, the form of Contract between the Owner and Contractor shall be the CMAA Standard Form of Contract Between Owner and Contractor, CMAA Document A-2 (2005 Edition). The General Conditions for the Project shall be the CMAA General Conditions of the Construction Contract Between Owner and Contractor, CMAA Document A-3 (2005 Edition).

1.4 Relationship of the CM to Other Project Participants

1.4.1 Working Relationship: In providing the CM's services described in this Agreement, the CM shall endeavor to maintain, on behalf of the Owner, a working relationship with the Contractor and Designer.

1.4.2 Limitations: Nothing in this Agreement shall be construed to mean that the CM assumes any of the responsibilities or duties of the Contractor or the Designer. The Contractor will be solely responsible for construction means, methods, techniques, sequences and procedures used in the construction of the Project and for the safety of its personnel, property, and its operations and for performing in accordance with the contract between the Owner and Contractor. The Designer is solely responsible for the design requirements and design criteria of the Project and shall perform in accordance with the Agreement between the Designer and the Owner. The CM's services shall be rendered compatibly and in cooperation with the services provided by the Designer under the Agreement between Owner and Designer. It is not intended that the services of the Designer and the CM be competitive or duplicative, but rather complementary. The CM will be entitled to rely upon the Designer for the proper performance of services undertaken by the Designer pursuant to the Agreement between Owner and the Designer.

ARTICLE 2
PROJECT DEFINITION

2.1 The term "Project", when used in this Agreement, shall be defined as all work to be furnished or provided in accordance with the Contract Documents prepared by the Designer.

CMAA Document A-1 (2005 Edition)

2.2 The Project name and location is as follows:

_____

_____

_____

_____

_____

_____

_____

2.3 The Project is intended for use as:

_____

_____

_____

_____

_____

_____

_____

_____

_____

_____

_____

_____

_____

_____

_____

2.4 The term "Contract Documents" means the Instruction to Bidders, the Contract, the General Conditions and any Supplemental Conditions furnished to the Contractor, the drawings and specifications furnished to the Contractor and all exhibits thereto, addenda, bulletins and change orders issued in accordance with the General Conditions to any of the above, and all other documents specified in Exhibit B of the Standard Form of Contract Between Owner and Contractor, CMAA Document A-2, 2005 edition.

ARTICLE 3
BASIC SERVICES

3.1 CM's Basic Services

3.1.1 Basic Services: The CM shall perform the Basic Services described in this Article. It is not required that the services be performed in the order in which they are described.

3.2 Pre-Design Phase

3.2.1 Project Management

3.2.1.1 Construction Management Plan: The CM shall prepare a Construction Management Plan for the Project and shall make recommendations to the plan throughout the duration of the Project, as may be appropriate. In preparing the Construction Management Plan, the CM shall consider the Owner's schedule, budget and general design requirements for the Project. The CM shall then develop various alternatives for the scheduling and management of the Project and shall make recommendations to the Owner. The Construction Management Plan shall be presented to the Owner for acceptance.

3.2.1.2 Designer Selection: The CM shall assist the Owner in the selection of a Designer by developing lists of potential firms, developing criteria for selection, preparing and transmitting the requests for proposal, assisting in conducting interviews, evaluating candidates and making recommendations.

3.2.1.3 Designer Contract Preparation: The CM shall assist the Owner in review and preparation of the Agreement between the Owner and Designer.

3.2.1.4 Designer Orientation: The CM shall conduct, or assist the Owner in conducting, a Designer orientation session during which the Designer shall receive information regarding the Project scope, schedule, budget, and administrative requirements.

3.2.2 Time Management

3.2.2.1 Master Schedule: In accordance with the Construction Management Plan, the CM shall prepare a Master Schedule for the Project. The Master Schedule shall specify the proposed starting and finishing dates for each major project activity. The CM shall submit the Master Schedule to the Owner for acceptance.

3.2.2.2 Design Phase Milestone Schedule: After the Owner accepts the Master Schedule the CM shall prepare the Milestone Schedule for the Design Phase, which shall be used for judging progress during the Design Phase.

CMAA Document A-1 (2005 Edition)

3.2.3 Cost Management

3.2.3.1 Construction Market Survey: The CM shall conduct a Construction Market Survey to provide current information regarding the general availability of local construction services, labor, material and equipment costs and the economic factors related to the construction of the Project. A report of the Construction Market Survey shall be provided to the Owner and Designer.

3.2.3.2 Project and Construction Budget: Based on the Construction Management Plan and the Construction Market Survey, the CM shall prepare a Project and Construction Budget based on the separate divisions of the Work required for the Project and shall identify contingencies for design and construction. The CM shall review the budget with the Owner and Designer and the CM shall submit the Project and Construction Budget to the Owner for acceptance. The Project and Construction Budget shall be revised by the CM as directed by the Owner.

3.2.3.3 Preliminary Estimate and Budget Analysis: The CM shall analyze and report to the Owner and the Designer the estimated cost of various design and construction alternatives, including CM's assumptions in preparing its analysis, a variance analysis between budget and preliminary estimate, and recommendations for any adjustments to the budget. As a part of the cost analysis, the CM shall consider costs related to efficiency, usable life, maintenance, energy and operation.

3.2.4 Management Information System (MIS)

3.2.4.1 Establishing the Project MIS: The CM shall develop a MIS in order to establish communication between the Owner, CM, Designer, Contractor and other parties involved with the Project. In developing the MIS, the CM shall interview the Owner's key personnel, the Designer and others in order to determine the type of information for reporting, the reporting format and the desired frequency for distribution of the various reports.

3.2.4.2 Design Phase Procedure: The MIS shall include procedures for reporting, communications and administration during the Design Phase.

3.3 Design Phase

3.3.1 Project Management

3.3.1.1 Revisions to the Construction Management Plan: During the Design Phase the CM shall make recommendations to the Owner regarding revisions to the Construction Management Plan. The Construction Management Plan shall include a description of the various bid packages recommended for the Project. Revisions approved by the Owner shall be incorporated into the Construction Management Plan.

3.3.1.2 Project Conference: At the start of the Design Phase, the CM shall conduct a Project Conference attended by the Designer, the Owner and others as necessary. During the Project Conference the CM shall review the Construction Management Plan, the Master Schedule, Design Phase Milestone Schedule, the Project and Construction Budget and the MIS.

3.3.1.3 Design Phase Information: The CM shall monitor the Designer's compliance with the Construction Management Plan and the MIS, and the CM shall coordinate and expedite the flow of information between the Owner, Designer and others as necessary.

3.3.1.4 Progress Meetings: The CM shall conduct periodic progress meetings attended by the Owner, Designer and others. Such meetings shall serve as a forum for the exchange of information concerning the Project and the review of design progress. The CM shall prepare and distribute minutes of these meetings to the Owner, Designer and others as necessary.

3.3.1.5 Review of Design Documents: The CM shall review the design documents and make recommendations to the Owner and Designer as to constructibility, scheduling, and time of construction; as to clarity, consistency, and coordination of documentation among Contractors; and as to the separation of the Project into contracts for various categories of the Work. In addition, the CM shall give to the Designer all data of which it or the Owner is aware concerning patents or copyrights for inclusion in Contract Documents. The recommendations resulting from such review shall be provided to the Owner and Designer in writing or as notations

CMAA Document A-1 (2005 Edition)

on the design documents. In making reviews and recommendations as to design documentation or design matters the CM shall not be responsible for providing nor will the CM have control over the Project design, design requirements, design criteria or the substance of contents of the design documents. By performing the reviews and making recommendations described herein, the CM shall not be deemed to be acting in a manner so as to assume responsibility or liability, in whole or in part, for any aspect of the project design, design requirements, design criteria or the substance or contents of the design documents. The CM's actions in making such reviews and recommendations as provided herein are to be advisory only to the Owner and to the Designer.

3.3.1.6 Owner's Design Reviews: The CM shall expedite the Owner's design reviews by compiling and conveying the Owner's review comments to the Designer.

3.3.1.7 Approvals by Regulatory Agencies: The CM shall coordinate transmittal of documents to regulatory agencies for review and shall advise the Owner of potential problems resulting from such reviews and suggested solutions regarding completion of such reviews.

3.3.1.8 Other Contract Conditions: The CM shall assist the Owner to prepare the Supplemental Conditions of the Construction Contract and separate General Conditions for materials or equipment procurement contracts to meet the specific requirements of the Project, and shall provide these to the Designer for inclusion in the Contract Documents.

3.3.1.9 Project Funding: The CM shall assist the Owner in preparing documents concerning the Project and Construction Budget for use in obtaining or reporting on Project funding. The documents shall be prepared in a format approved the Owner.

3.3.2 Time Management

3.3.2.1 Revisions to the Master Schedule: While performing the services provided in Paragraphs 3.3.1.1, 3.3.1.2 and as necessary during the Design Phase, the CM shall recommend revisions to the Master Schedule. The Owner shall issue, as needed, change orders to the appropriate parties to implement the Master Schedule revisions.

3.3.2.2 Monitoring the Design Phase Milestone Schedule: While performing the services provided in Paragraphs 3.3.1.3 and 3.3.1.4, the CM shall monitor compliance with the Design Phase Milestone Schedule.

3.3.2.3 Pre-Bid Construction Schedules: Prior to transmitting Contract Documents to bidders, the CM shall prepare a Pre-Bid Construction Schedule for each part of the Project and make the schedule available to the bidders during the Procurement Phase.

3.3.3 Cost Management

3.3.3.1 Cost Control: The CM shall prepare an estimate of the construction cost for each submittal of design drawings and specifications from the Designer. This estimate shall include a contingency acceptable to the Owner, CM and the Designer for construction costs appropriate for the type and location of the Project and the extent to which the design has progressed. The Owner recognizes that the CM will perform in accordance with the standard of care established in this Agreement and that the CM has no control over the costs of labor, materials, equipment or services furnished by others, or over the Contractor's methods of determining prices, or over competitive bidding or market prices. Accordingly, the CM does not represent or guarantee that proposals, bids or actual construction costs will not vary from budget figures included in the Construction Management Plan as amended from time to time. If the budget figure is exceeded, the Owner will give written consent to increasing the budget, or authorize negotiations or rebidding of the Project within a reasonable time, or cooperate with the CM and Designer to revise the Project's general scope, extent or character in keeping with the Project's design requirements and sound design practices, or modify the design requirements appropriately. Instead of the foregoing, the Owner may abandon the Project and terminate this Agreement in accordance with Article 10. The estimate for each submittal shall be accompanied by a report to the Owner and Designer identifying variances from the Project and Construction Budget. The CM shall facilitate decisions by the Owner and Designer when changes to the design are required to remain within the Project and Construction Budget.

3.3.3.2 Project and Construction Budget Revision: The CM shall make recommendations to the Owner concerning revisions to the Project and Construction Budget that may result from design changes.

3.3.3.3 Value Engineering Studies: The CM shall provide value engineering recommendations to the Owner and Designer on major construction components, including cost evaluations of alternative materials and systems.

3.3.4 Management Information Systems (MIS)

3.3.4.1 Schedule Reports: In conjunction with the services provided by Paragraph 3.3.2.2, the CM shall prepare and distribute schedule maintenance reports that shall compare actual progress with scheduled progress for the Design Phase and the overall Project and shall make recommendations to the Owner for corrective action

3.3.4.2 Project Cost Reports: The CM shall prepare and distribute Project cost reports that shall indicate actual or estimated costs compared to the Project and Construction Budget and shall make recommendations to the Owner for corrective action.

3.3.4.3 Cash Flow Report: The CM shall periodically prepare and distribute a cash flow report.

3.3.4.4 Design Phase Change Report: The CM shall prepare and distribute Design Phase change reports that shall list all Owner-approved changes as of the date of the report and shall state the effect of the changes on the Project and Construction Budget and the Master Schedule.

3.4 Procurement Phase

3.4.1 Project Management

3.4.1.1 Prequalifying Bidders: The CM shall assist the Owner in developing lists of possible bidders and in prequalifying bidders. This service shall include preparation and distribution of questionnaires; receiving and analyzing completed questionnaires; interviewing possible bidders, bonding agents and financial institutions; and preparing recommendations for the Owner. The CM shall prepare a list of bidders for each bid package and transmit to the Owner for approval.

3.4.1.2 Bidder's Interest Campaign: The CM shall conduct a telephone and correspondence campaign to attempt to increase interest among qualified bidders.

3.4.1.3 Notices and Advertisements: The CM shall assist the Owner in preparing and placing notices and advertisements to solicit bids for the Project.

3.4.1.4 Delivery of Bid Documents: The CM shall expedite the delivery of Bid Documents to the bidders. The CM shall obtain the documents from the Designer and arrange for printing, binding, wrapping and delivery to the bidders. The CM shall maintain a list of bidders receiving Bid Documents.

3.4.1.5 Pre-Bid Conference: In conjunction with the Owner and Designer, the CM shall conduct pre-bid conferences. These conferences shall be forums for the Owner, CM and Designer to explain the Project requirements to the bidders, including information concerning schedule requirements, time and cost control requirements, access requirements, contractor interfaces, the Owner's administrative requirements and technical information.

3.4.1.6 Information to Bidders: The CM shall develop and coordinate procedures to provide answers to bidder's questions. All answers shall be in the form of addenda.

3.4.1.7 Addenda: The CM shall receive from the Designer a copy of all addenda. The CM shall review addenda for constructibility, for effect on the Project and Construction Budget, scheduling and time of construction, and for consistency with the related provisions as documented in the Bid Documents. The CM shall distribute a copy of all addenda to each bidder receiving Bid Documents.

CMAA Document A-1 (2005 Edition)

3.4.1.8 Bid Opening and Recommendations: The CM shall assist the Owner in the bid opening and shall evaluate the bids for responsiveness and price. The CM shall make recommendations to the Owner concerning the acceptance or rejection of bids.

3.4.1.9 Post-Bid Conference: The CM shall conduct a post-bid conference to review Contract award procedures, schedules, Project staffing and other pertinent issues.

3.4.1.10 Construction Contracts: The CM shall assist the Owner in the assembly, delivery and execution of the Contract Documents. The CM shall issue to the Contractor on behalf of the Owner the Notice of Award and the Notice to Proceed.

3.4.2 Time Management

3.4.2.1 Pre-Bid Construction Schedule: The CM shall emphasize to the bidders their responsibilities regarding the Pre-Bid Construction Schedule specified in the Instructions to Bidders or the Contract Documents.

3.4.2.2 Master Schedule: The CM shall recommend to the Owner any appropriate revisions to the Master Schedule. Following acceptance by the Owner of such revisions, the CM shall provide a copy of the Master Schedule to the Designer and to the bidders.

3.4.3 Cost Management

3.4.3.1 Estimates for Addenda: The CM shall prepare an estimate of costs for all Addenda and shall submit a copy of the estimate to the Designer and to the Owner for approval.

3.4.3.2 Analyzing Bids: Upon receipt of the bids, the CM shall evaluate the bids, including alternate bid prices and unit prices, and shall make a recommendation to the Owner regarding the award of the Construction Contract.

3.4.4 Management Information System (MIS)

3.4.4.1 Schedule Maintenance Reports: The CM shall prepare and distribute schedule maintenance reports during the Procurement Phase. The reports shall compare the actual bid and award dates to scheduled bid and award dates and shall summarize the progress of the Project.

3.4.4.2 Project Cost Reports: The CM shall prepare and distribute project cost reports during the Procurement Phase. The reports shall compare actual contract award prices for the Project with those contemplated by the Project and Construction Budget.

3.4.4.3 Cash Flow Reports: The CM shall prepare and distribute cash flow reports during the Procurement Phase. The reports shall be based on actual contract award prices and estimated other construction costs for the duration of the Project.

3.5 Construction Phase

3.5.1 Project Management

3.5.1.1 Pre-Construction Conference: In consultation with the Owner and Designer, the CM shall conduct a Pre-Construction Conference during which the CM shall review the Project reporting procedures and other requirements for performance of the Work..

3.5.1.2 Permits, Bonds and Insurance: The CM shall verify that the Contractor has provided evidence that required permits, bonds, and insurance have been obtained. Such action by the CM shall not relieve the Contractor of its responsibility to comply with the provisions of the Contract Documents.

3.5.1.3 On-Site Management and Construction Phase Communication Procedures: The CM shall provide and maintain a management team on the Project site to provide contract administration as an agent of the Owner, and the CM shall establish and implement coordination and communication procedures among the CM, Owner, Designer and Contractor.

3.5.1.4 Contract Administration Procedures: The CM shall establish and implement procedures for reviewing and processing requests for clarifications and interpretations of the Contract Documents; shop drawings, samples and other submittals; contract schedule adjustments; change order proposals; written proposals for substitutions; payment applications; and the maintenance of logs. As the Owner's representative at the construction site, the CM shall be the party to whom all such information shall be submitted.

CMAA Document A-1 (2005 Edition)

3.5.1.5 <u>Review of Requests for Information, Shop Drawings, Samples, and Other Submittals:</u> The CM shall examine the Contractor's requests for information, shop drawings, samples, and other submittals, and Designer's reply or other action concerning them, to determine the anticipated effect on compliance with the Project requirements, the Project and Construction Budget, and the Master Schedule. The CM shall forward to the Designer for review, approval or rejection, as appropriate, the request for clarification or interpretation, shop drawing, sample, or other submittal, along with the CM's comments. The CM's comments shall not relate to design considerations, but rather to matters of cost, scheduling and time of construction, and clarity, consistency, and coordination in documentation. The CM shall receive from the Designer and transmit to the Contractor, all information so received from the Designer.

3.5.1.6 <u>Project Site Meetings:</u> Periodically the CM shall conduct meetings at the Project site with each Contractor, and the CM shall conduct coordination meetings with the Contractor, the Owner and the Designer. The CM shall prepare and distribute minutes to all attendees, the Owner and Designer.

3.5.1.7 <u>Coordination of Other Independent Consultants:</u> Technical inspection and testing provided by others shall be coordinated by the CM. The CM shall receive a copy of all inspection and testing reports and shall provide a copy of such reports to the Designer. The CM shall not be responsible for providing, nor shall the CM control, the actual performance of technical inspection and testing. The CM is performing a coordination function only and the CM is not acting in a manner so as to assume responsibility or liability, in whole or in part, for all or any part of such inspection and testing.

3.5.1.8 <u>Minor Variations in the Work:</u> The CM may authorize minor variations in the Work from the requirements of the Contract Documents that do not involve an adjustment in the Contract price or time and which are consistent with the overall intent of the Contract Documents. The CM shall provide to the Designer copies of such authorizations.

3.5.1.9 <u>Change Orders:</u> The CM shall establish and implement a change order control system. All changes to the Contract between the Owner and Contractor shall be only by change orders executed by the Owner.

3.5.1.9.1 All proposed Owner-initiated changes shall first be described in detail by the CM in a request for a proposal issued to the Contractor. The request shall be accompanied by drawings and specifications prepared by the Designer. In response to the request for a proposal, the Contractor shall submit to the CM for evaluation detailed information concerning the price and time adjustments, if any, as may be necessary to perform the proposed change order Work. The CM shall review the Contractor's proposal, shall discuss the proposed change order with the Contractor, and endeavor to determine the Contractor's basis for the price and time proposed to perform the changed Work.

3.5.1.9.2 The CM shall review the contents of all Contractor requested changes to the Contract time or price, endeavor to determine the cause of the request, and assemble and evaluate information concerning the request. The CM shall provide to the Designer a copy of each change request, and the CM shall in its evaluations of the Contractor's request consider the Designer's comments regarding the proposed changes.

3.5.1.9.3 The CM shall make recommendations to the Owner regarding all proposed change orders. At the Owner's direction, the CM shall prepare and issue to the Contractor appropriate change order documents. The CM shall provide to the Designer copies of all approved change orders.

3.5.1.10 <u>Subsurface and Physical Conditions:</u> Whenever the Contractor notifies the CM that a surface or subsurface condition at or contiguous to the site is encountered that differs from what the Contractor is entitled to rely upon or from what is indicated or referred to in the Contract Documents, or that may require a change in the Contract Documents, the CM shall notify the Designer. The CM shall receive from the Designer and transmit to the Contractor all information necessary to specify any design changes required to be responsive to the differing or changed condition and, if necessary, shall prepare a change order as indicated in Paragraph 3.5.1.9.

CMAA Document A-1 (2005 Edition)

3.5.1.11 <u>Quality Review:</u> The CM shall establish and implement a program to monitor the quality of the Work. The purpose of the program shall be to assist in guarding the Owner against Work by the Contractor that does not conform to the requirements of the Contract Documents. The CM shall reject any portion of the Work and transmit to the Owner and Contractor a notice of nonconforming Work when it is the opinion of the CM, Owner, or Designer that such Work does not conform to the requirements of the Contract Documents. Except for minor variations as described in Paragraph 3.5.1.8, the CM is not authorized to change, revoke, alter, enlarge, relax or release any requirements of the Contract Documents or to approve or accept any portion of the Work not conforming with the requirements of the Contract Documents. Communication between the CM and Contractor with regard to quality review shall not in any way be construed as binding the CM or Owner or releasing the Contractor from performing in accordance with the terms of the Contract Documents. The CM will not be responsible for, nor does the CM control, the means, methods, techniques, sequences and procedures of construction for the Project. It is understood that the CM's action in providing quality review under this Agreement is a service of the CM for the sole benefit of the Owner and by performing as provided herein, the CM is not acting in a manner so as to assume responsibility of liability, in whole or in part, for all or any part of the construction for the Project. No action taken by the CM shall relieve the Contractor from its obligation to perform the Work in strict conformity with the requirements of the Contract Documents, and in strict conformity with all other applicable laws, rules and regulations.

3.5.1.12 <u>Contractor's Safety Program:</u> The CM shall require each Contractor that will perform Work at the site to prepare and submit to the CM for general review a safety program, as required by the Contract Documents. The CM shall review each safety program to determine that the programs of the various Contractors performing Work at the site, as submitted, provide for coordination among the Contractors of their respective programs. The CM shall not be responsible for any Contractor's implementation of or compliance with its safety programs, or for initiating, maintaining, monitoring or supervising the implementation of such programs or the procedures and precautions associated therewith, or for the coordination of any of the above with the other Contractors performing the Work at the site. The CM shall not be

responsible for the adequacy or completeness of any Contractor's safety programs, procedures or precautions.

3.5.1.13 <u>Disputes Between Contractor and Owner:</u> The CM shall render to the Owner in writing within a reasonable time decisions concerning disputes between the Contractor and the Owner relating to acceptability of the Work, or the interpretation of the requirements of the Contract Documents pertaining to the furnishing and performing of the Work.

3.5.1.14 <u>Operation and Maintenance Materials:</u> The CM shall receive from the Contractor operation and maintenance manuals, warranties and guarantees for materials and equipment installed in the Project. The CM shall deliver this information to the Owner and shall provide a copy of the information to the Designer.

3.5.1.15 <u>Substantial Completion:</u> The CM shall determine when the Project and the Contractor's Work is substantially complete. In consultation with the Designer, the CM shall, prior to issuing a certificate of substantial completion, prepare a list of incomplete Work or Work which does not conform to the requirements of the Contract Documents. This list shall be attached to the certificate of substantial completion.

3.5.1.16 <u>Final Completion:</u> In consultation with the Designer, the CM shall determine when the Project and the Contractor's Work is finally completed, shall issue a certificate of final completion and shall provide to the Owner a written recommendation regarding payment to the Contractor.

3.5.2 <u>Time Management</u>

3.5.2.1 <u>Master Schedule:</u> The CM shall adjust and update the Master Schedule and distribute copies to the Owner and Designer. All adjustments to the Master Schedule shall be made for the benefit of the Project.

3.5.2.2 <u>Contractor's Construction Schedule:</u> The CM shall review the Contractor's Construction Schedule and shall verify that the schedule is prepared in accordance with the requirements of the Contract Documents and that it establishes completion dates that comply with the requirements of the Master Schedule.

CMAA Document A-1 (2005 Edition)

3.5.2.3 Construction Schedule Report: The CM shall, on a monthly basis, review the progress of construction of the Contractor, shall evaluate the percentage complete of each construction activity as indicated in the Contractor's Construction Schedule and shall review such percentages with the Contractor. This evaluation shall serve as data for input to the periodic Construction Schedule report that shall be prepared and distributed to the Contractor, Owner and Designer by the CM. The report shall indicate the actual progress compared to scheduled progress and shall serve as the basis for the progress payments to the Contractor. The CM shall advise and make recommendations to the Owner concerning the alternative courses of action that the Owner may take in its efforts to achieve Contract compliance by the Contractor.

3.5.2.4 Effect of Change Orders on the Schedule: Prior to the issuance of a change order, the CM shall determine and advise the Owner as to the effect on the Master Schedule of the change. The CM shall verify that activities and adjustments of time, if any, required by approved change orders have been incorporated into the Contractor's Construction Schedule.

3.5.2.5 Recovery Schedules: The CM may require the Contractor to prepare and submit a recovery schedule as specified in the Contract Documents.

3.5.3 Cost Management

3.5.3.1 Schedule of Values (Each Contract): The CM shall, in participation with the Contractor, determine a schedule of values for the construction Contract. The schedule of values shall be the basis for the allocation of the Contract price to the activities shown on the Contractor's Construction Schedule.

3.5.3.2 Allocation of Cost to the Contractor's Construction Schedule: The Contractor's Construction Schedule shall have the total Contract price allocated by the Contractor among the Contractor's scheduled activities so that each of the Contractor's activities shall be allocated a price and the sum of the prices of the activities shall equal the total Contract price. The CM shall review the Contract price allocations and verify that such allocations are made in accordance with the requirements of the Contract Documents. Progress payments to the Contractor shall be based on the Contractor's

percentage of completion of the scheduled activities as set out in the Construction Schedule reports and the Contractor's compliance with the requirements of the Contract Documents.

3.5.3.3 Effect of Change Orders on Cost: The CM shall advise the Owner as to the effect on the Project and Construction Budget of all proposed and approved change orders.

3.5.3.4 Cost Records: In instances when a lump sum or unit price is not determined prior to the Owner's authorization to the Contractor to perform change order Work, the CM shall request from the Contractor records of the cost of payroll, materials and equipment incurred and the amount of payments to each subcontractor by the Contractor in performing the Work.

3.5.3.5 Trade-off Studies: The CM shall provide trade-off studies for various minor construction components. The results of these studies shall be in report form and distributed to the Owner and Designer.

3.5.3.6 Progress Payments: The CM shall review the payment applications submitted by the Contractor and determine whether the amount requested reflects the progress of the Contractor's Work. The CM shall make appropriate adjustments to each payment application and shall prepare and forward to the Owner a progress payment report. The report shall state the total Contract price, payments to date, current payment requested, retainage and actual amounts owed for the current period. Included in this report shall be a Certificate of Payment that shall be signed by the CM and delivered to the Owner.

3.5.4 Management Information System (MIS)

3.5.4.1 Schedule Maintenance Reports: The CM shall prepare and distribute schedule maintenance reports during the Construction Phase. The reports shall compare the projected completion dates to scheduled completion dates of each separate contract and to the Master Schedule for the Project.

CMAA Document A-1 (2005 Edition)

3.5.4.2 Project Cost Reports: The CM shall prepare and distribute Project cost reports during the Construction Phase. The reports shall compare actual Project costs to the Project and Construction Budget.

3.5.4.3 Project and Construction Budget Revisions: The CM shall make recommendations to the Owner concerning changes that may result in revisions to the Project and Construction Budget. Copies of the recommendations shall be provided to the Designer.

3.5.4.4 Cash Flow Reports: The CM shall periodically prepare and distribute cash flow reports during the construction phase. The reports shall compare actual cash flow to planned cash flow.

3.5.4.5 Progress Payment Reports (Each Contract): The CM shall prepare and distribute the Progress Payment reports. The reports shall state the total Contract price, payment to date, current payment requested, retainage, and amounts owed for the period. A portion of this report shall be a recommendation of payment that shall be signed by the CM and delivered to the Owner for use by the Owner in making payments to the Contractor.

3.5.4.6 Change Order Reports: The CM shall periodically during the construction phase prepare and distribute change order reports. The report shall list all Owner-approved change orders by number, a brief description of the change order work, the cost established in the change order and percent of completion of the change order work. The report shall also include similar information for potential change orders of which the CM may be aware.

3.6 Post-Construction Phase

3.6.1 Project Management

3.6.1.1 Record Documents: The CM shall coordinate and expedite submittals of information from the Contractor to the Designer for preparation of record drawings and specifications, and shall coordinate and expedite the transmittal of such record documents to the Owner.

3.6.1.2 Operation and Maintenance Materials and Certificates: Prior to the final completion of the Project, the CM shall compile manufacturers' operations and maintenance manuals, warranties and guarantees, and certificates, and index and bind such documents in an organized manner. This information shall then be provided to the Owner.

3.6.1.3 Occupancy Permit: The CM shall assist the Owner in obtaining an occupancy permit by coordinating final testing, preparing and submitting documentation to governmental agencies, and accompanying governmental officials during inspections of the Project.

3.6.2 Time Management

3.6.2.1 Occupancy Plan: The CM shall prepare an occupancy plan that shall include a schedule for location for furniture, equipment and the Owner's personnel. This schedule shall be provided to the Owner.

3.6.3 Cost Management

3.6.3.1 Change Orders: The CM shall continue during the post-construction phase to provide services related to change orders as specified in Paragraph 3.5.3.3.

3.6.4 Management Information Systems (MIS)

3.6.4.1 Close Out Reports: At the conclusion of the Project, the CM shall prepare and deliver to the Owner final Project accounting and close out reports.

3.6.4.2 MIS Reports for Occupancy: The CM shall prepare and distribute reports associated with the occupancy plan.

ARTICLE 4
ADDITIONAL SERVICES

4.1 At the request of the Owner, the CM shall perform Additional Services and the CM shall be compensated for same as provided in Article 8 of this Agreement. The CM shall be obligated to perform Additional Services only after the Owner and CM have executed a written amendment to this Agreement providing for performance of such services. Additional Services may include, but are not limited to:

CMAA Document A-1 (2005 Edition)

4.1.1 Services during the design or construction phases related to investigation, appraisal or evaluation of surface or subsurface conditions at or contiguous to the site or other existing conditions, facilities, or equipment that differs from what is indicated in the Contract Documents, or determination of the accuracy of existing drawings or other information furnished by the Owner;

4.1.2 Services related to the procurement, storage, maintenance and installation of the Owner-furnished equipment, materials, supplies and furnishings;

4.1.3 Services related to determination of space needs;

4.1.4 Preparation of space programs;

4.1.5 Services related to building site investigations and analysis;

4.1.6 Services related to tenant or rental spaces;

4.1.7 Preparation of a Project financial feasibility study;

4.1.8 Preparation of financial, accounting or MIS reports not provided under Basic Services;

4.1.9 Performance of technical inspection and testing;

4.1.10 Preparation of an operations and maintenance manual;

4.1.11 Services related to recruiting and training of maintenance personnel;

4.1.12 Services provided in respect of a dispute between the Owner and the Contractor after the CM has rendered its decision thereon in accordance with Paragraph 3.5.1.13;

4.1.13 Performing warranty inspections during the warranty period of the Project;

4.1.14 Consultation regarding replacement of Work or property damaged by fire or other cause during construction and furnishing services in connection with the replacement of such;

4.1.15 Service made necessary by the default of the Contractor;

4.1.16 Preparation for and serving as a witness in connection with any public or private hearing or arbitration, mediation or legal proceeding;

4.1.17 Assisting the Owner in public relations activities, including preparing information for and attending public meetings; and

4.1.18 Assisting the Owner with procurement and preparation of contracts in connection with the occupancy of the Project, and providing personnel to oversee the location of furniture and equipment;

4.1.19 Services related to the initial operation of any equipment such as start-up, testing, adjusting and balancing.

4.1.20 Any other services not otherwise included in this Agreement.

ARTICLE 5
DURATION OF THE CONSTRUCTION
MANAGER'S SERVICES

5.1 The commencement date for the CM's Basic Services shall be the date of the execution of this Agreement.

5.2 The duration of the CM's Basic Services under this Agreement shall be _____ consecutive calendar days from the commencement date.

5.3 The duration of the CM's Basic Services may be changed only as specified in Article 6.

CMAA Document A-1 (2005 Edition)

ARTICLE 6
CHANGES IN THE CONSTRUCTION MANAGER'S BASIC SERVICES AND COMPENSATION

6.1 Owner Changes

6.1.1 The Owner, without invalidating this Agreement, may make changes in the CM's Basic Services specified in Article 3 of this Agreement. The CM shall promptly notify the Owner of changes that increase or decrease the CM's compensation or the duration of the CM's Basic Services or both.

6.1.2 If the scope or the duration of the CM's Basic Services is changed, the CM's compensation shall be adjusted equitably. A written proposal indicating the change in compensation for a change in the scope or duration of Basic Services shall be provided by the CM to the Owner within thirty (30) days of the occurrence of the event giving rise to such request. The amount of the change in compensation to be paid shall be determined on the basis of the CM's cost and a customary and reasonable adjustment in the CM's Fixed Fee, Lump Sum, or multipliers and rates consistent with the provisions of Article 8.

6.2 Authorization

6.2.1 Changes in CM's Basic Services and entitlement to additional compensation or a change in duration of this Agreement shall be made by a written amendment to this Agreement executed by the Owner and the CM. The amendment shall be executed by the Owner and CM prior to the CM performing the services required by the amendment.

6.2.2 The CM shall proceed to perform the services required by the amendment only after receiving written notice from the Owner directing the CM to proceed.

6.3 Invoices for Additional Compensation

6.3.1 The CM shall submit invoices for additional compensation with its invoice for Basic Services and payment shall be made pursuant to the provisions of Article 8 of this Agreement.

ARTICLE 7
OWNER'S RESPONSIBILITIES

7.1 The Owner shall provide to the CM complete information regarding the Owner's knowledge of and requirements for the Project. The Owner shall be responsible for the accuracy and completeness of all reports, data, and other information furnished pursuant to this Paragraph 7.1. The CM may use and rely on the information furnished by the Owner in performing services under this Agreement, and on the reports, data, and other information furnished by the Owner to the Designer.

7.2 The Owner shall be responsible for the presence at the site of any asbestos, PCB's, petroleum, hazardous materials and radioactive materials, and the consequences of such presence.

7.3 The Owner shall examine information submitted by the CM and shall render decisions pertaining thereto promptly.

7.4 The Owner shall furnish legal, accounting and insurance counseling services as may be necessary for the Project.

7.5 The Owner shall furnish insurance for the Project as specified in Article 9.

7.6 If the Owner observes or otherwise becomes aware of any fault or defect in the Project or CM's services or any Work that does not comply with the requirements of the Contract Documents, the Owner shall give prompt written notice thereof to the CM.

7.7 The Owner shall furnish required information and approvals and perform its responsibilities and activities in a timely manner to facilitate orderly progress of the Work in cooperation with the CM consistent with this Agreement and in accordance with the planning and scheduling requirements and budgetary restraints of the Project as determined by the CM.

7.8 The Owner shall retain a Designer whose services, duties and responsibilities shall be described in a written agreement between the Owner and Designer. The services, duties, and responsibilities of the Designer set out in the agreement

CMAA Document A-1 (2005 Edition)

between the Owner and Designer shall be compatible and consistent with this Agreement and the Contract Documents. The Owner shall, in its agreement with the Designer, require that the Designer perform its services in cooperation with the CM, consistent with this Agreement and in accordance with the planning, scheduling and budgetary requirements of the Project as determined by the Owner and documented by the CM. The terms and conditions of the agreement between the Owner and the Designer shall not be changed or waived without written consent of the CM, whose consent shall not be unreasonably withheld.

7.9 The Owner shall approve the Project and construction budget and any subsequent revisions as provided in Paragraph 3.2.3.2 of this Agreement.

7.10 The Owner shall cause any and all agreements between the Owner and others to be compatible and consistent with this Agreement. Each of the agreements shall include waiver of subrogation and shall expressly recognize the CM as the Owner's agent in providing the CM's Basic and Additional Services specified in this Agreement.

7.11 At the request of the CM, sufficient copies of the Contract Documents shall be furnished by the Owner at the Owner's expense.

7.12 The Owner shall in a timely manner secure, submit and pay for necessary approvals, easements, assessments, permits and charges required for the construction, use or occupancy of permanent structures or for permanent changes in existing facilities.

7.13 The Owner shall furnish evidence satisfactory to the CM that sufficient funds are available and committed for the entire cost of the Project. Unless such reasonable evidence is furnished, the CM is not required to commence the CM's services and may, if such evidence is not presented within a reasonable time, suspend the services specified in this Agreement upon fifteen (15) days written notice to the Owner. In such event, the CM shall be compensated in the manner provided in Paragraph 10.2.

7.14 The Owner, its representatives and consultants shall communicate with the Contractor only through the CM.

7.15 The Owner shall send to the CM and shall require the Designer to send to the CM copies of all notices and communications sent to or received by the Owner or the Designer relating to the Project. During the construction phase of the Project, the Owner shall require that the Contractor submits all notices and communications relating to the Project directly to the CM.

7.16 The Owner shall designate, in writing, an officer, employee or other authorized representatives to act in the Owner's behalf with respect to the project. This representative shall have the authority to approve changes in the scope of the Project and shall be available during working hours and as often as may be required to render decisions and to furnish information in a timely manner.

7.17 The Owner shall make payments to the Contractor as recommended by the CM on the basis of the Contractor's applications for payment.

7.18 In the case of the termination of the Designer's services, the Owner shall appoint a new Designer who shall be acceptable to the CM and whose responsibilities with respect to the Project and status under the new Agreement with the Owner shall be similar to that of the Designer under the Owner-Designer Agreement and the Contract Documents.

Introduction to Basic Epidemiology and Principles of Statistics

Cross-Sectional Studies (Surveys)

These examine the relationship between a disease or other health-related characteristic and other variables of interest (as) that exist in a population at a given time. The presence or absence (or the level) of a characteristic is examined in each member of the study population or in a representative sample. These studies are used to obtain information not routinely available from surveillance or case series. Cross-sectional studies provide no information on the temporal sequence of cause and effect. In surveys examining the association between an exposure and an outcome, both are measured simultaneously and it is often hard to determine whether the exposure preceded the outcome or vice versa.

Surveys may simply describe characteristics or behaviors within a study population (malaria prevalence, vaccine coverage); or may be used to examine potential risk factors (e.g., how those who receive vaccination differ from those who do not). In general, surveys measure the situation at a given moment—prevalence—rather than the occurrence of new events—incidence.

Systematic Error (Bias)

Bias occurs when there is a tendency to produce results that differ in a systematic manner from the true values. A study with small systematic bias is said to have high accuracy. Bias (or systematic error) may lead to over- or underestimation of the strength of an association. The sources of bias in epidemiology are many and over 30 specific types of bias have been identified. The main biases are:

Selection bias

Information bias

Bias due to confounding

Selection bias

Selection bias occurs when there is a systematic difference between the characteristics of the people selected for a study, or who agree to participate, and the characteristics of those who are not selected, or who do not agree to participate (e.g., in a study limited to volunteers).

Information bias (also called observation bias)

Information bias occurs when there are quality (accuracy) problems in the collection, recording, coding or analysis of data among comparison groups. Interviewers might, for example, interview the cases with more diligence than the interview control, or a person with a disease may recall previous exposures better than persons who are healthy (this type of bias is called *recall bias*). Although selection bias or information bias can usually be corrected at the time of analysis, it is best to think about possible sources of bias at the time of the study design so that they can be minimized or avoided.

Bias due to confounding

In a study of the association between exposure to a cause (or risk factor or protecting factor) and the occurrence of the disease, confounding can occur when another factor exists in the study population and is associated both with the disease and the initial factor being studied. A problem arises if this second extraneous factor is unequally distributed among the exposure subgroups. Confounding occurs when the effects of two protective or risk factors have not been separated and it is therefore incorrectly concluded that the effect is due to one variable rather than the other. For instance, in a study of the association between tobacco smoking and lung cancer, age would be a confounding factor if the average ages of the nonsmoking and smoking groups in the study population were very different, since lung cancer incidence increases with age. Suppose one wishes to study the relationship between income and malaria, *it*[1] is likely that a higher income protects against malaria (e.g., people with a high income are more likely to buy drugs for malaria prophylaxis). It is also known that, in that community, income is associated both with the use of bed nets. The relationship between income and malaria is thus affected by the relationship between bed nets and income. In other words, bed nets confound the relationship between income and malaria. Such biases can be controlled for in the analysis if appropriate information has been collected during the study on potential confounding variables, and if each factor is properly analyzed and interpreted.[2]

While the above observations pertain to medical research, they are relevant to the nature of just about any research. The point is—one should take any statistics with a grain of salt, until such time as it can be adequately analyzed and certified as being (somewhat) accurate.

---

[1] Italics denote author's insertions

[2] Communicable Diseases Cluster Department of Control, Prevention and Eradication, Social Mobilization, and Training Unit, *Introduction to basic epidemiology and principles of statistics for tropical diseases control: Learner's Guide*, Updated July 2002 Trial Edition.

Recommended Standard (RS)-232-C

The RS-232-C was originally set to standardize the interconnections of terminals and host computers through public telephone networks. Modems were used to translate the digital data signals from the computer equipment to analog audio signals suitable for transmission on the telephone network, and back to digital signals at the receiving end.

In the mid- to late 1960s, nearly all serial links for remote access to computers were through a telephone line. Remote access to the large mainframes of the time was accomplished almost exclusively by using the telephone network.

At that time, each manufacturer of equipment used a different configuration for interfacing a data terminal equipment (DTE) with a data communications equipment (DCE). Cables, connectors and voltage levels were different and incompatible, thus the interconnection of two pieces of equipment made by two different companies required the use of voltage level converters, and the manufacturing of special cables and connectors.

In 1969, EIA with Bell Laboratories and other parties established a recommended standard for interfacing terminals and data communications equipment. The object of this standard was to simplify the interconnection of equipment manufactured by different firms.

The standard defines electrical, mechanical, and functional characteristics. The electrical characteristics include parameters such as voltage levels and cable impedance. The mechanical section describes the pin number assignments and plug. The connector itself, however, is not specified. The functional description defines the functions of the different electrical signals to be used.

This standard shortly became Recommended Standard number 232, revision C (RS-232-C) from the Electronic Industry Association, and a similar standard was available in Europe, developed by the Comite Consultatif Internatinale de Telegraphie et Telephonie (CCITT), and known as functional description (V.24) and electrical specifications (V.28). RS-232-C was widely adopted by manufacturers of terminals and computer equipment.

In the 1980s, the rapidly growing microcomputer industry found the RS-232-C standard cheap (compared to parallel connections) and suitable for connecting peripheral equipment to microcomputers. RS-232-C quickly became a standard for connecting microcomputers to printers, plotters, backup tape devices, terminals, programmed equipment, and other microcomputers.[1]

---

[1]http://www2.rad.com/networks/1995/rs232/hist.htm#hist

The Spearin Doctrine

248 U.S. 132

UNITED STATES

v.

SPEARIN

SPEARIN

UNITED STATES

SUPREME COURT OF THE UNITED STATES

Argued November 14, 15, 1918

December 9, 1918

JUDGES: White, McKenna, Holmes, Day, Van Devanter, Pitney, Brandeis, Clarke; McReynolds took no part in the consideration or decision of the case.

OPINION: MR. JUSTICE BRANDEIS delivered the opinion of the court.

Spearin brought this suit in the Court of Claims, demanding a balance alleged to be due for work done under a contract to construct a dry-dock and also damages for its annulment. Judgment was entered for him in the sum of $141,180.86; (51 Ct. Cl. 155) and both parties appealed to this court. The Government contends that Spearin is entitled to recover only $7,907.98. Spearin claims the additional sum of $63,658.70.

First. The decision to be made on the Government's appeal depends upon whether or not it was entitled to annul the contract. The facts essential to a determination of the question are these:

Spearin contracted to build for $757,800 a dry-dock at the Brooklyn Navy Yard in accordance with plans and specifications which had been prepared by the

Government. The site selected by it was intersected by a 6-foot brick sewer; and it was necessary to divert and relocate a section thereof before the work of constructing the drydock could begin. The plans and specifications provided that the contractor should do the work and prescribed the dimensions, material, and location of the section to be substituted. All the prescribed requirements were fully complied with by Spearin; and the substituted section was accepted by the Government as satisfactory. It was located about 37 to 50 feet from the proposed excavation for the dry-dock; but a large part of the new section was within the area set aside as space within which the contractor's operations were to be carried on. Both before and after the diversion of the 6-foot sewer, it connected, within the Navy Yard but outside the space reserved for work on the dry-dock, with a 7-foot sewer which emptied into Wallabout Basin.

About a year after this relocation of the 6-foot sewer there occurred a sudden and heavy downpour of rain coincident with a high tide. This forced the water up the sewer for a considerable distance to a depth of 2 feet or more. Internal pressure broke the 6-foot sewer as so relocated, at several places; and the excavation of the dry-dock was flooded. Upon investigation, it was discovered that there was a dam from 5 to $5 \times 1/2$ feet high in the 7-foot sewer; and that dam, by diverting to the 6-foot sewer the greater part of the water, had caused the internal pressure, which broke it. Both sewers were a part of the city sewerage system; but the dam was not shown either on the city's plan, nor on the Government's plans and blueprints, which were submitted to Spearin. On them the 7-foot sewer appeared as unobstructed. The Government officials concerned with the letting of the contract and construction of the dry-dock did not know of the existence of the dam. The site selected for the dry-dock was low ground; and during some years prior to making the contract sued on, the sewers had, from time to time, overflowed to the knowledge of these Government officials and others. But the fact had not been communicated to Spearin by anyone. He had, before entering into the contract, made a superficial examination of the premises and sought from the civil engineer's office at the Navy Yard information concerning the conditions and probable cost of the work; but he had made no special examination of the sewers nor special enquiry into the possibility of the work being flooded thereby; and had no information on the subject.

Promptly after the breaking of the sewer Spearin notified the Government that he considered the sewers under existing plans a menace to the work and that he would not resume operations unless the Government either made good or assumed responsibility for the damage that had already occurred and either made such changes in the sewer system as would remove the danger or assumed responsibility for the damage which might thereafter be occasioned by the insufficient capacity and the location and design of the existing sewers. The estimated cost of restoring the sewer was $3,875. But it was unsafe to both Spearin and the Government's property to proceed with the work with the 6-foot sewer in its then condition. The Government insisted that the responsibility for remedying existing conditions rested with the contractor. After fifteen months spent in investigation and fruitless correspondence, the Secretary of the Navy annulled the contract and took possession of the plant and materials on the site. Later the dry-dock, under radically changed and enlarged plans, was completed by other contractors, the Government having first discontinued the use of the 6-foot intersecting sewer and then reconstructed it by modifying size, shape and material so as to remove all danger of its breaking from internal pressure. Up to that time $210,939.18 had been expended by Spearin on the work; and he had received from the Government on account thereof $129,758.32. The court found that if he had been allowed to complete the contract he would have earned a profit of $60,000, and its judgment included that sum.

The general rules of law applicable to these facts are well settled. Where one agrees to do, for a fixed sum, a thing possible to be performed, he will not be excused or become entitled to additional compensation, because unforeseen difficulties are encountered. *Day v. United States*, 245 U.S. 159; *Phoenix Bridge Co. v. United States*, 211 U.S. 188. Thus one who undertakes to erect a structure upon a particular site, assumes ordinarily the risk of subsidence of the soil. *Simpson v. United States*, 172 U.S. 372; *Dermott v. Jones*, 2 Wall. 1. But if the contractor is bound to build according to plans and specifications prepared by the owner, the contractor will not be responsible for the consequences of defects in the plans and specifications. *MacKnight Flintic Stone Co. v. The Mayor*, 160 N.Y. 72; *Filbert v. Philadelphia*, 181 Pa. St. 530; *Bentley v. State*, 73 Wisconsin, 416. See *Sundstrom v. New York*, 213 N.Y. 68. This responsibility of the owner is not overcome by the usual clauses requiring builders to visit the site, to check the plans, and to inform themselves of the requirements of the work, as is shown by *Christie v. United States*, 237 U.S. 234; *Hollerbach v. United States*, 233 U.S. 165, and *United States v. Utah & c. Stage Co.*, 199 U.S. 414, 424, where it was held that the contractor should be relieved, if he was misled by erroneous statements in the specifications.

In the case at bar, the sewer, as well as the other structures, was to be built in accordance with the plans and specifications furnished by the Government. The construction of the sewer constituted as much an integral part of the contract as did the construction of any part of the dry-dock proper. It was as necessary as any other work in the preparation for the foundation. It involved no separate contract and no separate consideration. The contention of the Government that the present case is to be distinguished from the *Bentley Case, supra*, and other similar cases, on the ground that the contract with reference to the sewer is purely collateral, is clearly without merit. The risk of the existing system proving adequate might have rested upon Spearin, if the contract for the dry-dock had not contained the provision for relocation of the 6-foot sewer. But the insertion of the articles prescribing the character, dimensions and location of the sewer imported a warranty that, if the specifications were complied with, the sewer would be adequate. This implied warranty is not overcome by the general clauses requiring the contractor, to examine the site, [n1] to check up the plans, [n2] and to assume responsibility for the work until completion and acceptance. [n3] The obligation to examine the site did not impose upon him the duty of making a diligent enquiry into the history of the locality with a view to determining, at his peril, whether the sewer specifically prescribed by the Government would prove adequate. The duty to check plans did not impose the obligation to pass upon their adequacy to accomplish the purpose in view. And the provision concerning contractor's responsibility cannot be construed as abridging rights arising under specific provisions of the contract.

n1 "271. *Examination of site.*   Intending bidders are expected to examine the site of the proposed dry-dock and inform themselves thoroughly of the actual conditions and requirements before submitting proposals."

n2 "25. *Checking plans and dimensions; lines and levels.*   The contractor shall check all plans furnished him immediately upon their receipt and promptly notify the civil engineer in charge of any discrepancies discovered therein. . . . The contractor will be held responsible for the lines and levels of his work, and he must combine all materials properly, so that the completed structure shall conform to the true intent and meaning of the plans and specifications."

n3 "21. *Contractor's responsibility.*   The contractor shall be responsible for the entire work and every part thereof, until completion and final acceptance by the Chief of Bureau of Yards and Docks, and for all tools, appliances, and property of every description used in connection therewith . . . ."

Neither § 3744 of the Revised Statutes, which provides [138] that contracts of the Navy Department shall be reduced to writing, nor the parol evidence rule, precludes reliance upon a warranty implied by law. See *Kellogg Bridge Co. v. Hamilton*, 110 U.S. 108.   The breach of warranty, followed by the Government's repudiation of all responsibility for the past and for making working conditions safe in the future, justified Spearin in refusing to resume the work. He was not obliged to restore the sewer and to proceed, at his peril, with the construction of the dry-dock. When the Government refused to assume the responsibility, he might have terminated the contract himself, *Anvil Mining Co. v. Humble*, 153 U.S. 540, 551–552; but he did not. When the Government annulled the contract without justification, it became liable for all damages resulting from its breach. Both the main and the cross-appeal raise questions as to the amount recoverable.

The Government contends that Spearin should, as requested, have repaired the sewer and proceeded with the work; and that having declined to do so, he should be denied all recovery except $7,907.98, which represents the proceeds of that part of the plant which the Government sold plus the value of that retained by it. But Spearin was under no obligation to repair the sewer and proceed with the work, while the Government denied responsibility for providing and refused to provide sewer conditions safe for the work. When it wrongfully annulled the contract, Spearin became entitled to compensation for all losses resulting from its breach.

Spearin insists that he should be allowed the additional sum of $63,658.70, because, as he alleges, the lower court awarded him (in addition to $60,000 for profits) not the difference between his proper expenditures and his receipts from the Government, but the difference between such receipts and the value of the work, materials, and plant (as reported by a naval board appointed by the defendant). [*139] Language in the findings of fact concerning damages lends possibly some warrant for that contention; but the discussion of the subject in the opinion makes it clear that the rule enunciated in *United States v. Behan*, 110 U.S. 338, which claimant invokes, was adopted and correctly applied by the court.

The judgment of the Court of Claims is, therefore, Affirmed.

Index

ABOUT THE AUTHOR

Derek Graham has more than 20 years of experience in construction and construction project management. Currently an independent consultant in the New York City high-end residential sector as an owner's representative, quality control inspector/specialist, planner, and expert witness, he has also worked extensively in the commercial and hospitality sectors. Mr. Graham is skilled in all aspects of construction, including building trades, cost estimating, contract negotiation, troubleshooting, financial reporting, and crisis management.